Garfield
FAT CAT 3-PACK
VOLUME 6

BY
JIM DAVIS

BALLANTINE BOOKS · NEW YORK

1996, 2011 Ballantine Books Trade Paperback Edition

Copyright © 2011 by PAWS, Inc. All Rights Reserved.
GARFIELD ROUNDS OUT copyright © 1988, 2008 by PAWS, Inc. All Rights Reserved.
GARFIELD CHEWS THE FAT copyright © 1989, 2008 by PAWS, Inc. All Rights Reserved.
GARFIELD GOES TO WAIST copyright © 1990, 2009 by PAWS, Inc. All Rights Reserved.
"GARFIELD" and the GARFIELD characters are registered and unregistered trademarks of PAWS, Inc.

Published in the United States by Ballantine Books, an imprint of The Random House Publishing Group,
a division of Random House, Inc., New York.

BALLANTINE and colophon are registered trademarks of Random House, Inc.

Originally published as three separate volumes, in both black and white and color, as *Garfield Rounds Out*,
Garfield Chews the Fat, and *Garfield Goes to Waist*. This compilation was originally published in black and
white in 1996.

ISBN 978-0-345-52420-1

Printed in the United States of America

www.ballantinebooks.com

First Colorized Edition

9 8 7 6 5 4 3 2

Garfield
rounds out

BY JIM DAVIS

Ballantine Books • **New York**

GARFIELD'S SCALE OF INTELLIGENCE

0 ———→   1000

amoeba | slug | dog | not-too-bright rock | chicken | monkey | man | food processor | cat

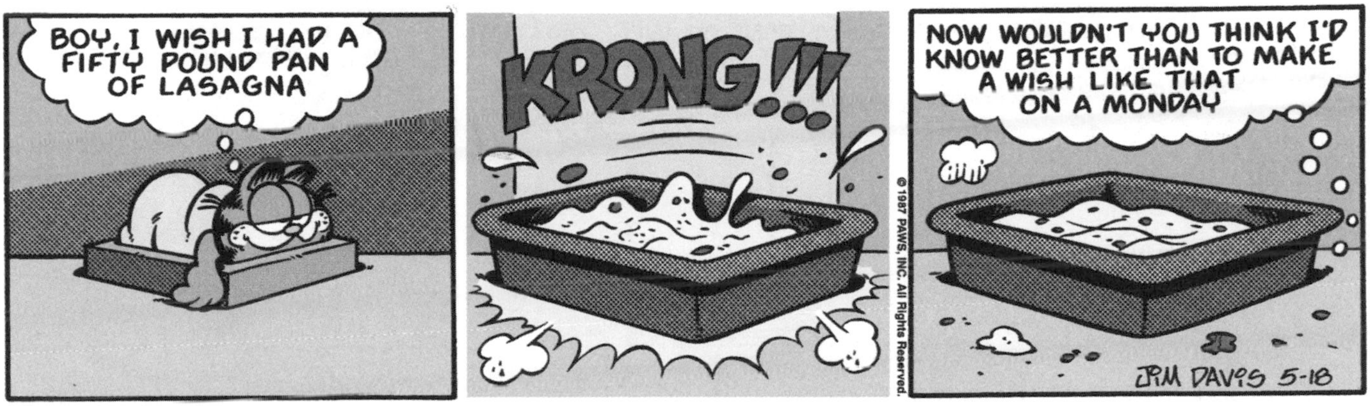
BOY, I WISH I HAD A FIFTY POUND PAN OF LASAGNA
KRONG!!!
© 1987 PAWS, INC. All Rights Reserved.
NOW WOULDN'T YOU THINK I'D KNOW BETTER THAN TO MAKE A WISH LIKE THAT ON A MONDAY
JIM DAVIS 5-18

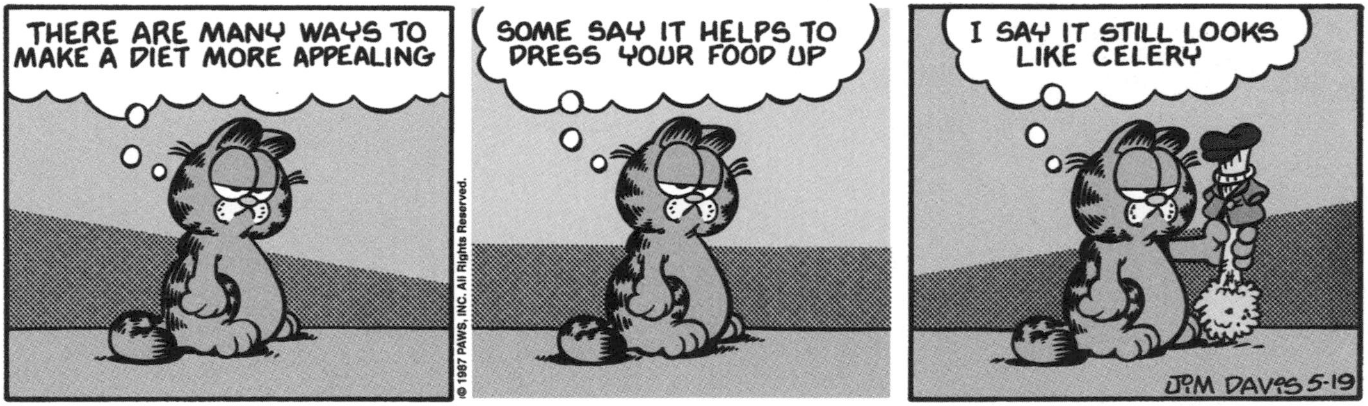
THERE ARE MANY WAYS TO MAKE A DIET MORE APPEALING
© 1987 PAWS, INC. All Rights Reserved.
SOME SAY IT HELPS TO DRESS YOUR FOOD UP
I SAY IT STILL LOOKS LIKE CELERY
JIM DAVIS 5-19

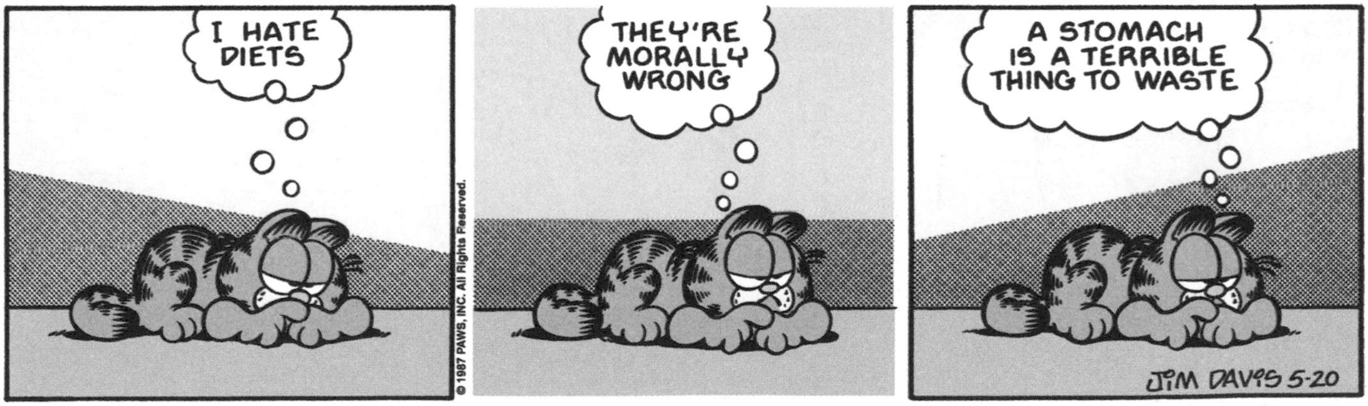
I HATE DIETS
© 1987 PAWS, INC. All Rights Reserved.
THEY'RE MORALLY WRONG
A STOMACH IS A TERRIBLE THING TO WASTE
JIM DAVIS 5-20

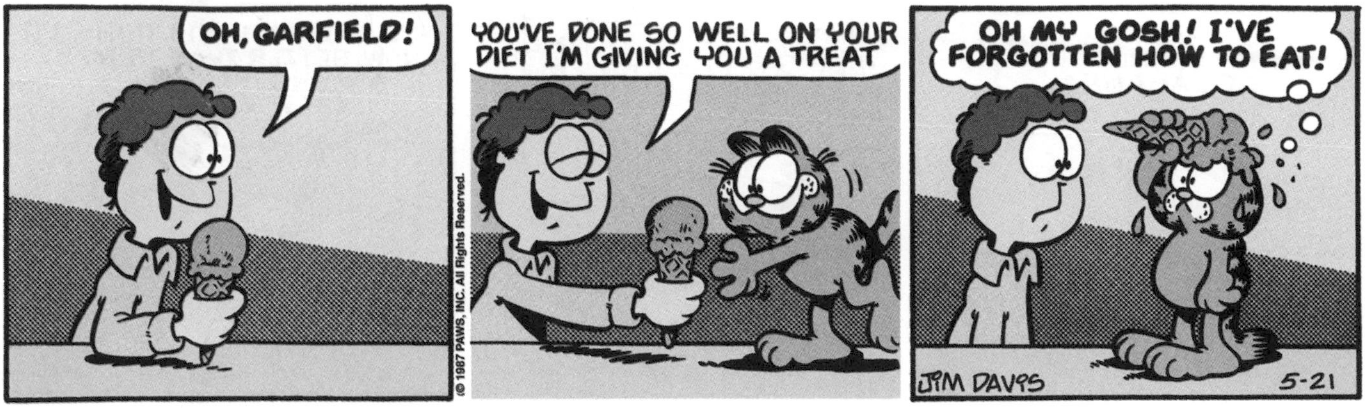
OH, GARFIELD!
YOU'VE DONE SO WELL ON YOUR DIET I'M GIVING YOU A TREAT
© 1987 PAWS, INC. All Rights Reserved.
OH MY GOSH! I'VE FORGOTTEN HOW TO EAT!
JIM DAVIS
5-21

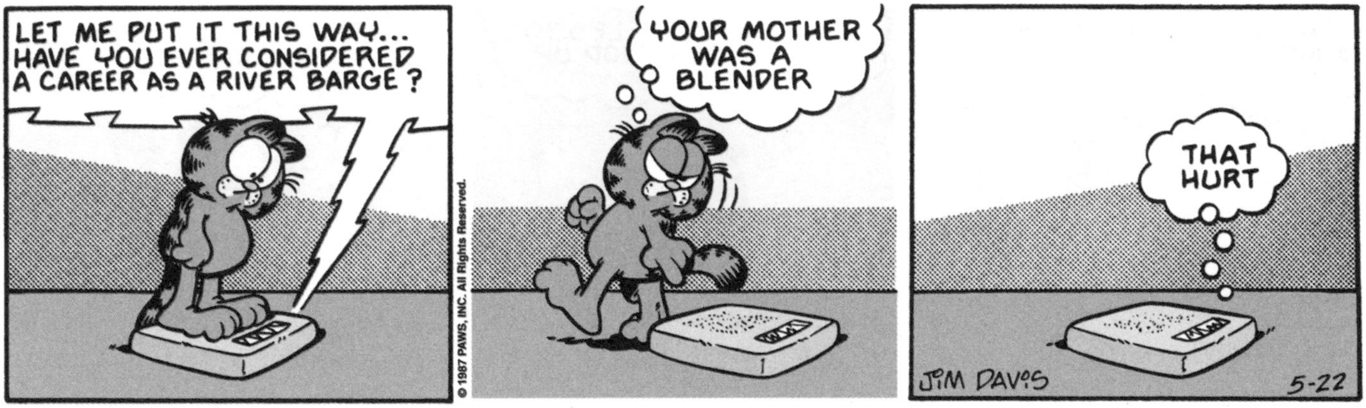
LET ME PUT IT THIS WAY... HAVE YOU EVER CONSIDERED A CAREER AS A RIVER BARGE ?
© 1987 PAWS, INC. All Rights Reserved.
YOUR MOTHER WAS A BLENDER
THAT HURT
JIM DAVIS
5-22

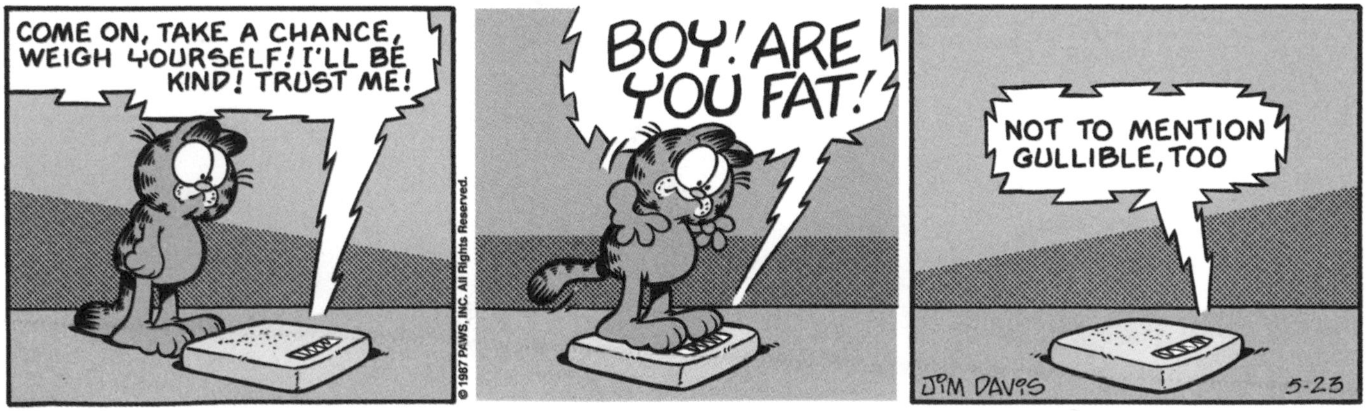
COME ON, TAKE A CHANCE, WEIGH YOURSELF! I'LL BE KIND! TRUST ME!
© 1987 PAWS, INC. All Rights Reserved.
BOY! ARE YOU FAT!
NOT TO MENTION GULLIBLE, TOO
JIM DAVIS
5-23

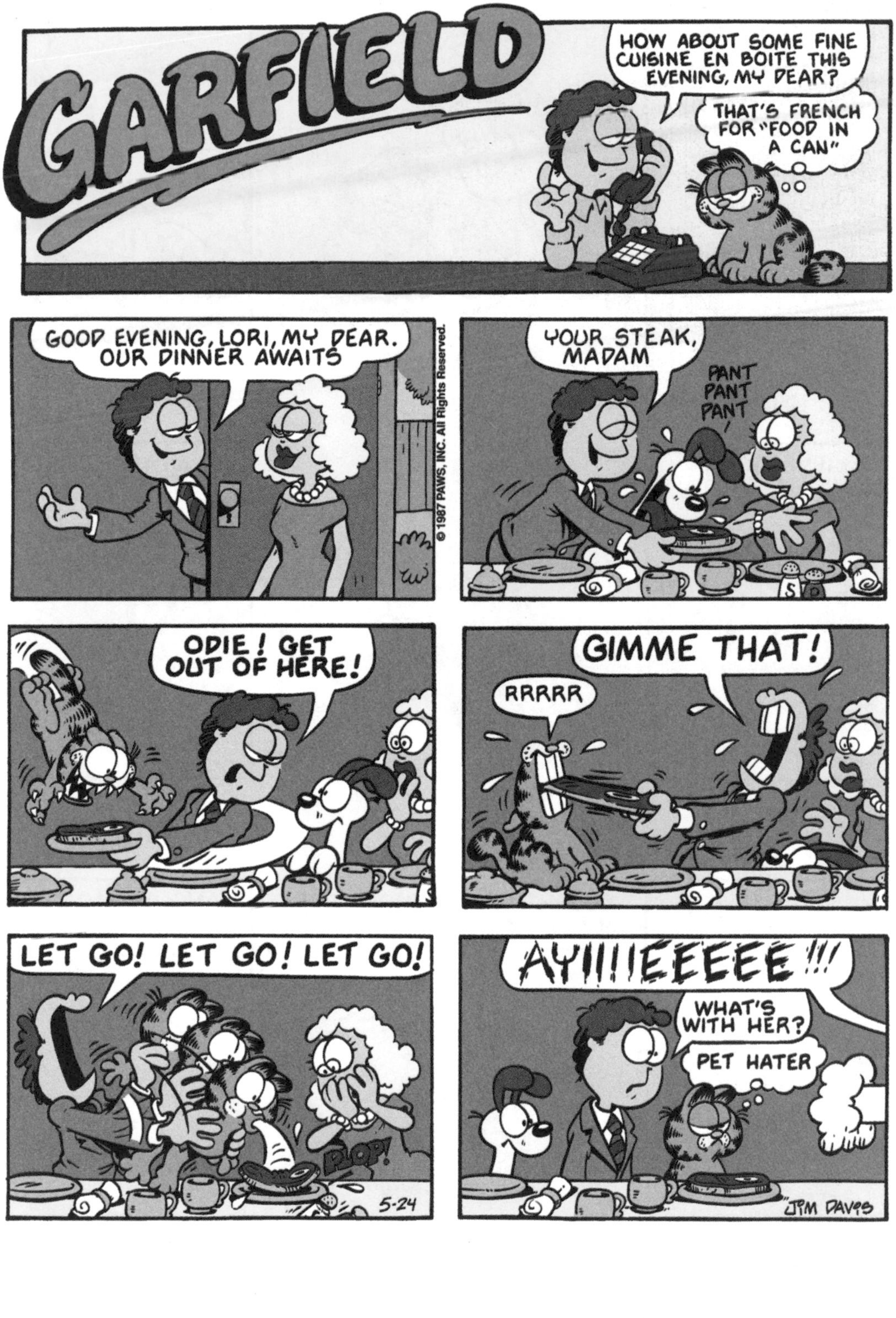
GARFIELD
HOW ABOUT SOME FINE CUISINE EN BOITE THIS EVENING, MY DEAR?
THAT'S FRENCH FOR "FOOD IN A CAN"
GOOD EVENING, LORI, MY DEAR. OUR DINNER AWAITS
© 1987 PAWS, INC. All Rights Reserved.
YOUR STEAK, MADAM
PANT PANT PANT
ODIE! GET OUT OF HERE!
GIMME THAT!
RRRRR
LET GO! LET GO! LET GO!
PLOP!
5-24
AYIIIIEEEEE!!!
WHAT'S WITH HER?
PET HATER
JIM DAVIS

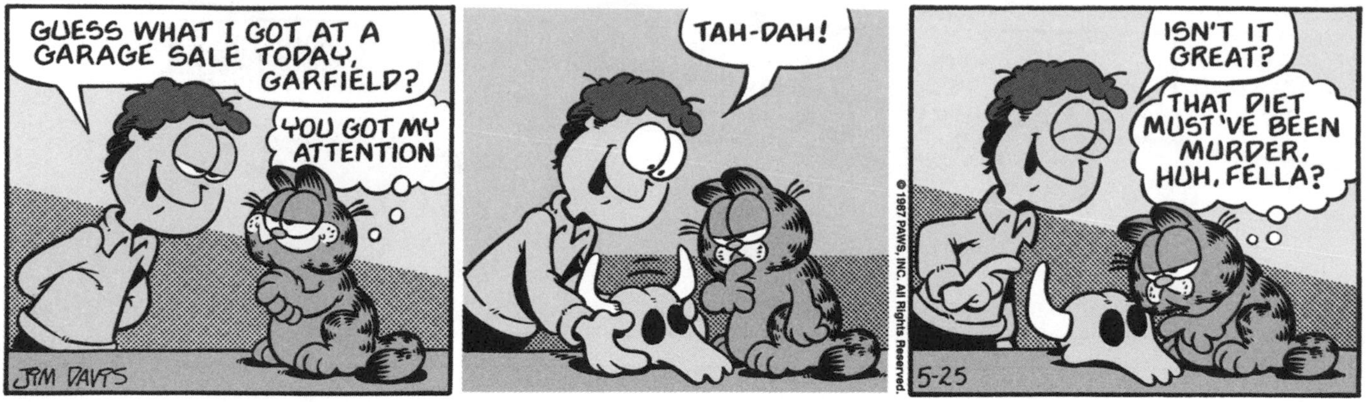
GUESS WHAT I GOT AT A GARAGE SALE TODAY, GARFIELD?
YOU GOT MY ATTENTION
JIM DAVIS
TAH-DAH!
© 1987 PAWS, INC. All Rights Reserved.
ISN'T IT GREAT?
THAT DIET MUST'VE BEEN MURDER, HUH, FELLA?
5-25

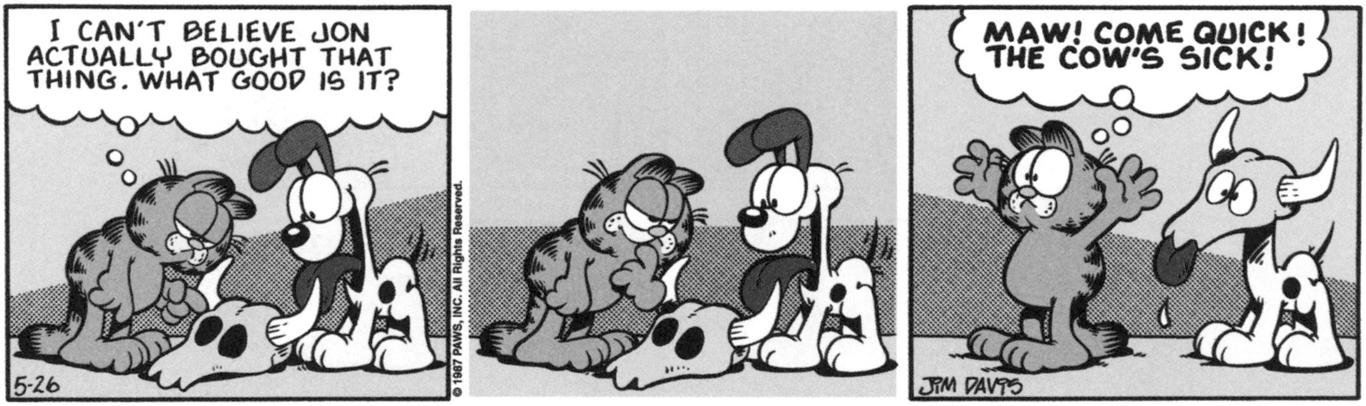
I CAN'T BELIEVE JON ACTUALLY BOUGHT THAT THING. WHAT GOOD IS IT?
5-26
© 1987 PAWS, INC. All Rights Reserved.
MAW! COME QUICK! THE COW'S SICK!
JIM DAVIS

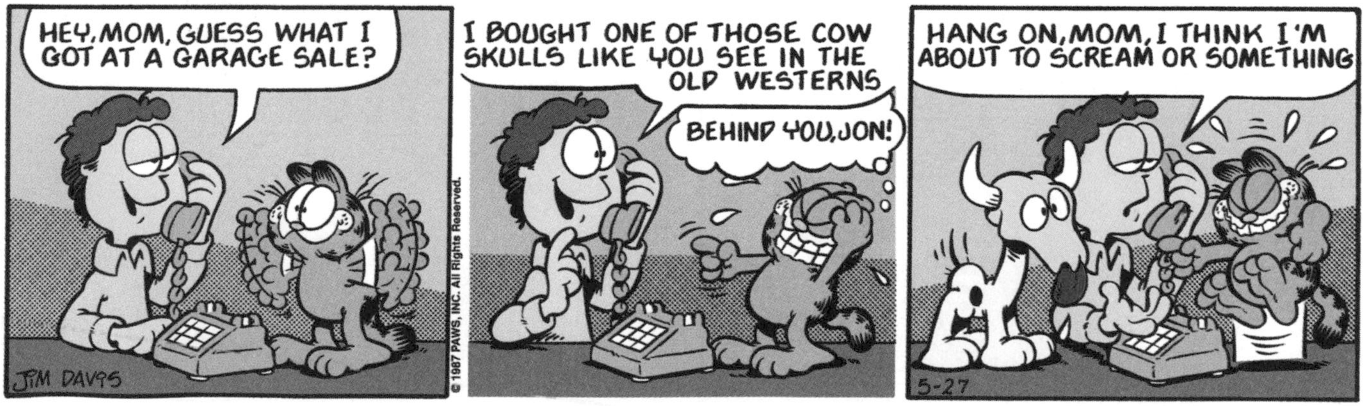
HEY, MOM, GUESS WHAT I GOT AT A GARAGE SALE?
JIM DAVIS
© 1987 PAWS, INC. All Rights Reserved.
I BOUGHT ONE OF THOSE COW SKULLS LIKE YOU SEE IN THE OLD WESTERNS
BEHIND YOU, JON!
HANG ON, MOM, I THINK I'M ABOUT TO SCREAM OR SOMETHING
5-27

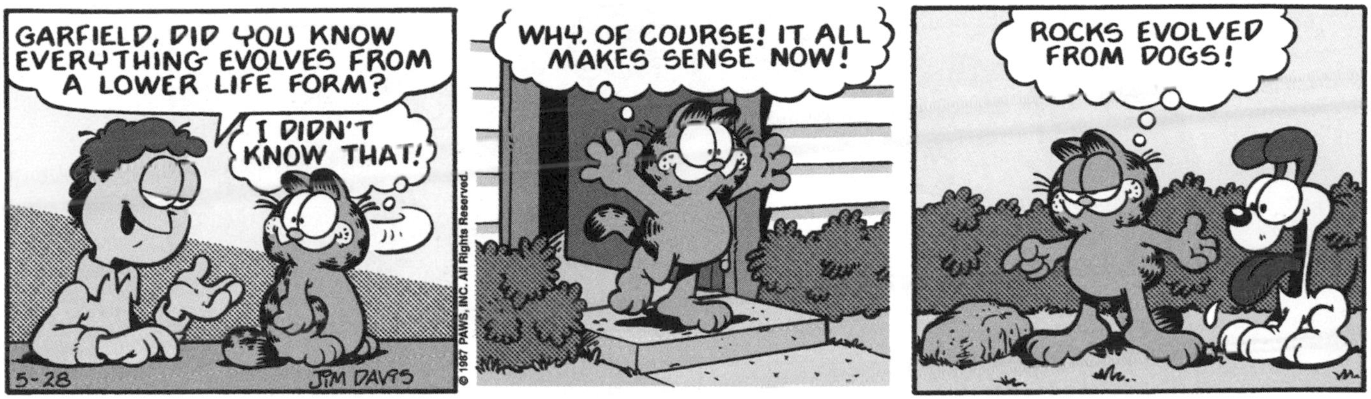
GARFIELD, DID YOU KNOW EVERYTHING EVOLVES FROM A LOWER LIFE FORM?
I DIDN'T KNOW THAT!
5-28
JIM DAVIS
© 1987 PAWS, INC. All Rights Reserved.
WHY, OF COURSE! IT ALL MAKES SENSE NOW!
ROCKS EVOLVED FROM DOGS!

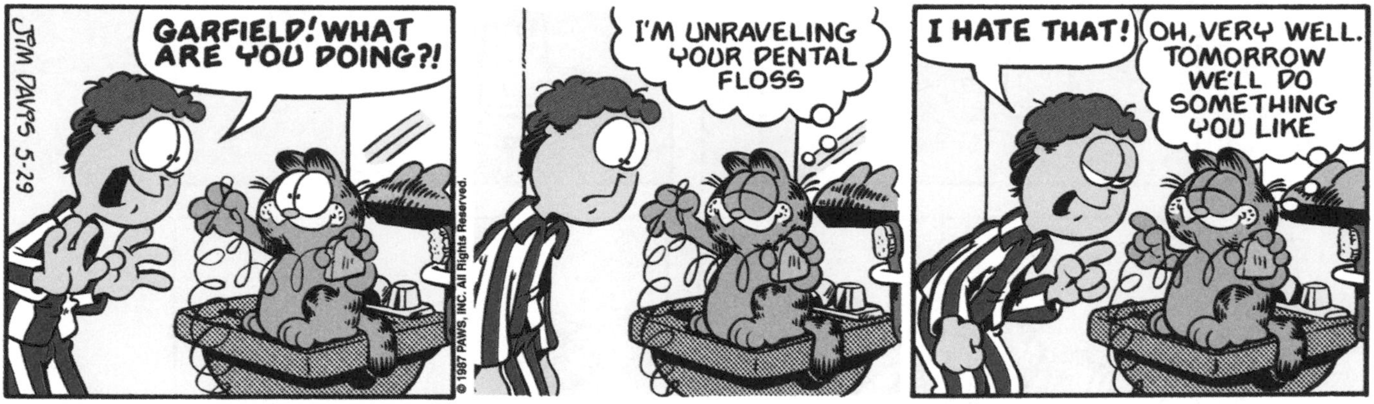
JIM DAVIS 5-29
GARFIELD! WHAT ARE YOU DOING?!
© 1987 PAWS, INC. All Rights Reserved.
I'M UNRAVELING YOUR DENTAL FLOSS
I HATE THAT!
OH, VERY WELL. TOMORROW WE'LL DO SOMETHING YOU LIKE

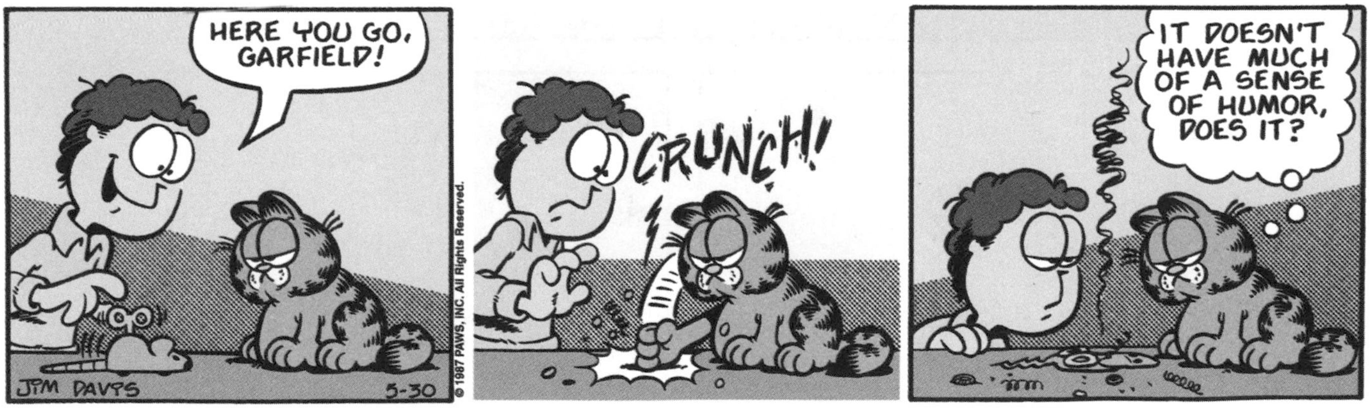
HERE YOU GO, GARFIELD!
JIM DAVIS
5-30
© 1987 PAWS, INC. All Rights Reserved.
CRUNCH!
IT DOESN'T HAVE MUCH OF A SENSE OF HUMOR, DOES IT?

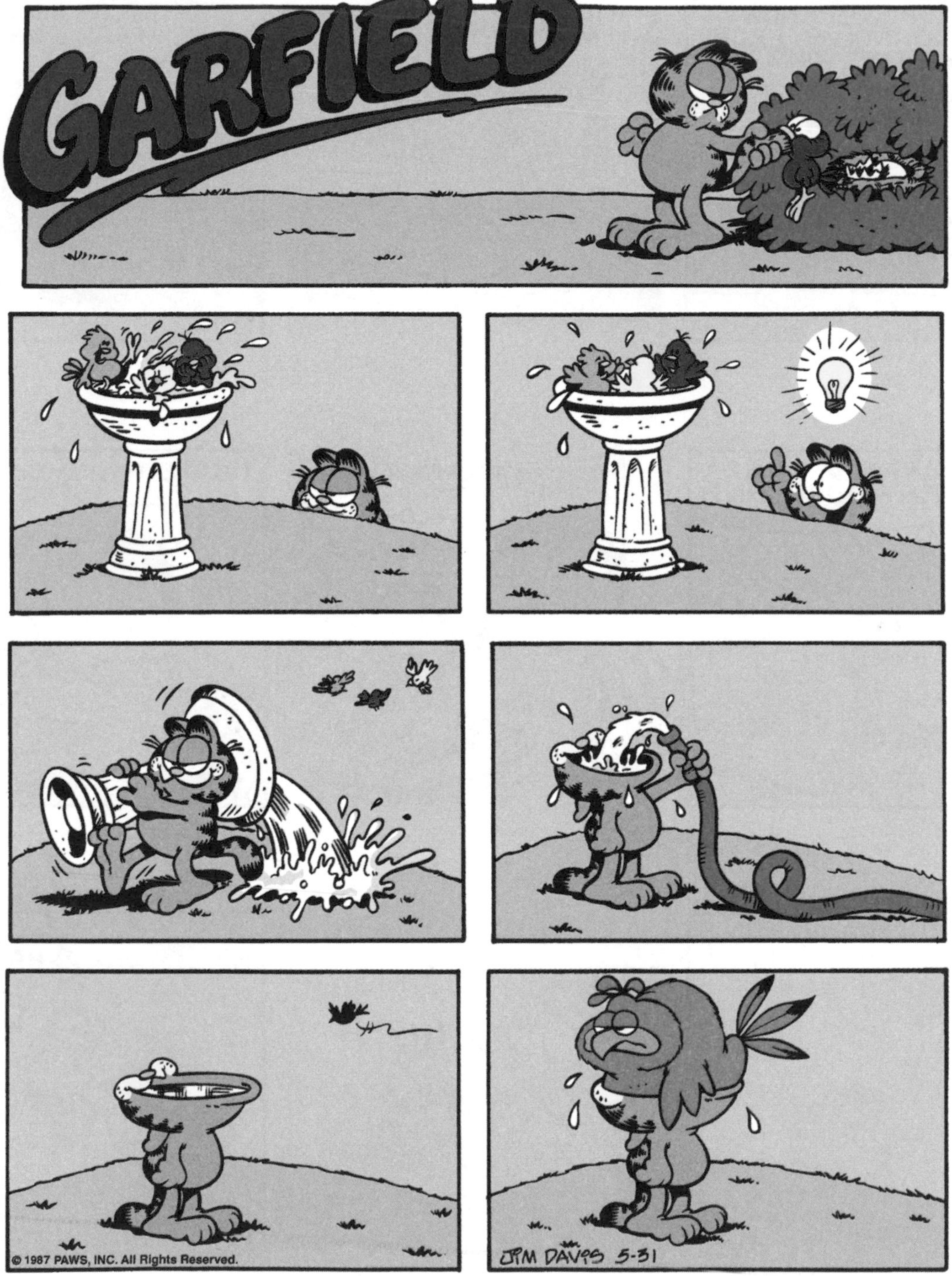
GARFIELD
© 1987 PAWS, INC. All Rights Reserved.
JIM DAVIS 5-31

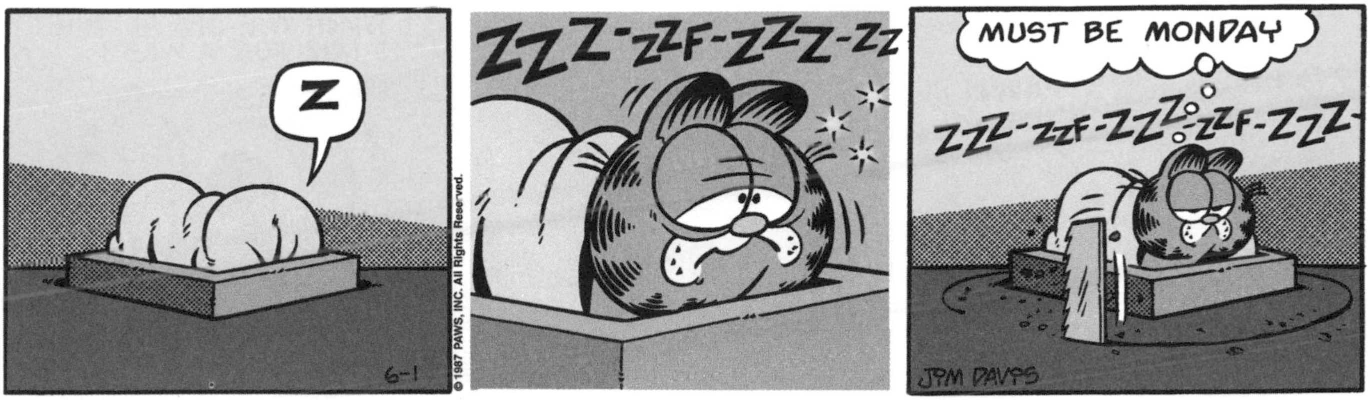
Z
ZZZ-ZZF-ZZZ-ZZ
MUST BE MONDAY
ZZZ-ZZF-ZZZ-ZZF-ZZZ-
© 1987 PAWS, INC. All Rights Reserved.
6-1
JIM DAVIS

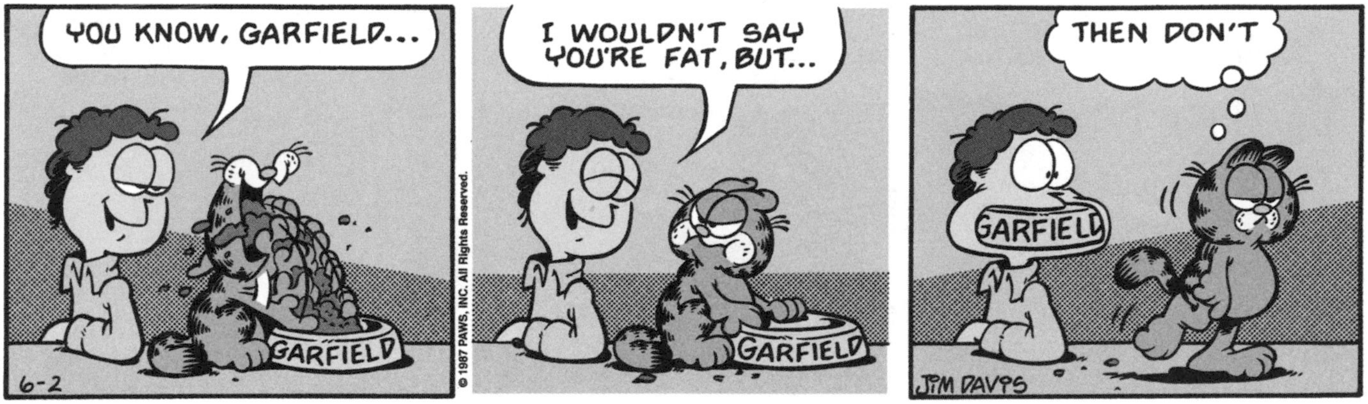
YOU KNOW, GARFIELD...
GARFIELD
I WOULDN'T SAY YOU'RE FAT, BUT...
GARFIELD
THEN DON'T
GARFIELD
© 1987 PAWS, INC. All Rights Reserved.
6-2
JIM DAVIS

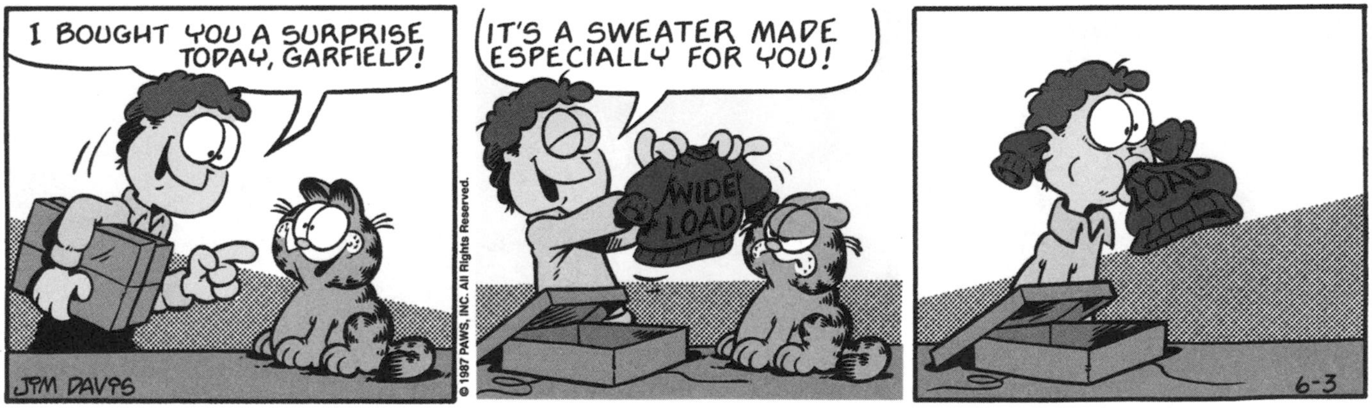
I BOUGHT YOU A SURPRISE TODAY, GARFIELD!
IT'S A SWEATER MADE ESPECIALLY FOR YOU!
WIDE LOAD
LOAD
© 1987 PAWS, INC. All Rights Reserved.
JIM DAVIS
6-3

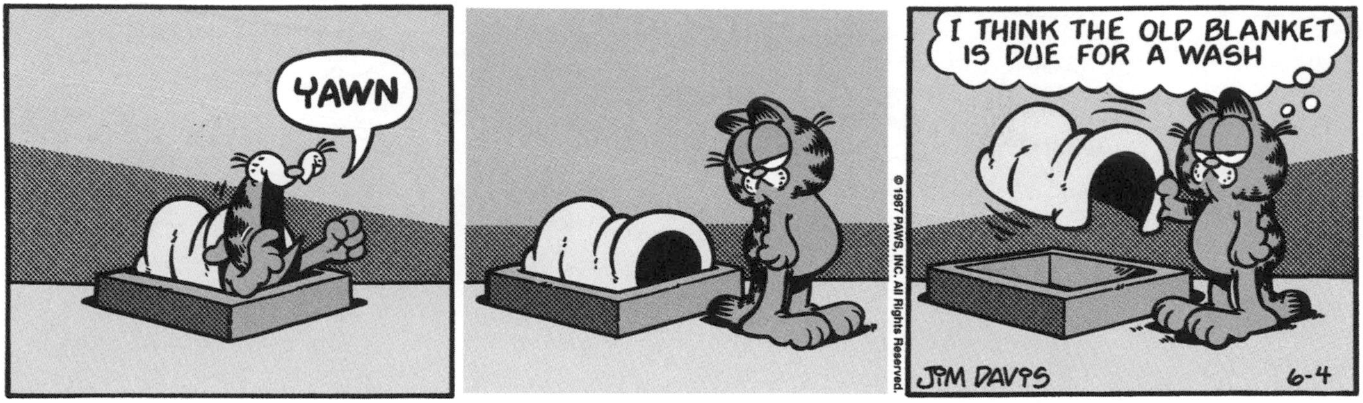
YAWN
© 1987 PAWS, INC. All Rights Reserved.
I THINK THE OLD BLANKET IS DUE FOR A WASH
JIM DAVIS
6-4

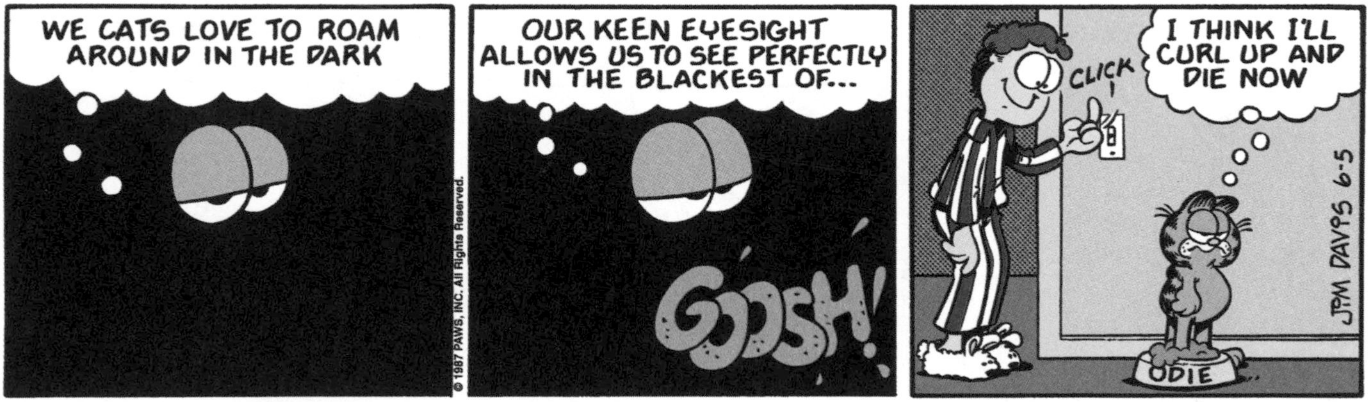
WE CATS LOVE TO ROAM AROUND IN THE DARK
© 1987 PAWS, INC. All Rights Reserved.
OUR KEEN EYESIGHT ALLOWS US TO SEE PERFECTLY IN THE BLACKEST OF...
GOOSH!
CLICK
I THINK I'LL CURL UP AND DIE NOW
JIM DAVIS 6-5
ODIE

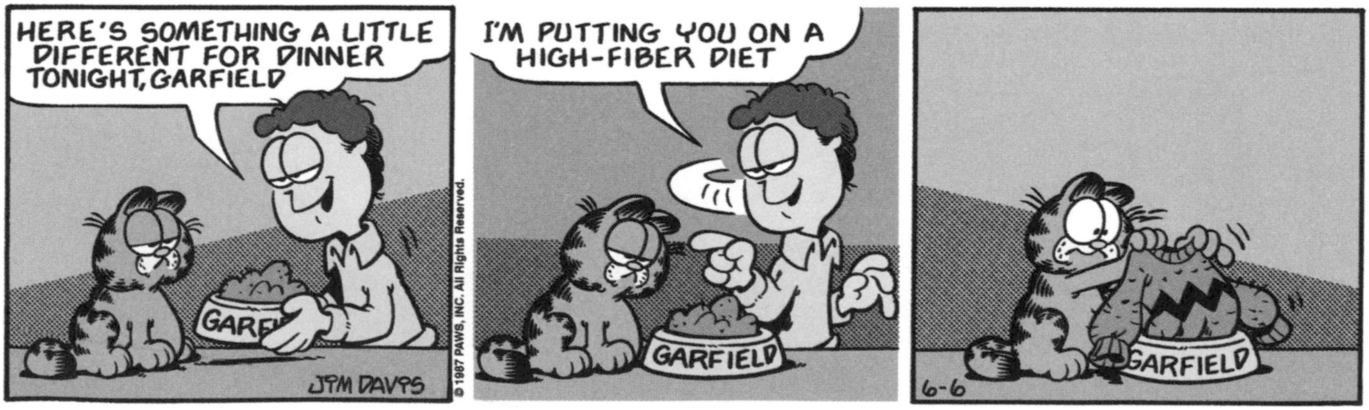
HERE'S SOMETHING A LITTLE DIFFERENT FOR DINNER TONIGHT, GARFIELD
JIM DAVIS
© 1987 PAWS, INC. All Rights Reserved.
I'M PUTTING YOU ON A HIGH-FIBER DIET
GARFIELD
GARFIELD
6-6

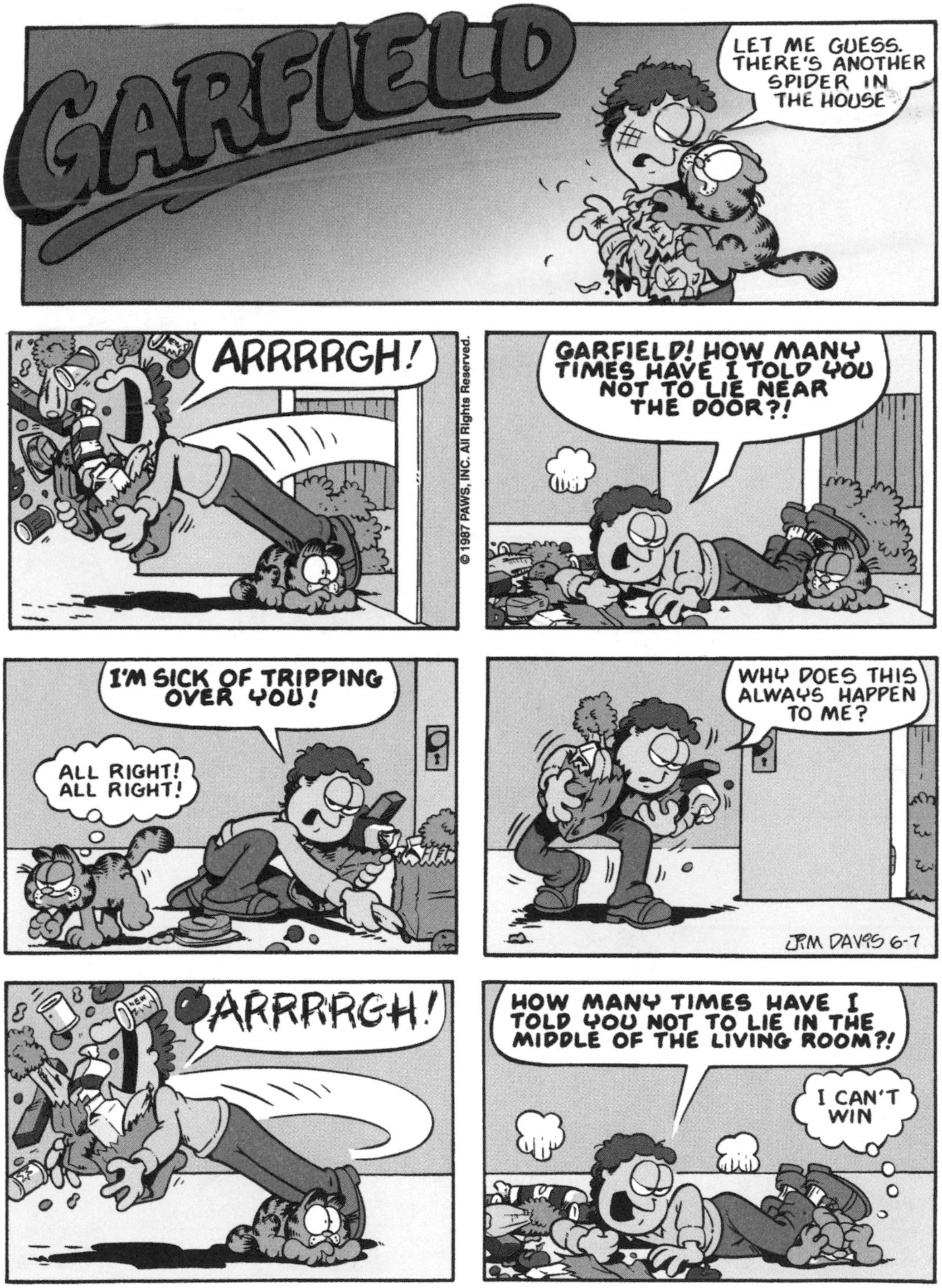
GARFIELD
LET ME GUESS. THERE'S ANOTHER SPIDER IN THE HOUSE
ARRRRGH!
© 1987 PAWS, INC. All Rights Reserved.
GARFIELD! HOW MANY TIMES HAVE I TOLD YOU NOT TO LIE NEAR THE DOOR?!
I'M SICK OF TRIPPING OVER YOU!
ALL RIGHT! ALL RIGHT!
WHY DOES THIS ALWAYS HAPPEN TO ME?
JIM DAVIS 6-7
ARRRRGH!
HOW MANY TIMES HAVE I TOLD YOU NOT TO LIE IN THE MIDDLE OF THE LIVING ROOM?!
I CAN'T WIN

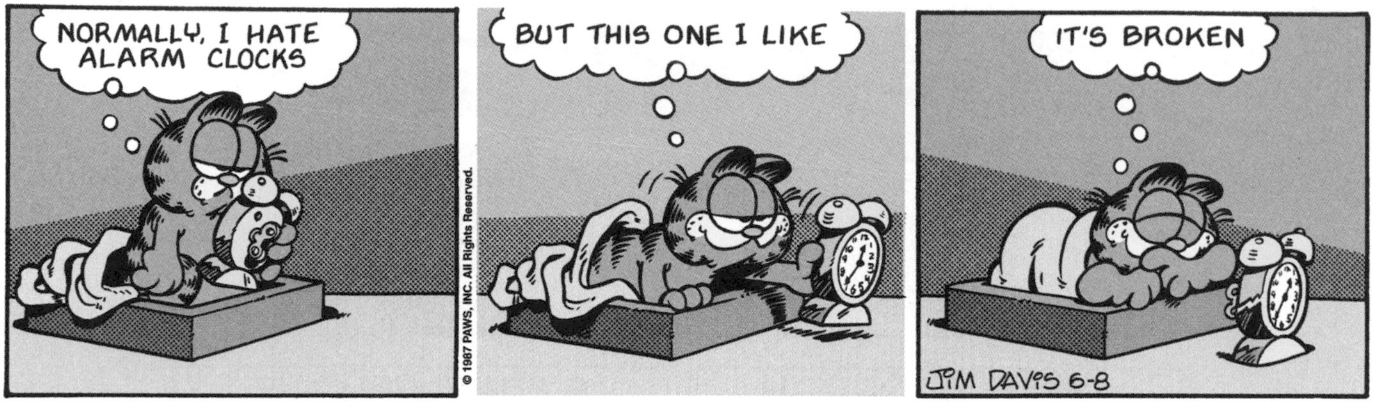
NORMALLY, I HATE ALARM CLOCKS
© 1987 PAWS, INC. All Rights Reserved.
BUT THIS ONE I LIKE
IT'S BROKEN
JIM DAVIS 6-8

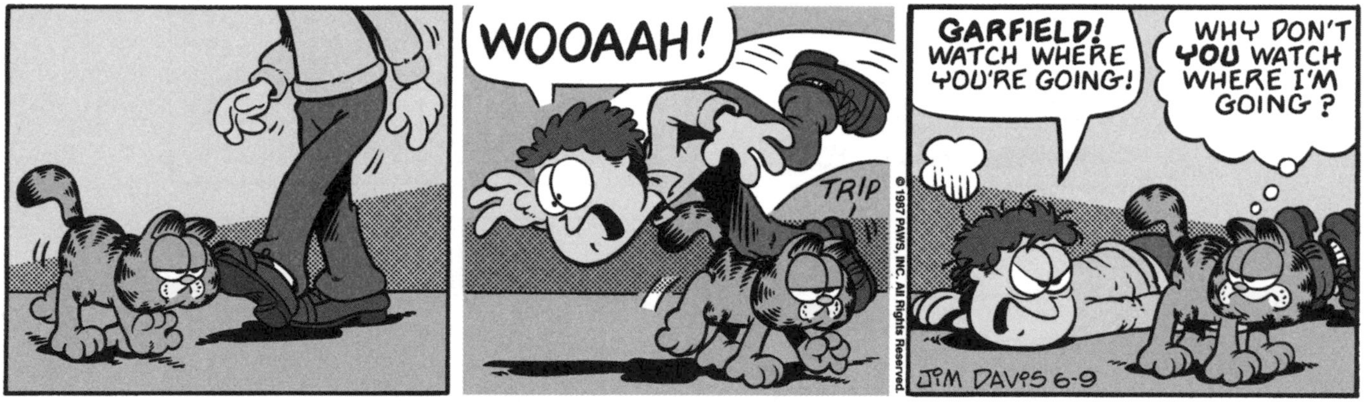
WOOAAH!
TRIP
© 1987 PAWS, INC. All Rights Reserved.
GARFIELD! WATCH WHERE YOU'RE GOING!
WHY DON'T YOU WATCH WHERE I'M GOING?
JIM DAVIS 6-9

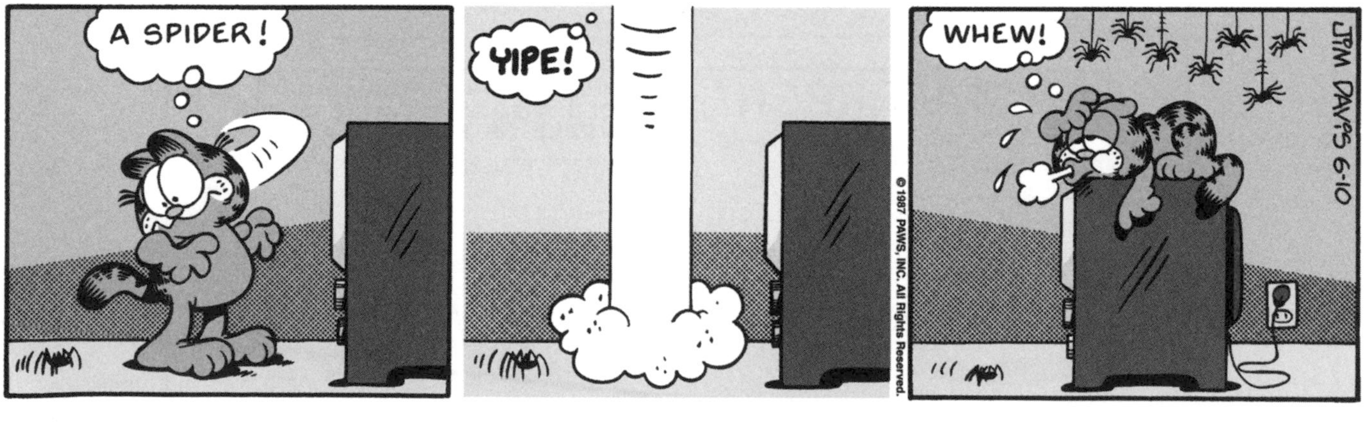
A SPIDER!
YIPE!
© 1987 PAWS, INC. All Rights Reserved.
WHEW!
JIM DAVIS 6-10

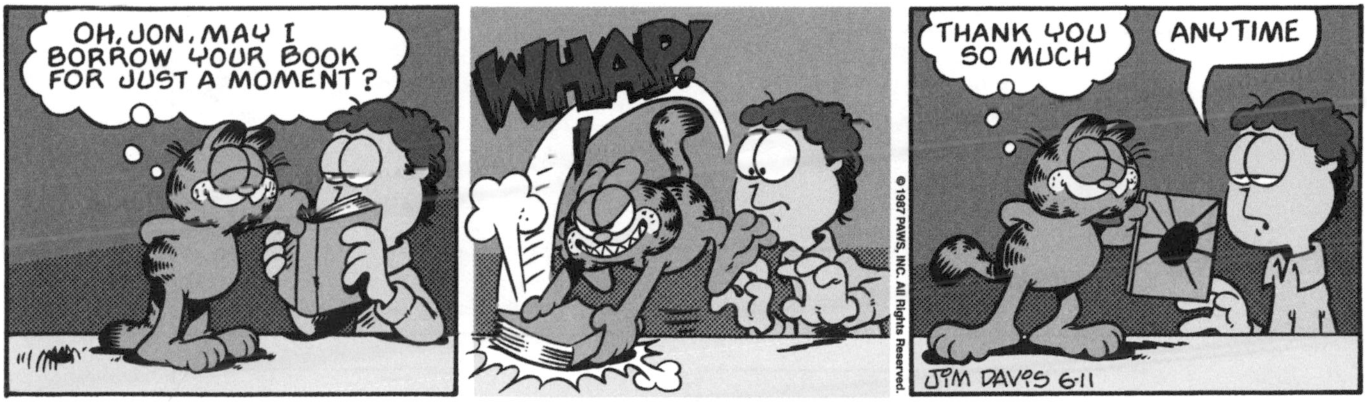
OH, JON, MAY I BORROW YOUR BOOK FOR JUST A MOMENT?
WHAP!
THANK YOU SO MUCH
ANYTIME
JIM DAVIS 6-11

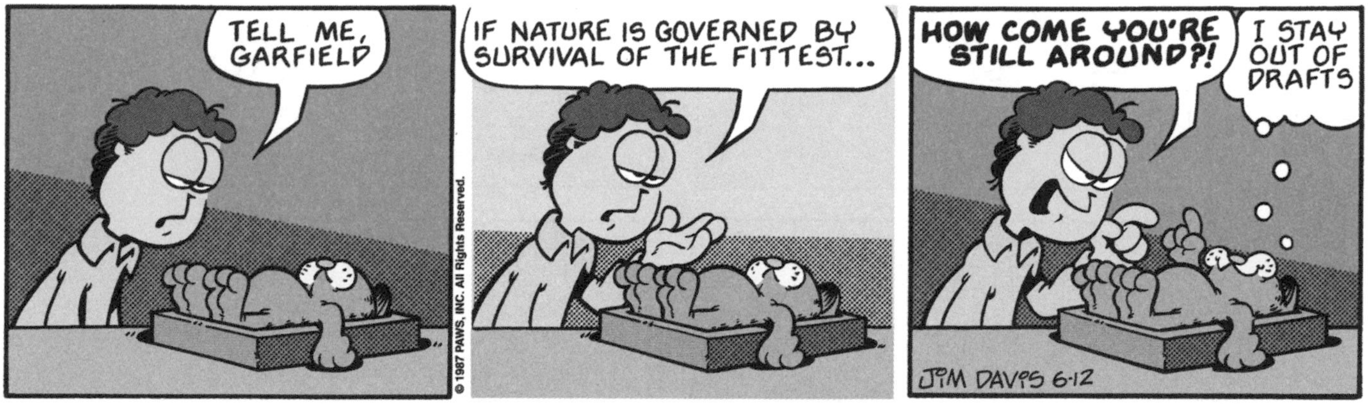
TELL ME, GARFIELD
IF NATURE IS GOVERNED BY SURVIVAL OF THE FITTEST...
HOW COME YOU'RE STILL AROUND?!
I STAY OUT OF DRAFTS
JIM DAVIS 6-12

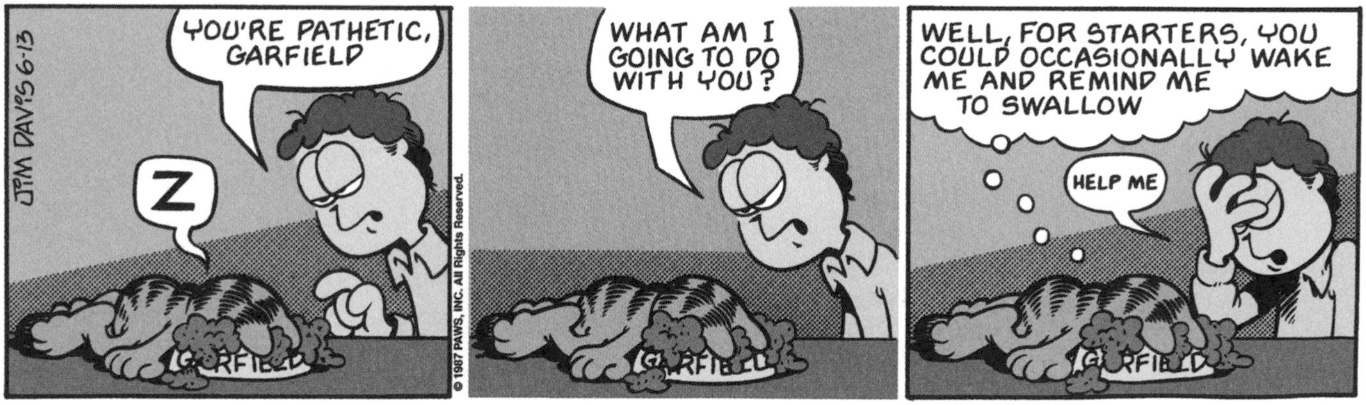
JIM DAVIS 6-13
YOU'RE PATHETIC, GARFIELD
Z
WHAT AM I GOING TO DO WITH YOU?
WELL, FOR STARTERS, YOU COULD OCCASIONALLY WAKE ME AND REMIND ME TO SWALLOW
HELP ME

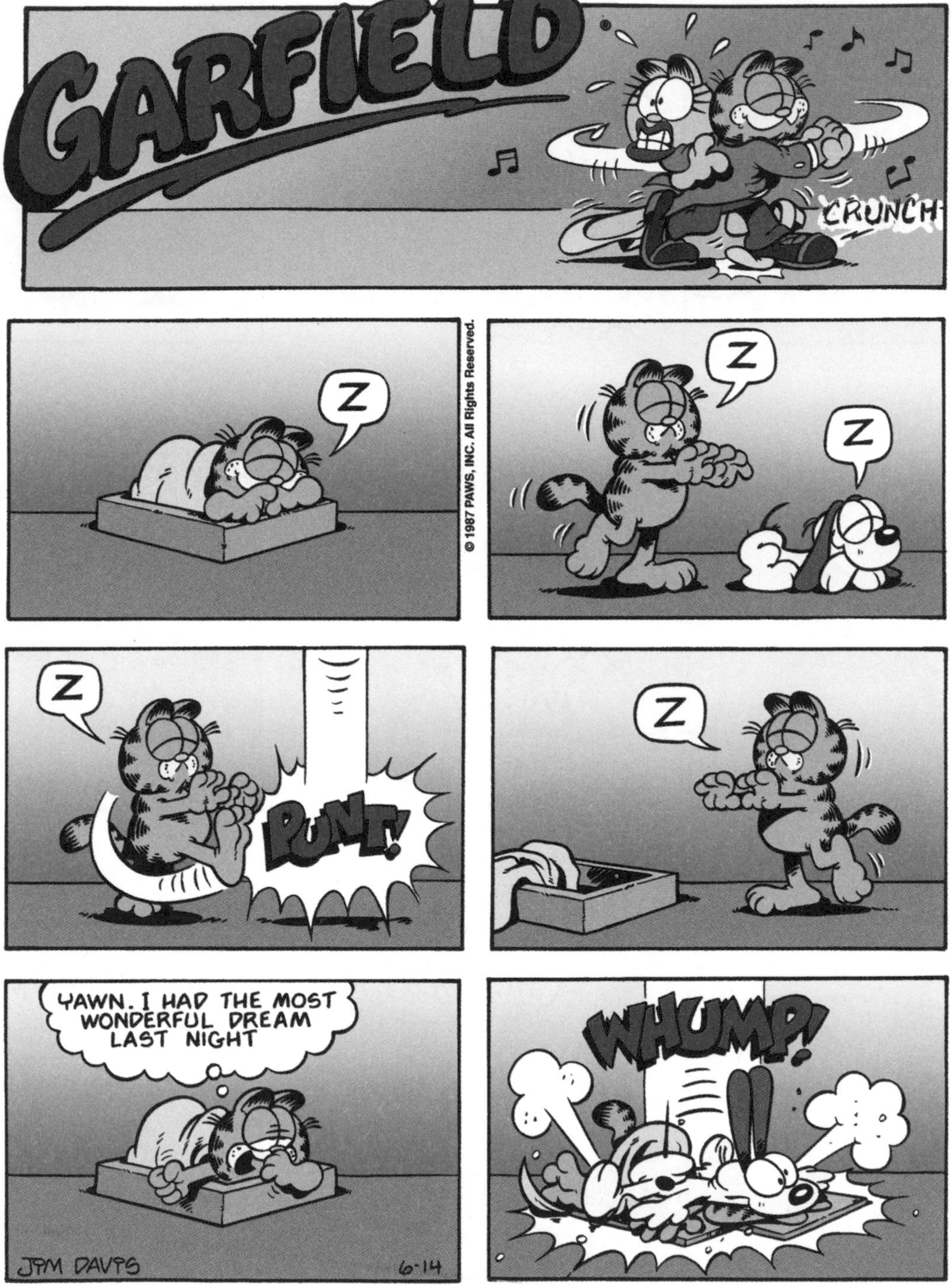
GARFIELD
CRUNCH
Z
© 1987 PAWS, INC. All Rights Reserved.
Z
Z
Z
PUNT!
Z
YAWN. I HAD THE MOST WONDERFUL DREAM LAST NIGHT
WHUMP!
JIM DAVIS
6-14

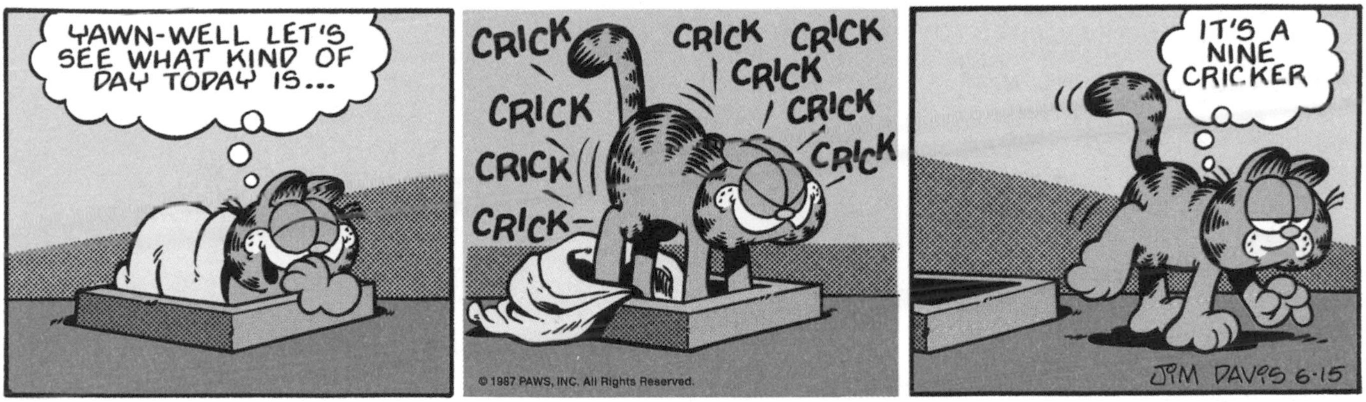
YAWN-WELL LET'S SEE WHAT KIND OF DAY TODAY IS...
CRICK CRICK CRICK CRICK CRICK CRICK CRICK CRICK CRICK
© 1987 PAWS, INC. All Rights Reserved.
IT'S A NINE CRICKER
JIM DAVIS 6-15

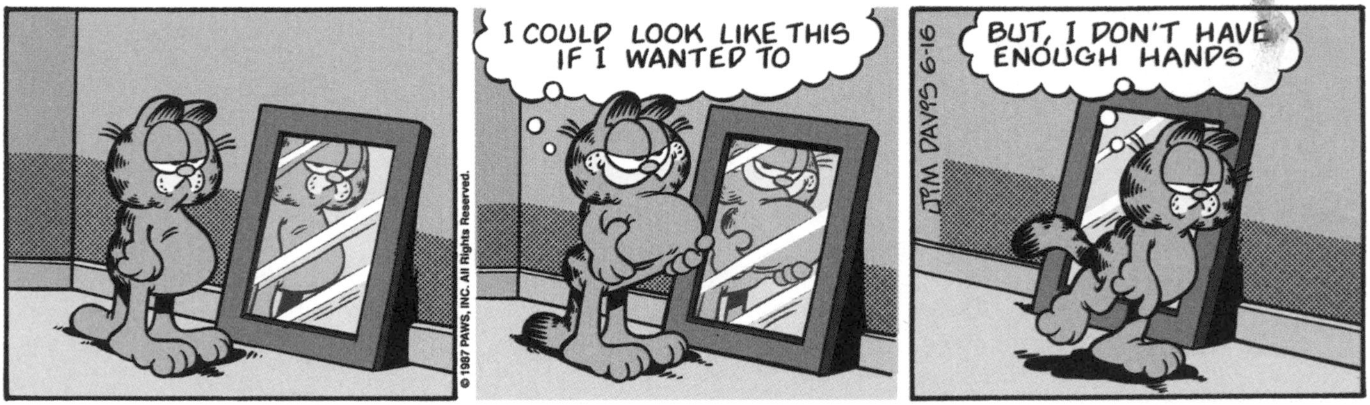
© 1987 PAWS, INC. All Rights Reserved.
I COULD LOOK LIKE THIS IF I WANTED TO
JIM DAVIS 6-16
BUT, I DON'T HAVE ENOUGH HANDS

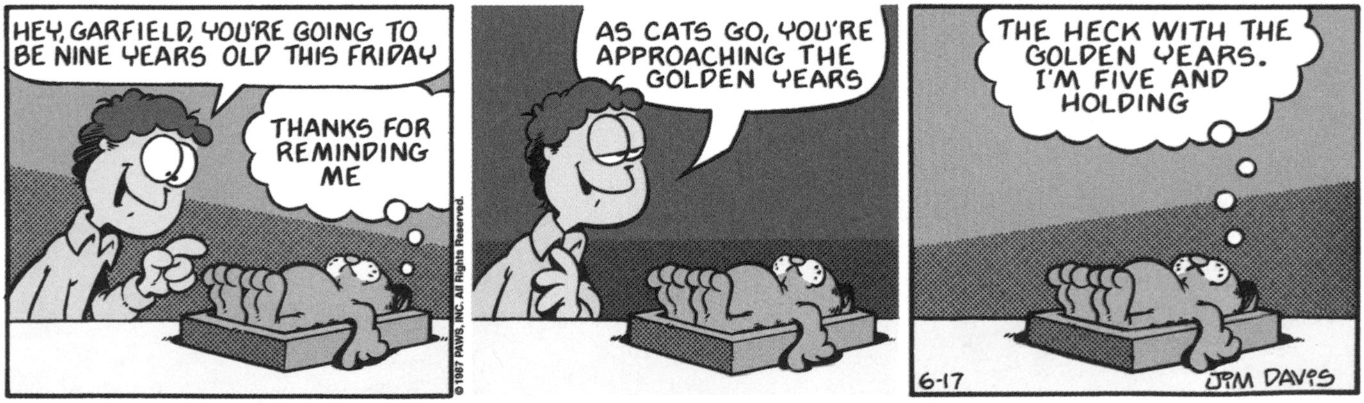
HEY, GARFIELD, YOU'RE GOING TO BE NINE YEARS OLD THIS FRIDAY
THANKS FOR REMINDING ME
© 1987 PAWS, INC. All Rights Reserved.
AS CATS GO, YOU'RE APPROACHING THE GOLDEN YEARS
THE HECK WITH THE GOLDEN YEARS. I'M FIVE AND HOLDING
6-17
JIM DAVIS

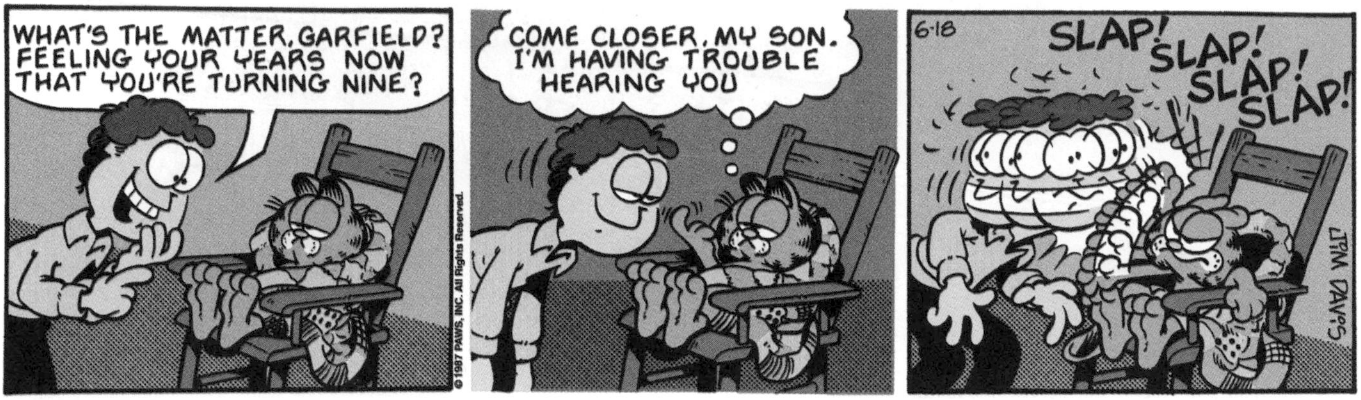
WHAT'S THE MATTER, GARFIELD? FEELING YOUR YEARS NOW THAT YOU'RE TURNING NINE?
© 1987 PAWS, INC. All Rights Reserved.
COME CLOSER, MY SON. I'M HAVING TROUBLE HEARING YOU
6-18
SLAP! SLAP! SLAP! SLAP!
JIM DAVIS

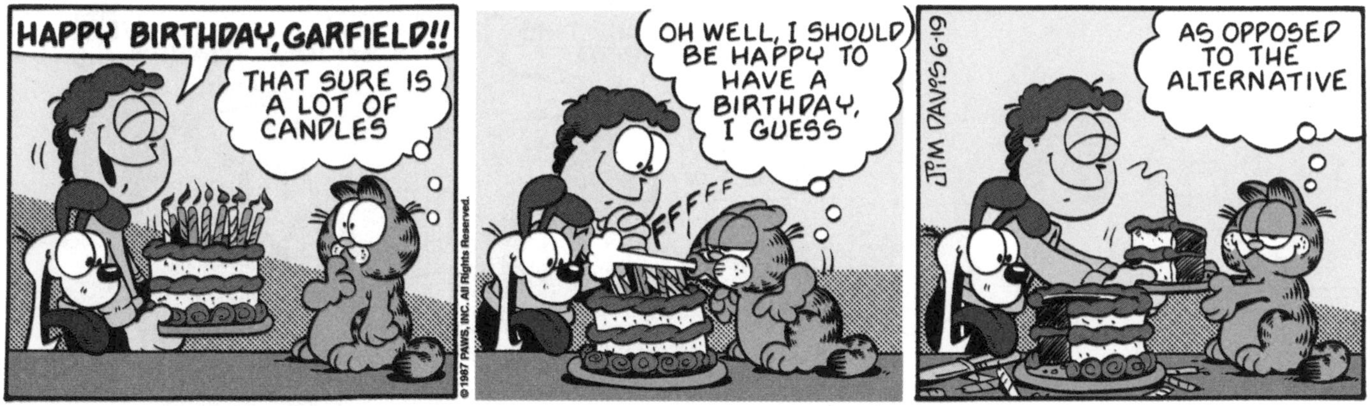
HAPPY BIRTHDAY, GARFIELD!!
THAT SURE IS A LOT OF CANDLES
© 1987 PAWS, INC. All Rights Reserved.
OH WELL, I SHOULD BE HAPPY TO HAVE A BIRTHDAY, I GUESS
FFFFF
JIM DAVIS 6-19
AS OPPOSED TO THE ALTERNATIVE

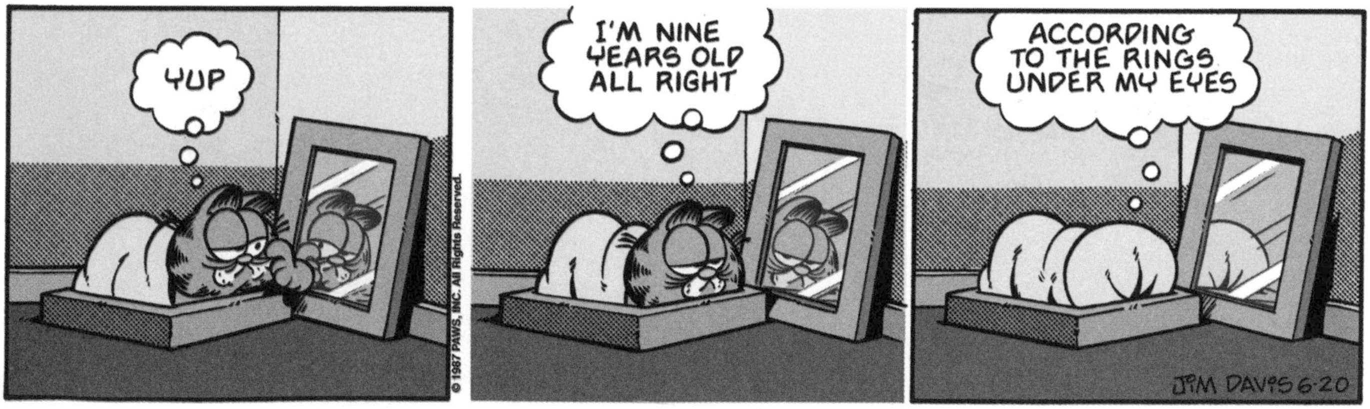
YUP
© 1987 PAWS, INC. All Rights Reserved.
I'M NINE YEARS OLD ALL RIGHT
ACCORDING TO THE RINGS UNDER MY EYES
JIM DAVIS 6-20

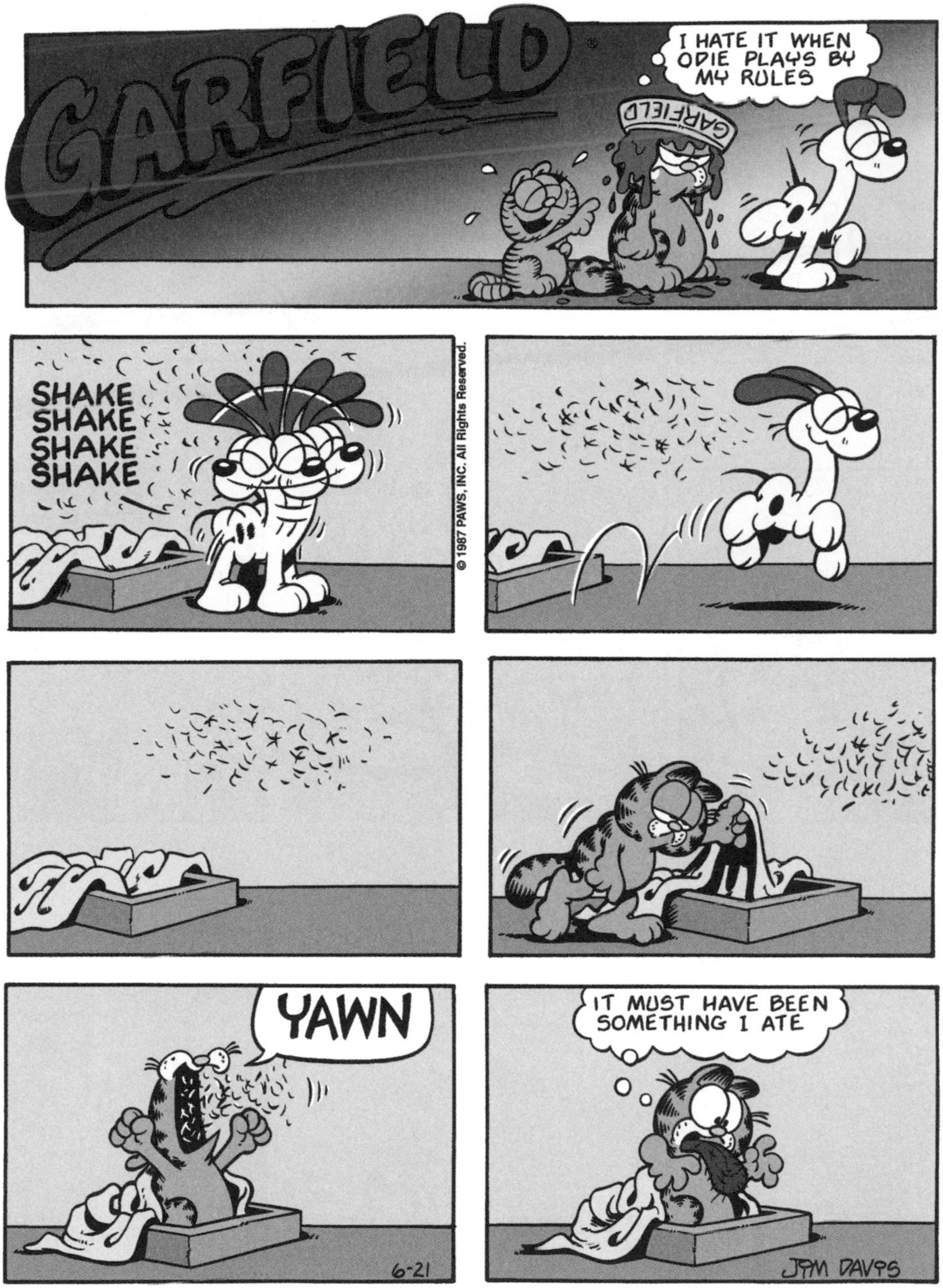
GARFIELD
I HATE IT WHEN ODIE PLAYS BY MY RULES
GARFIELD
SHAKE SHAKE SHAKE SHAKE
© 1987 PAWS, INC. All Rights Reserved.
YAWN
6-21
IT MUST HAVE BEEN SOMETHING I ATE
JIM DAVIS

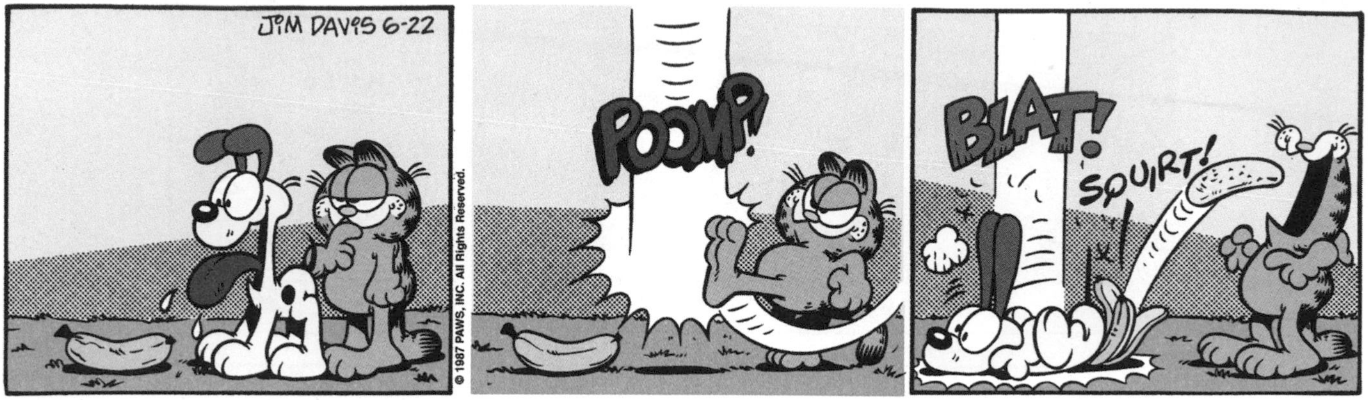
JIM DAVIS 6-22
© 1987 PAWS, INC. All Rights Reserved.
POOMP!
BLAT!
SQUIRT!

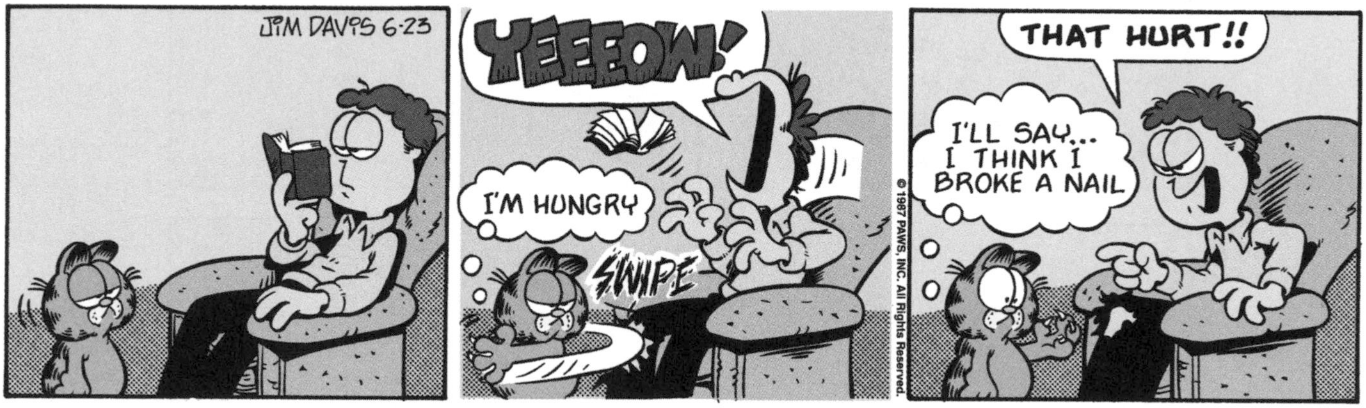
JIM DAVIS 6-23
YEEEOW!
I'M HUNGRY
SWIPE
© 1987 PAWS, INC. All Rights Reserved.
THAT HURT!!
I'LL SAY... I THINK I BROKE A NAIL

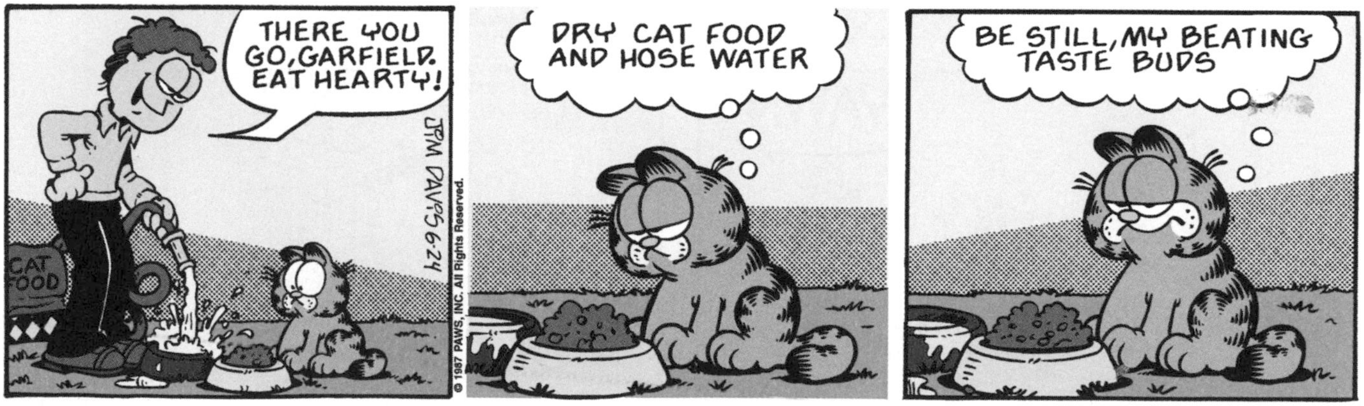
THERE YOU GO, GARFIELD. EAT HEARTY!
CAT FOOD
JIM DAVIS 6-24
© 1987 PAWS, INC. All Rights Reserved.
DRY CAT FOOD AND HOSE WATER
BE STILL, MY BEATING TASTE BUDS

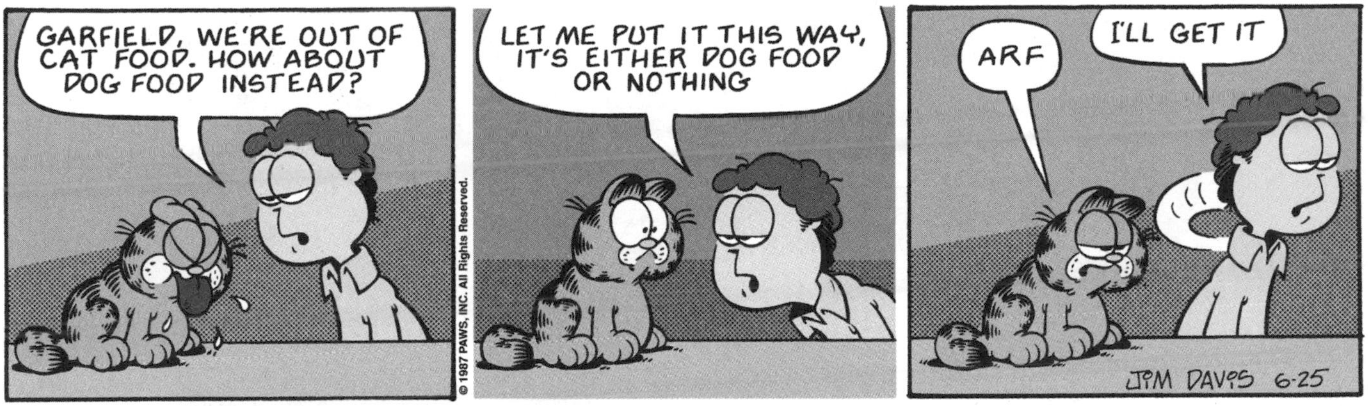
GARFIELD, WE'RE OUT OF CAT FOOD. HOW ABOUT DOG FOOD INSTEAD?
© 1987 PAWS, INC. All Rights Reserved.
LET ME PUT IT THIS WAY, IT'S EITHER DOG FOOD OR NOTHING
ARF
I'LL GET IT
JIM DAVIS 6-25

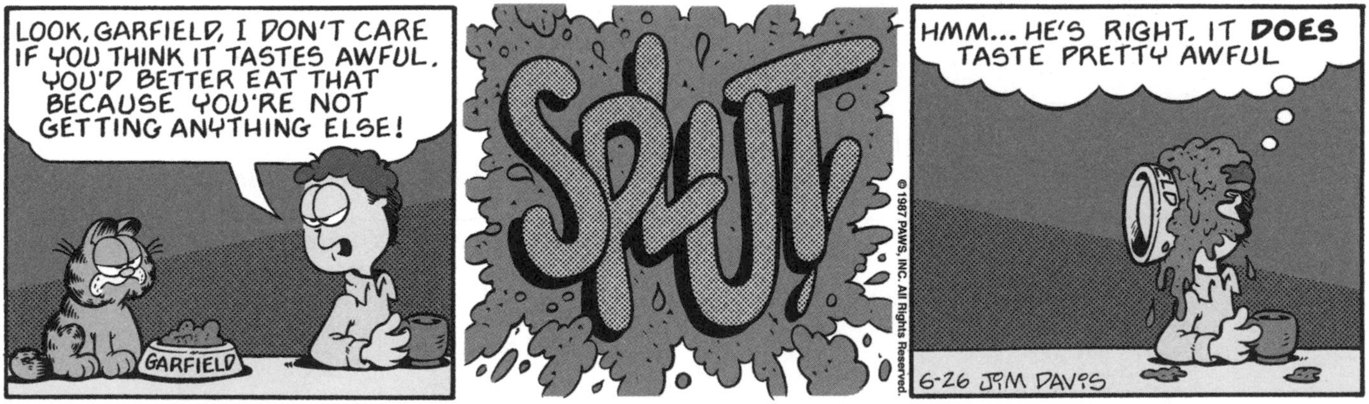
LOOK, GARFIELD, I DON'T CARE IF YOU THINK IT TASTES AWFUL. YOU'D BETTER EAT THAT BECAUSE YOU'RE NOT GETTING ANYTHING ELSE!
GARFIELD
SPLUT
© 1987 PAWS, INC. All Rights Reserved.
HMM... HE'S RIGHT. IT **DOES** TASTE PRETTY AWFUL
6-26 JIM DAVIS

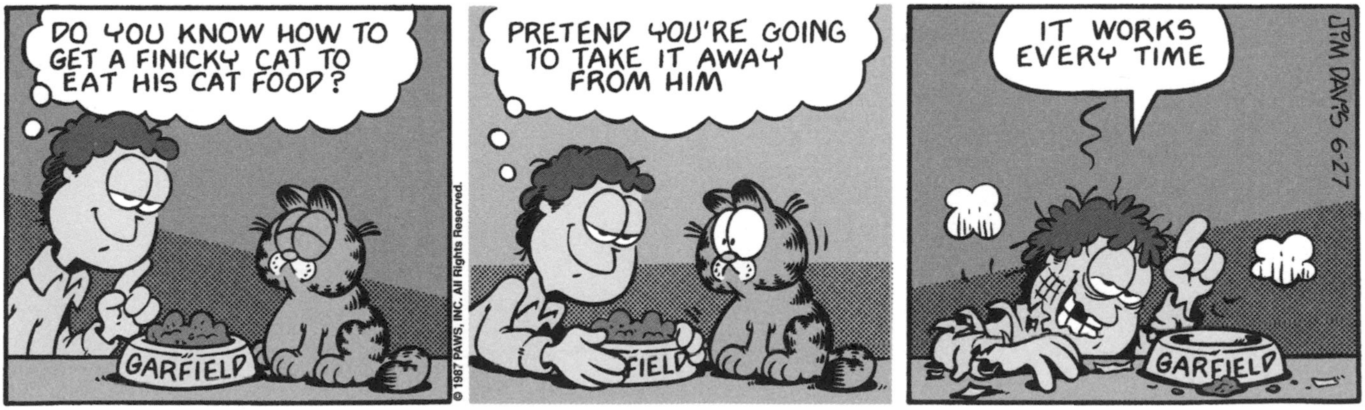
DO YOU KNOW HOW TO GET A FINICKY CAT TO EAT HIS CAT FOOD?
GARFIELD
© 1987 PAWS, INC. All Rights Reserved.
PRETEND YOU'RE GOING TO TAKE IT AWAY FROM HIM
IT WORKS EVERY TIME
GARFIELD
JIM DAVIS 6-27

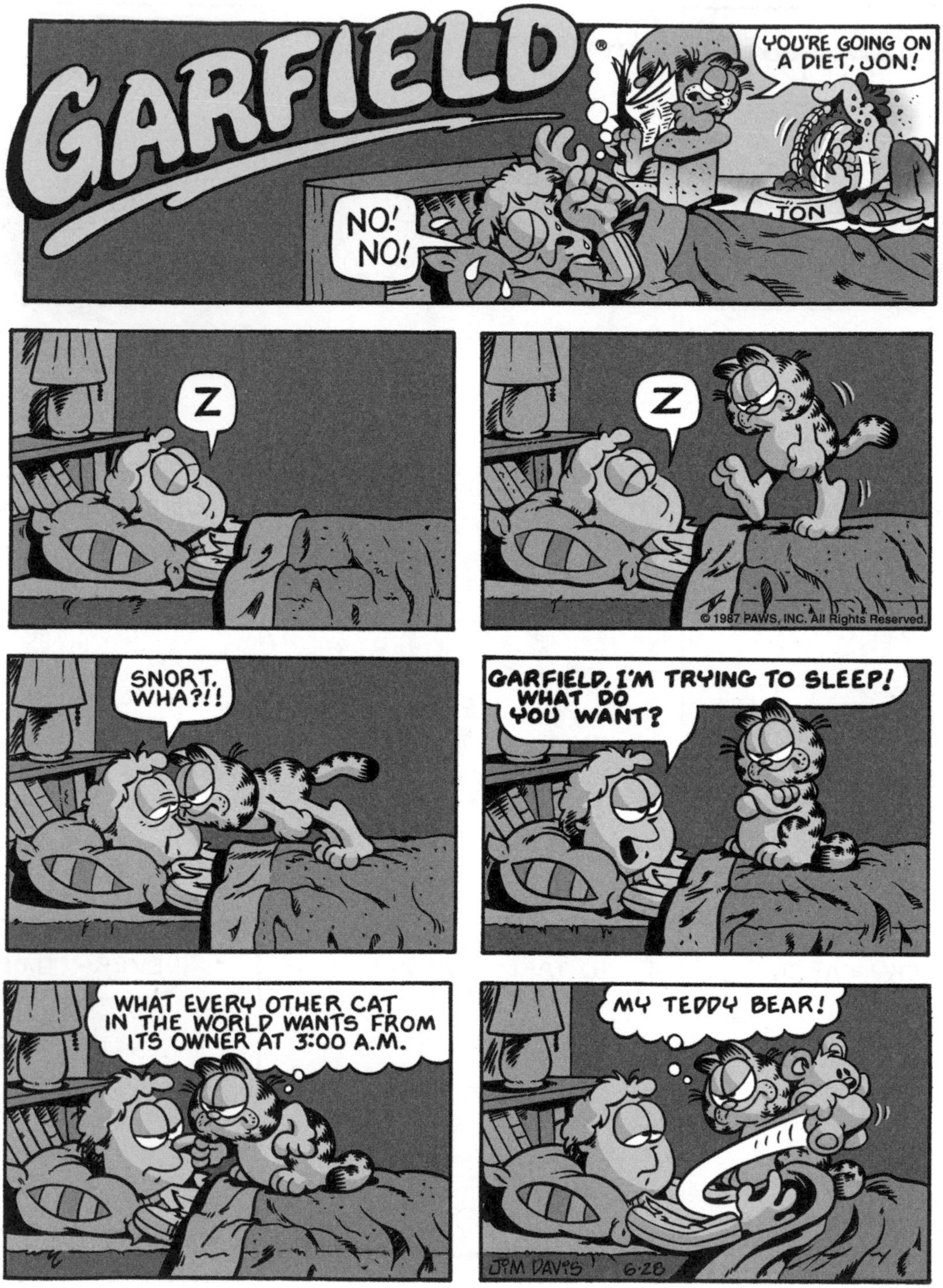
GARFIELD
YOU'RE GOING ON A DIET, JON!
JON
NO! NO!
Z
Z
© 1987 PAWS, INC. All Rights Reserved.
SNORT. WHA?!!
GARFIELD, I'M TRYING TO SLEEP! WHAT DO YOU WANT?
WHAT EVERY OTHER CAT IN THE WORLD WANTS FROM ITS OWNER AT 3:00 A.M.
MY TEDDY BEAR!
JIM DAVIS 6·28

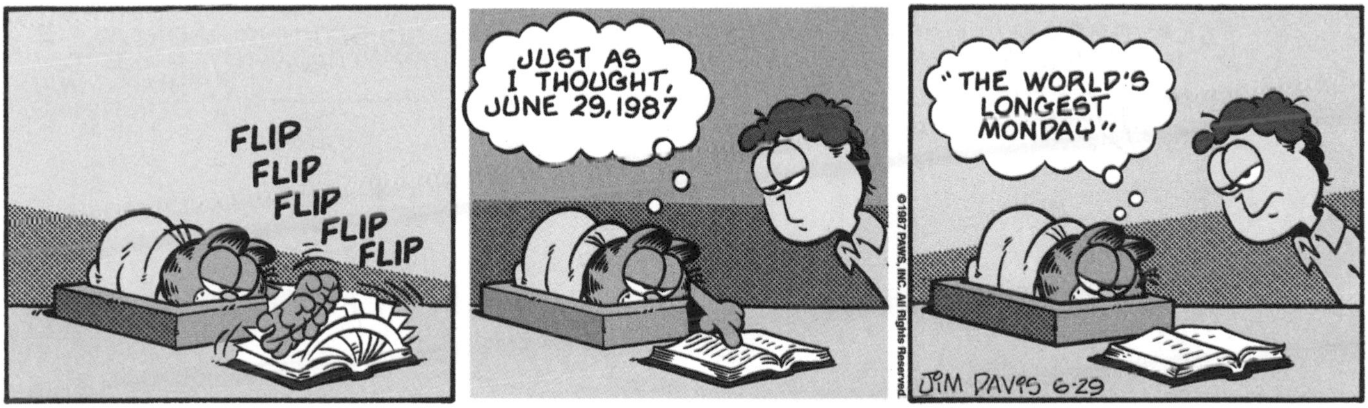
FLIP
FLIP
FLIP
FLIP
FLIP
JUST AS I THOUGHT, JUNE 29, 1987
"THE WORLD'S LONGEST MONDAY"
© 1987 PAWS, INC. All Rights Reserved.
JIM DAVIS 6-29

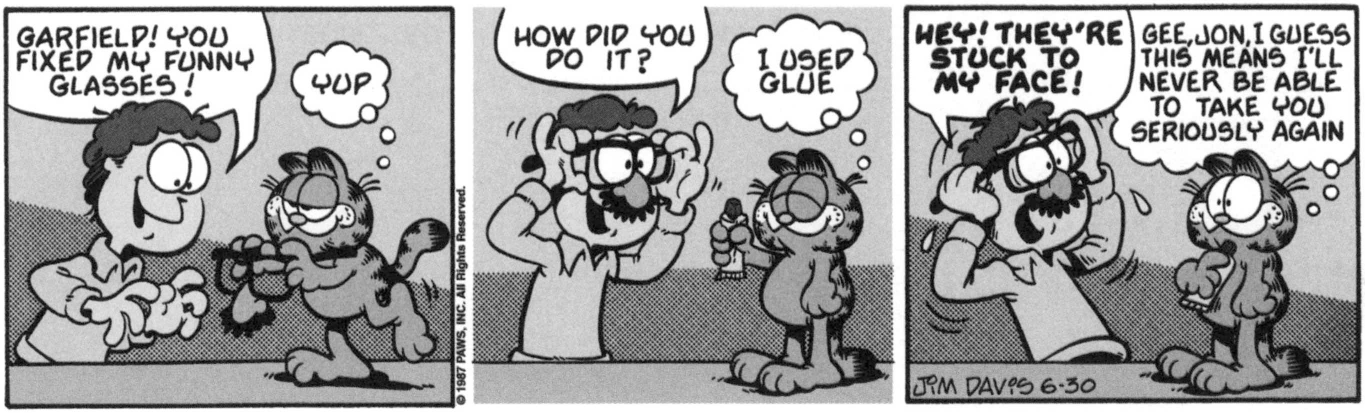
GARFIELD! YOU FIXED MY FUNNY GLASSES!
YUP
© 1987 PAWS, INC. All Rights Reserved.
HOW DID YOU DO IT?
I USED GLUE
HEY! THEY'RE STUCK TO MY FACE!
GEE, JON, I GUESS THIS MEANS I'LL NEVER BE ABLE TO TAKE YOU SERIOUSLY AGAIN
JIM DAVIS 6-30

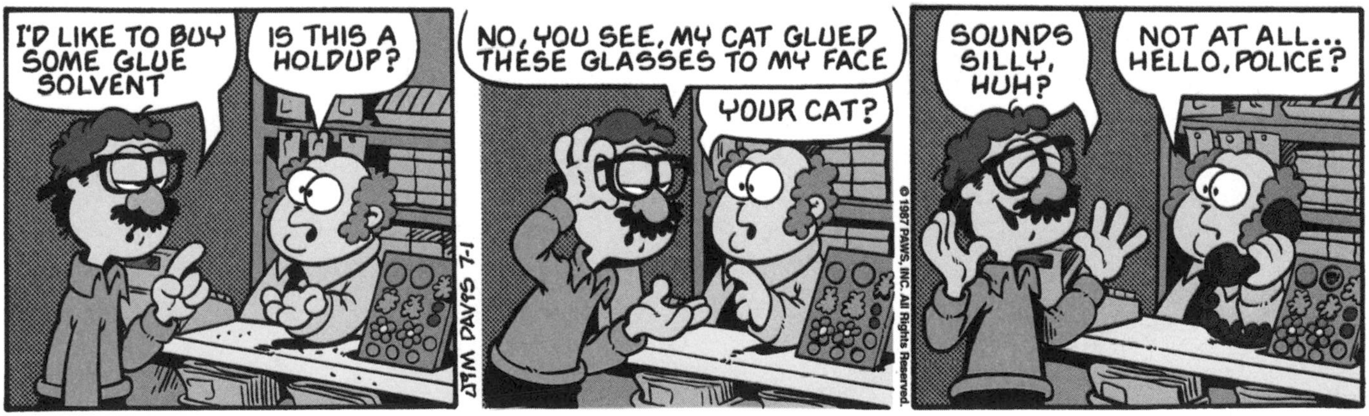
I'D LIKE TO BUY SOME GLUE SOLVENT
IS THIS A HOLDUP?
JIM DAVIS 7-1
NO, YOU SEE, MY CAT GLUED THESE GLASSES TO MY FACE
YOUR CAT?
© 1987 PAWS, INC. All Rights Reserved.
SOUNDS SILLY, HUH?
NOT AT ALL... HELLO, POLICE?

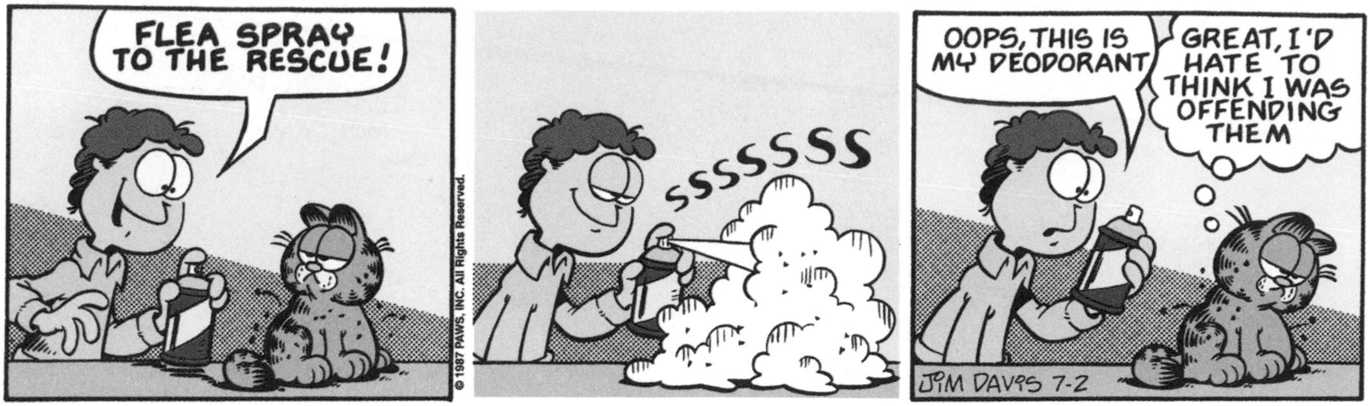
FLEA SPRAY TO THE RESCUE!
SSSSSSS
OOPS, THIS IS MY DEODORANT
GREAT, I'D HATE TO THINK I WAS OFFENDING THEM
JIM DAVIS 7-2

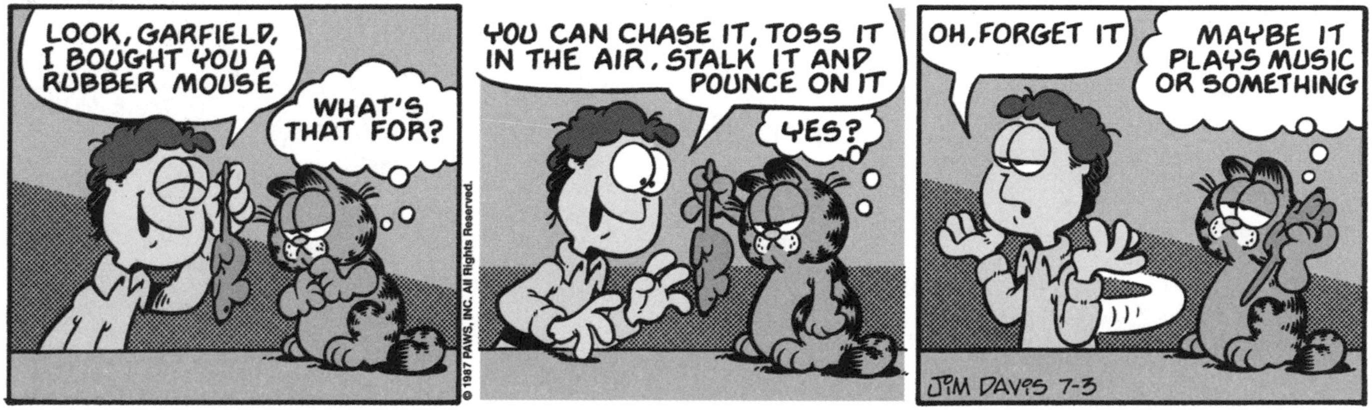
LOOK, GARFIELD, I BOUGHT YOU A RUBBER MOUSE
WHAT'S THAT FOR?
YOU CAN CHASE IT, TOSS IT IN THE AIR, STALK IT AND POUNCE ON IT
YES?
OH, FORGET IT
MAYBE IT PLAYS MUSIC OR SOMETHING
JIM DAVIS 7-3

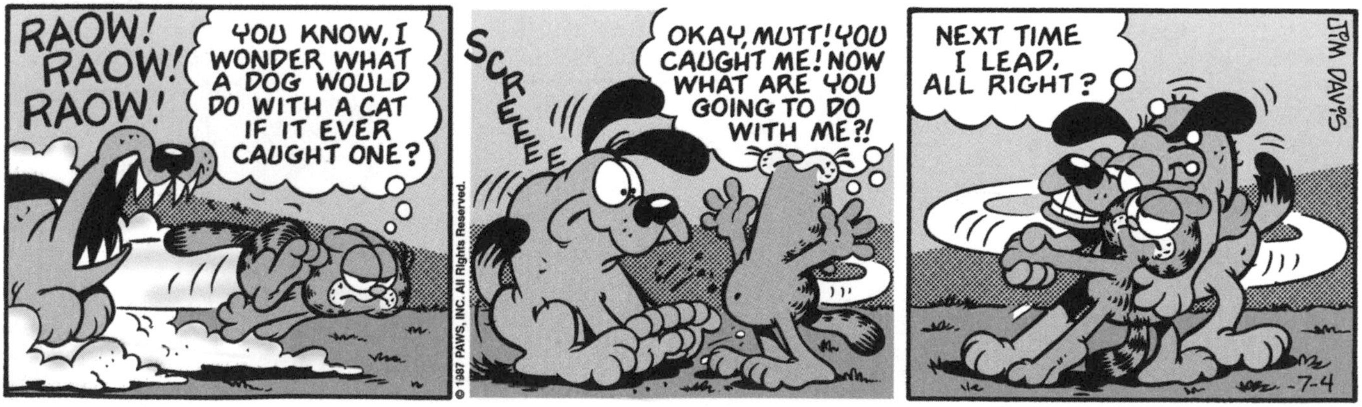
RAOW! RAOW! RAOW!
YOU KNOW, I WONDER WHAT A DOG WOULD DO WITH A CAT IF IT EVER CAUGHT ONE?
SCREEEE
OKAY, MUTT! YOU CAUGHT ME! NOW WHAT ARE YOU GOING TO DO WITH ME?!
NEXT TIME I LEAD, ALL RIGHT?
JIM DAVIS
7-4

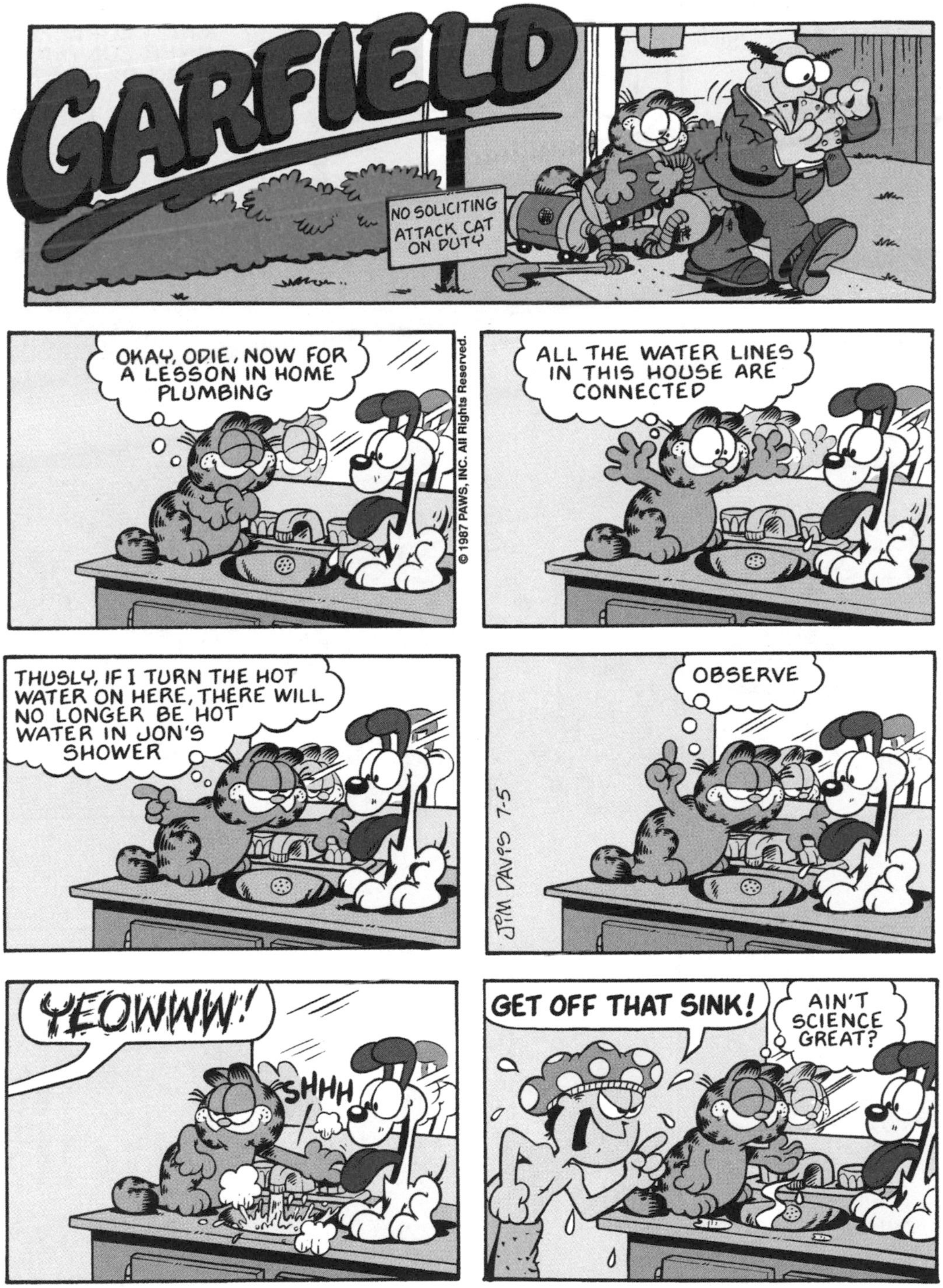
GARFIELD
NO SOLICITING
ATTACK CAT
ON DUTY
OKAY, ODIE, NOW FOR A LESSON IN HOME PLUMBING
© 1987 PAWS, INC. All Rights Reserved.
ALL THE WATER LINES IN THIS HOUSE ARE CONNECTED
THUSLY, IF I TURN THE HOT WATER ON HERE, THERE WILL NO LONGER BE HOT WATER IN JON'S SHOWER
JIM DAVIS 7-5
OBSERVE
YEOWWW!
SHHH
GET OFF THAT SINK!
AIN'T SCIENCE GREAT?

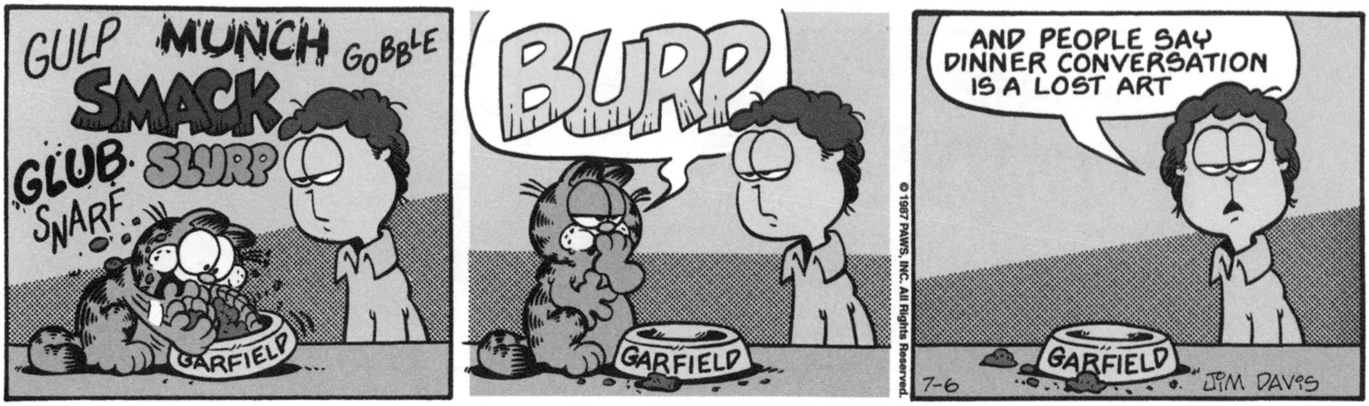
GULP
MUNCH
GOBBLE
SMACK
GLUB
SLURP
SNARF
BURP
AND PEOPLE SAY DINNER CONVERSATION IS A LOST ART
© 1987 PAWS, INC. All Rights Reserved.
7-6
JIM DAVIS

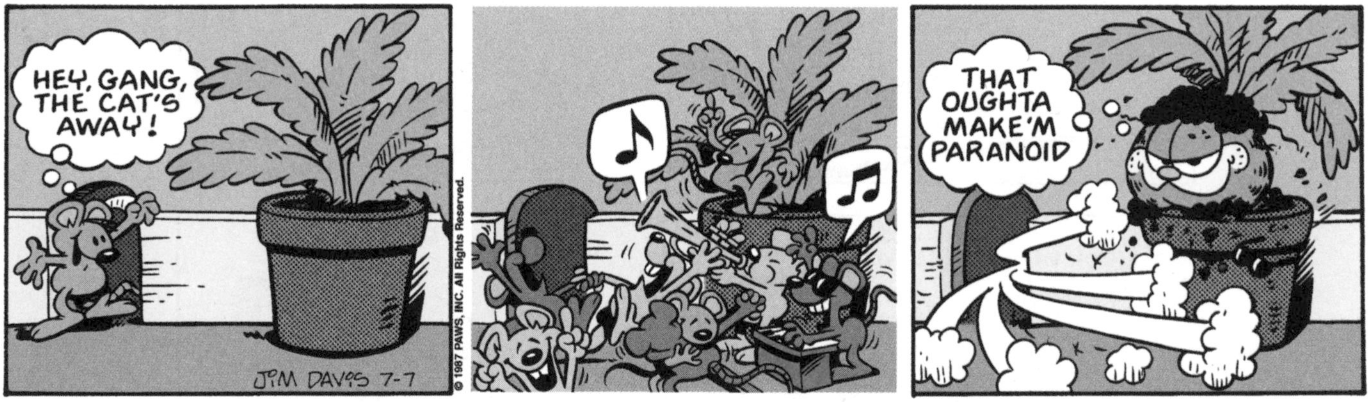
HEY, GANG, THE CAT'S AWAY!
JIM DAVIS 7-7
© 1987 PAWS, INC. All Rights Reserved.
THAT OUGHTA MAKE'M PARANOID

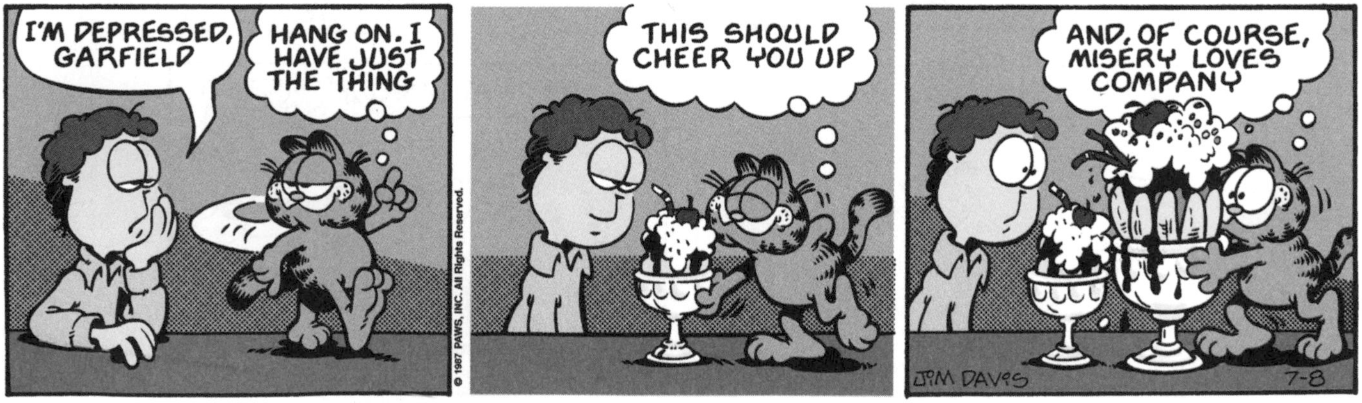
I'M DEPRESSED, GARFIELD
HANG ON. I HAVE JUST THE THING
© 1987 PAWS, INC. All Rights Reserved.
THIS SHOULD CHEER YOU UP
AND, OF COURSE, MISERY LOVES COMPANY
JIM DAVIS
7-8

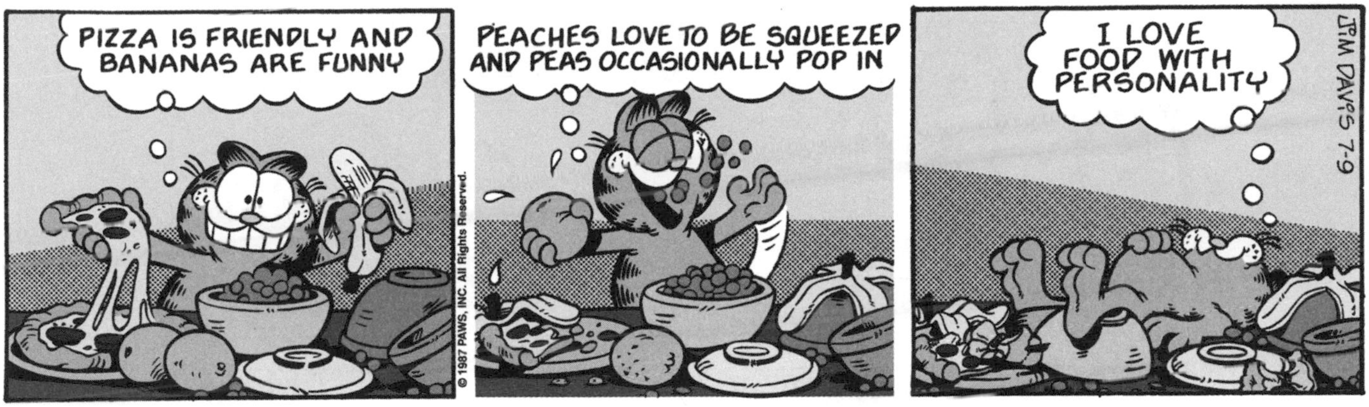
PIZZA IS FRIENDLY AND BANANAS ARE FUNNY
© 1987 PAWS, INC. All Rights Reserved.
PEACHES LOVE TO BE SQUEEZED AND PEAS OCCASIONALLY POP IN
I LOVE FOOD WITH PERSONALITY
JIM DAVIS 7-9

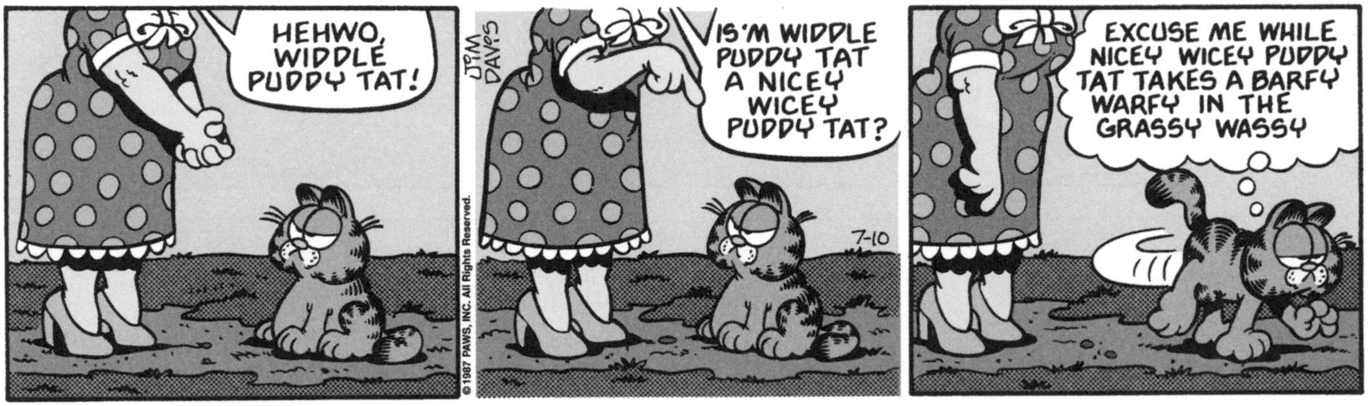
HEHWO, WIDDLE PUDDY TAT!
© 1987 PAWS, INC. All Rights Reserved.
JIM DAVIS
IS'M WIDDLE PUDDY TAT A NICEY WICEY PUDDY TAT?
7-10
EXCUSE ME WHILE NICEY WICEY PUDDY TAT TAKES A BARFY WARFY IN THE GRASSY WASSY

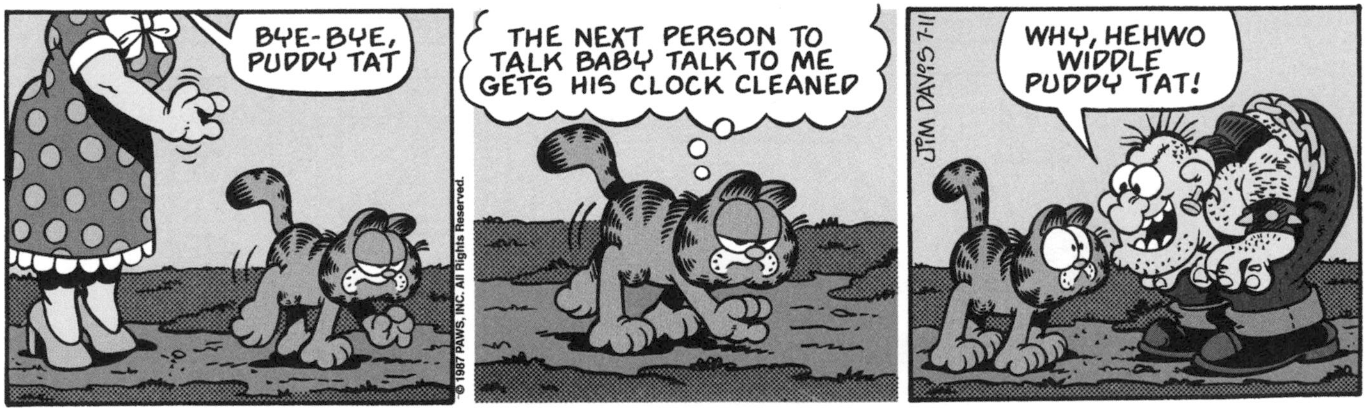
BYE-BYE, PUDDY TAT
© 1987 PAWS, INC. All Rights Reserved.
THE NEXT PERSON TO TALK BABY TALK TO ME GETS HIS CLOCK CLEANED
JIM DAVIS 7-11
WHY, HEHWO WIDDLE PUDDY TAT!

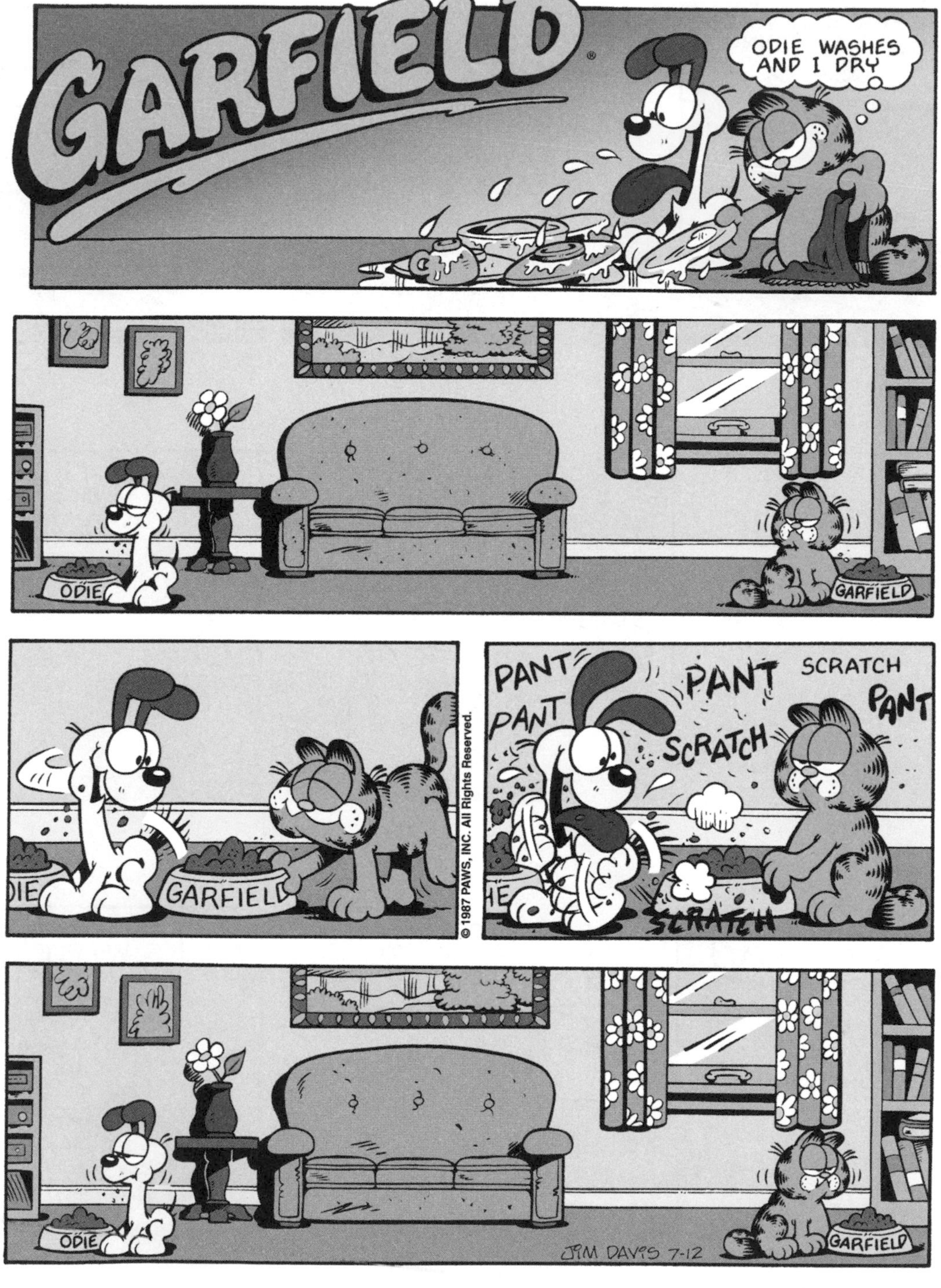
GARFIELD
ODIE WASHES AND I DRY
ODIE
GARFIELD
DIE
GARFIELD
© 1987 PAWS, INC. All Rights Reserved.
PANT
PANT
PANT
SCRATCH
SCRATCH
PANT
SCRATCH
ODIE
GARFIELD
JIM DAVIS 7-12

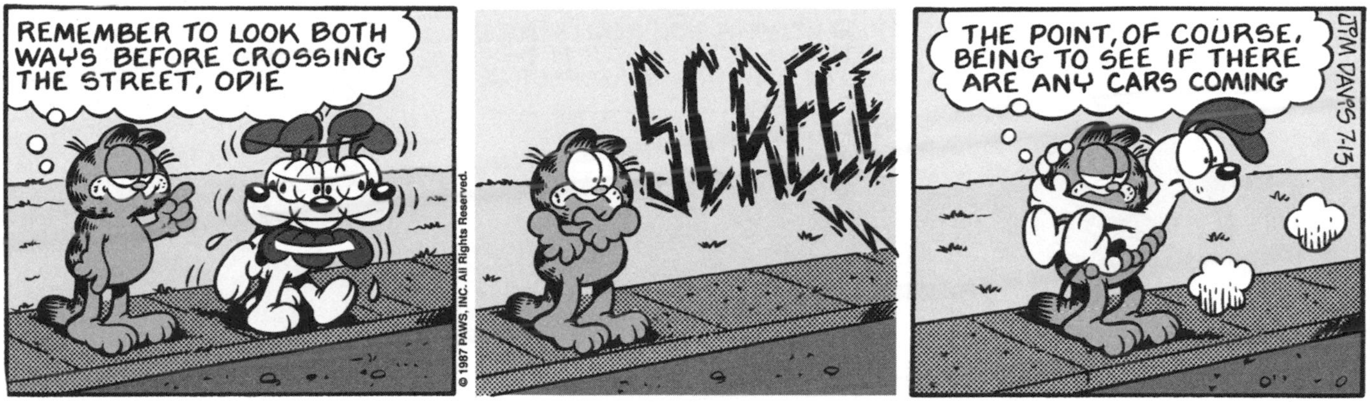
REMEMBER TO LOOK BOTH WAYS BEFORE CROSSING THE STREET, ODIE
© 1987 PAWS, INC. All Rights Reserved.
SCREEE
THE POINT, OF COURSE, BEING TO SEE IF THERE ARE ANY CARS COMING
JIM DAVIS 7-13

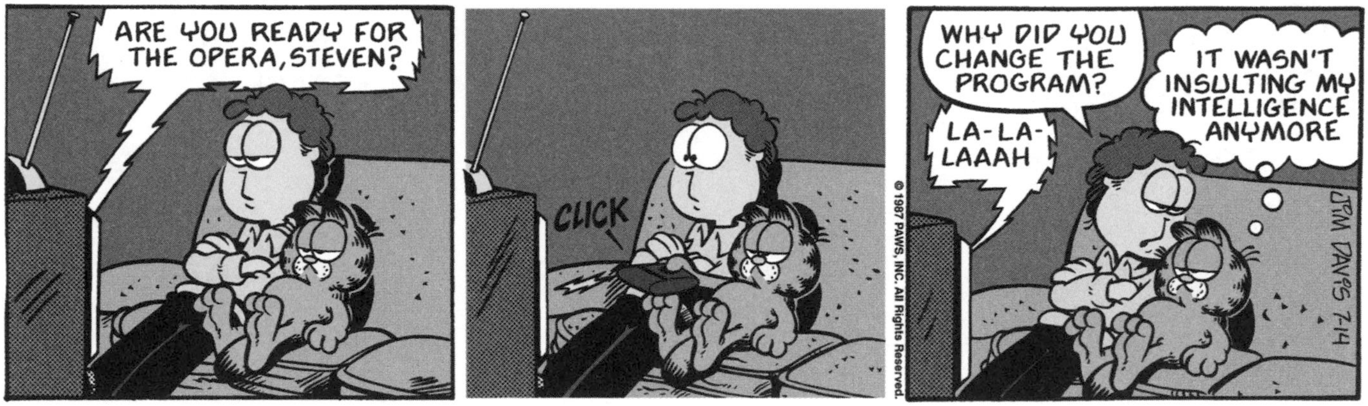
ARE YOU READY FOR THE OPERA, STEVEN?
CLICK
© 1987 PAWS, INC. All Rights Reserved.
WHY DID YOU CHANGE THE PROGRAM?
LA-LA-LAAAH
IT WASN'T INSULTING MY INTELLIGENCE ANYMORE
JIM DAVIS 7-14

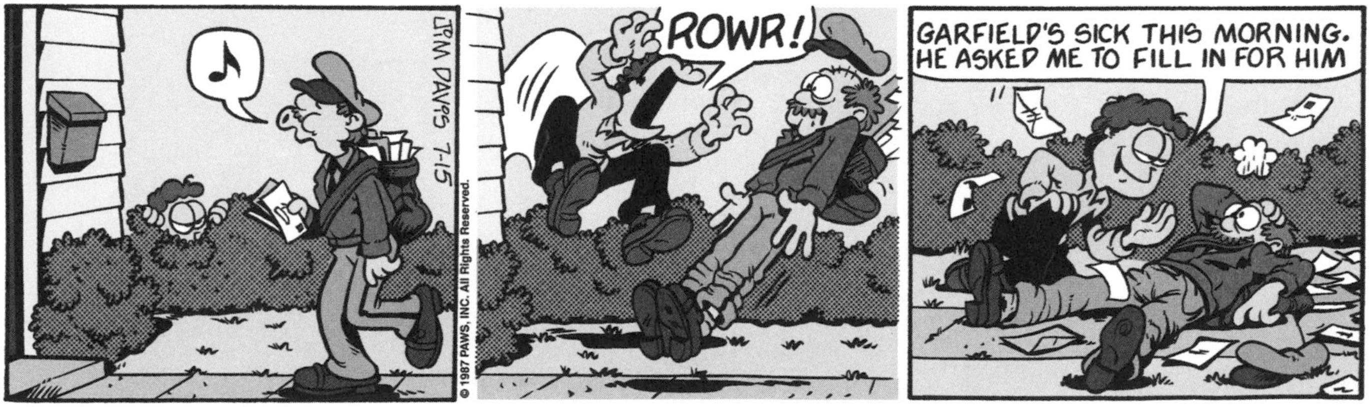
♪
JIM DAVIS 7-15
© 1987 PAWS, INC. All Rights Reserved.
ROWR!
GARFIELD'S SICK THIS MORNING. HE ASKED ME TO FILL IN FOR HIM

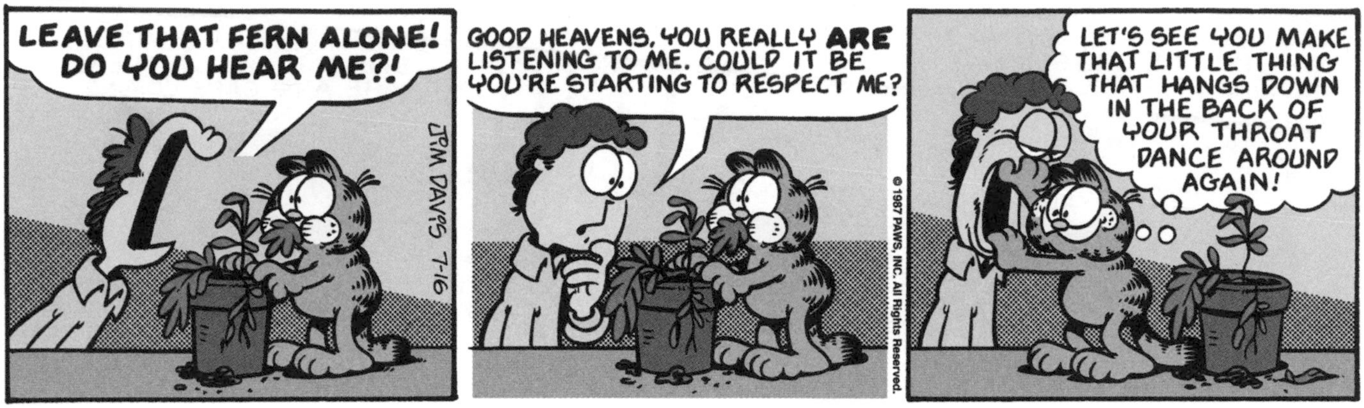
LEAVE THAT FERN ALONE! DO YOU HEAR ME?!
JIM DAVIS 7-16
GOOD HEAVENS, YOU REALLY **ARE** LISTENING TO ME. COULD IT BE YOU'RE STARTING TO RESPECT ME?
© 1987 PAWS, INC. All Rights Reserved.
LET'S SEE YOU MAKE THAT LITTLE THING THAT HANGS DOWN IN THE BACK OF YOUR THROAT DANCE AROUND AGAIN!

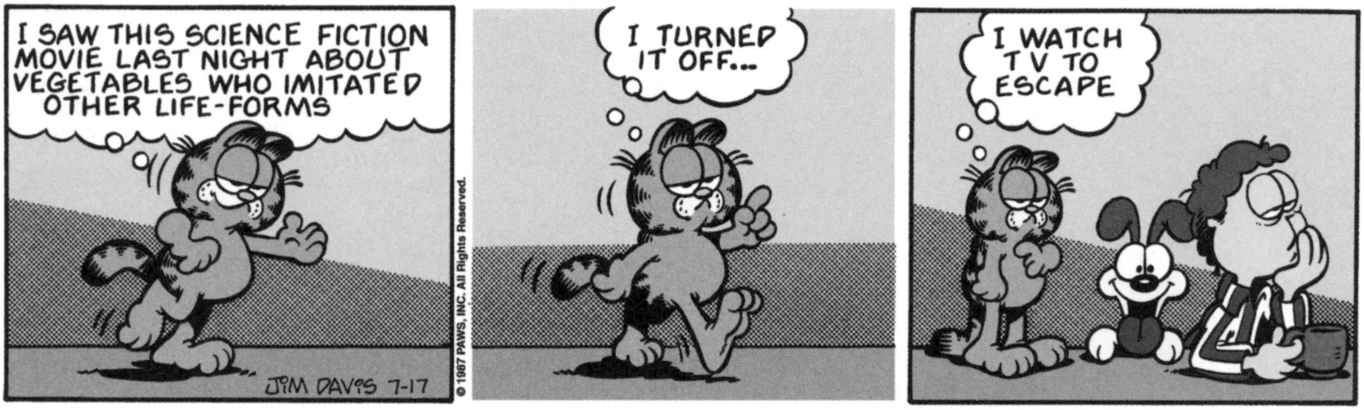
I SAW THIS SCIENCE FICTION MOVIE LAST NIGHT ABOUT VEGETABLES WHO IMITATED OTHER LIFE-FORMS
JIM DAVIS 7-17
© 1987 PAWS, INC. All Rights Reserved.
I TURNED IT OFF...
I WATCH TV TO ESCAPE

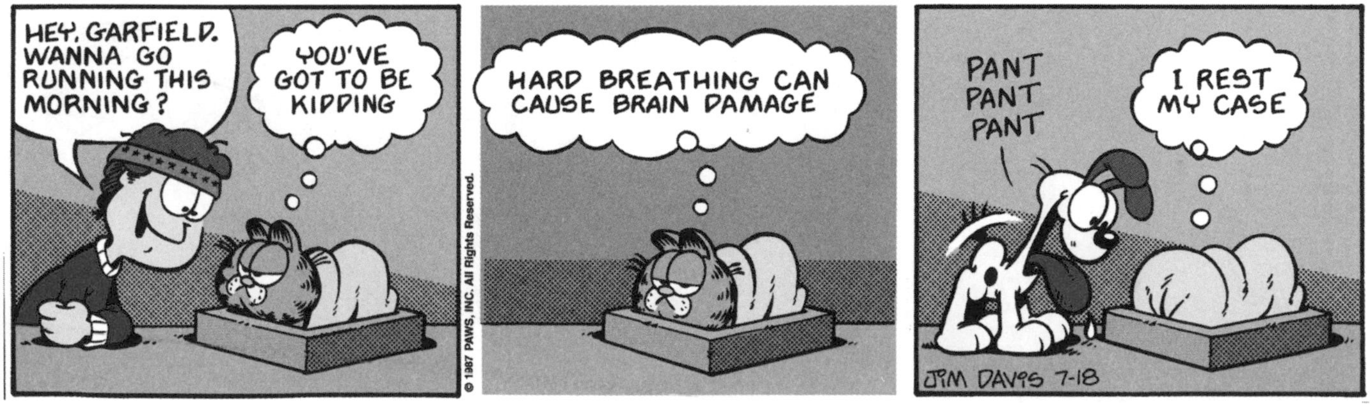
HEY, GARFIELD. WANNA GO RUNNING THIS MORNING?
YOU'VE GOT TO BE KIDDING
© 1987 PAWS, INC. All Rights Reserved.
HARD BREATHING CAN CAUSE BRAIN DAMAGE
PANT PANT PANT
I REST MY CASE
JIM DAVIS 7-18

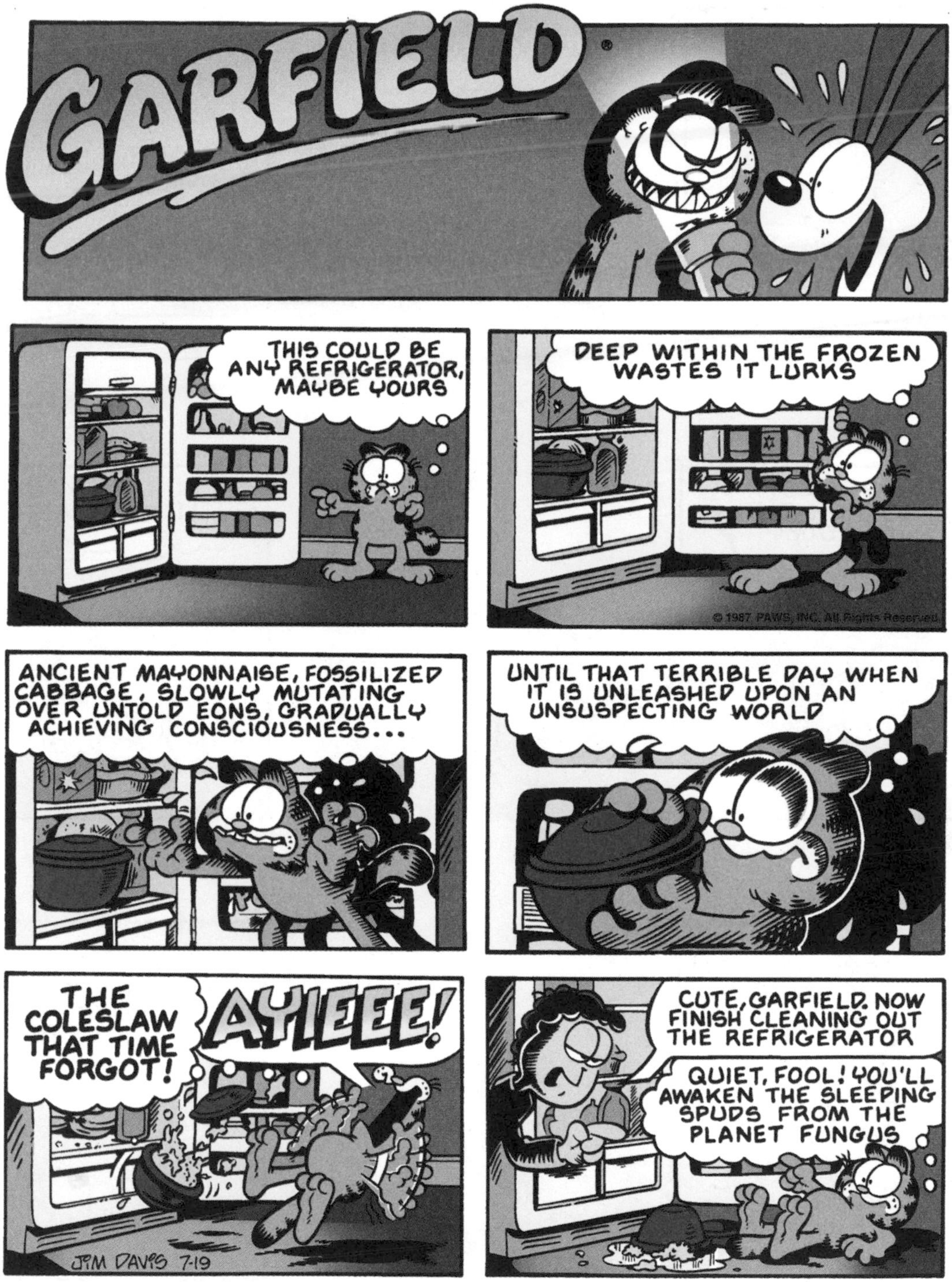
GARFIELD
THIS COULD BE ANY REFRIGERATOR, MAYBE YOURS
DEEP WITHIN THE FROZEN WASTES IT LURKS
© 1987 PAWS, INC. All Rights Reserved
ANCIENT MAYONNAISE, FOSSILIZED CABBAGE, SLOWLY MUTATING OVER UNTOLD EONS, GRADUALLY ACHIEVING CONSCIOUSNESS...
UNTIL THAT TERRIBLE DAY WHEN IT IS UNLEASHED UPON AN UNSUSPECTING WORLD
THE COLESLAW THAT TIME FORGOT!
AYIEEEE!
JIM DAVIS 7-19
CUTE, GARFIELD. NOW FINISH CLEANING OUT THE REFRIGERATOR
QUIET, FOOL! YOU'LL AWAKEN THE SLEEPING SPUDS FROM THE PLANET FUNGUS

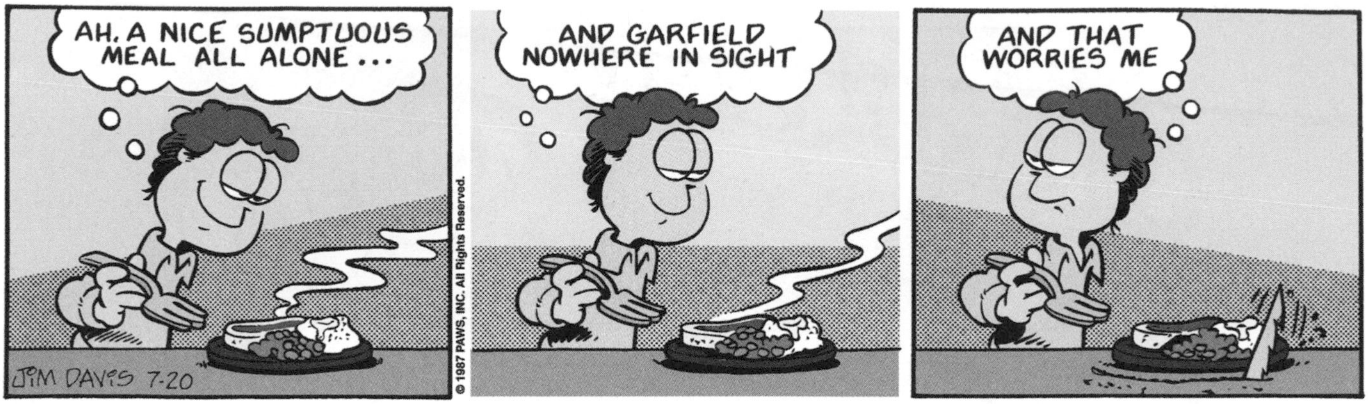
AH, A NICE SUMPTUOUS MEAL ALL ALONE...
AND GARFIELD NOWHERE IN SIGHT
AND THAT WORRIES ME
JIM DAVIS 7-20
© 1987 PAWS, INC. All Rights Reserved.

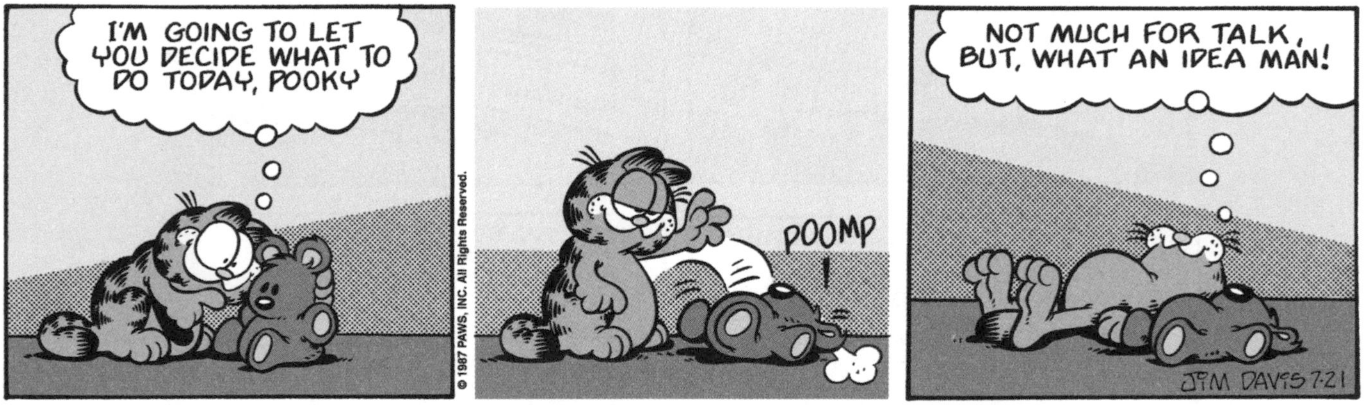
I'M GOING TO LET YOU DECIDE WHAT TO DO TODAY, POOKY
POOMP
!
NOT MUCH FOR TALK, BUT, WHAT AN IDEA MAN!
JIM DAVIS 7-21
© 1987 PAWS, INC. All Rights Reserved.

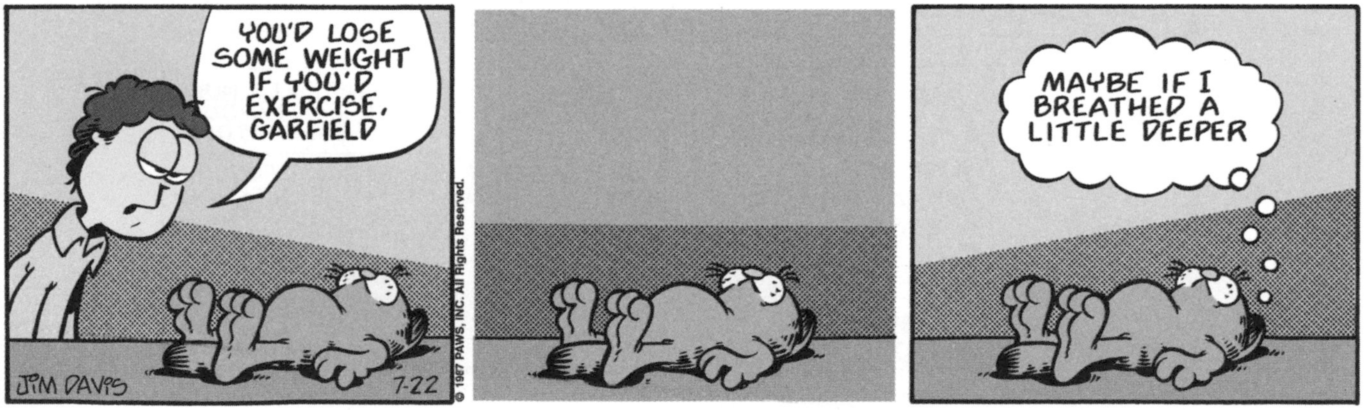
YOU'D LOSE SOME WEIGHT IF YOU'D EXERCISE, GARFIELD
MAYBE IF I BREATHED A LITTLE DEEPER
JIM DAVIS 7-22
© 1987 PAWS, INC. All Rights Reserved.

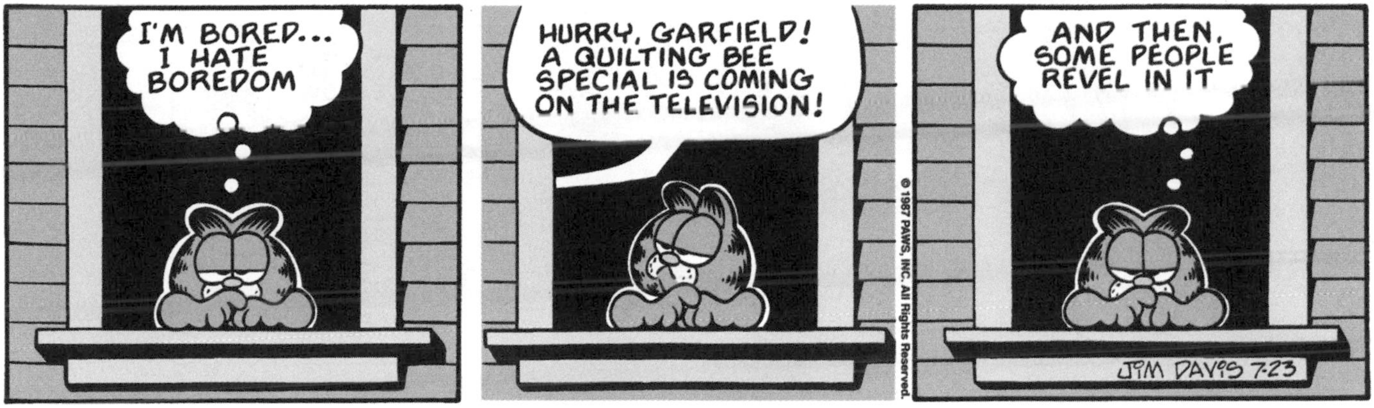
I'M BORED... I HATE BOREDOM
HURRY, GARFIELD! A QUILTING BEE SPECIAL IS COMING ON THE TELEVISION!
© 1987 PAWS, INC. All Rights Reserved.
AND THEN, SOME PEOPLE REVEL IN IT
JIM DAVIS 7-23

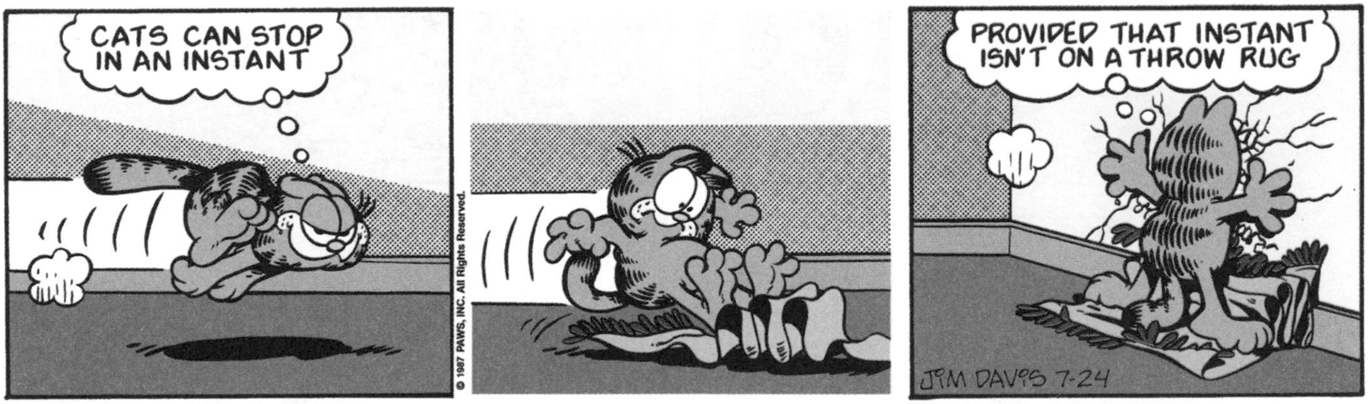
CATS CAN STOP IN AN INSTANT
© 1987 PAWS, INC. All Rights Reserved.
PROVIDED THAT INSTANT ISN'T ON A THROW RUG
JIM DAVIS 7-24

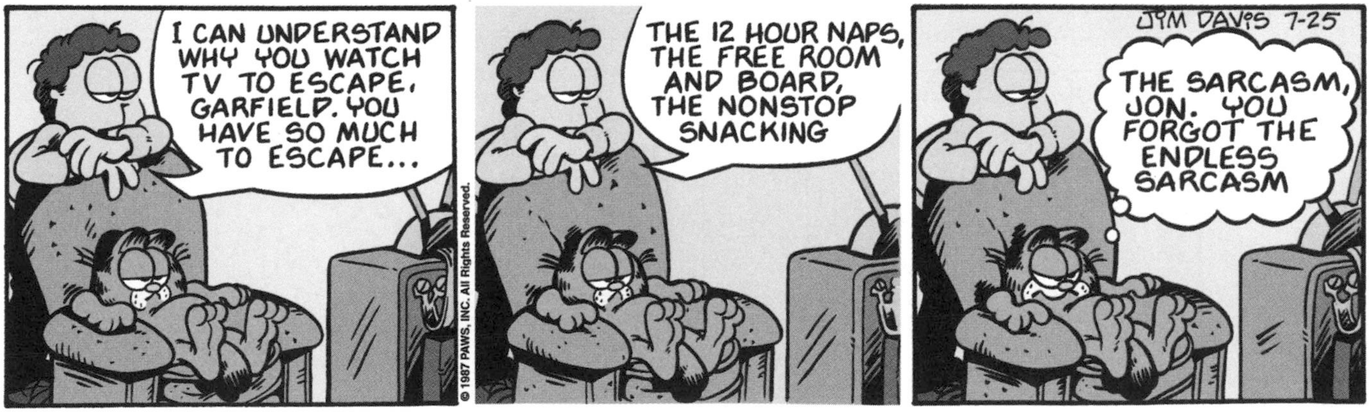
I CAN UNDERSTAND WHY YOU WATCH TV TO ESCAPE, GARFIELD. YOU HAVE SO MUCH TO ESCAPE...
© 1987 PAWS, INC. All Rights Reserved.
THE 12 HOUR NAPS, THE FREE ROOM AND BOARD, THE NONSTOP SNACKING
JIM DAVIS 7-25
THE SARCASM, JON. YOU FORGOT THE ENDLESS SARCASM

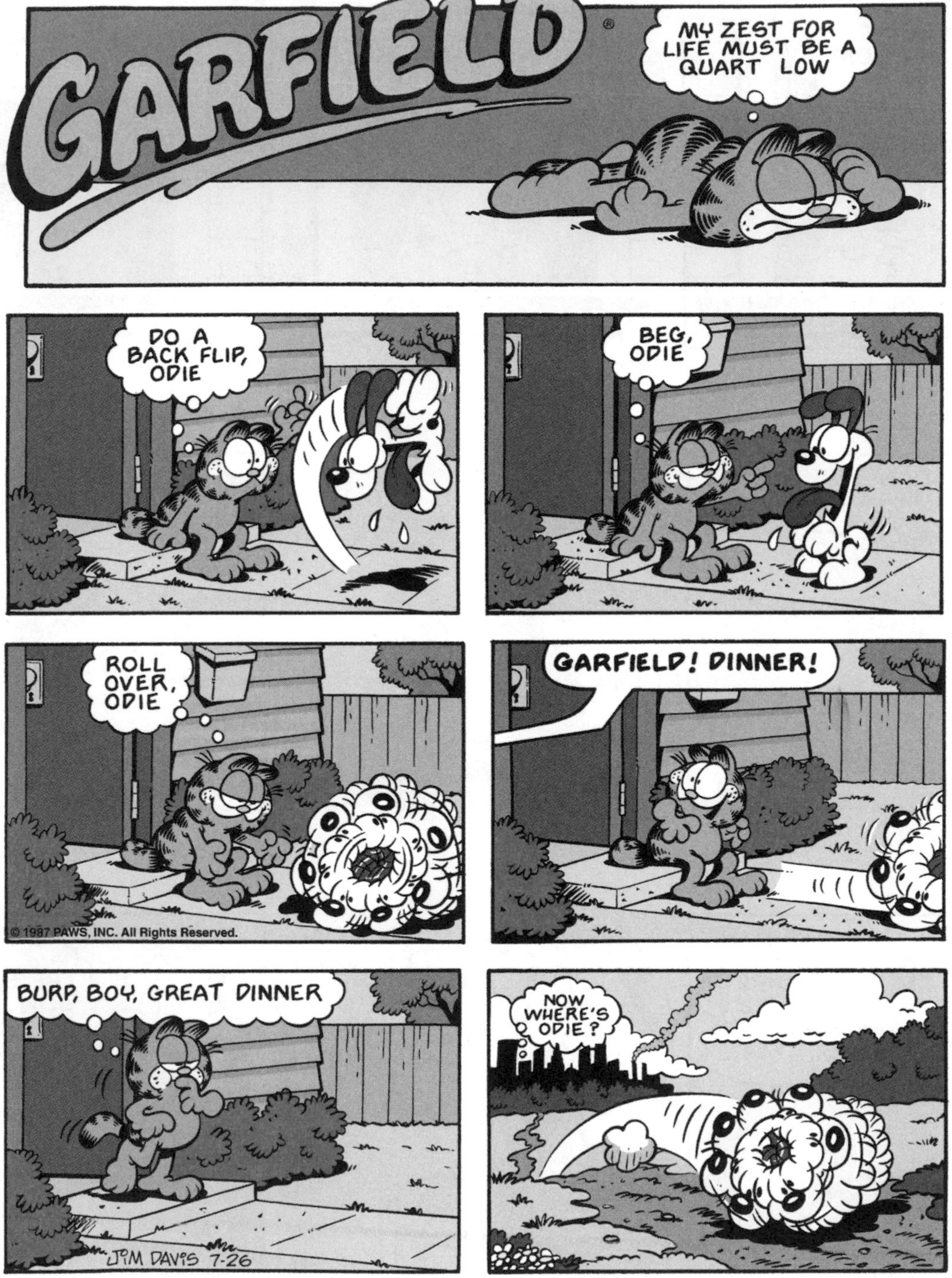
GARFIELD®
MY ZEST FOR LIFE MUST BE A QUART LOW
DO A BACK FLIP, ODIE
BEG, ODIE
ROLL OVER, ODIE
GARFIELD! DINNER!
BURP, BOY, GREAT DINNER
NOW WHERE'S ODIE?
JIM DAVIS 7-26

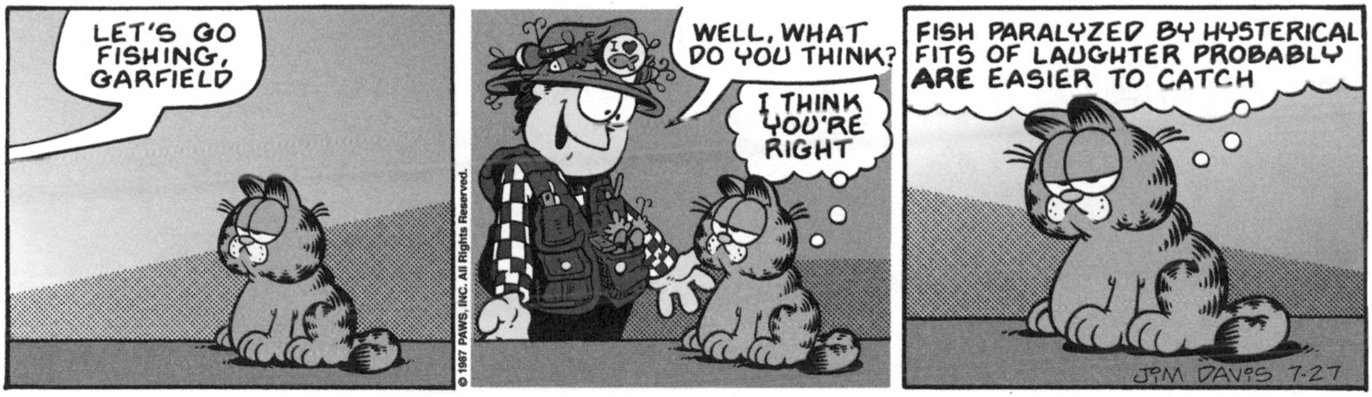
LET'S GO FISHING, GARFIELD
WELL, WHAT DO YOU THINK?
I THINK YOU'RE RIGHT
© 1987 PAWS, INC. All Rights Reserved.
FISH PARALYZED BY HYSTERICAL FITS OF LAUGHTER PROBABLY **ARE** EASIER TO CATCH
JIM DAVIS 7-27

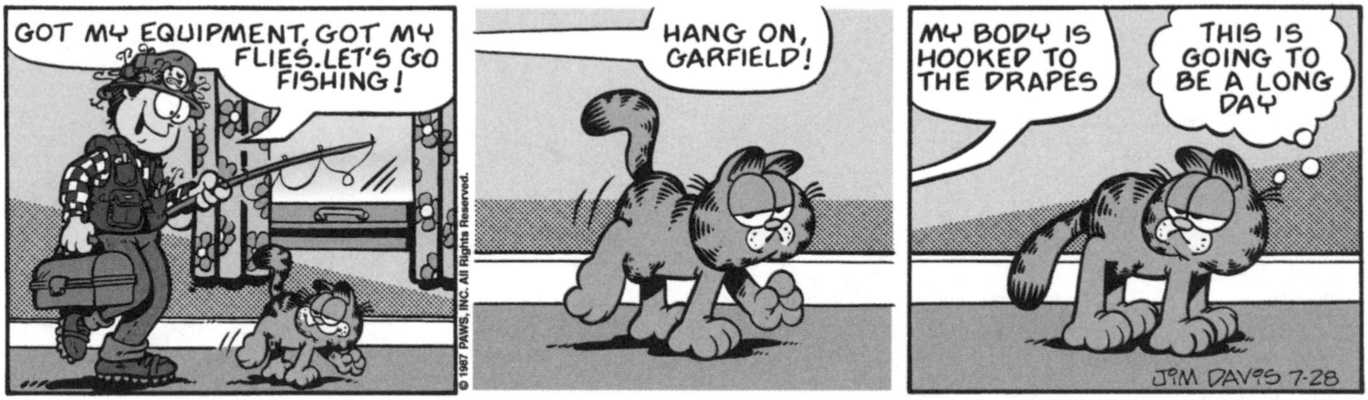
GOT MY EQUIPMENT, GOT MY FLIES. LET'S GO FISHING!
© 1987 PAWS, INC. All Rights Reserved.
HANG ON, GARFIELD!
MY BODY IS HOOKED TO THE DRAPES
THIS IS GOING TO BE A LONG DAY
JIM DAVIS 7-28

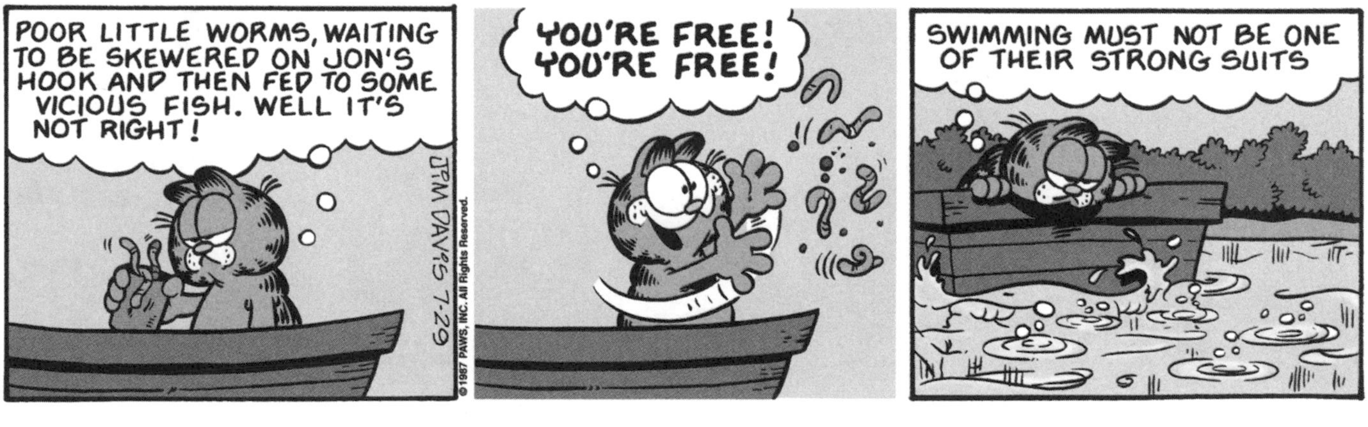
POOR LITTLE WORMS, WAITING TO BE SKEWERED ON JON'S HOOK AND THEN FED TO SOME VICIOUS FISH. WELL IT'S NOT RIGHT!
JIM DAVIS 7-29
© 1987 PAWS, INC. All Rights Reserved.
YOU'RE FREE! YOU'RE FREE!
SWIMMING MUST NOT BE ONE OF THEIR STRONG SUITS

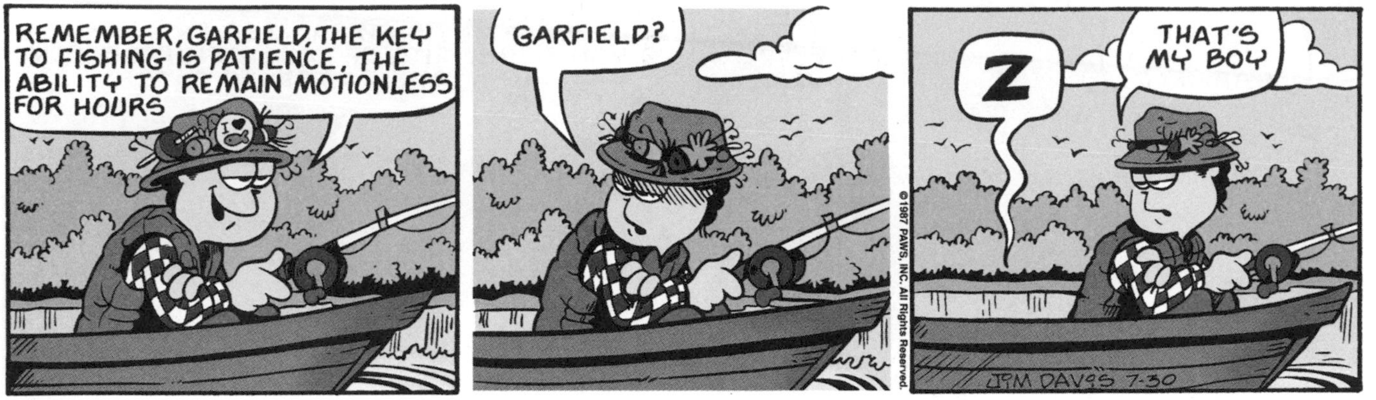
REMEMBER, GARFIELD, THE KEY TO FISHING IS PATIENCE, THE ABILITY TO REMAIN MOTIONLESS FOR HOURS
GARFIELD?
Z
THAT'S MY BOY
JIM DAVIS 7-30
© 1987 PAWS, INC. All Rights Reserved.

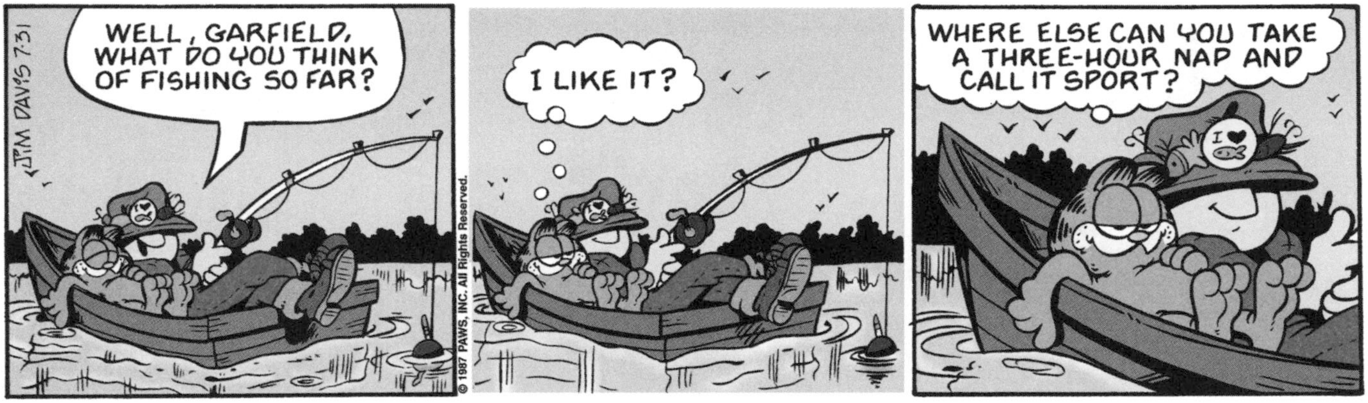
JIM DAVIS 7-31
WELL, GARFIELD, WHAT DO YOU THINK OF FISHING SO FAR?
I LIKE IT?
WHERE ELSE CAN YOU TAKE A THREE-HOUR NAP AND CALL IT SPORT?
© 1987 PAWS, INC. All Rights Reserved.

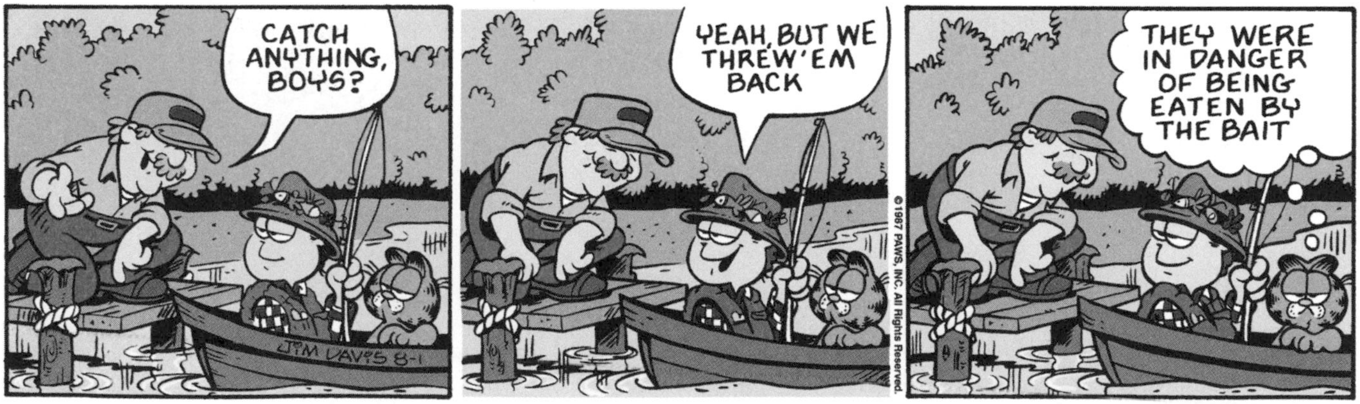
CATCH ANYTHING, BOYS?
YEAH, BUT WE THREW 'EM BACK
THEY WERE IN DANGER OF BEING EATEN BY THE BAIT
JIM DAVIS 8-1
© 1987 PAWS, INC. All Rights Reserved.

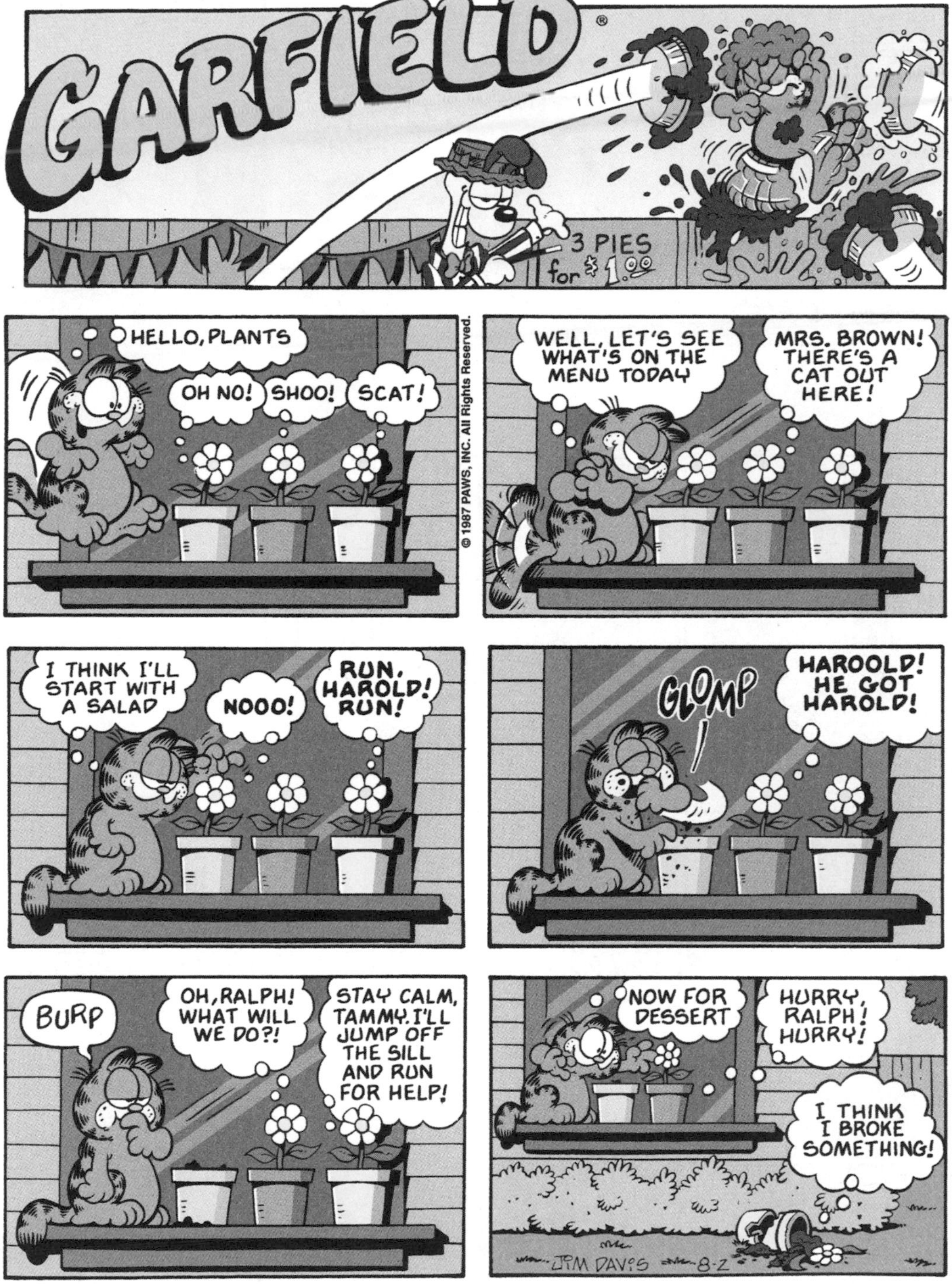
GARFIELD®
3 PIES for $1.00
HELLO, PLANTS
OH NO!
SHOO!
SCAT!
WELL, LET'S SEE WHAT'S ON THE MENU TODAY
MRS. BROWN! THERE'S A CAT OUT HERE!
I THINK I'LL START WITH A SALAD
NOOO!
RUN, HAROLD! RUN!
GLOMP
HAROOLD! HE GOT HAROLD!
BURP
OH, RALPH! WHAT WILL WE DO?!
STAY CALM, TAMMY. I'LL JUMP OFF THE SILL AND RUN FOR HELP!
NOW FOR DESSERT
HURRY, RALPH! HURRY!
I THINK I BROKE SOMETHING!
JIM DAVIS 8-2

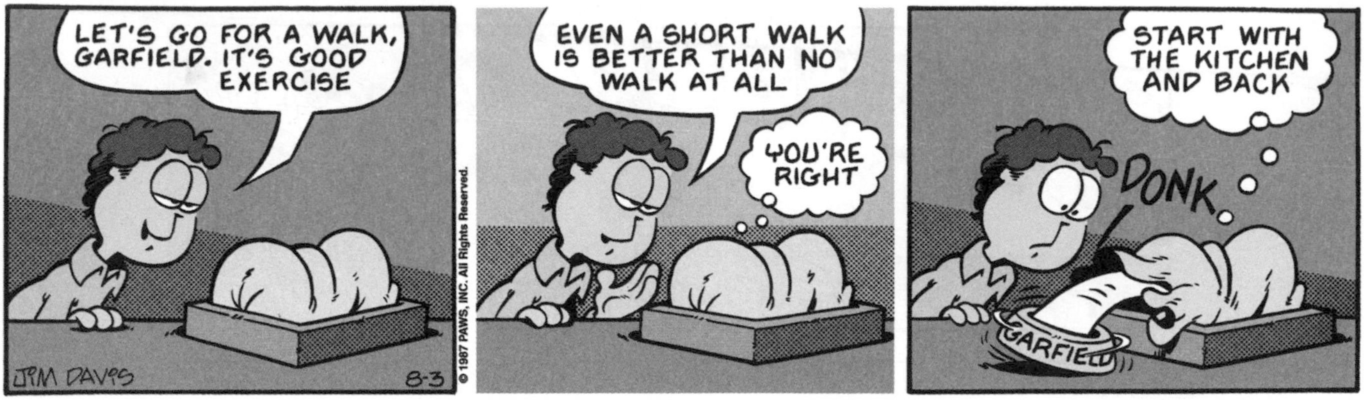
LET'S GO FOR A WALK, GARFIELD. IT'S GOOD EXERCISE
JIM DAVIS 8-3
© 1987 PAWS, INC. All Rights Reserved.
EVEN A SHORT WALK IS BETTER THAN NO WALK AT ALL
YOU'RE RIGHT
START WITH THE KITCHEN AND BACK
DONK
GARFIELD

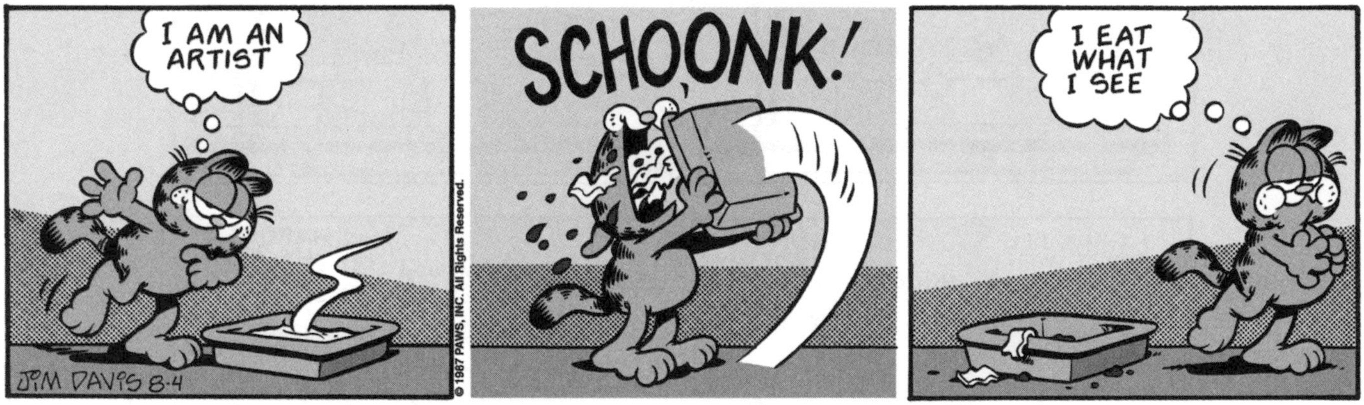
I AM AN ARTIST
JIM DAVIS 8-4
© 1987 PAWS, INC. All Rights Reserved.
SCHOONK!
I EAT WHAT I SEE

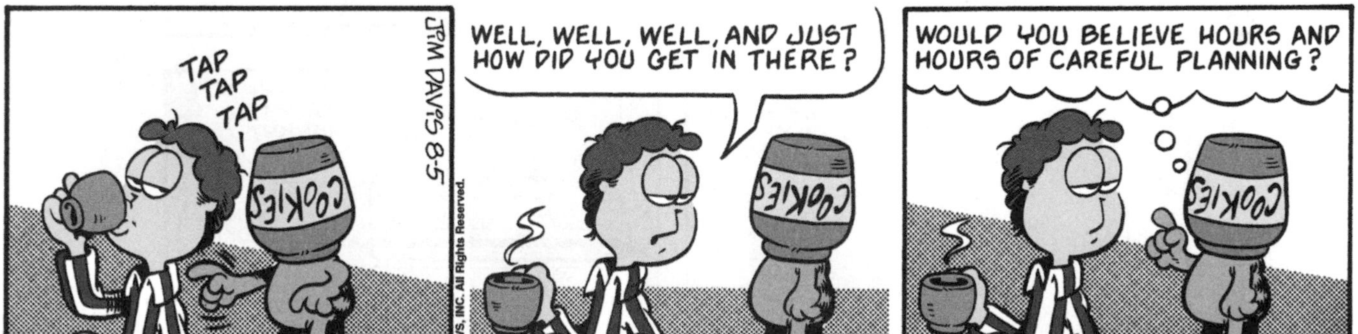
TAP TAP TAP
JIM DAVIS 8-5
© 1987 PAWS, INC. All Rights Reserved.
WELL, WELL, WELL, AND JUST HOW DID YOU GET IN THERE?
WOULD YOU BELIEVE HOURS AND HOURS OF CAREFUL PLANNING?

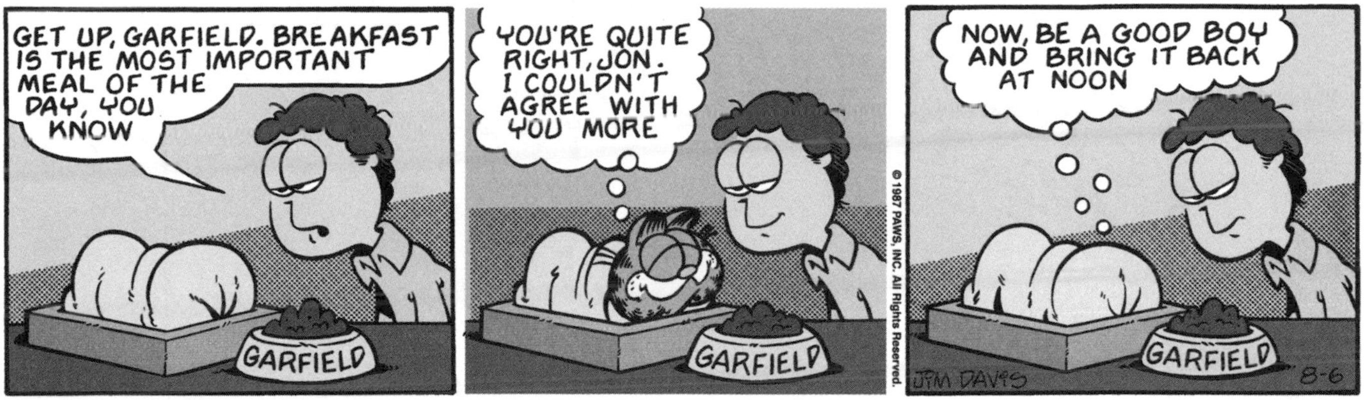
GET UP, GARFIELD. BREAKFAST IS THE MOST IMPORTANT MEAL OF THE DAY, YOU KNOW
GARFIELD
YOU'RE QUITE RIGHT, JON. I COULDN'T AGREE WITH YOU MORE
GARFIELD
© 1987 PAWS, INC. All Rights Reserved.
NOW, BE A GOOD BOY AND BRING IT BACK AT NOON
GARFIELD
JIM DAVIS
8-6

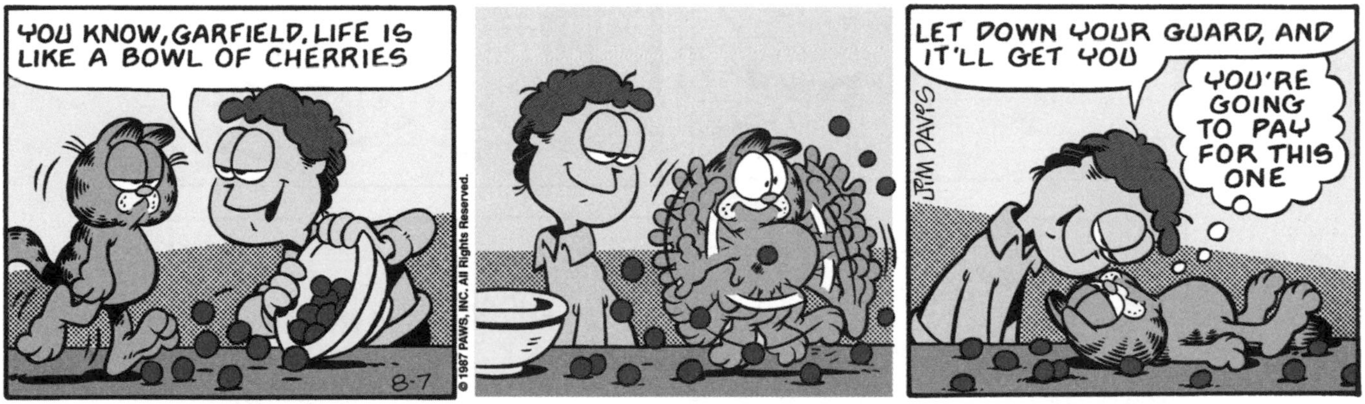
YOU KNOW, GARFIELD, LIFE IS LIKE A BOWL OF CHERRIES
8-7
© 1987 PAWS, INC. All Rights Reserved.
LET DOWN YOUR GUARD, AND IT'LL GET YOU
YOU'RE GOING TO PAY FOR THIS ONE
JIM DAVIS

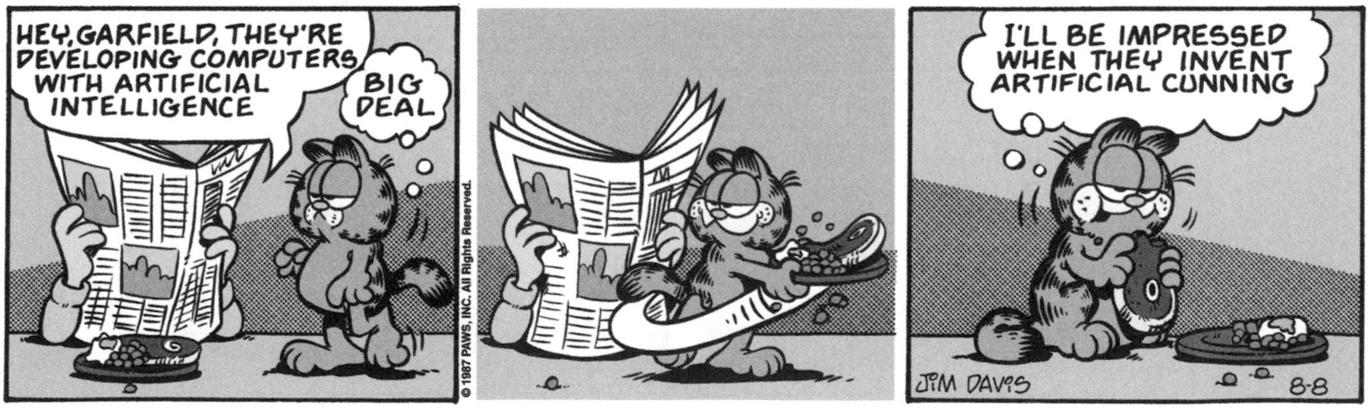
HEY, GARFIELD, THEY'RE DEVELOPING COMPUTERS WITH ARTIFICIAL INTELLIGENCE
BIG DEAL
© 1987 PAWS, INC. All Rights Reserved.
I'LL BE IMPRESSED WHEN THEY INVENT ARTIFICIAL CUNNING
JIM DAVIS
8-8

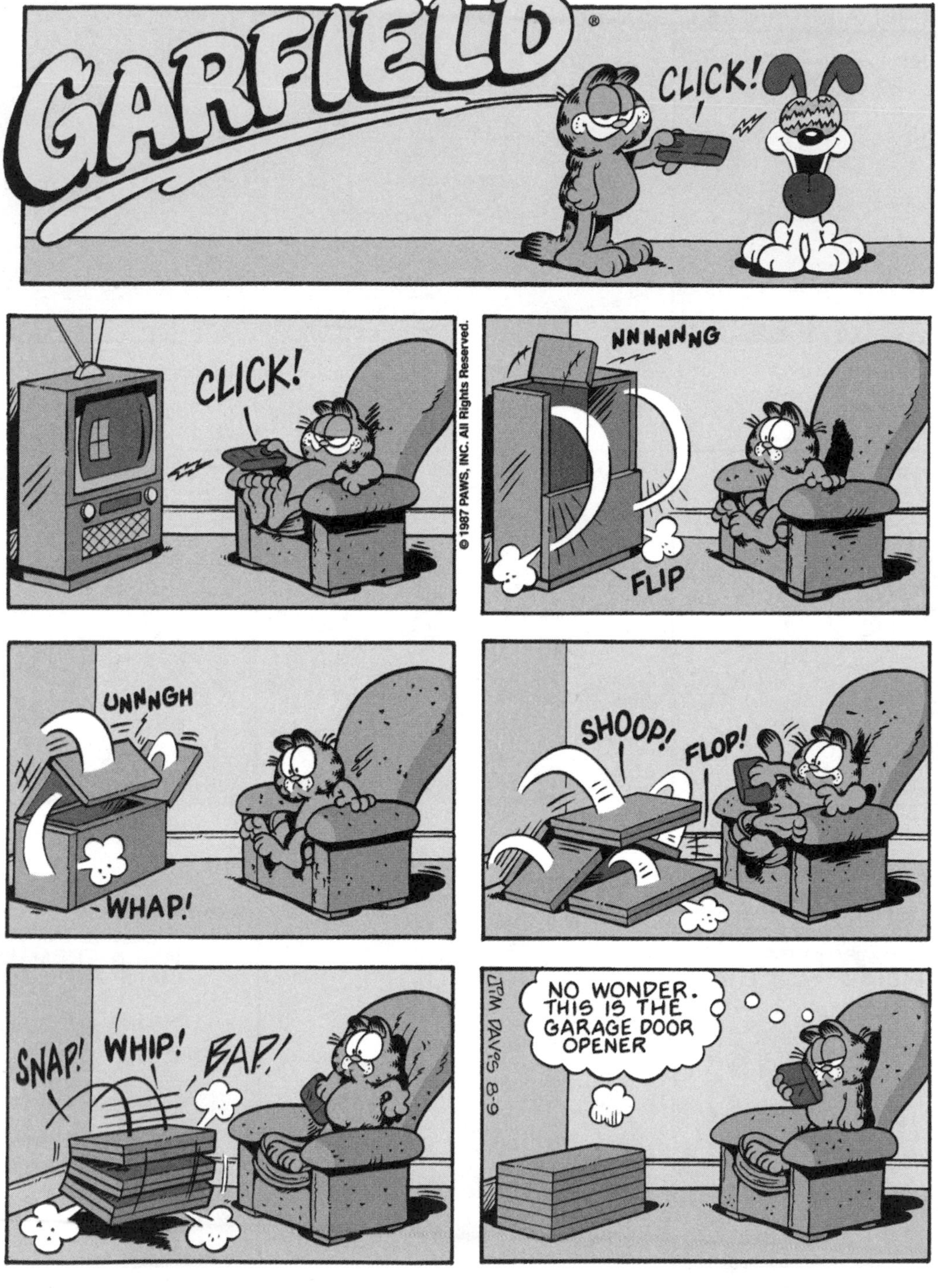
GARFIELD
CLICK!
CLICK!
© 1987 PAWS, INC. All Rights Reserved.
NNNNNNG
FLIP
UNNNGH
WHAP!
SHOOP!
FLOP!
SNAP!
WHIP!
BAP!
JIM DAVIS 8-9
NO WONDER. THIS IS THE GARAGE DOOR OPENER

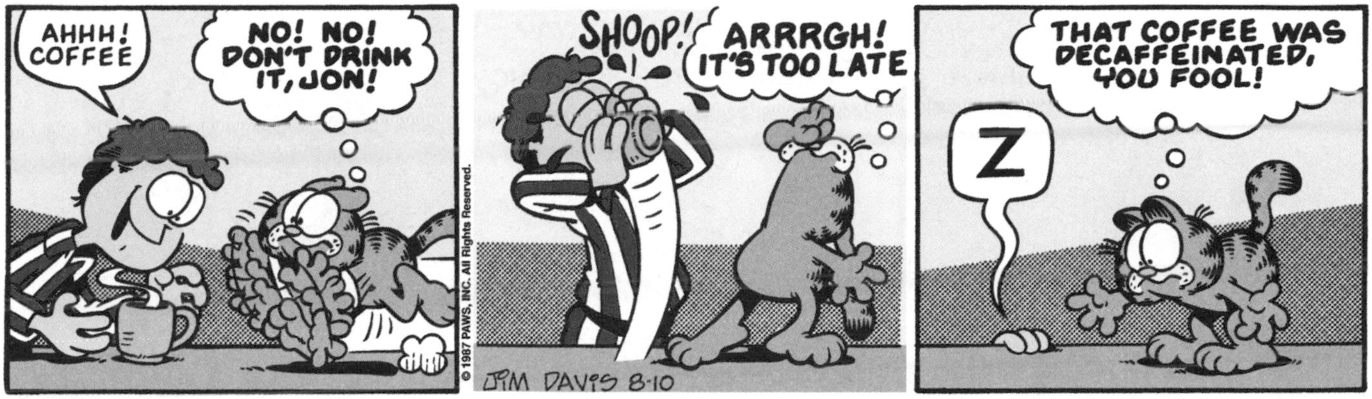
AHHH! COFFEE
NO! NO! DON'T DRINK IT, JON!
SHOOP!
ARRRGH! IT'S TOO LATE
Z
THAT COFFEE WAS DECAFFEINATED, YOU FOOL!
© 1987 PAWS, INC. All Rights Reserved.
JIM DAVIS 8-10

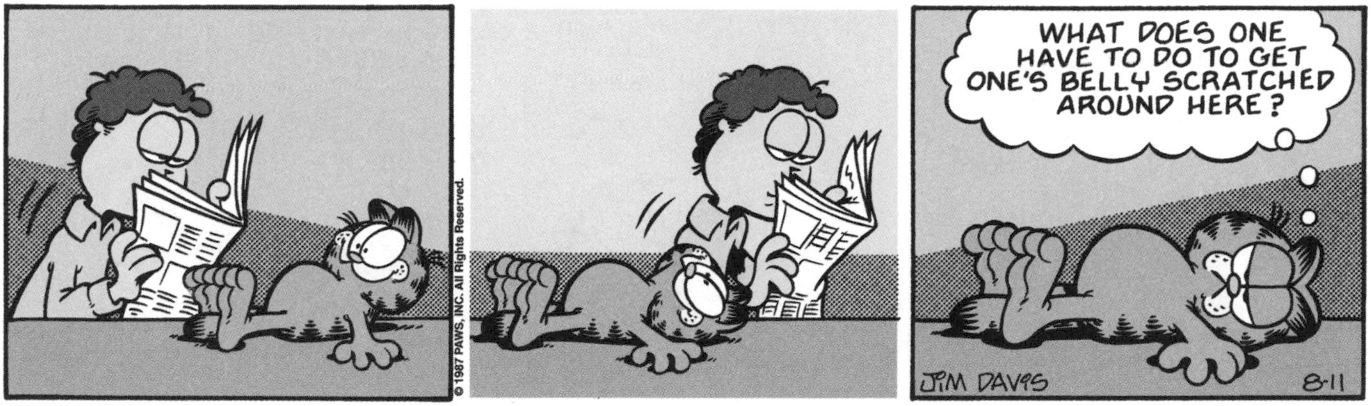
WHAT DOES ONE HAVE TO DO TO GET ONE'S BELLY SCRATCHED AROUND HERE?
© 1987 PAWS, INC. All Rights Reserved.
JIM DAVIS
8-11

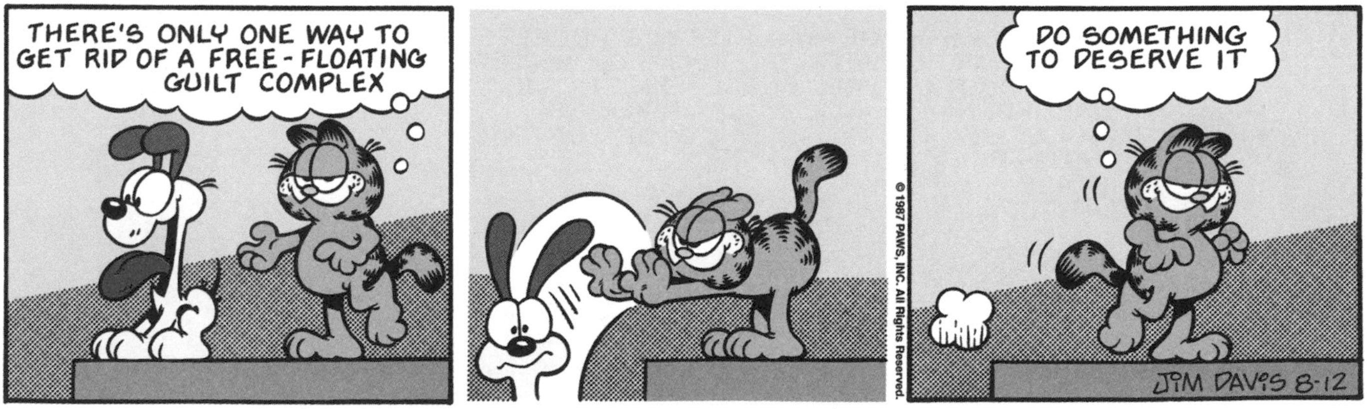
THERE'S ONLY ONE WAY TO GET RID OF A FREE-FLOATING GUILT COMPLEX
DO SOMETHING TO DESERVE IT
© 1987 PAWS, INC. All Rights Reserved.
JIM DAVIS 8-12

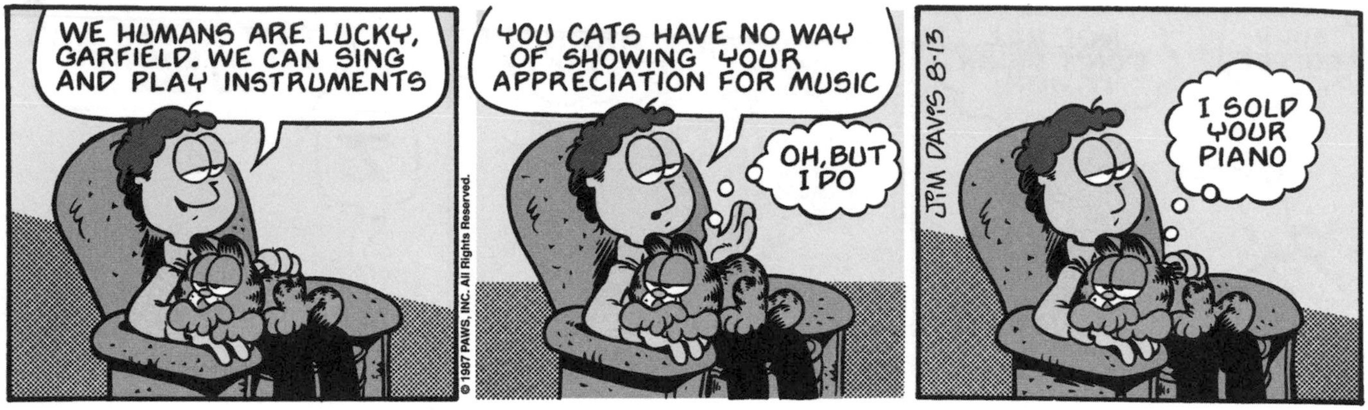
WE HUMANS ARE LUCKY, GARFIELD. WE CAN SING AND PLAY INSTRUMENTS
© 1987 PAWS, INC. All Rights Reserved.
YOU CATS HAVE NO WAY OF SHOWING YOUR APPRECIATION FOR MUSIC
OH, BUT I DO
JIM DAVIS 8-13
I SOLD YOUR PIANO

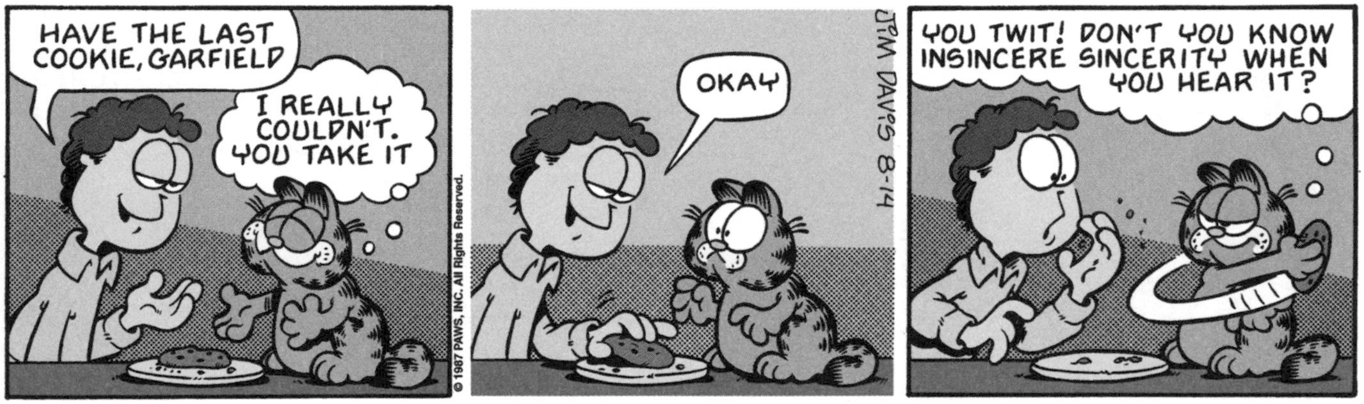
HAVE THE LAST COOKIE, GARFIELD
I REALLY COULDN'T. YOU TAKE IT
© 1987 PAWS, INC. All Rights Reserved.
OKAY
JIM DAVIS 8-14
YOU TWIT! DON'T YOU KNOW INSINCERE SINCERITY WHEN YOU HEAR IT?

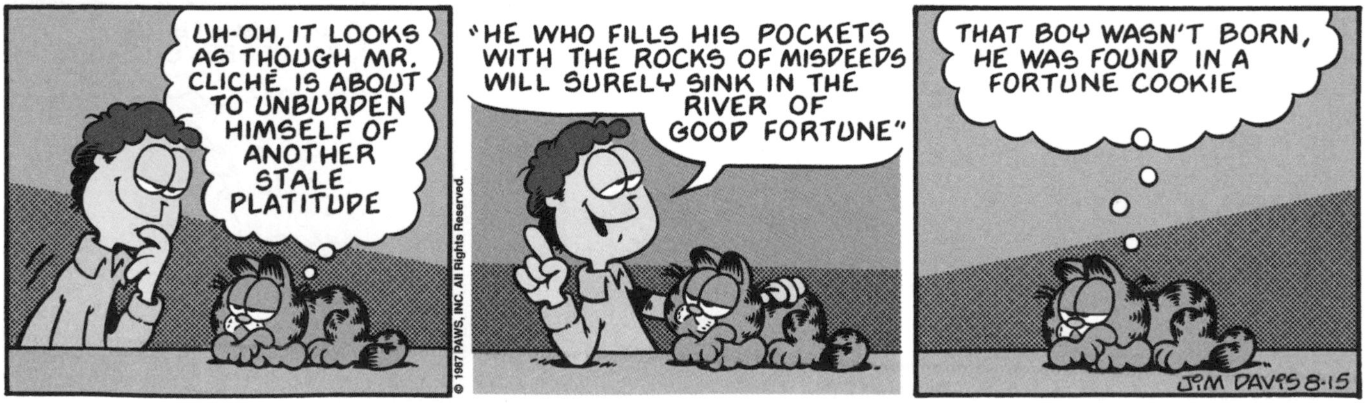
UH-OH, IT LOOKS AS THOUGH MR. CLICHÉ IS ABOUT TO UNBURDEN HIMSELF OF ANOTHER STALE PLATITUDE
© 1987 PAWS, INC. All Rights Reserved.
"HE WHO FILLS HIS POCKETS WITH THE ROCKS OF MISDEEDS WILL SURELY SINK IN THE RIVER OF GOOD FORTUNE"
THAT BOY WASN'T BORN, HE WAS FOUND IN A FORTUNE COOKIE
JIM DAVIS 8-15

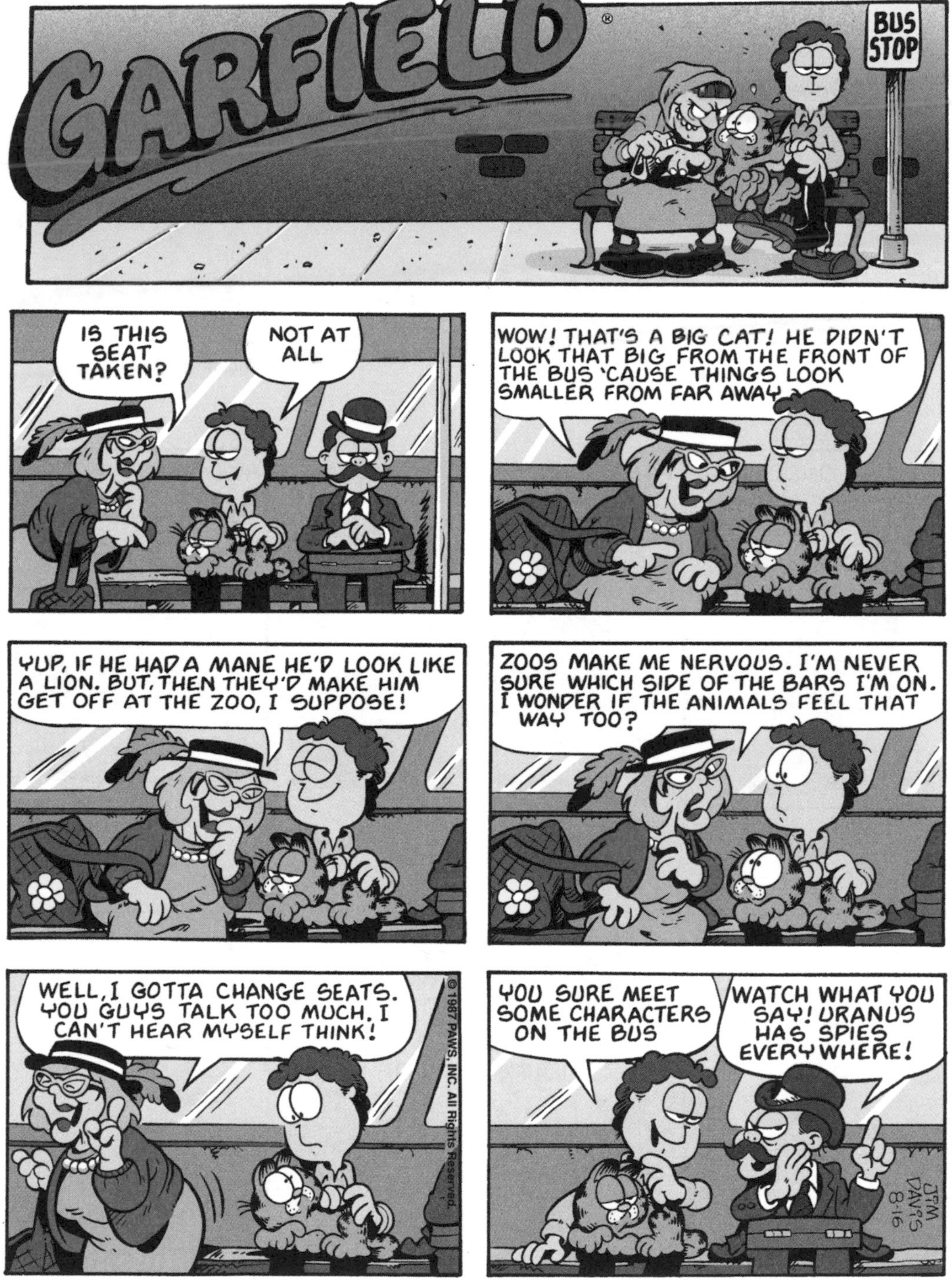
GARFIELD®
BUS STOP
IS THIS SEAT TAKEN?
NOT AT ALL
WOW! THAT'S A BIG CAT! HE DIDN'T LOOK THAT BIG FROM THE FRONT OF THE BUS 'CAUSE THINGS LOOK SMALLER FROM FAR AWAY
YUP, IF HE HAD A MANE HE'D LOOK LIKE A LION. BUT, THEN THEY'D MAKE HIM GET OFF AT THE ZOO, I SUPPOSE!
ZOOS MAKE ME NERVOUS. I'M NEVER SURE WHICH SIDE OF THE BARS I'M ON. I WONDER IF THE ANIMALS FEEL THAT WAY TOO?
WELL, I GOTTA CHANGE SEATS. YOU GUYS TALK TOO MUCH. I CAN'T HEAR MYSELF THINK!
© 1987 PAWS, INC. All Rights Reserved.
YOU SURE MEET SOME CHARACTERS ON THE BUS
WATCH WHAT YOU SAY! URANUS HAS SPIES EVERYWHERE!
JIM DAVIS 8-16

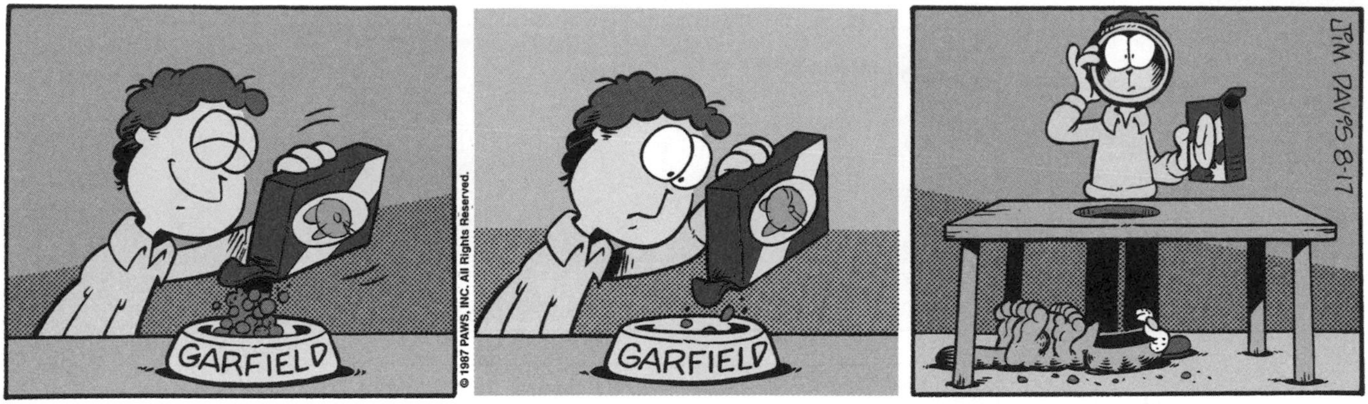
GARFIELD
GARFIELD
© 1987 PAWS, INC. All Rights Reserved.
JIM DAVIS 8-17

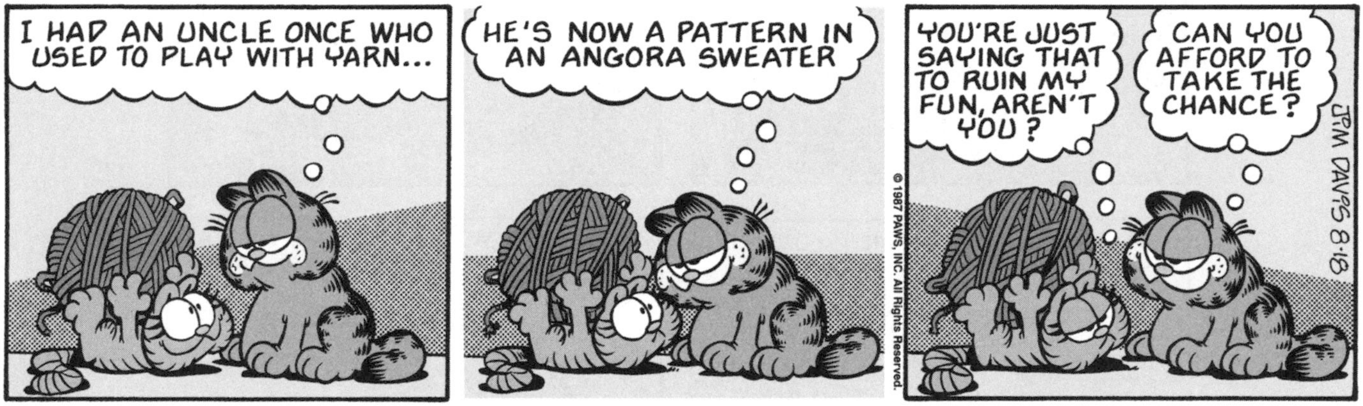
I HAD AN UNCLE ONCE WHO USED TO PLAY WITH YARN...
HE'S NOW A PATTERN IN AN ANGORA SWEATER
YOU'RE JUST SAYING THAT TO RUIN MY FUN, AREN'T YOU?
CAN YOU AFFORD TO TAKE THE CHANCE?
© 1987 PAWS, INC. All Rights Reserved.
JIM DAVIS 8-18

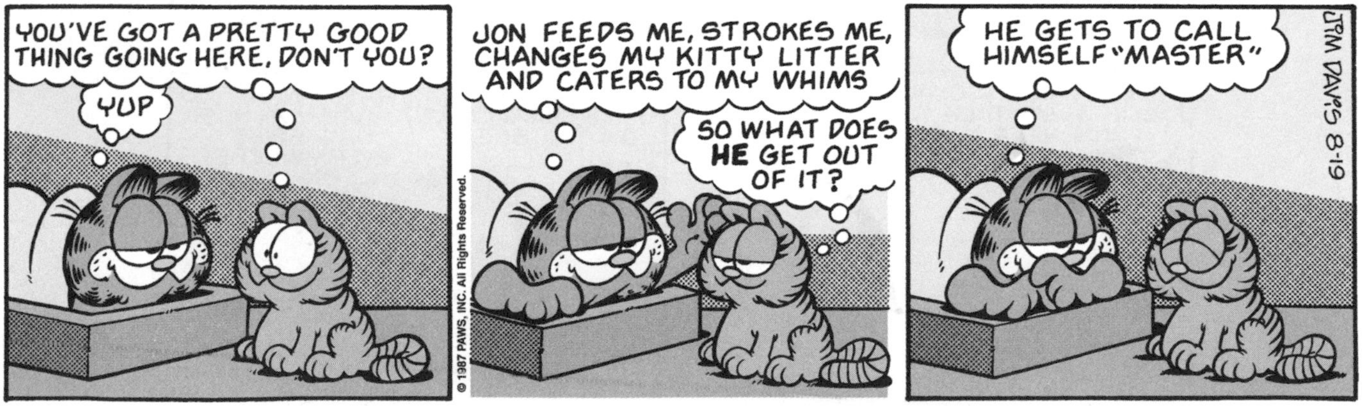
YOU'VE GOT A PRETTY GOOD THING GOING HERE, DON'T YOU?
YUP
JON FEEDS ME, STROKES ME, CHANGES MY KITTY LITTER AND CATERS TO MY WHIMS
SO WHAT DOES **HE** GET OUT OF IT?
HE GETS TO CALL HIMSELF "MASTER"
© 1987 PAWS, INC. All Rights Reserved.
JIM DAVIS 8-19

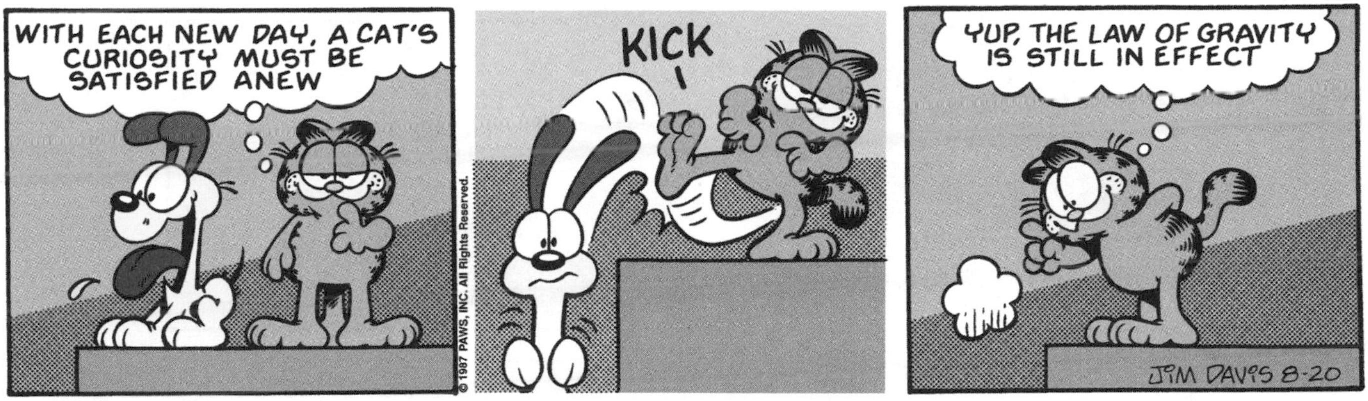
WITH EACH NEW DAY, A CAT'S CURIOSITY MUST BE SATISFIED ANEW
KICK
© 1987 PAWS, INC. All Rights Reserved.
YUP, THE LAW OF GRAVITY IS STILL IN EFFECT
JIM DAVIS 8-20

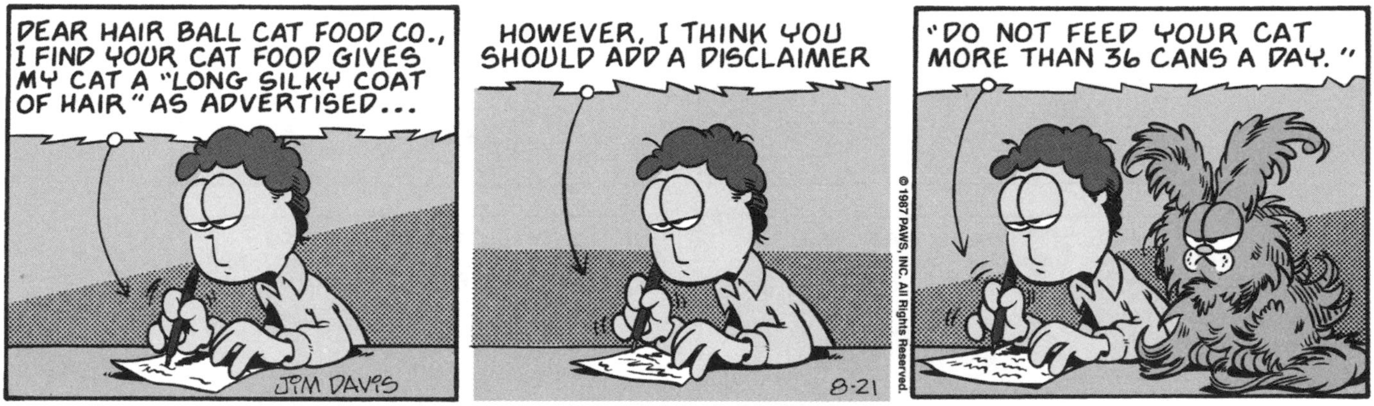
DEAR HAIR BALL CAT FOOD CO., I FIND YOUR CAT FOOD GIVES MY CAT A "LONG SILKY COAT OF HAIR" AS ADVERTISED...
JIM DAVIS
HOWEVER, I THINK YOU SHOULD ADD A DISCLAIMER
8-21
© 1987 PAWS, INC. All Rights Reserved.
"DO NOT FEED YOUR CAT MORE THAN 36 CANS A DAY."

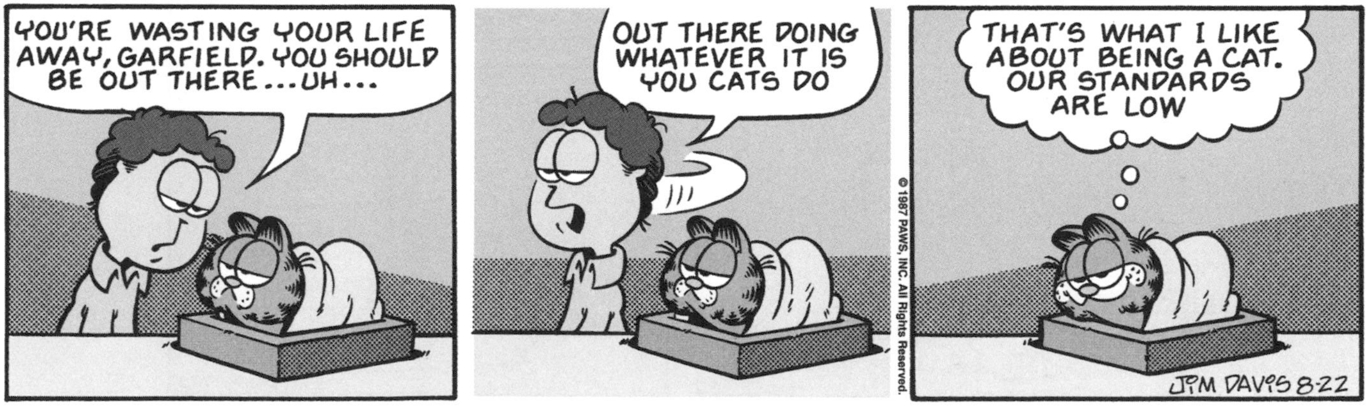
YOU'RE WASTING YOUR LIFE AWAY, GARFIELD. YOU SHOULD BE OUT THERE...UH...
OUT THERE DOING WHATEVER IT IS YOU CATS DO
© 1987 PAWS, INC. All Rights Reserved.
THAT'S WHAT I LIKE ABOUT BEING A CAT. OUR STANDARDS ARE LOW
JIM DAVIS 8-22

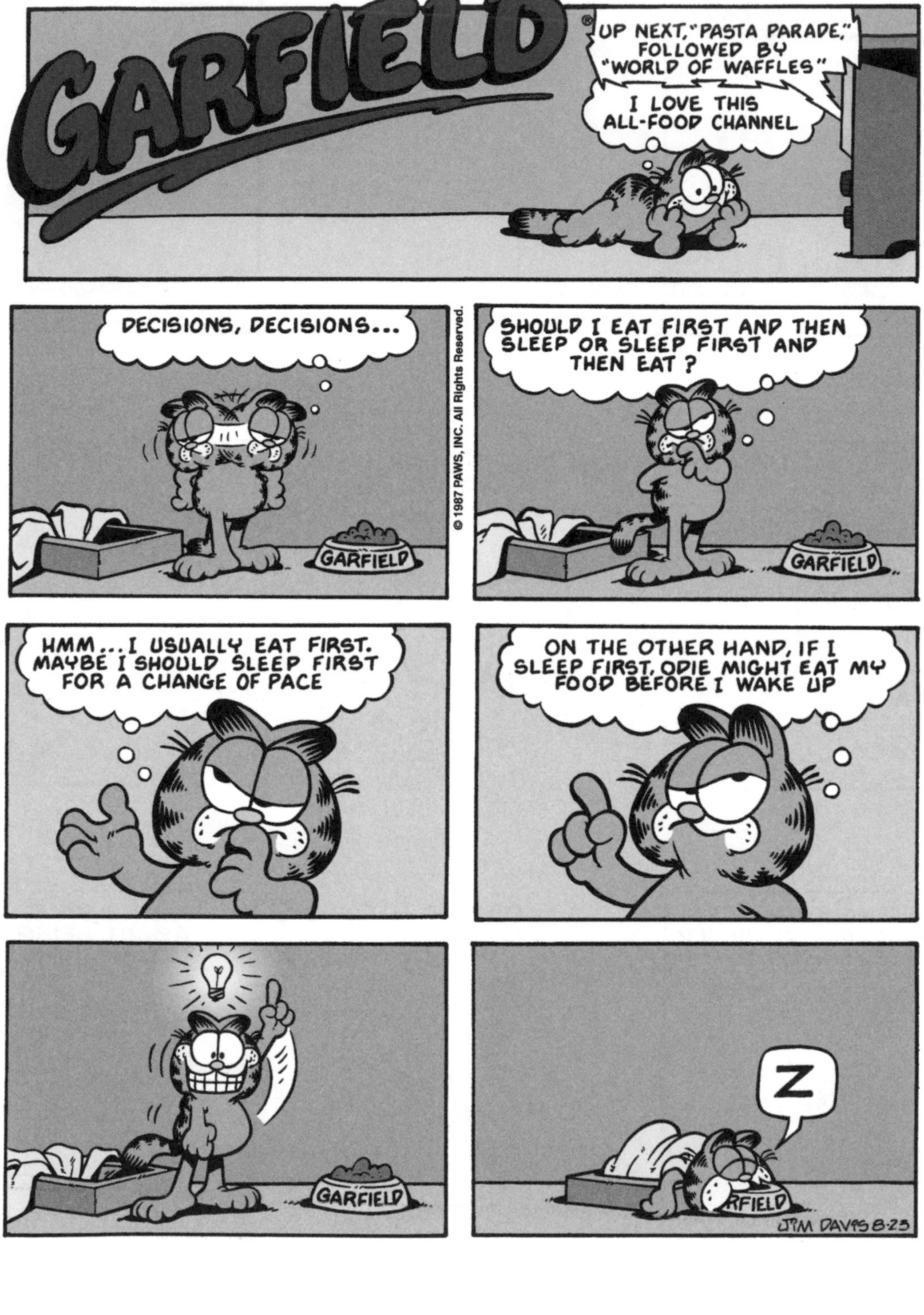
GARFIELD®
UP NEXT, "PASTA PARADE," FOLLOWED BY "WORLD OF WAFFLES"
I LOVE THIS ALL-FOOD CHANNEL
DECISIONS, DECISIONS...
GARFIELD
© 1987 PAWS, INC. All Rights Reserved.
SHOULD I EAT FIRST AND THEN SLEEP OR SLEEP FIRST AND THEN EAT ?
GARFIELD
HMM... I USUALLY EAT FIRST. MAYBE I SHOULD SLEEP FIRST FOR A CHANGE OF PACE
ON THE OTHER HAND, IF I SLEEP FIRST, ODIE MIGHT EAT MY FOOD BEFORE I WAKE UP
GARFIELD
Z
RFIELD
JIM DAVIS 8-23

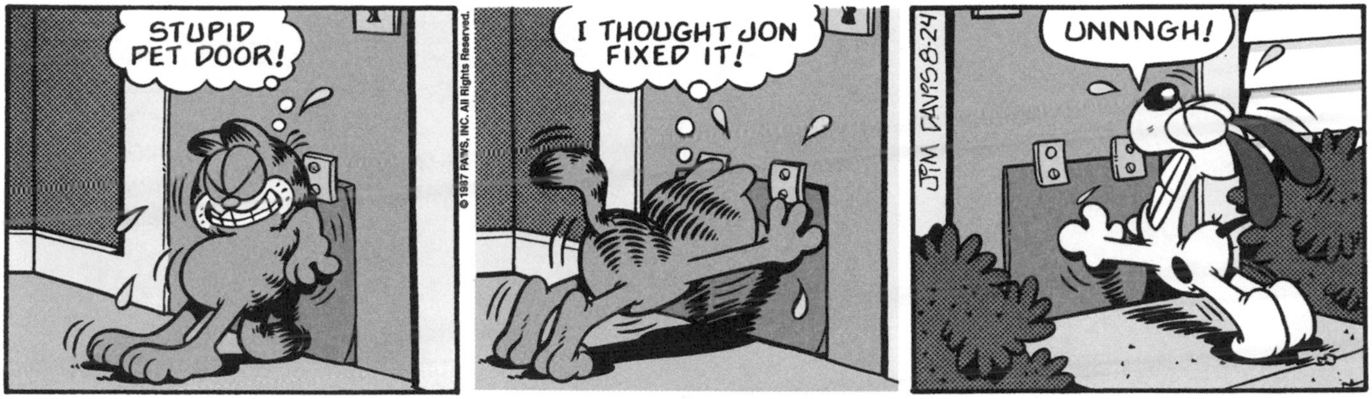
STUPID PET DOOR!
© 1987 PAWS, INC. All Rights Reserved.
I THOUGHT JON FIXED IT!
JIM DAVIS 8-24
UNNNGH!

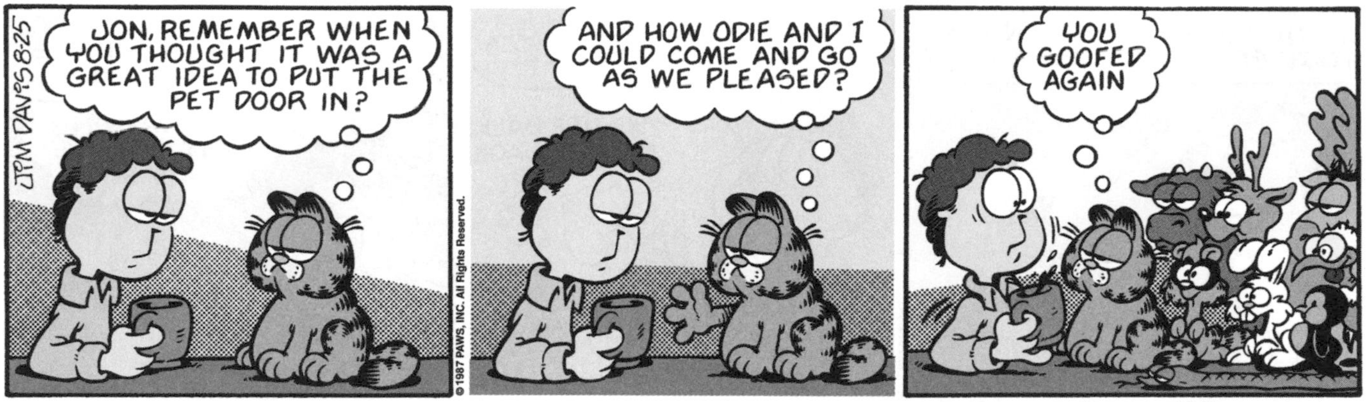
JIM DAVIS 8-25
JON, REMEMBER WHEN YOU THOUGHT IT WAS A GREAT IDEA TO PUT THE PET DOOR IN?
© 1987 PAWS, INC. All Rights Reserved.
AND HOW ODIE AND I COULD COME AND GO AS WE PLEASED?
YOU GOOFED AGAIN

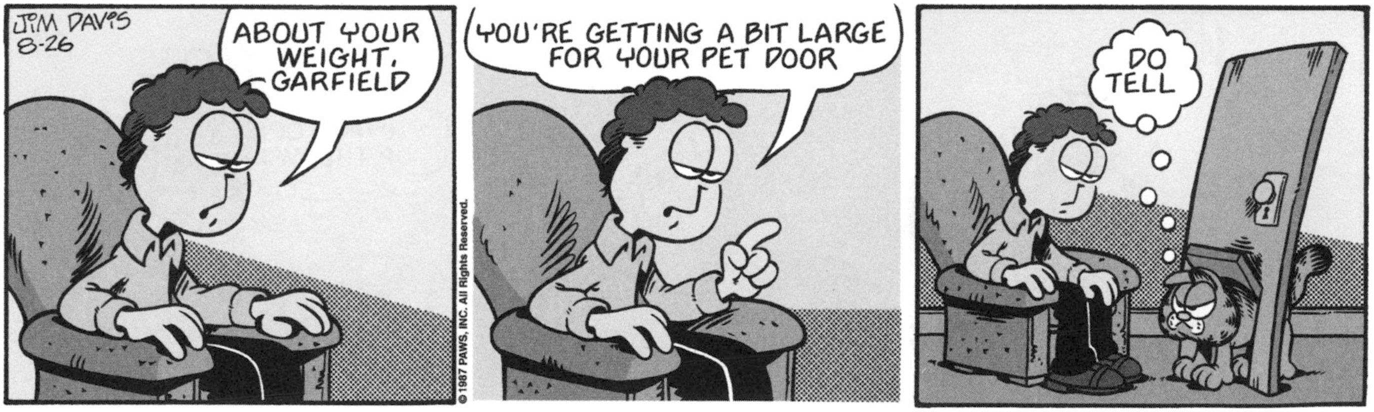
JIM DAVIS 8-26
ABOUT YOUR WEIGHT, GARFIELD
© 1987 PAWS, INC. All Rights Reserved.
YOU'RE GETTING A BIT LARGE FOR YOUR PET DOOR
DO TELL

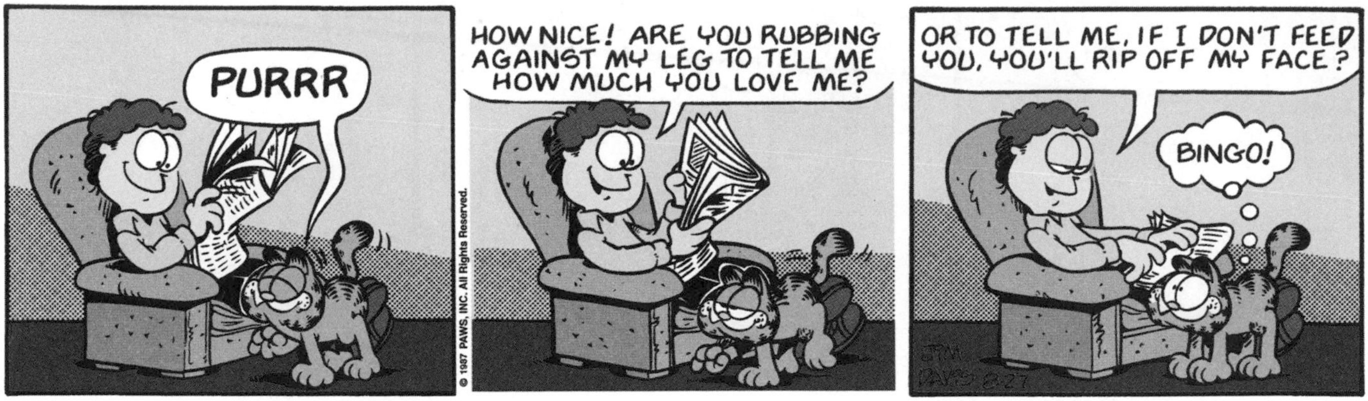
PURRR
HOW NICE! ARE YOU RUBBING AGAINST MY LEG TO TELL ME HOW MUCH YOU LOVE ME?
OR TO TELL ME, IF I DON'T FEED YOU, YOU'LL RIP OFF MY FACE?
BINGO!
© 1987 PAWS, INC. All Rights Reserved.

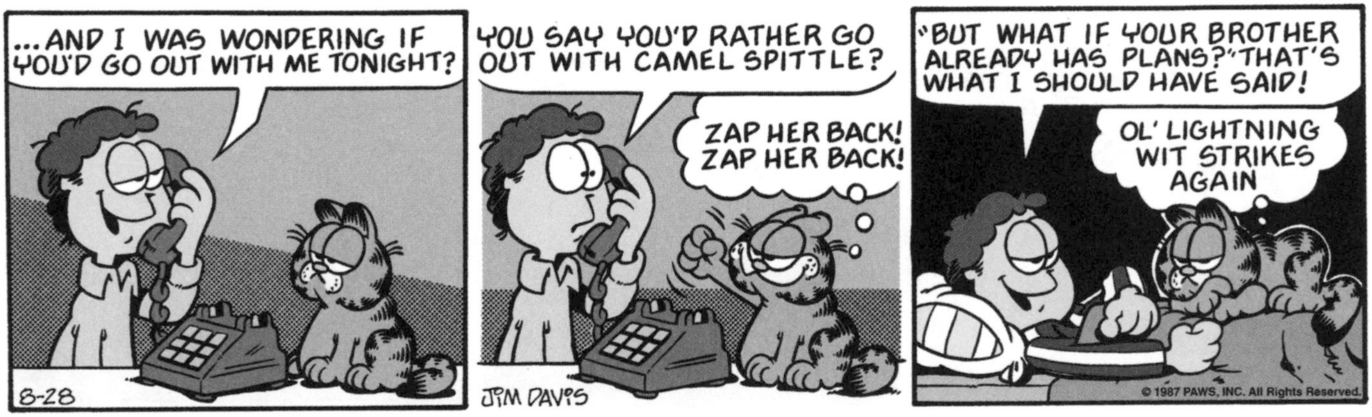
...AND I WAS WONDERING IF YOU'D GO OUT WITH ME TONIGHT?
8-28
YOU SAY YOU'D RATHER GO OUT WITH CAMEL SPITTLE?
ZAP HER BACK! ZAP HER BACK!
JIM DAVIS
"BUT WHAT IF YOUR BROTHER ALREADY HAS PLANS?" THAT'S WHAT I SHOULD HAVE SAID!
OL' LIGHTNING WIT STRIKES AGAIN
© 1987 PAWS, INC. All Rights Reserved.

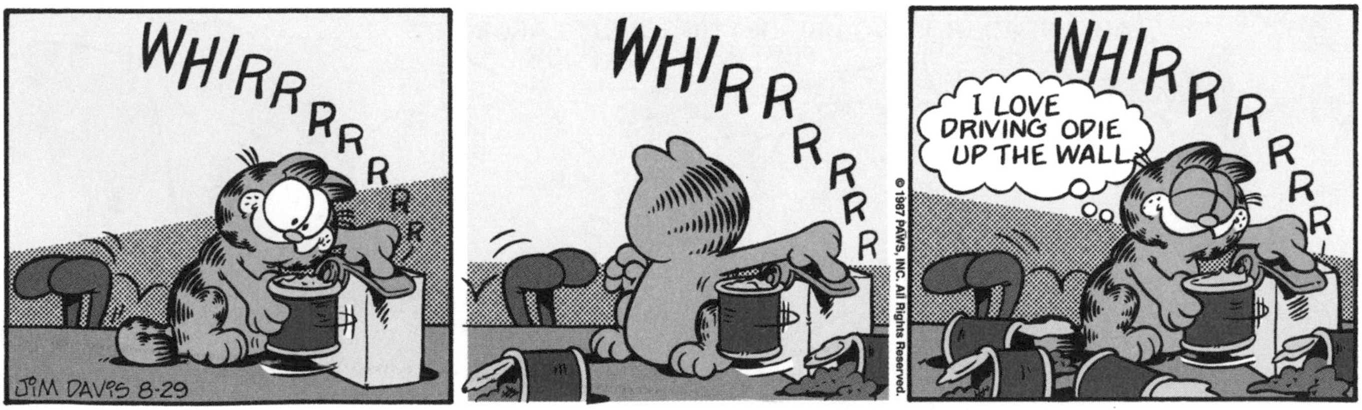
WHIRRRRRRR
JIM DAVIS 8-29
WHIRRRRRR
© 1987 PAWS, INC. All Rights Reserved.
WHIRRRRRRR
I LOVE DRIVING ODIE UP THE WALL

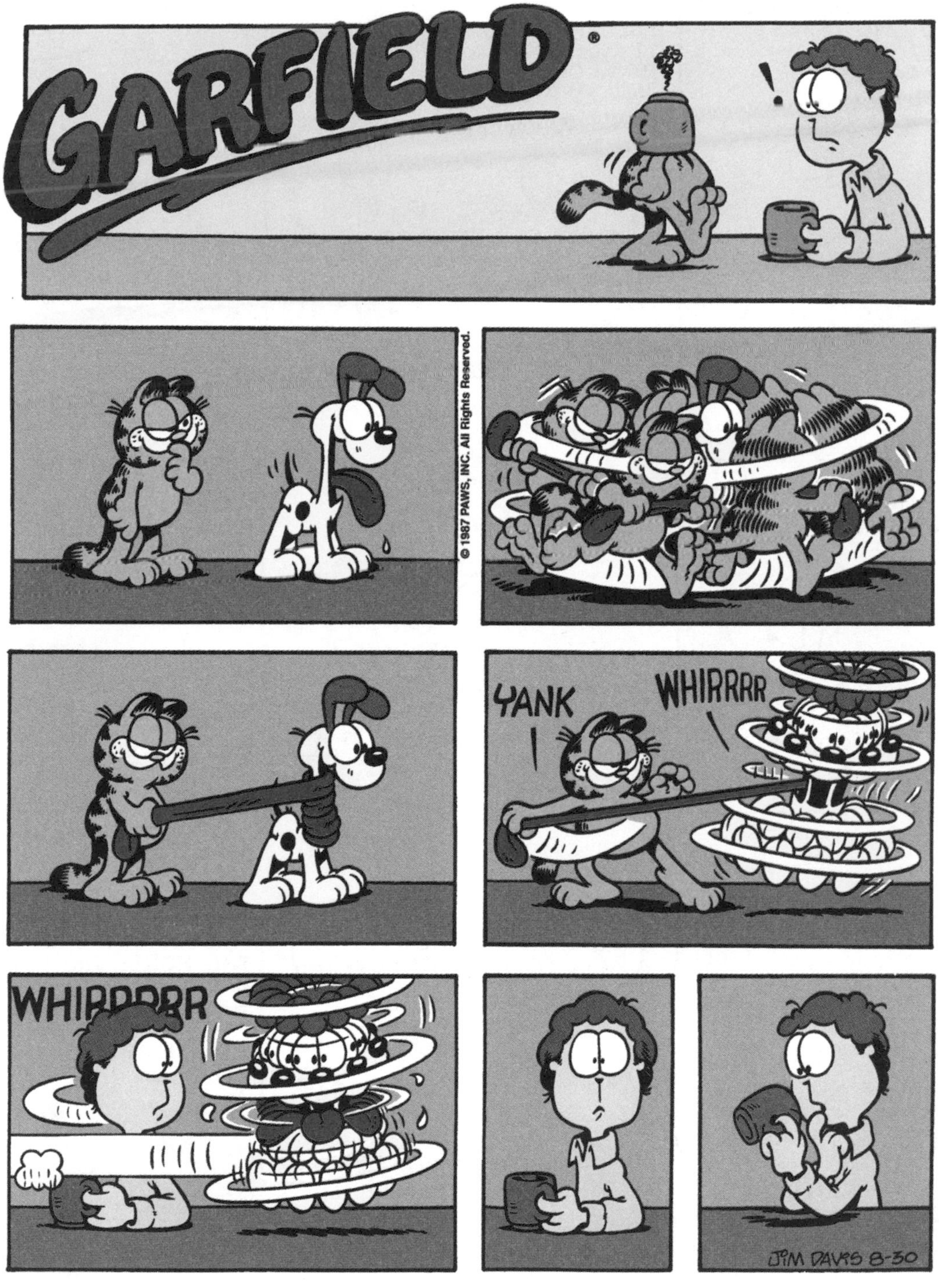
GARFIELD®
!
© 1987 PAWS, INC. All Rights Reserved.
YANK
WHIRRRR
WHIRRRRR
JIM DAVIS 8-30

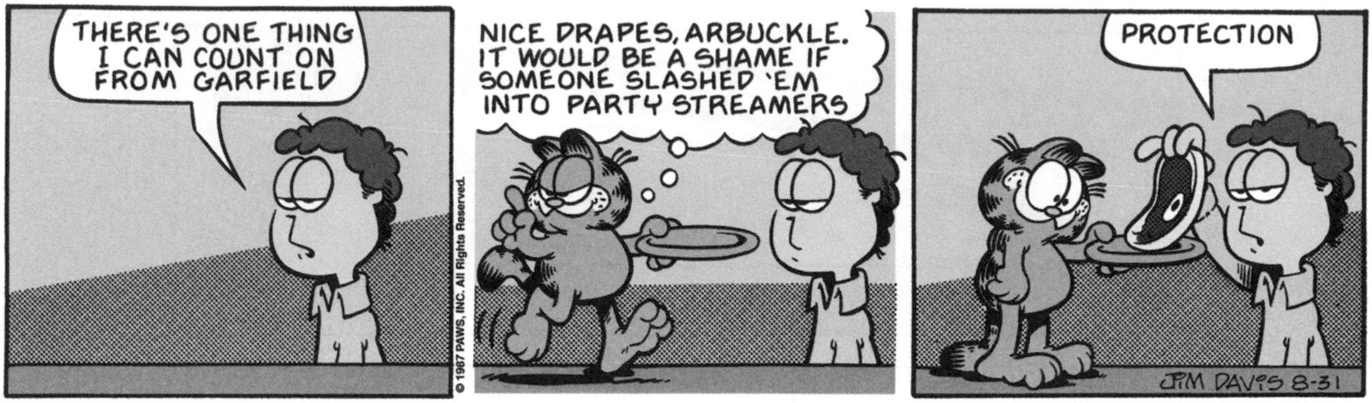
THERE'S ONE THING I CAN COUNT ON FROM GARFIELD
NICE DRAPES, ARBUCKLE. IT WOULD BE A SHAME IF SOMEONE SLASHED 'EM INTO PARTY STREAMERS
PROTECTION
JIM DAVIS 8-31
© 1987 PAWS, INC. All Rights Reserved.

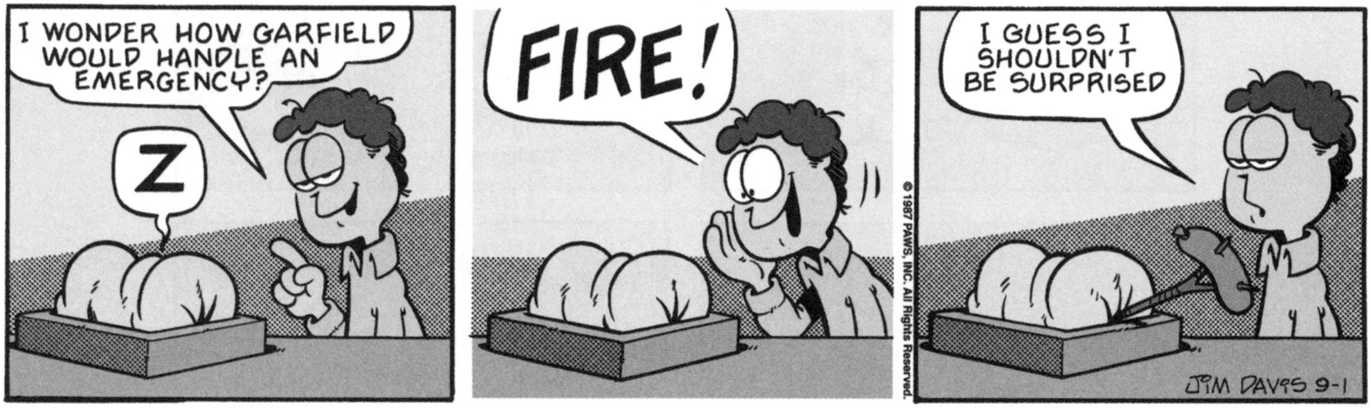
I WONDER HOW GARFIELD WOULD HANDLE AN EMERGENCY?
Z
FIRE!
I GUESS I SHOULDN'T BE SURPRISED
JIM DAVIS 9-1
© 1987 PAWS, INC. All Rights Reserved.

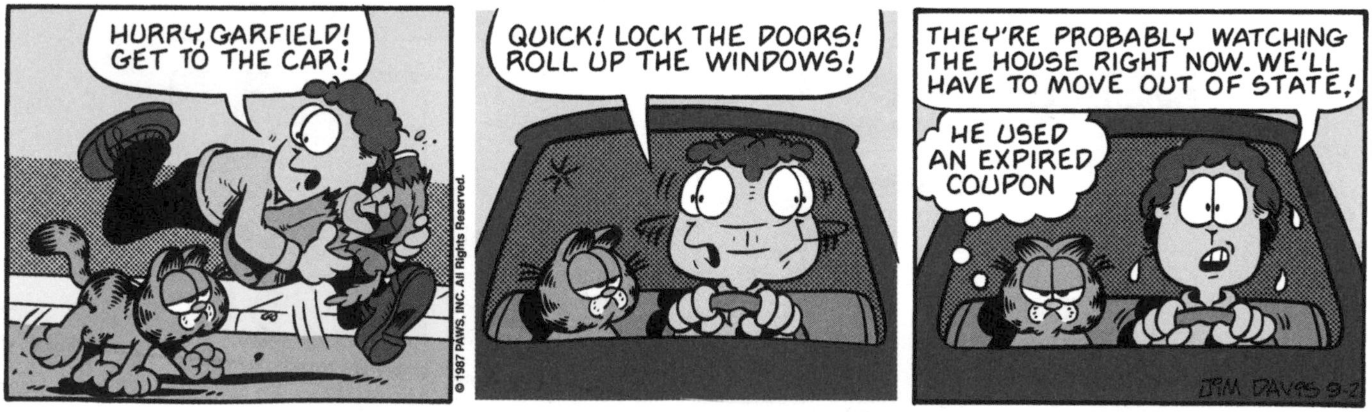
HURRY, GARFIELD! GET TO THE CAR!
QUICK! LOCK THE DOORS! ROLL UP THE WINDOWS!
THEY'RE PROBABLY WATCHING THE HOUSE RIGHT NOW. WE'LL HAVE TO MOVE OUT OF STATE!
HE USED AN EXPIRED COUPON
JIM DAVIS 9-2
© 1987 PAWS, INC. All Rights Reserved.

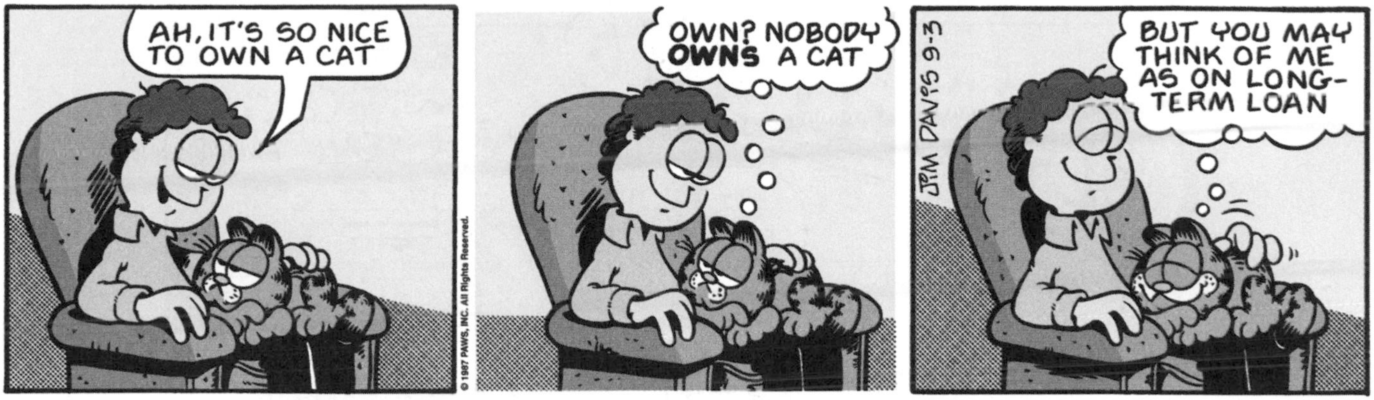
AH, IT'S SO NICE TO OWN A CAT
OWN? NOBODY **OWNS** A CAT
JIM DAVIS 9-3
BUT YOU MAY THINK OF ME AS ON LONG-TERM LOAN

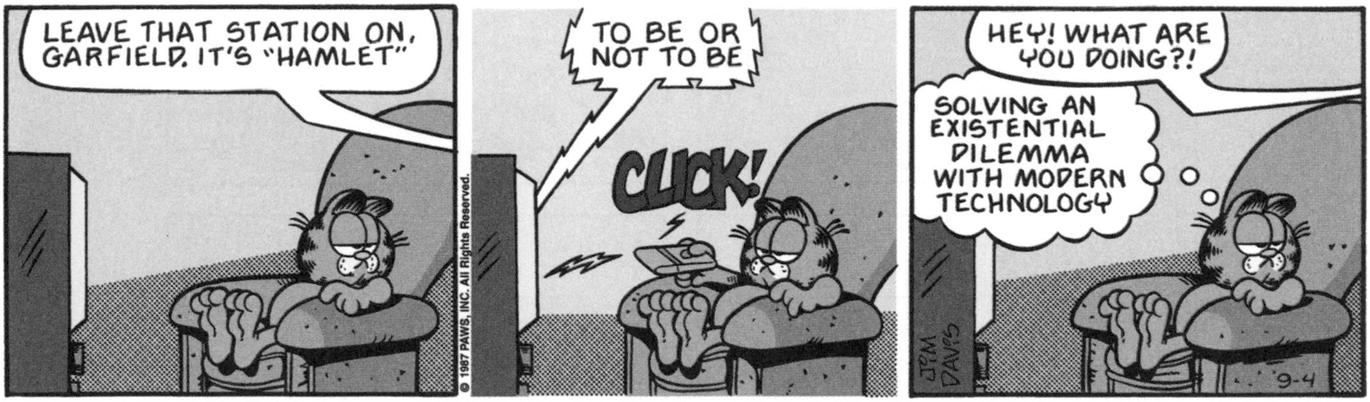
LEAVE THAT STATION ON, GARFIELD. IT'S "HAMLET"
TO BE OR NOT TO BE
CLICK!
HEY! WHAT ARE YOU DOING?!
SOLVING AN EXISTENTIAL DILEMMA WITH MODERN TECHNOLOGY
JIM DAVIS
9-4

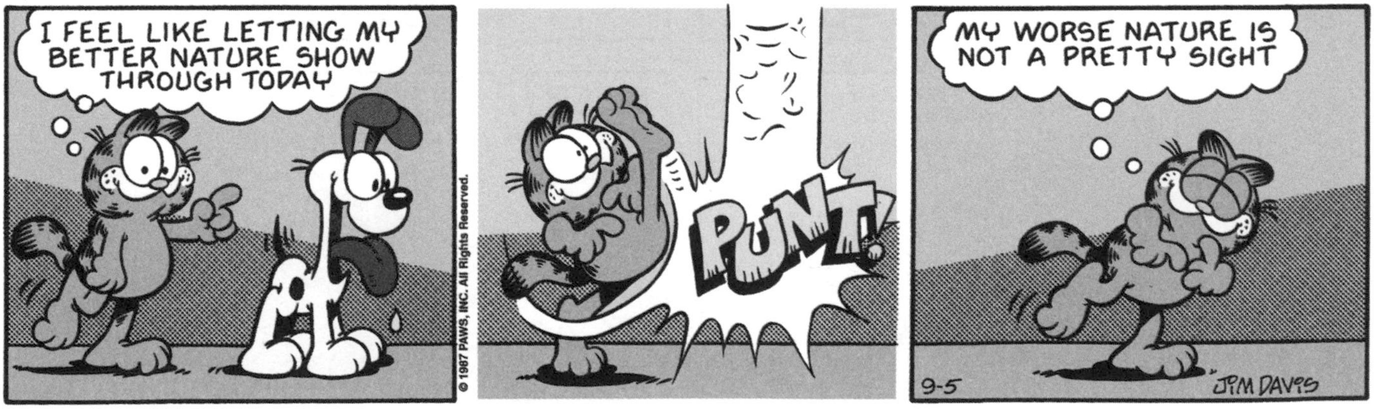
I FEEL LIKE LETTING MY BETTER NATURE SHOW THROUGH TODAY
PUNT!
MY WORSE NATURE IS NOT A PRETTY SIGHT
9-5
JIM DAVIS

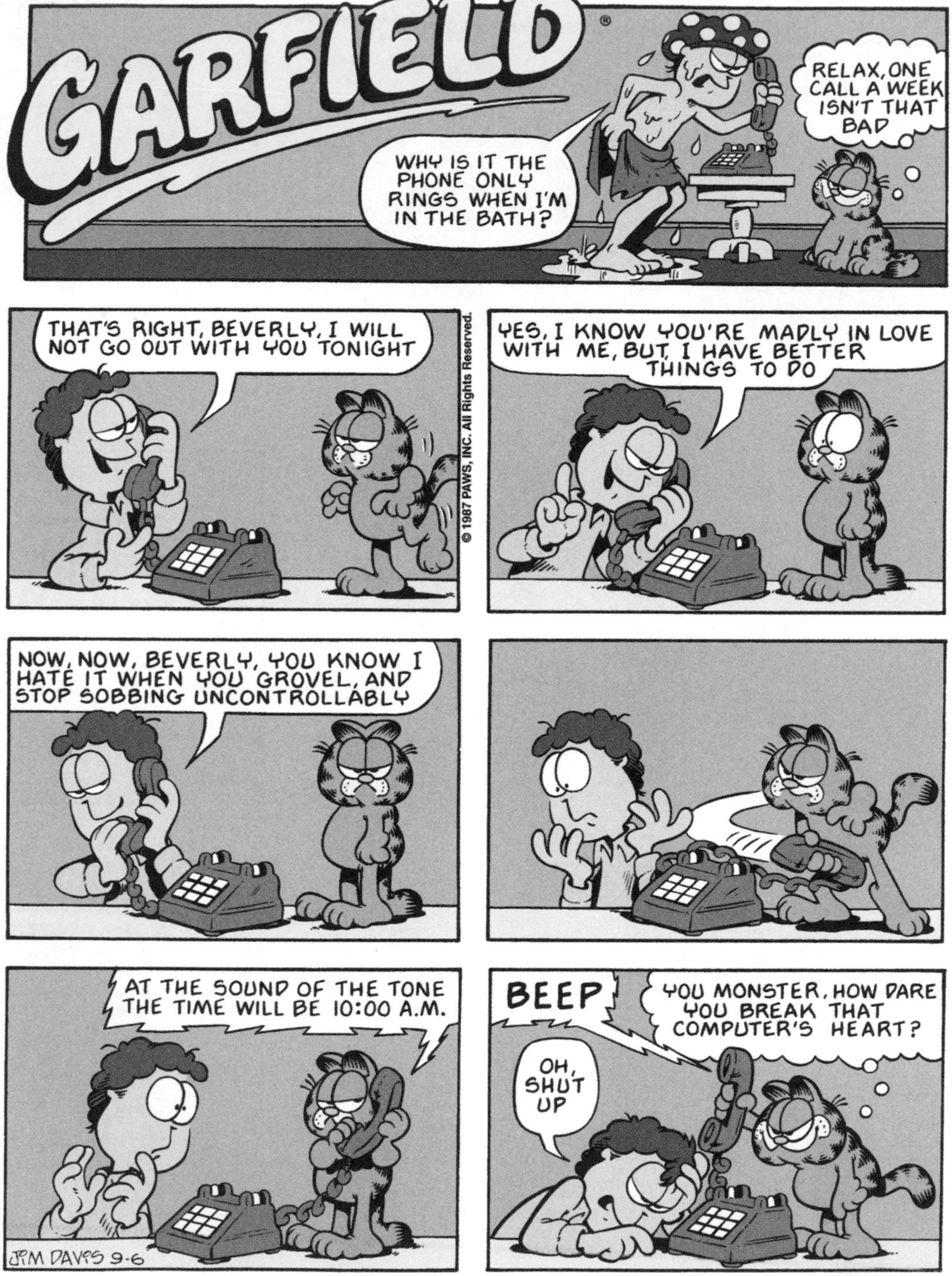
GARFIELD
WHY IS IT THE PHONE ONLY RINGS WHEN I'M IN THE BATH?
RELAX, ONE CALL A WEEK ISN'T THAT BAD
THAT'S RIGHT, BEVERLY, I WILL NOT GO OUT WITH YOU TONIGHT
© 1987 PAWS, INC. All Rights Reserved.
YES, I KNOW YOU'RE MADLY IN LOVE WITH ME, BUT, I HAVE BETTER THINGS TO DO
NOW, NOW, BEVERLY, YOU KNOW I HATE IT WHEN YOU GROVEL, AND STOP SOBBING UNCONTROLLABLY
AT THE SOUND OF THE TONE THE TIME WILL BE 10:00 A.M.
JIM DAVIS 9-6
BEEP
YOU MONSTER, HOW DARE YOU BREAK THAT COMPUTER'S HEART?
OH, SHUT UP

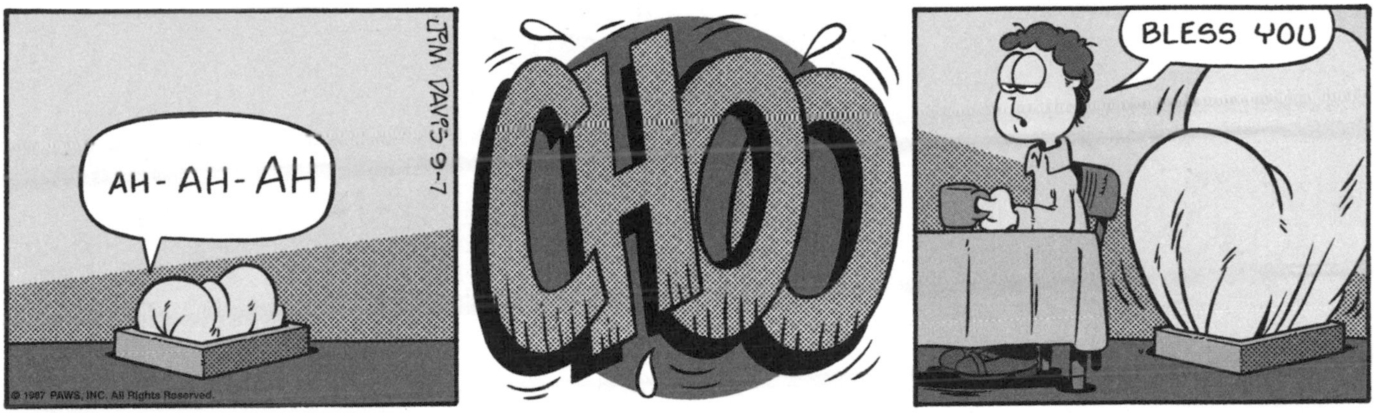
JIM DAVIS 9-7
AH- AH- AH
© 1987 PAWS, INC. All Rights Reserved.
CHOO
BLESS YOU

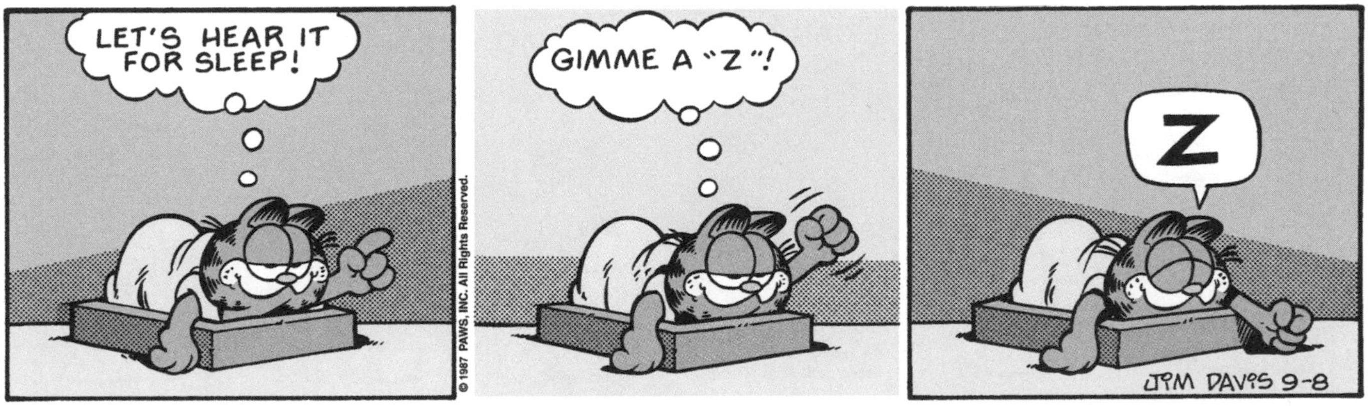
LET'S HEAR IT FOR SLEEP!
© 1987 PAWS, INC. All Rights Reserved.
GIMME A "Z"!
Z
JIM DAVIS 9-8

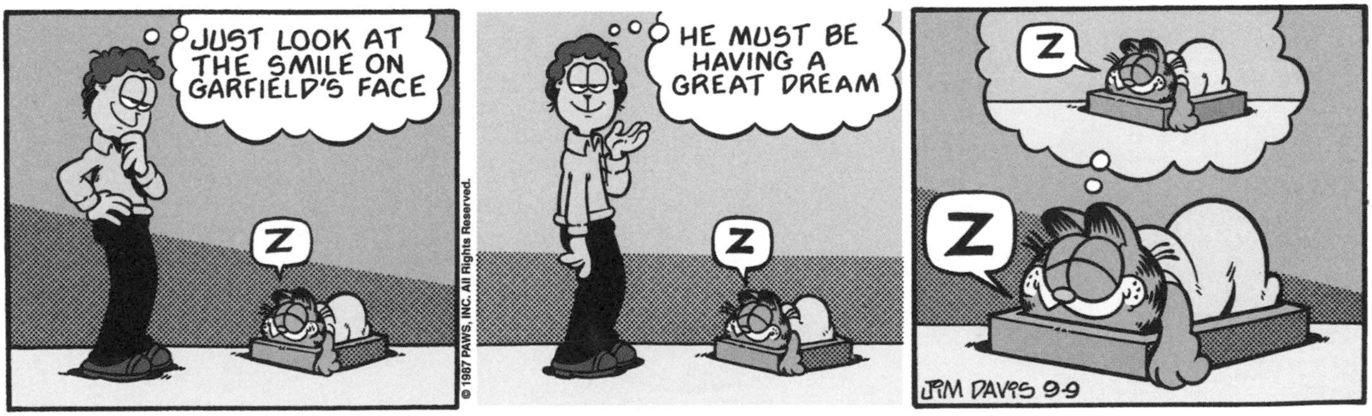
JUST LOOK AT THE SMILE ON GARFIELD'S FACE
Z
© 1987 PAWS, INC. All Rights Reserved.
HE MUST BE HAVING A GREAT DREAM
Z
Z
Z
JIM DAVIS 9-9

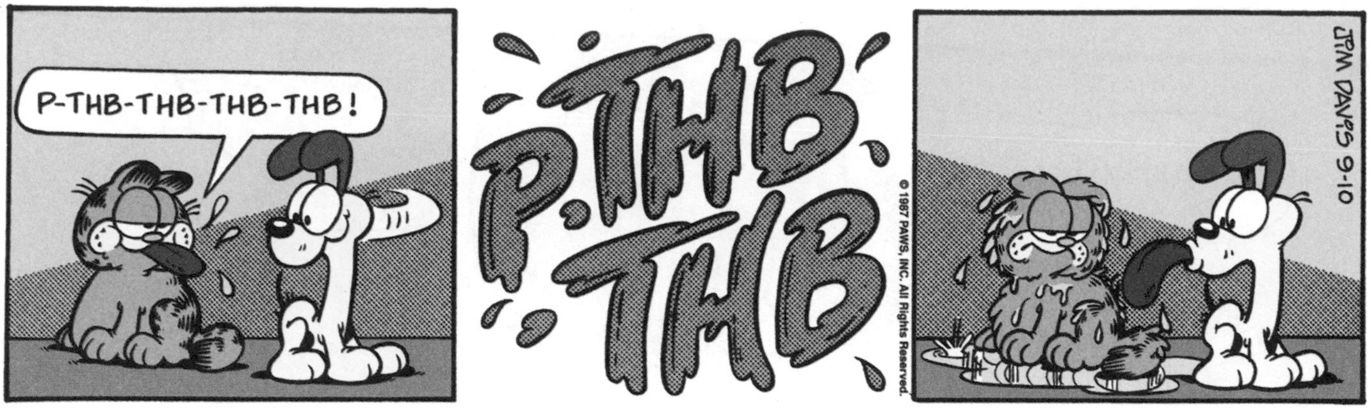
P-THB-THB-THB-THB!
P-THB THB
© 1987 PAWS, INC. All Rights Reserved.
JIM DAVIS 9-10

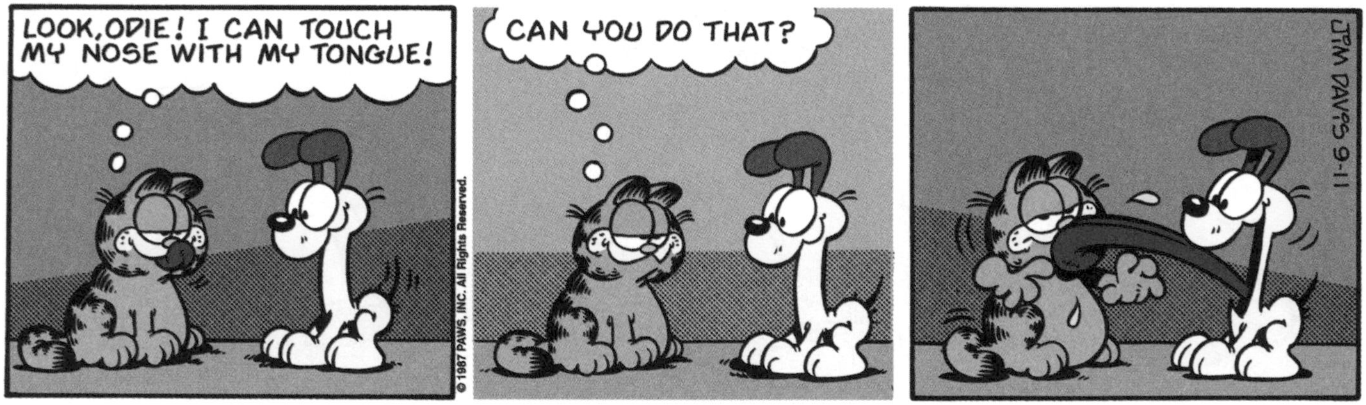
LOOK, ODIE! I CAN TOUCH MY NOSE WITH MY TONGUE!
© 1987 PAWS, INC. All Rights Reserved.
CAN YOU DO THAT?
JIM DAVIS 9-11

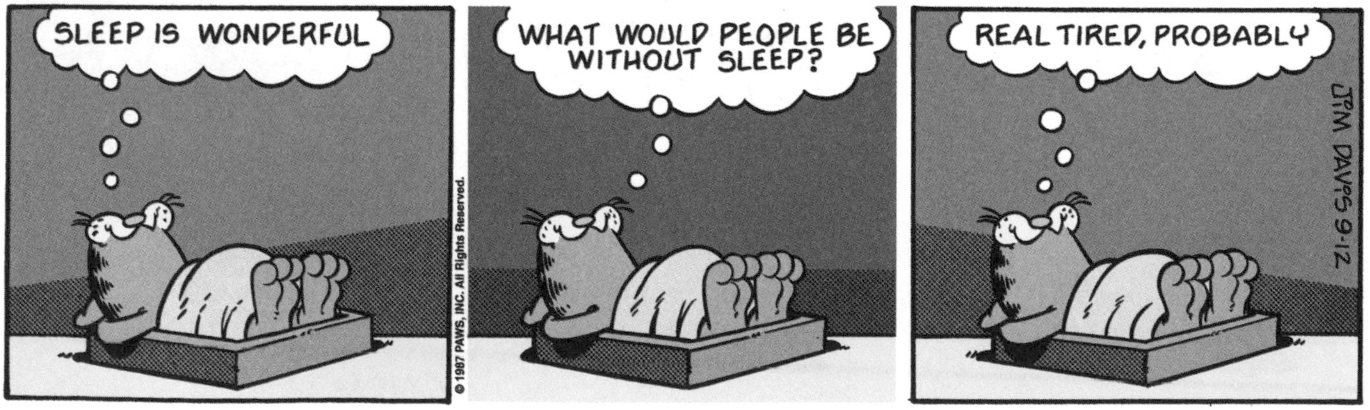
SLEEP IS WONDERFUL
© 1987 PAWS, INC. All Rights Reserved.
WHAT WOULD PEOPLE BE WITHOUT SLEEP?
REAL TIRED, PROBABLY
JIM DAVIS 9-12

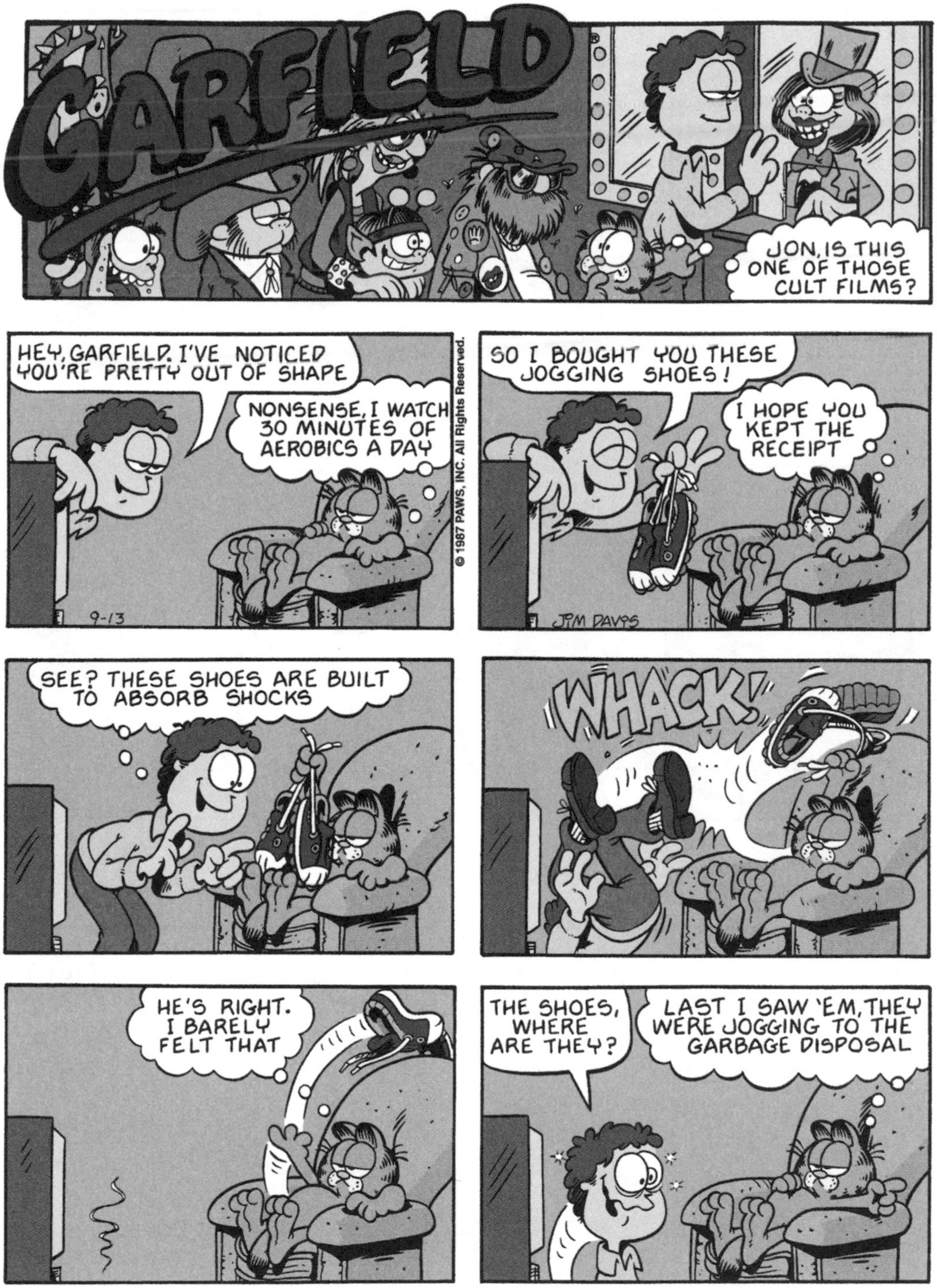
GARFIELD
JON, IS THIS ONE OF THOSE CULT FILMS?
HEY, GARFIELD. I'VE NOTICED YOU'RE PRETTY OUT OF SHAPE
NONSENSE, I WATCH 30 MINUTES OF AEROBICS A DAY
9-13
© 1987 PAWS, INC. All Rights Reserved.
SO I BOUGHT YOU THESE JOGGING SHOES!
I HOPE YOU KEPT THE RECEIPT
JIM DAVIS
SEE? THESE SHOES ARE BUILT TO ABSORB SHOCKS
WHACK!
HE'S RIGHT. I BARELY FELT THAT
THE SHOES, WHERE ARE THEY?
LAST I SAW 'EM, THEY WERE JOGGING TO THE GARBAGE DISPOSAL

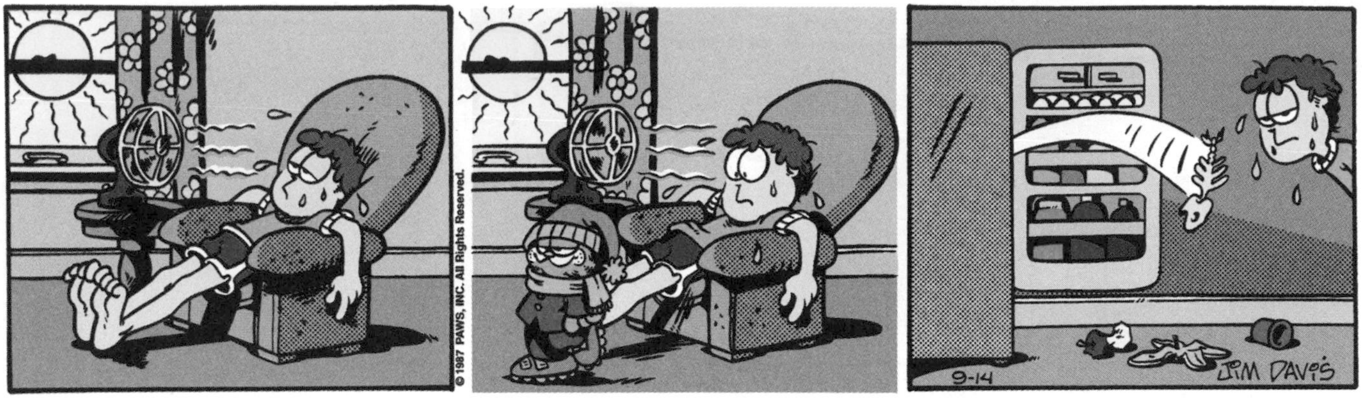
© 1987 PAWS, INC. All Rights Reserved.
9-14
JIM DAVIS

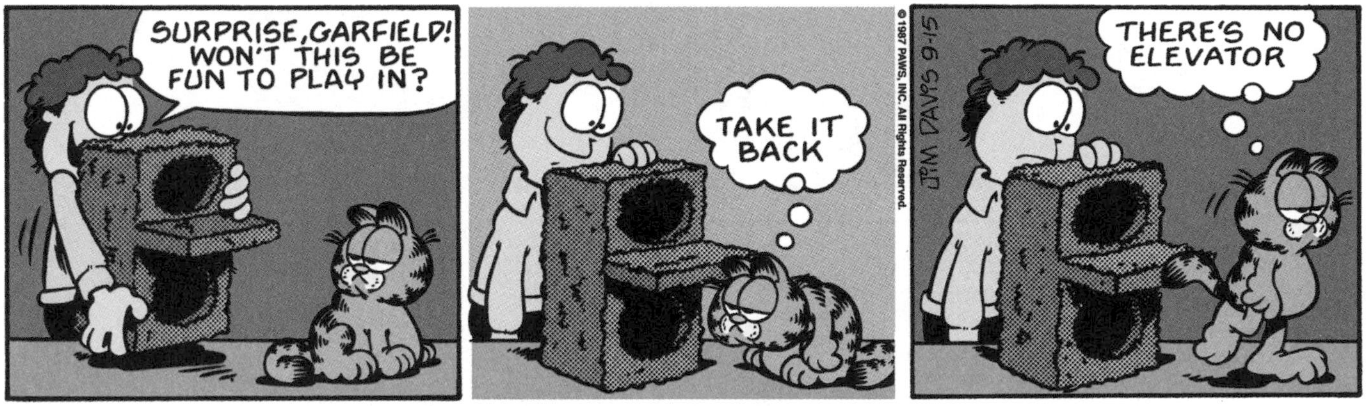
SURPRISE, GARFIELD! WON'T THIS BE FUN TO PLAY IN?
TAKE IT BACK
© 1987 PAWS, INC. All Rights Reserved.
JIM DAVIS 9-15
THERE'S NO ELEVATOR

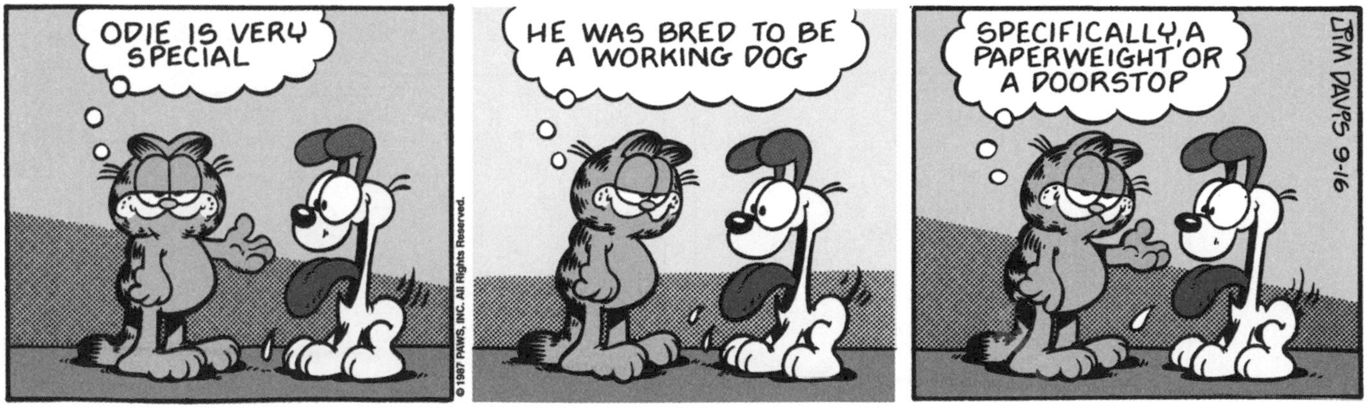
ODIE IS VERY SPECIAL
© 1987 PAWS, INC. All Rights Reserved.
HE WAS BRED TO BE A WORKING DOG
SPECIFICALLY, A PAPERWEIGHT OR A DOORSTOP
JIM DAVIS 9-16

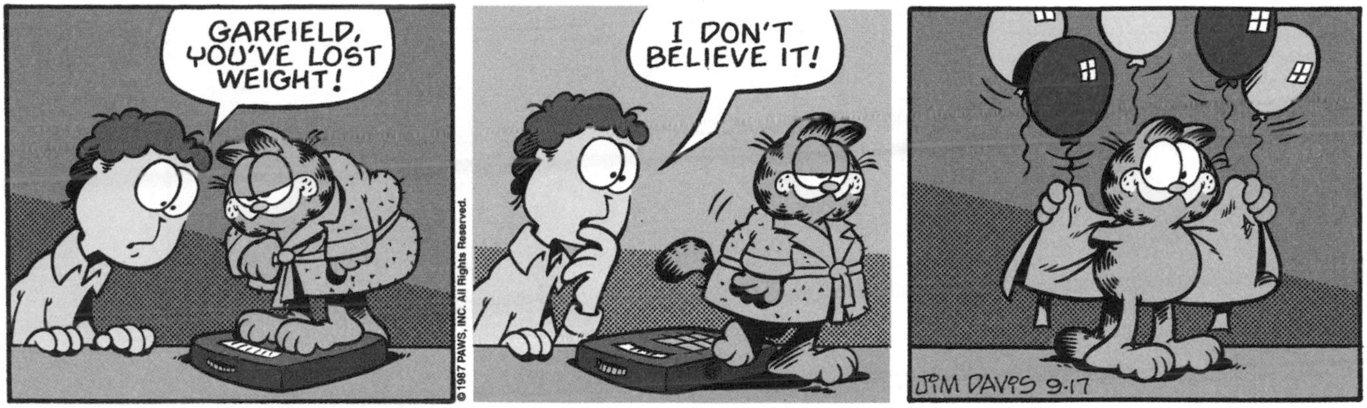
GARFIELD, YOU'VE LOST WEIGHT!
© 1987 PAWS, INC. All Rights Reserved.
I DON'T BELIEVE IT!
JIM DAVIS 9-17

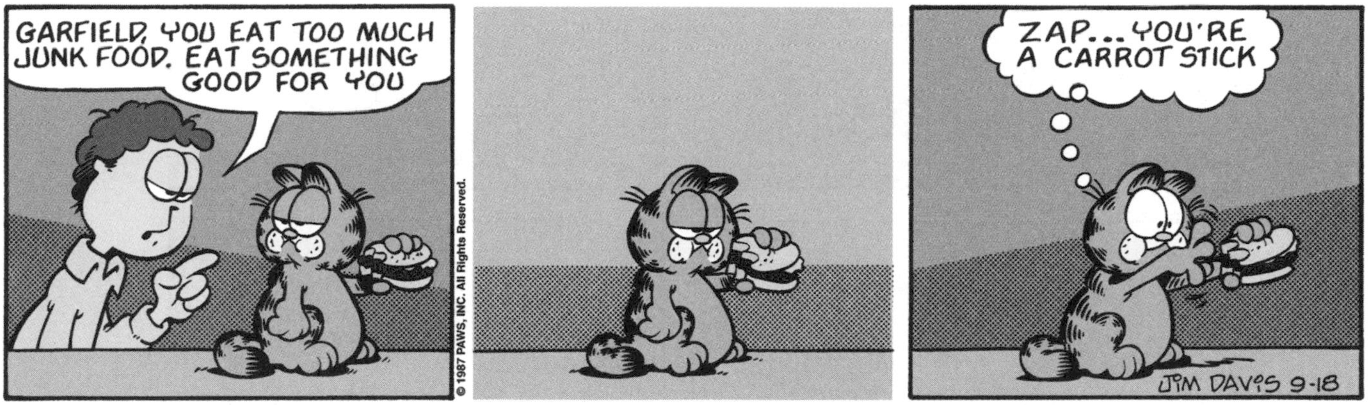
GARFIELD, YOU EAT TOO MUCH JUNK FOOD. EAT SOMETHING GOOD FOR YOU
© 1987 PAWS, INC. All Rights Reserved.
ZAP... YOU'RE A CARROT STICK
JIM DAVIS 9-18

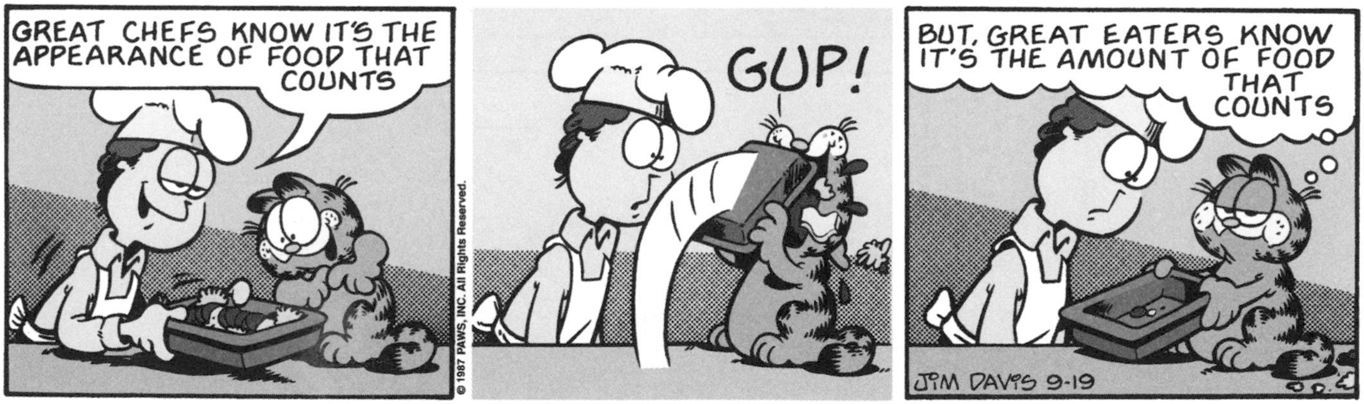
GREAT CHEFS KNOW IT'S THE APPEARANCE OF FOOD THAT COUNTS
© 1987 PAWS, INC. All Rights Reserved.
GUP!
BUT, GREAT EATERS KNOW IT'S THE AMOUNT OF FOOD THAT COUNTS
JIM DAVIS 9-19

GARFIELD®
NO, PLEASE DON'T DO IT, IN THE NAME OF HUMANITY!!
WHUMP!
© 1987 PAWS, INC. All Rights Reserved.
HAW! HAW! HAW! HAW!
ZIP!
WHUMP!
HAW! HAW! HAW!
REBA! COME HERE AND LOOK AT THIS, BUT YOU'D BETTER CINCH UP YOUR CORSET FIRST!
JIM DAVIS 9-20

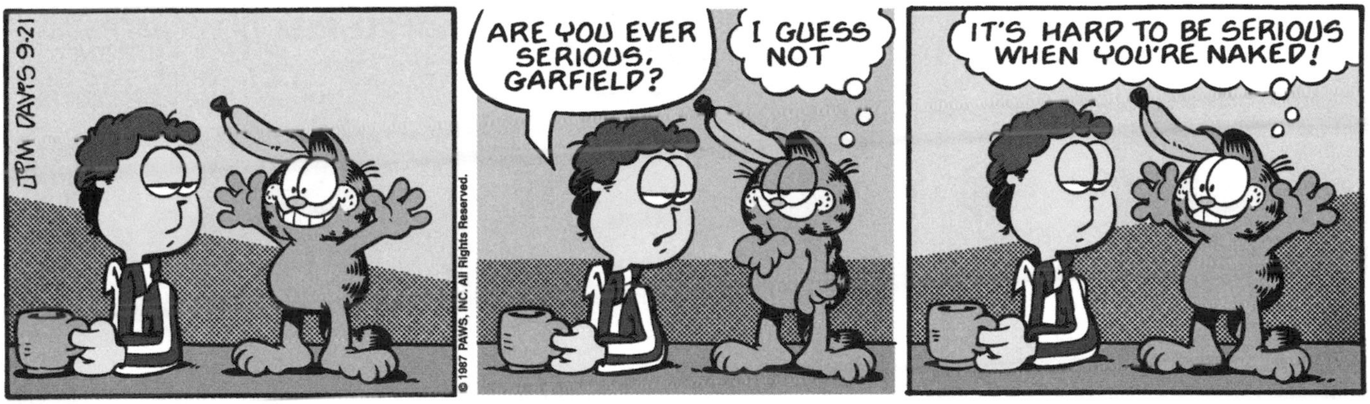
JIM DAVIS 9-21
© 1987 PAWS, INC. All Rights Reserved.
ARE YOU EVER SERIOUS, GARFIELD?
I GUESS NOT
IT'S HARD TO BE SERIOUS WHEN YOU'RE NAKED!

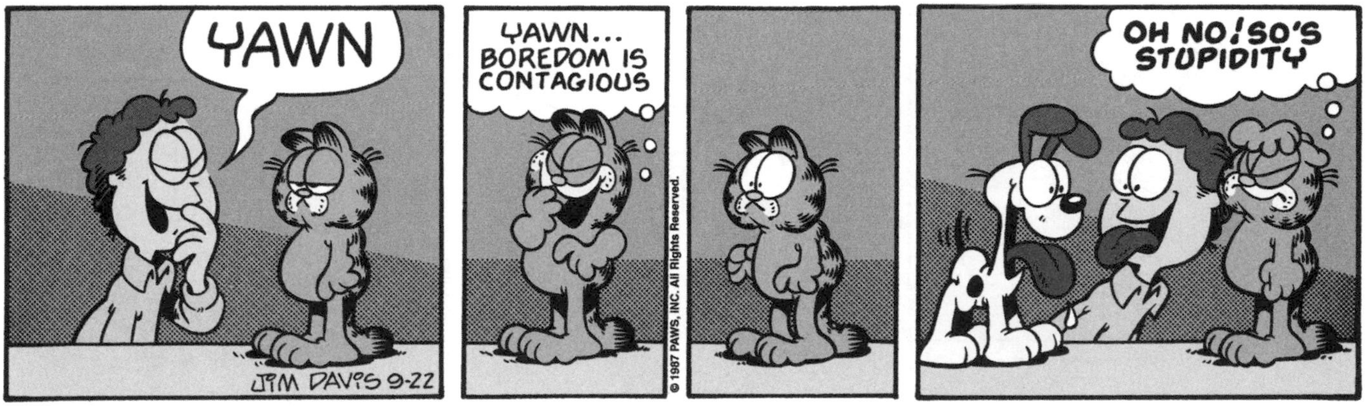
YAWN
JIM DAVIS 9-22
YAWN... BOREDOM IS CONTAGIOUS
© 1987 PAWS, INC. All Rights Reserved.
OH NO! SO'S STUPIDITY

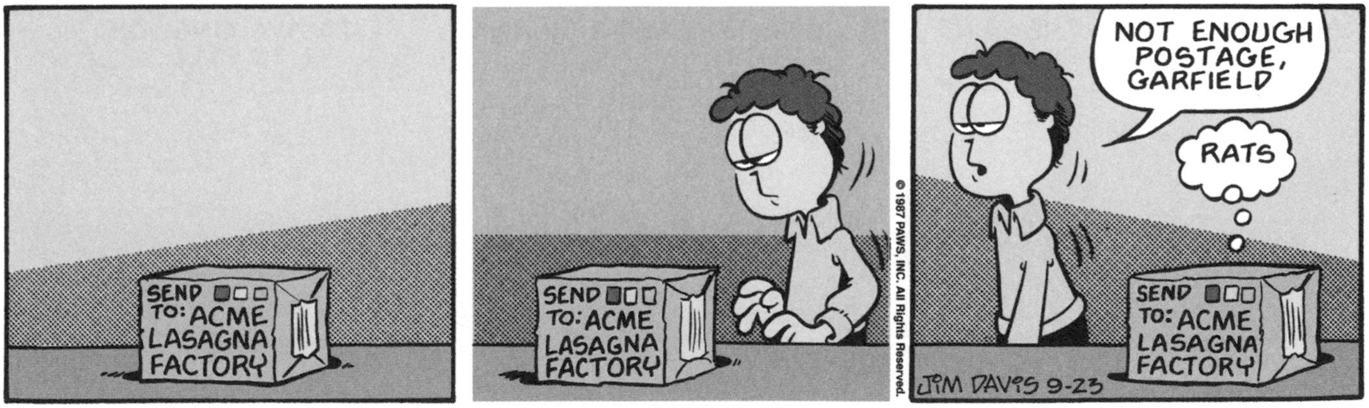
SEND TO: ACME LASAGNA FACTORY
SEND TO: ACME LASAGNA FACTORY
© 1987 PAWS, INC. All Rights Reserved.
NOT ENOUGH POSTAGE, GARFIELD
RATS
SEND TO: ACME LASAGNA FACTORY
JIM DAVIS 9-23

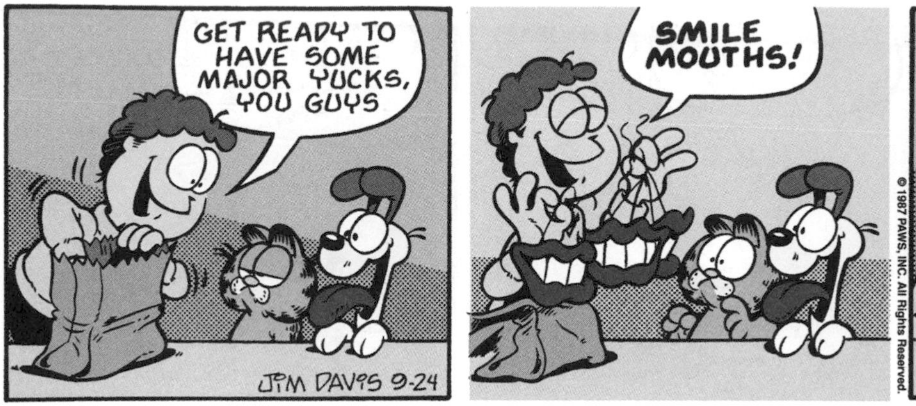
GET READY TO HAVE SOME MAJOR YUCKS, YOU GUYS
JIM DAVIS 9-24
SMILE MOUTHS!
© 1987 PAWS, INC. All Rights Reserved.
HEE HEE!
I'LL KEEP HIM LAUGHING WHILE YOU GET THE AUTHORITIES

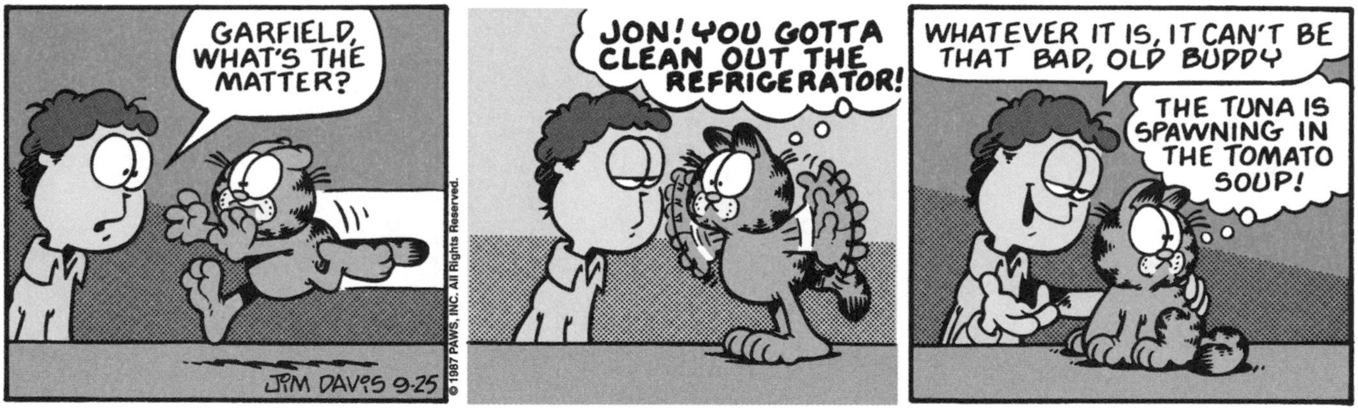
GARFIELD, WHAT'S THE MATTER?
JIM DAVIS 9-25
© 1987 PAWS, INC. All Rights Reserved.
JON! YOU GOTTA CLEAN OUT THE REFRIGERATOR!
WHATEVER IT IS, IT CAN'T BE THAT BAD, OLD BUDDY
THE TUNA IS SPAWNING IN THE TOMATO SOUP!

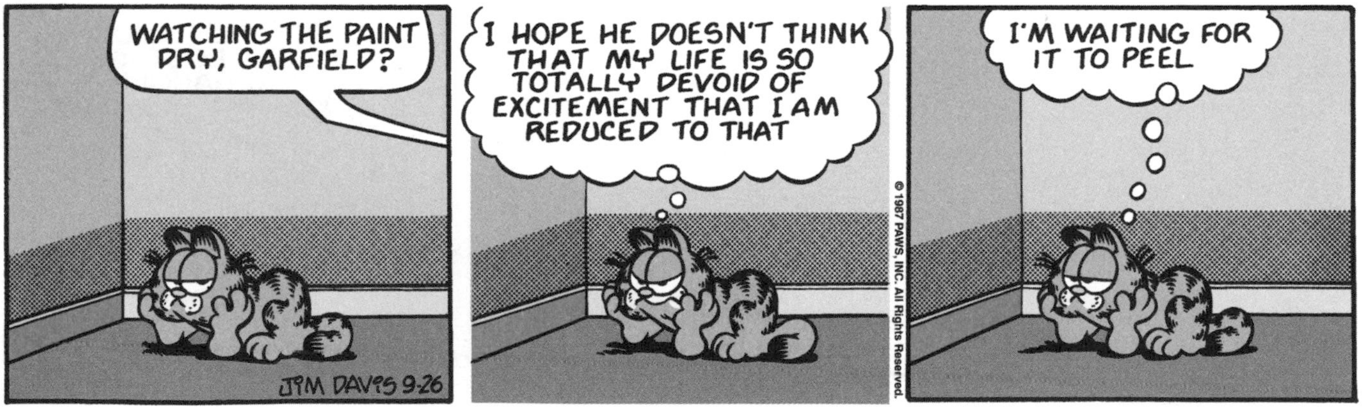
WATCHING THE PAINT DRY, GARFIELD?
JIM DAVIS 9-26
I HOPE HE DOESN'T THINK THAT MY LIFE IS SO TOTALLY DEVOID OF EXCITEMENT THAT I AM REDUCED TO THAT
© 1987 PAWS, INC. All Rights Reserved.
I'M WAITING FOR IT TO PEEL

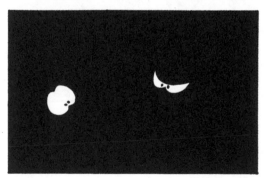

A HUNGRY VULTURE PERCHES ABOVE HIS PREY, SILENTLY, PATIENTLY, WAITING FOR HIS MEAL TO DRAW ITS LAST BREATH

CLICK

CLICK

STOP THAT! YOU KNOW I HATE THAT!

NO MORE VULTURES!

NO MORE VULTURES

9-27

Z

A VORACIOUS ALLIGATOR STEALTHILY GLIDES TOWARD THE FINGERS OF AN UNWARY RIVER TRAVELER

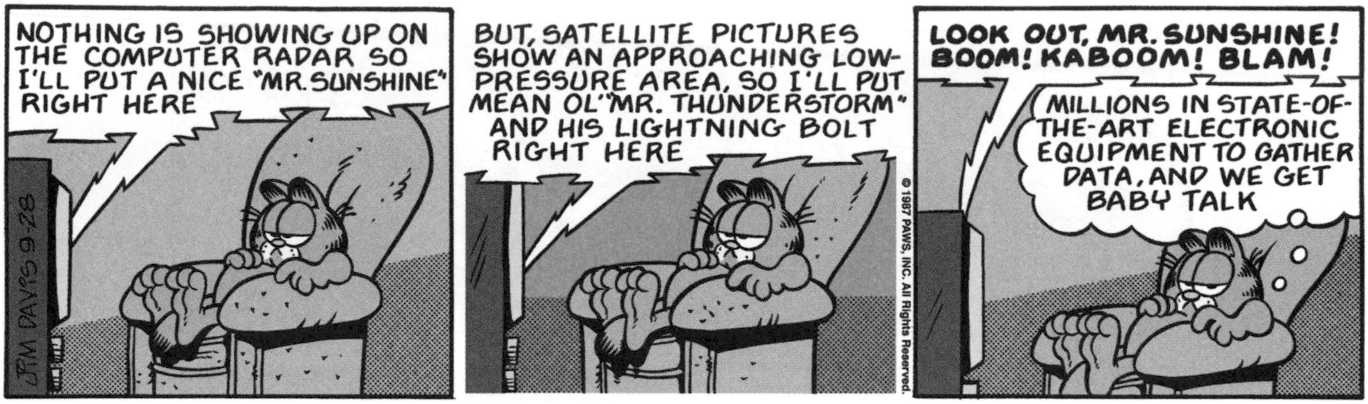
NOTHING IS SHOWING UP ON THE COMPUTER RADAR SO I'LL PUT A NICE "MR. SUNSHINE" RIGHT HERE
JIM DAVIS 9-28
BUT, SATELLITE PICTURES SHOW AN APPROACHING LOW-PRESSURE AREA, SO I'LL PUT MEAN OL' "MR. THUNDERSTORM" AND HIS LIGHTNING BOLT RIGHT HERE
© 1987 PAWS, INC. All Rights Reserved.
LOOK OUT, MR. SUNSHINE! BOOM! KABOOM! BLAM!
MILLIONS IN STATE-OF-THE-ART ELECTRONIC EQUIPMENT TO GATHER DATA, AND WE GET BABY TALK

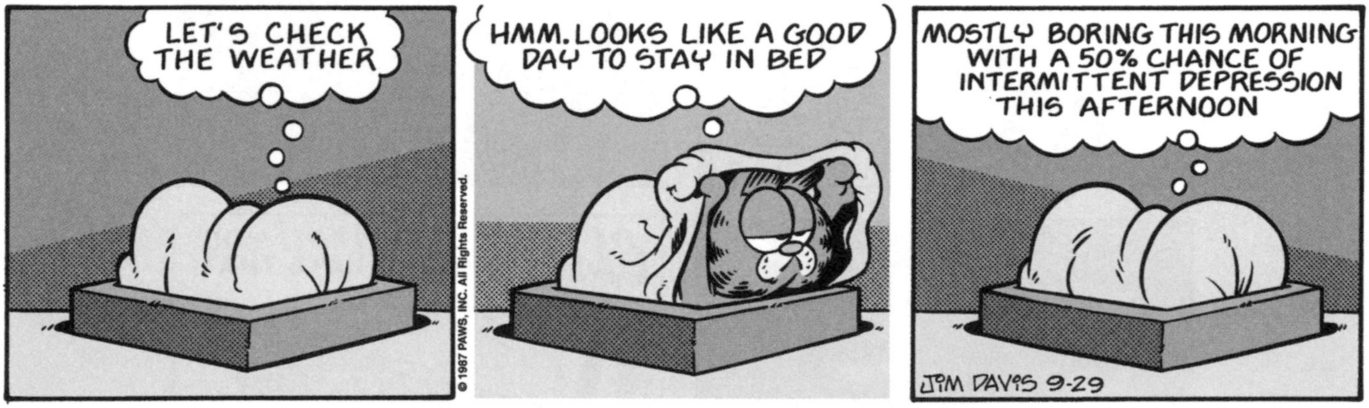
LET'S CHECK THE WEATHER
© 1987 PAWS, INC. All Rights Reserved.
HMM. LOOKS LIKE A GOOD DAY TO STAY IN BED
MOSTLY BORING THIS MORNING WITH A 50% CHANCE OF INTERMITTENT DEPRESSION THIS AFTERNOON
JIM DAVIS 9-29

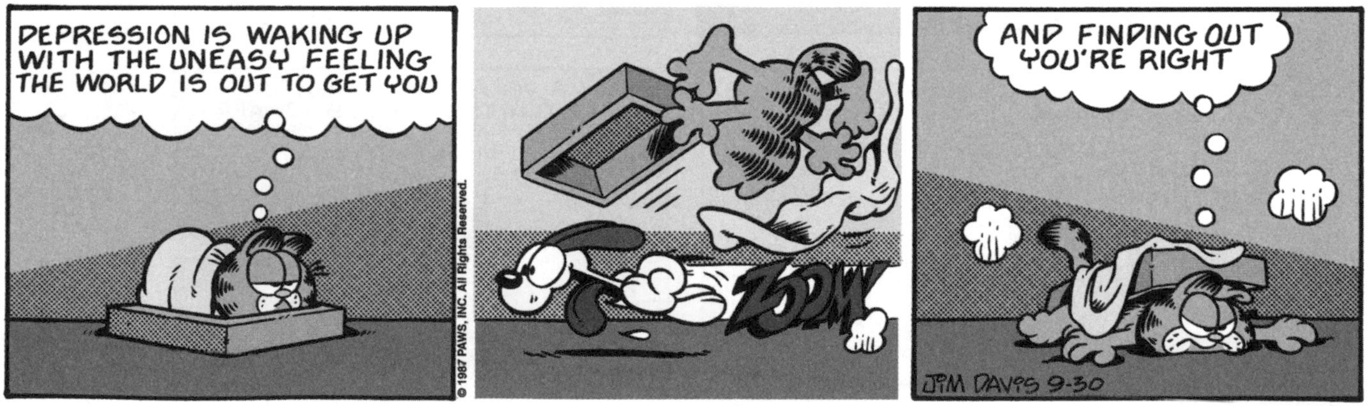
DEPRESSION IS WAKING UP WITH THE UNEASY FEELING THE WORLD IS OUT TO GET YOU
© 1987 PAWS, INC. All Rights Reserved.
ZOOM
AND FINDING OUT YOU'RE RIGHT
JIM DAVIS 9-30

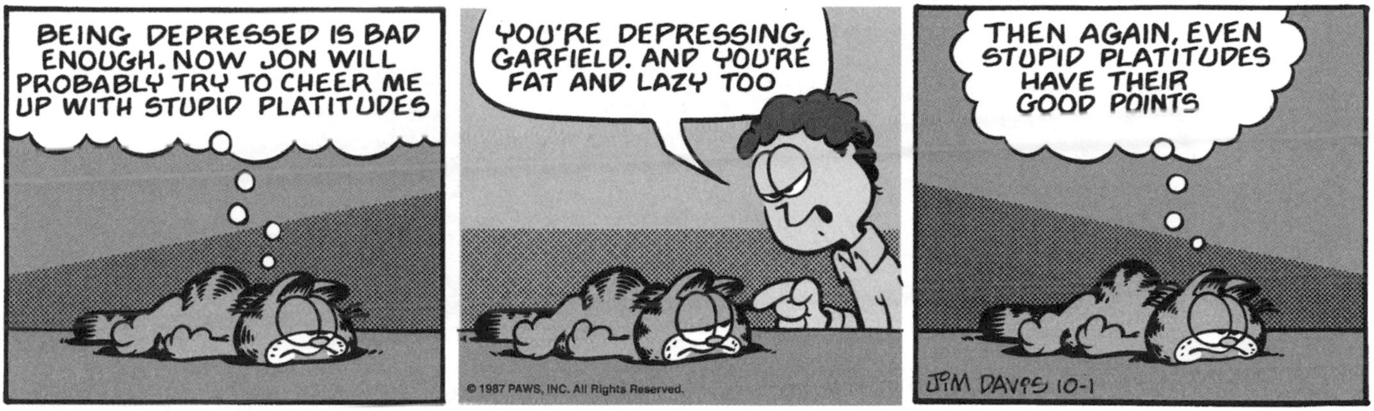
BEING DEPRESSED IS BAD ENOUGH. NOW JON WILL PROBABLY TRY TO CHEER ME UP WITH STUPID PLATITUDES
YOU'RE DEPRESSING, GARFIELD. AND YOU'RE FAT AND LAZY TOO
© 1987 PAWS, INC. All Rights Reserved.
THEN AGAIN, EVEN STUPID PLATITUDES HAVE THEIR GOOD POINTS
JIM DAVIS 10-1

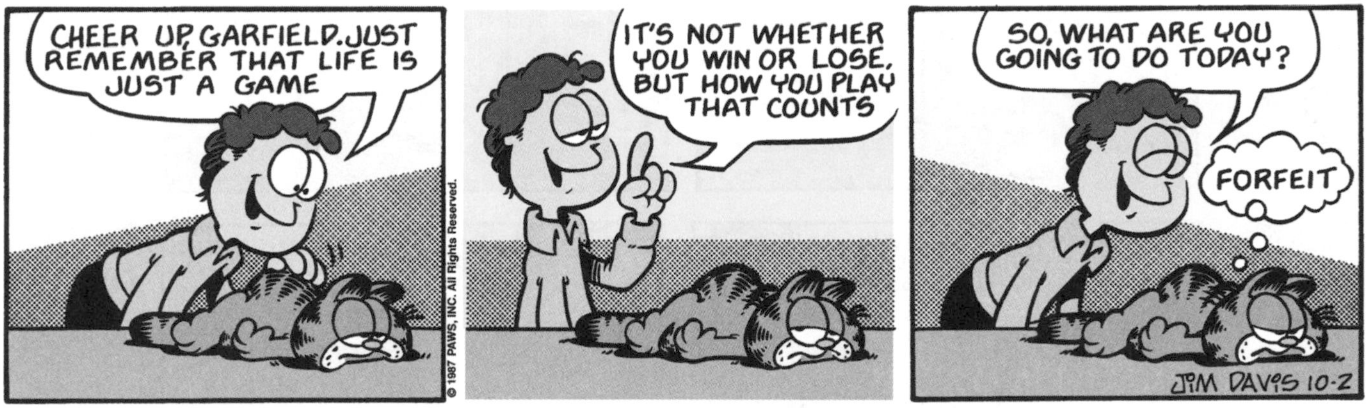
CHEER UP, GARFIELD. JUST REMEMBER THAT LIFE IS JUST A GAME
© 1987 PAWS, INC. All Rights Reserved.
IT'S NOT WHETHER YOU WIN OR LOSE, BUT HOW YOU PLAY THAT COUNTS
SO, WHAT ARE YOU GOING TO DO TODAY?
FORFEIT
JIM DAVIS 10-2

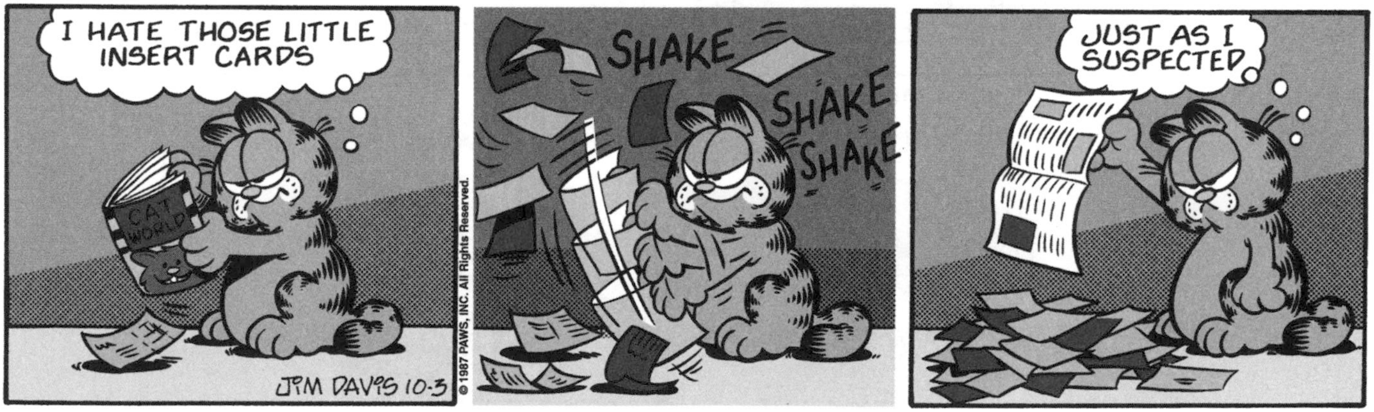
I HATE THOSE LITTLE INSERT CARDS
CAT WORLD
JIM DAVIS 10-3
© 1987 PAWS, INC. All Rights Reserved.
SHAKE
SHAKE
SHAKE
JUST AS I SUSPECTED

GARFIELD
CAN WE BE OF ASSISTANCE?
THAT STUPID DOG NEXT DOOR IS IN FOR A **BIG** SURPRISE
WHEN HE COMES BY, HE WILL MISTAKE THE MIRROR FOR ME
© 1987 PAWS, INC. All Rights Reserved.
THEN HE WILL ATTACK AND FALL INTO THIS PIT
THEN THIS NET WILL FALL ON HIM
THEN THIS CEMENT MIXER WILL TIP, SEALING THAT SUCKER UP FOR ABOUT TEN MILLION YEARS
WAIT! WAIT! GO BACK AND COME IN AGAIN!
JIM DAVIS 10-4

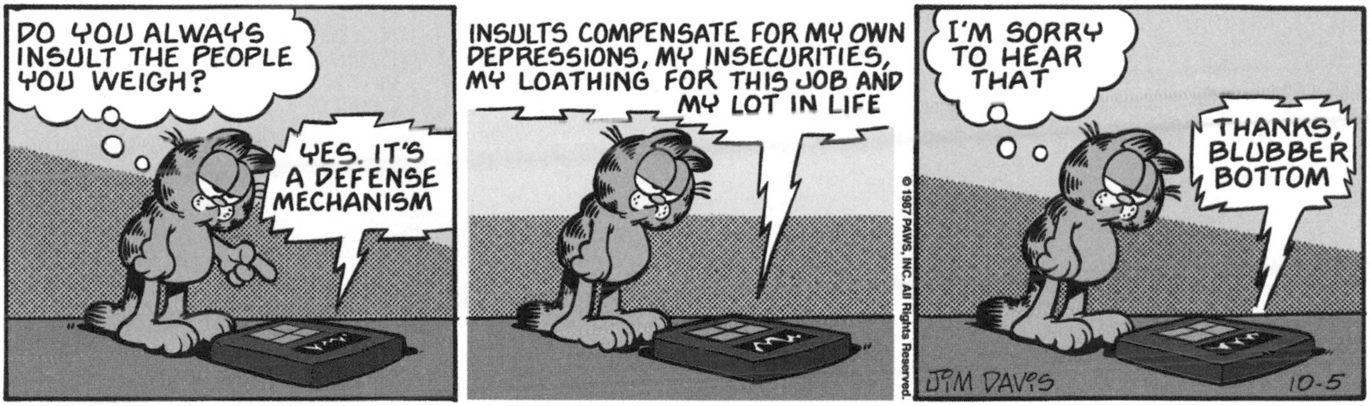
DO YOU ALWAYS INSULT THE PEOPLE YOU WEIGH?
YES. IT'S A DEFENSE MECHANISM
INSULTS COMPENSATE FOR MY OWN DEPRESSIONS, MY INSECURITIES, MY LOATHING FOR THIS JOB AND MY LOT IN LIFE
© 1987 PAWS, INC. All Rights Reserved.
I'M SORRY TO HEAR THAT
THANKS, BLUBBER BOTTOM
JIM DAVIS
10-5

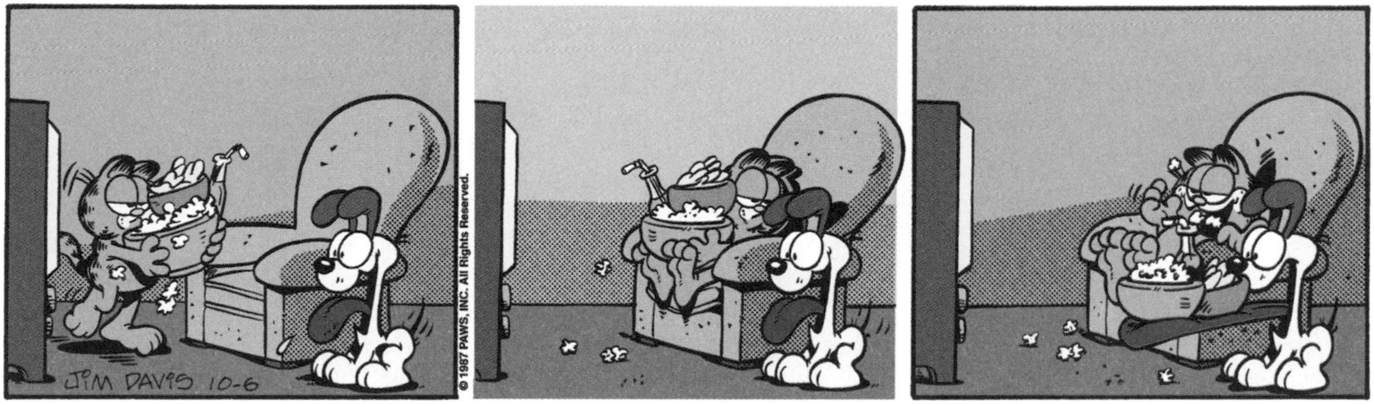
JIM DAVIS 10-6
© 1987 PAWS, INC. All Rights Reserved.

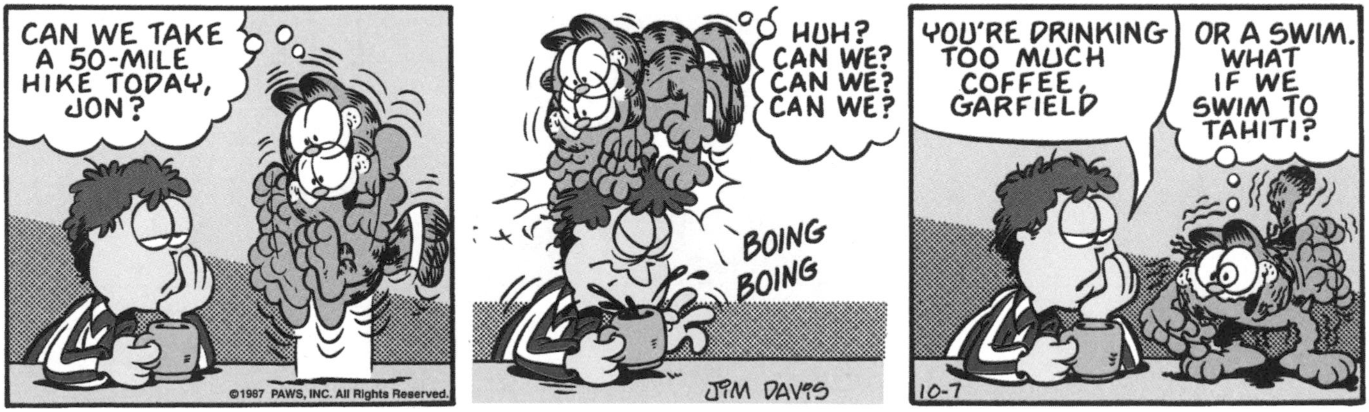
CAN WE TAKE A 50-MILE HIKE TODAY, JON?
©1987 PAWS, INC. All Rights Reserved.
HUH? CAN WE? CAN WE? CAN WE?
BOING
BOING
JIM DAVIS
YOU'RE DRINKING TOO MUCH COFFEE, GARFIELD
OR A SWIM. WHAT IF WE SWIM TO TAHITI?
10-7

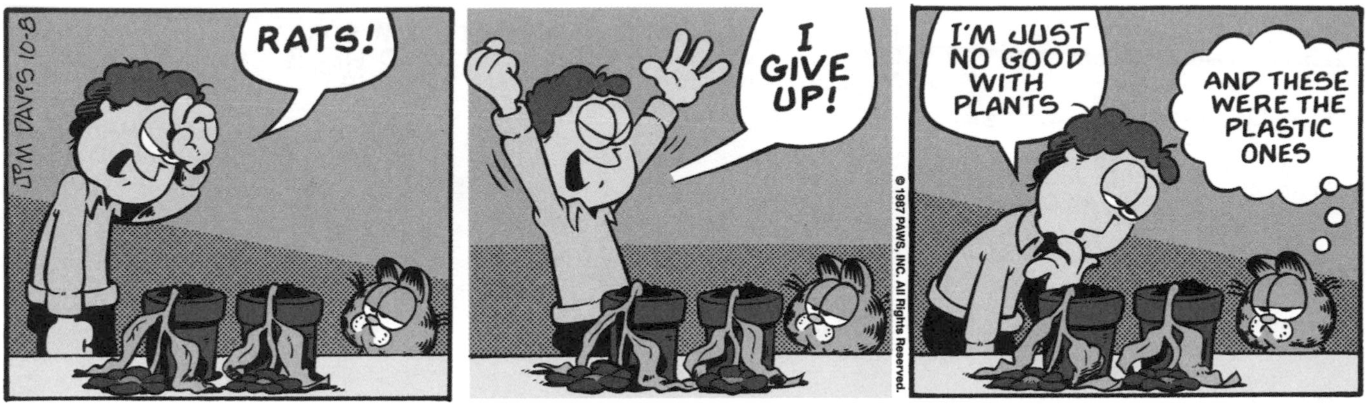
JIM DAVIS 10-8
RATS!
I GIVE UP!
© 1987 PAWS, INC. All Rights Reserved.
I'M JUST NO GOOD WITH PLANTS
AND THESE WERE THE PLASTIC ONES

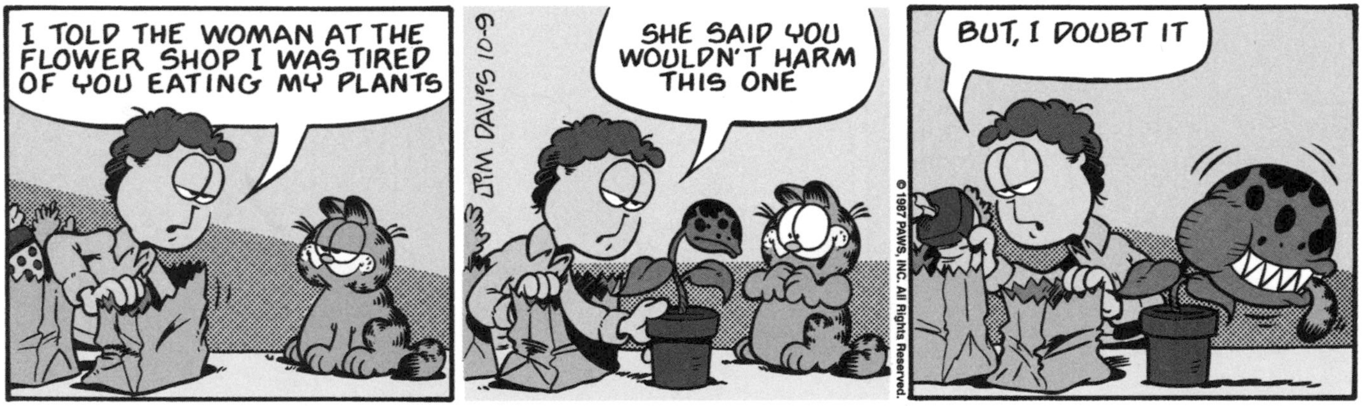
I TOLD THE WOMAN AT THE FLOWER SHOP I WAS TIRED OF YOU EATING MY PLANTS
JIM DAVIS 10-9
SHE SAID YOU WOULDN'T HARM THIS ONE
© 1987 PAWS, INC. All Rights Reserved.
BUT, I DOUBT IT

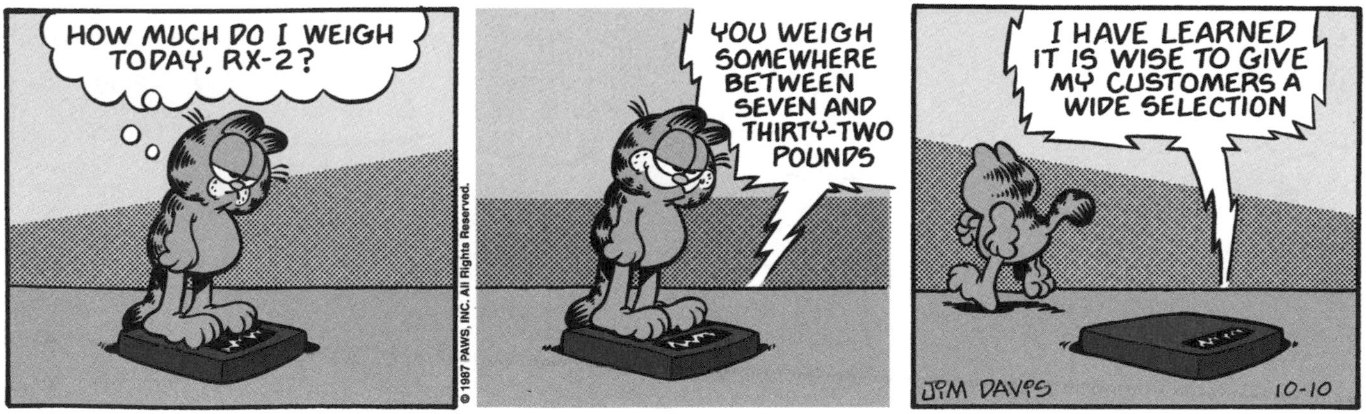
HOW MUCH DO I WEIGH TODAY, RX-2?
© 1987 PAWS, INC. All Rights Reserved.
YOU WEIGH SOMEWHERE BETWEEN SEVEN AND THIRTY-TWO POUNDS
I HAVE LEARNED IT IS WISE TO GIVE MY CUSTOMERS A WIDE SELECTION
JIM DAVIS
10-10

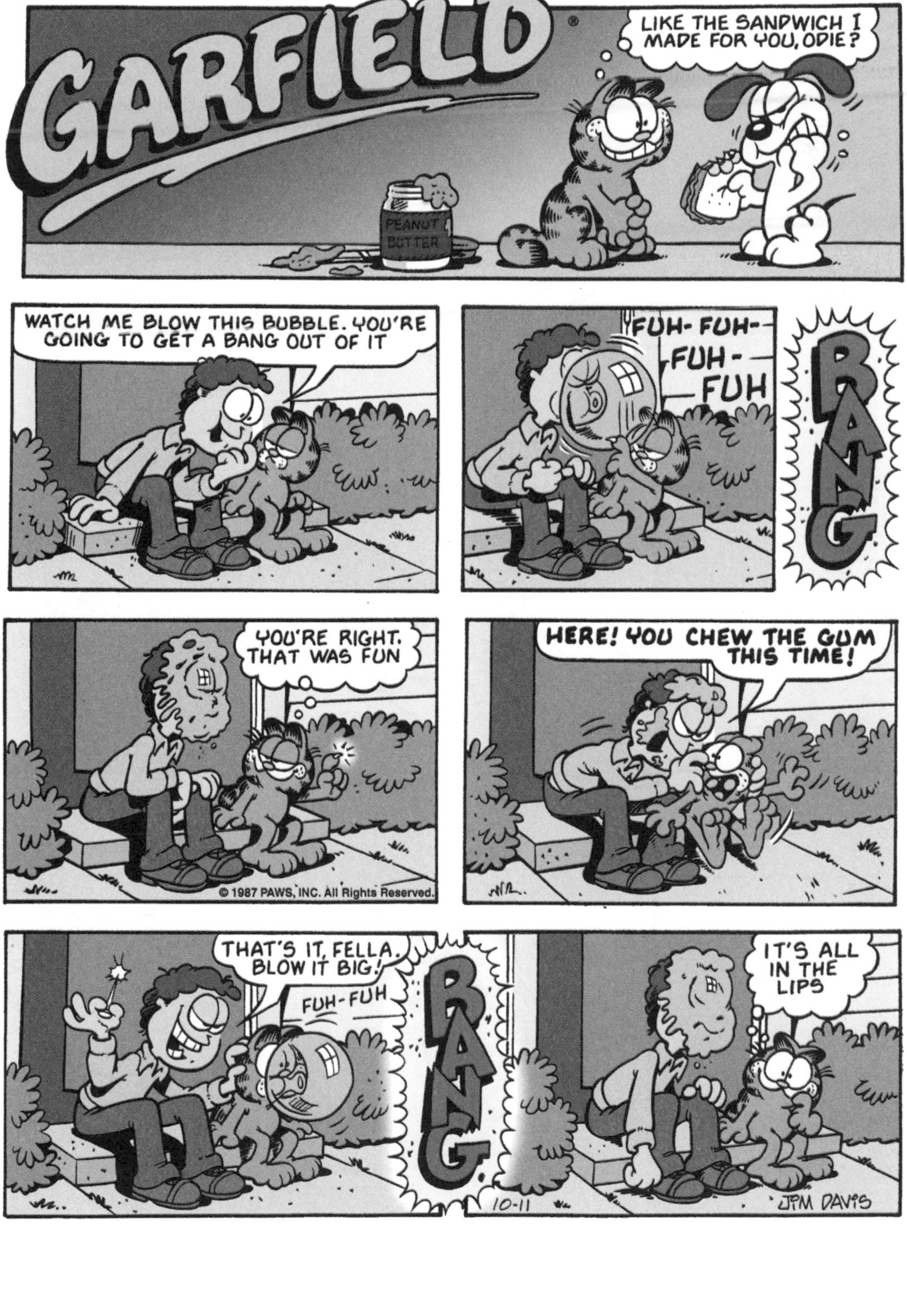
GARFIELD
LIKE THE SANDWICH I MADE FOR YOU, ODIE?
PEANUT BUTTER
WATCH ME BLOW THIS BUBBLE. YOU'RE GOING TO GET A BANG OUT OF IT
FUH-FUH-FUH-FUH
BANG
YOU'RE RIGHT. THAT WAS FUN
© 1987 PAWS, INC. All Rights Reserved.
HERE! YOU CHEW THE GUM THIS TIME!
THAT'S IT, FELLA. BLOW IT BIG!
FUH-FUH
BANG
IT'S ALL IN THE LIPS
10-11
JIM DAVIS

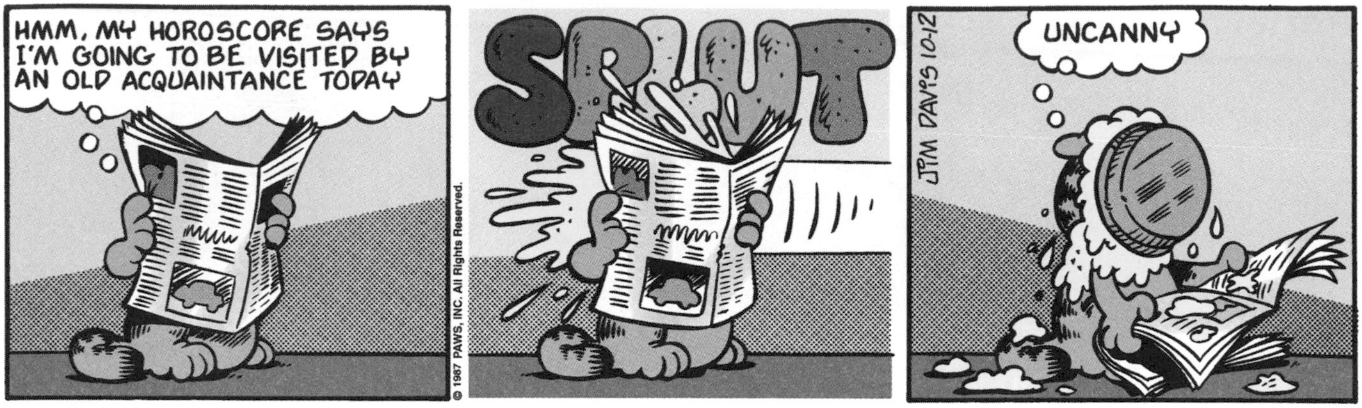
HMM, MY HOROSCOPE SAYS I'M GOING TO BE VISITED BY AN OLD ACQUAINTANCE TODAY
SPLUT
JIM DAVIS 10-12
UNCANNY

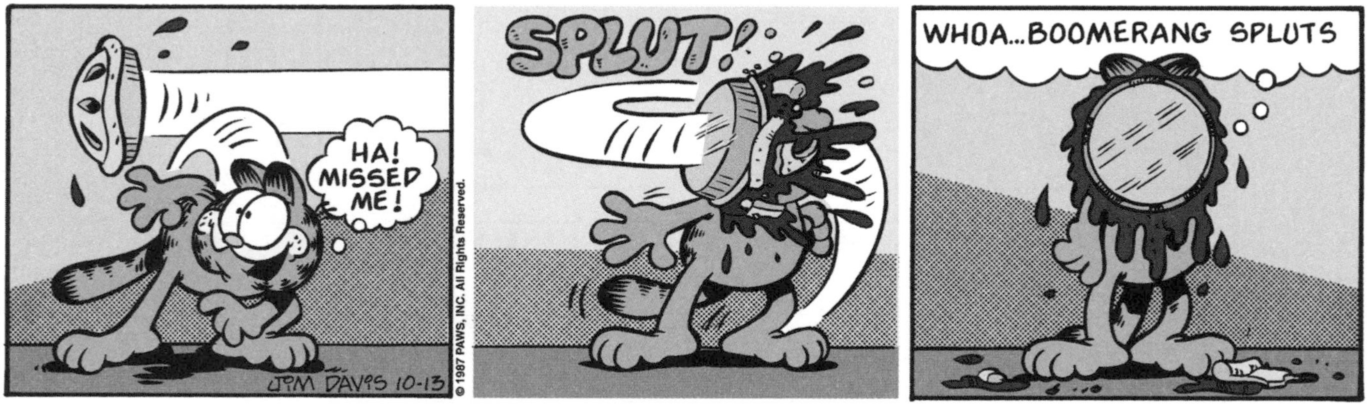
HA! MISSED ME!
JIM DAVIS 10-13
SPLUT!
WHOA...BOOMERANG SPLUTS

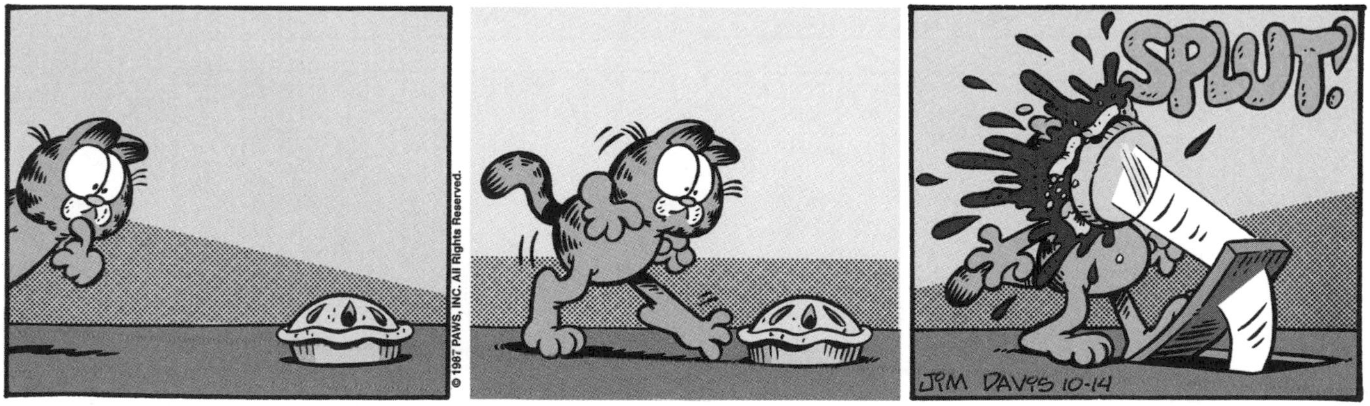
SPLUT!
JIM DAVIS 10-14

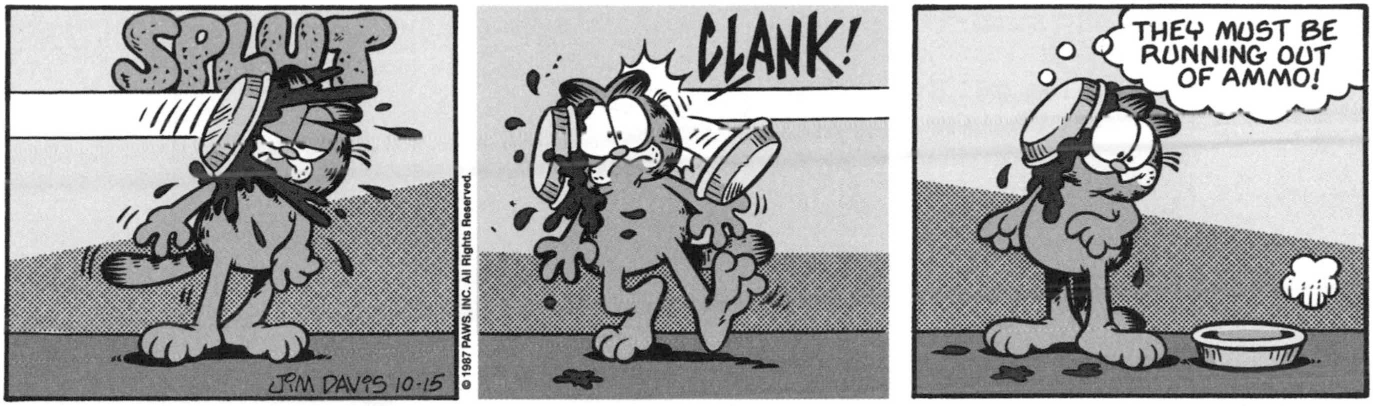
SPLUT
JIM DAVIS 10-15
© 1987 PAWS, INC. All Rights Reserved.
CLANK!
THEY MUST BE RUNNING OUT OF AMMO!

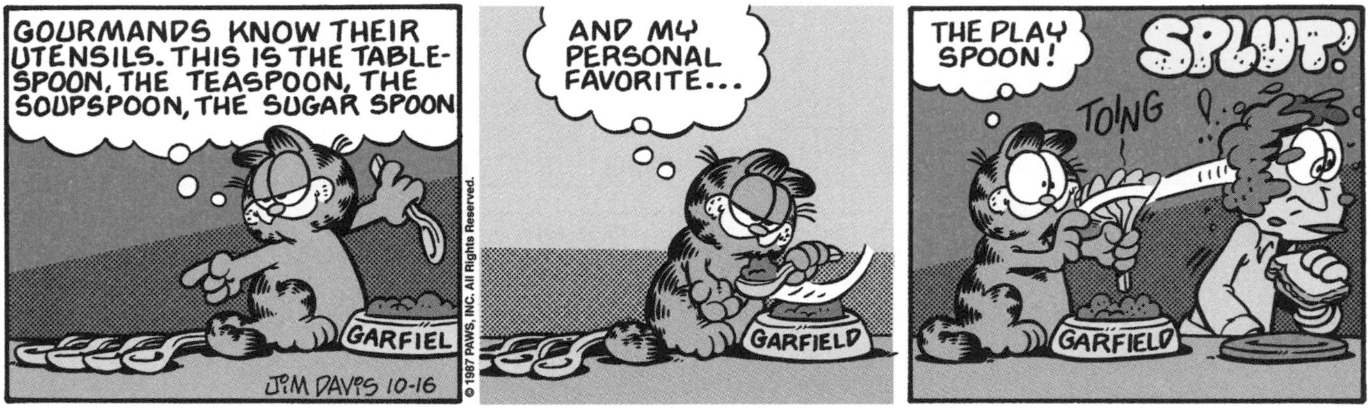
GOURMANDS KNOW THEIR UTENSILS. THIS IS THE TABLESPOON, THE TEASPOON, THE SOUPSPOON, THE SUGAR SPOON
GARFIEL
JIM DAVIS 10-16
© 1987 PAWS, INC. All Rights Reserved.
AND MY PERSONAL FAVORITE...
GARFIELD
THE PLAY SPOON!
SPLUT!
TOING
GARFIELD

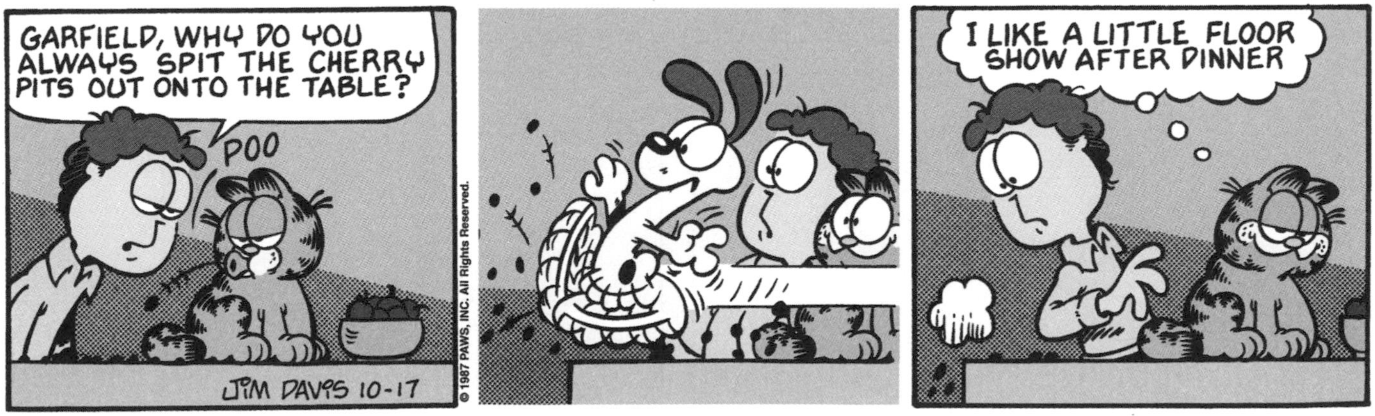
GARFIELD, WHY DO YOU ALWAYS SPIT THE CHERRY PITS OUT ONTO THE TABLE?
POO
JIM DAVIS 10-17
© 1987 PAWS, INC. All Rights Reserved.
I LIKE A LITTLE FLOOR SHOW AFTER DINNER

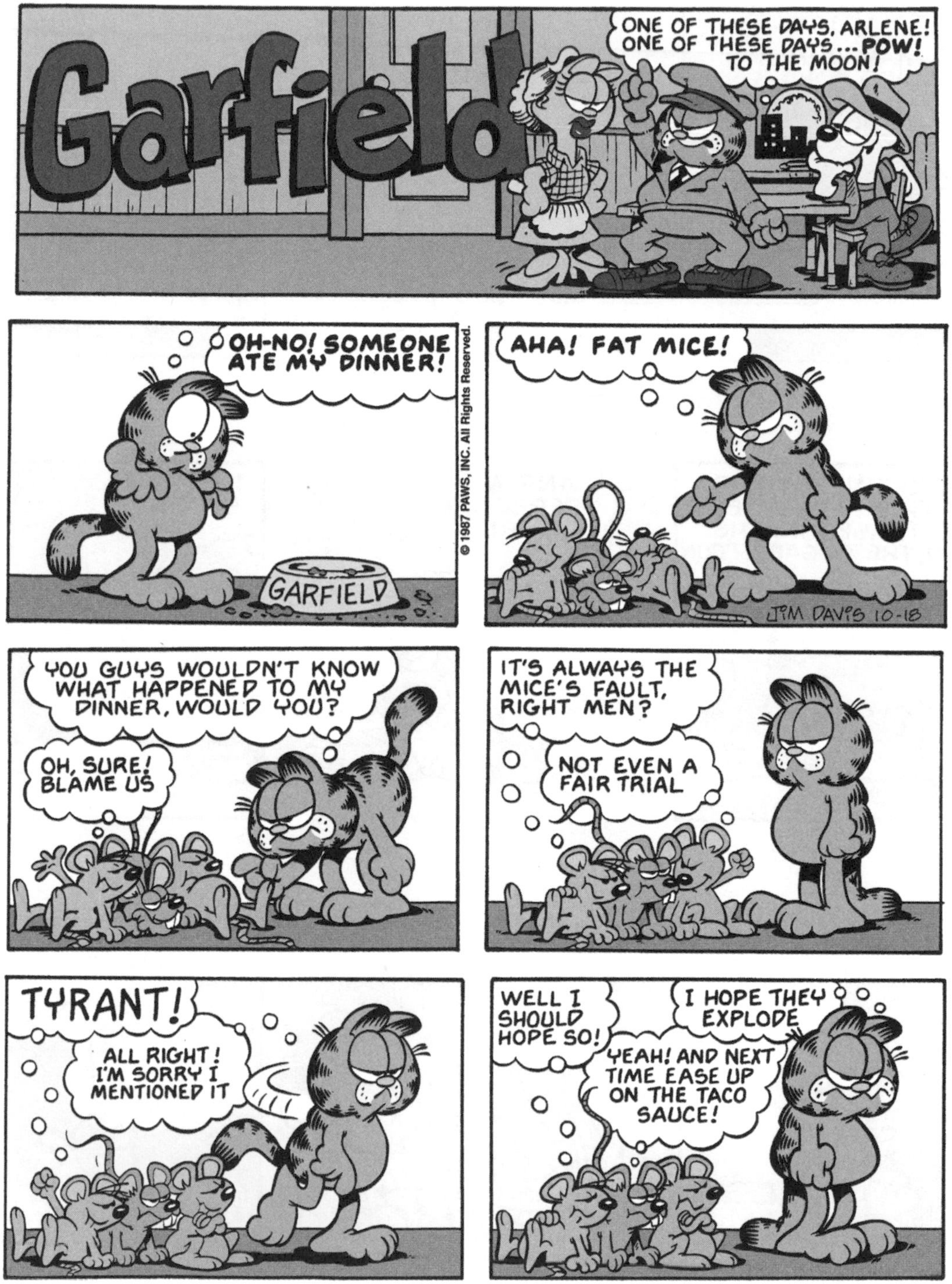
Garfield
ONE OF THESE DAYS, ARLENE! ONE OF THESE DAYS... POW! TO THE MOON!
OH-NO! SOMEONE ATE MY DINNER!
GARFIELD
AHA! FAT MICE!
JIM DAVIS 10-18
YOU GUYS WOULDN'T KNOW WHAT HAPPENED TO MY DINNER, WOULD YOU?
OH, SURE! BLAME US
IT'S ALWAYS THE MICE'S FAULT, RIGHT MEN?
NOT EVEN A FAIR TRIAL
TYRANT!
ALL RIGHT! I'M SORRY I MENTIONED IT
WELL I SHOULD HOPE SO!
I HOPE THEY EXPLODE
YEAH! AND NEXT TIME EASE UP ON THE TACO SAUCE!

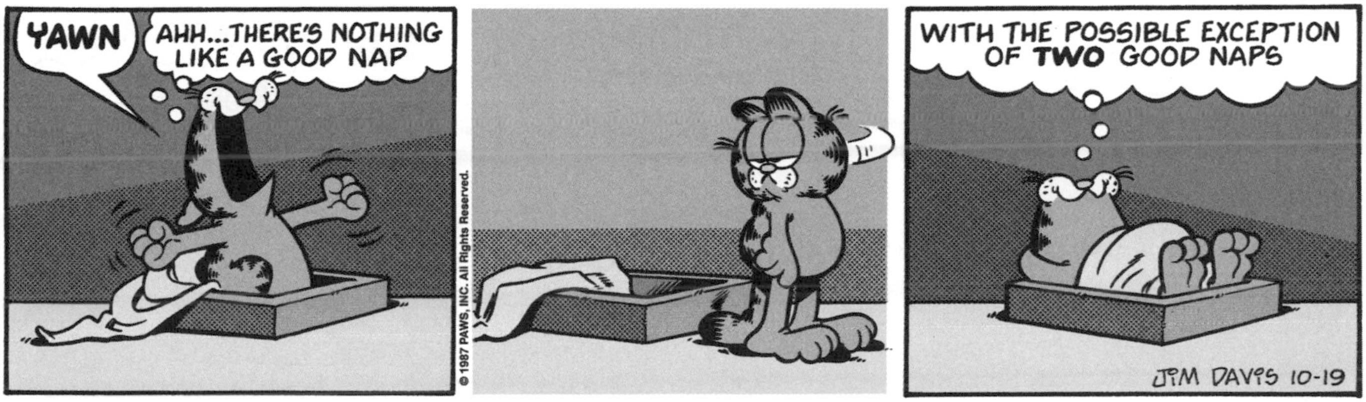
YAWN
AHH...THERE'S NOTHING LIKE A GOOD NAP
© 1987 PAWS, INC. All Rights Reserved.
WITH THE POSSIBLE EXCEPTION OF TWO GOOD NAPS
JIM DAVIS 10-19

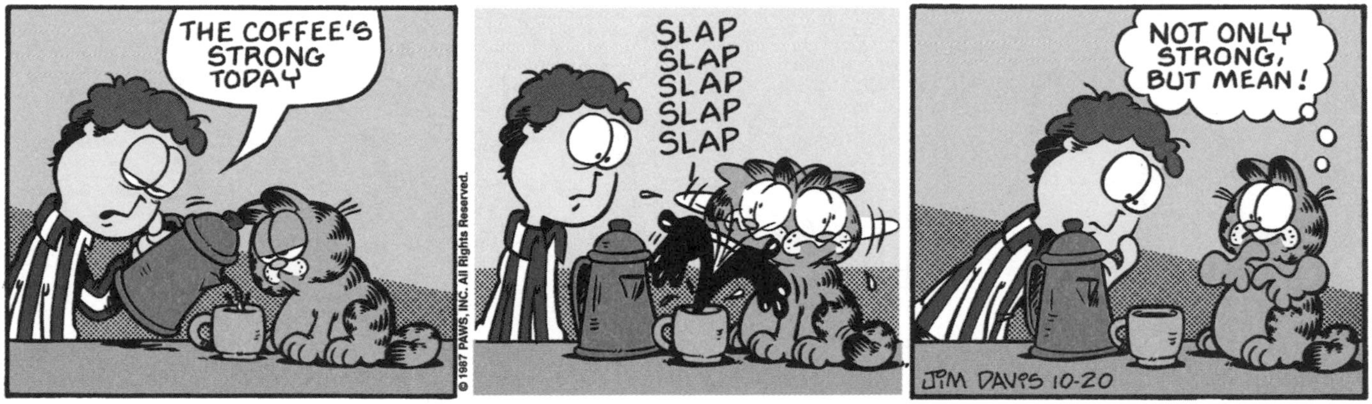
THE COFFEE'S STRONG TODAY
© 1987 PAWS, INC. All Rights Reserved.
SLAP SLAP SLAP SLAP SLAP
NOT ONLY STRONG, BUT MEAN!
JIM DAVIS 10-20

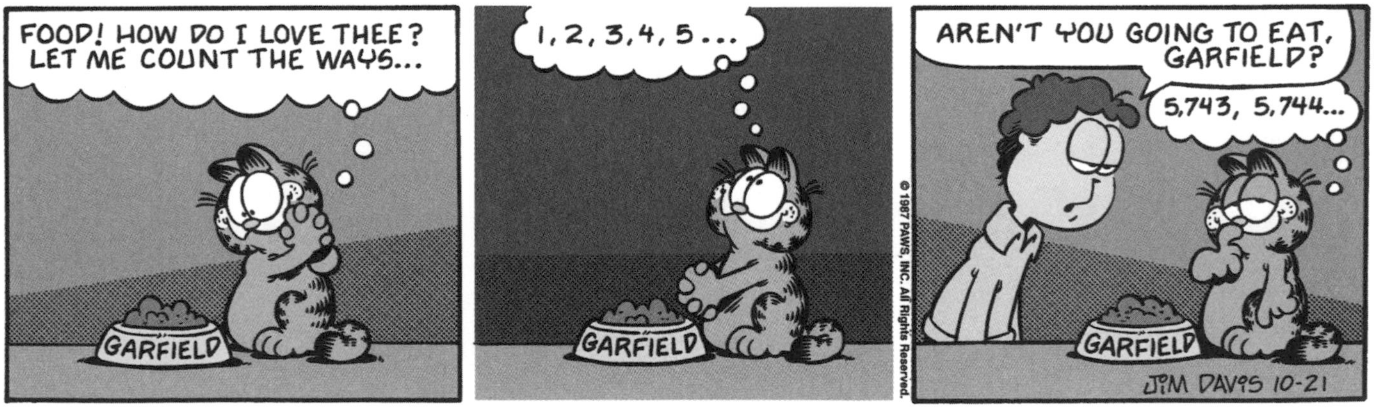
FOOD! HOW DO I LOVE THEE? LET ME COUNT THE WAYS...
GARFIELD
1, 2, 3, 4, 5 ...
GARFIELD
© 1987 PAWS, INC. All Rights Reserved.
AREN'T YOU GOING TO EAT, GARFIELD?
5,743, 5,744...
GARFIELD
JIM DAVIS 10-21

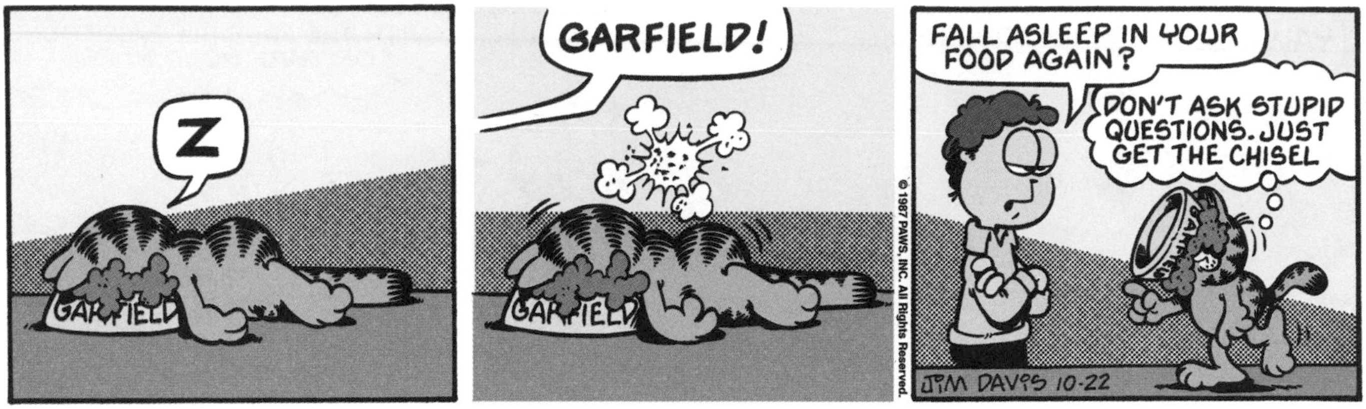
Z
GARFIELD!
FALL ASLEEP IN YOUR FOOD AGAIN?
DON'T ASK STUPID QUESTIONS. JUST GET THE CHISEL
GARFIELD
JIM DAVIS 10-22
© 1987 PAWS, INC. All Rights Reserved.

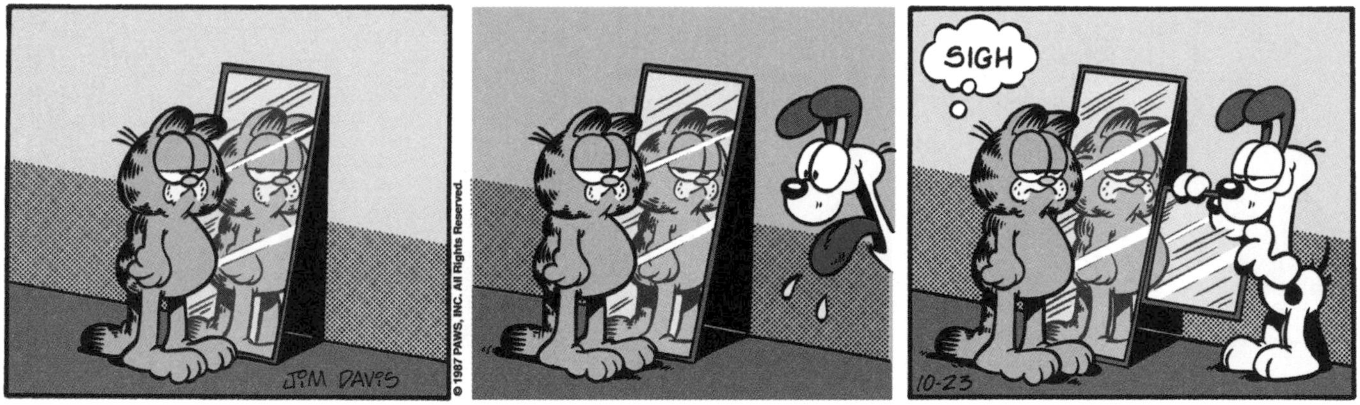
JIM DAVIS
© 1987 PAWS, INC. All Rights Reserved.
SIGH
10-23

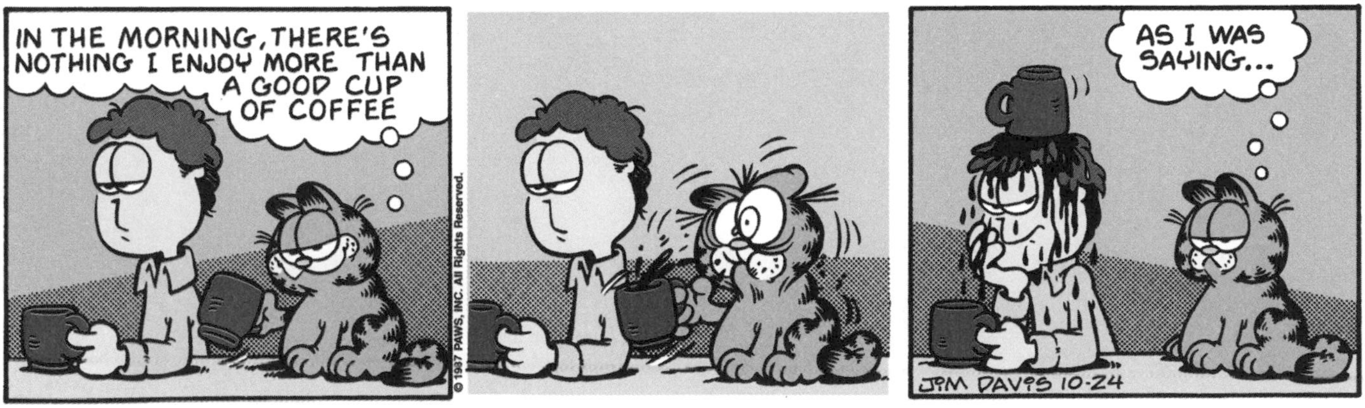
IN THE MORNING, THERE'S NOTHING I ENJOY MORE THAN A GOOD CUP OF COFFEE
© 1937 PAWS, INC. All Rights Reserved.
AS I WAS SAYING...
JIM DAVIS 10-24

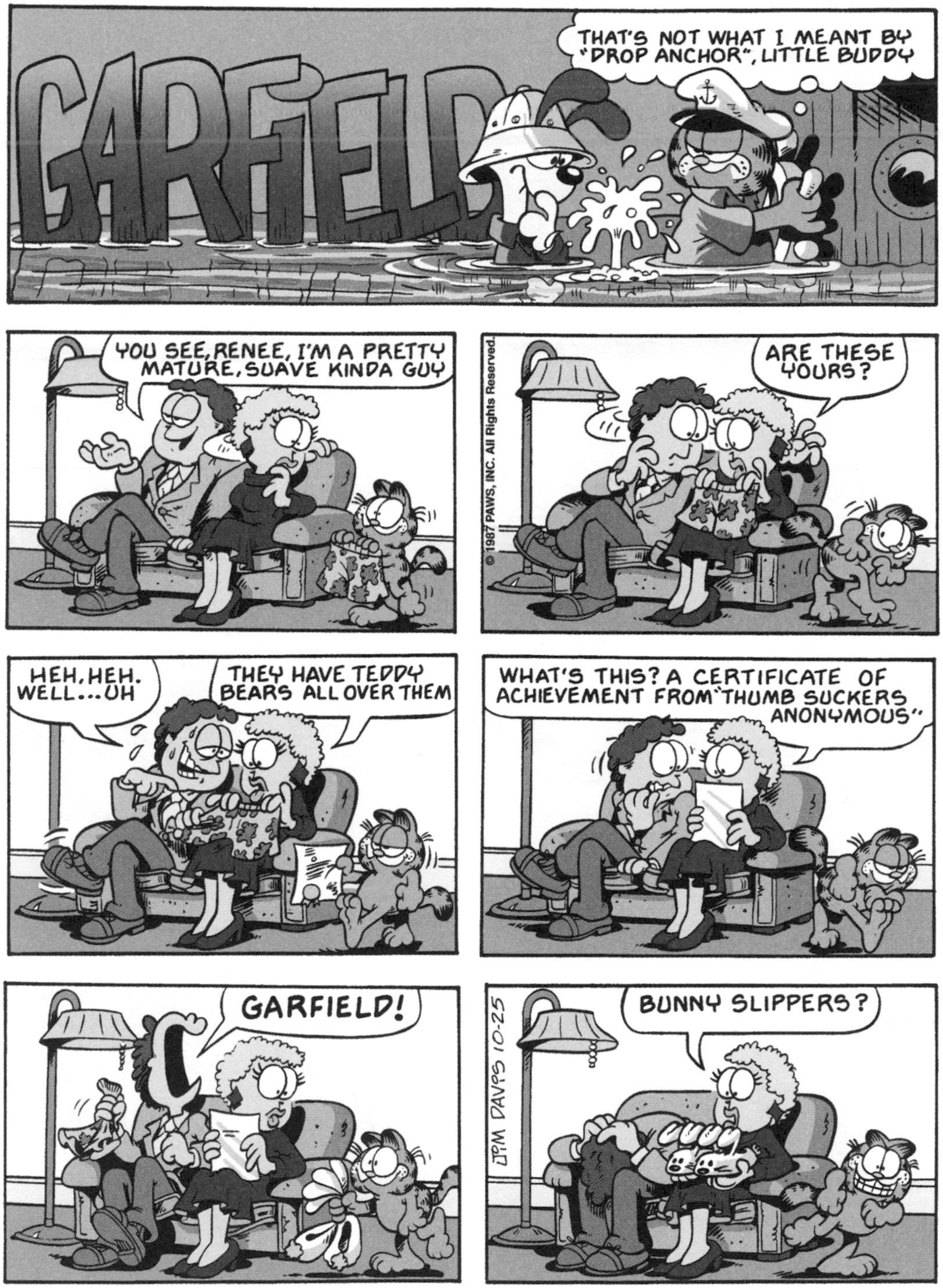
GARFIELD
THAT'S NOT WHAT I MEANT BY "DROP ANCHOR", LITTLE BUDDY
YOU SEE, RENEE, I'M A PRETTY MATURE, SUAVE KINDA GUY
© 1987 PAWS, INC. All Rights Reserved.
ARE THESE YOURS?
THEY HAVE TEDDY BEARS ALL OVER THEM
HEH, HEH. WELL...UH
WHAT'S THIS? A CERTIFICATE OF ACHIEVEMENT FROM "THUMB SUCKERS ANONYMOUS"
GARFIELD!
JIM DAVIS 10-25
BUNNY SLIPPERS?

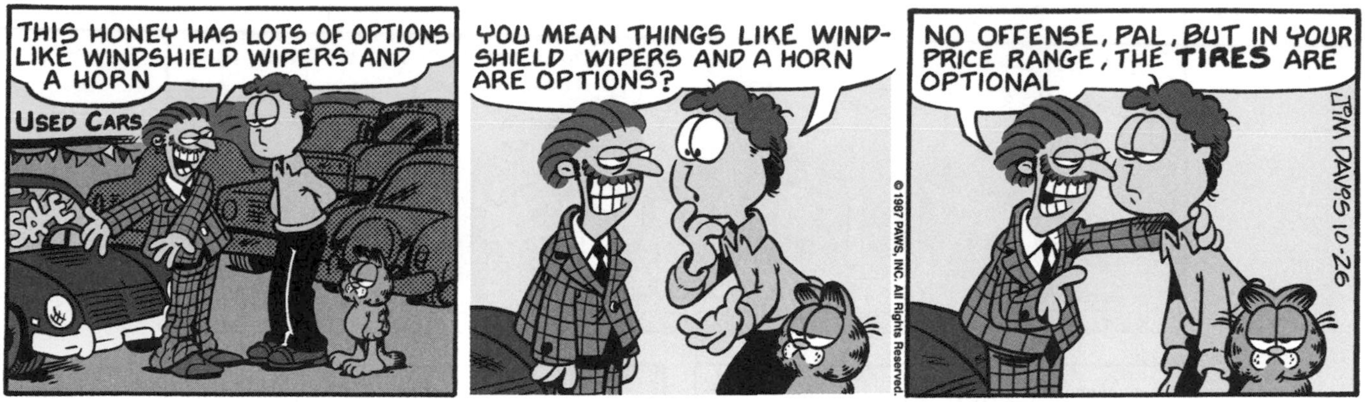
THIS HONEY HAS LOTS OF OPTIONS LIKE WINDSHIELD WIPERS AND A HORN
USED CARS
YOU MEAN THINGS LIKE WIND-SHIELD WIPERS AND A HORN ARE OPTIONS?
© 1987 PAWS, INC. All Rights Reserved.
NO OFFENSE, PAL, BUT IN YOUR PRICE RANGE, THE **TIRES** ARE OPTIONAL
JIM DAVIS 10-26

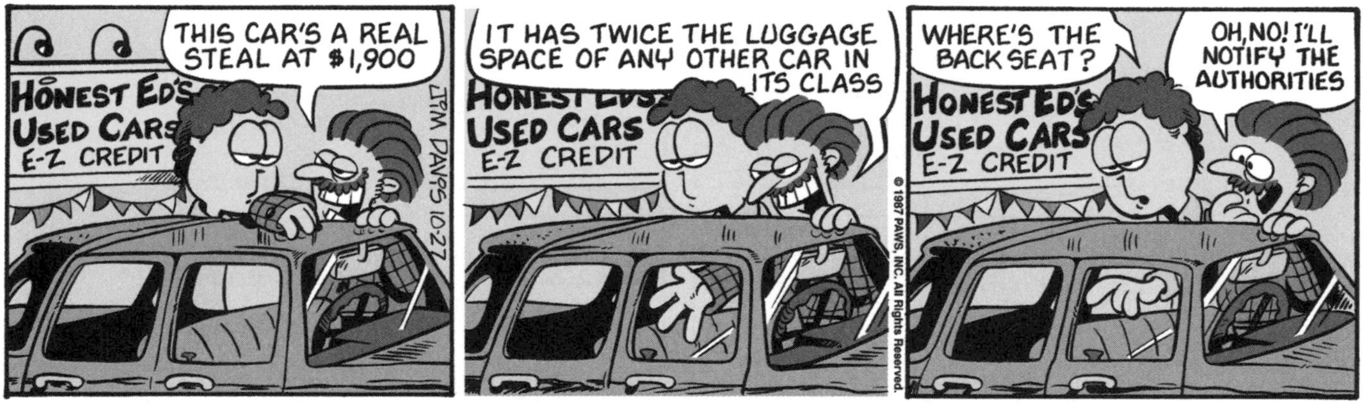
THIS CAR'S A REAL STEAL AT $1,900
HONEST ED'S USED CARS E-Z CREDIT
JIM DAVIS 10-27
IT HAS TWICE THE LUGGAGE SPACE OF ANY OTHER CAR IN ITS CLASS
© 1987 PAWS, INC. All Rights Reserved.
WHERE'S THE BACK SEAT?
OH, NO! I'LL NOTIFY THE AUTHORITIES

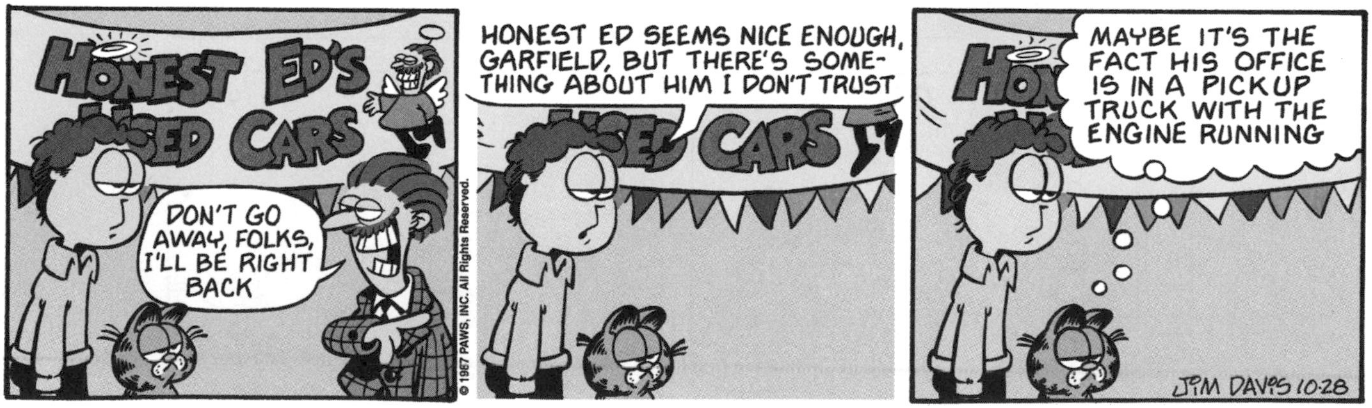
HONEST ED'S USED CARS
DON'T GO AWAY, FOLKS, I'LL BE RIGHT BACK
© 1987 PAWS, INC. All Rights Reserved.
HONEST ED SEEMS NICE ENOUGH, GARFIELD, BUT THERE'S SOME-THING ABOUT HIM I DON'T TRUST
MAYBE IT'S THE FACT HIS OFFICE IS IN A PICKUP TRUCK WITH THE ENGINE RUNNING
JIM DAVIS 10-28

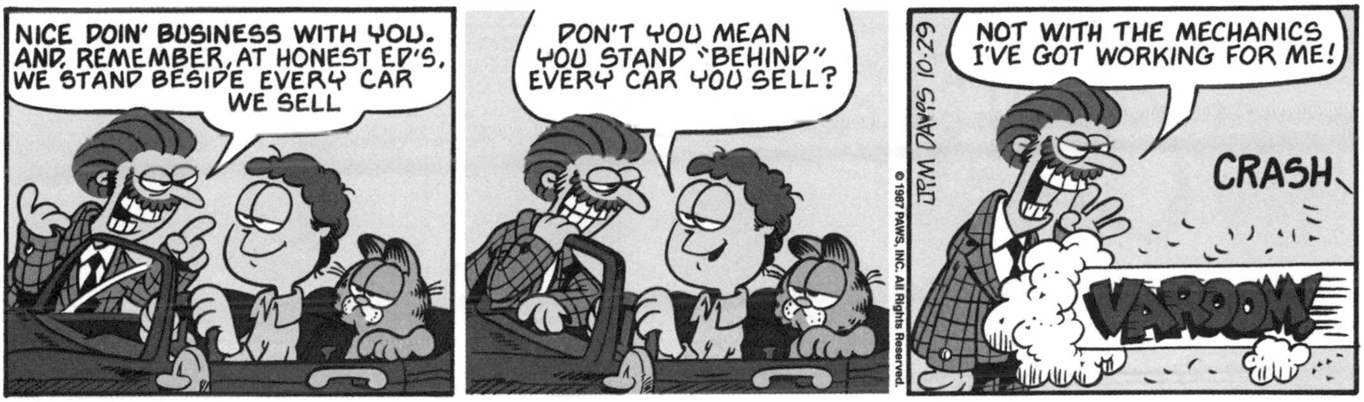
NICE DOIN' BUSINESS WITH YOU. AND, REMEMBER, AT HONEST ED'S, WE STAND BESIDE EVERY CAR WE SELL
DON'T YOU MEAN YOU STAND "BEHIND" EVERY CAR YOU SELL?
© 1987 PAWS, INC. All Rights Reserved.
JIM DAVIS 10-29
NOT WITH THE MECHANICS I'VE GOT WORKING FOR ME!
CRASH
VAROOM!

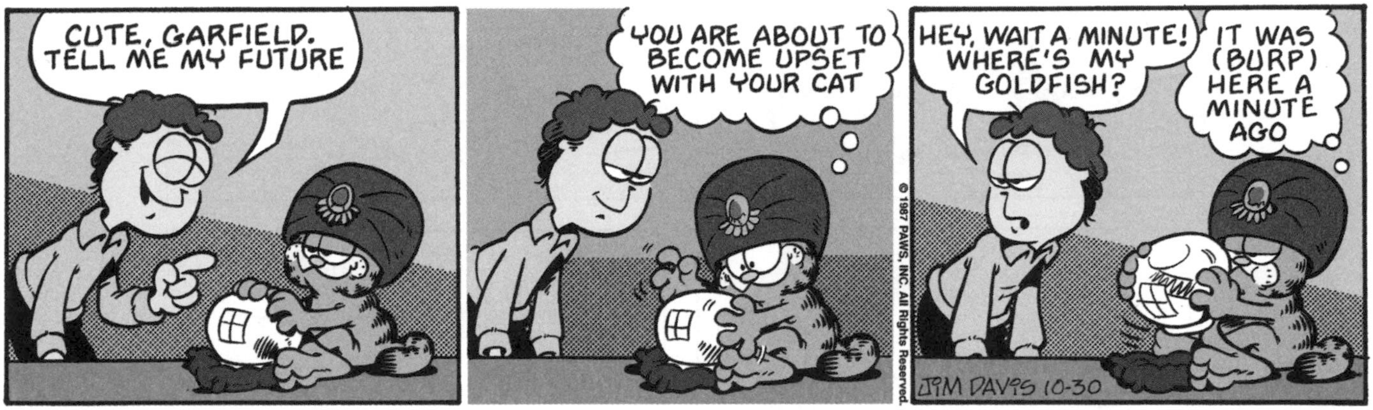
CUTE, GARFIELD. TELL ME MY FUTURE
YOU ARE ABOUT TO BECOME UPSET WITH YOUR CAT
© 1987 PAWS, INC. All Rights Reserved.
HEY, WAIT A MINUTE! WHERE'S MY GOLDFISH?
IT WAS (BURP) HERE A MINUTE AGO
JIM DAVIS 10-30

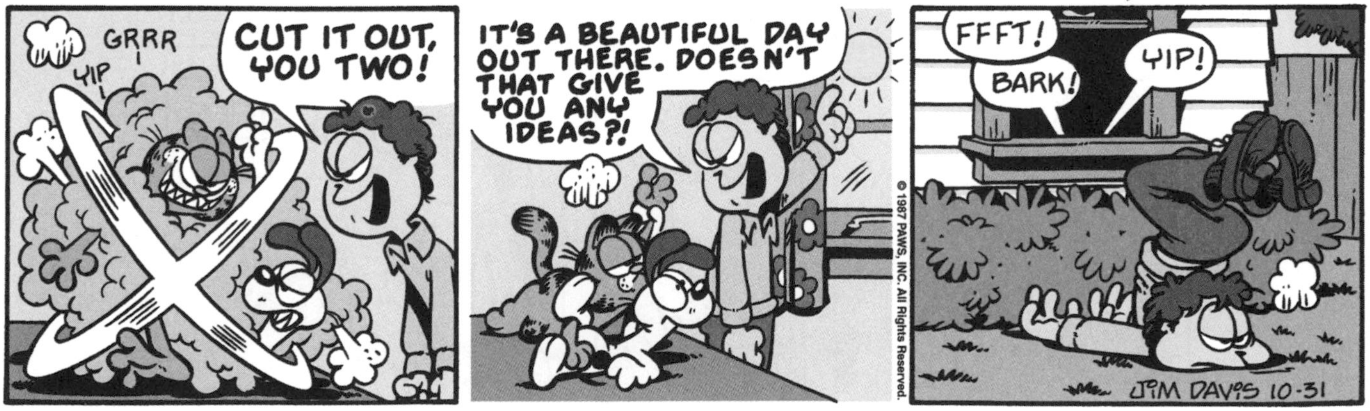
GRRR
YIP
CUT IT OUT, YOU TWO!
IT'S A BEAUTIFUL DAY OUT THERE. DOESN'T THAT GIVE YOU ANY IDEAS?!
© 1987 PAWS, INC. All Rights Reserved.
FFFT!
BARK!
YIP!
JIM DAVIS 10-31

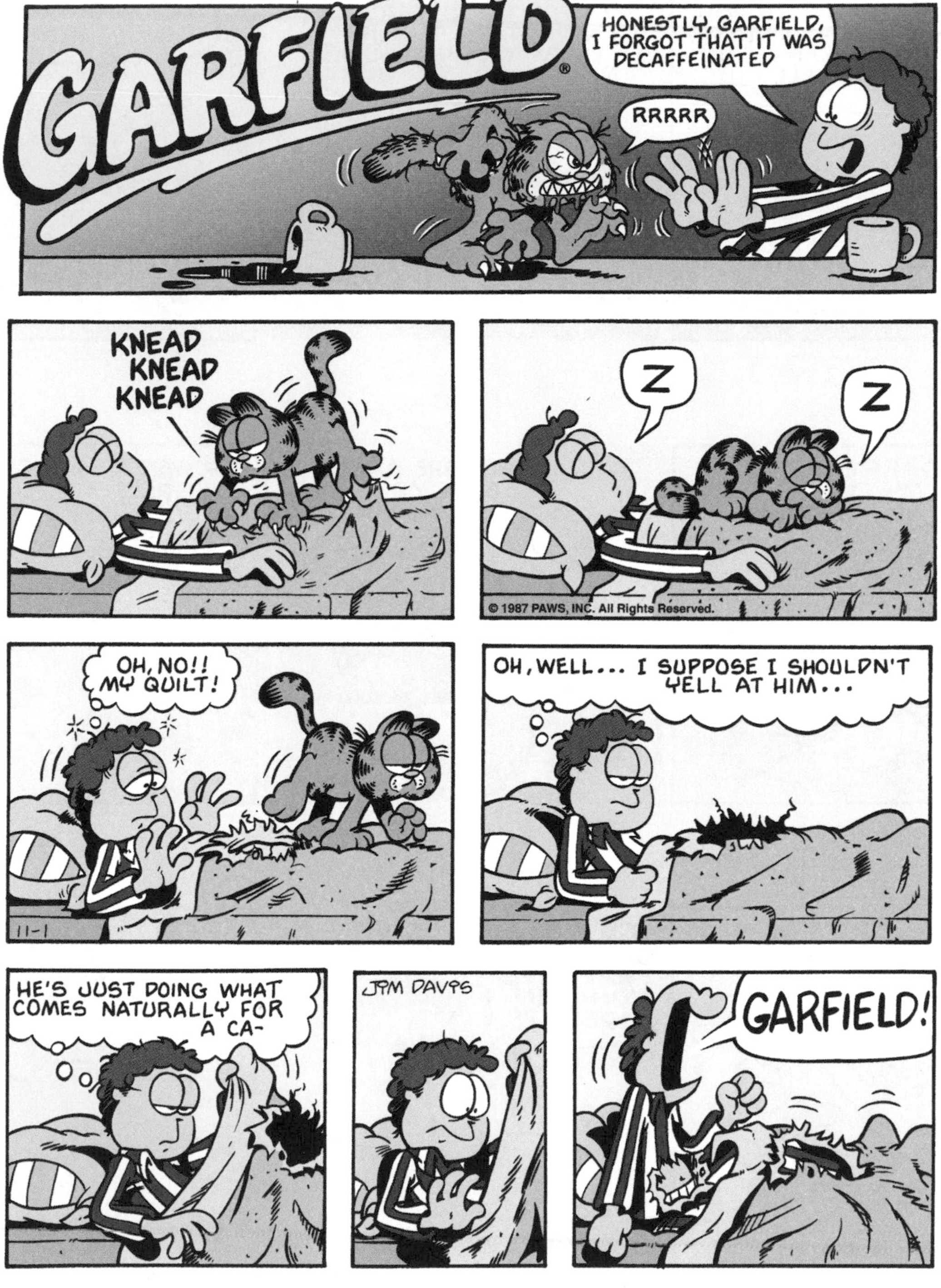
GARFIELD®
HONESTLY, GARFIELD, I FORGOT THAT IT WAS DECAFFEINATED
RRRRR
KNEAD KNEAD KNEAD
Z
Z
© 1987 PAWS, INC. All Rights Reserved.
OH, NO!! MY QUILT!
11-1
OH, WELL... I SUPPOSE I SHOULDN'T YELL AT HIM...
HE'S JUST DOING WHAT COMES NATURALLY FOR A CA-
JIM DAVIS
GARFIELD!

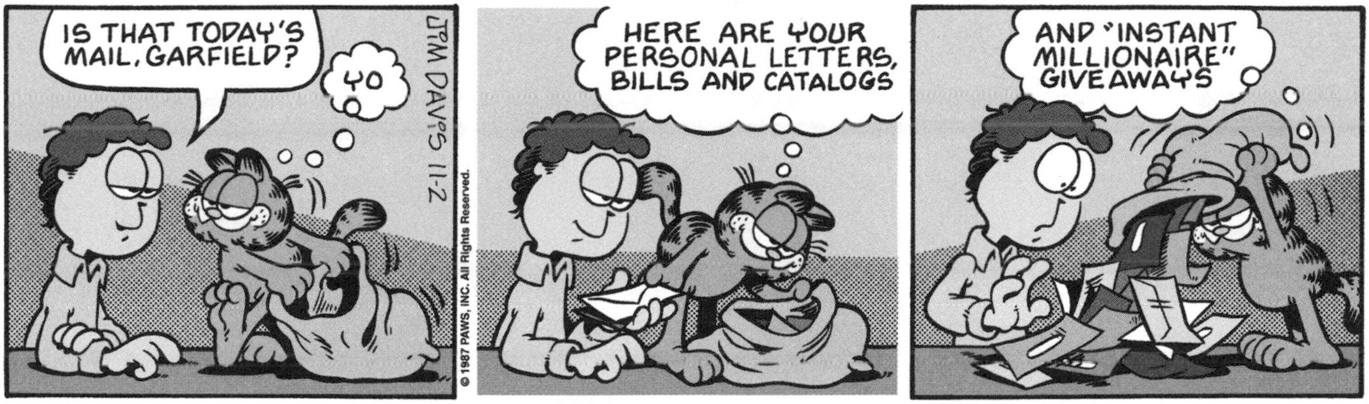
IS THAT TODAY'S MAIL, GARFIELD?
YO
JIM DAVIS 11-2
© 1987 PAWS, INC. All Rights Reserved.
HERE ARE YOUR PERSONAL LETTERS, BILLS AND CATALOGS
AND "INSTANT MILLIONAIRE" GIVEAWAYS

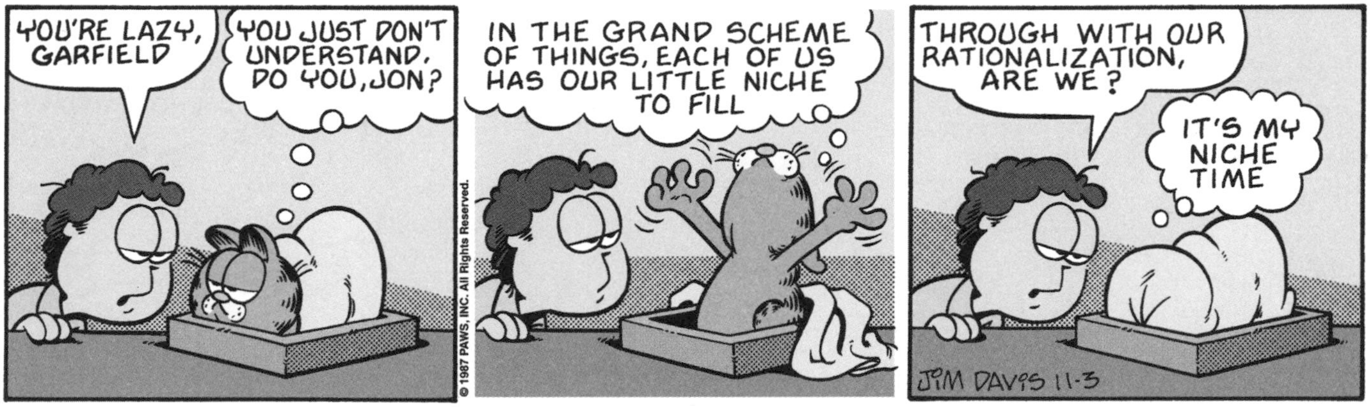
YOU'RE LAZY, GARFIELD
YOU JUST DON'T UNDERSTAND, DO YOU, JON?
© 1987 PAWS, INC. All Rights Reserved.
IN THE GRAND SCHEME OF THINGS, EACH OF US HAS OUR LITTLE NICHE TO FILL
THROUGH WITH OUR RATIONALIZATION, ARE WE?
IT'S MY NICHE TIME
JIM DAVIS 11-3

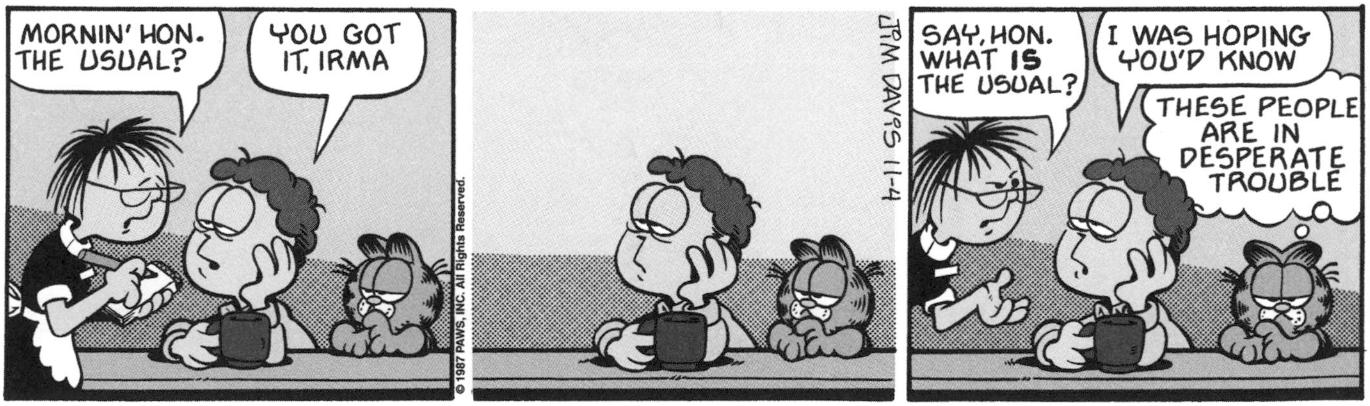
MORNIN' HON. THE USUAL?
YOU GOT IT, IRMA
© 1987 PAWS, INC. All Rights Reserved.
JIM DAVIS 11-4
SAY, HON. WHAT **IS** THE USUAL?
I WAS HOPING YOU'D KNOW
THESE PEOPLE ARE IN DESPERATE TROUBLE

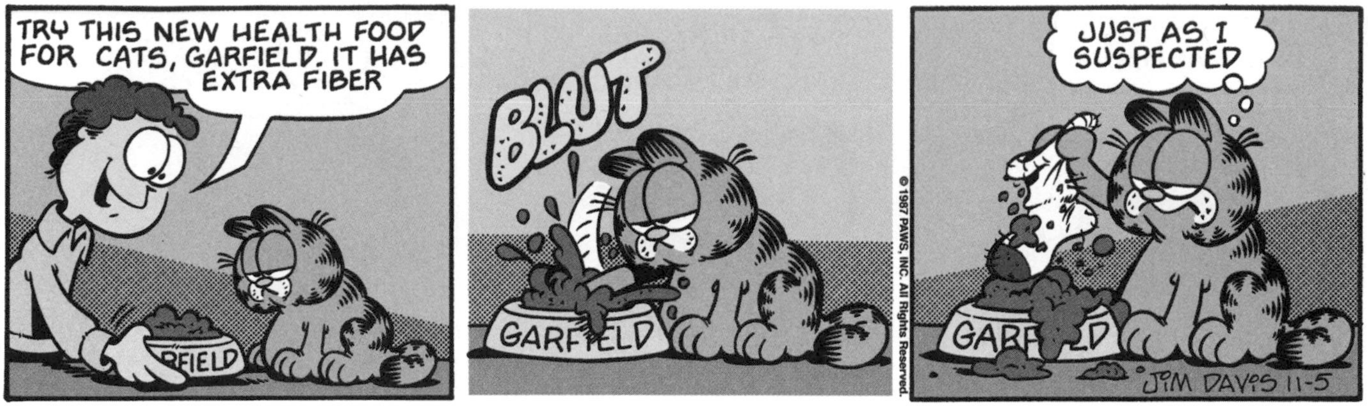
TRY THIS NEW HEALTH FOOD FOR CATS, GARFIELD. IT HAS EXTRA FIBER
RFIELD
BLUT
GARFIELD
© 1987 PAWS, INC. All Rights Reserved.
JUST AS I SUSPECTED
GARF LD
JIM DAVIS 11-5

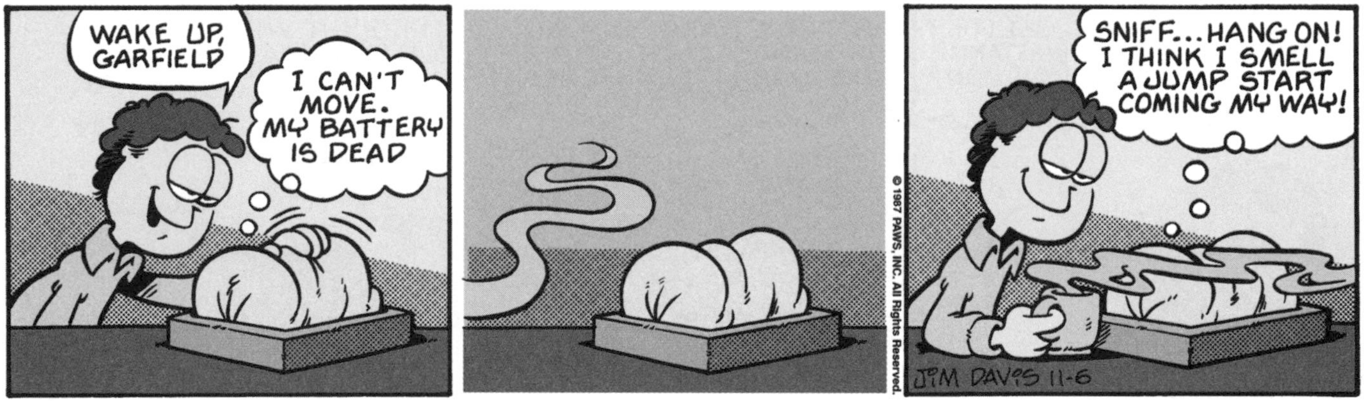
WAKE UP, GARFIELD
I CAN'T MOVE. MY BATTERY IS DEAD
© 1987 PAWS, INC. All Rights Reserved.
SNIFF...HANG ON! I THINK I SMELL A JUMP START COMING MY WAY!
JIM DAVIS 11-6

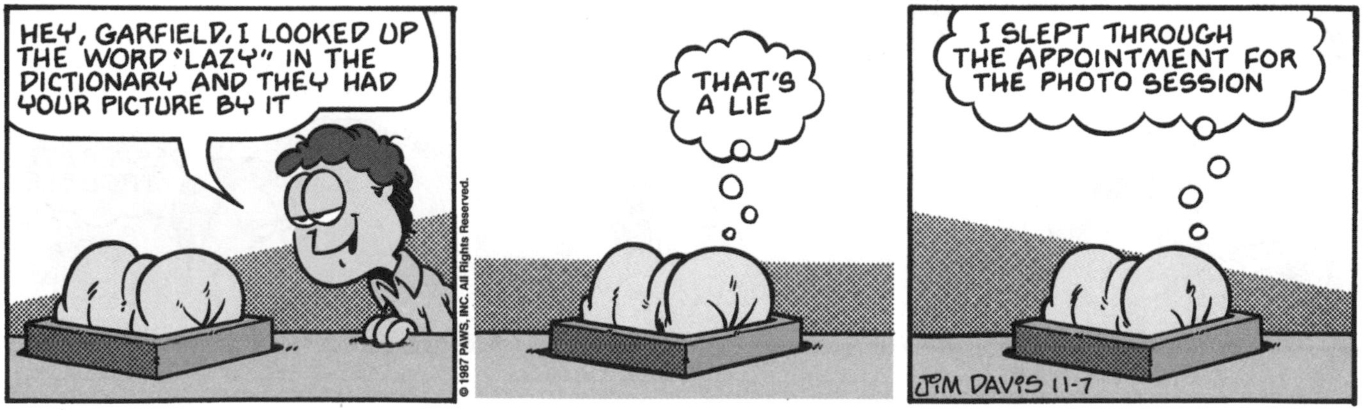
HEY, GARFIELD, I LOOKED UP THE WORD "LAZY" IN THE DICTIONARY AND THEY HAD YOUR PICTURE BY IT
© 1987 PAWS, INC. All Rights Reserved.
THAT'S A LIE
I SLEPT THROUGH THE APPOINTMENT FOR THE PHOTO SESSION
JIM DAVIS 11-7

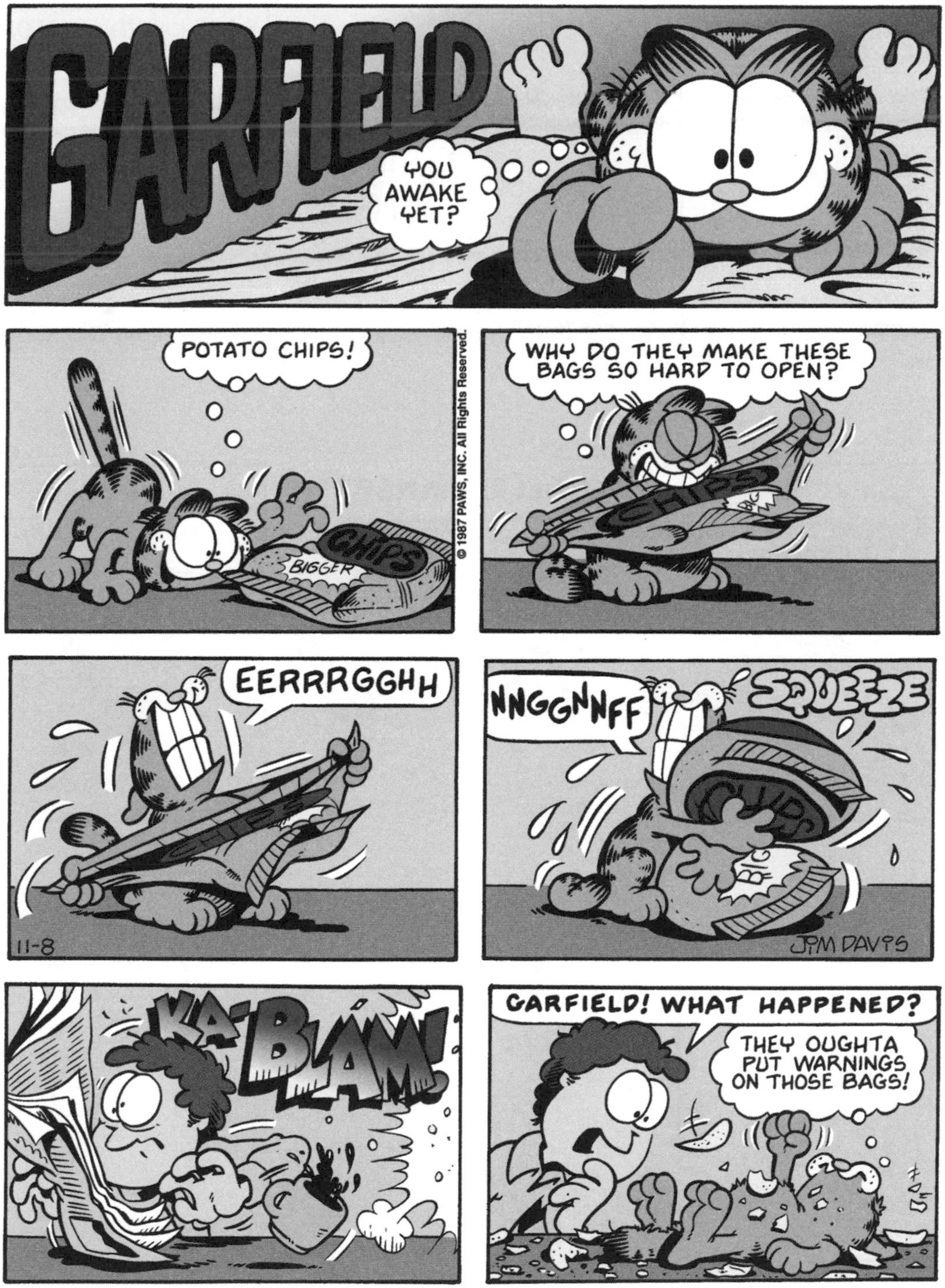
GARFIELD
YOU AWAKE YET?
POTATO CHIPS!
CHIPS
BIGGER
© 1987 PAWS, INC. All Rights Reserved.
WHY DO THEY MAKE THESE BAGS SO HARD TO OPEN?
CHIPS
EERRRGGHH
11-8
NNGGNNFF
SQUEEZE
JIM DAVIS
KA-BLAM!
GARFIELD! WHAT HAPPENED?
THEY OUGHTA PUT WARNINGS ON THOSE BAGS!

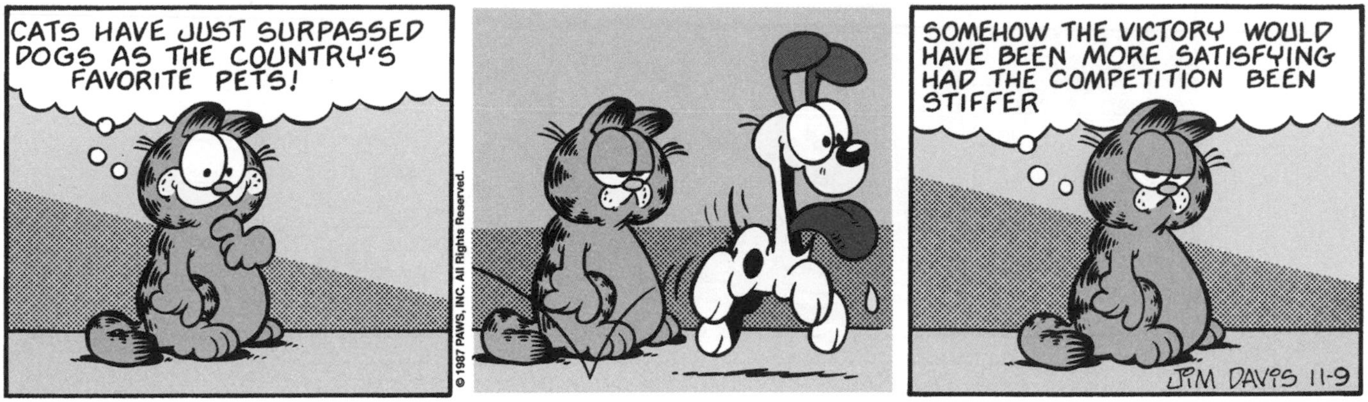
CATS HAVE JUST SURPASSED DOGS AS THE COUNTRY'S FAVORITE PETS!
© 1987 PAWS, INC. All Rights Reserved.
SOMEHOW THE VICTORY WOULD HAVE BEEN MORE SATISFYING HAD THE COMPETITION BEEN STIFFER
JIM DAVIS 11-9

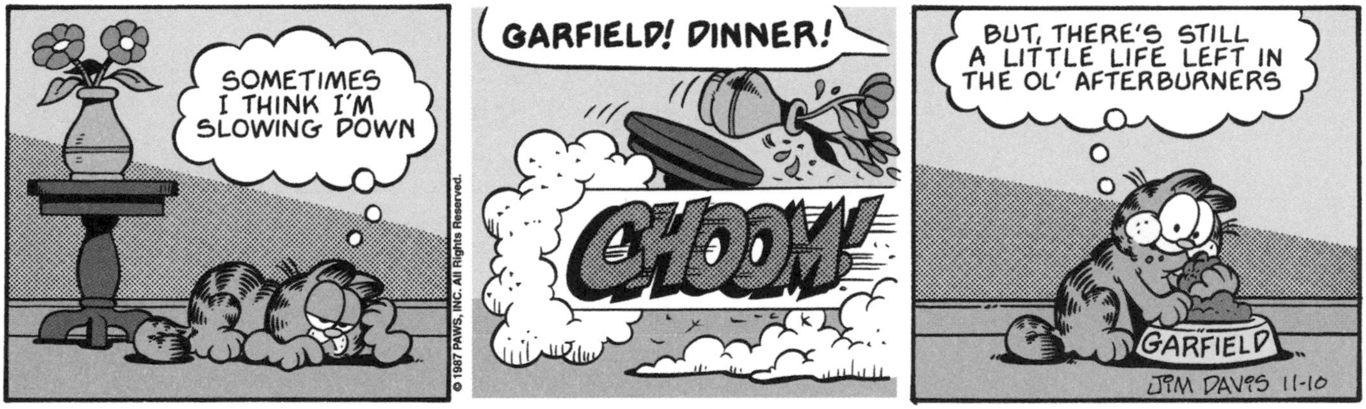
SOMETIMES I THINK I'M SLOWING DOWN
© 1987 PAWS, INC. All Rights Reserved.
GARFIELD! DINNER!
CHOOM!
BUT, THERE'S STILL A LITTLE LIFE LEFT IN THE OL' AFTERBURNERS
GARFIELD
JIM DAVIS 11-10

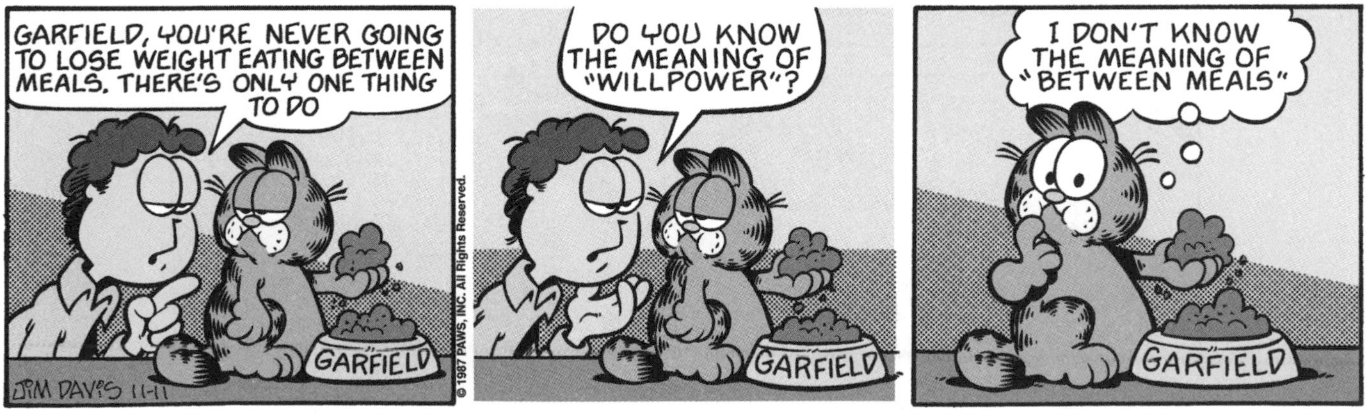
GARFIELD, YOU'RE NEVER GOING TO LOSE WEIGHT EATING BETWEEN MEALS. THERE'S ONLY ONE THING TO DO
GARFIELD
JIM DAVIS 11-11
© 1987 PAWS, INC. All Rights Reserved.
DO YOU KNOW THE MEANING OF "WILLPOWER"?
GARFIELD
I DON'T KNOW THE MEANING OF "BETWEEN MEALS"
GARFIELD

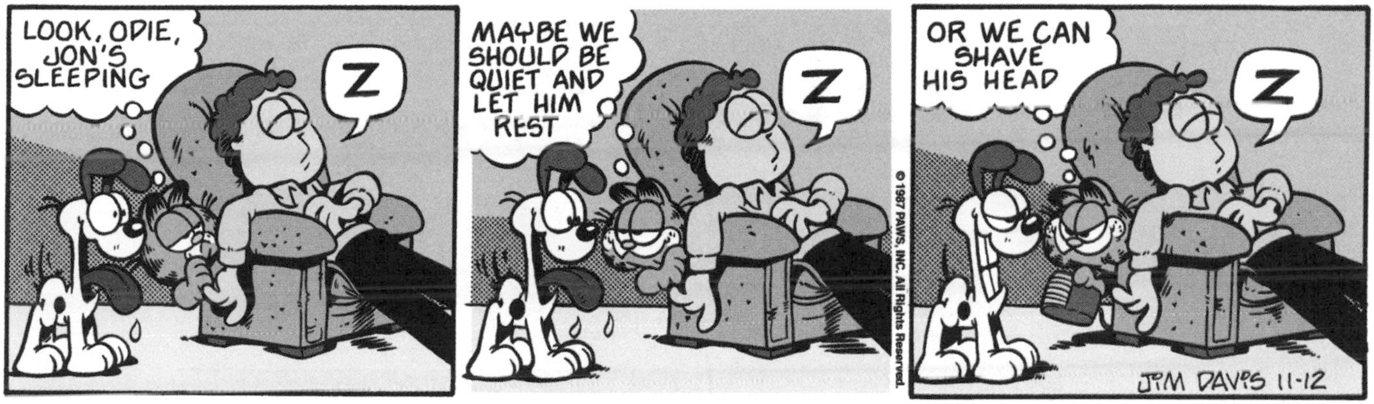
LOOK, ODIE, JON'S SLEEPING
Z
MAYBE WE SHOULD BE QUIET AND LET HIM REST
Z
© 1987 PAWS, INC. All Rights Reserved.
OR WE CAN SHAVE HIS HEAD
Z
JIM DAVIS 11-12

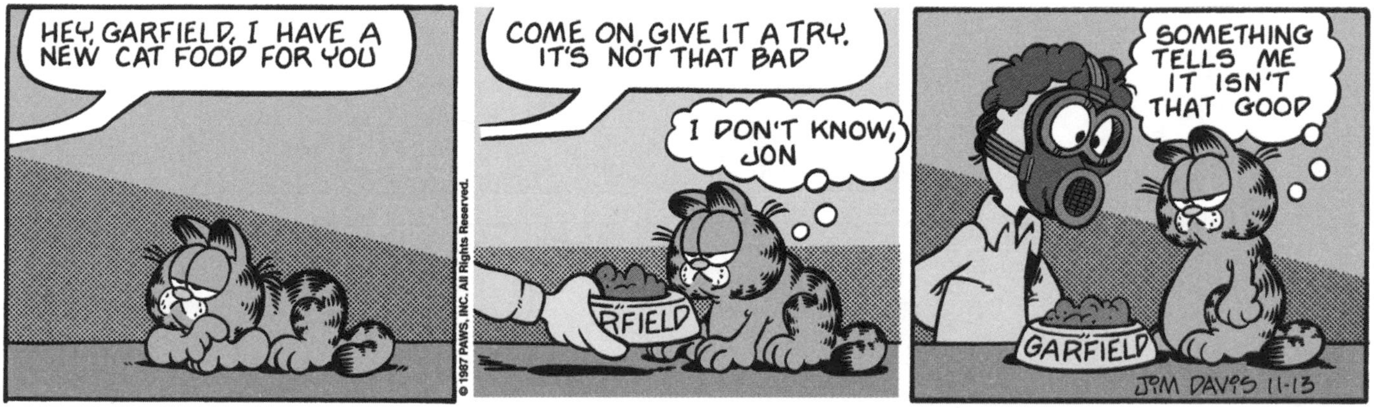
HEY, GARFIELD, I HAVE A NEW CAT FOOD FOR YOU
© 1987 PAWS, INC. All Rights Reserved.
COME ON, GIVE IT A TRY. IT'S NOT THAT BAD
I DON'T KNOW, JON
RFIELD
SOMETHING TELLS ME IT ISN'T THAT GOOD
GARFIELD
JIM DAVIS 11-13

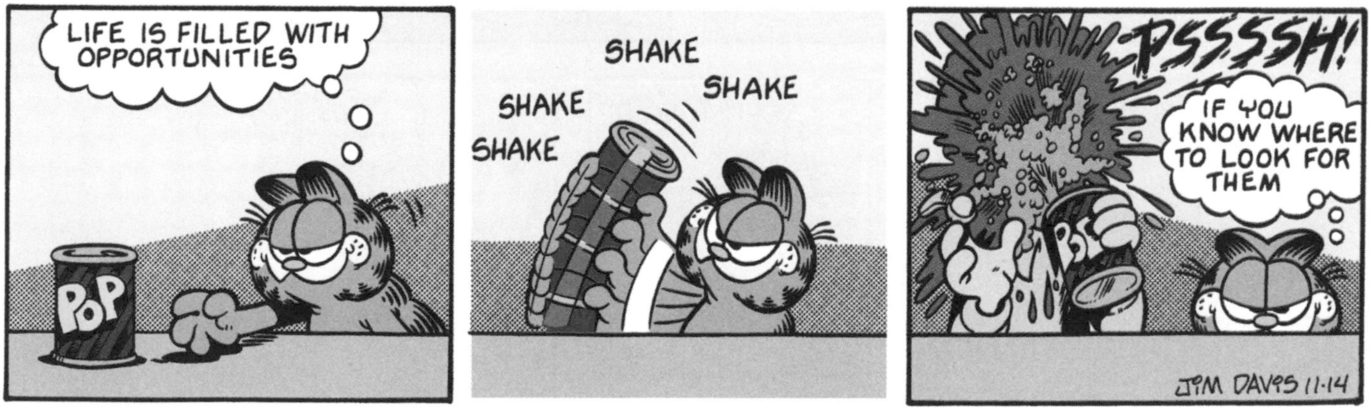
LIFE IS FILLED WITH OPPORTUNITIES
POP
SHAKE
SHAKE
SHAKE
SHAKE
PSSSSH!
IF YOU KNOW WHERE TO LOOK FOR THEM
JIM DAVIS 11-14

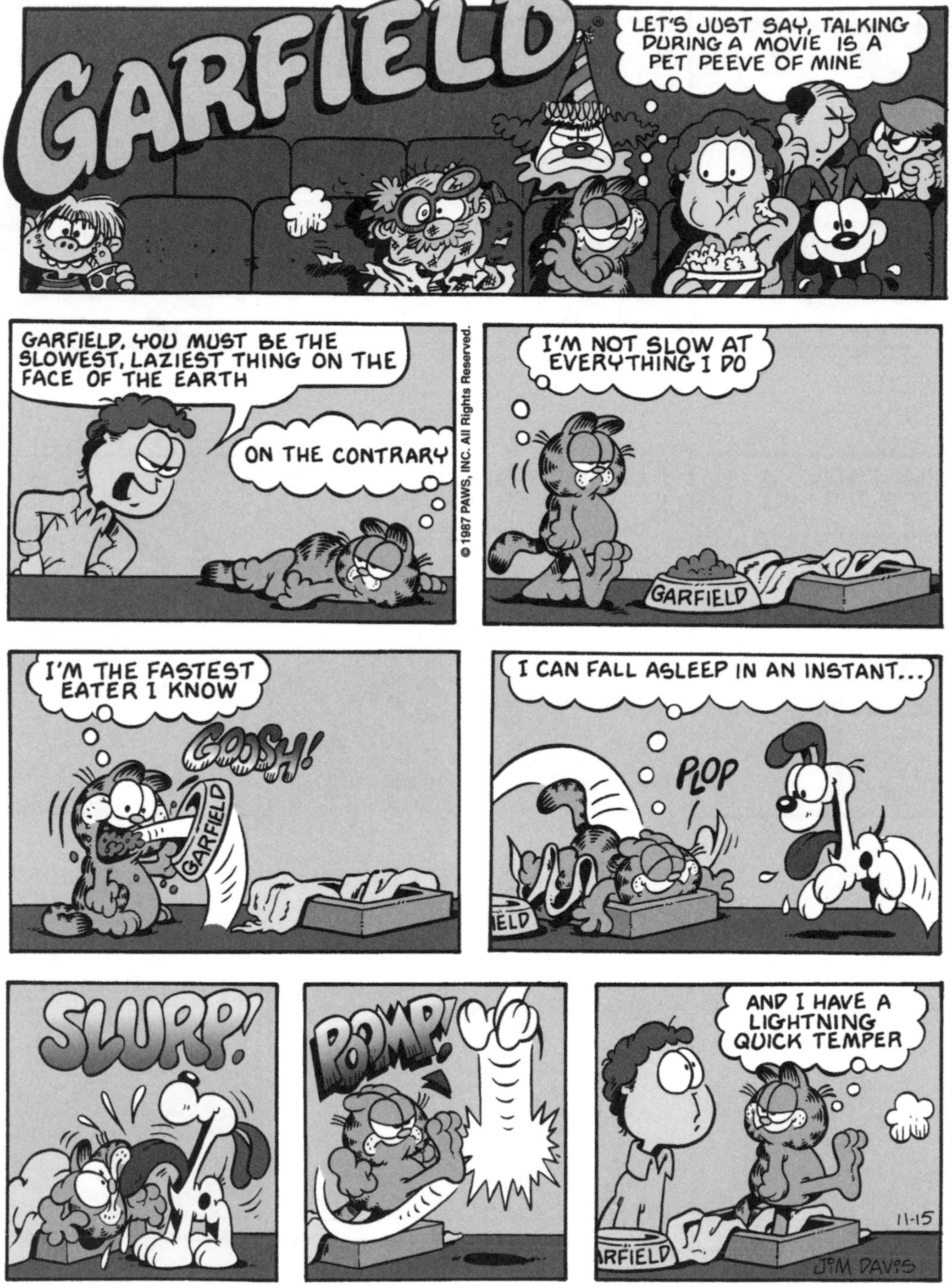

GARFIELD
LET'S JUST SAY, TALKING DURING A MOVIE IS A PET PEEVE OF MINE
GARFIELD, YOU MUST BE THE SLOWEST, LAZIEST THING ON THE FACE OF THE EARTH
ON THE CONTRARY
© 1987 PAWS, INC. All Rights Reserved.
I'M NOT SLOW AT EVERYTHING I DO
GARFIELD
I'M THE FASTEST EATER I KNOW
GOOSH!
GARFIELD
I CAN FALL ASLEEP IN AN INSTANT...
PLOP
SLURP!
POMP!
AND I HAVE A LIGHTNING QUICK TEMPER
11-15
RFIELD
JIM DAVIS

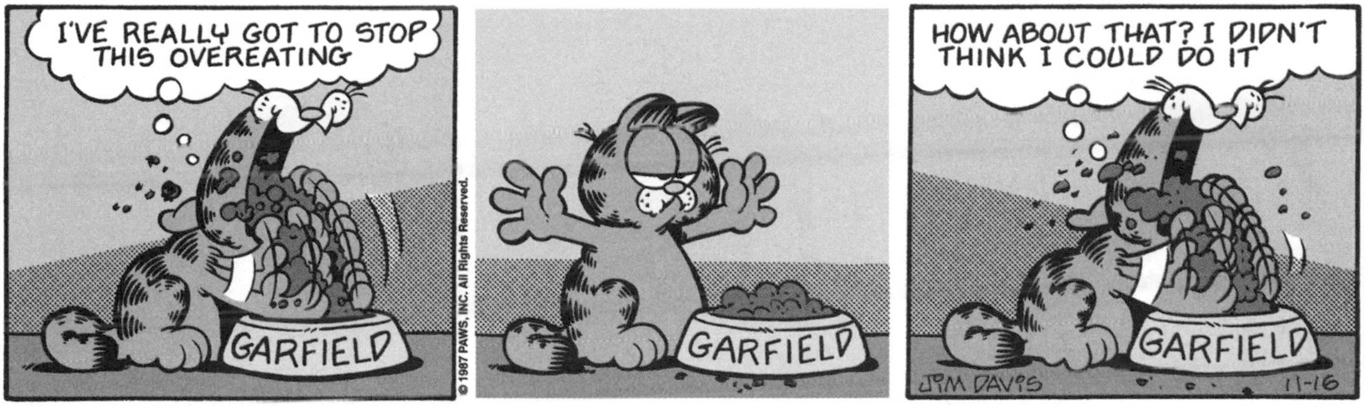
I'VE REALLY GOT TO STOP THIS OVEREATING
GARFIELD
© 1987 PAWS, INC. All Rights Reserved.
GARFIELD
HOW ABOUT THAT? I DIDN'T THINK I COULD DO IT
GARFIELD
JIM DAVIS 11-16

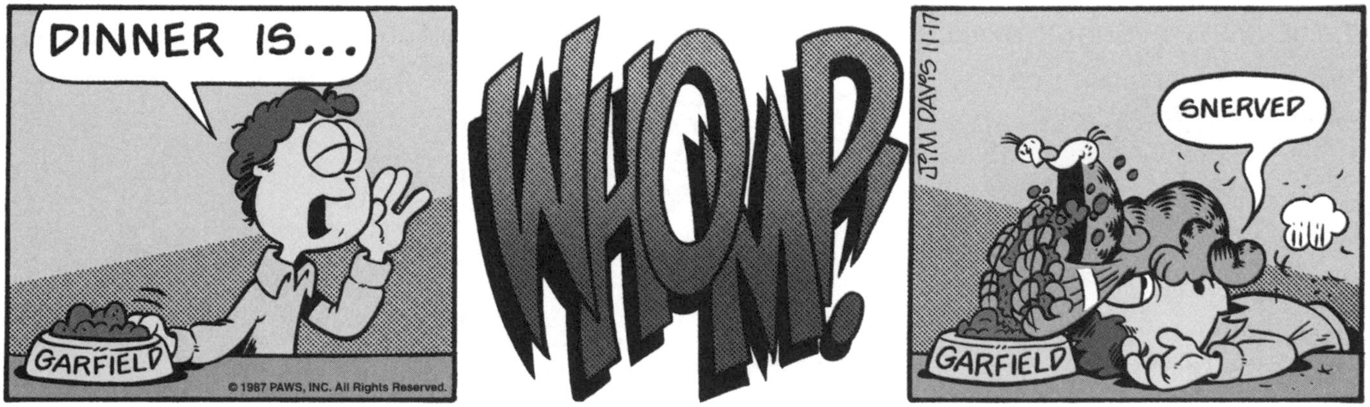
DINNER IS...
GARFIELD
© 1987 PAWS, INC. All Rights Reserved.
WHOMP!
JIM DAVIS 11-17
SNERVED
GARFIELD

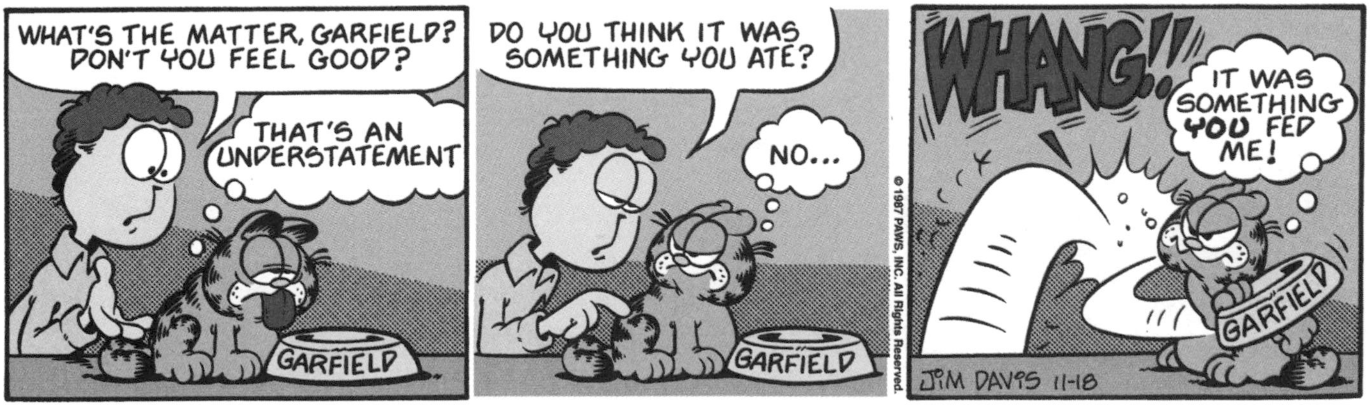
WHAT'S THE MATTER, GARFIELD? DON'T YOU FEEL GOOD?
THAT'S AN UNDERSTATEMENT
GARFIELD
DO YOU THINK IT WAS SOMETHING YOU ATE?
NO...
GARFIELD
© 1987 PAWS, INC. All Rights Reserved.
WHANG!!
IT WAS SOMETHING YOU FED ME!
GARFIELD
JIM DAVIS 11-18

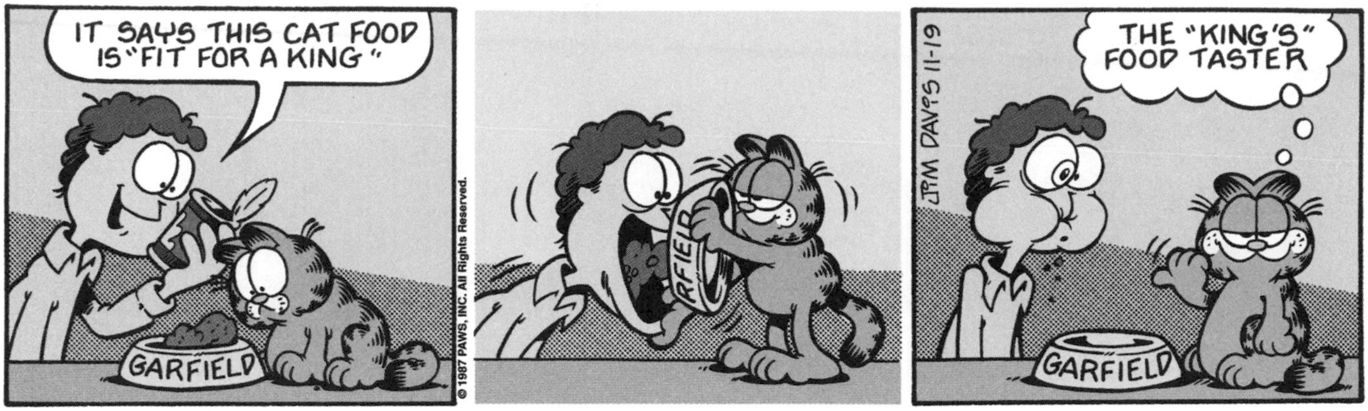
IT SAYS THIS CAT FOOD IS "FIT FOR A KING"
GARFIELD
© 1987 PAWS, INC. All Rights Reserved.
RFIELD
JIM DAVIS 11-19
THE "KING'S" FOOD TASTER
GARFIELD

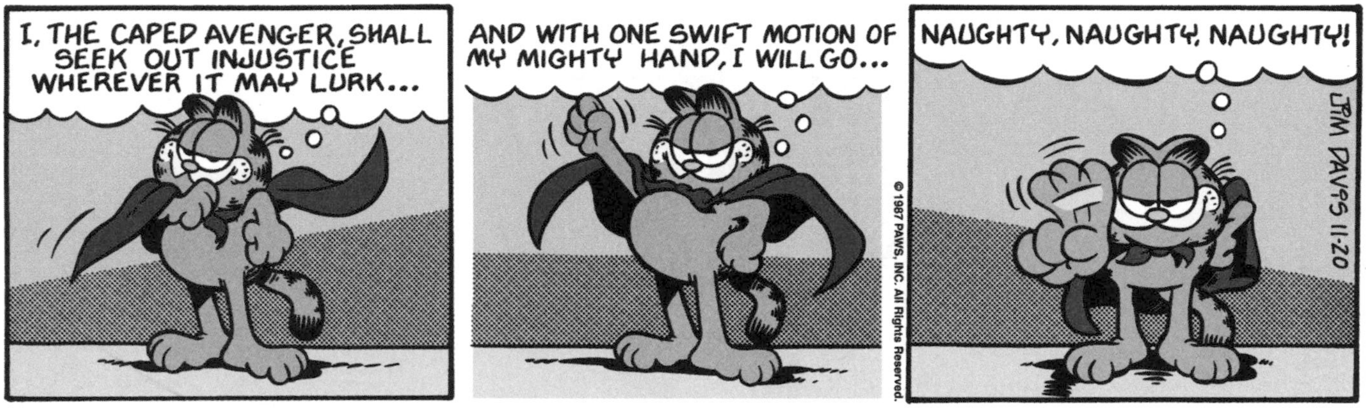
I, THE CAPED AVENGER, SHALL SEEK OUT INJUSTICE WHEREVER IT MAY LURK...
AND WITH ONE SWIFT MOTION OF MY MIGHTY HAND, I WILL GO...
© 1987 PAWS, INC. All Rights Reserved.
NAUGHTY, NAUGHTY, NAUGHTY!
JIM DAVIS 11-20

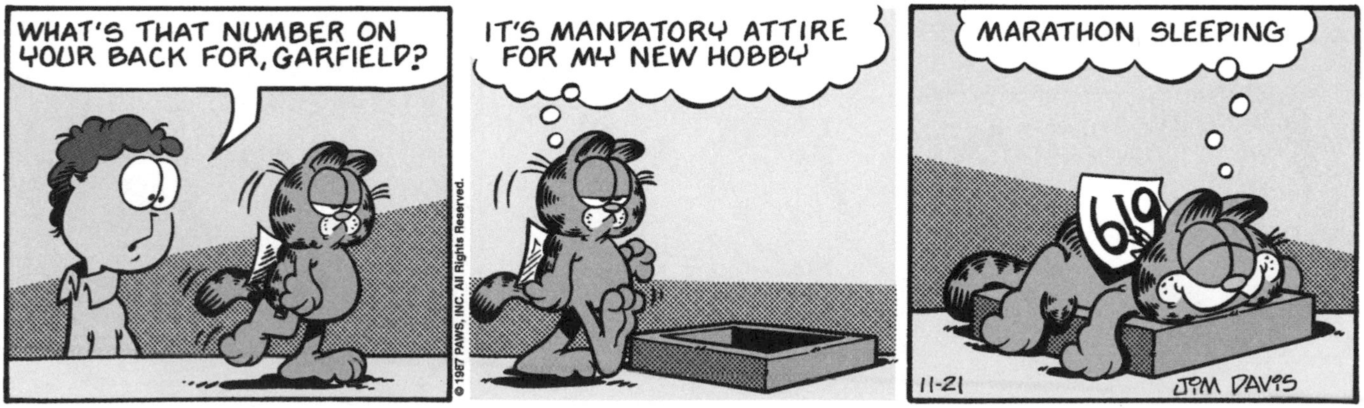
WHAT'S THAT NUMBER ON YOUR BACK FOR, GARFIELD?
© 1987 PAWS, INC. All Rights Reserved.
IT'S MANDATORY ATTIRE FOR MY NEW HOBBY
MARATHON SLEEPING
619
11-21
JIM DAVIS

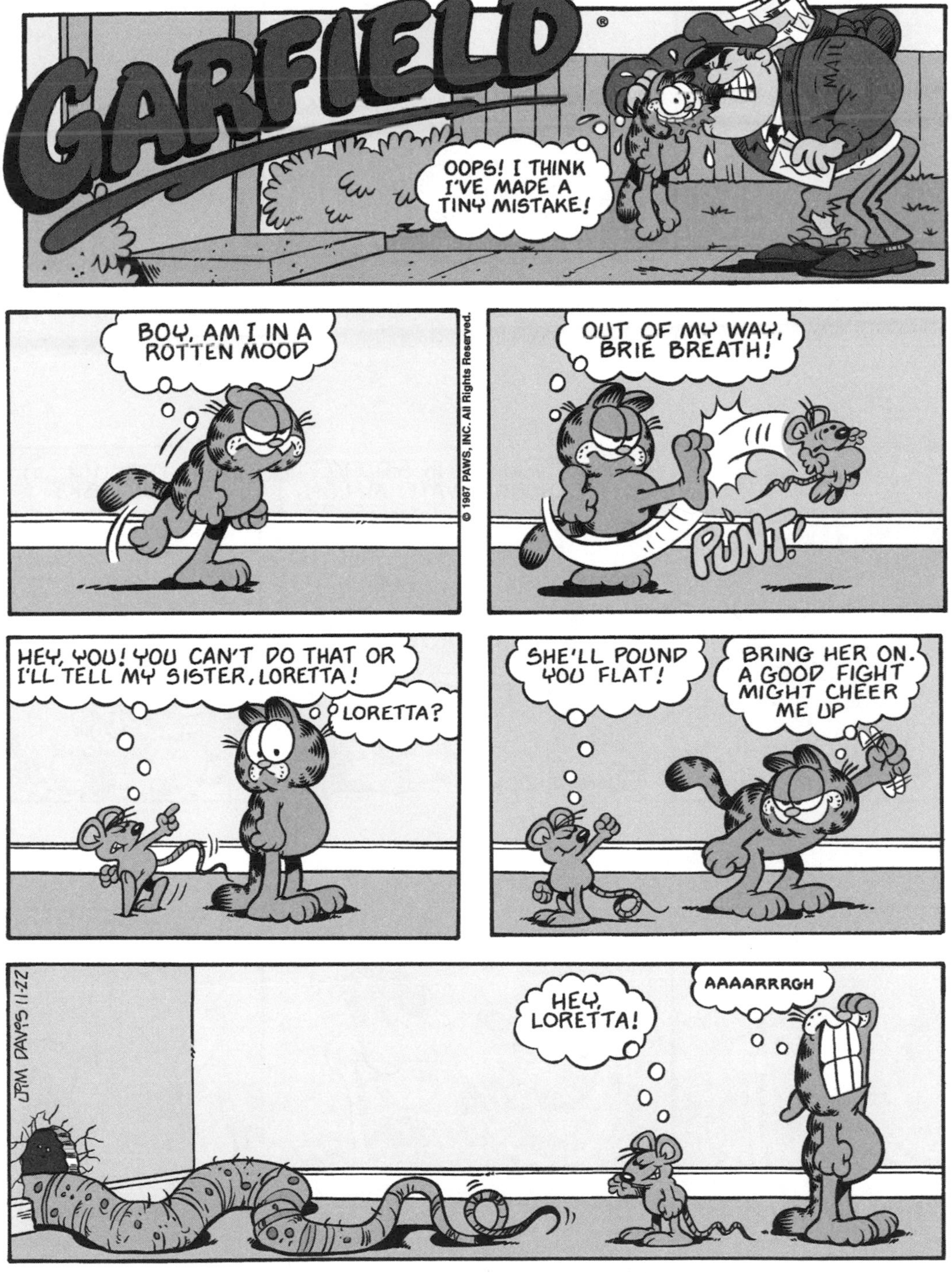
GARFIELD®
OOPS! I THINK I'VE MADE A TINY MISTAKE!
BOY, AM I IN A ROTTEN MOOD
© 1987 PAWS, INC. All Rights Reserved.
OUT OF MY WAY, BRIE BREATH!
PUNT!
HEY, YOU! YOU CAN'T DO THAT OR I'LL TELL MY SISTER, LORETTA!
LORETTA?
SHE'LL POUND YOU FLAT!
BRING HER ON. A GOOD FIGHT MIGHT CHEER ME UP
JPM DAVPS 11-22
HEY, LORETTA!
AAAARRRGH

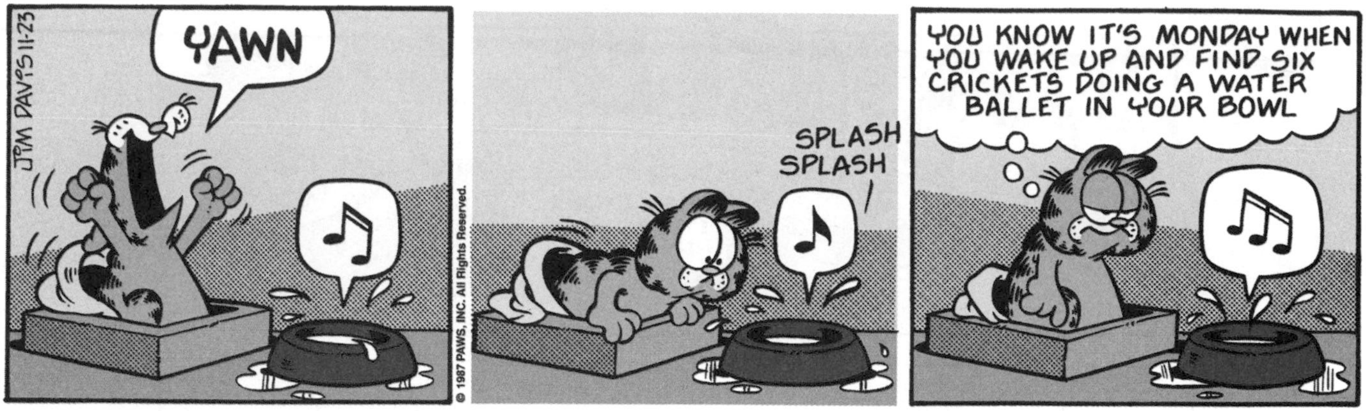
JIM DAVIS 11-23
YAWN
SPLASH SPLASH
YOU KNOW IT'S MONDAY WHEN YOU WAKE UP AND FIND SIX CRICKETS DOING A WATER BALLET IN YOUR BOWL
© 1987 PAWS, INC. All Rights Reserved.

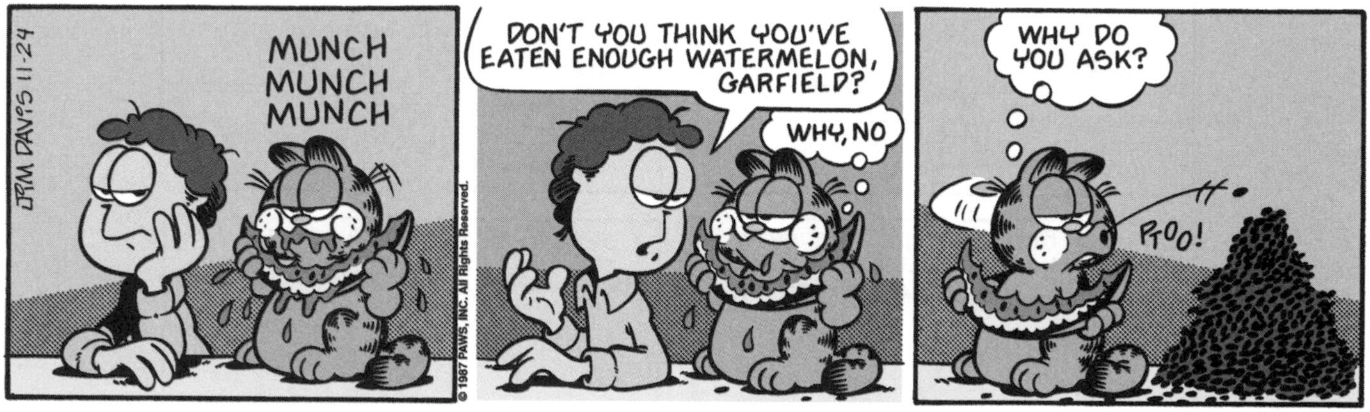
JIM DAVIS 11-24
MUNCH MUNCH MUNCH
DON'T YOU THINK YOU'VE EATEN ENOUGH WATERMELON, GARFIELD?
WHY, NO
WHY DO YOU ASK?
PTOO!
© 1987 PAWS, INC. All Rights Reserved.

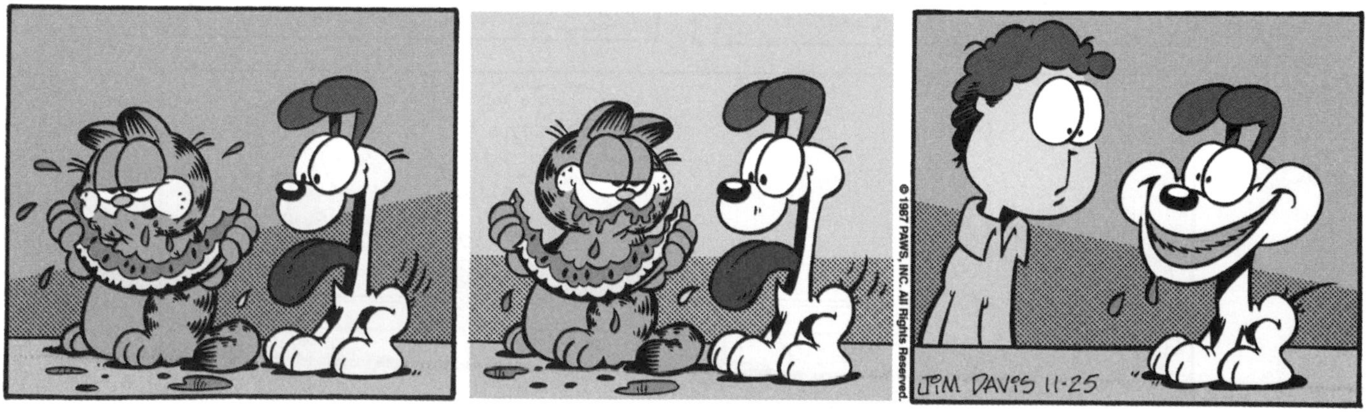
© 1987 PAWS, INC. All Rights Reserved.
JIM DAVIS 11-25

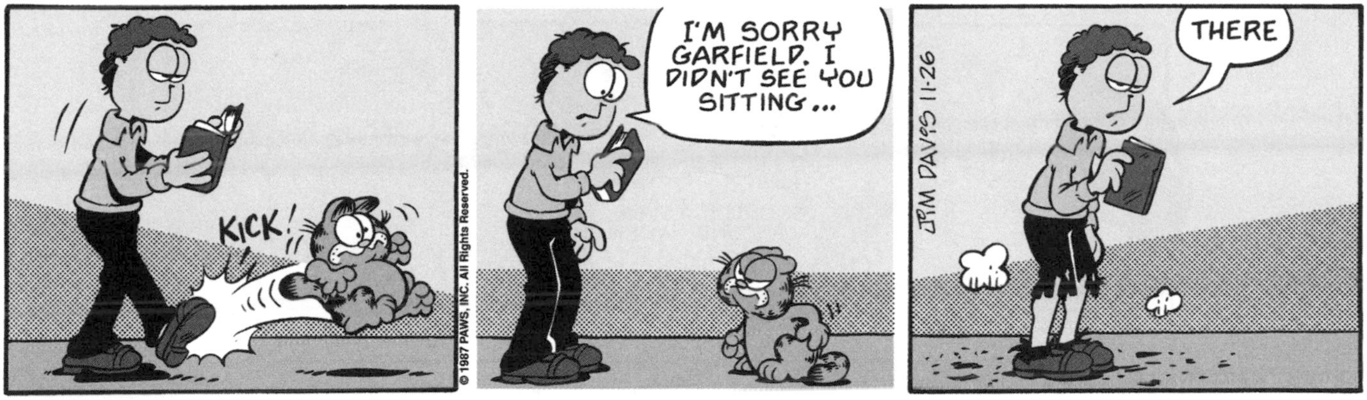
KICK!
© 1987 PAWS, INC. All Rights Reserved.
I'M SORRY GARFIELD. I DIDN'T SEE YOU SITTING...
JIM DAVIS 11-26
THERE

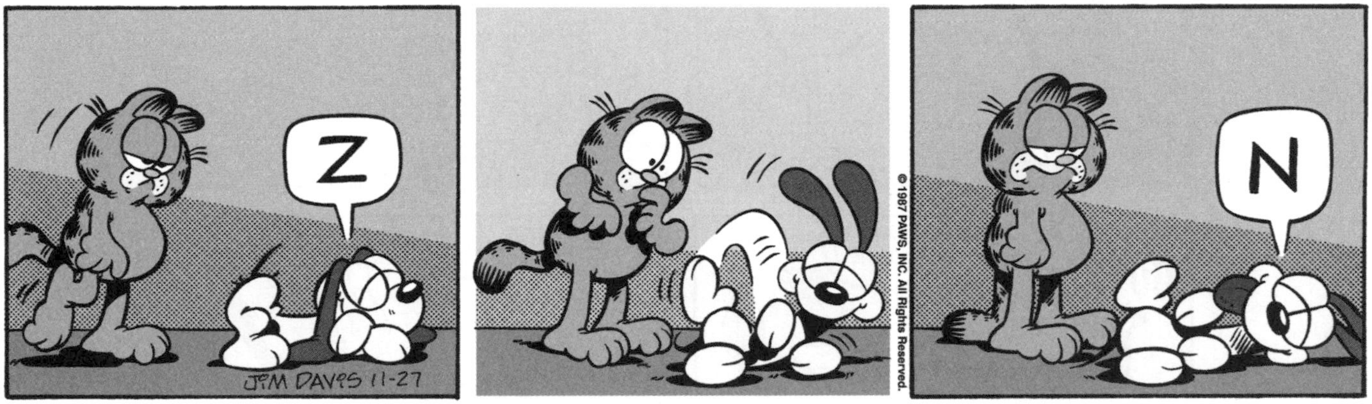
Z
JIM DAVIS 11-27
© 1987 PAWS, INC. All Rights Reserved.
N

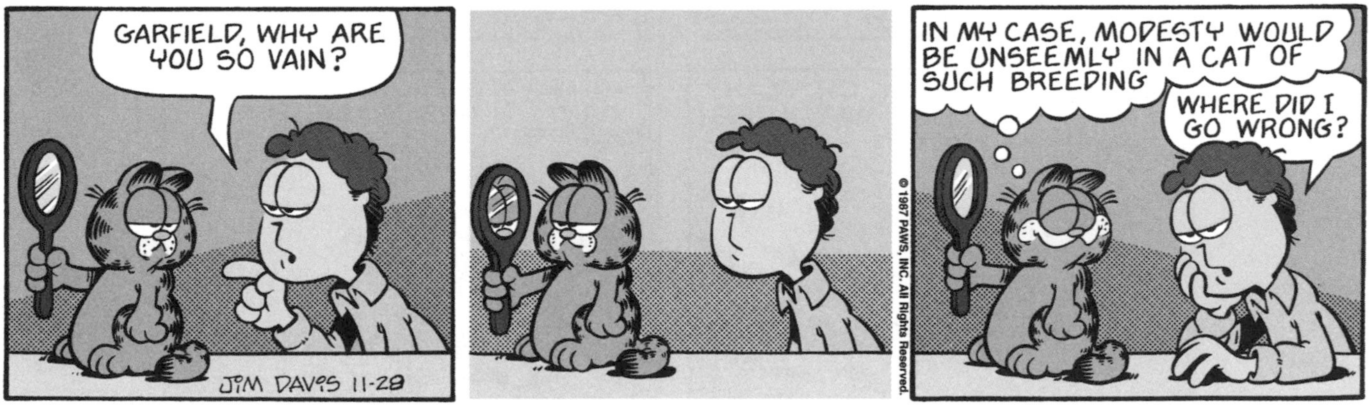
GARFIELD, WHY ARE YOU SO VAIN?
JIM DAVIS 11-28
© 1987 PAWS, INC. All Rights Reserved.
IN MY CASE, MODESTY WOULD BE UNSEEMLY IN A CAT OF SUCH BREEDING
WHERE DID I GO WRONG?

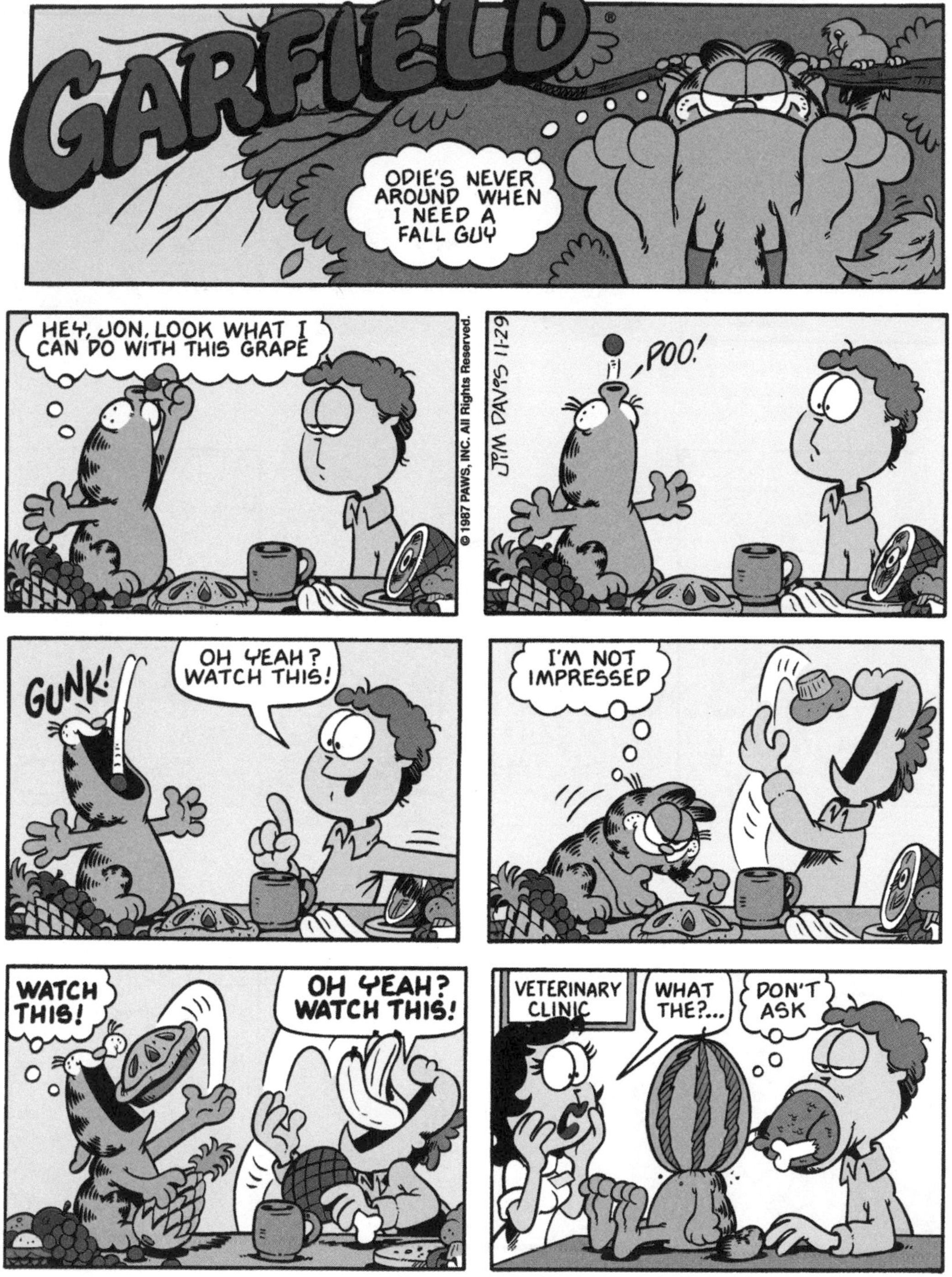
GARFIELD
ODIE'S NEVER AROUND WHEN I NEED A FALL GUY
HEY, JON, LOOK WHAT I CAN DO WITH THIS GRAPE
© 1987 PAWS, INC. All Rights Reserved.
JPM DAVIS 11-29
POO!
GUNK!
OH YEAH? WATCH THIS!
I'M NOT IMPRESSED
WATCH THIS!
OH YEAH? WATCH THIS!
VETERINARY CLINIC
WHAT THE?...
DON'T ASK

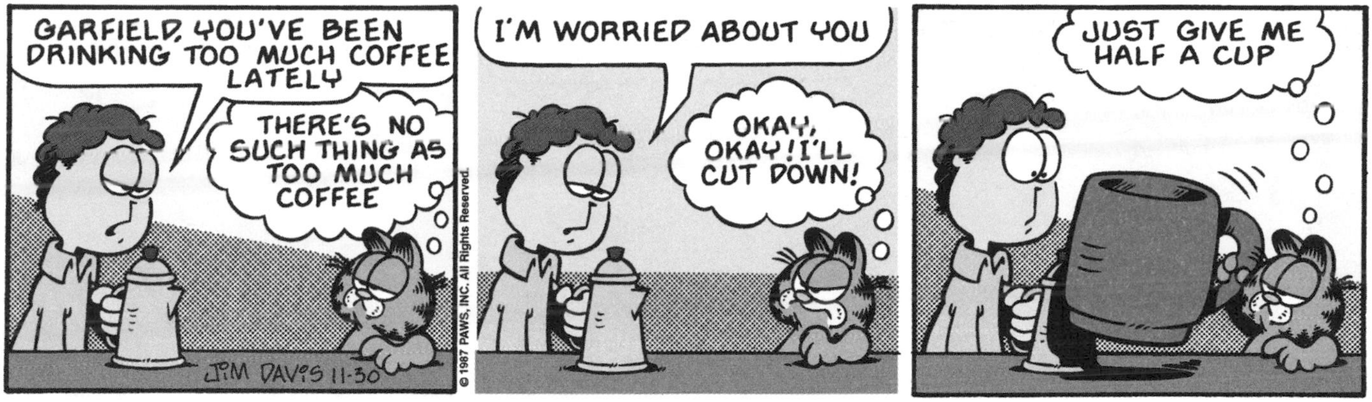
GARFIELD, YOU'VE BEEN DRINKING TOO MUCH COFFEE LATELY
THERE'S NO SUCH THING AS TOO MUCH COFFEE
JIM DAVIS 11-30
© 1987 PAWS, INC. All Rights Reserved.
I'M WORRIED ABOUT YOU
OKAY, OKAY! I'LL CUT DOWN!
JUST GIVE ME HALF A CUP

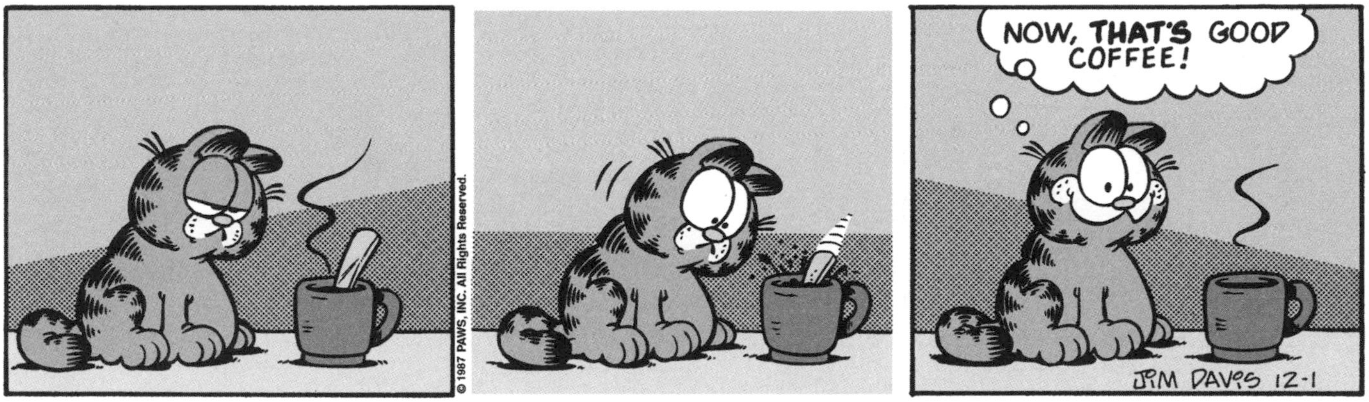
© 1987 PAWS, INC. All Rights Reserved.
NOW, THAT'S GOOD COFFEE!
JIM DAVIS 12-1

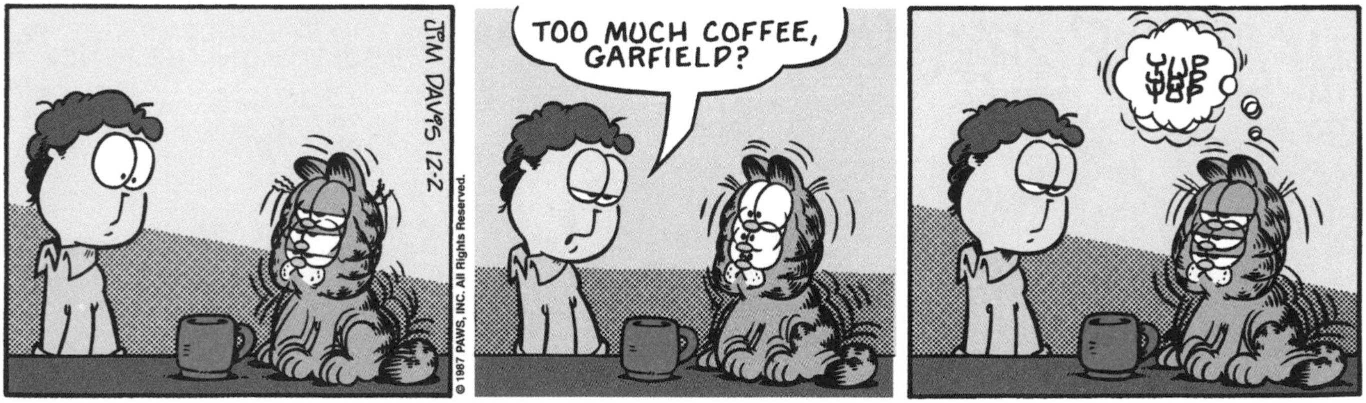
JIM DAVIS 12-2
© 1987 PAWS, INC. All Rights Reserved.
TOO MUCH COFFEE, GARFIELD?
YUP YUP YUP

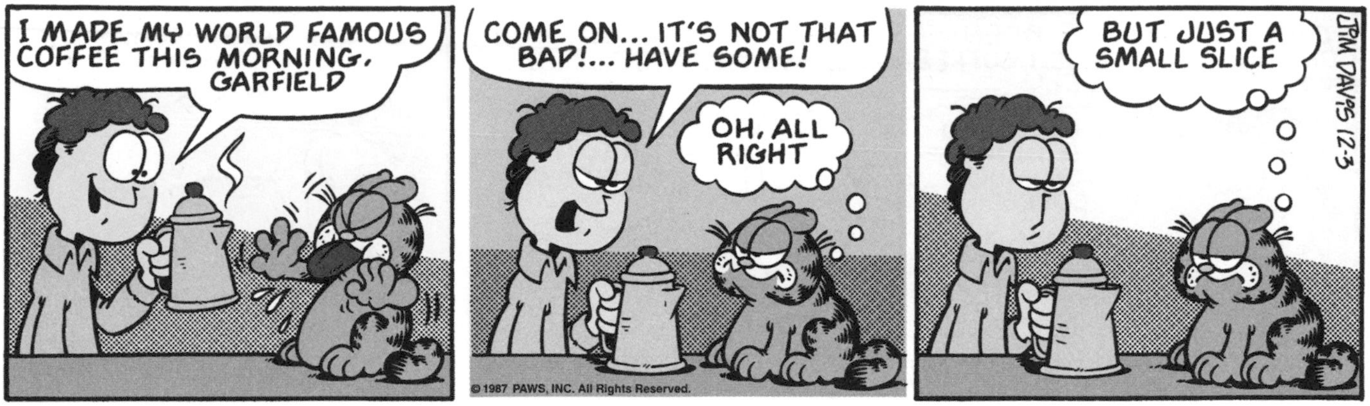
I MADE MY WORLD FAMOUS COFFEE THIS MORNING, GARFIELD
COME ON... IT'S NOT THAT BAD!... HAVE SOME!
OH, ALL RIGHT
BUT JUST A SMALL SLICE
© 1987 PAWS, INC. All Rights Reserved.
JIM DAVIS 12-3

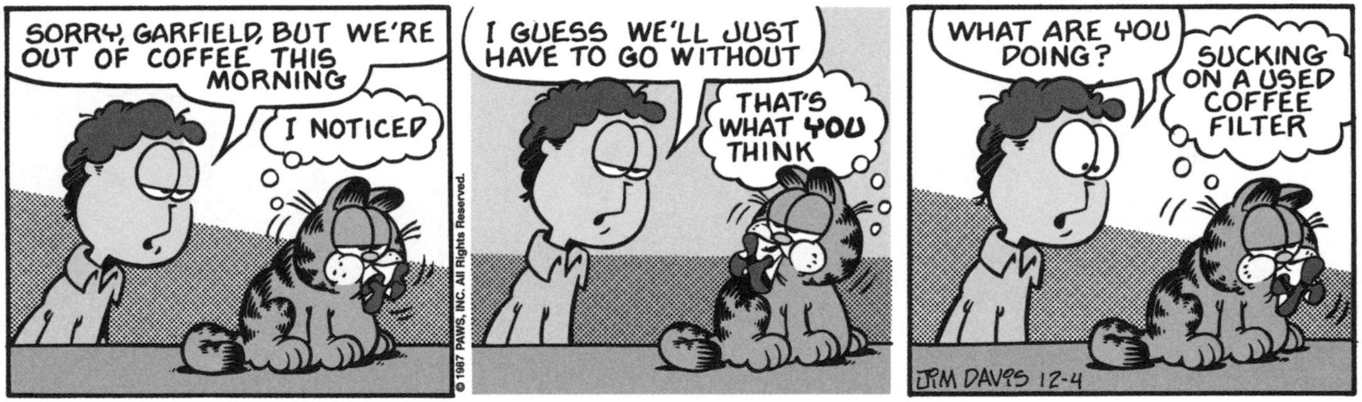
SORRY, GARFIELD, BUT WE'RE OUT OF COFFEE THIS MORNING
I NOTICED
I GUESS WE'LL JUST HAVE TO GO WITHOUT
THAT'S WHAT YOU THINK
WHAT ARE YOU DOING?
SUCKING ON A USED COFFEE FILTER
© 1987 PAWS, INC. All Rights Reserved.
JIM DAVIS 12-4

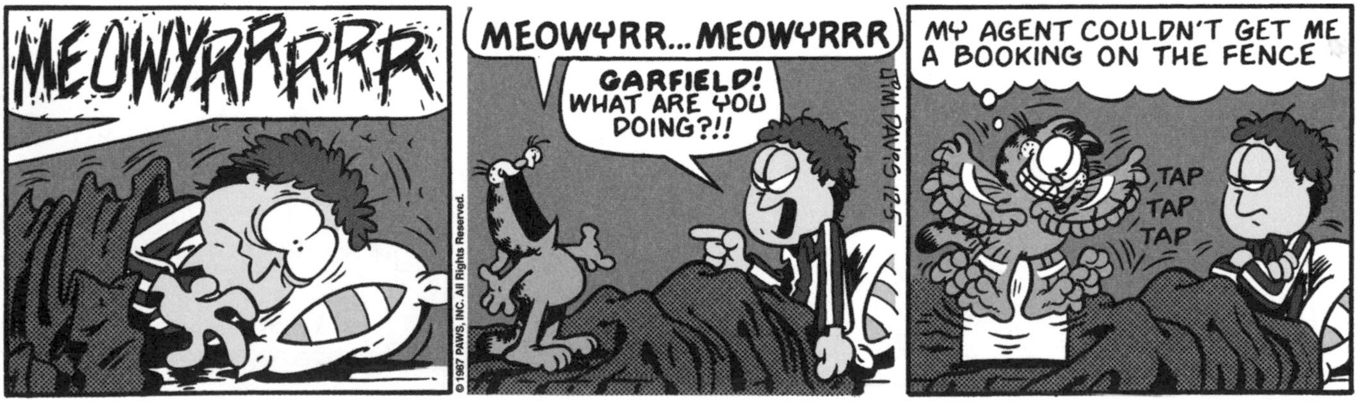
MEOWYRRRRR
MEOWYRR... MEOWYRRR
GARFIELD! WHAT ARE YOU DOING?!!
MY AGENT COULDN'T GET ME A BOOKING ON THE FENCE
TAP TAP TAP
© 1987 PAWS, INC. All Rights Reserved.
JIM DAVIS 12-5

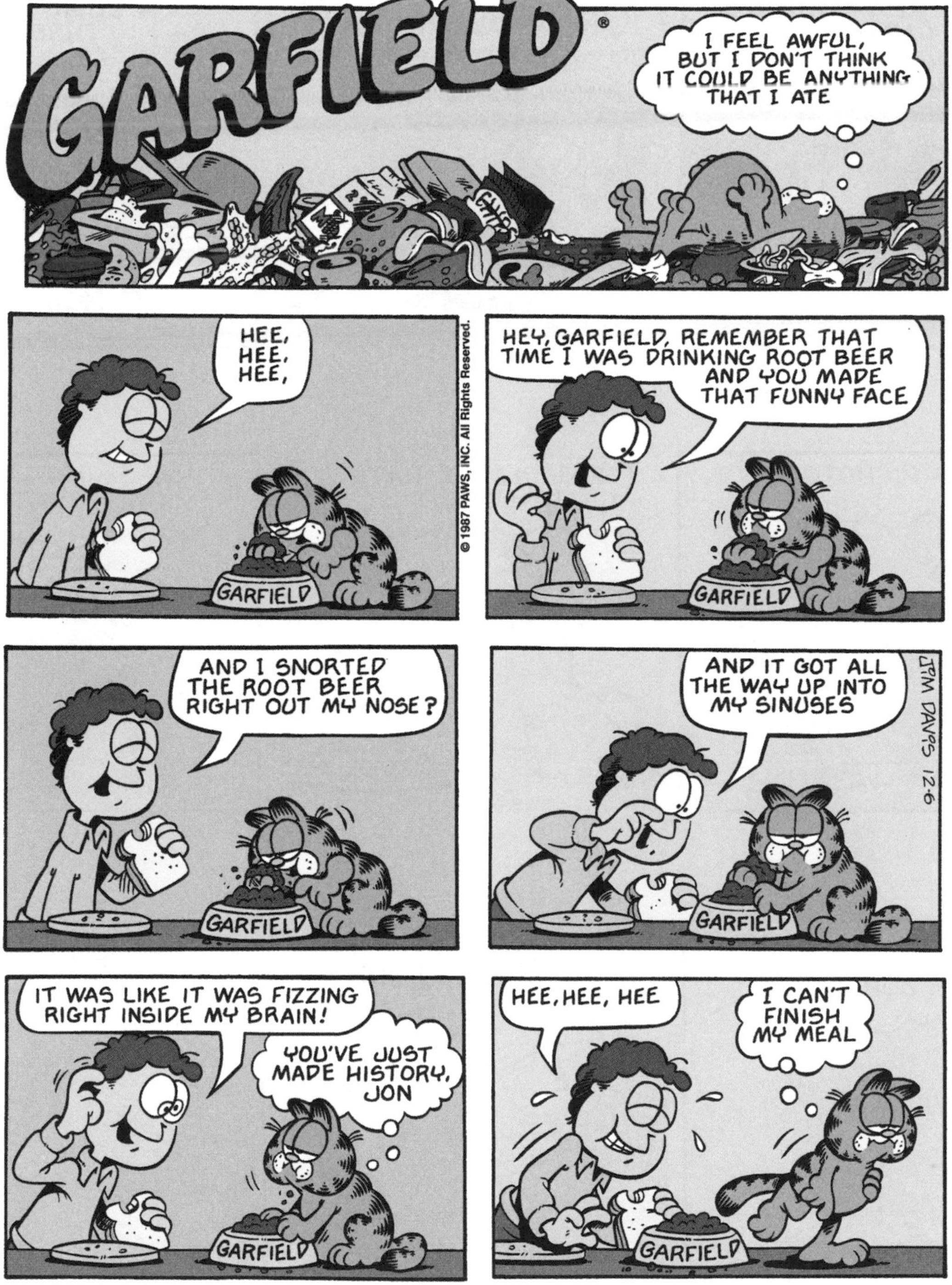
GARFIELD®
I FEEL AWFUL, BUT I DON'T THINK IT COULD BE ANYTHING THAT I ATE
HEE, HEE, HEE,
GARFIELD
© 1987 PAWS, INC. All Rights Reserved.
HEY, GARFIELD, REMEMBER THAT TIME I WAS DRINKING ROOT BEER AND YOU MADE THAT FUNNY FACE
GARFIELD
AND I SNORTED THE ROOT BEER RIGHT OUT MY NOSE?
GARFIELD
AND IT GOT ALL THE WAY UP INTO MY SINUSES
JIM DAVIS 12-6
GARFIELD
IT WAS LIKE IT WAS FIZZING RIGHT INSIDE MY BRAIN!
YOU'VE JUST MADE HISTORY, JON
GARFIELD
HEE, HEE, HEE
I CAN'T FINISH MY MEAL
GARFIELD

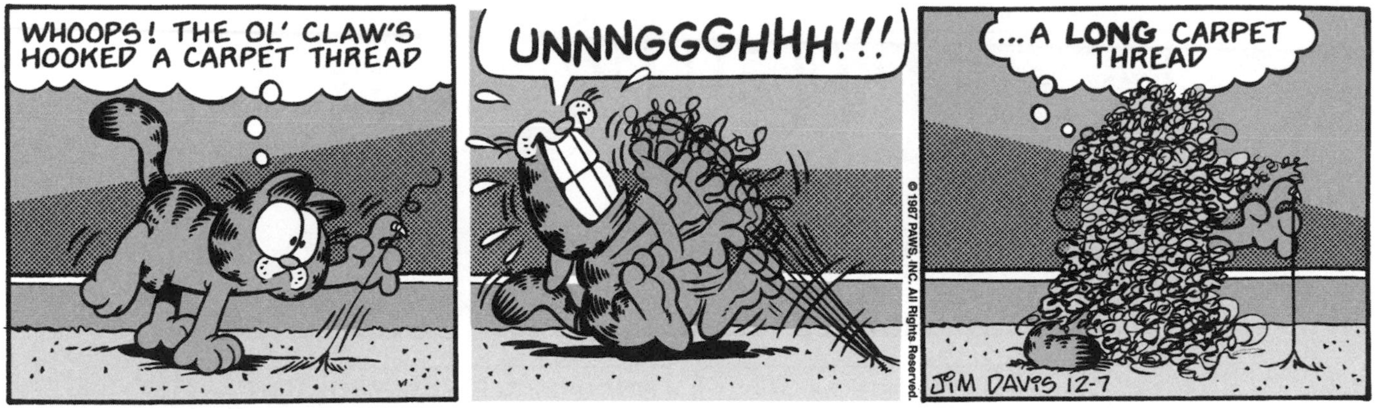
WHOOPS! THE OL' CLAW'S HOOKED A CARPET THREAD
UNNNGGGHHH!!!
...A LONG CARPET THREAD
© 1987 PAWS, INC. All Rights Reserved.
JIM DAVIS 12-7

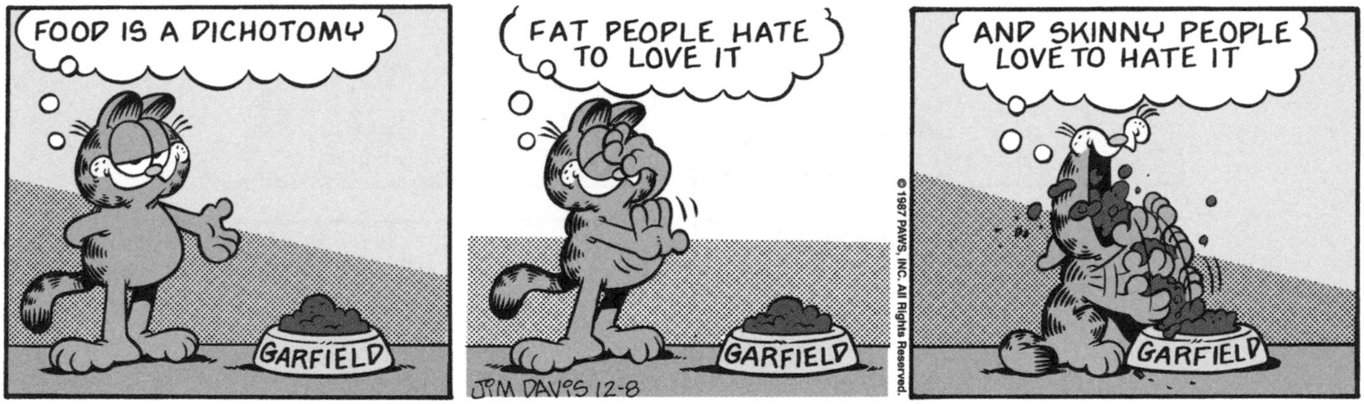
FOOD IS A DICHOTOMY
FAT PEOPLE HATE TO LOVE IT
AND SKINNY PEOPLE LOVE TO HATE IT
GARFIELD
GARFIELD
GARFIELD
JIM DAVIS 12-8
© 1987 PAWS, INC. All Rights Reserved.

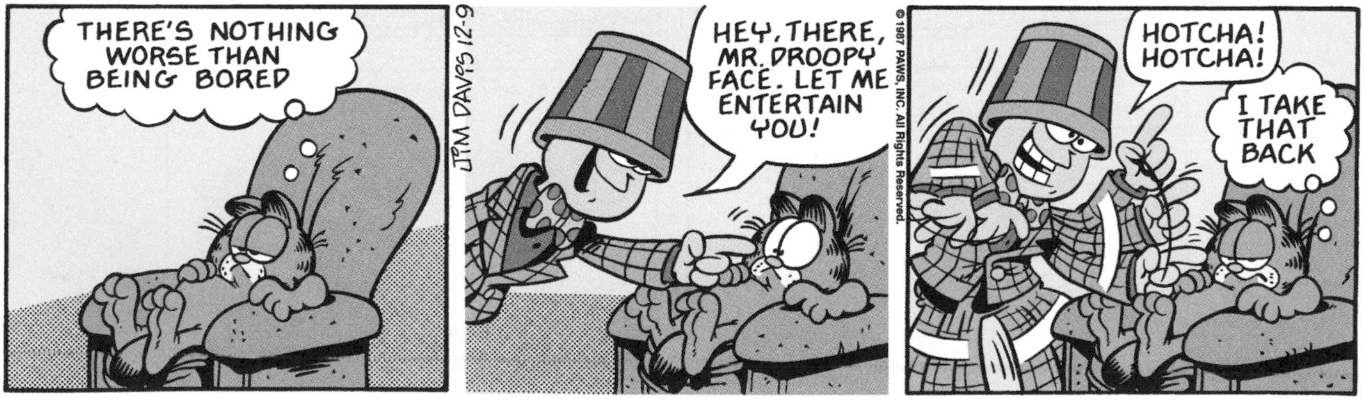
THERE'S NOTHING WORSE THAN BEING BORED
JIM DAVIS 12-9
HEY, THERE, MR. DROOPY FACE. LET ME ENTERTAIN YOU!
© 1987 PAWS, INC. All Rights Reserved.
HOTCHA! HOTCHA!
I TAKE THAT BACK

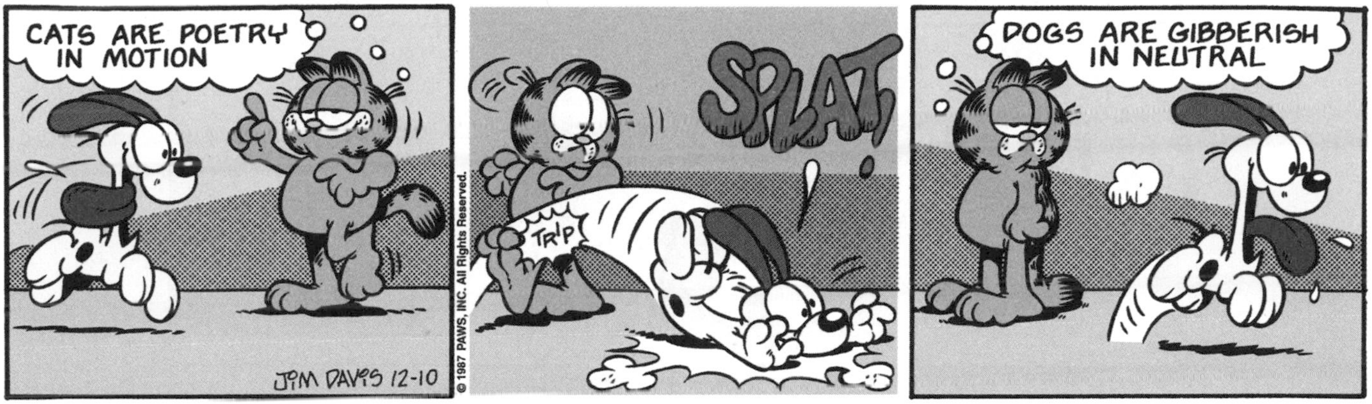
CATS ARE POETRY IN MOTION
JIM DAVIS 12-10
© 1987 PAWS, INC. All Rights Reserved.
TRIP
SPLAT
DOGS ARE GIBBERISH IN NEUTRAL

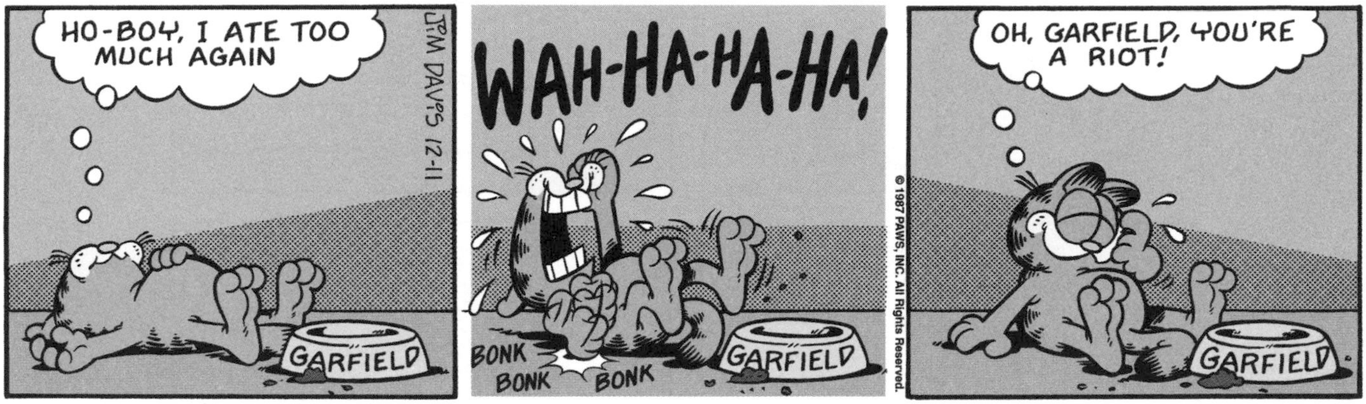
HO-BOY, I ATE TOO MUCH AGAIN
JIM DAVIS 12-11
GARFIELD
WAH-HA-HA-HA!
BONK
BONK
BONK
GARFIELD
© 1987 PAWS, INC. All Rights Reserved.
OH, GARFIELD, YOU'RE A RIOT!
GARFIELD

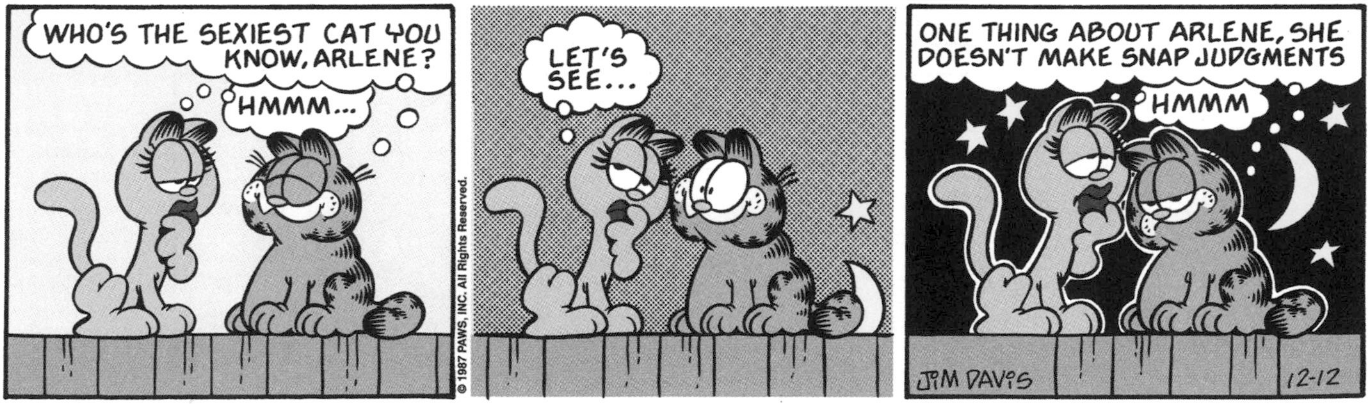
WHO'S THE SEXIEST CAT YOU KNOW, ARLENE?
HMMM...
© 1987 PAWS, INC. All Rights Reserved.
LET'S SEE...
ONE THING ABOUT ARLENE, SHE DOESN'T MAKE SNAP JUDGMENTS
HMMM
JIM DAVIS
12-12

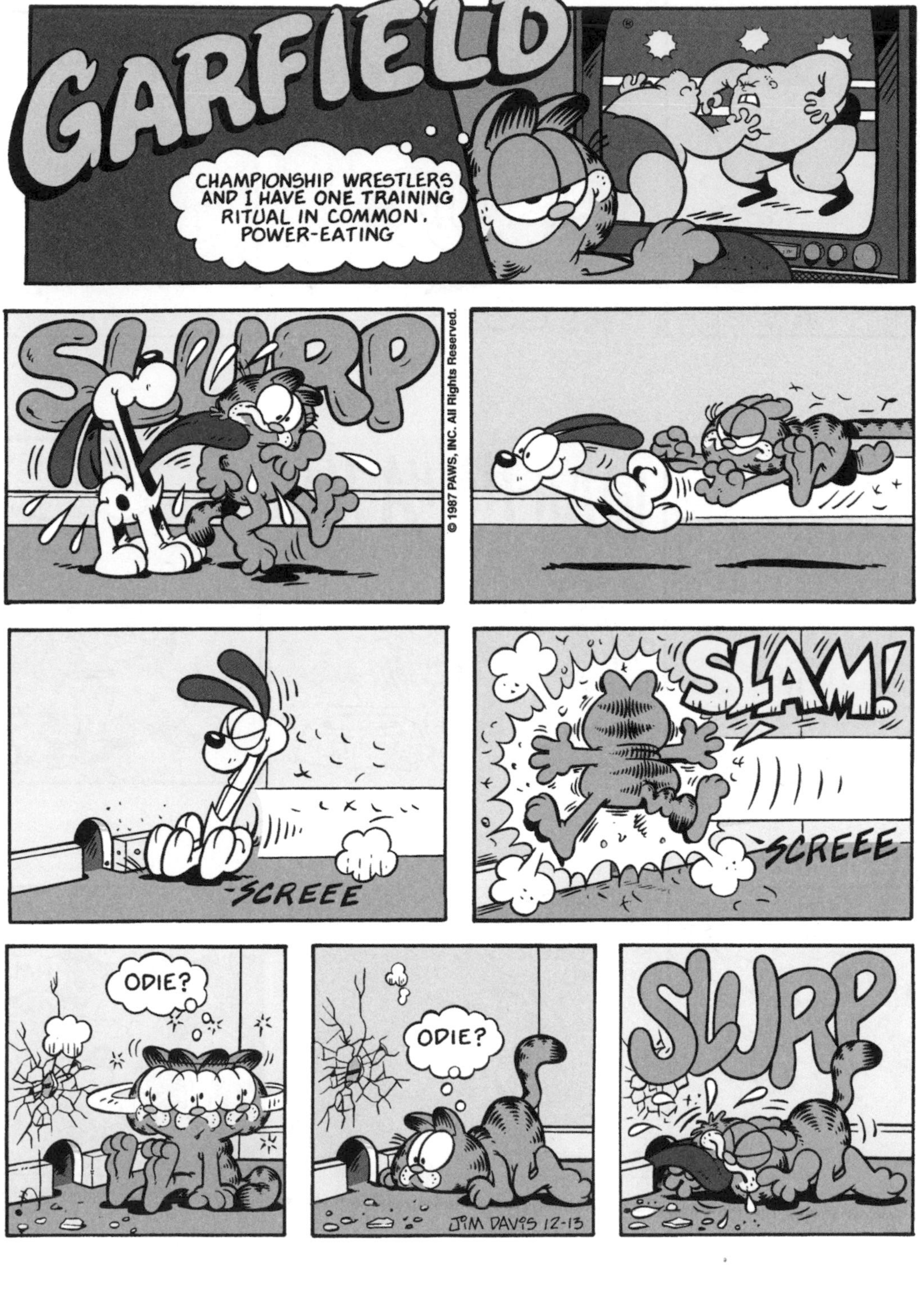
GARFIELD
CHAMPIONSHIP WRESTLERS AND I HAVE ONE TRAINING RITUAL IN COMMON. POWER-EATING
SLURP
© 1987 PAWS, INC. All Rights Reserved.
SCREEE
SLAM!
SCREEE
ODIE?
ODIE?
JIM DAVIS 12-13
SLURP

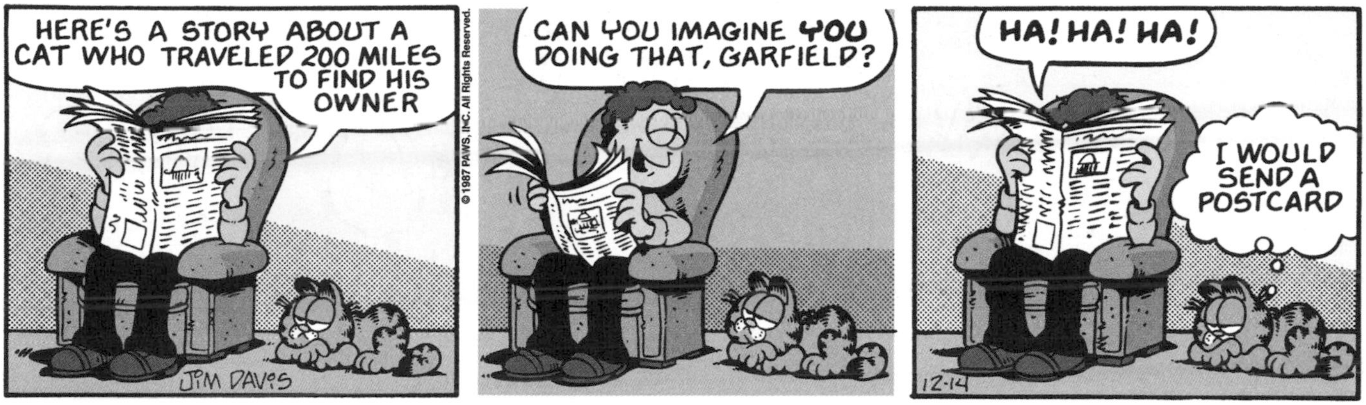
HERE'S A STORY ABOUT A CAT WHO TRAVELED 200 MILES TO FIND HIS OWNER
JIM DAVIS
© 1987 PAWS, INC. All Rights Reserved.
CAN YOU IMAGINE YOU DOING THAT, GARFIELD?
HA! HA! HA!
I WOULD SEND A POSTCARD
12-14

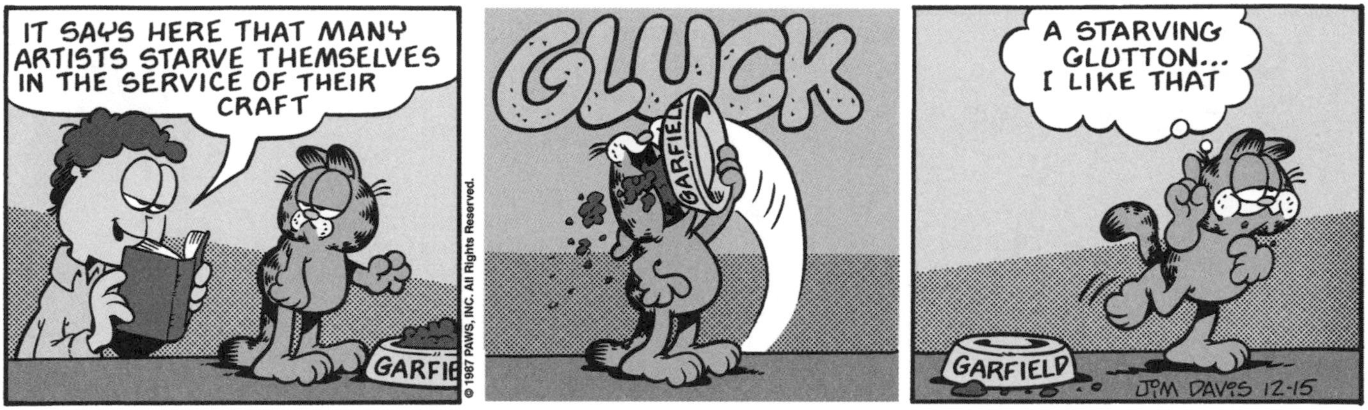
IT SAYS HERE THAT MANY ARTISTS STARVE THEMSELVES IN THE SERVICE OF THEIR CRAFT
GARFIE
© 1987 PAWS, INC. All Rights Reserved.
GLUCK
GARFIEL
A STARVING GLUTTON... I LIKE THAT
GARFIELD
JIM DAVIS 12-15

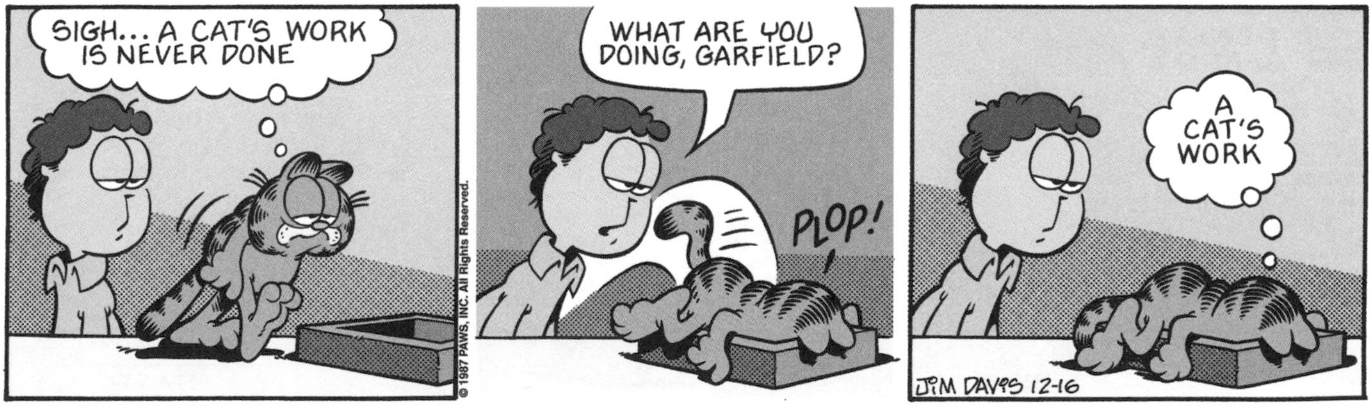
SIGH... A CAT'S WORK IS NEVER DONE
© 1987 PAWS, INC. All Rights Reserved.
WHAT ARE YOU DOING, GARFIELD?
PLOP!
A CAT'S WORK
JIM DAVIS 12-16

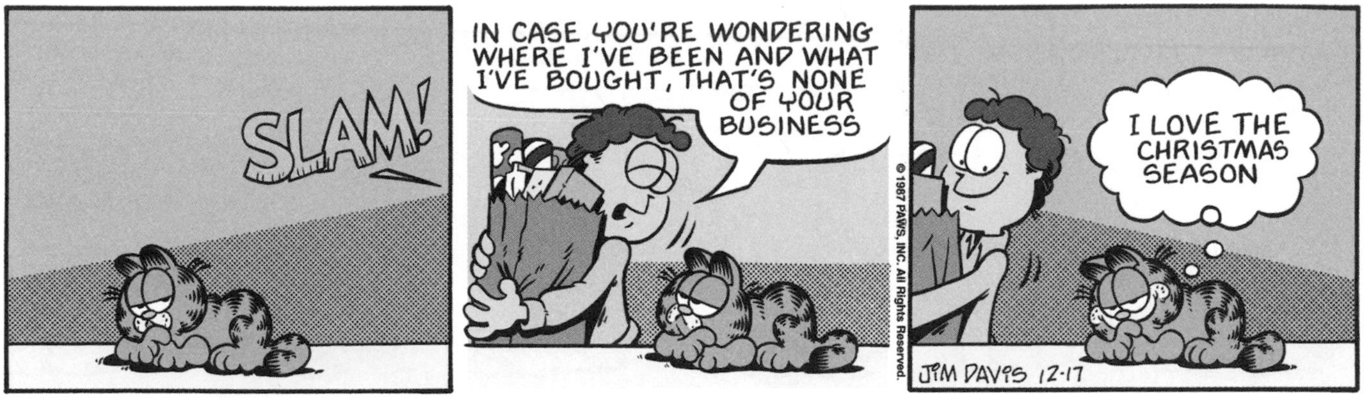
SLAM!
IN CASE YOU'RE WONDERING WHERE I'VE BEEN AND WHAT I'VE BOUGHT, THAT'S NONE OF YOUR BUSINESS
© 1987 PAWS, INC. All Rights Reserved.
I LOVE THE CHRISTMAS SEASON
JIM DAVIS 12-17

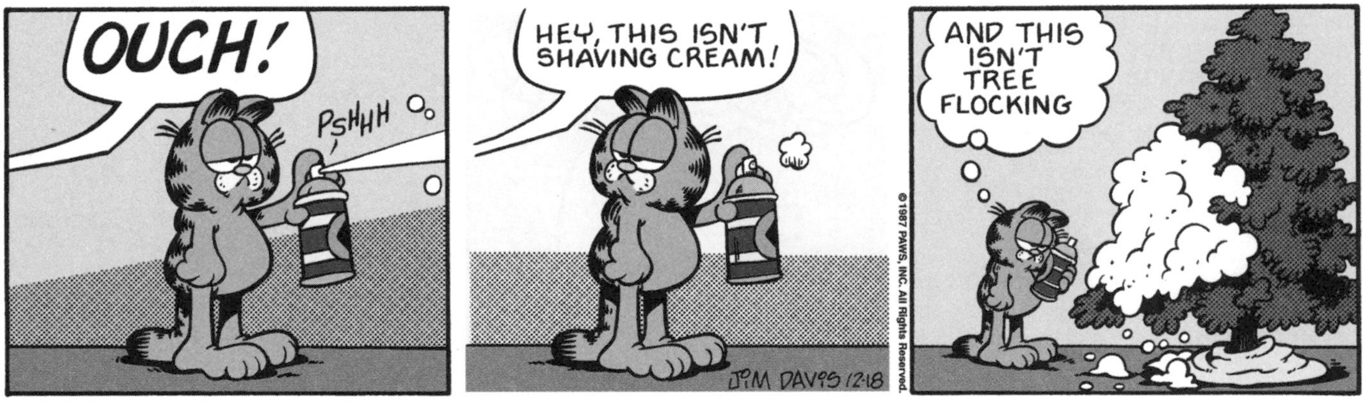
OUCH!
PSHHH
HEY, THIS ISN'T SHAVING CREAM!
JIM DAVIS 12-18
© 1987 PAWS, INC. All Rights Reserved.
AND THIS ISN'T TREE FLOCKING

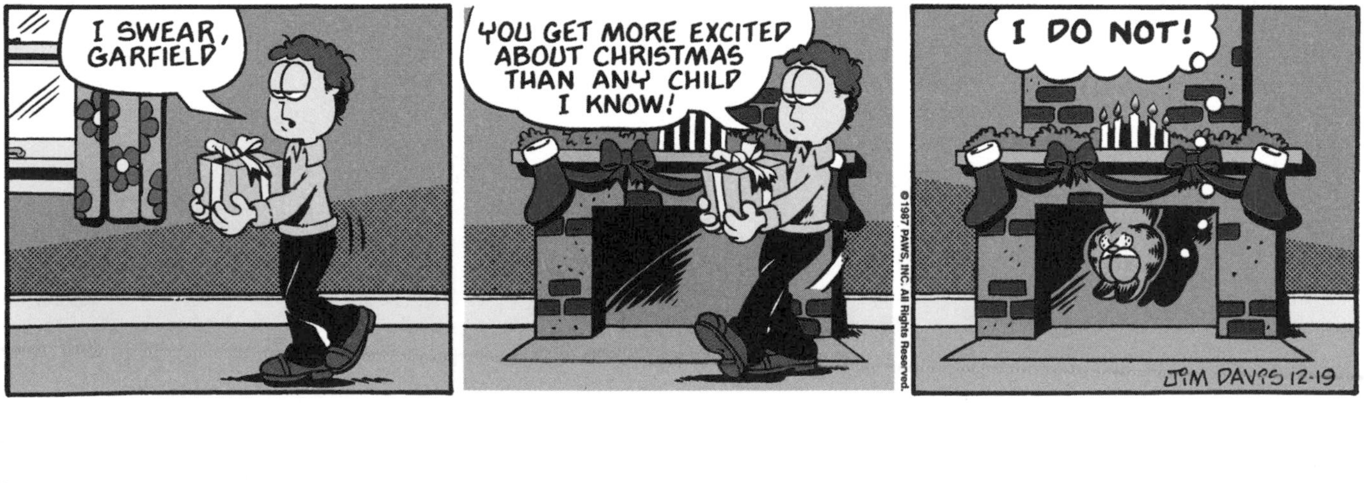
I SWEAR, GARFIELD
YOU GET MORE EXCITED ABOUT CHRISTMAS THAN ANY CHILD I KNOW!
© 1987 PAWS, INC. All Rights Reserved.
I DO NOT!
JIM DAVIS 12-19

Garfield
chews the fat

BY JIM DAVIS

Ballantine Books • **New York**

THE GARFIELD WORKOUT

DO THESE EXERCISES EVERY DAY, AND YOU'LL SOON BE IN THE SAME SHAPE AS GARFIELD!

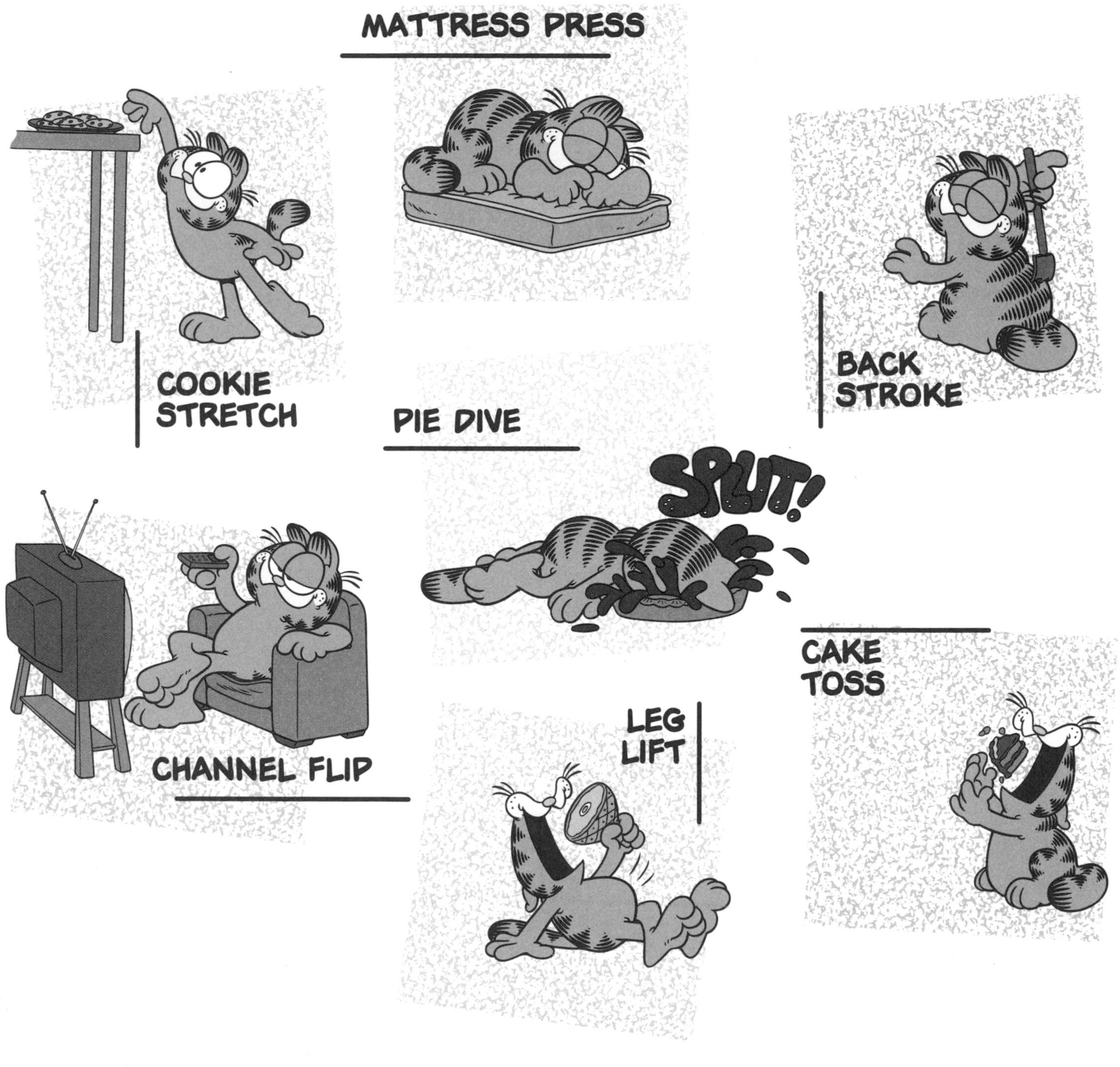
MATTRESS PRESS
COOKIE STRETCH
BACK STROKE
PIE DIVE
SPLUT!
CHANNEL FLIP
LEG LIFT
CAKE TOSS

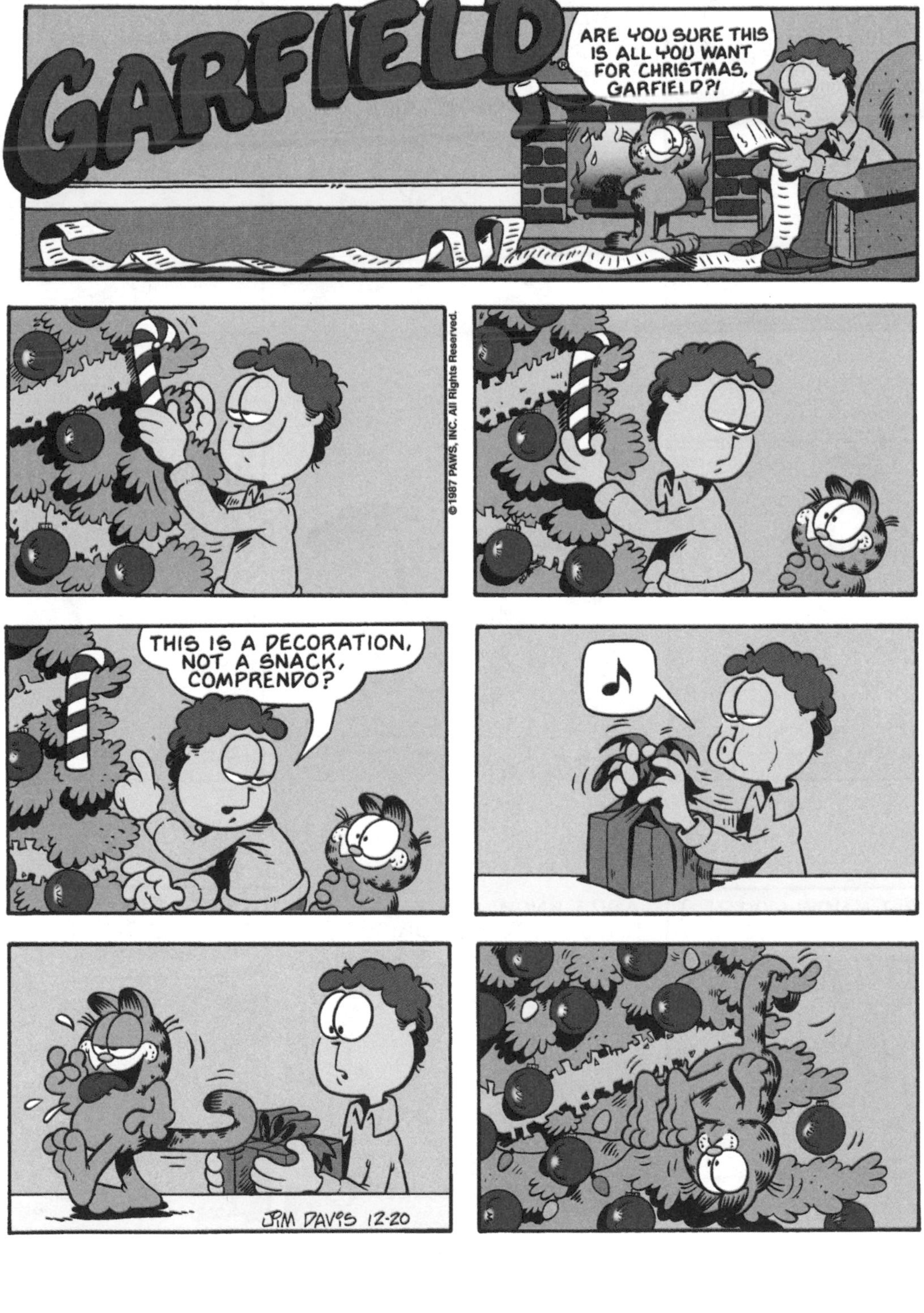
GARFIELD®
ARE YOU SURE THIS IS ALL YOU WANT FOR CHRISTMAS, GARFIELD?!
© 1987 PAWS, INC. All Rights Reserved.
THIS IS A DECORATION, NOT A SNACK, COMPRENDO?
♪
JIM DAVIS 12-20

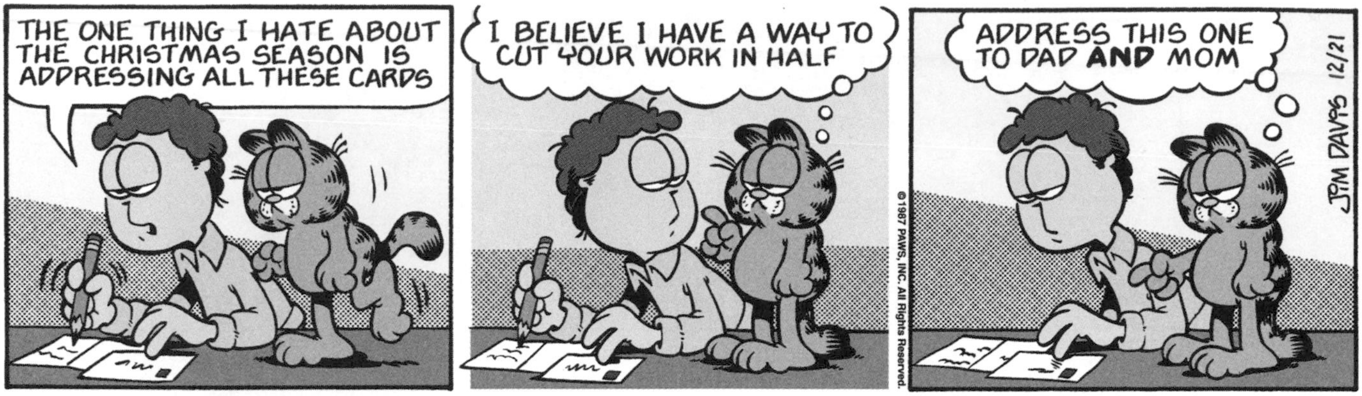
THE ONE THING I HATE ABOUT THE CHRISTMAS SEASON IS ADDRESSING ALL THESE CARDS
I BELIEVE I HAVE A WAY TO CUT YOUR WORK IN HALF
©1987 PAWS, INC. All Rights Reserved.
ADDRESS THIS ONE TO DAD **AND** MOM
JIM DAVIS 12/21

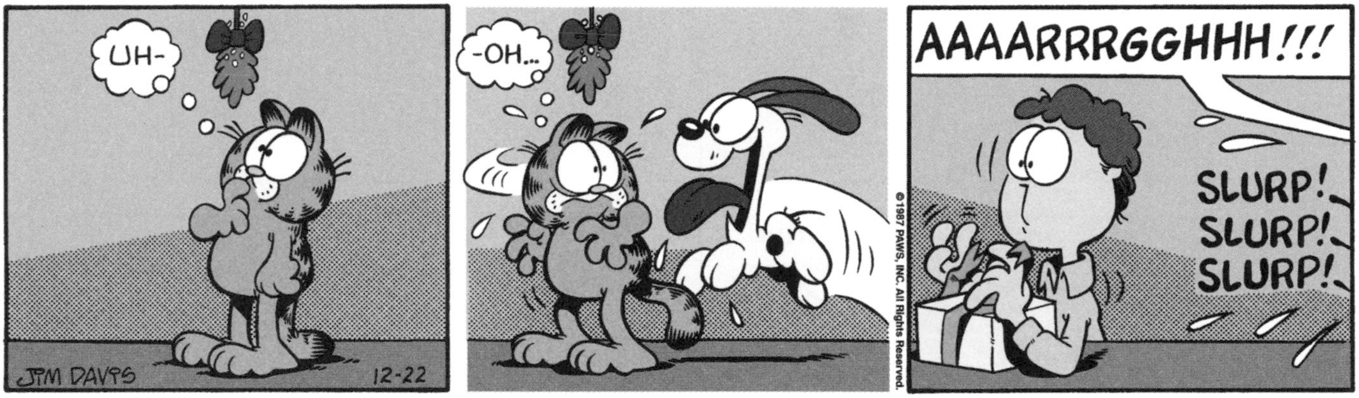
UH-
JIM DAVIS 12-22
-OH...
©1987 PAWS, INC. All Rights Reserved.
AAAARRRGGHHH!!!
SLURP!
SLURP!
SLURP!

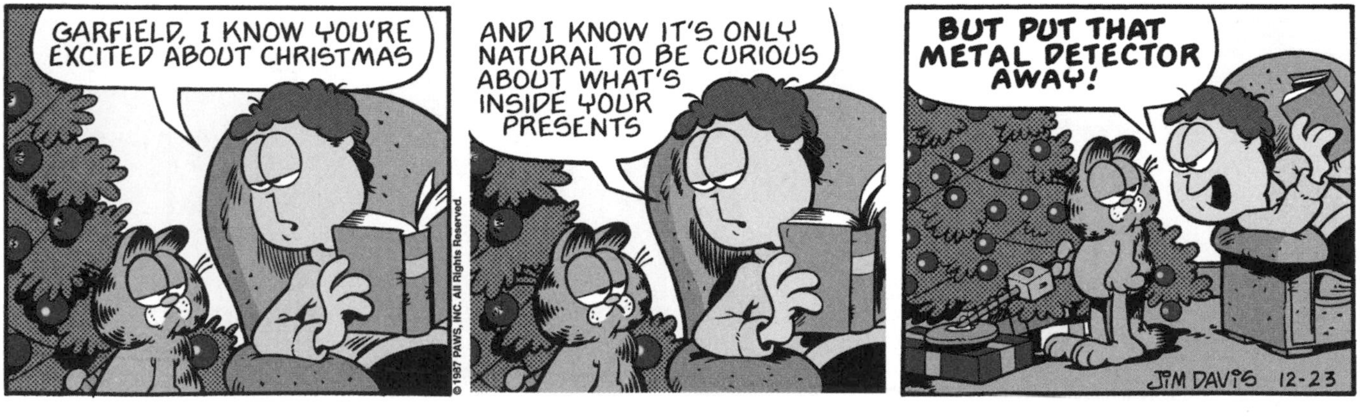
GARFIELD, I KNOW YOU'RE EXCITED ABOUT CHRISTMAS
©1987 PAWS, INC. All Rights Reserved.
AND I KNOW IT'S ONLY NATURAL TO BE CURIOUS ABOUT WHAT'S INSIDE YOUR PRESENTS
BUT PUT THAT METAL DETECTOR AWAY!
JIM DAVIS 12-23

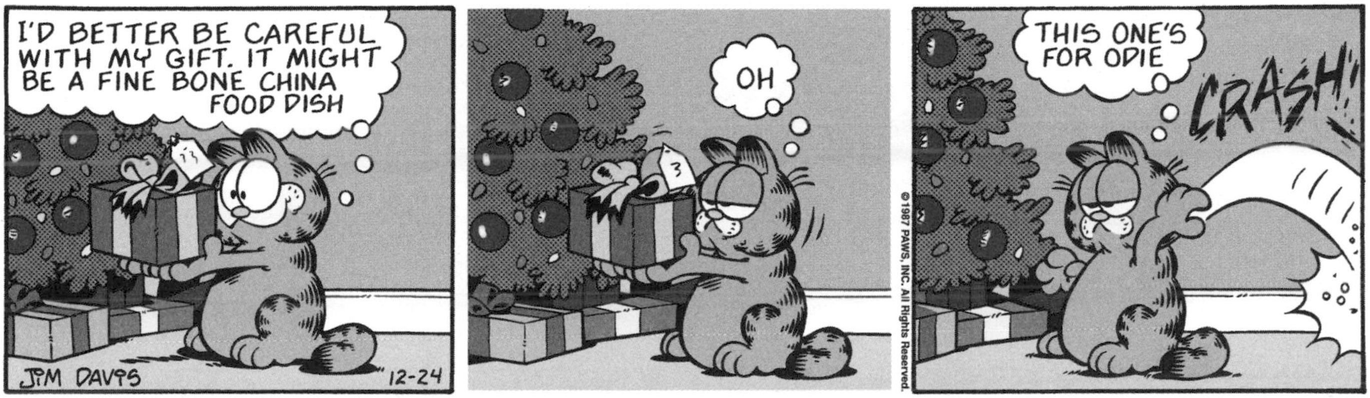
I'D BETTER BE CAREFUL WITH MY GIFT. IT MIGHT BE A FINE BONE CHINA FOOD DISH
JIM DAVIS 12-24
OH
© 1987 PAWS, INC. All Rights Reserved.
THIS ONE'S FOR ODIE
CRASH!

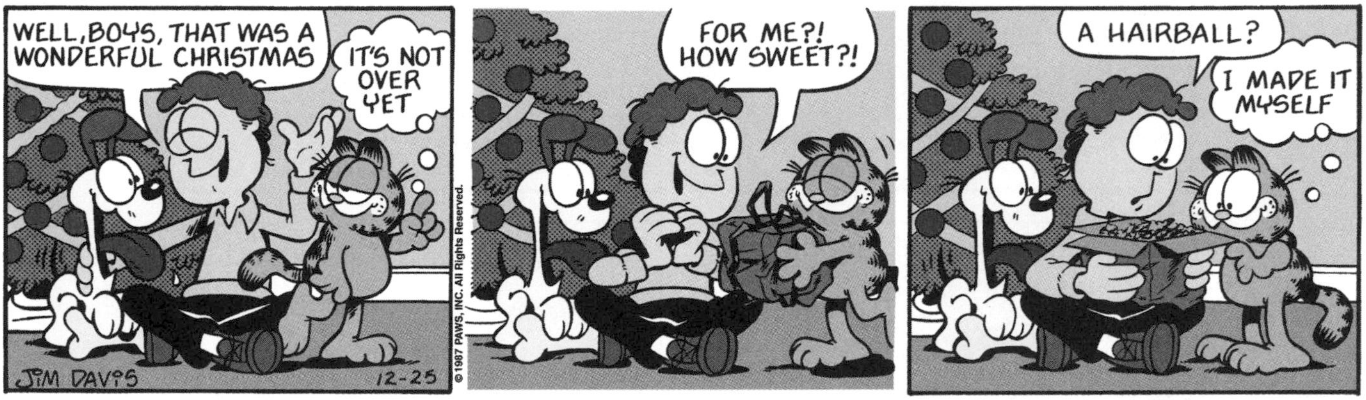
WELL, BOYS, THAT WAS A WONDERFUL CHRISTMAS
IT'S NOT OVER YET
JIM DAVIS 12-25
© 1987 PAWS, INC. All Rights Reserved.
FOR ME?! HOW SWEET?!
A HAIRBALL?
I MADE IT MYSELF

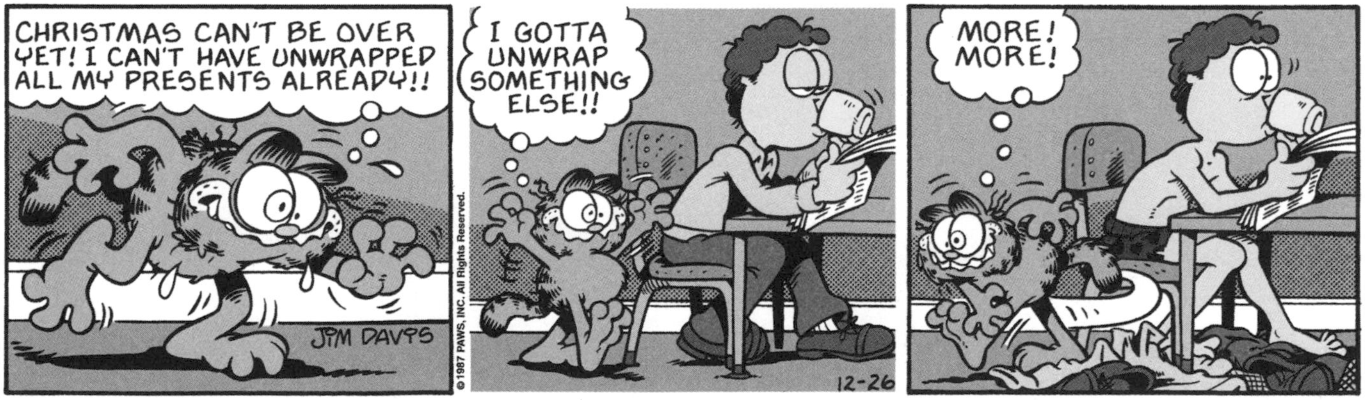
CHRISTMAS CAN'T BE OVER YET! I CAN'T HAVE UNWRAPPED ALL MY PRESENTS ALREADY!!
JIM DAVIS
© 1987 PAWS, INC. All Rights Reserved.
I GOTTA UNWRAP SOMETHING ELSE!!
12-26
MORE! MORE!

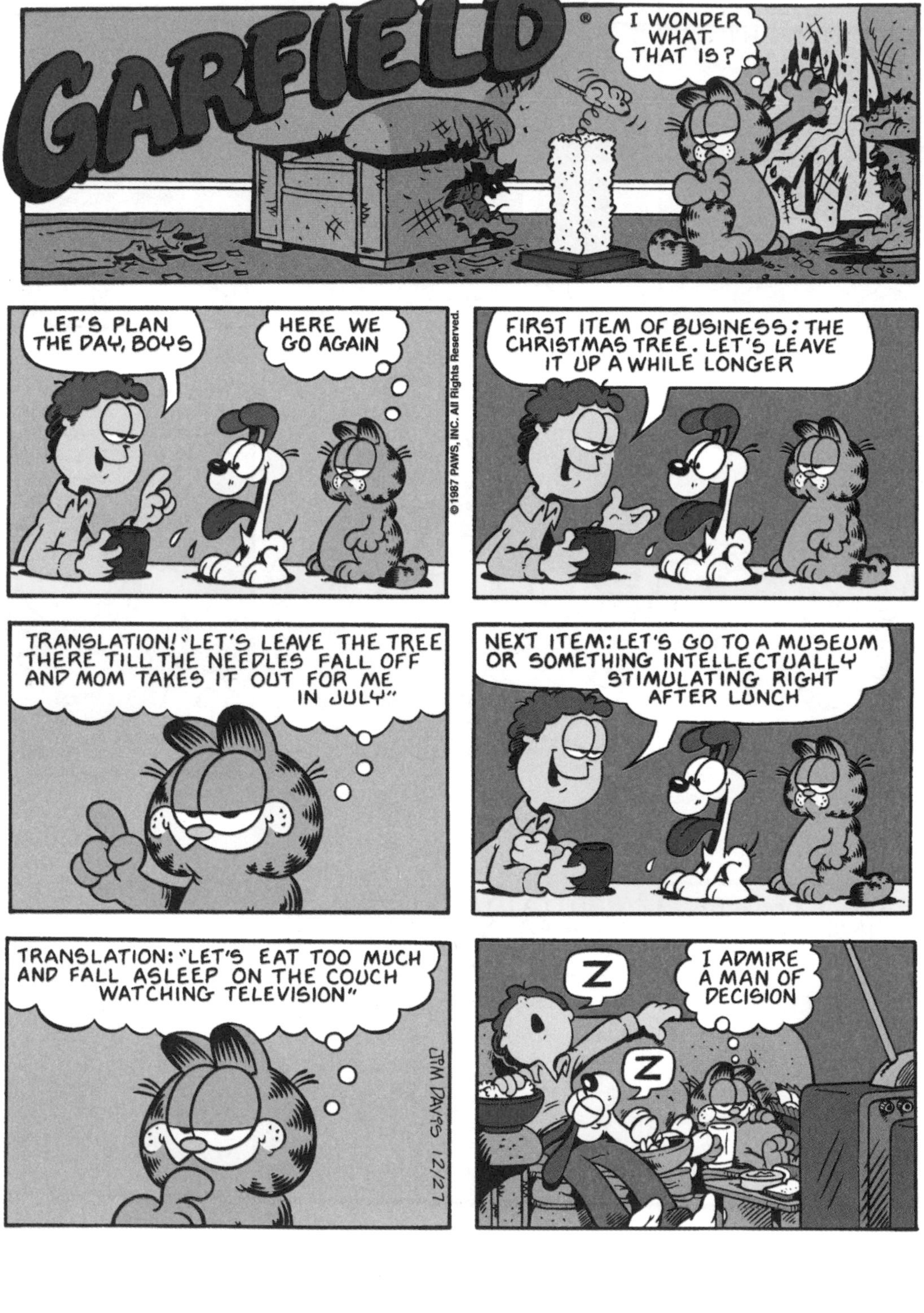
GARFIELD®
I WONDER WHAT THAT IS?
LET'S PLAN THE DAY, BOYS
HERE WE GO AGAIN
© 1987 PAWS, INC. All Rights Reserved.
FIRST ITEM OF BUSINESS: THE CHRISTMAS TREE. LET'S LEAVE IT UP A WHILE LONGER
TRANSLATION! "LET'S LEAVE THE TREE THERE TILL THE NEEDLES FALL OFF AND MOM TAKES IT OUT FOR ME IN JULY"
NEXT ITEM: LET'S GO TO A MUSEUM OR SOMETHING INTELLECTUALLY STIMULATING RIGHT AFTER LUNCH
TRANSLATION: "LET'S EAT TOO MUCH AND FALL ASLEEP ON THE COUCH WATCHING TELEVISION"
JIM DAVIS 12/27
Z
I ADMIRE A MAN OF DECISION
Z

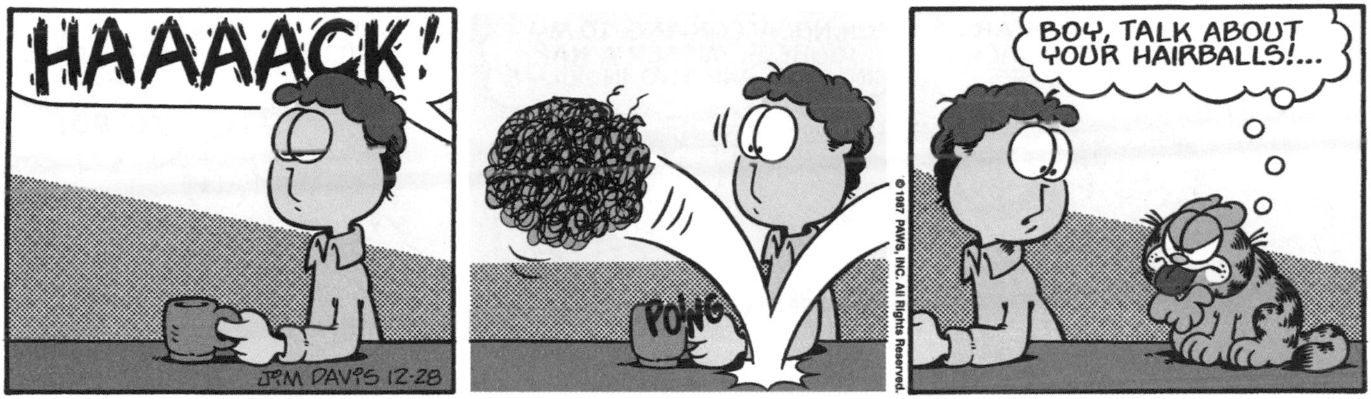
HAAAACK!
POING
BOY, TALK ABOUT YOUR HAIRBALLS!...
JIM DAVIS 12-28
© 1987 PAWS, INC. All Rights Reserved.

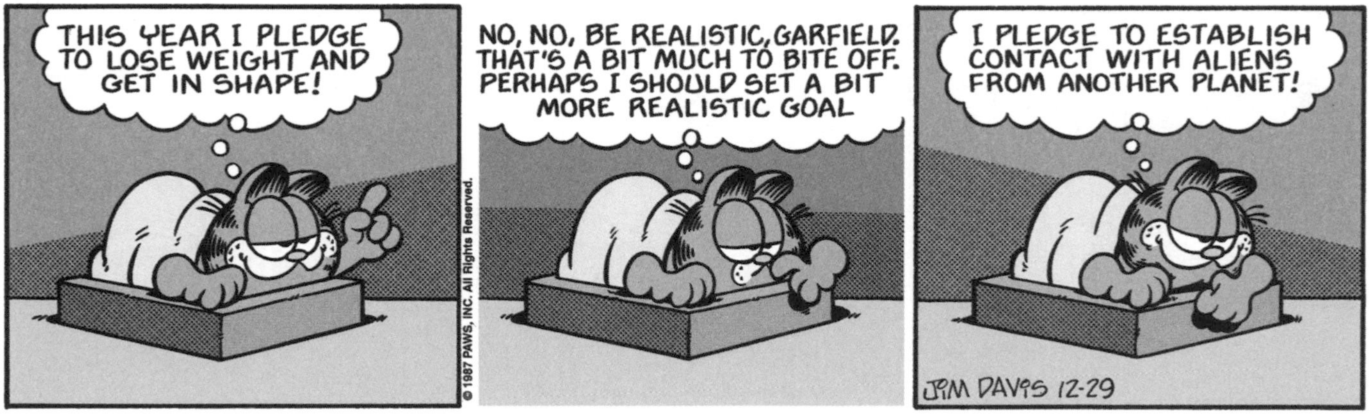
THIS YEAR I PLEDGE TO LOSE WEIGHT AND GET IN SHAPE!
© 1987 PAWS, INC. All Rights Reserved.
NO, NO, BE REALISTIC, GARFIELD. THAT'S A BIT MUCH TO BITE OFF. PERHAPS I SHOULD SET A BIT MORE REALISTIC GOAL
I PLEDGE TO ESTABLISH CONTACT WITH ALIENS FROM ANOTHER PLANET!
JIM DAVIS 12-29

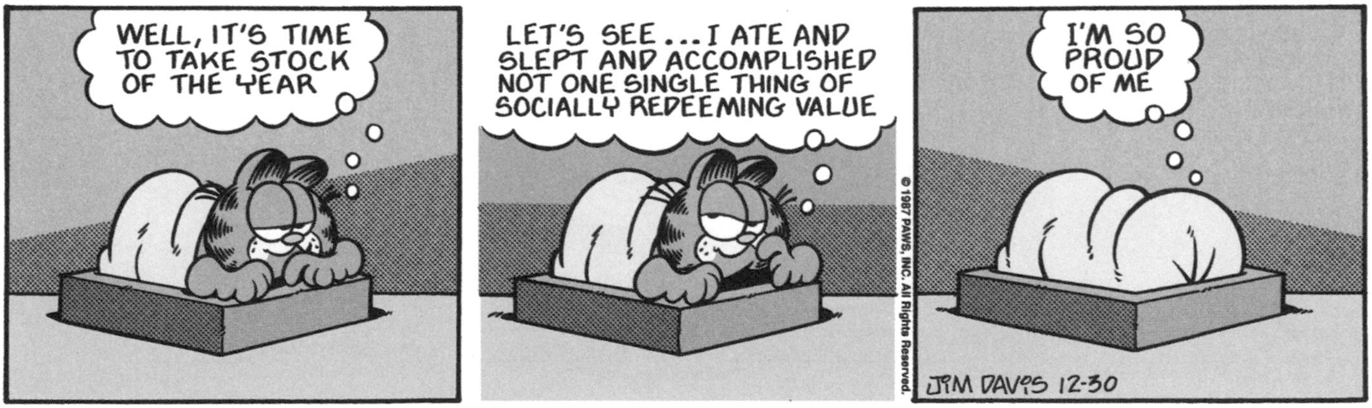
WELL, IT'S TIME TO TAKE STOCK OF THE YEAR
LET'S SEE ... I ATE AND SLEPT AND ACCOMPLISHED NOT ONE SINGLE THING OF SOCIALLY REDEEMING VALUE
© 1987 PAWS, INC. All Rights Reserved.
I'M SO PROUD OF ME
JIM DAVIS 12-30

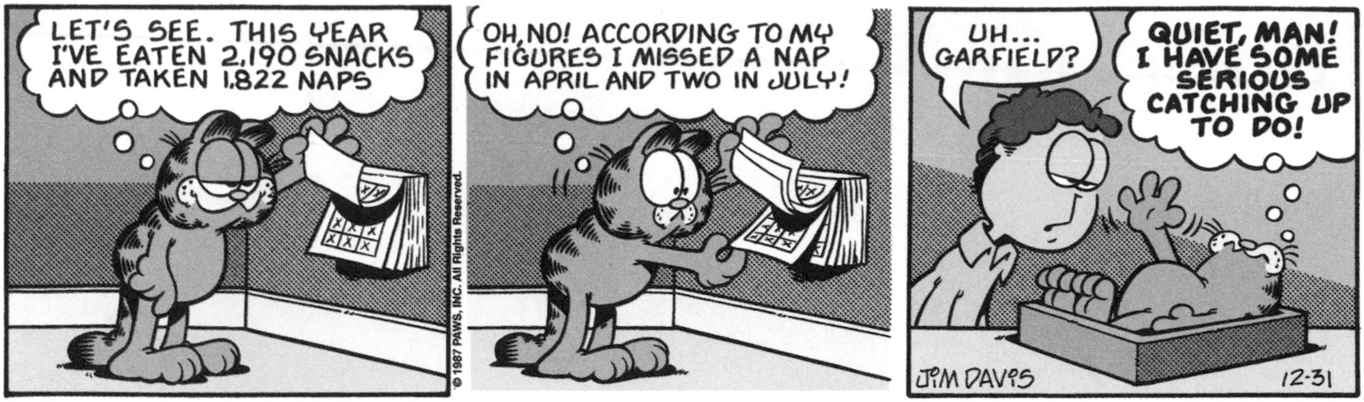
LET'S SEE. THIS YEAR I'VE EATEN 2,190 SNACKS AND TAKEN 1,822 NAPS
© 1987 PAWS, INC. All Rights Reserved.
OH, NO! ACCORDING TO MY FIGURES I MISSED A NAP IN APRIL AND TWO IN JULY!
UH... GARFIELD?
QUIET, MAN! I HAVE SOME SERIOUS CATCHING UP TO DO!
JIM DAVIS
12-31

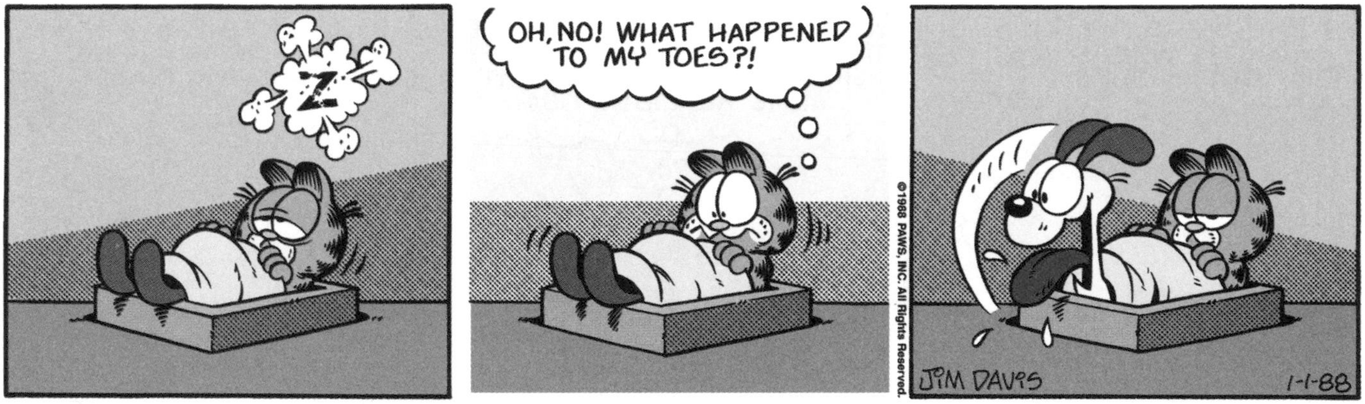
Z
OH, NO! WHAT HAPPENED TO MY TOES?!
© 1988 PAWS, INC. All Rights Reserved.
JIM DAVIS
1-1-88

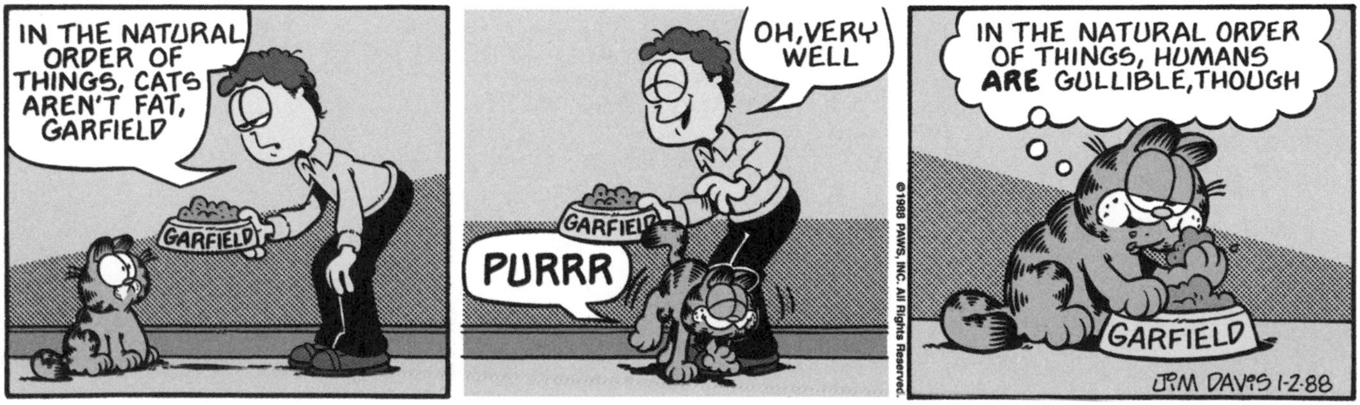
IN THE NATURAL ORDER OF THINGS, CATS AREN'T FAT, GARFIELD
GARFIELD
OH, VERY WELL
GARFIELD
PURRR
© 1988 PAWS, INC. All Rights Reserved.
IN THE NATURAL ORDER OF THINGS, HUMANS ARE GULLIBLE, THOUGH
GARFIELD
JIM DAVIS 1-2-88

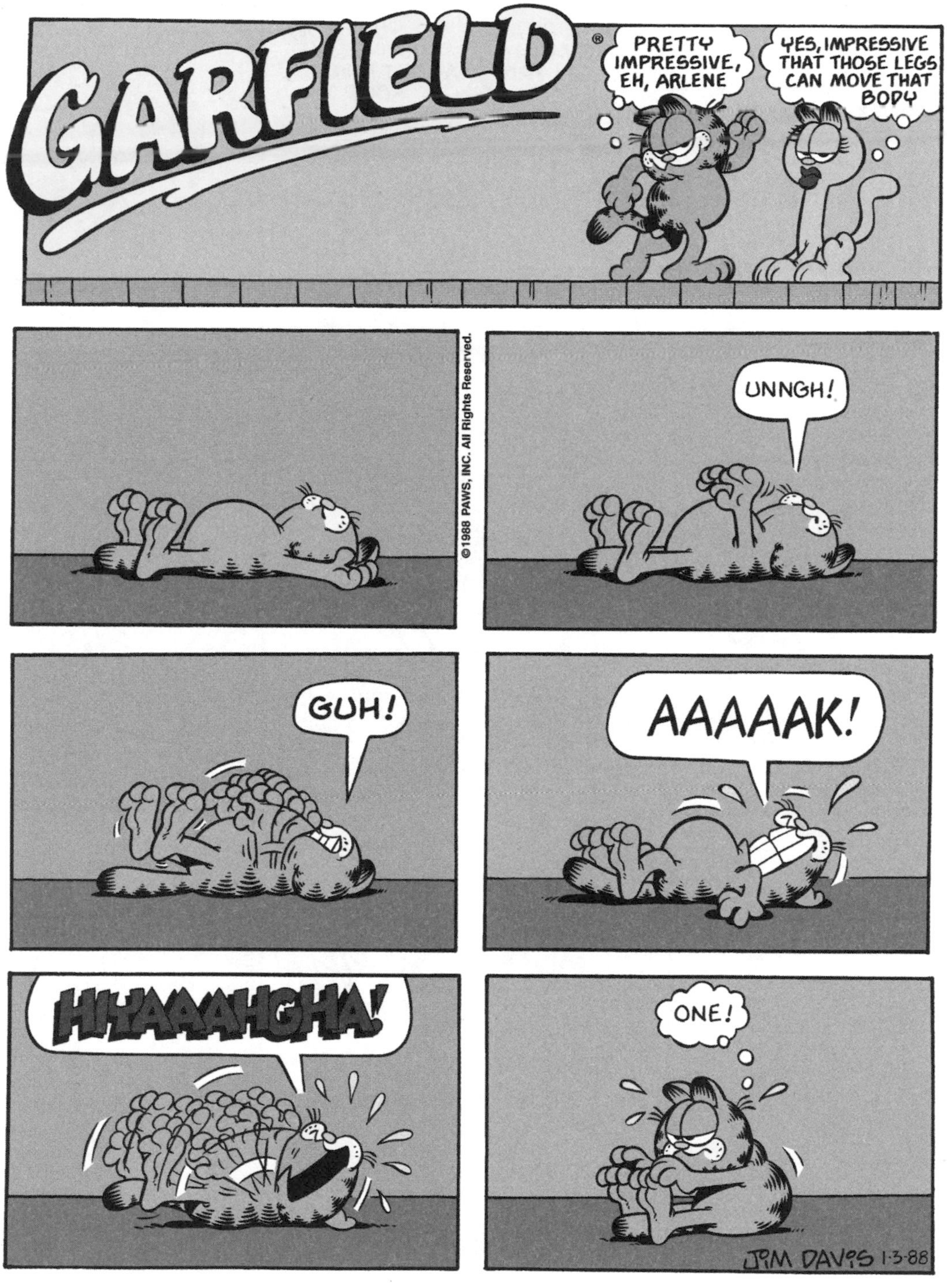
GARFIELD®
PRETTY IMPRESSIVE, EH, ARLENE
YES, IMPRESSIVE THAT THOSE LEGS CAN MOVE THAT BODY
UNNGH!
GUH!
AAAAAK!
HIYAAAHGHA!
ONE!
JIM DAVIS 1-3-88

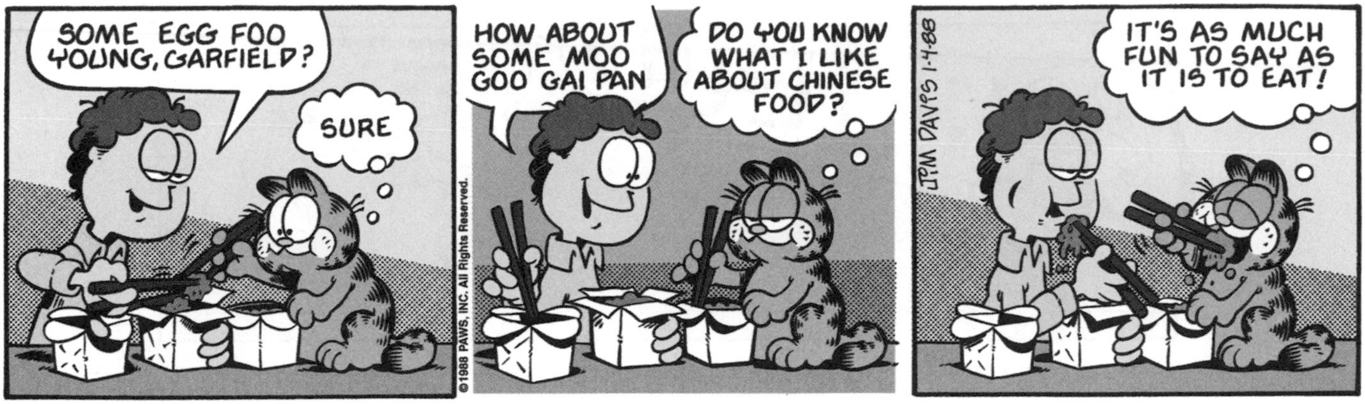
SOME EGG FOO YOUNG, GARFIELD?
SURE
©1988 PAWS, INC. All Rights Reserved.
HOW ABOUT SOME MOO GOO GAI PAN
DO YOU KNOW WHAT I LIKE ABOUT CHINESE FOOD?
JIM DAVIS 1-4-88
IT'S AS MUCH FUN TO SAY AS IT IS TO EAT!

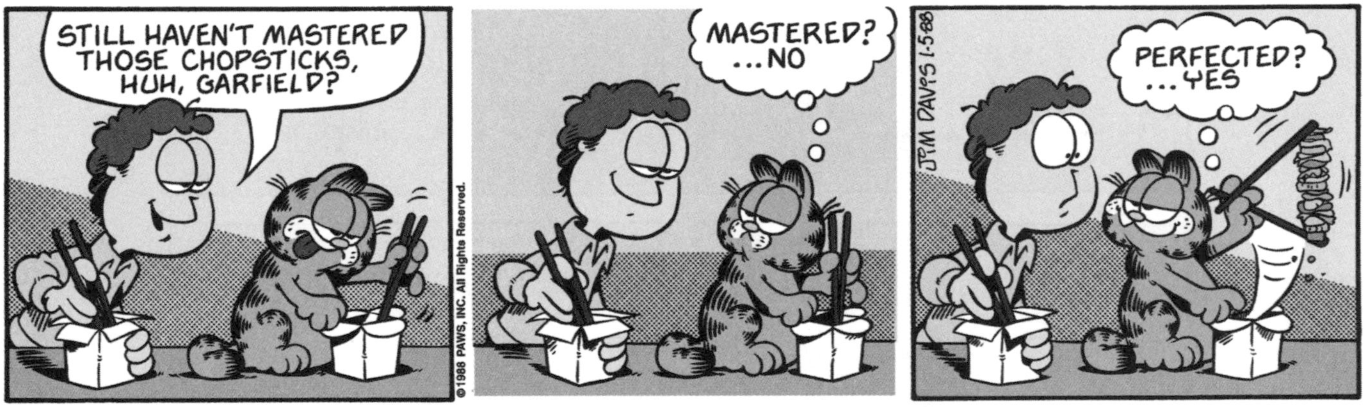
STILL HAVEN'T MASTERED THOSE CHOPSTICKS, HUH, GARFIELD?
©1988 PAWS, INC. All Rights Reserved.
MASTERED? ...NO
JIM DAVIS 1-5-88
PERFECTED? ...YES

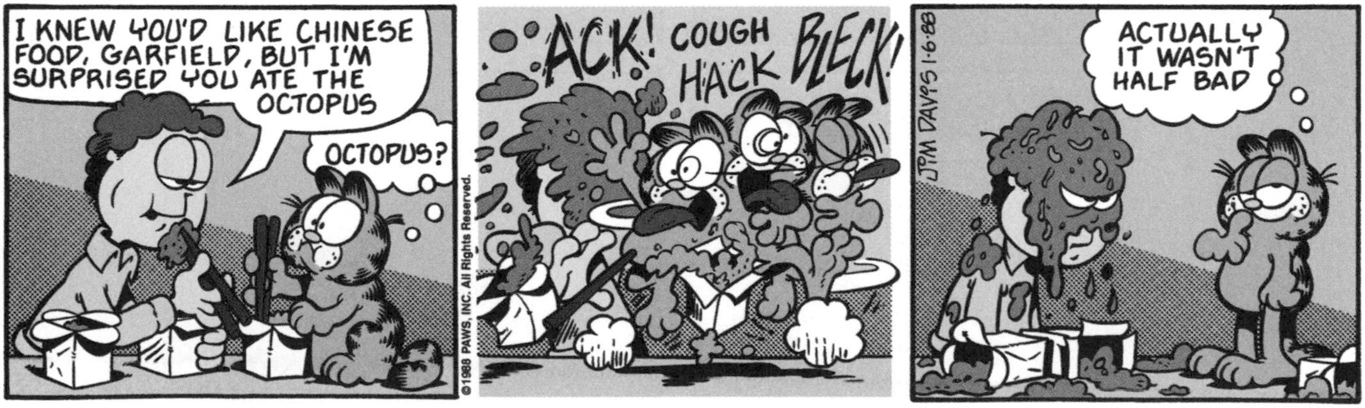
I KNEW YOU'D LIKE CHINESE FOOD, GARFIELD, BUT I'M SURPRISED YOU ATE THE OCTOPUS
OCTOPUS?
©1988 PAWS, INC. All Rights Reserved.
ACK! COUGH HACK BLECK!
JIM DAVIS 1-6-88
ACTUALLY IT WASN'T HALF BAD

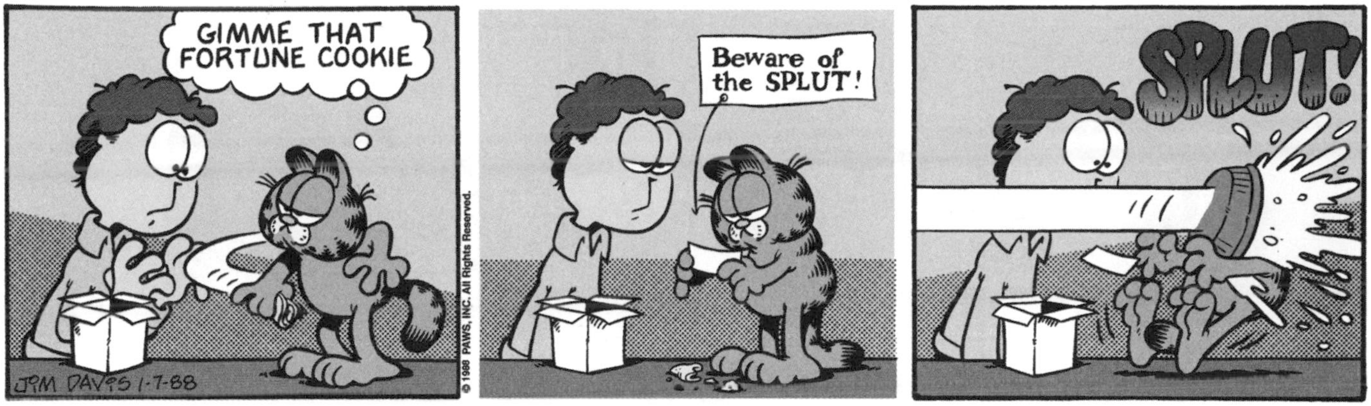
GIMME THAT FORTUNE COOKIE
JIM DAVIS 1-7-88
© 1988 PAWS, INC. All Rights Reserved.
Beware of the SPLUT!
SPLUT!

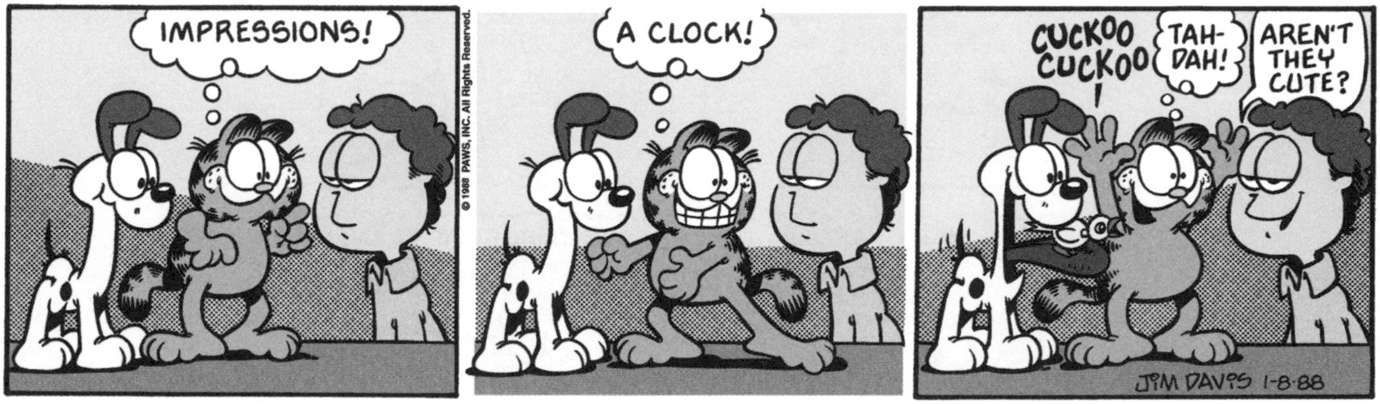
IMPRESSIONS!
© 1988 PAWS, INC. All Rights Reserved.
A CLOCK!
CUCKOO CUCKOO
TAH-DAH!
AREN'T THEY CUTE?
JIM DAVIS 1-8-88

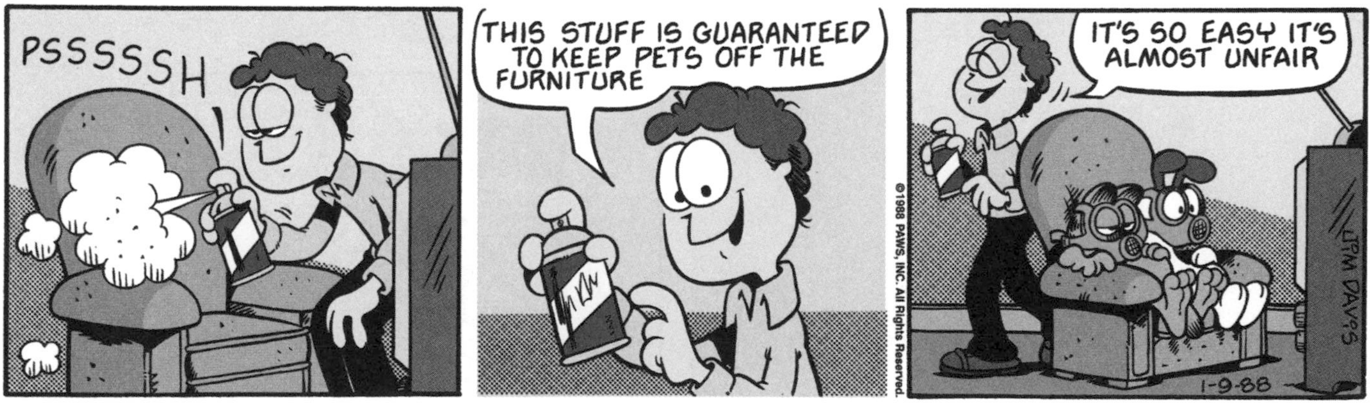
PSSSSSH
THIS STUFF IS GUARANTEED TO KEEP PETS OFF THE FURNITURE
© 1988 PAWS, INC. All Rights Reserved.
IT'S SO EASY IT'S ALMOST UNFAIR
JIM DAVIS
1-9-88

GARFIELD®
MOND
I CAN FEEL MONDAY CREEPING UP
Presenting...
RIP VAN GARFIELD
THE STORY OF A CATNAP...
Z
THAT LASTED 50 YEARS!
FOR THE FIRST TIME IN MY LIFE, I FEEL RESTED!
SOME THINGS HAD CHANGED...
ROOF! ROOF!
SOME THINGS HADN'T CHANGED...
HOW ABOUT A DATE, DOC?
NO WAY!
AND SOME THINGS HAD **REALLY** CHANGED!
SET THE TABLE, MOM! HERE'S A JUICY ONE!
POOF!
THAT'S IT! NO MORE PIZZA AFTER MIDNIGHT
© 1988 PAWS, INC. All Rights Reserved.
JIM DAVIS 1-10

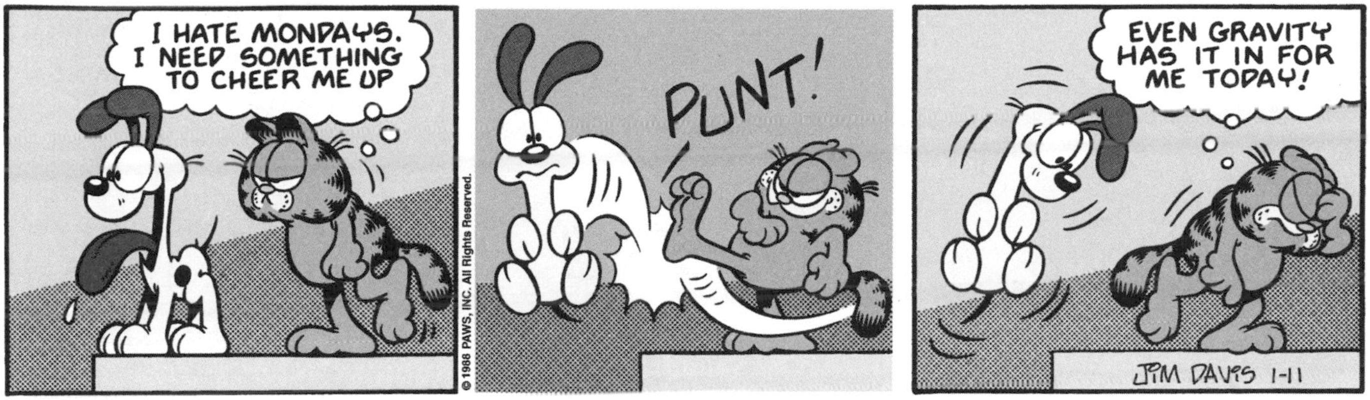
I HATE MONDAYS. I NEED SOMETHING TO CHEER ME UP
© 1988 PAWS, INC. All Rights Reserved.
PUNT!
EVEN GRAVITY HAS IT IN FOR ME TODAY!
JIM DAVIS 1-11

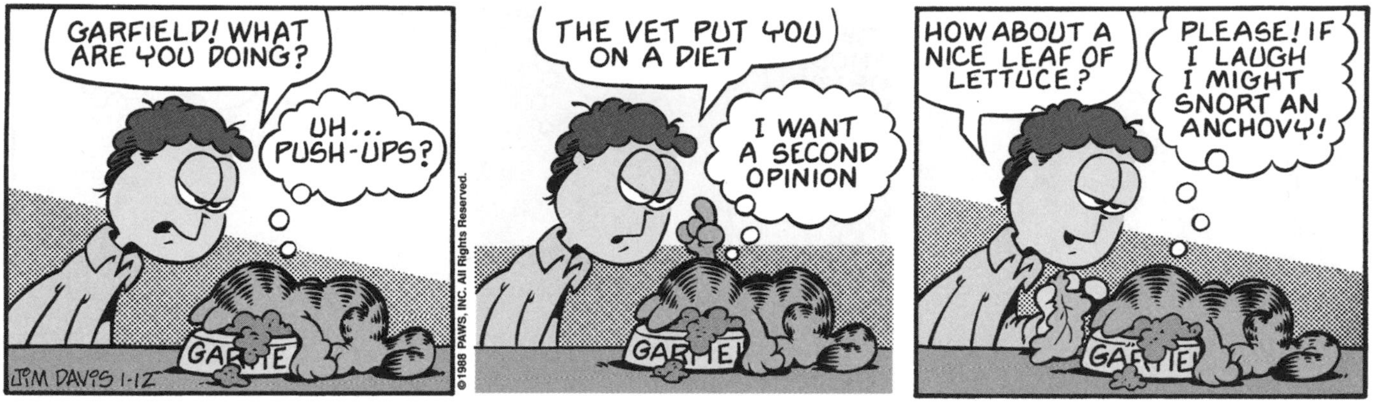
GARFIELD! WHAT ARE YOU DOING?
UH... PUSH-UPS?
JIM DAVIS 1-12
© 1988 PAWS, INC. All Rights Reserved.
THE VET PUT YOU ON A DIET
I WANT A SECOND OPINION
HOW ABOUT A NICE LEAF OF LETTUCE?
PLEASE! IF I LAUGH I MIGHT SNORT AN ANCHOVY!

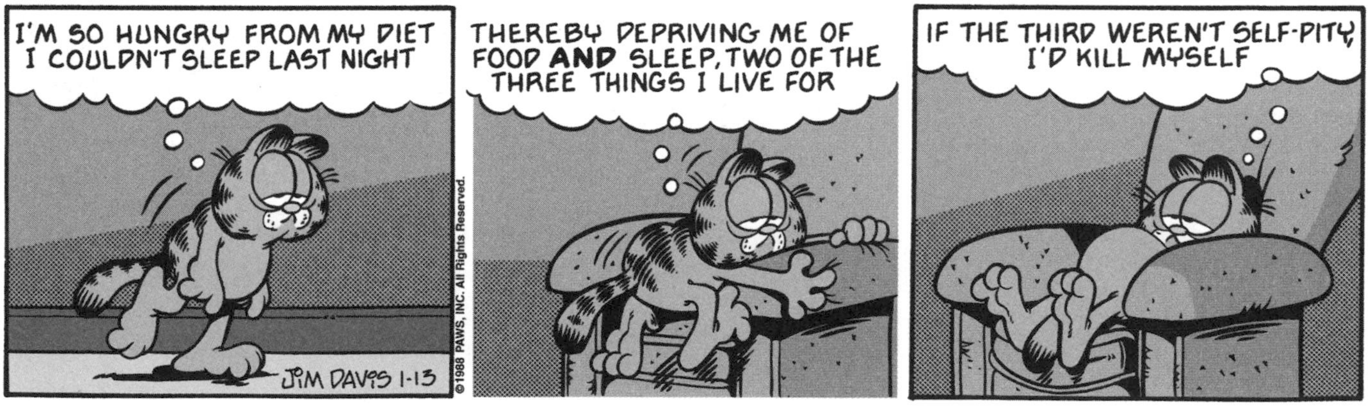
I'M SO HUNGRY FROM MY DIET I COULDN'T SLEEP LAST NIGHT
JIM DAVIS 1-13
© 1988 PAWS, INC. All Rights Reserved.
THEREBY DEPRIVING ME OF FOOD **AND** SLEEP, TWO OF THE THREE THINGS I LIVE FOR
IF THE THIRD WEREN'T SELF-PITY, I'D KILL MYSELF

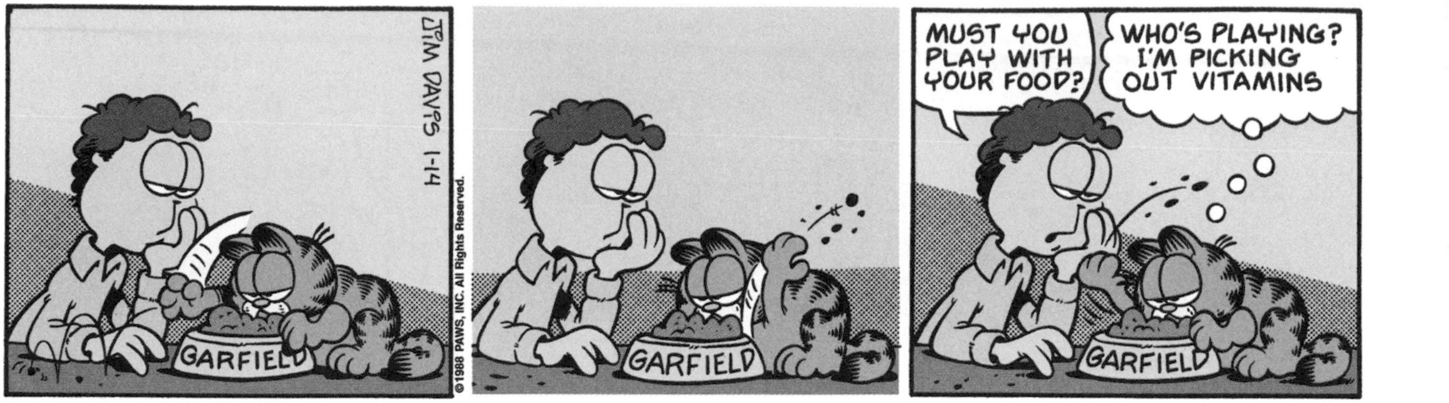
JIM DAVIS 1-14
© 1988 PAWS, INC. All Rights Reserved.
GARFIELD
GARFIELD
MUST YOU PLAY WITH YOUR FOOD?
WHO'S PLAYING? I'M PICKING OUT VITAMINS
GARFIELD

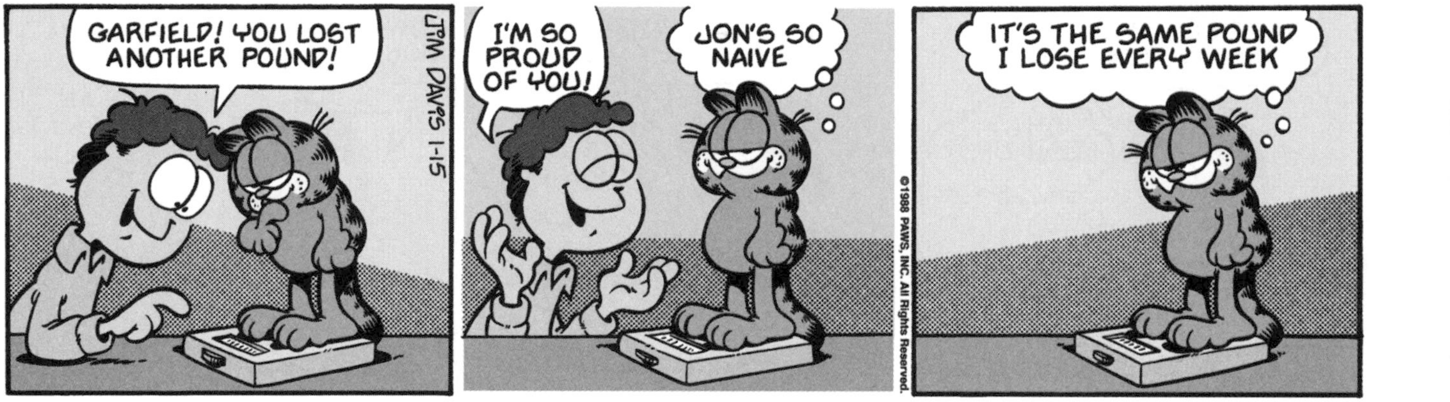
GARFIELD! YOU LOST ANOTHER POUND!
JIM DAVIS 1-15
I'M SO PROUD OF YOU!
JON'S SO NAIVE
© 1988 PAWS, INC. All Rights Reserved.
IT'S THE SAME POUND I LOSE EVERY WEEK

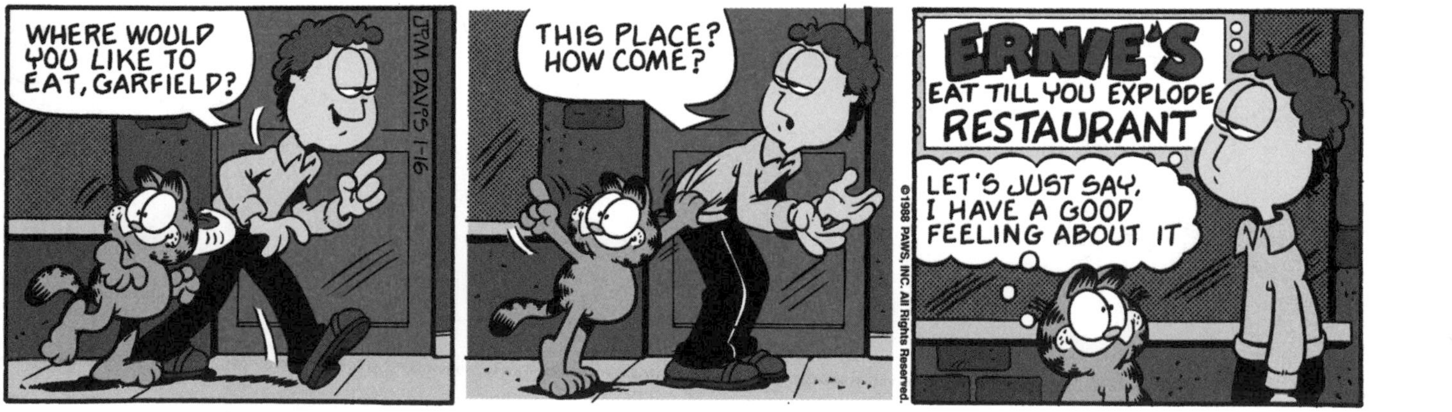
WHERE WOULD YOU LIKE TO EAT, GARFIELD?
JIM DAVIS 1-16
THIS PLACE? HOW COME?
© 1988 PAWS, INC. All Rights Reserved.
ERNIE'S
EAT TILL YOU EXPLODE
RESTAURANT
LET'S JUST SAY, I HAVE A GOOD FEELING ABOUT IT

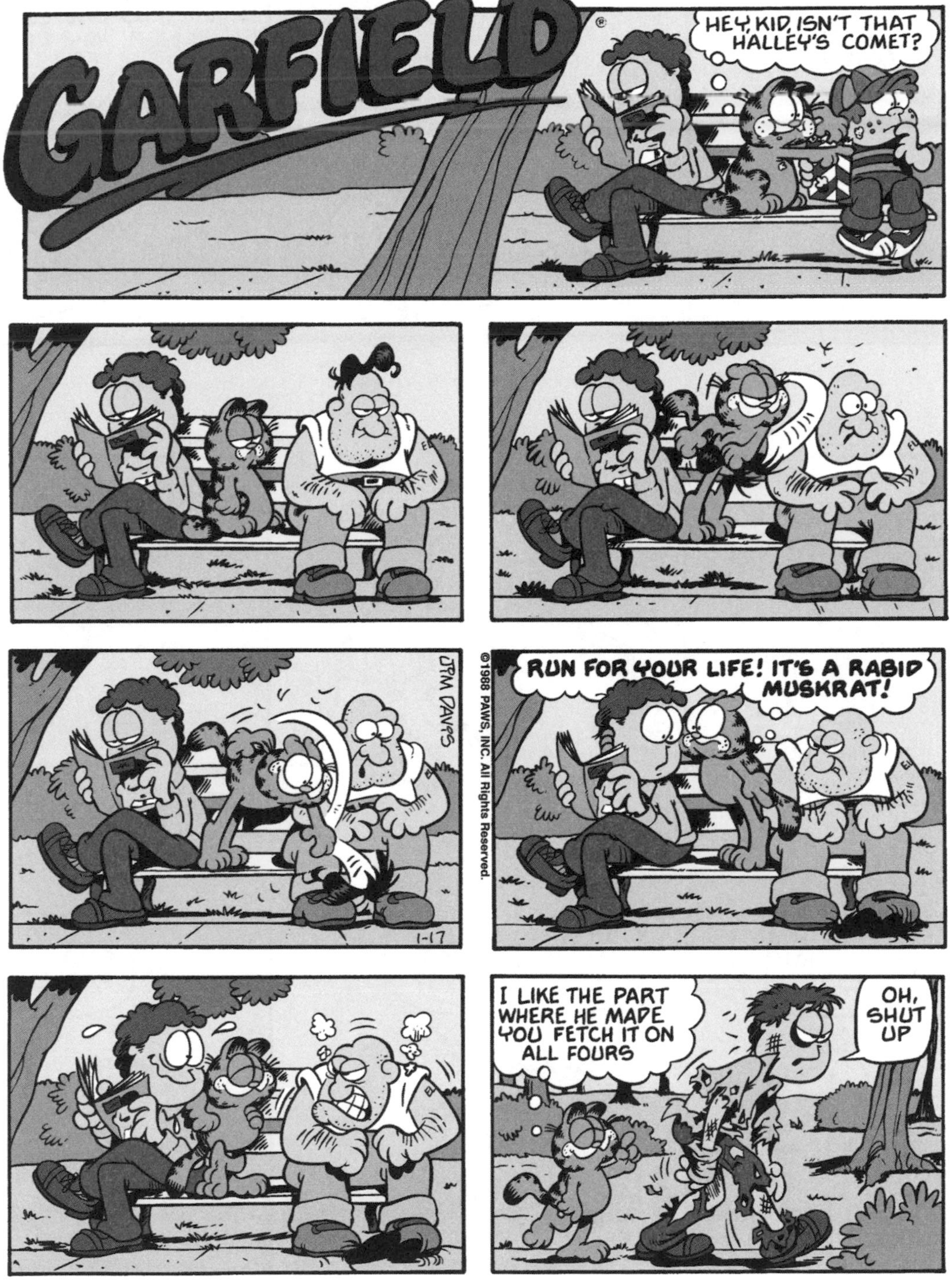
GARFIELD
HEY, KID, ISN'T THAT HALLEY'S COMET?
JIM DAVIS
1-17
© 1988 PAWS, INC. All Rights Reserved.
RUN FOR YOUR LIFE! IT'S A RABID MUSKRAT!
I LIKE THE PART WHERE HE MADE YOU FETCH IT ON ALL FOURS
OH, SHUT UP

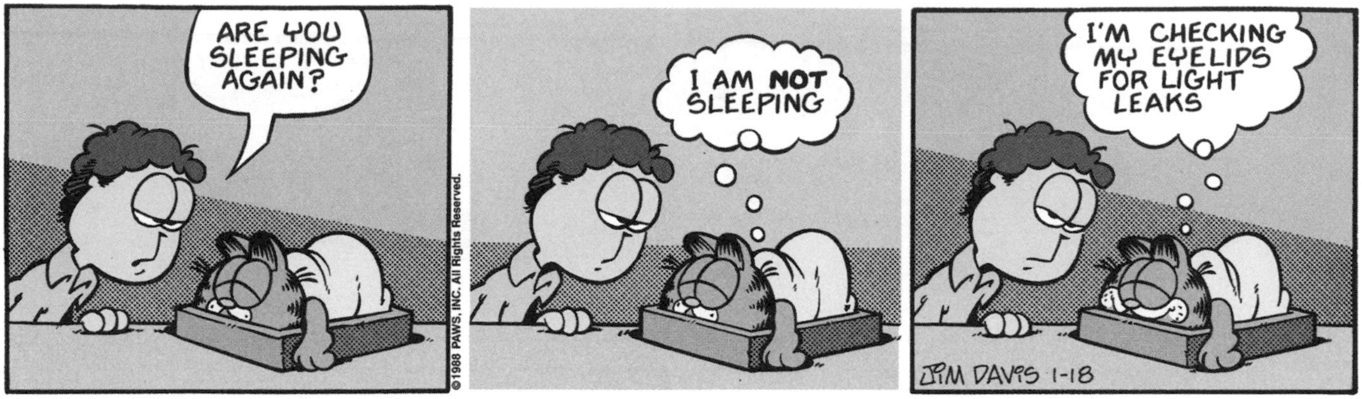
ARE YOU SLEEPING AGAIN?
I AM NOT SLEEPING
I'M CHECKING MY EYELIDS FOR LIGHT LEAKS
JIM DAVIS 1-18
©1988 PAWS, INC. All Rights Reserved.

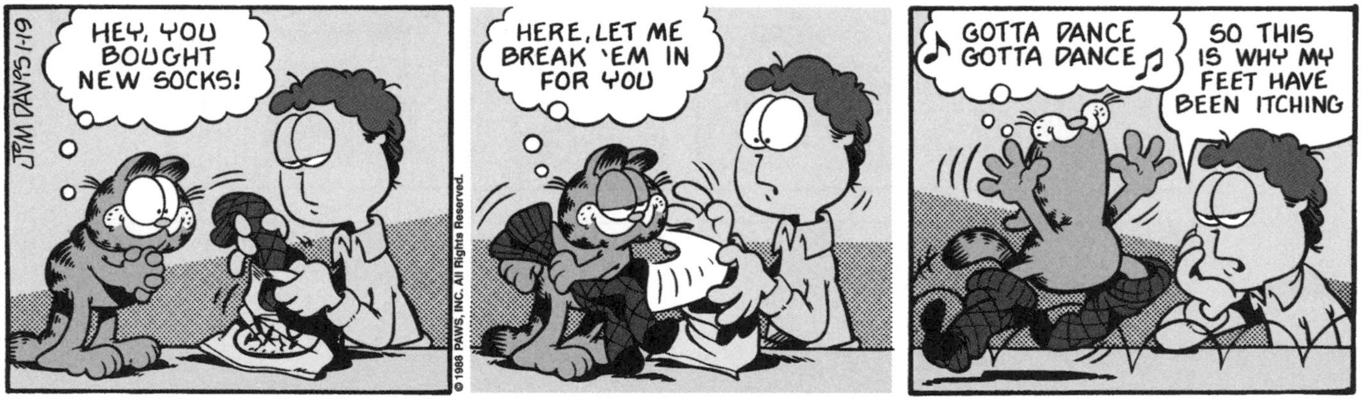
JIM DAVIS 1-19
HEY, YOU BOUGHT NEW SOCKS!
©1988 PAWS, INC. All Rights Reserved.
HERE, LET ME BREAK 'EM IN FOR YOU
GOTTA DANCE GOTTA DANCE
SO THIS IS WHY MY FEET HAVE BEEN ITCHING

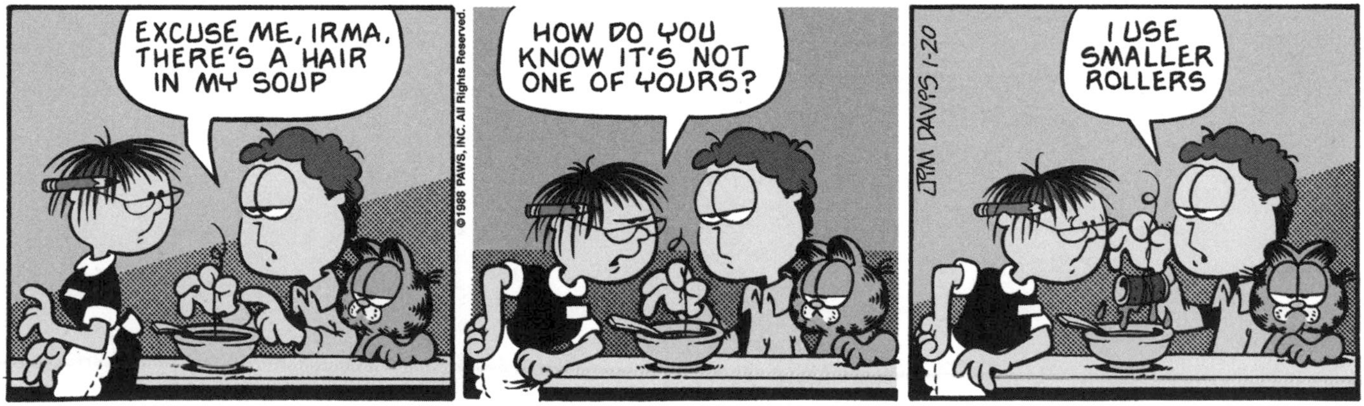
EXCUSE ME, IRMA, THERE'S A HAIR IN MY SOUP
©1988 PAWS, INC. All Rights Reserved.
HOW DO YOU KNOW IT'S NOT ONE OF YOURS?
JIM DAVIS 1-20
I USE SMALLER ROLLERS

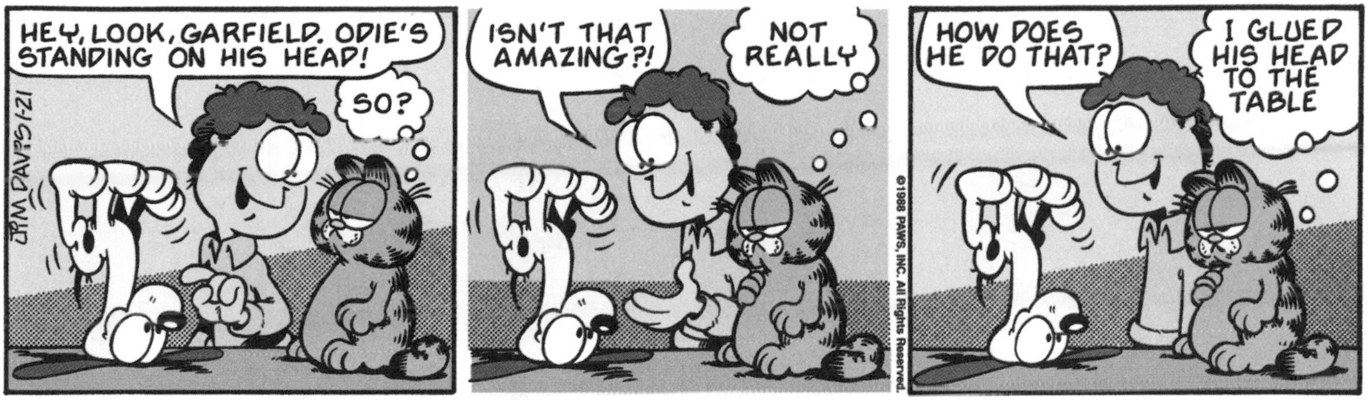
HEY, LOOK, GARFIELD. ODIE'S STANDING ON HIS HEAD!
SO?
ISN'T THAT AMAZING?!
NOT REALLY
HOW DOES HE DO THAT?
I GLUED HIS HEAD TO THE TABLE
JIM DAVIS 1-21
©1988 PAWS, INC. All Rights Reserved.

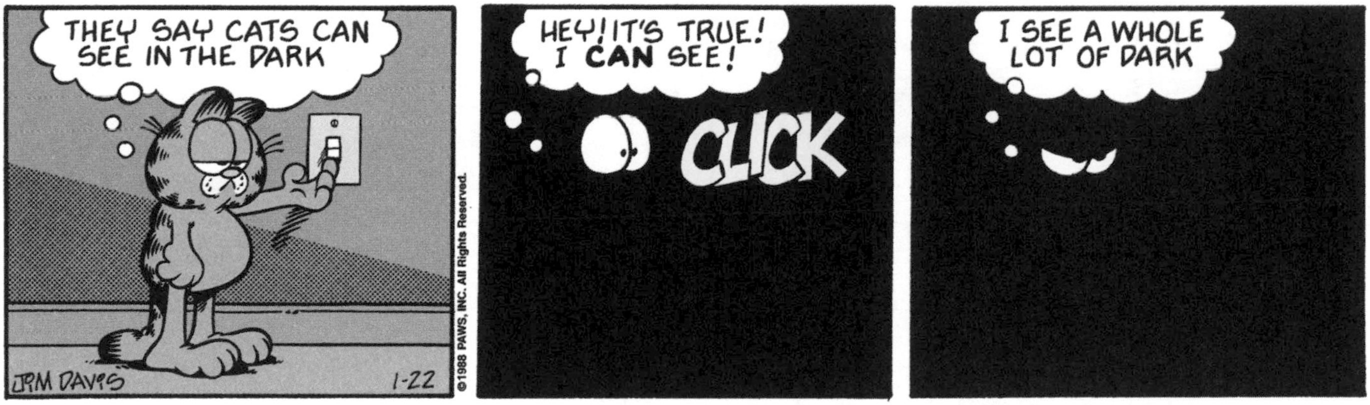
THEY SAY CATS CAN SEE IN THE DARK
JIM DAVIS 1-22
©1988 PAWS, INC. All Rights Reserved.
HEY! IT'S TRUE! I CAN SEE!
CLICK
I SEE A WHOLE LOT OF DARK

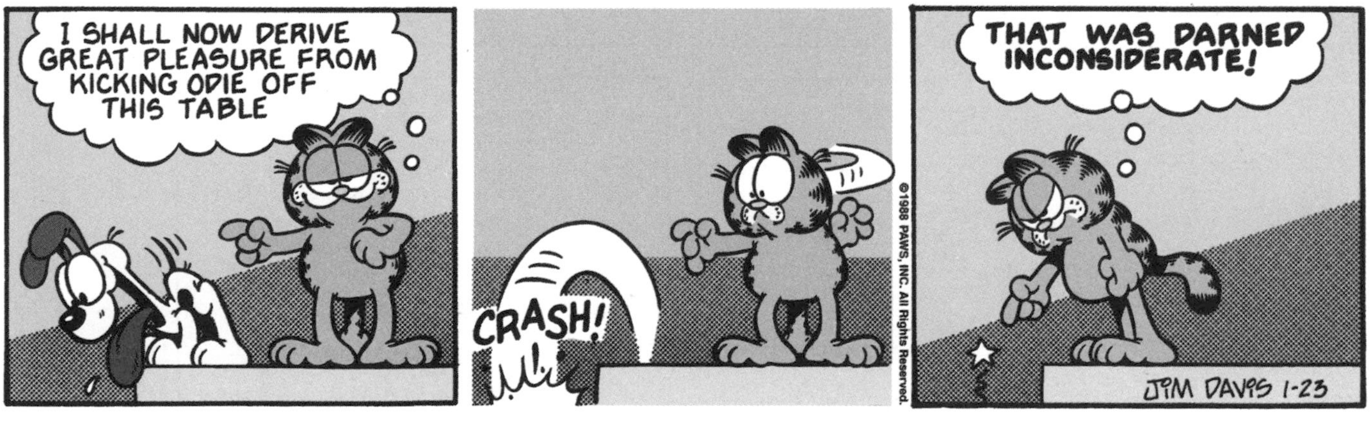
I SHALL NOW DERIVE GREAT PLEASURE FROM KICKING ODIE OFF THIS TABLE
CRASH!
©1988 PAWS, INC. All Rights Reserved.
THAT WAS DARNED INCONSIDERATE!
JIM DAVIS 1-23

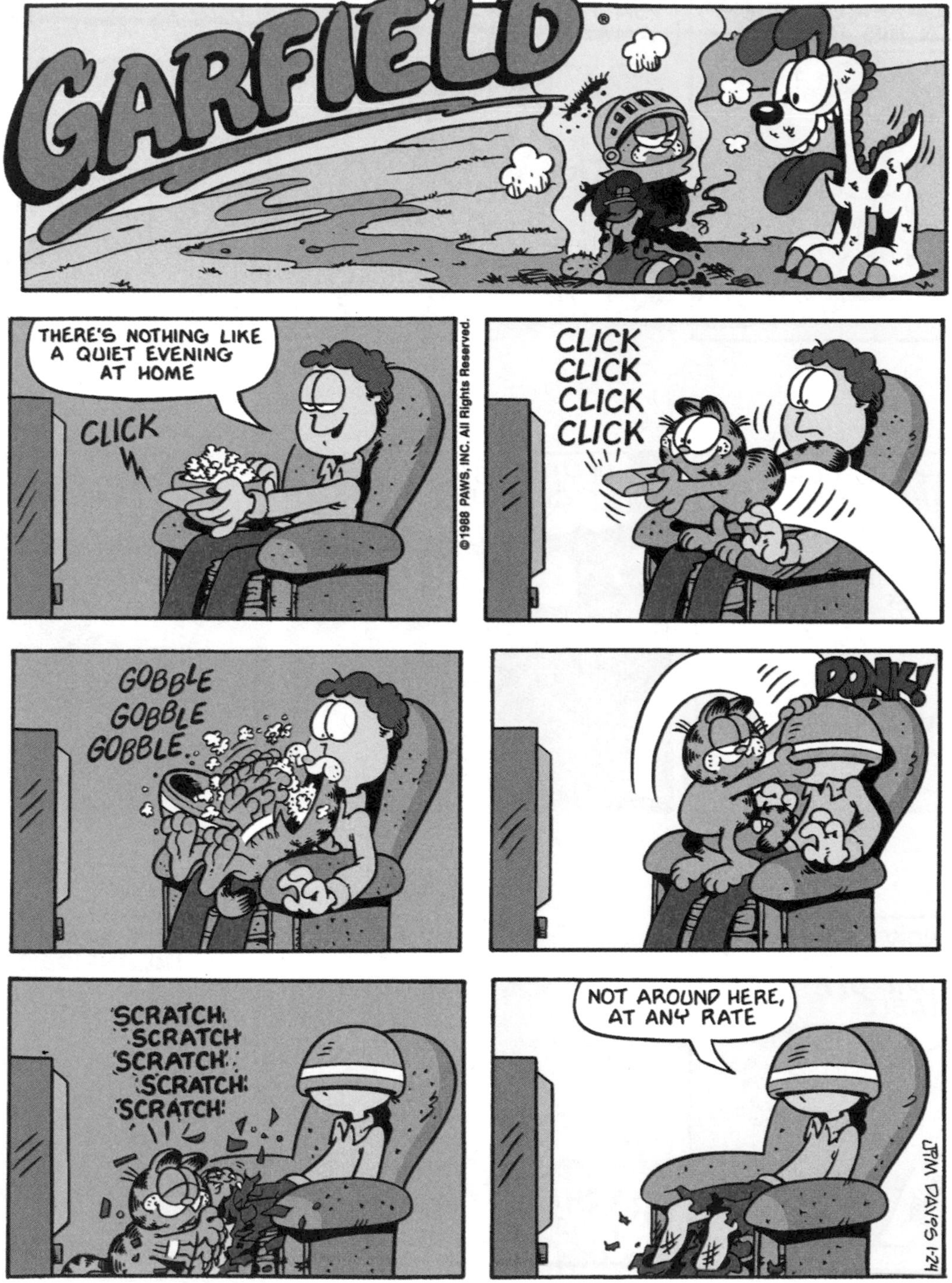
GARFIELD®
THERE'S NOTHING LIKE A QUIET EVENING AT HOME
CLICK
©1988 PAWS, INC. All Rights Reserved.
CLICK CLICK CLICK CLICK
GOBBLE GOBBLE GOBBLE...
DONK!
SCRATCH SCRATCH SCRATCH SCRATCH SCRATCH
NOT AROUND HERE, AT ANY RATE
JIM DAVIS 1-24

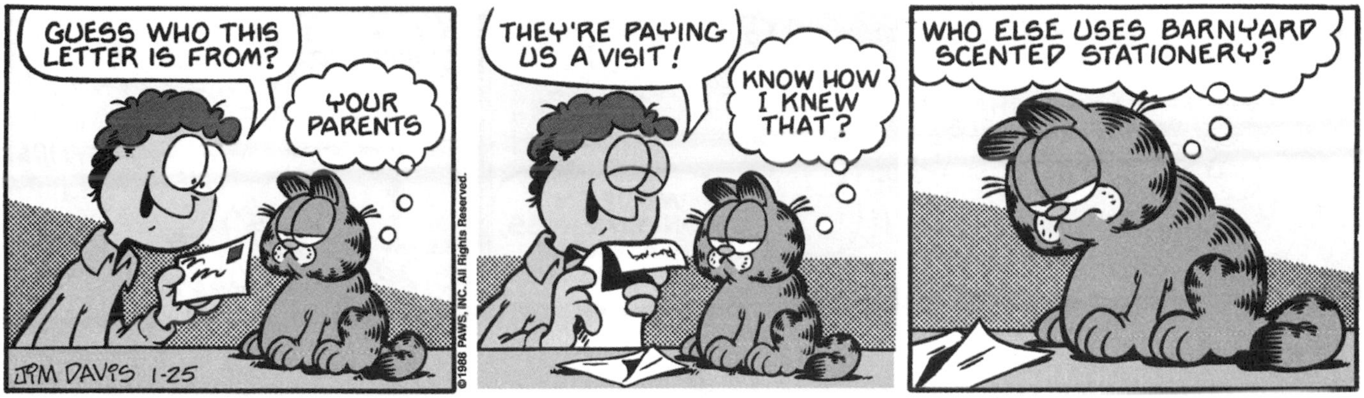
GUESS WHO THIS LETTER IS FROM?
YOUR PARENTS
JIM DAVIS 1-25
©1988 PAWS, INC. All Rights Reserved.
THEY'RE PAYING US A VISIT!
KNOW HOW I KNEW THAT?
WHO ELSE USES BARNYARD SCENTED STATIONERY?

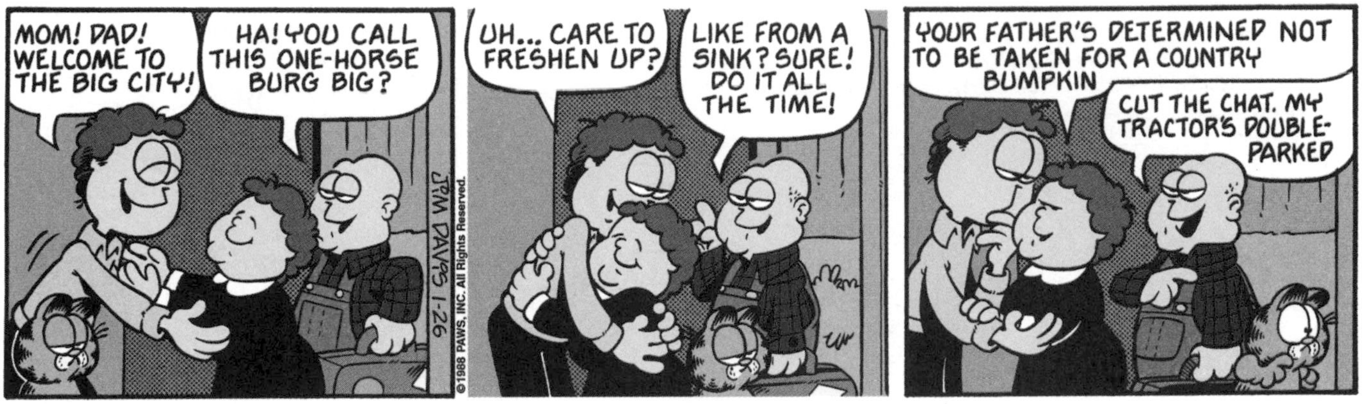
MOM! DAD! WELCOME TO THE BIG CITY!
HA! YOU CALL THIS ONE-HORSE BURG BIG?
JIM DAVIS 1-26
©1988 PAWS, INC. All Rights Reserved.
UH... CARE TO FRESHEN UP?
LIKE FROM A SINK? SURE! DO IT ALL THE TIME!
YOUR FATHER'S DETERMINED NOT TO BE TAKEN FOR A COUNTRY BUMPKIN
CUT THE CHAT. MY TRACTOR'S DOUBLE-PARKED

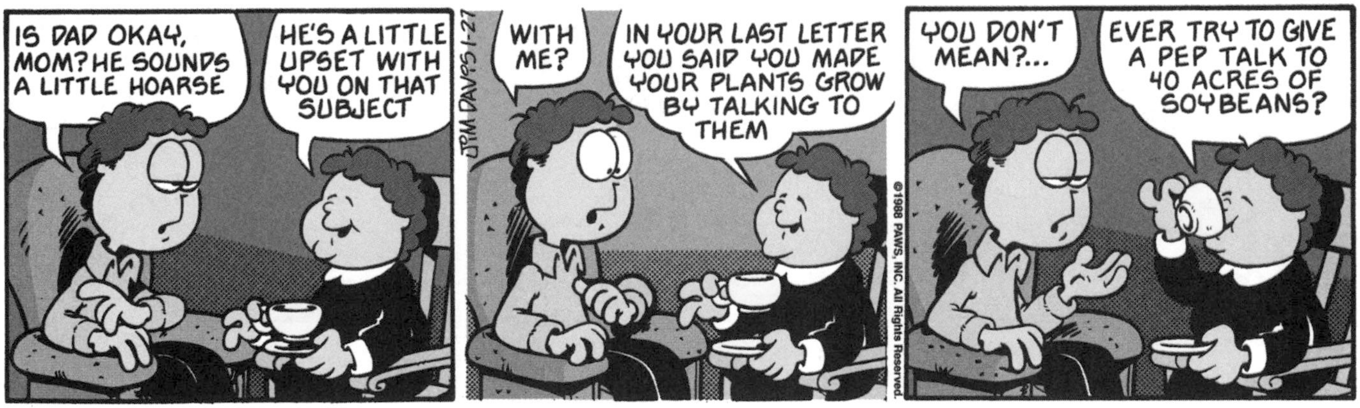
IS DAD OKAY, MOM? HE SOUNDS A LITTLE HOARSE
HE'S A LITTLE UPSET WITH YOU ON THAT SUBJECT
JIM DAVIS 1-27
WITH ME?
IN YOUR LAST LETTER YOU SAID YOU MADE YOUR PLANTS GROW BY TALKING TO THEM
©1988 PAWS, INC. All Rights Reserved.
YOU DON'T MEAN?...
EVER TRY TO GIVE A PEP TALK TO 40 ACRES OF SOYBEANS?

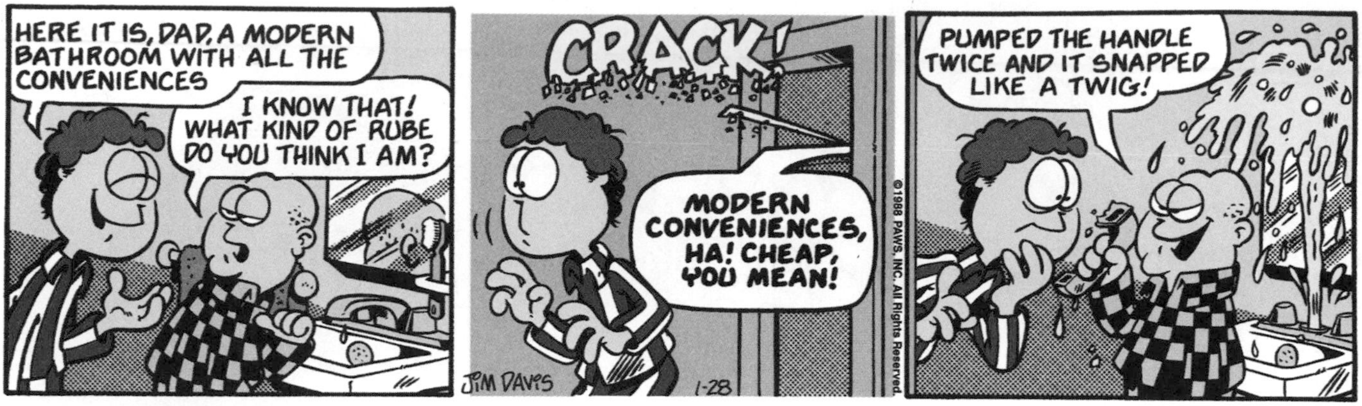
HERE IT IS, DAD, A MODERN BATHROOM WITH ALL THE CONVENIENCES
I KNOW THAT! WHAT KIND OF RUBE DO YOU THINK I AM?
CRACK!
MODERN CONVENIENCES, HA! CHEAP, YOU MEAN!
JIM DAVIS 1-28
©1988 PAWS, INC. All Rights Reserved.
PUMPED THE HANDLE TWICE AND IT SNAPPED LIKE A TWIG!

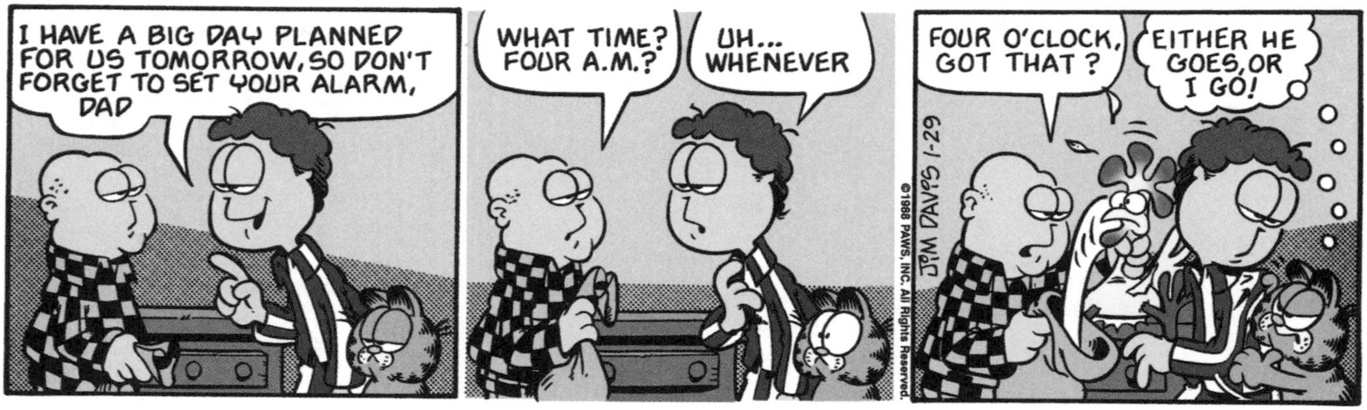
I HAVE A BIG DAY PLANNED FOR US TOMORROW, SO DON'T FORGET TO SET YOUR ALARM, DAD
WHAT TIME? FOUR A.M.?
UH... WHENEVER
JIM DAVIS 1-29
©1988 PAWS, INC. All Rights Reserved.
FOUR O'CLOCK, GOT THAT?
EITHER HE GOES, OR I GO!

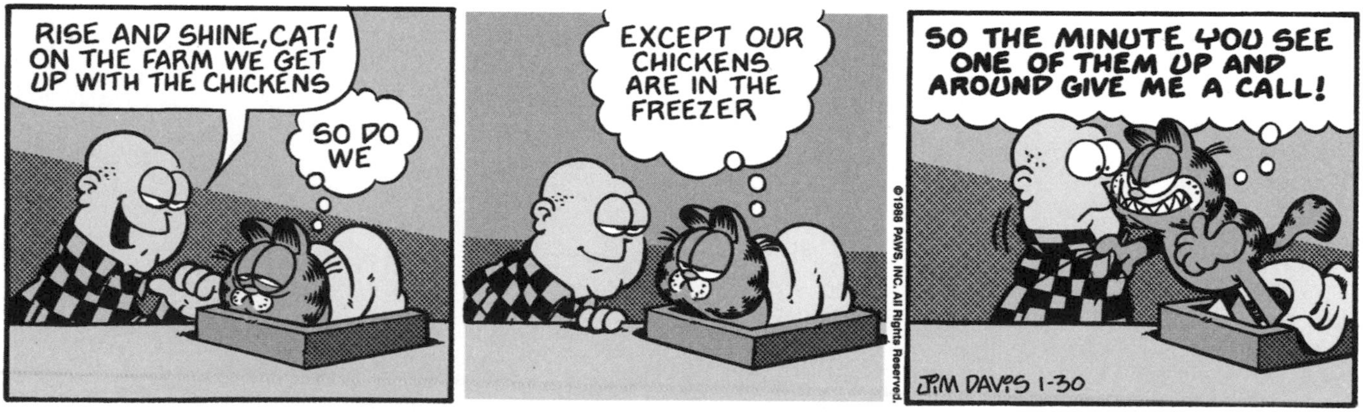
RISE AND SHINE, CAT! ON THE FARM WE GET UP WITH THE CHICKENS
SO DO WE
EXCEPT OUR CHICKENS ARE IN THE FREEZER
©1988 PAWS, INC. All Rights Reserved.
SO THE MINUTE YOU SEE ONE OF THEM UP AND AROUND GIVE ME A CALL!
JIM DAVIS 1-30

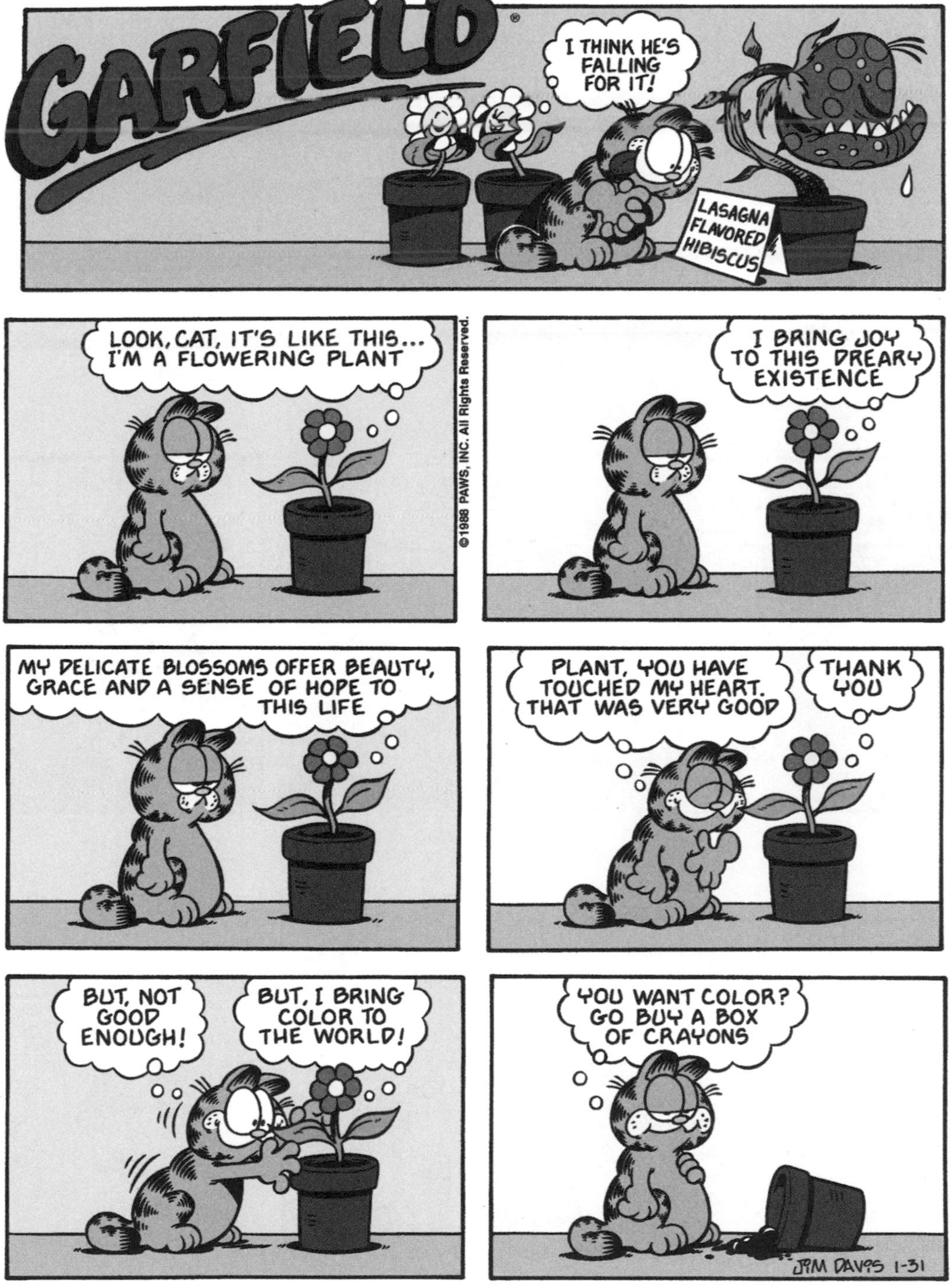
GARFIELD
I THINK HE'S FALLING FOR IT!
LASAGNA FLAVORED HIBISCUS
LOOK, CAT, IT'S LIKE THIS... I'M A FLOWERING PLANT
©1988 PAWS, INC. All Rights Reserved.
I BRING JOY TO THIS DREARY EXISTENCE
MY DELICATE BLOSSOMS OFFER BEAUTY, GRACE AND A SENSE OF HOPE TO THIS LIFE
PLANT, YOU HAVE TOUCHED MY HEART. THAT WAS VERY GOOD
THANK YOU
BUT, NOT GOOD ENOUGH!
BUT, I BRING COLOR TO THE WORLD!
YOU WANT COLOR? GO BUY A BOX OF CRAYONS
JIM DAVIS 1-31

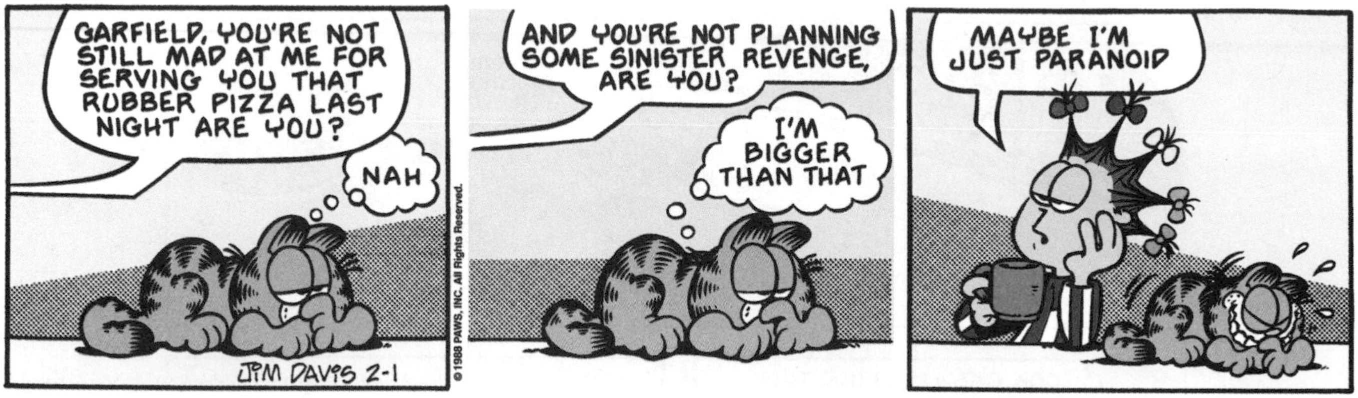
GARFIELD, YOU'RE NOT STILL MAD AT ME FOR SERVING YOU THAT RUBBER PIZZA LAST NIGHT ARE YOU?
NAH
JIM DAVIS 2-1
©1988 PAWS, INC. All Rights Reserved.
AND YOU'RE NOT PLANNING SOME SINISTER REVENGE, ARE YOU?
I'M BIGGER THAN THAT
MAYBE I'M JUST PARANOID

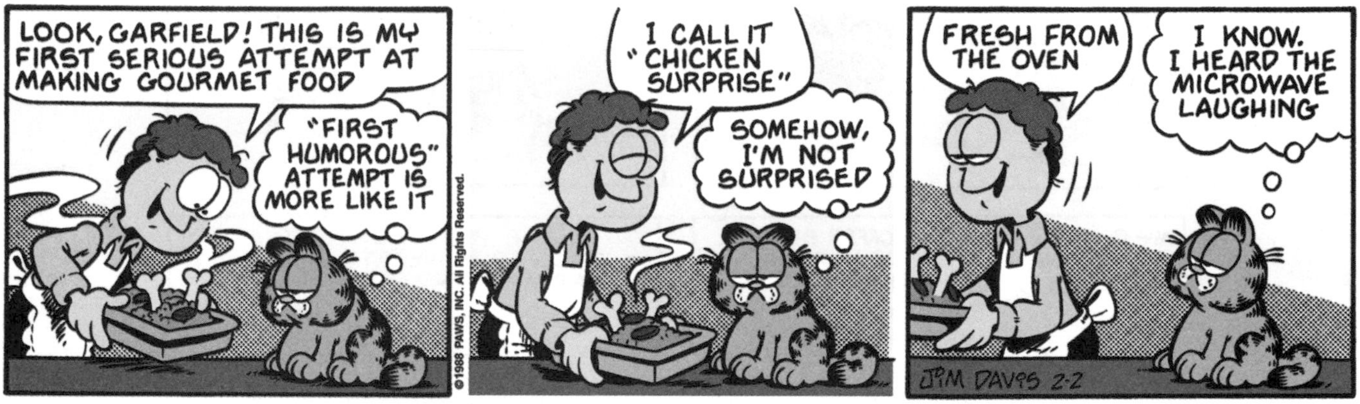
LOOK, GARFIELD! THIS IS MY FIRST SERIOUS ATTEMPT AT MAKING GOURMET FOOD
"FIRST HUMOROUS" ATTEMPT IS MORE LIKE IT
©1988 PAWS, INC. All Rights Reserved.
I CALL IT "CHICKEN SURPRISE"
SOMEHOW, I'M NOT SURPRISED
FRESH FROM THE OVEN
I KNOW. I HEARD THE MICROWAVE LAUGHING
JIM DAVIS 2-2

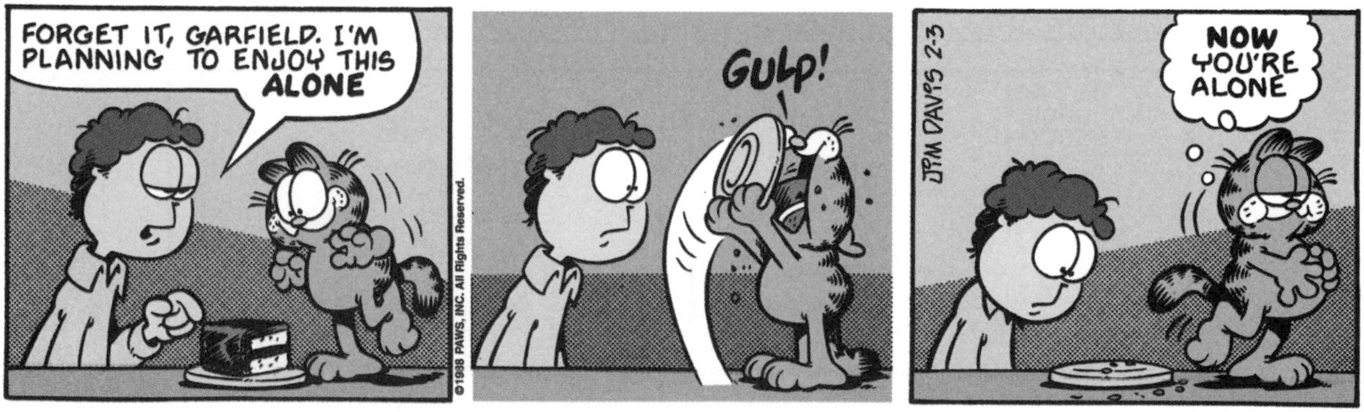
FORGET IT, GARFIELD. I'M PLANNING TO ENJOY THIS ALONE
©1988 PAWS, INC. All Rights Reserved.
GULP!
JIM DAVIS 2-3
NOW YOU'RE ALONE

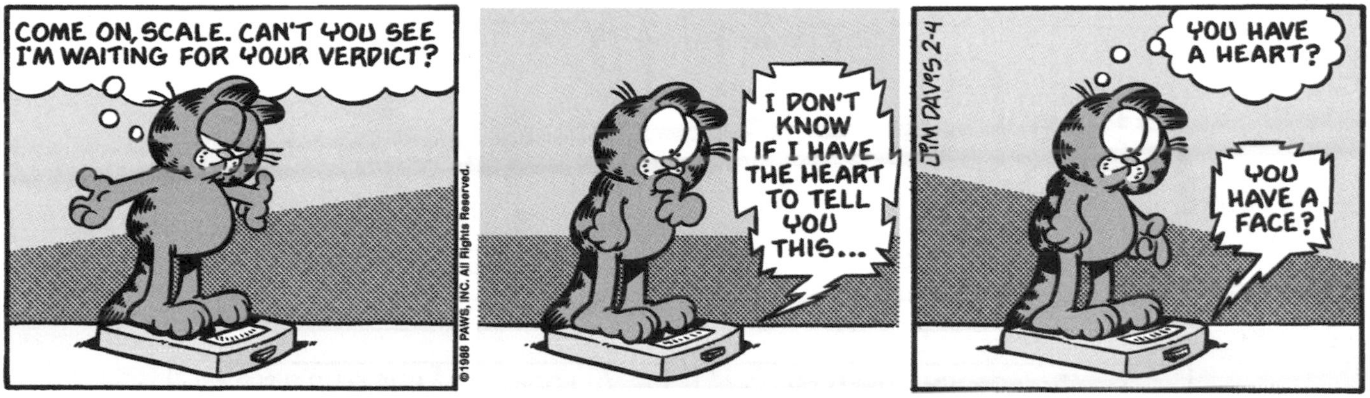
COME ON, SCALE. CAN'T YOU SEE I'M WAITING FOR YOUR VERDICT?
©1988 PAWS, INC. All Rights Reserved.
I DON'T KNOW IF I HAVE THE HEART TO TELL YOU THIS...
JIM DAVIS 2-4
YOU HAVE A HEART?
YOU HAVE A FACE?

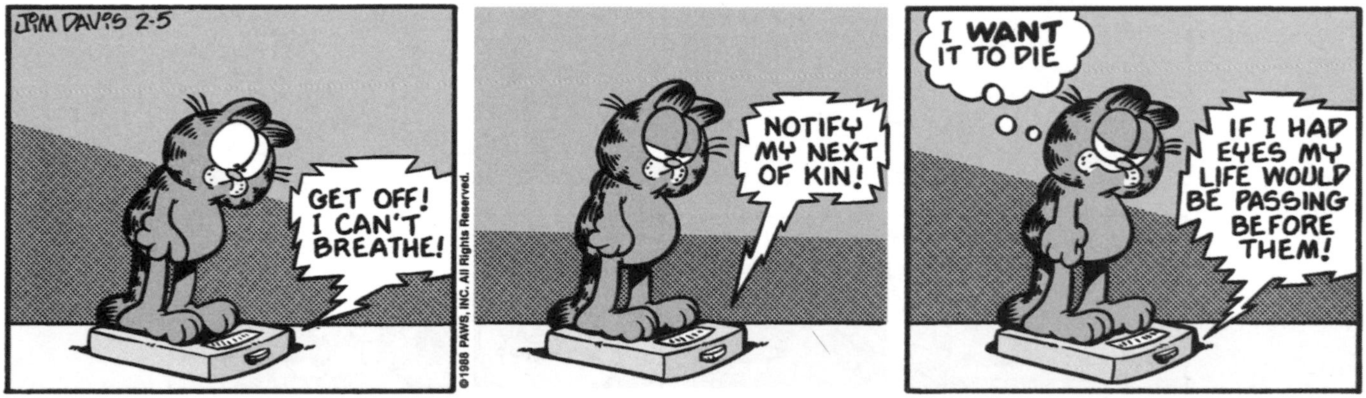
JIM DAVIS 2-5
GET OFF! I CAN'T BREATHE!
©1988 PAWS, INC. All Rights Reserved.
NOTIFY MY NEXT OF KIN!
I WANT IT TO DIE
IF I HAD EYES MY LIFE WOULD BE PASSING BEFORE THEM!

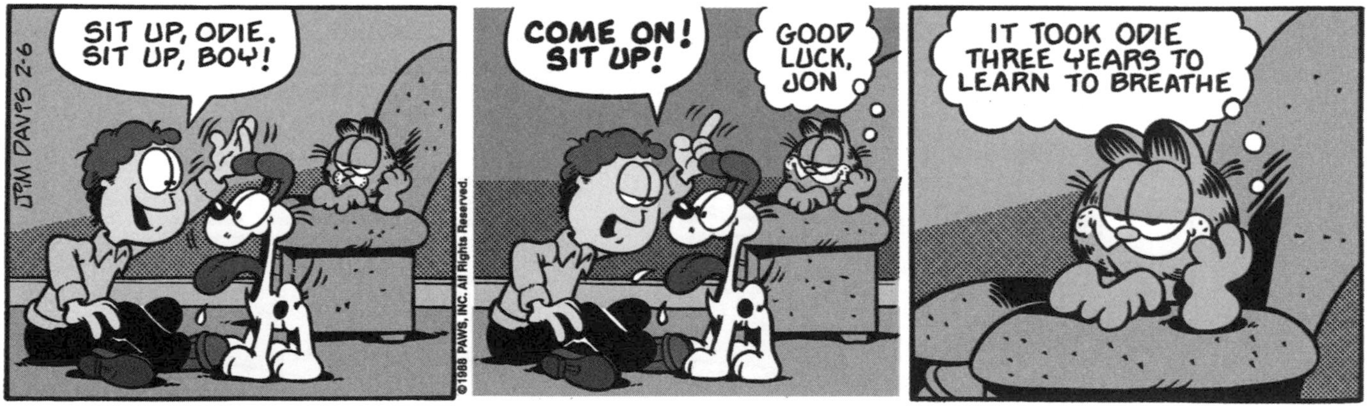
JIM DAVIS 2-6
SIT UP, ODIE. SIT UP, BOY!
©1988 PAWS, INC. All Rights Reserved.
COME ON! SIT UP!
GOOD LUCK, JON
IT TOOK ODIE THREE YEARS TO LEARN TO BREATHE

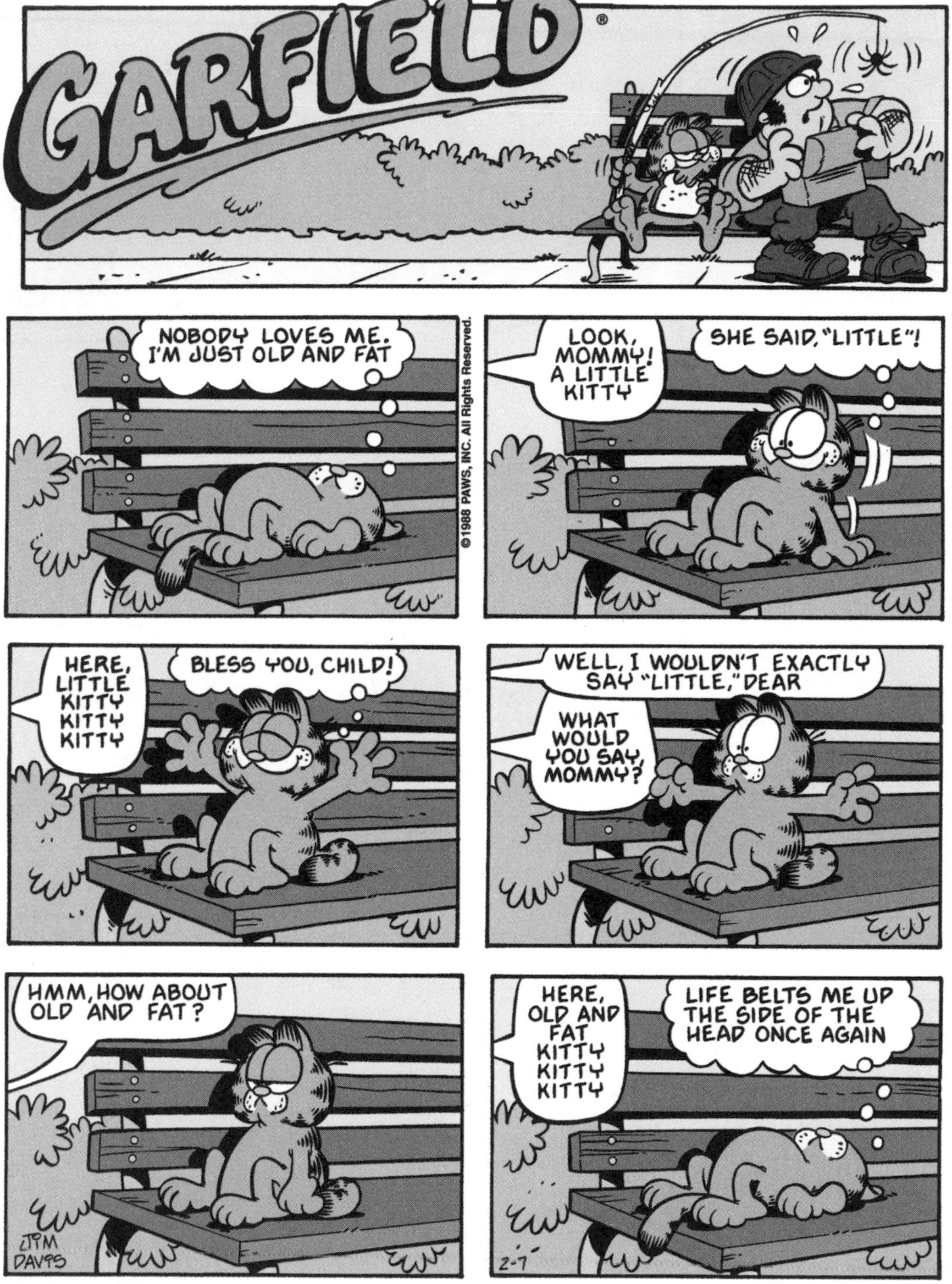
GARFIELD
NOBODY LOVES ME. I'M JUST OLD AND FAT
©1988 PAWS, INC. All Rights Reserved.
LOOK, MOMMY! A LITTLE KITTY
SHE SAID, "LITTLE"!
HERE, LITTLE KITTY KITTY KITTY
BLESS YOU, CHILD!
WELL, I WOULDN'T EXACTLY SAY "LITTLE," DEAR
WHAT WOULD YOU SAY, MOMMY?
HMM, HOW ABOUT OLD AND FAT?
HERE, OLD AND FAT KITTY KITTY KITTY
LIFE BELTS ME UP THE SIDE OF THE HEAD ONCE AGAIN
JIM DAVIS
2-7

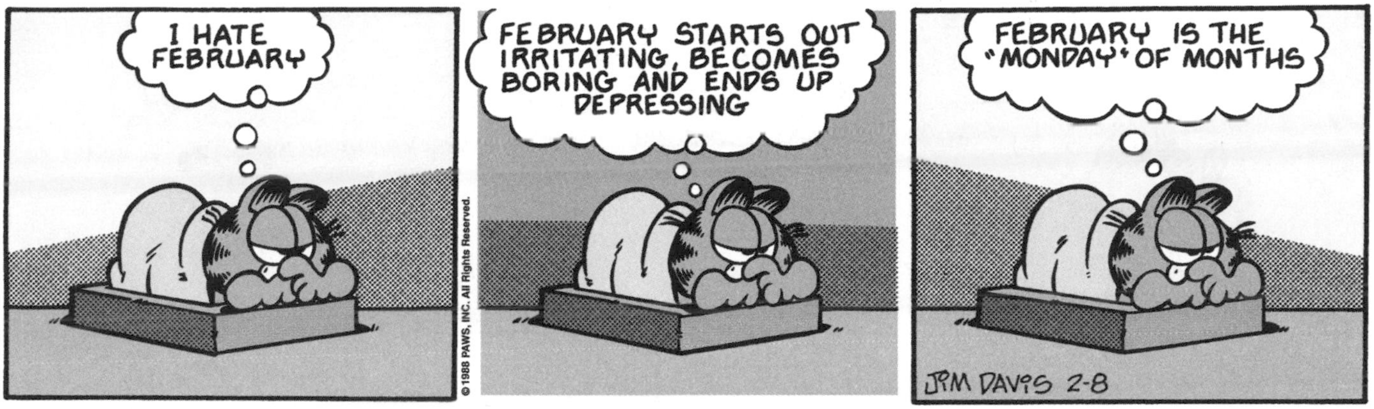
I HATE FEBRUARY
FEBRUARY STARTS OUT IRRITATING, BECOMES BORING AND ENDS UP DEPRESSING
FEBRUARY IS THE "MONDAY" OF MONTHS
© 1988 PAWS, INC. All Rights Reserved.
JIM DAVIS 2-8

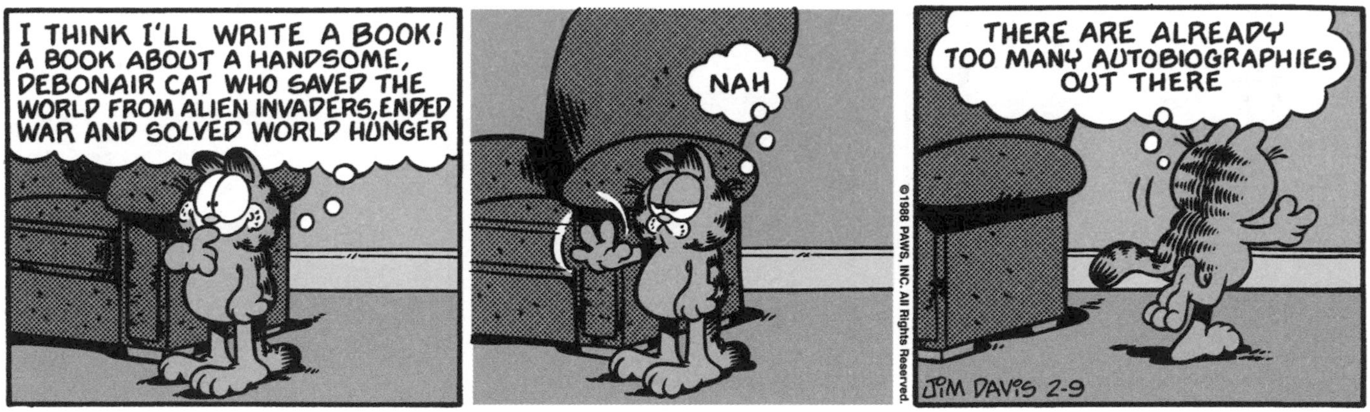
I THINK I'LL WRITE A BOOK! A BOOK ABOUT A HANDSOME, DEBONAIR CAT WHO SAVED THE WORLD FROM ALIEN INVADERS, ENDED WAR AND SOLVED WORLD HUNGER
NAH
THERE ARE ALREADY TOO MANY AUTOBIOGRAPHIES OUT THERE
© 1988 PAWS, INC. All Rights Reserved.
JIM DAVIS 2-9

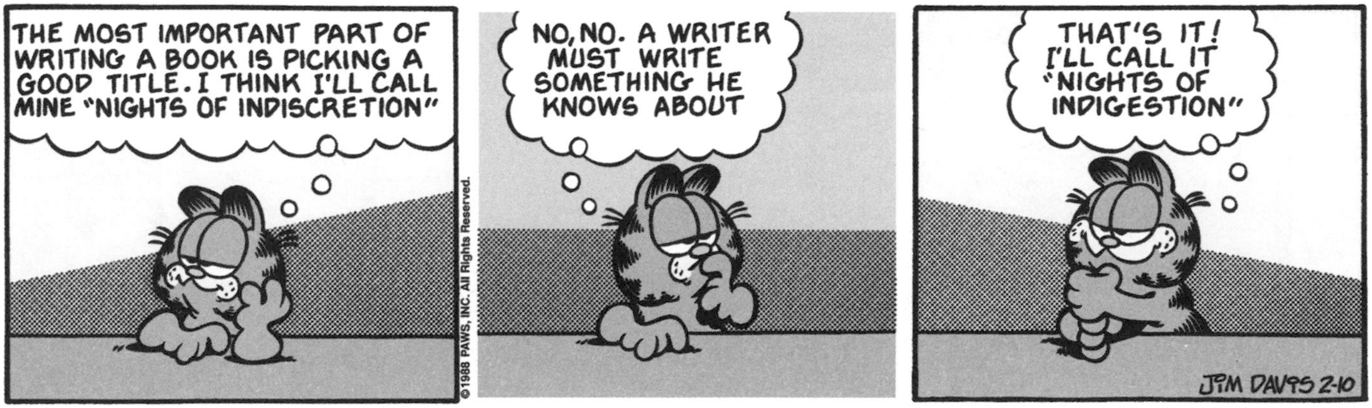
THE MOST IMPORTANT PART OF WRITING A BOOK IS PICKING A GOOD TITLE. I THINK I'LL CALL MINE "NIGHTS OF INDISCRETION"
NO, NO. A WRITER MUST WRITE SOMETHING HE KNOWS ABOUT
THAT'S IT! I'LL CALL IT "NIGHTS OF INDIGESTION"
© 1988 PAWS, INC. All Rights Reserved.
JIM DAVIS 2-10

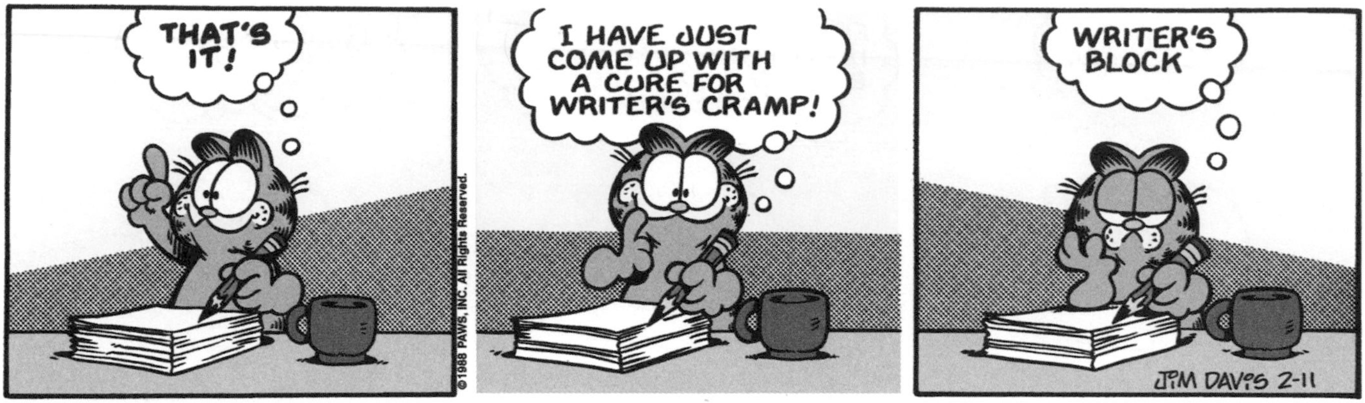
THAT'S IT!
I HAVE JUST COME UP WITH A CURE FOR WRITER'S CRAMP!
WRITER'S BLOCK
©1988 PAWS, INC. All Rights Reserved.
JIM DAVIS 2-11

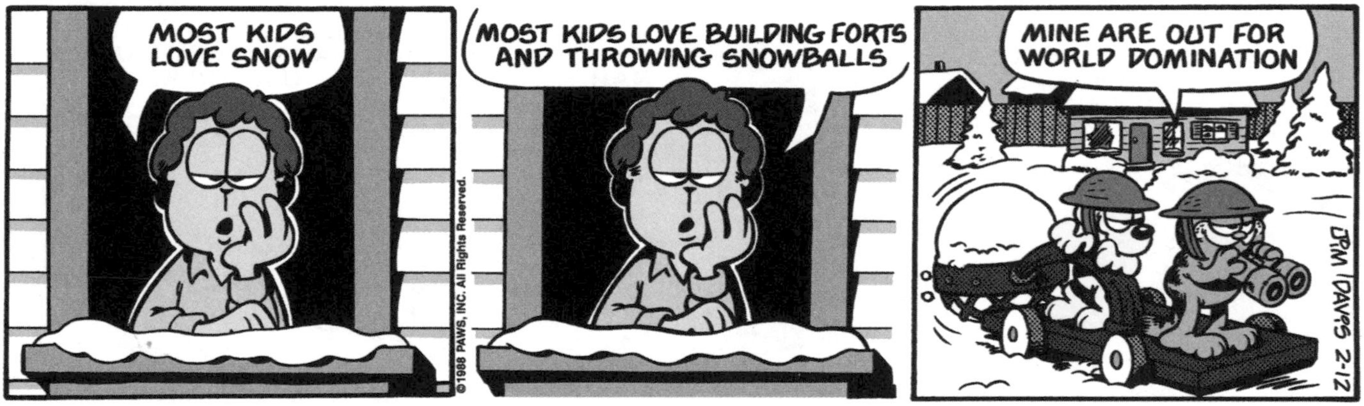
MOST KIDS LOVE SNOW
MOST KIDS LOVE BUILDING FORTS AND THROWING SNOWBALLS
MINE ARE OUT FOR WORLD DOMINATION
©1988 PAWS, INC. All Rights Reserved.
JIM DAVIS 2-12

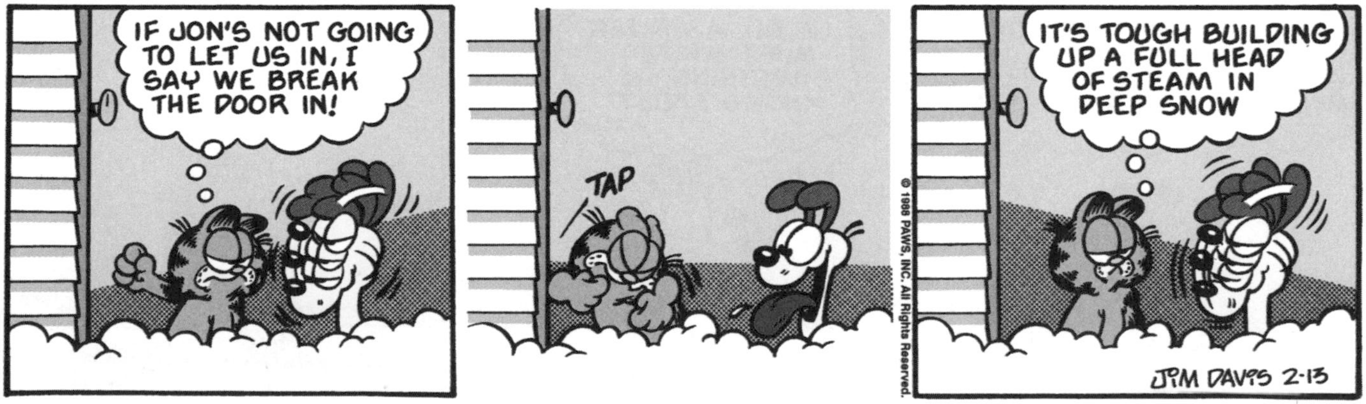
IF JON'S NOT GOING TO LET US IN, I SAY WE BREAK THE DOOR IN!
TAP
IT'S TOUGH BUILDING UP A FULL HEAD OF STEAM IN DEEP SNOW
©1988 PAWS, INC. All Rights Reserved.
JIM DAVIS 2-13

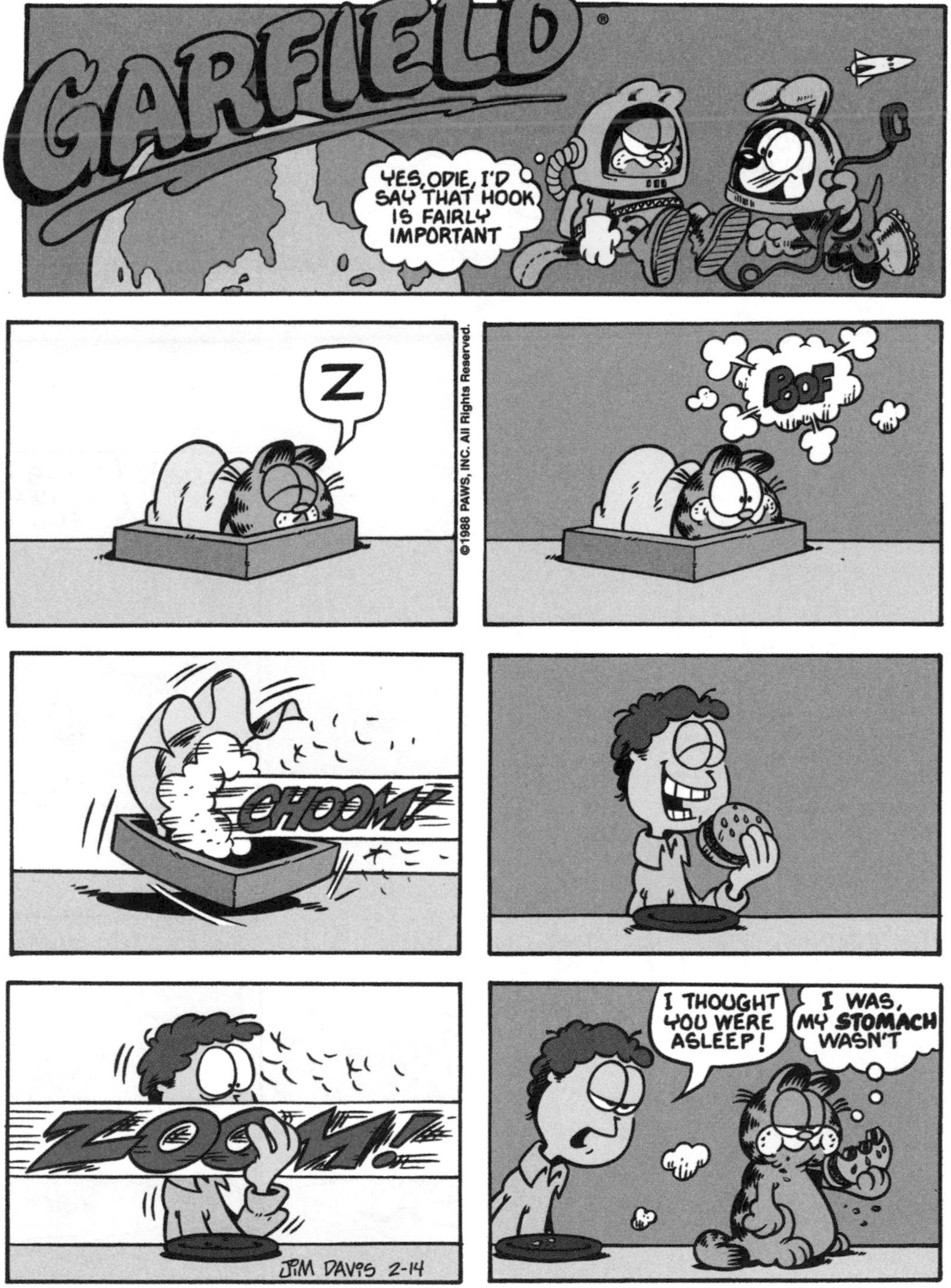
GARFIELD®
YES, ODIE, I'D SAY THAT HOOK IS FAIRLY IMPORTANT
©1988 PAWS, INC. All Rights Reserved.
Z
POOF
CHOOM!
ZOOM!
JIM DAVIS 2-14
I THOUGHT YOU WERE ASLEEP!
I WAS, MY STOMACH WASN'T

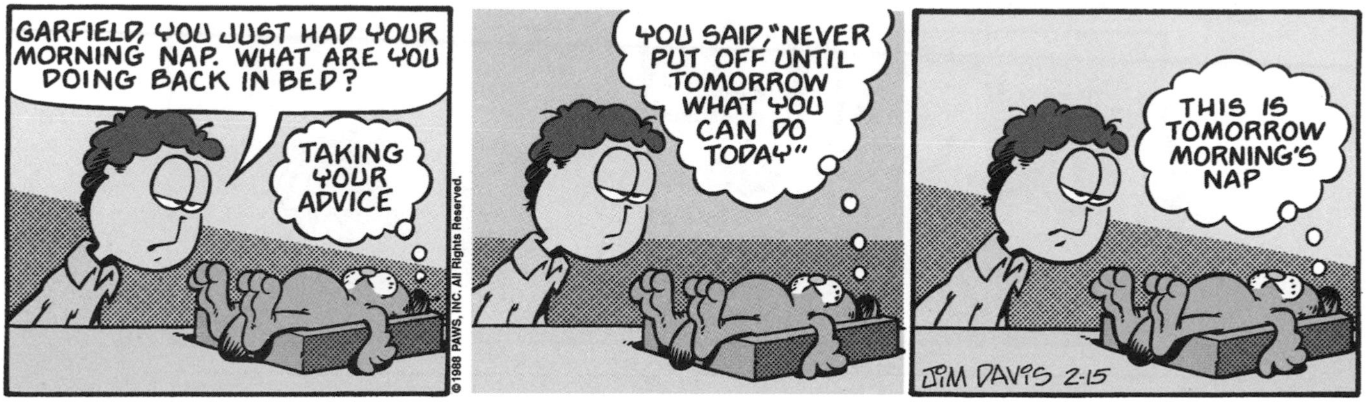
GARFIELD, YOU JUST HAD YOUR MORNING NAP. WHAT ARE YOU DOING BACK IN BED?
TAKING YOUR ADVICE
©1988 PAWS, INC. All Rights Reserved.
YOU SAID, "NEVER PUT OFF UNTIL TOMORROW WHAT YOU CAN DO TODAY"
THIS IS TOMORROW MORNING'S NAP
JIM DAVIS 2-15

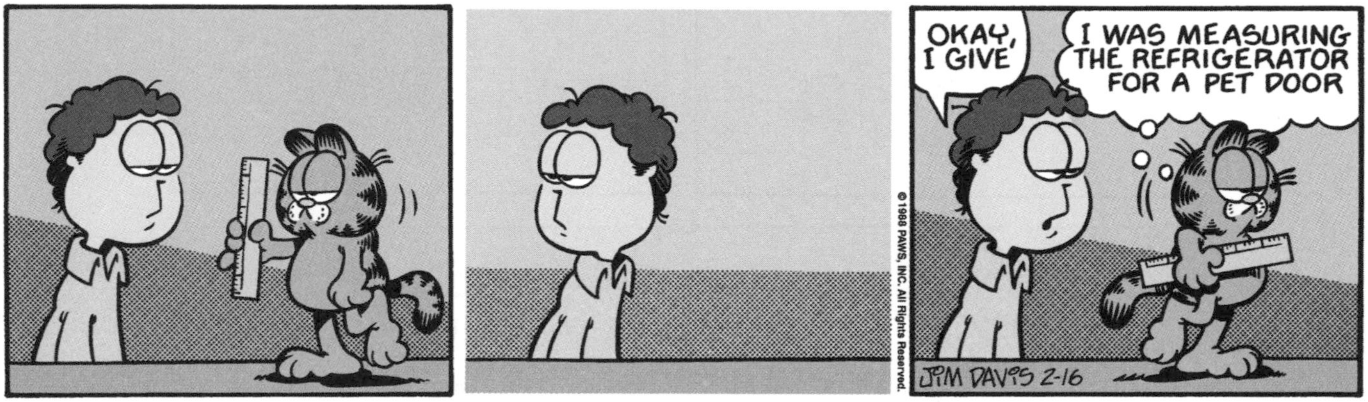
©1988 PAWS, INC. All Rights Reserved.
OKAY, I GIVE
I WAS MEASURING THE REFRIGERATOR FOR A PET DOOR
JIM DAVIS 2-16

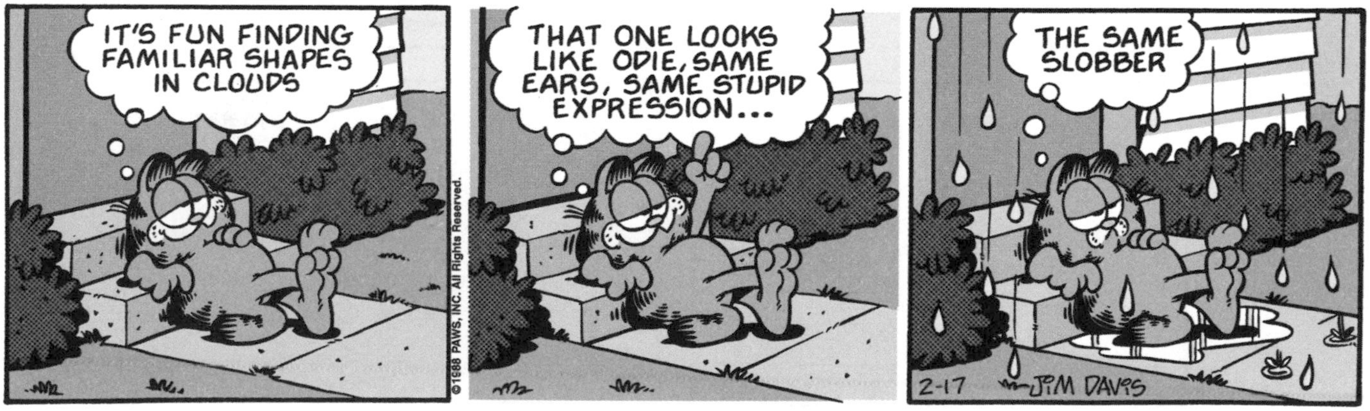
IT'S FUN FINDING FAMILIAR SHAPES IN CLOUDS
©1988 PAWS, INC. All Rights Reserved.
THAT ONE LOOKS LIKE ODIE, SAME EARS, SAME STUPID EXPRESSION...
THE SAME SLOBBER
2-17 JIM DAVIS

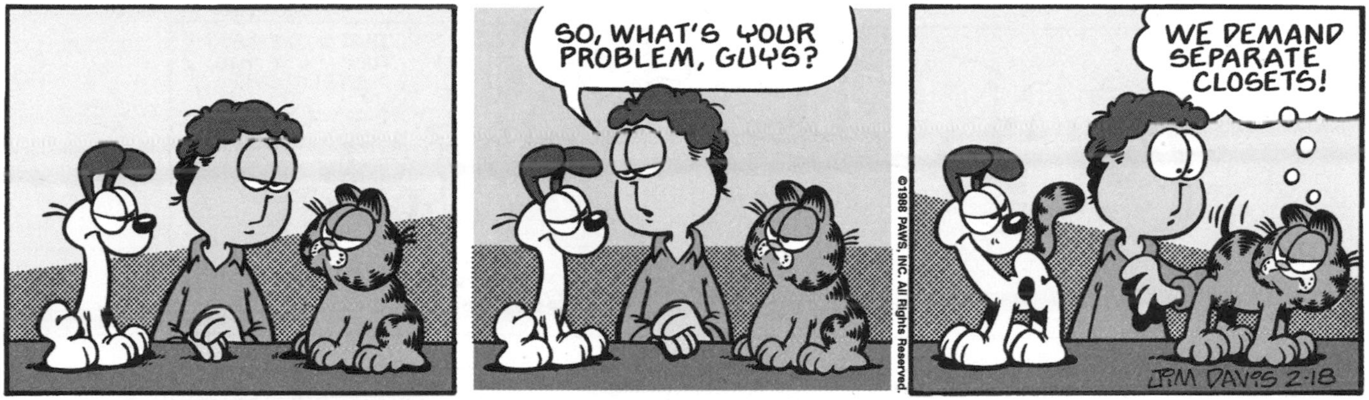
SO, WHAT'S YOUR PROBLEM, GUYS?
WE DEMAND SEPARATE CLOSETS!
©1988 PAWS, INC. All Rights Reserved.
JIM DAVIS 2-18

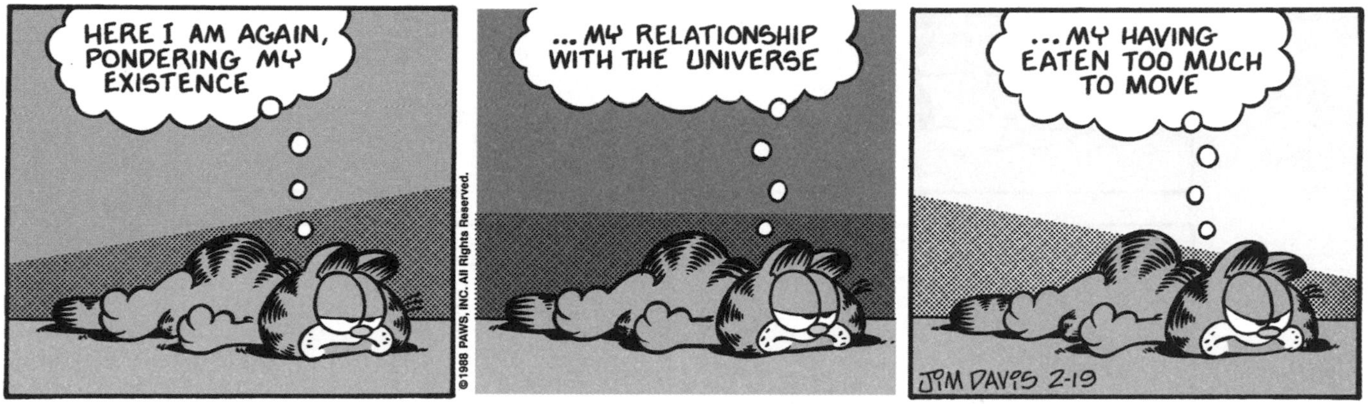
HERE I AM AGAIN, PONDERING MY EXISTENCE
... MY RELATIONSHIP WITH THE UNIVERSE
... MY HAVING EATEN TOO MUCH TO MOVE
©1988 PAWS, INC. All Rights Reserved.
JIM DAVIS 2-19

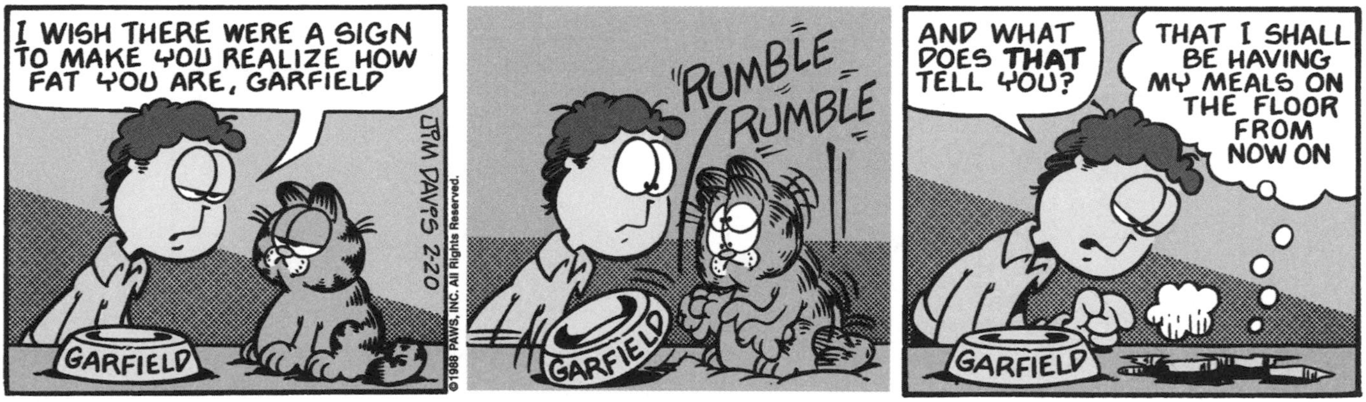
I WISH THERE WERE A SIGN TO MAKE YOU REALIZE HOW FAT YOU ARE, GARFIELD
GARFIELD
JIM DAVIS 2-20
©1988 PAWS, INC. All Rights Reserved.
RUMBLE RUMBLE
GARFIELD
AND WHAT DOES **THAT** TELL YOU?
THAT I SHALL BE HAVING MY MEALS ON THE FLOOR FROM NOW ON
GARFIELD

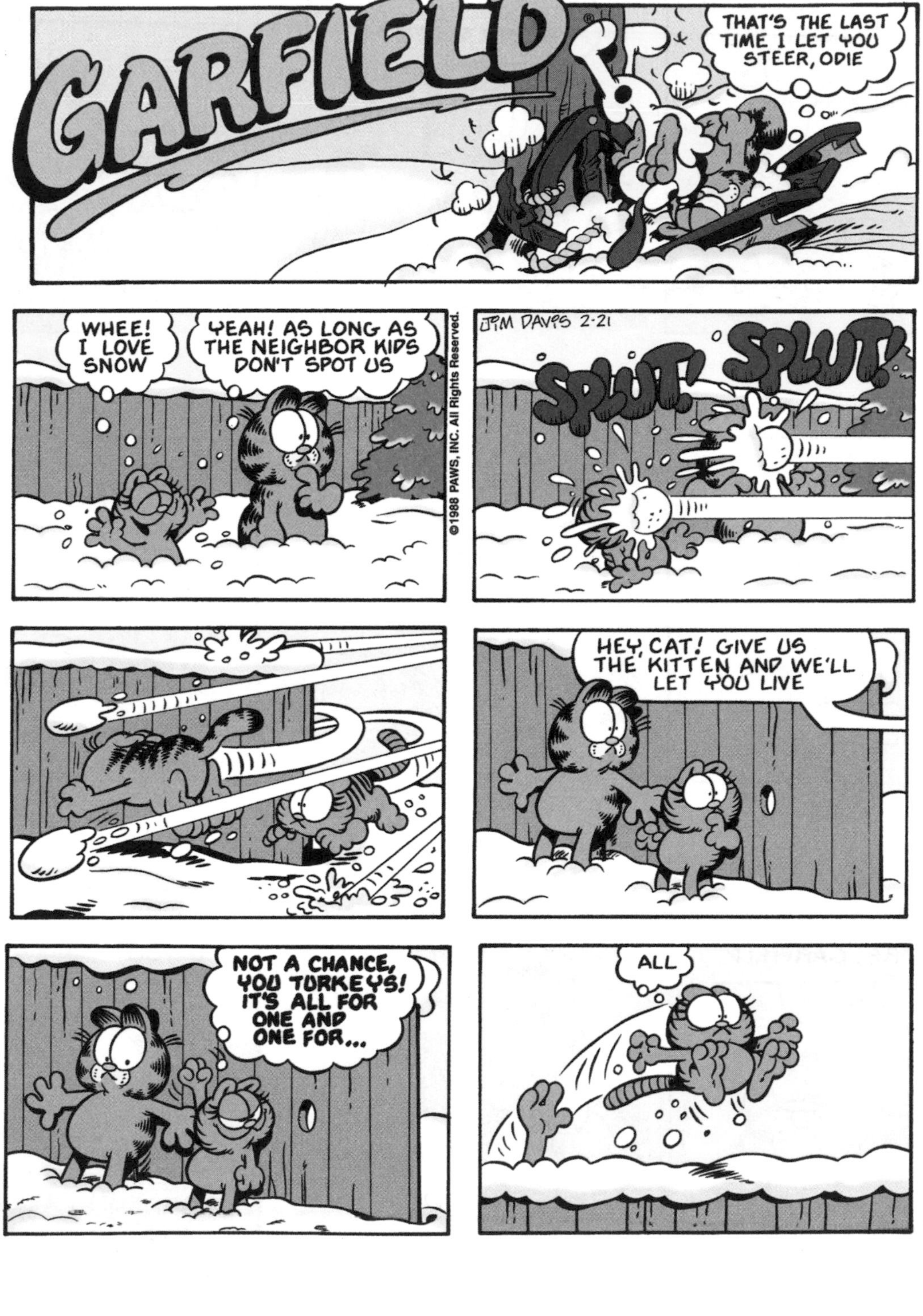
GARFIELD
THAT'S THE LAST TIME I LET YOU STEER, ODIE
WHEE! I LOVE SNOW
YEAH! AS LONG AS THE NEIGHBOR KIDS DON'T SPOT US
©1988 PAWS, INC. All Rights Reserved.
JIM DAVIS 2-21
SPLUT! SPLUT!
HEY, CAT! GIVE US THE KITTEN AND WE'LL LET YOU LIVE
NOT A CHANCE, YOU TURKEYS! IT'S ALL FOR ONE AND ONE FOR...
ALL

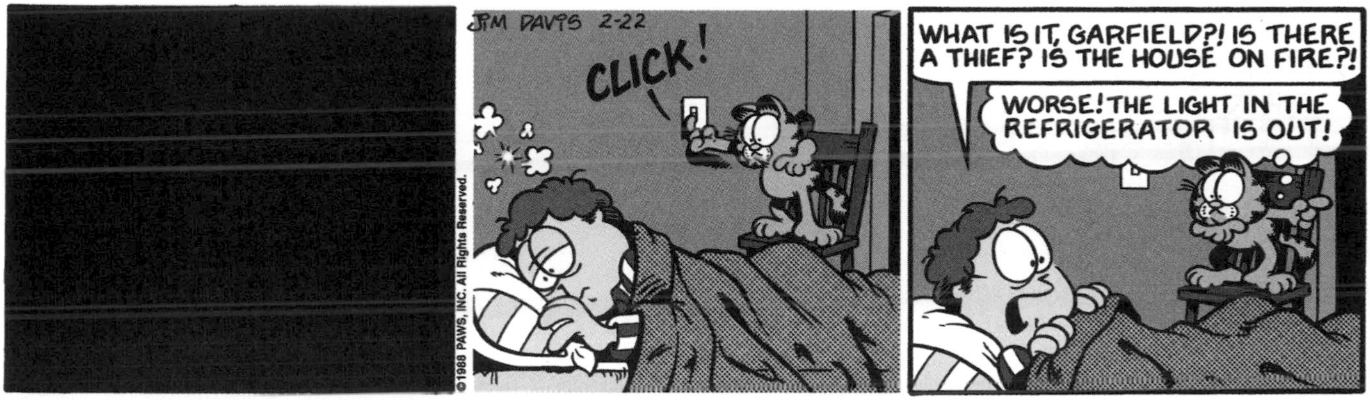
JIM DAVIS 2-22
CLICK!
©1988 PAWS, INC. All Rights Reserved.
WHAT IS IT, GARFIELD?! IS THERE A THIEF? IS THE HOUSE ON FIRE?!
WORSE! THE LIGHT IN THE REFRIGERATOR IS OUT!

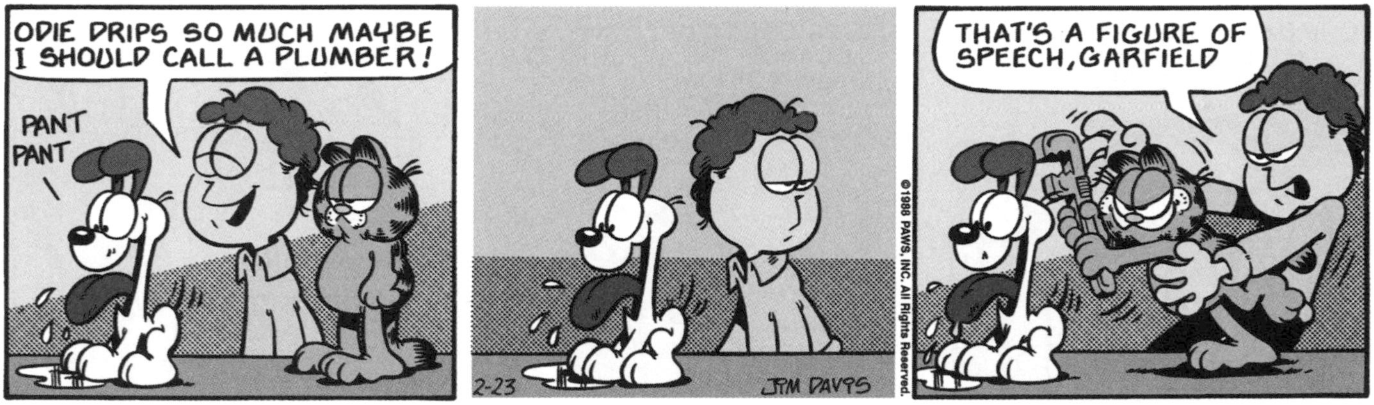
ODIE DRIPS SO MUCH MAYBE I SHOULD CALL A PLUMBER!
PANT PANT
2-23
JIM DAVIS
©1988 PAWS, INC. All Rights Reserved.
THAT'S A FIGURE OF SPEECH, GARFIELD

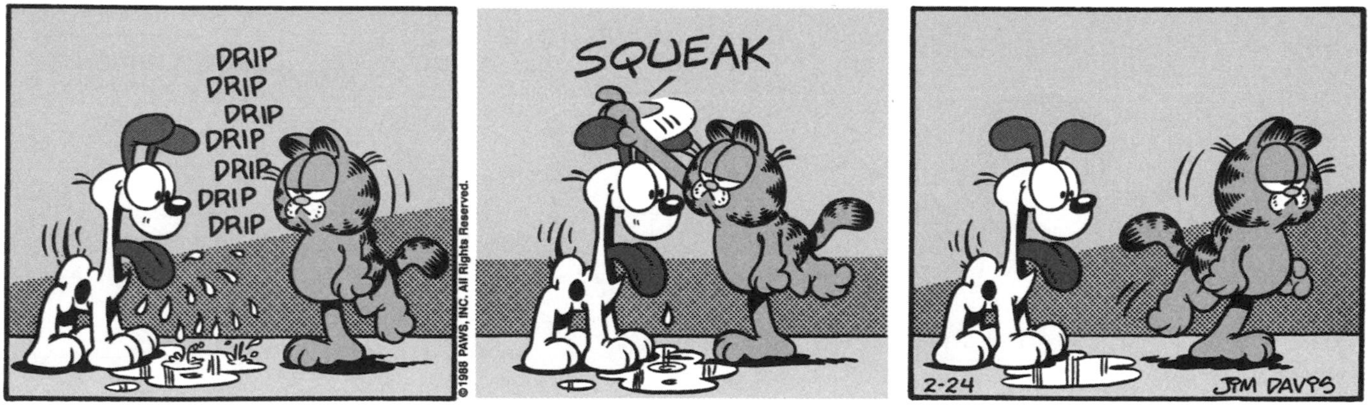
DRIP
DRIP
DRIP
DRIP
DRIP
DRIP
DRIP
©1988 PAWS, INC. All Rights Reserved.
SQUEAK
2-24
JIM DAVIS

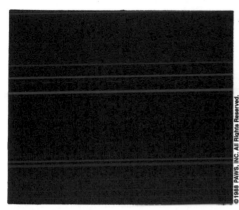

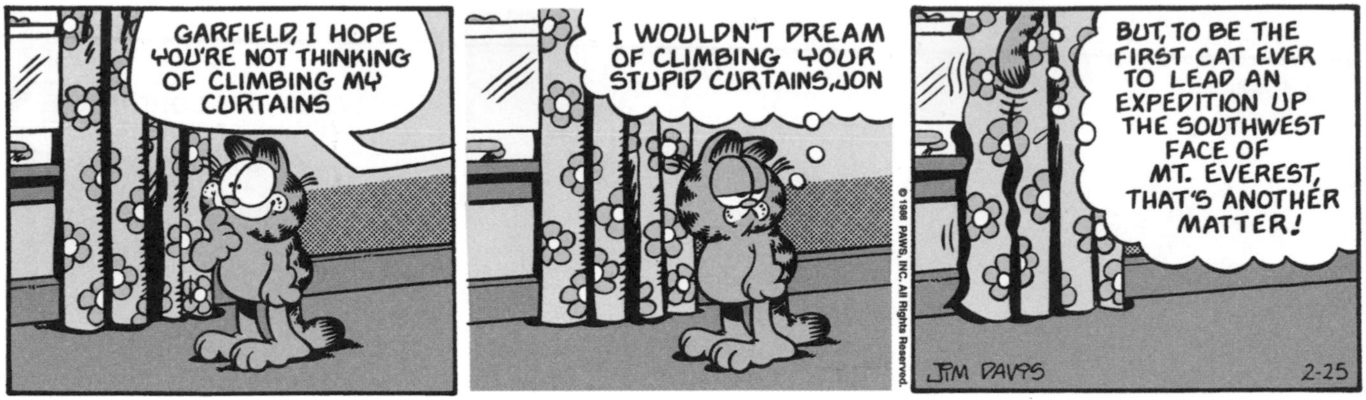
GARFIELD, I HOPE YOU'RE NOT THINKING OF CLIMBING MY CURTAINS
I WOULDN'T DREAM OF CLIMBING YOUR STUPID CURTAINS, JON
© 1988 PAWS, INC. All Rights Reserved.
BUT, TO BE THE FIRST CAT EVER TO LEAD AN EXPEDITION UP THE SOUTHWEST FACE OF MT. EVEREST, THAT'S ANOTHER MATTER!
JIM DAVIS
2-25

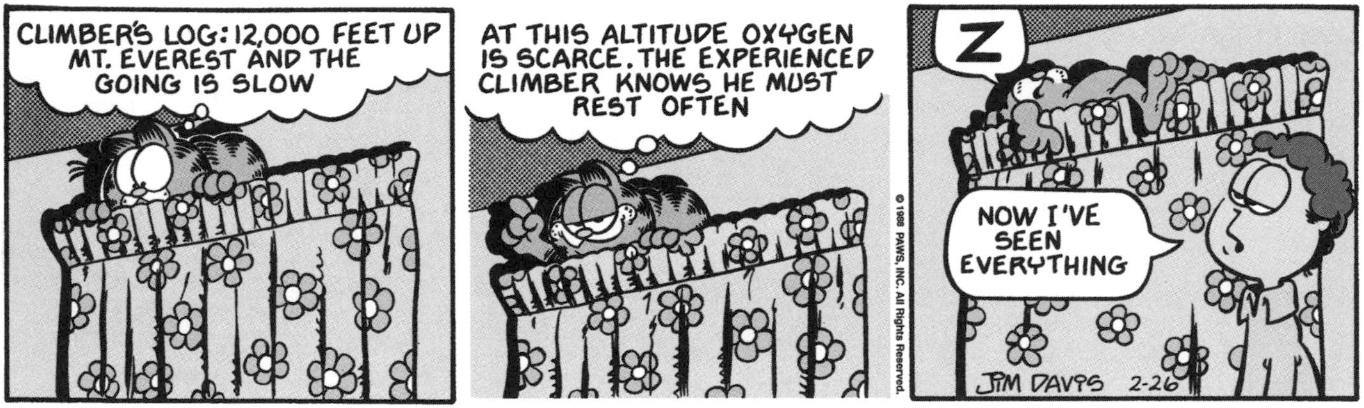
CLIMBER'S LOG: 12,000 FEET UP MT. EVEREST AND THE GOING IS SLOW
AT THIS ALTITUDE OXYGEN IS SCARCE. THE EXPERIENCED CLIMBER KNOWS HE MUST REST OFTEN
© 1988 PAWS, INC. All Rights Reserved.
Z
NOW I'VE SEEN EVERYTHING
JIM DAVIS
2-26

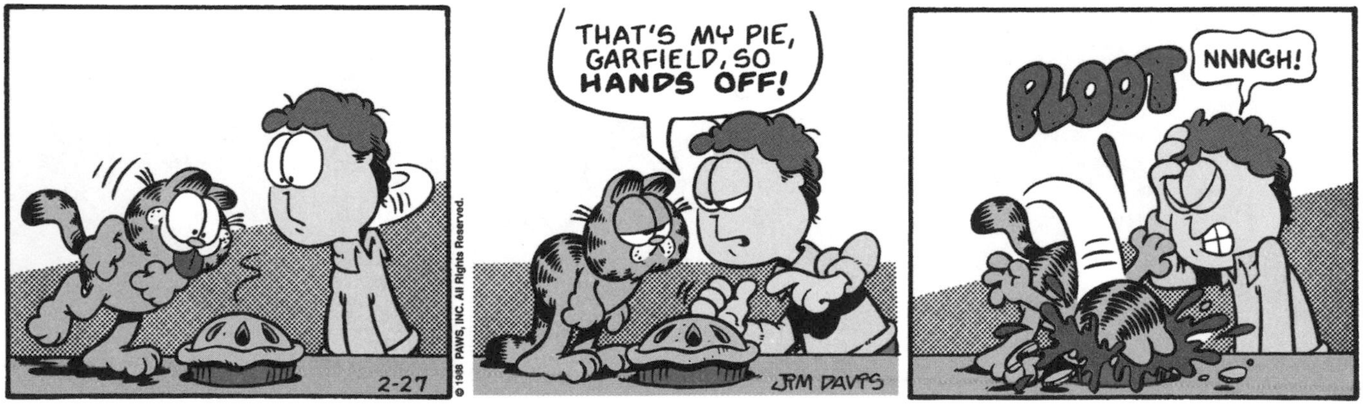
2-27
© 1988 PAWS, INC. All Rights Reserved.
THAT'S MY PIE, GARFIELD, SO **HANDS OFF!**
JIM DAVIS
PLOOT
NNNGH!

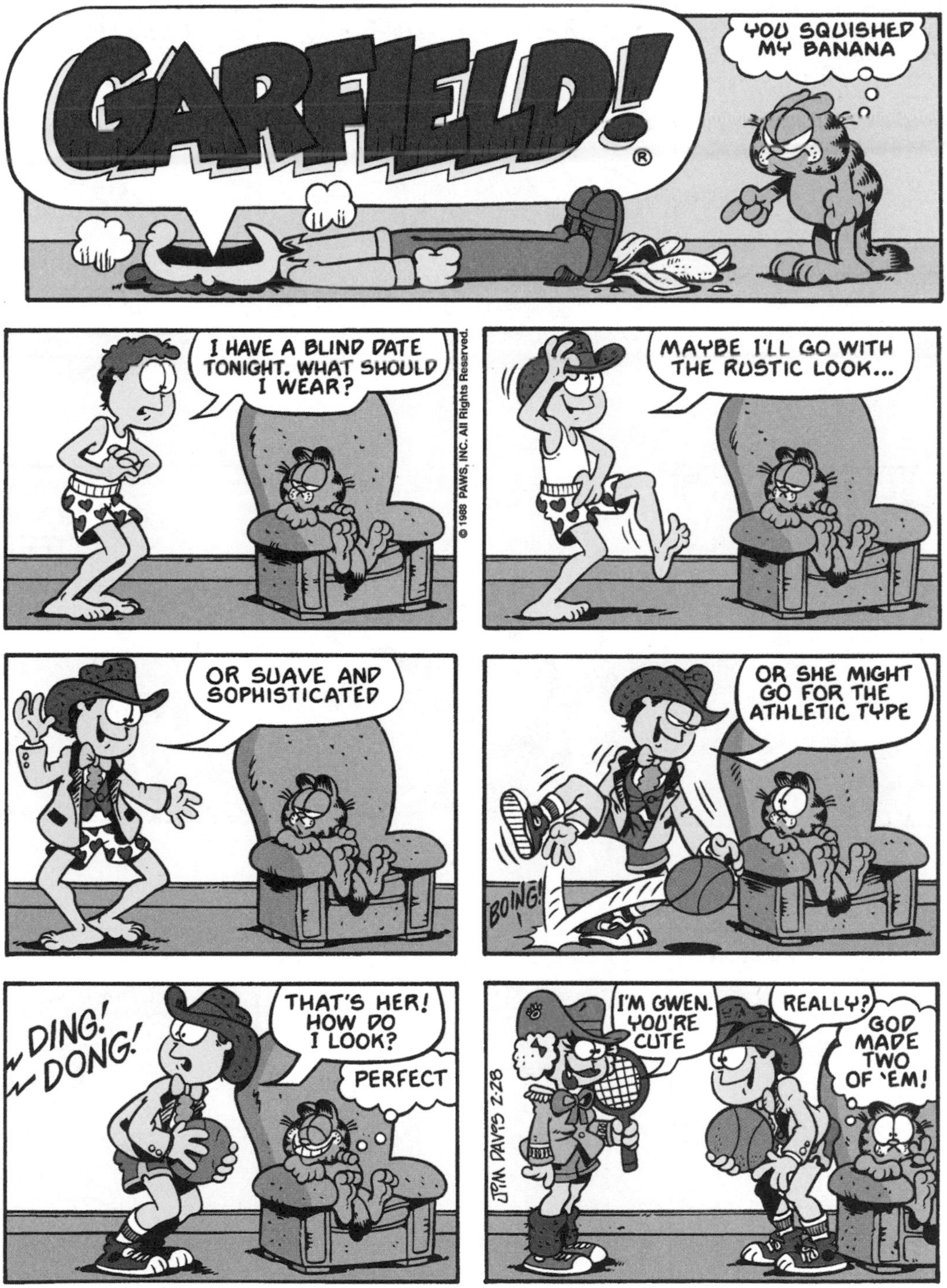

GARFIELD!
YOU SQUISHED MY BANANA
© 1988 PAWS, INC. All Rights Reserved.
I HAVE A BLIND DATE TONIGHT. WHAT SHOULD I WEAR?
MAYBE I'LL GO WITH THE RUSTIC LOOK...
OR SUAVE AND SOPHISTICATED
OR SHE MIGHT GO FOR THE ATHLETIC TYPE
BOING!
DING! DONG!
THAT'S HER! HOW DO I LOOK?
PERFECT
JIM DAVIS 2-28
I'M GWEN. YOU'RE CUTE
REALLY?
GOD MADE TWO OF 'EM!

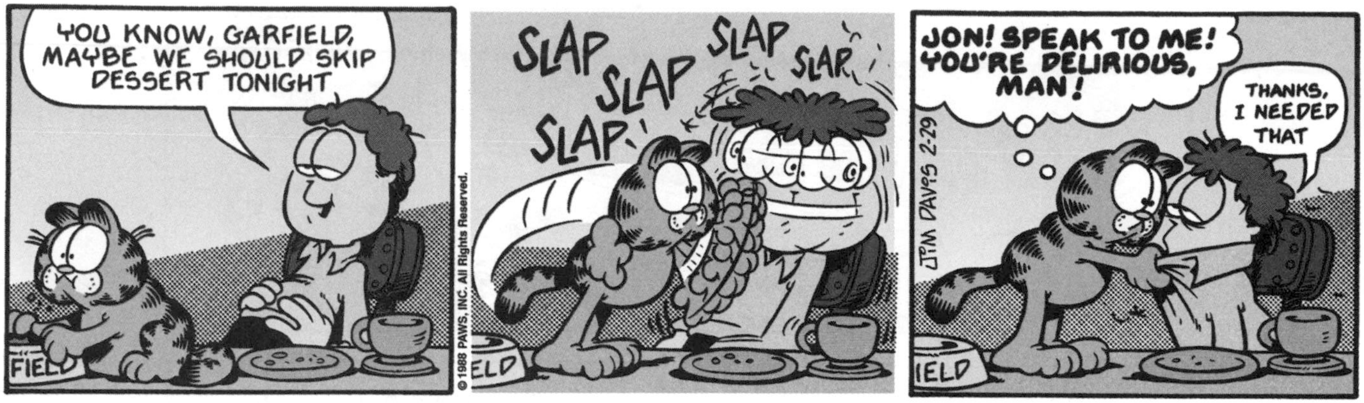
YOU KNOW, GARFIELD, MAYBE WE SHOULD SKIP DESSERT TONIGHT
SLAP SLAP SLAP SLAP SLAP
JON! SPEAK TO ME! YOU'RE DELIRIOUS, MAN!
THANKS, I NEEDED THAT
JIM DAVIS 2-29
© 1988 PAWS, INC. All Rights Reserved.

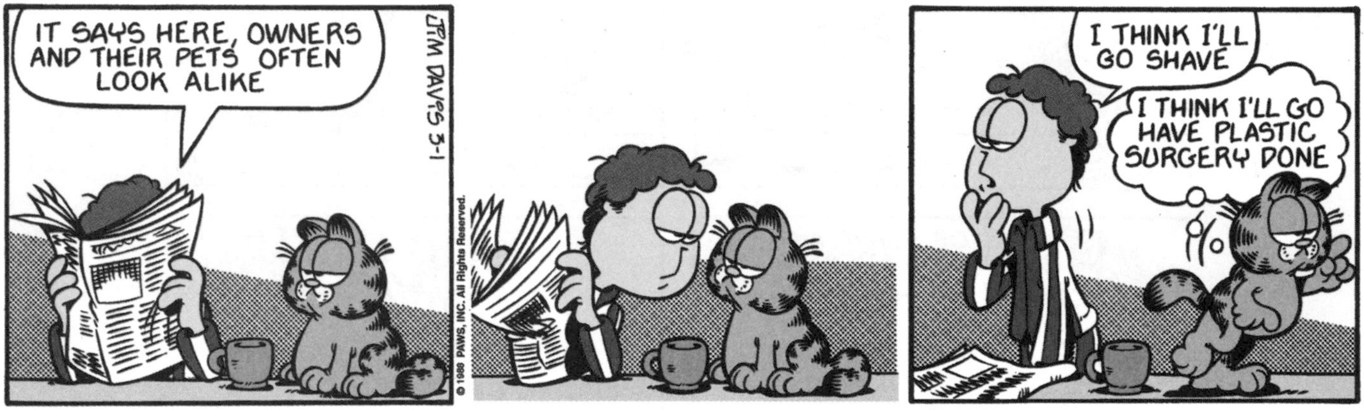
IT SAYS HERE, OWNERS AND THEIR PETS OFTEN LOOK ALIKE
I THINK I'LL GO SHAVE
I THINK I'LL GO HAVE PLASTIC SURGERY DONE
JIM DAVIS 3-1
© 1988 PAWS, INC. All Rights Reserved.

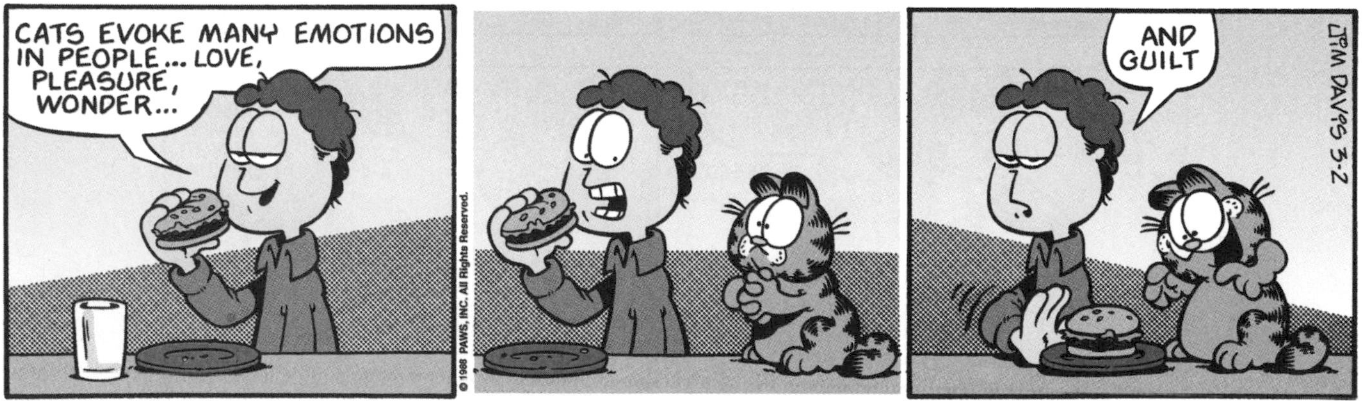
CATS EVOKE MANY EMOTIONS IN PEOPLE... LOVE, PLEASURE, WONDER...
AND GUILT
JIM DAVIS 3-2
© 1988 PAWS, INC. All Rights Reserved.

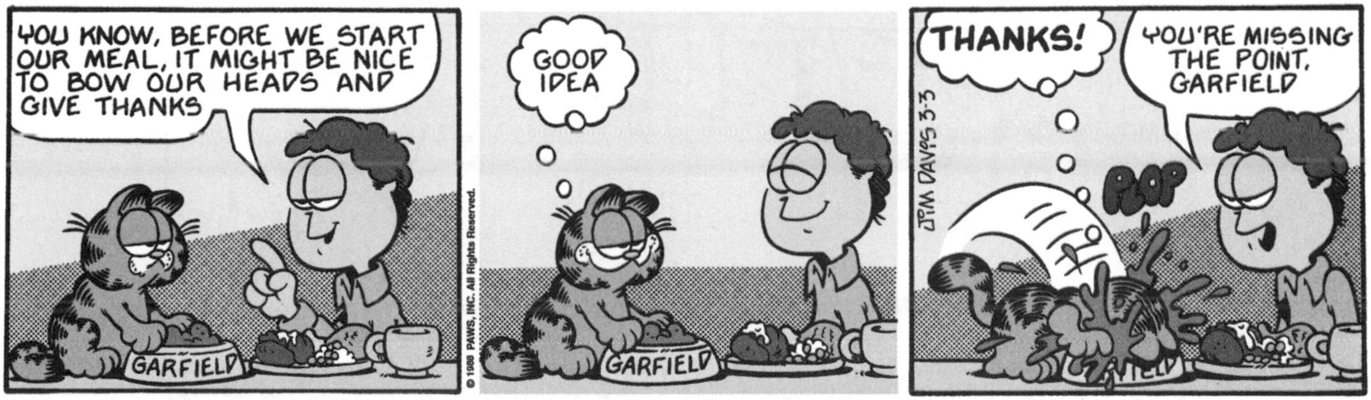
YOU KNOW, BEFORE WE START OUR MEAL, IT MIGHT BE NICE TO BOW OUR HEADS AND GIVE THANKS
GARFIELD
© 1988 PAWS, INC. All Rights Reserved.
GOOD IDEA
GARFIELD
THANKS!
YOU'RE MISSING THE POINT, GARFIELD
PLOP
JIM DAVIS 3-3

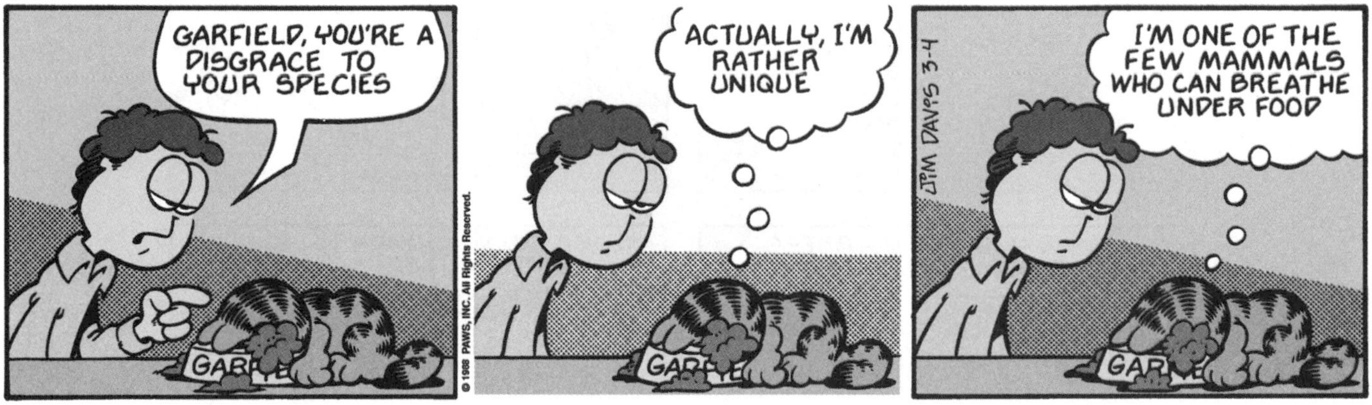
GARFIELD, YOU'RE A DISGRACE TO YOUR SPECIES
© 1988 PAWS, INC. All Rights Reserved.
ACTUALLY, I'M RATHER UNIQUE
JIM DAVIS 3-4
I'M ONE OF THE FEW MAMMALS WHO CAN BREATHE UNDER FOOD

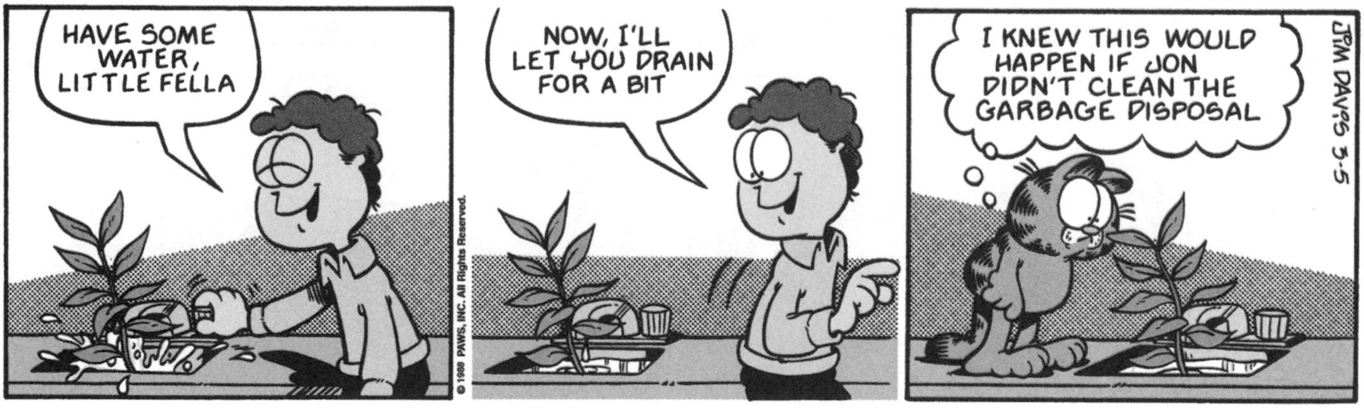
HAVE SOME WATER, LITTLE FELLA
© 1988 PAWS, INC. All Rights Reserved.
NOW, I'LL LET YOU DRAIN FOR A BIT
I KNEW THIS WOULD HAPPEN IF JON DIDN'T CLEAN THE GARBAGE DISPOSAL
JIM DAVIS 3-5

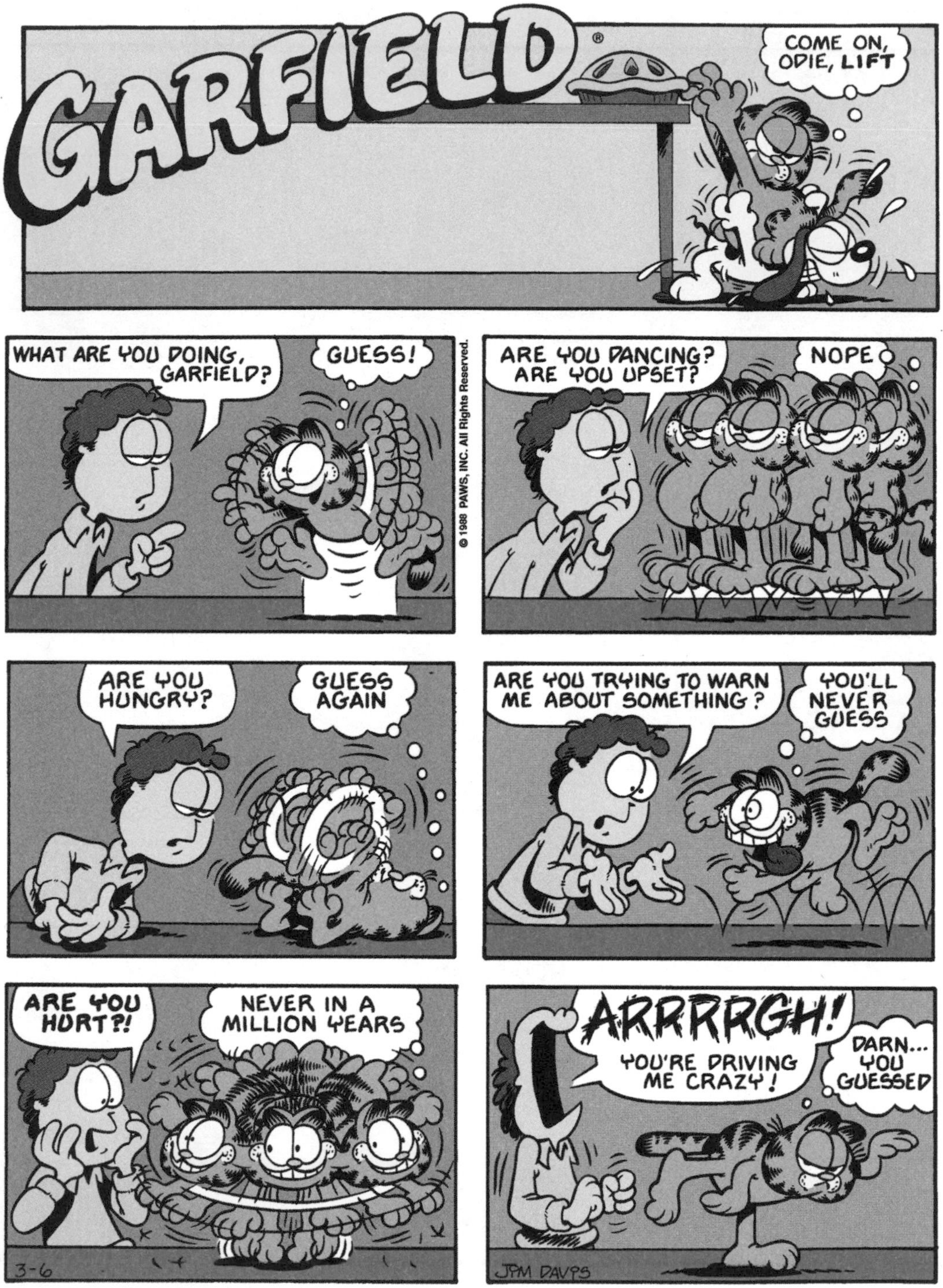
GARFIELD®
COME ON, ODIE, LIFT
© 1988 PAWS, INC. All Rights Reserved.
WHAT ARE YOU DOING, GARFIELD?
GUESS!
ARE YOU DANCING? ARE YOU UPSET?
NOPE
ARE YOU HUNGRY?
GUESS AGAIN
ARE YOU TRYING TO WARN ME ABOUT SOMETHING?
YOU'LL NEVER GUESS
ARE YOU HURT?!
NEVER IN A MILLION YEARS
3-6
ARRRRGH! YOU'RE DRIVING ME CRAZY!
DARN... YOU GUESSED
JPM DAVPS

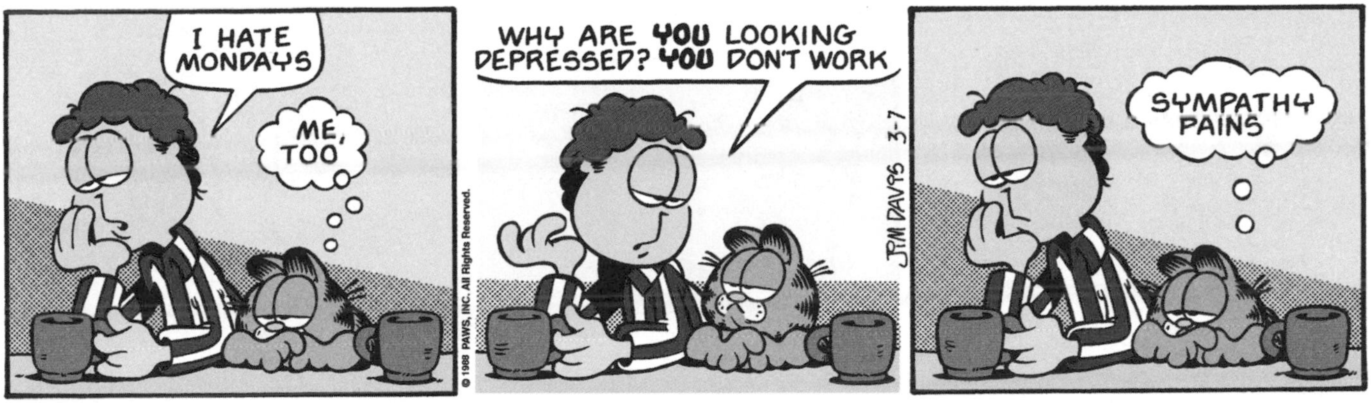
I HATE MONDAYS
ME, TOO
© 1988 PAWS, INC. All Rights Reserved.
WHY ARE YOU LOOKING DEPRESSED? YOU DON'T WORK
JIM DAVIS 3-7
SYMPATHY PAINS

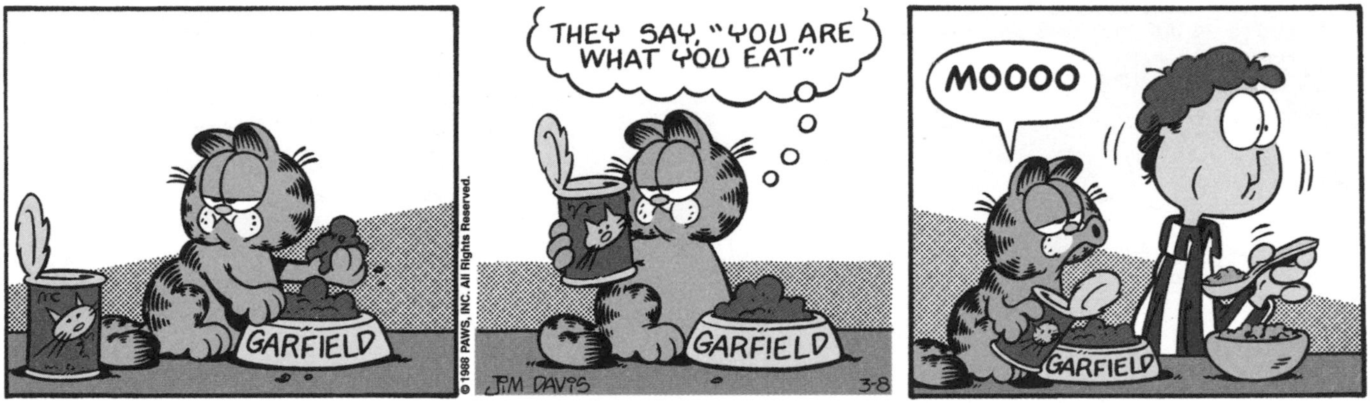
GARFIELD
© 1988 PAWS, INC. All Rights Reserved.
THEY SAY, "YOU ARE WHAT YOU EAT"
GARFIELD
JIM DAVIS
3-8
MOOOO
GARFIELD

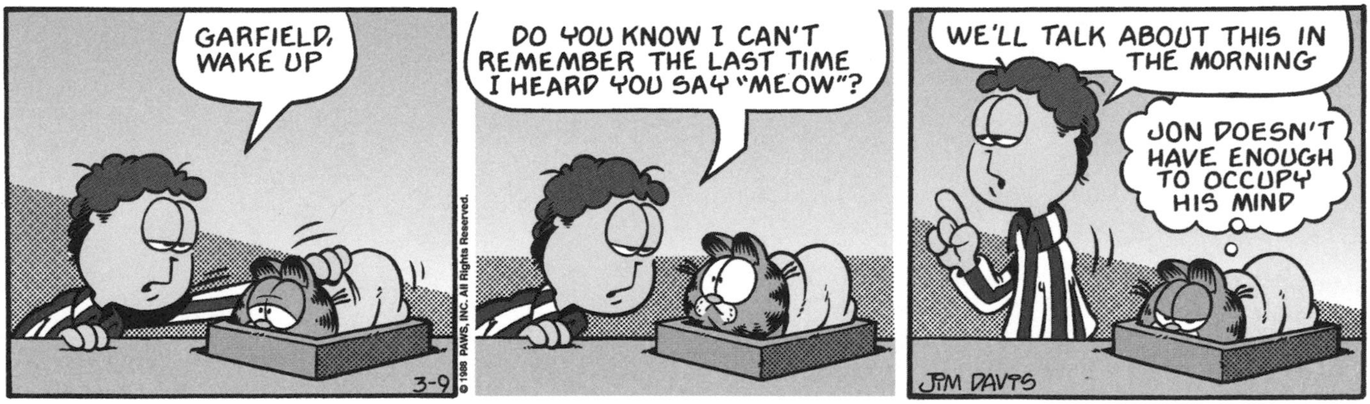
GARFIELD, WAKE UP
3-9
© 1988 PAWS, INC. All Rights Reserved.
DO YOU KNOW I CAN'T REMEMBER THE LAST TIME I HEARD YOU SAY "MEOW"?
WE'LL TALK ABOUT THIS IN THE MORNING
JON DOESN'T HAVE ENOUGH TO OCCUPY HIS MIND
JIM DAVIS

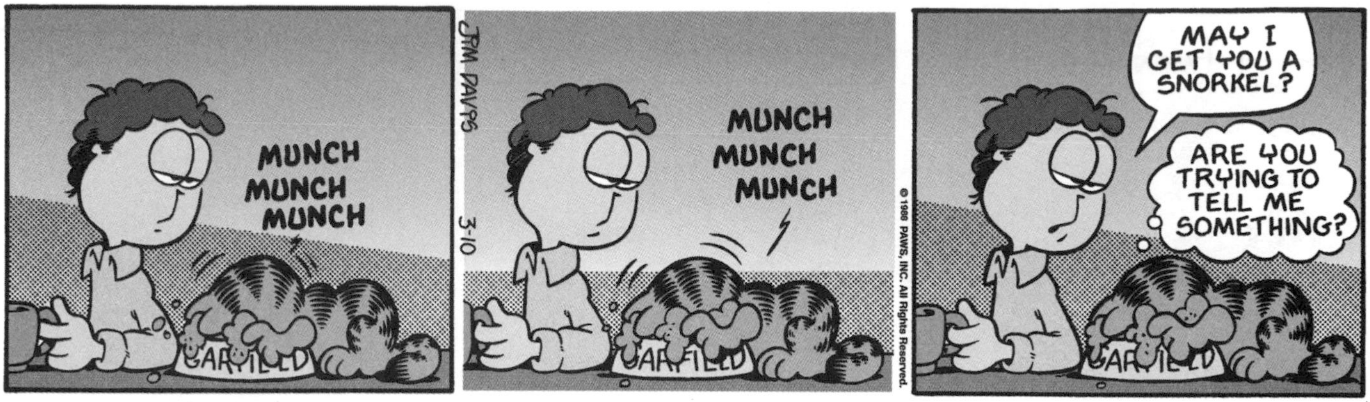
MUNCH MUNCH MUNCH
JIM DAVIS
3-10
MUNCH MUNCH MUNCH
© 1988 PAWS, INC. All Rights Reserved.
MAY I GET YOU A SNORKEL?
ARE YOU TRYING TO TELL ME SOMETHING?

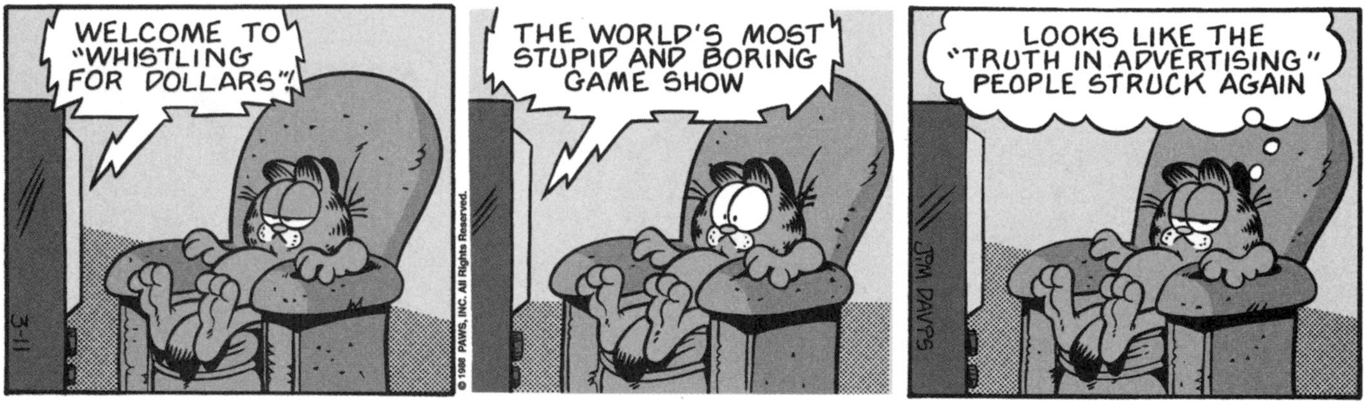
WELCOME TO "WHISTLING FOR DOLLARS"!
3-11
© 1988 PAWS, INC. All Rights Reserved.
THE WORLD'S MOST STUPID AND BORING GAME SHOW
LOOKS LIKE THE "TRUTH IN ADVERTISING" PEOPLE STRUCK AGAIN
JIM DAVIS

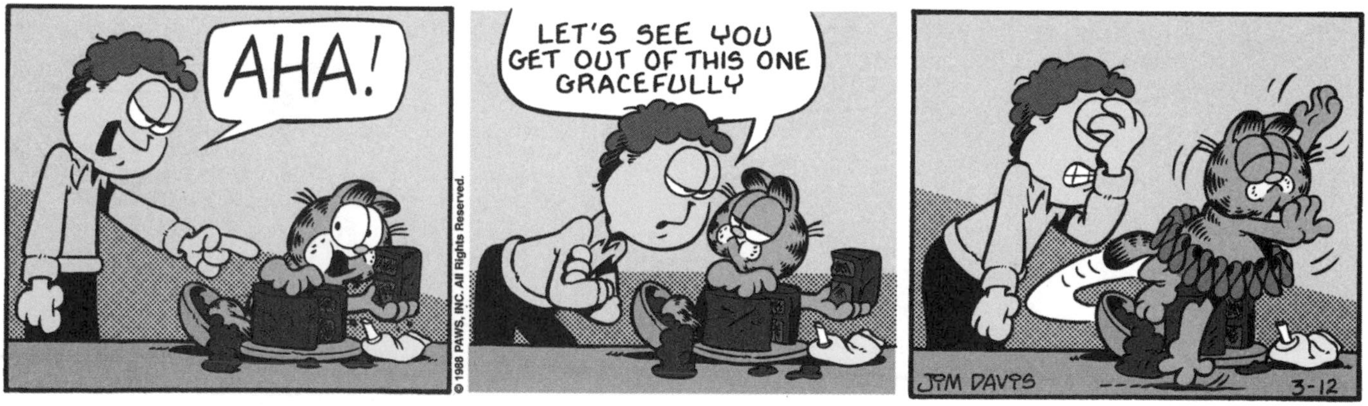
AHA!
© 1988 PAWS, INC. All Rights Reserved.
LET'S SEE YOU GET OUT OF THIS ONE GRACEFULLY
JIM DAVIS
3-12

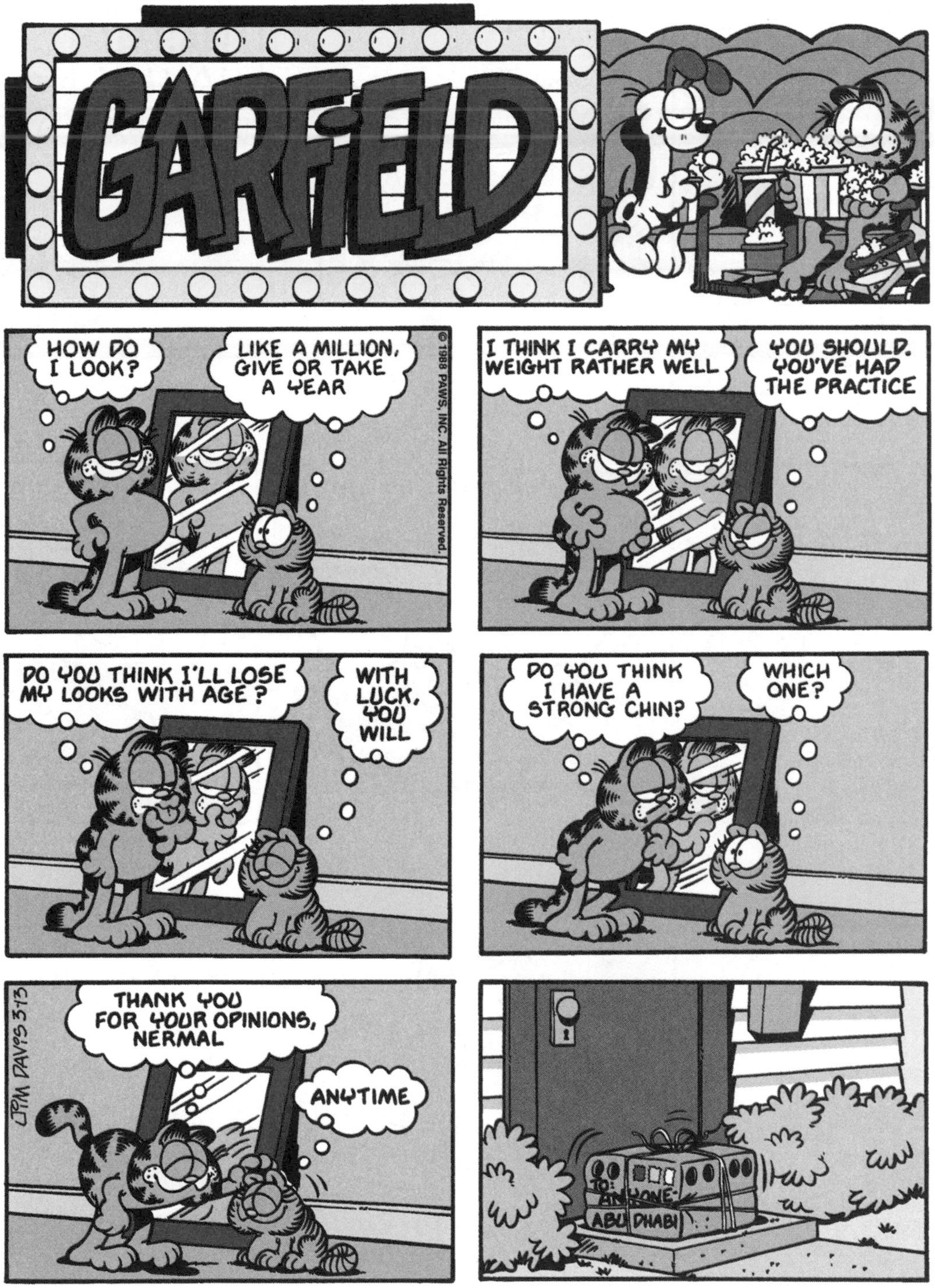
GARFIELD
HOW DO I LOOK?
LIKE A MILLION, GIVE OR TAKE A YEAR
© 1988 PAWS, INC. All Rights Reserved.
I THINK I CARRY MY WEIGHT RATHER WELL
YOU SHOULD. YOU'VE HAD THE PRACTICE
DO YOU THINK I'LL LOSE MY LOOKS WITH AGE ?
WITH LUCK, YOU WILL
DO YOU THINK I HAVE A STRONG CHIN?
WHICH ONE?
JIM DAVIS 3-13
THANK YOU FOR YOUR OPINIONS, NERMAL
ANYTIME
TO: ANYONE ABU DHABI

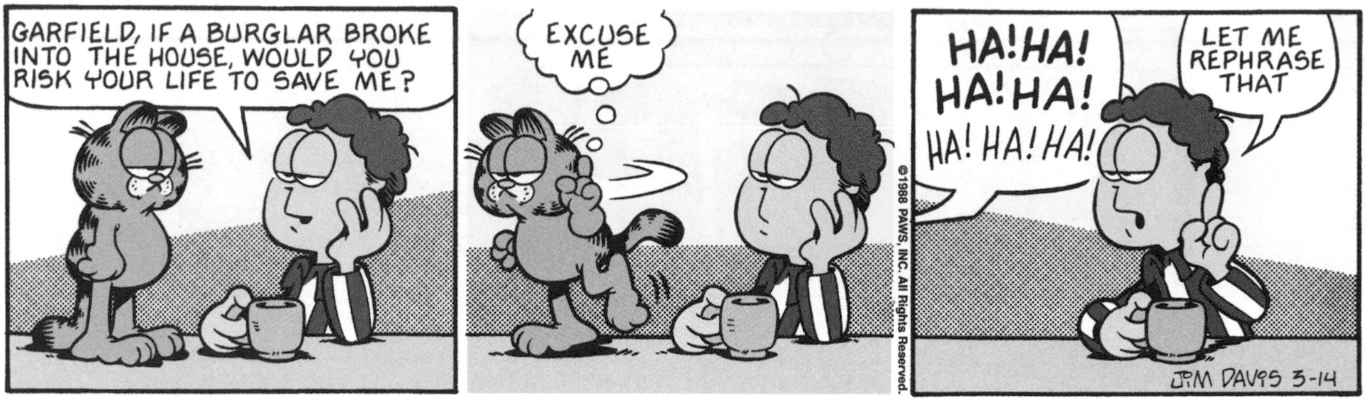
GARFIELD, IF A BURGLAR BROKE INTO THE HOUSE, WOULD YOU RISK YOUR LIFE TO SAVE ME?
EXCUSE ME
©1988 PAWS, INC. All Rights Reserved.
HA! HA! HA! HA! HA! HA! HA!
LET ME REPHRASE THAT
JIM DAVIS 3-14

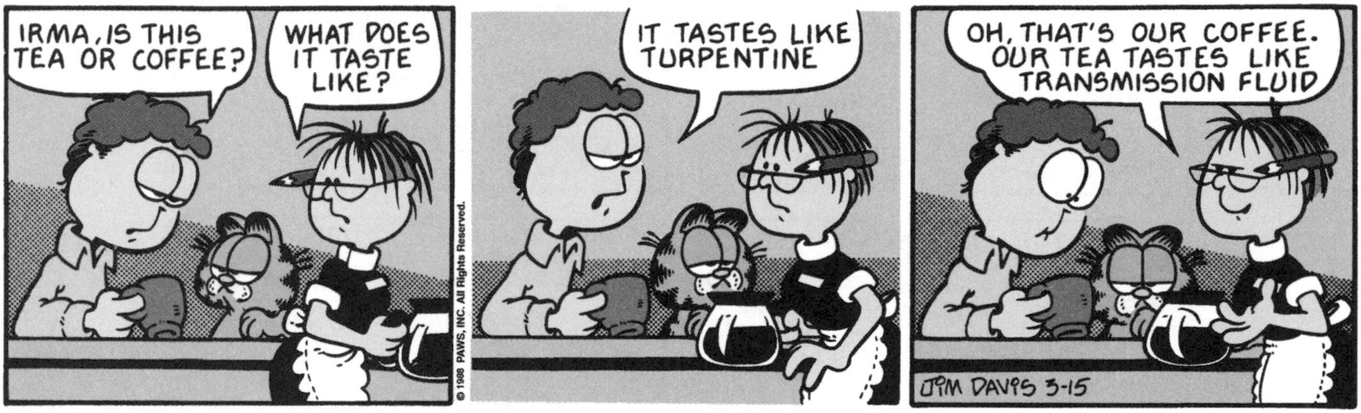
IRMA, IS THIS TEA OR COFFEE?
WHAT DOES IT TASTE LIKE?
© 1988 PAWS, INC. All Rights Reserved.
IT TASTES LIKE TURPENTINE
OH, THAT'S OUR COFFEE. OUR TEA TASTES LIKE TRANSMISSION FLUID
JIM DAVIS 3-15

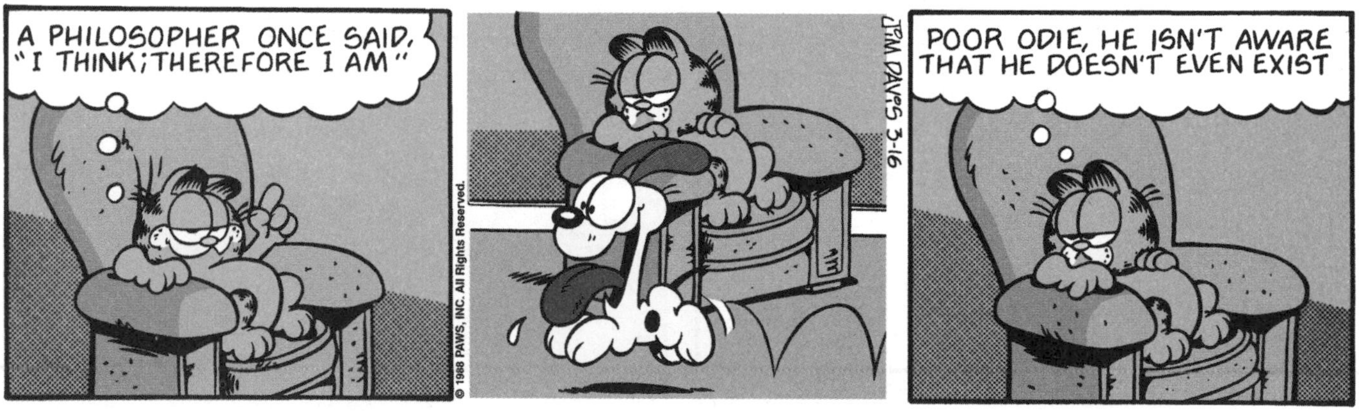
A PHILOSOPHER ONCE SAID, "I THINK; THEREFORE I AM"
© 1988 PAWS, INC. All Rights Reserved.
JIM DAVIS 3-16
POOR ODIE, HE ISN'T AWARE THAT HE DOESN'T EVEN EXIST

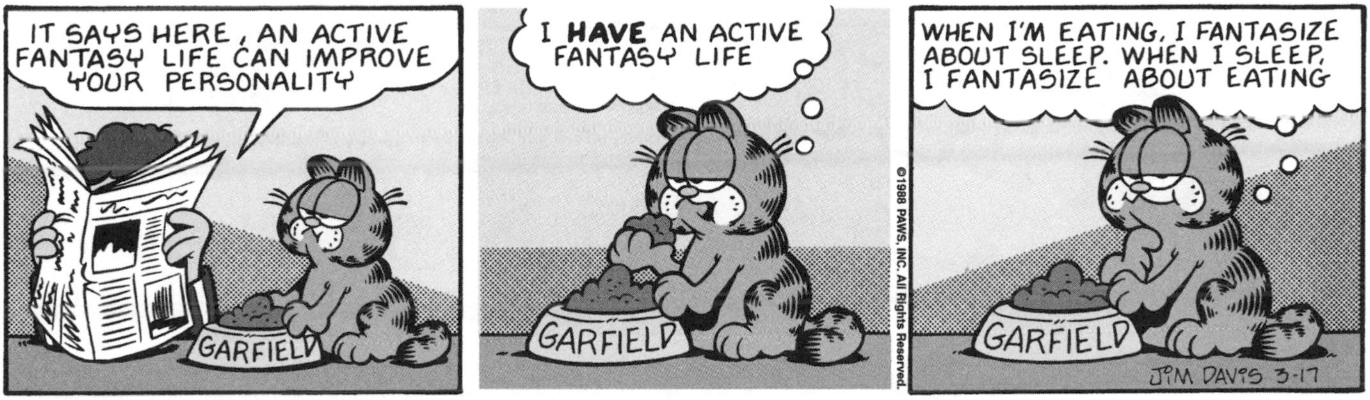
IT SAYS HERE, AN ACTIVE FANTASY LIFE CAN IMPROVE YOUR PERSONALITY
GARFIELD
I HAVE AN ACTIVE FANTASY LIFE
GARFIELD
©1988 PAWS, INC. All Rights Reserved.
WHEN I'M EATING, I FANTASIZE ABOUT SLEEP. WHEN I SLEEP, I FANTASIZE ABOUT EATING
GARFIELD
JIM DAVIS 3-17

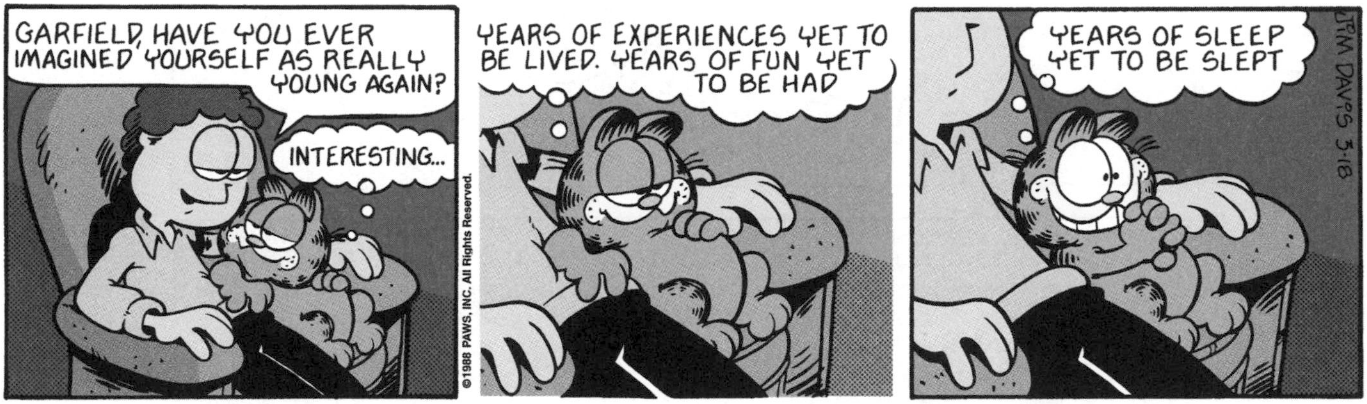
GARFIELD, HAVE YOU EVER IMAGINED YOURSELF AS REALLY YOUNG AGAIN?
INTERESTING...
©1988 PAWS, INC. All Rights Reserved.
YEARS OF EXPERIENCES YET TO BE LIVED. YEARS OF FUN YET TO BE HAD
YEARS OF SLEEP YET TO BE SLEPT
JIM DAVIS 3-18

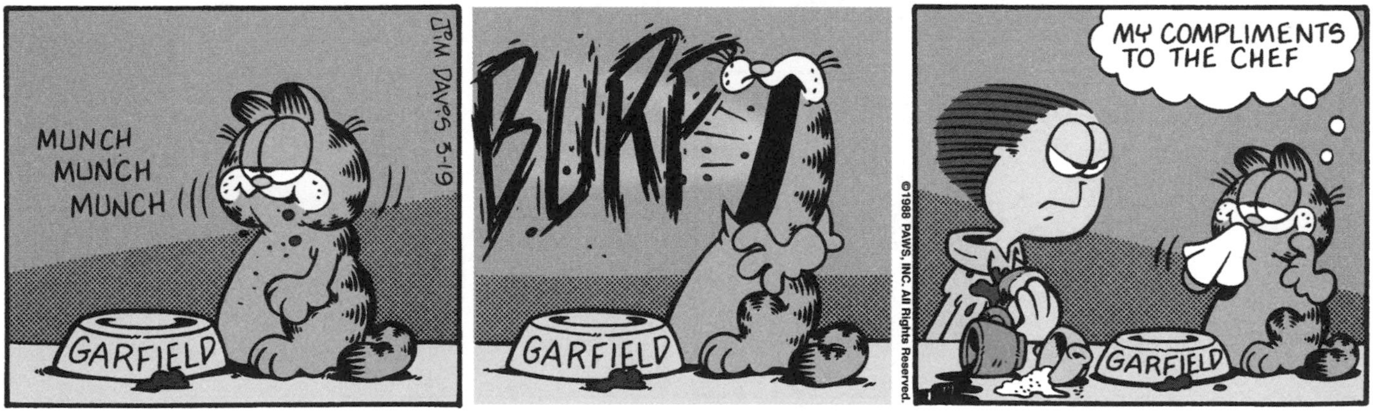
JIM DAVIS 3-19
MUNCH
MUNCH
MUNCH
GARFIELD
BURP
GARFIELD
©1988 PAWS, INC. All Rights Reserved.
MY COMPLIMENTS TO THE CHEF
GARFIELD

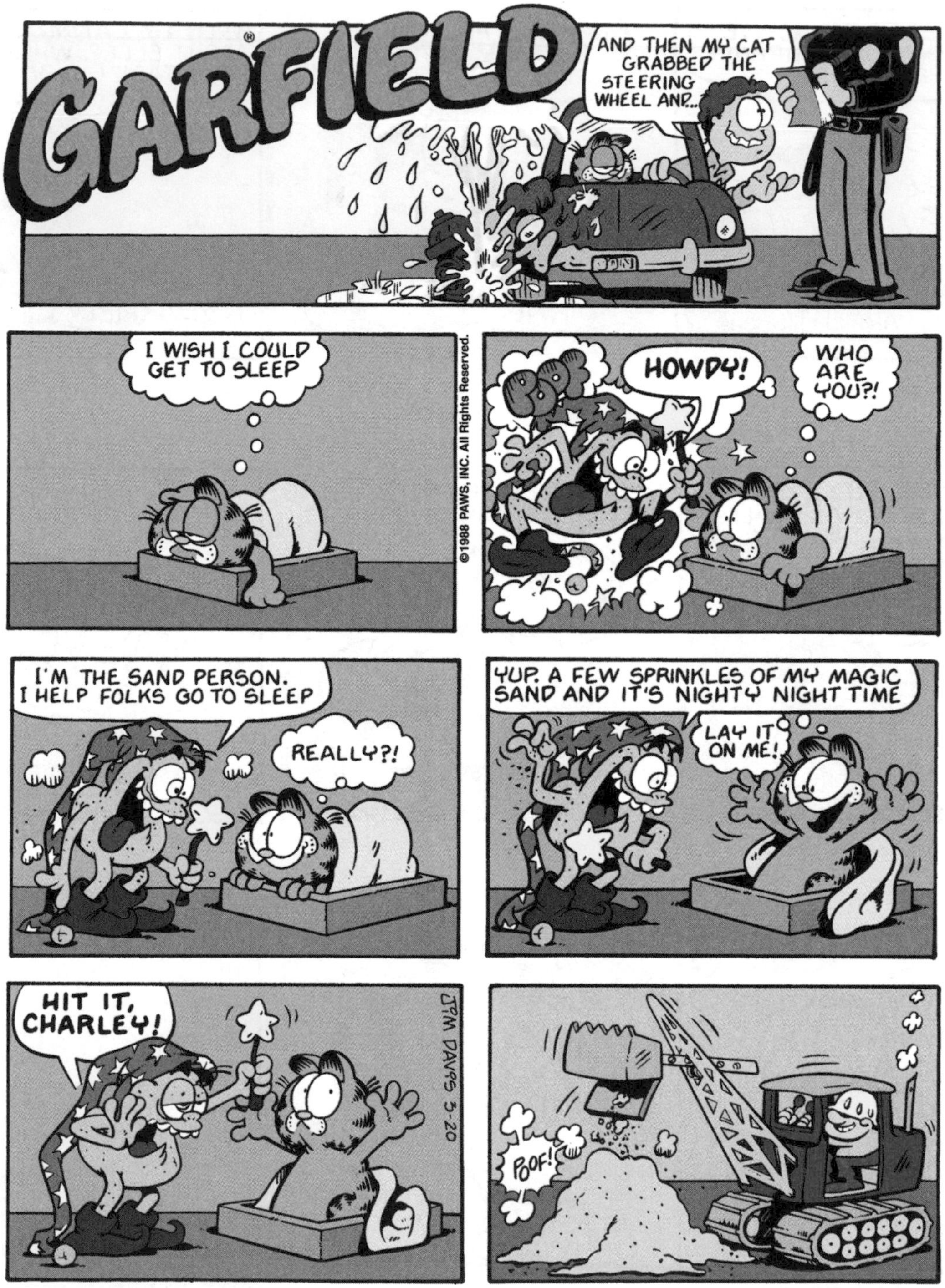
GARFIELD
AND THEN MY CAT GRABBED THE STEERING WHEEL AND...
I WISH I COULD GET TO SLEEP
HOWDY!
WHO ARE YOU?!
I'M THE SAND PERSON. I HELP FOLKS GO TO SLEEP
REALLY?!
YUP. A FEW SPRINKLES OF MY MAGIC SAND AND IT'S NIGHTY NIGHT TIME
LAY IT ON ME!
HIT IT, CHARLEY!
POOF!
JPM DAVPS 3-20

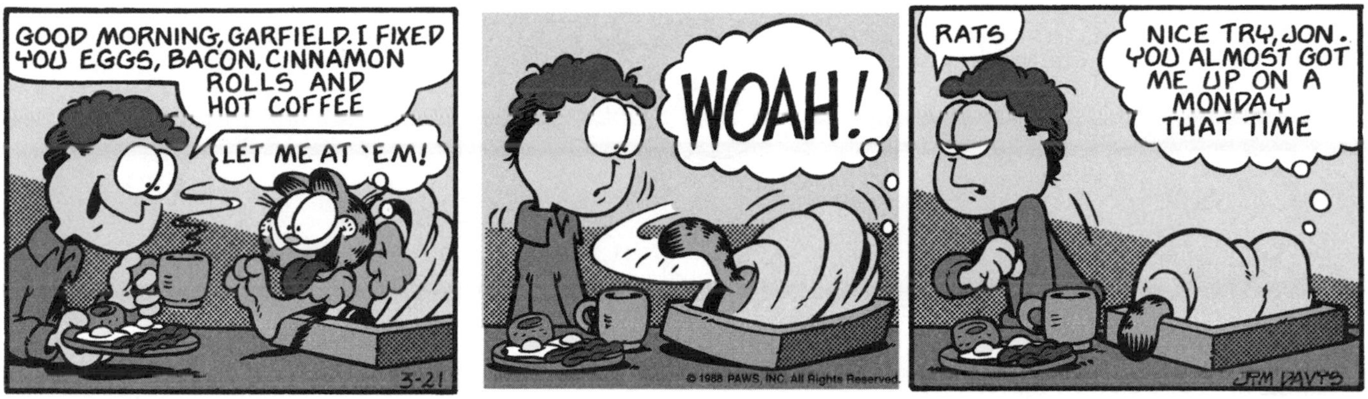
GOOD MORNING, GARFIELD. I FIXED YOU EGGS, BACON, CINNAMON ROLLS AND HOT COFFEE
LET ME AT 'EM!
3-21
WOAH!
© 1988 PAWS, INC. All Rights Reserved.
RATS
NICE TRY, JON. YOU ALMOST GOT ME UP ON A MONDAY THAT TIME
JIM DAVIS

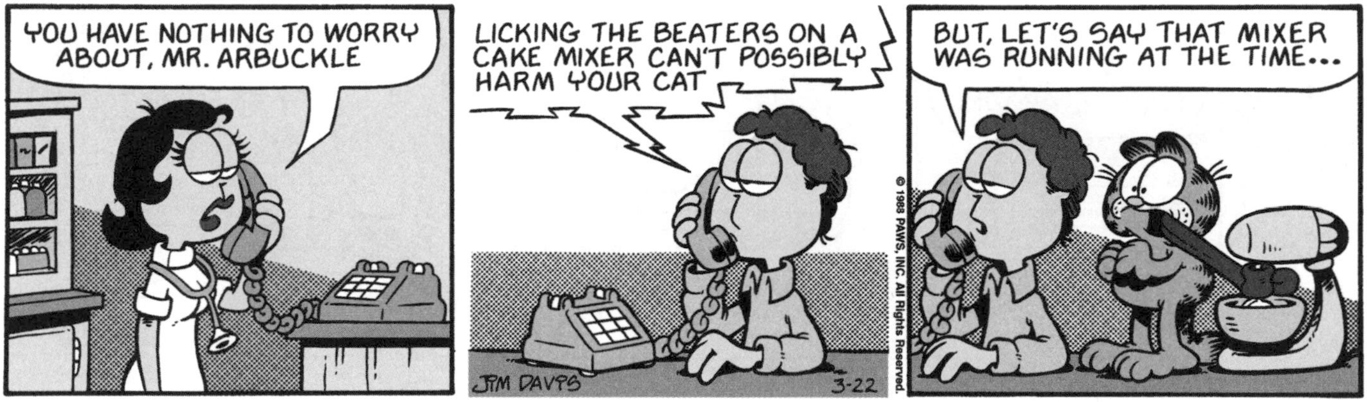
YOU HAVE NOTHING TO WORRY ABOUT, MR. ARBUCKLE
LICKING THE BEATERS ON A CAKE MIXER CAN'T POSSIBLY HARM YOUR CAT
JIM DAVIS
3-22
© 1988 PAWS, INC. All Rights Reserved.
BUT, LET'S SAY THAT MIXER WAS RUNNING AT THE TIME...

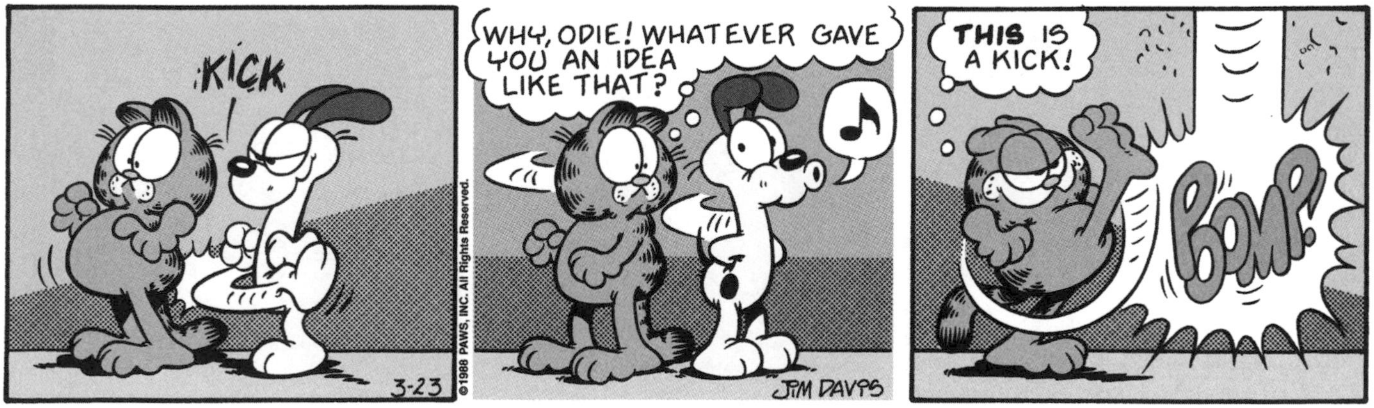
KICK
3-23
© 1988 PAWS, INC. All Rights Reserved.
WHY, ODIE! WHATEVER GAVE YOU AN IDEA LIKE THAT?
JIM DAVIS
THIS IS A KICK!
BOMP!

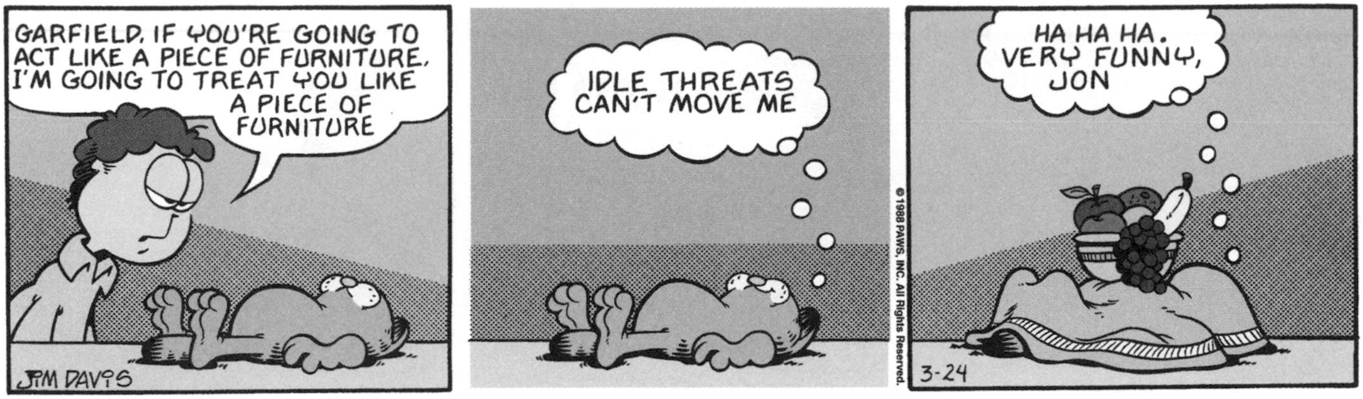
GARFIELD, IF YOU'RE GOING TO ACT LIKE A PIECE OF FURNITURE, I'M GOING TO TREAT YOU LIKE A PIECE OF FURNITURE
JIM DAVIS
IDLE THREATS CAN'T MOVE ME
© 1988 PAWS, INC. All Rights Reserved.
HA HA HA. VERY FUNNY, JON
3-24

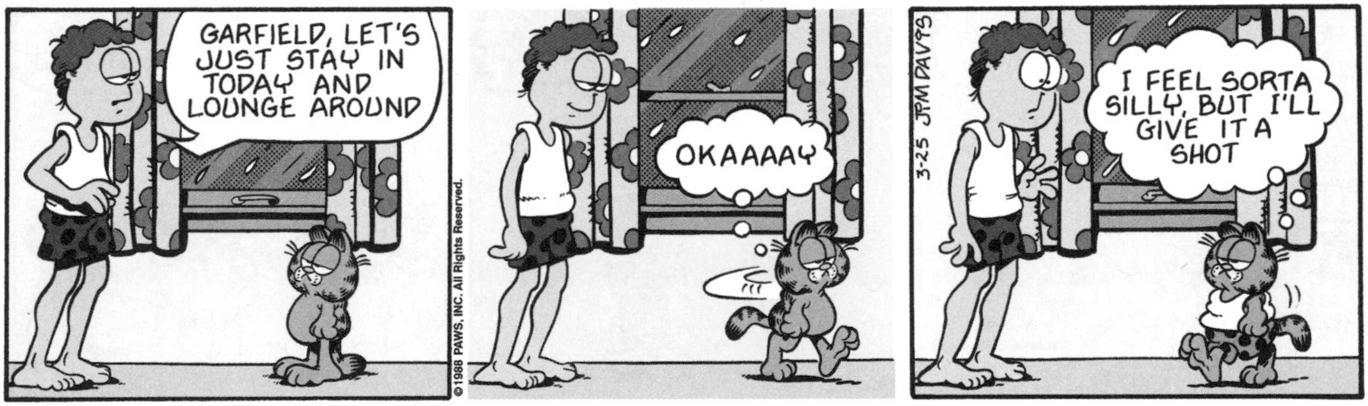
GARFIELD, LET'S JUST STAY IN TODAY AND LOUNGE AROUND
© 1988 PAWS, INC. All Rights Reserved.
OKAAAAY
3-25 JIM DAVIS
I FEEL SORTA SILLY, BUT I'LL GIVE IT A SHOT

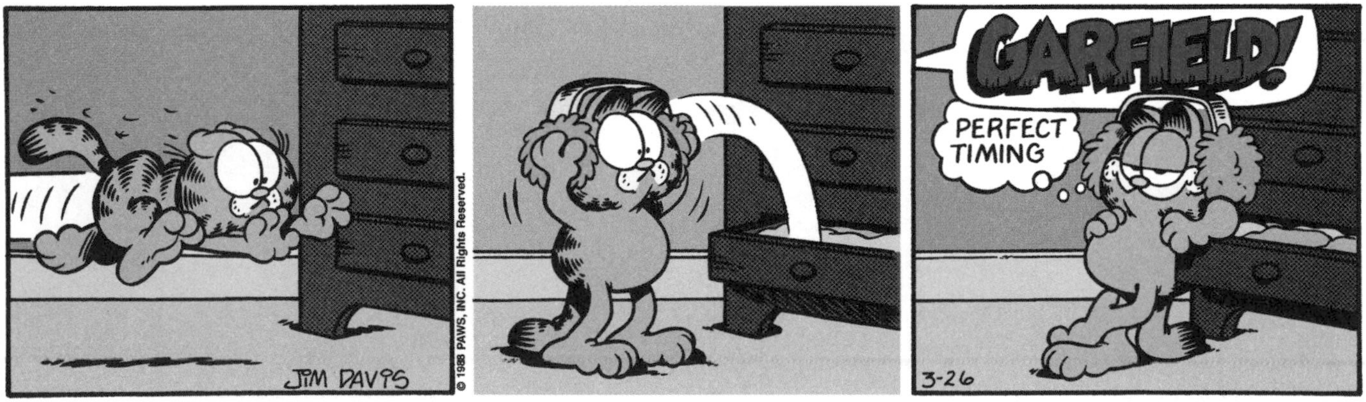
JIM DAVIS
© 1988 PAWS, INC. All Rights Reserved.
GARFIELD!
PERFECT TIMING
3-26

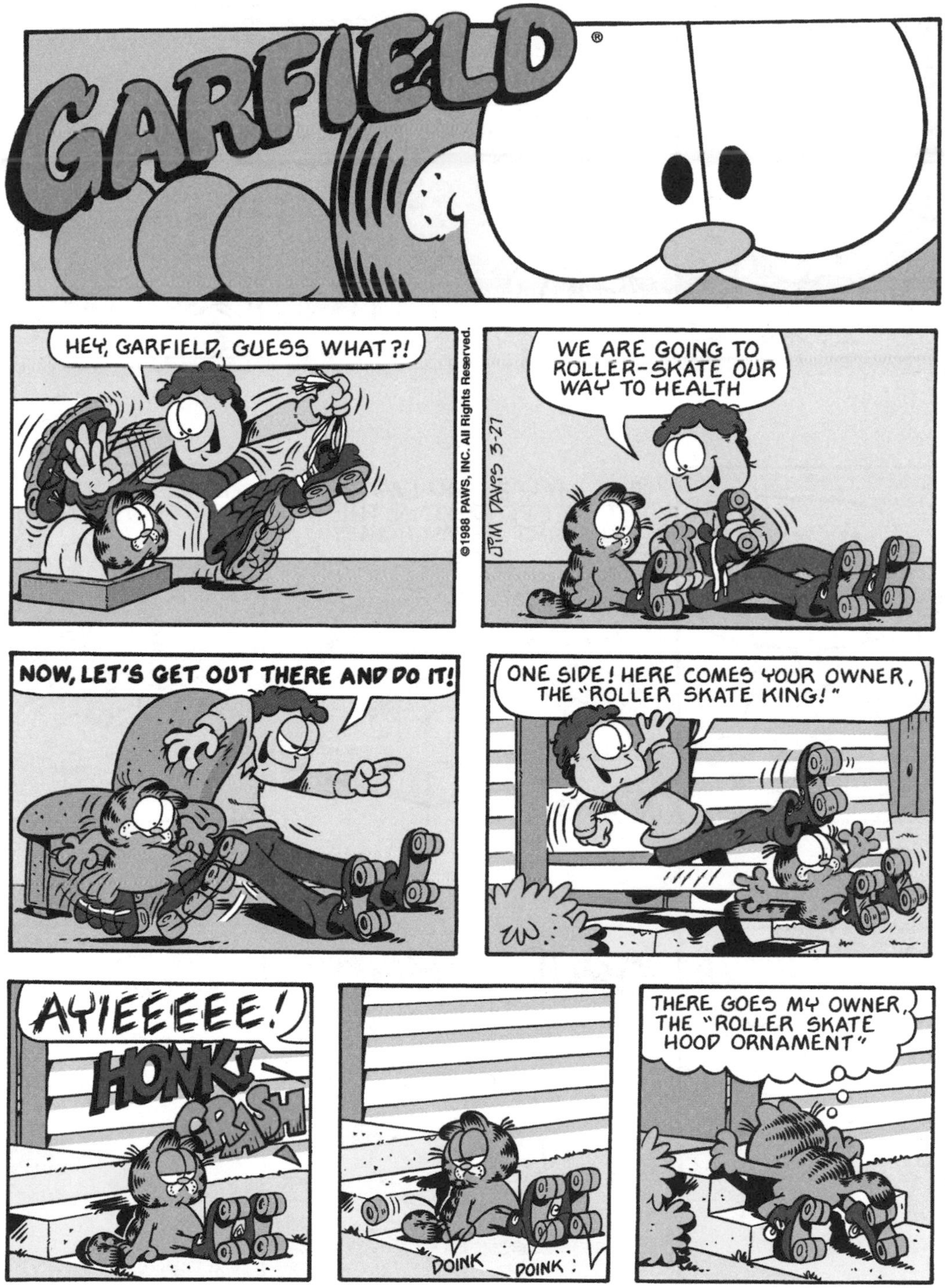

GARFIELD®
HEY, GARFIELD, GUESS WHAT?!
©1988 PAWS, INC. All Rights Reserved.
JPM DAVPS 3-27
WE ARE GOING TO ROLLER-SKATE OUR WAY TO HEALTH
NOW, LET'S GET OUT THERE AND DO IT!
ONE SIDE! HERE COMES YOUR OWNER, THE "ROLLER SKATE KING!"
AYIEEEEE!
HONK!
CRASH
DOINK
DOINK
THERE GOES MY OWNER, THE "ROLLER SKATE HOOD ORNAMENT"

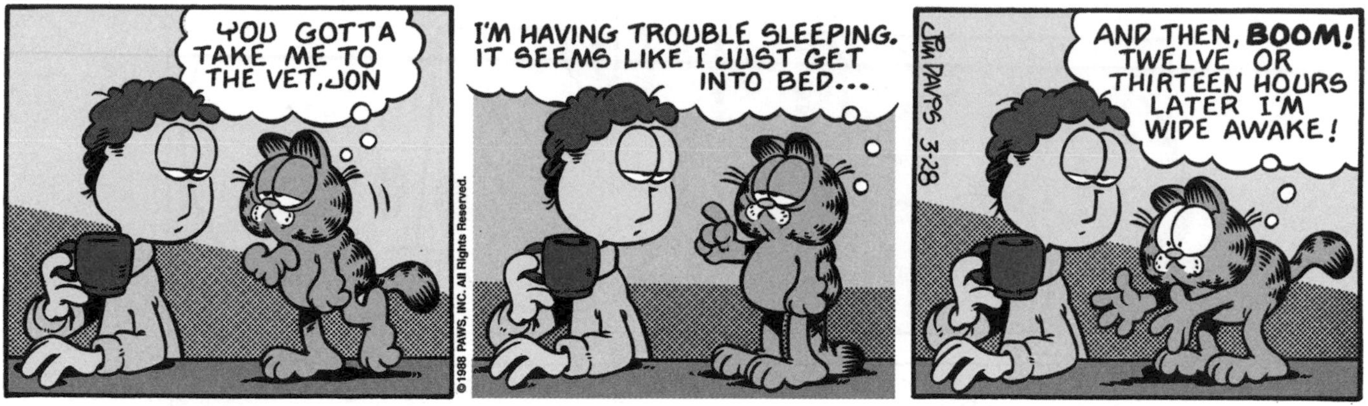
YOU GOTTA TAKE ME TO THE VET, JON
© 1988 PAWS, INC. All Rights Reserved.
I'M HAVING TROUBLE SLEEPING. IT SEEMS LIKE I JUST GET INTO BED...
JIM DAVIS 3-28
AND THEN, **BOOM!** TWELVE OR THIRTEEN HOURS LATER I'M WIDE AWAKE!

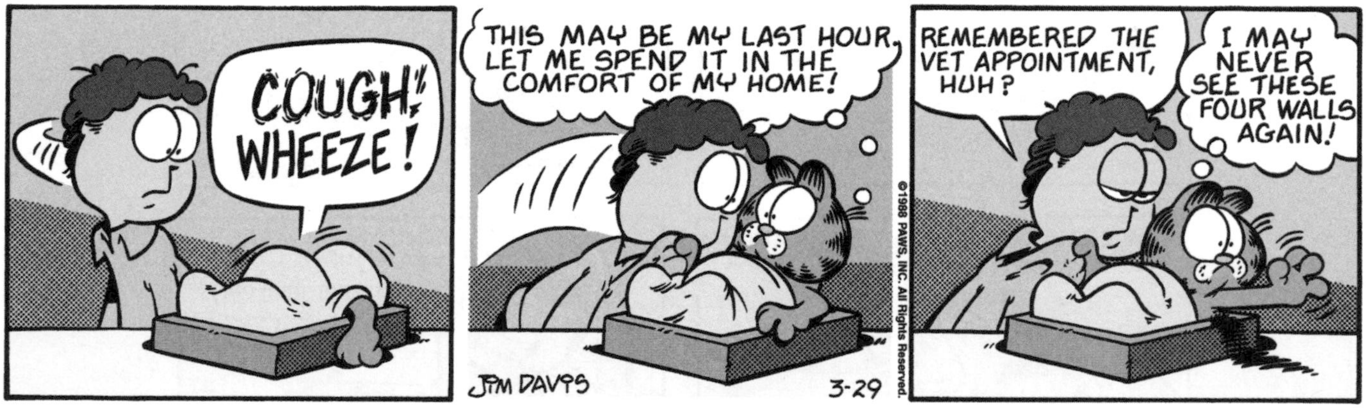
COUGH! WHEEZE!
THIS MAY BE MY LAST HOUR, LET ME SPEND IT IN THE COMFORT OF MY HOME!
JIM DAVIS
3-29
©1988 PAWS, INC. All Rights Reserved.
REMEMBERED THE VET APPOINTMENT, HUH?
I MAY NEVER SEE THESE FOUR WALLS AGAIN!

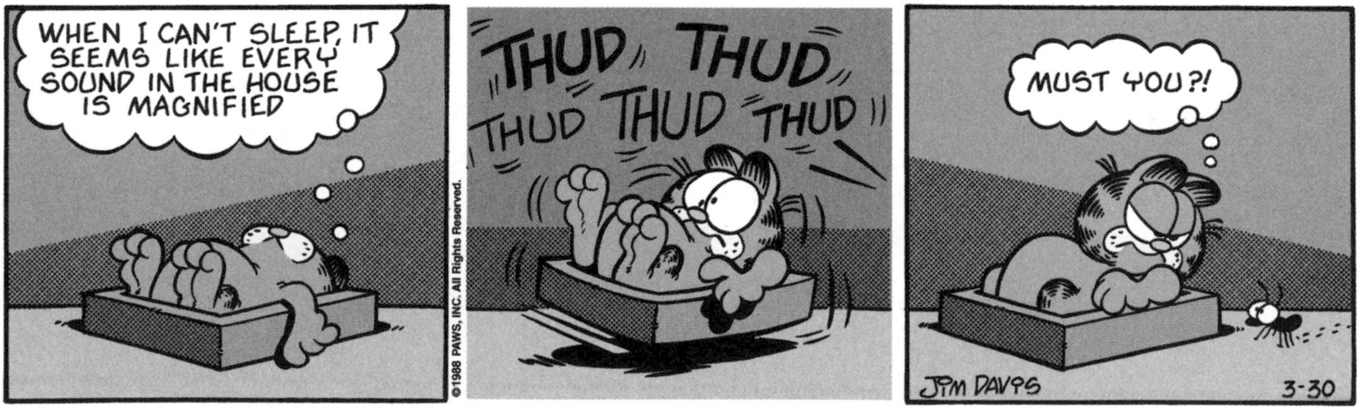
WHEN I CAN'T SLEEP, IT SEEMS LIKE EVERY SOUND IN THE HOUSE IS MAGNIFIED
©1988 PAWS, INC. All Rights Reserved.
THUD THUD THUD THUD THUD
MUST YOU?!
JIM DAVIS
3-30

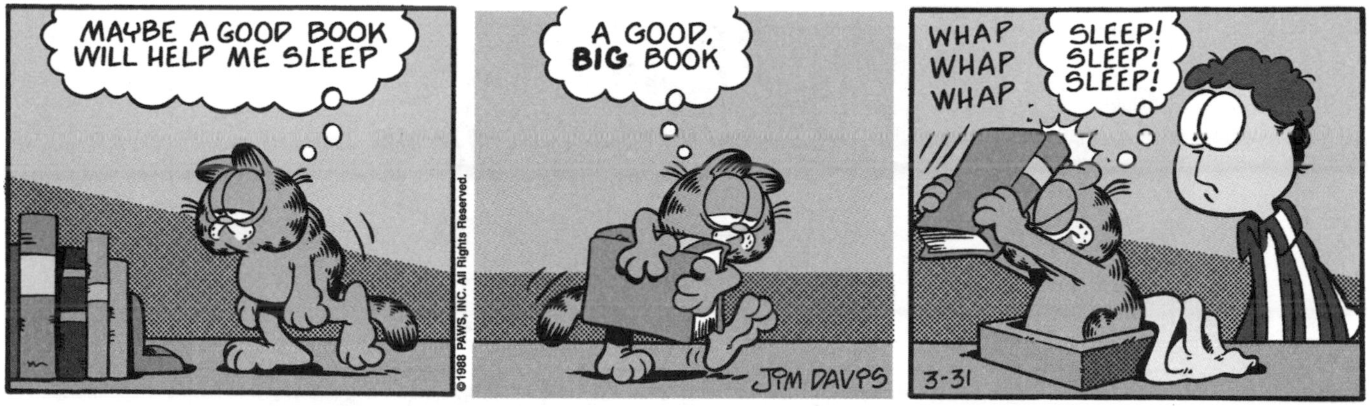
MAYBE A GOOD BOOK WILL HELP ME SLEEP
©1988 PAWS, INC. All Rights Reserved.
A GOOD, BIG BOOK
JIM DAVIS
WHAP WHAP WHAP
SLEEP! SLEEP! SLEEP!
3-31

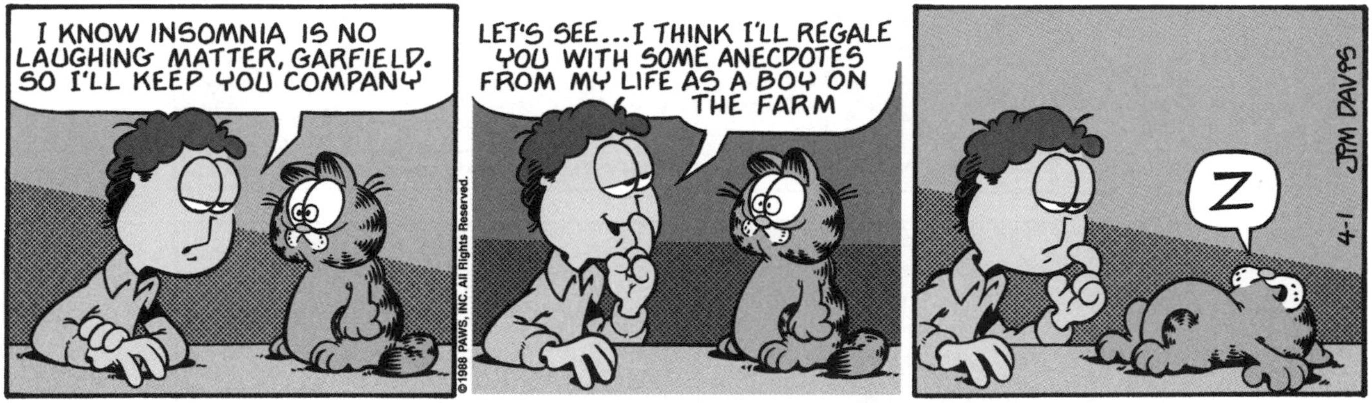
I KNOW INSOMNIA IS NO LAUGHING MATTER, GARFIELD. SO I'LL KEEP YOU COMPANY
©1988 PAWS, INC. All Rights Reserved.
LET'S SEE...I THINK I'LL REGALE YOU WITH SOME ANECDOTES FROM MY LIFE AS A BOY ON THE FARM
Z
JIM DAVIS
4-1

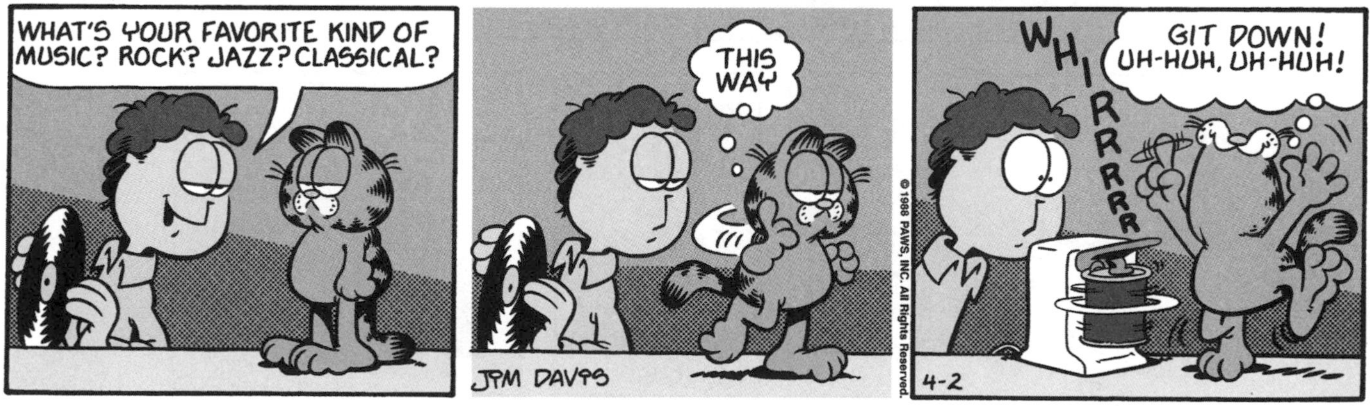
WHAT'S YOUR FAVORITE KIND OF MUSIC? ROCK? JAZZ? CLASSICAL?
THIS WAY
JIM DAVIS
©1988 PAWS, INC. All Rights Reserved.
WHIRRRRR
GIT DOWN! UH-HUH, UH-HUH!
4-2

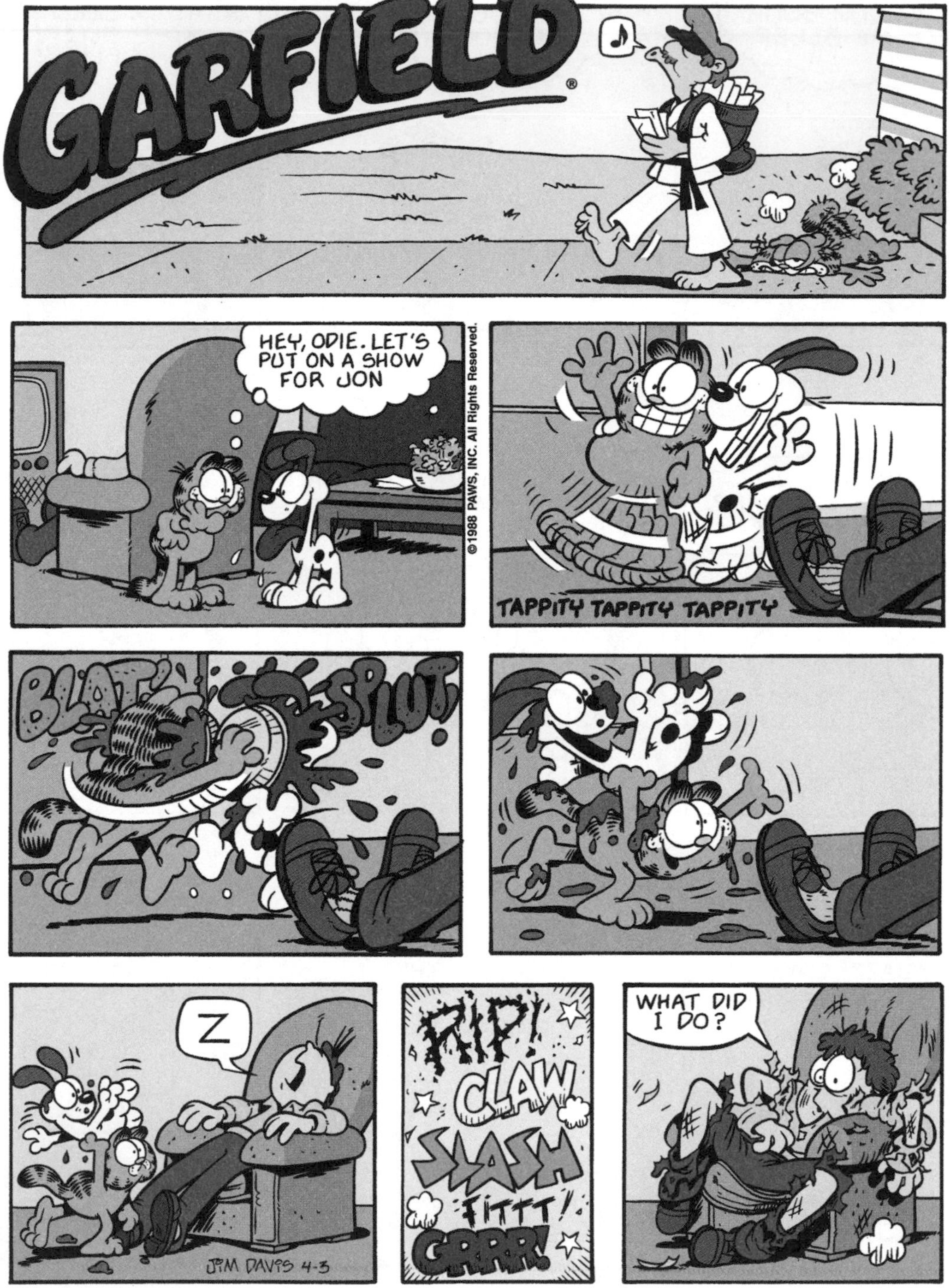
GARFIELD®
♪
HEY, ODIE. LET'S PUT ON A SHOW FOR JON
TAPPITY TAPPITY TAPPITY
BLAT!
SPLUT!
Z
JIM DAVIS 4-3
RIP!
CLAW
SLASH
FITTT!
GRRR!
WHAT DID I DO?

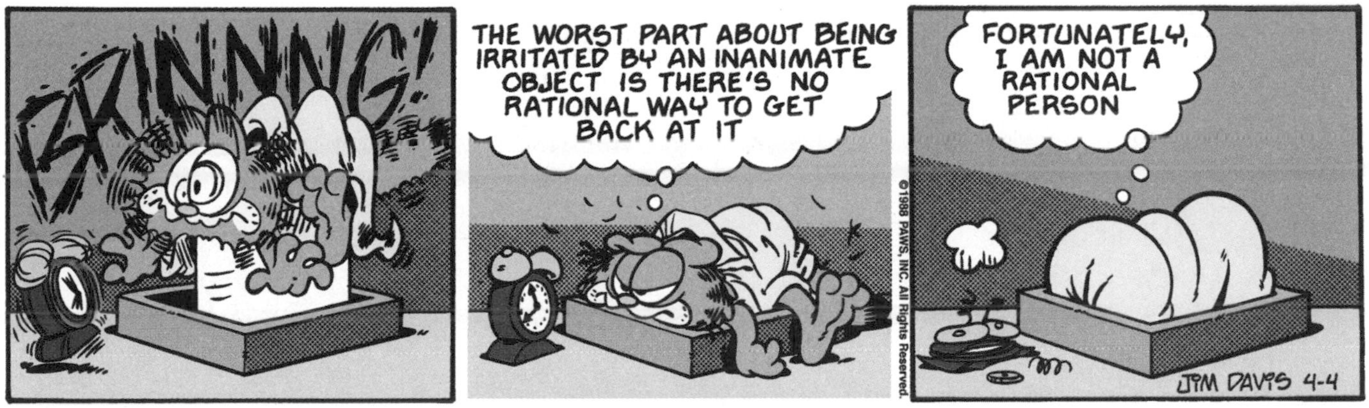
BRINNNG!
THE WORST PART ABOUT BEING IRRITATED BY AN INANIMATE OBJECT IS THERE'S NO RATIONAL WAY TO GET BACK AT IT
©1988 PAWS, INC. All Rights Reserved.
FORTUNATELY, I AM NOT A RATIONAL PERSON
JIM DAVIS 4-4

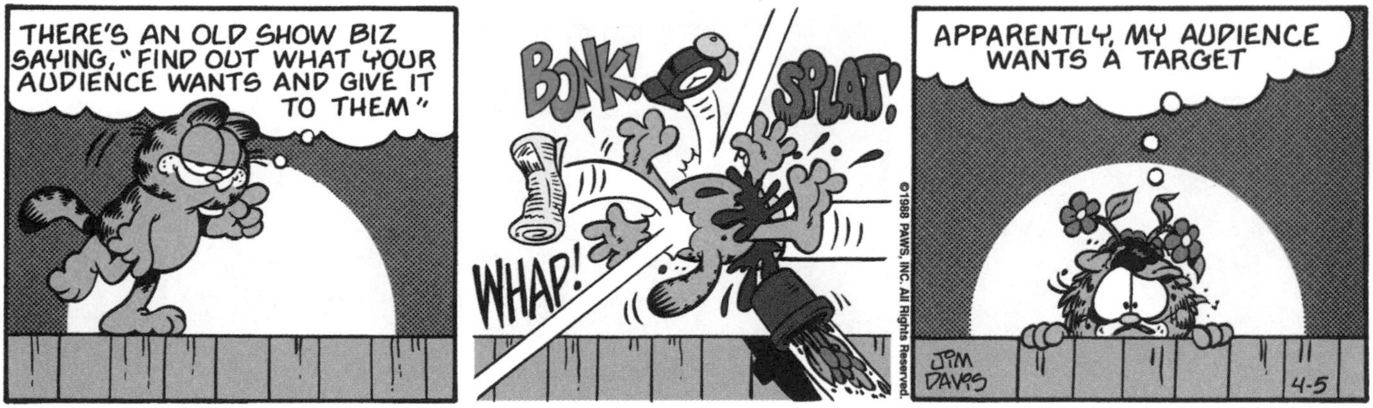
THERE'S AN OLD SHOW BIZ SAYING, "FIND OUT WHAT YOUR AUDIENCE WANTS AND GIVE IT TO THEM"
BONK!
SPLAT!
WHAP!
©1988 PAWS, INC. All Rights Reserved.
APPARENTLY, MY AUDIENCE WANTS A TARGET
JIM DAVIS
4-5

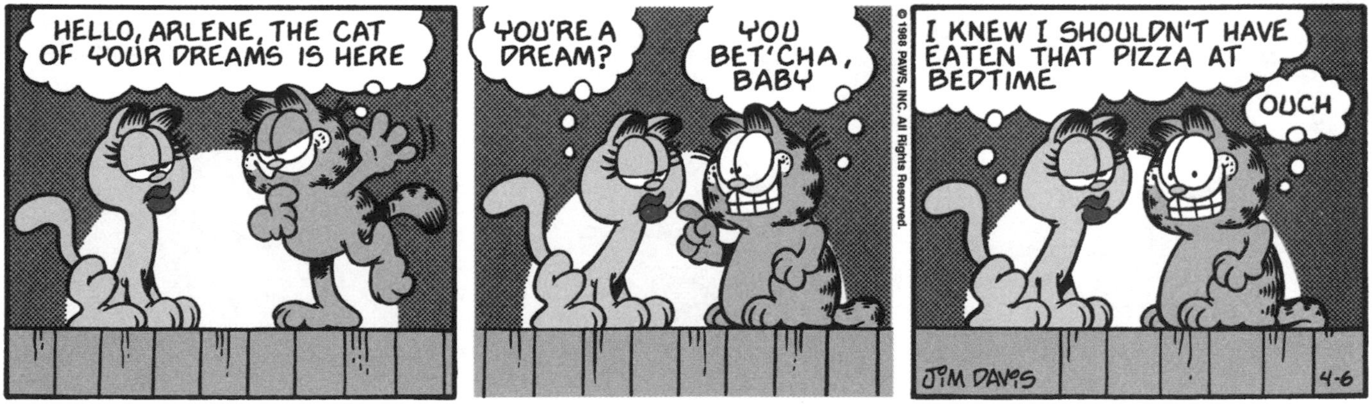
HELLO, ARLENE, THE CAT OF YOUR DREAMS IS HERE
YOU'RE A DREAM?
YOU BET'CHA, BABY
©1988 PAWS, INC. All Rights Reserved.
I KNEW I SHOULDN'T HAVE EATEN THAT PIZZA AT BEDTIME
OUCH
JIM DAVIS
4-6

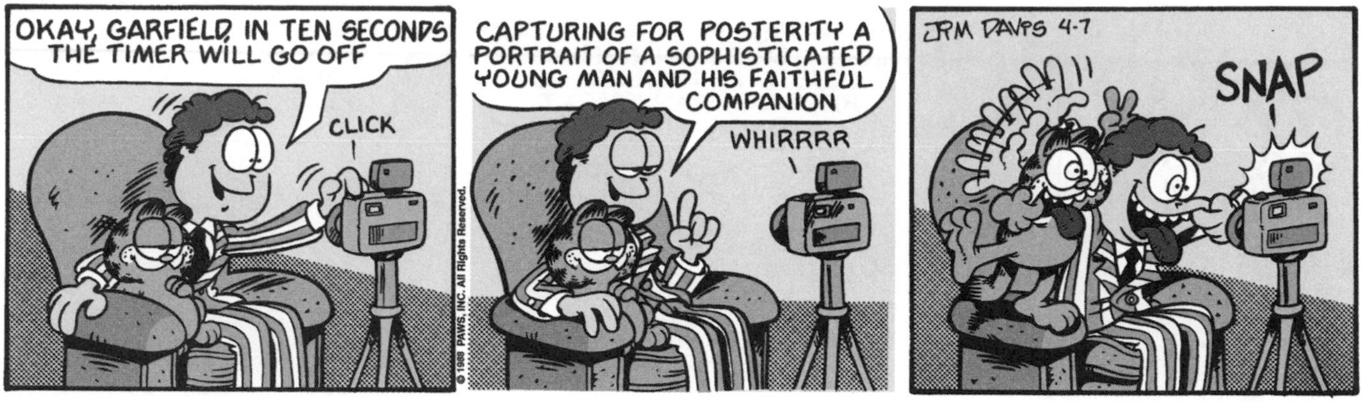
OKAY, GARFIELD, IN TEN SECONDS THE TIMER WILL GO OFF
CLICK
CAPTURING FOR POSTERITY A PORTRAIT OF A SOPHISTICATED YOUNG MAN AND HIS FAITHFUL COMPANION
WHIRRRR
© 1988 PAWS, INC. All Rights Reserved.
JIM DAVIS 4-7
SNAP

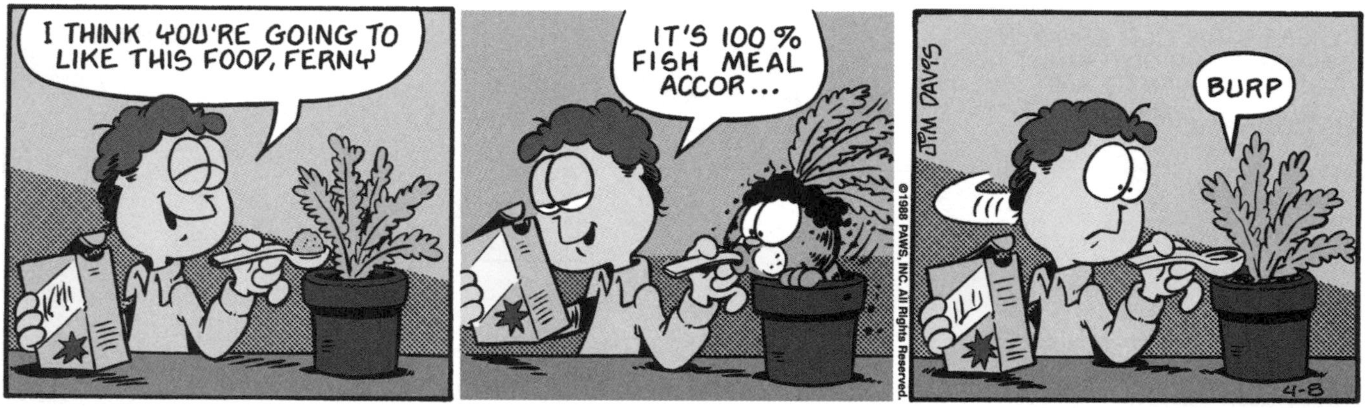
I THINK YOU'RE GOING TO LIKE THIS FOOD, FERNY
IT'S 100% FISH MEAL ACCOR...
© 1988 PAWS, INC. All Rights Reserved.
JIM DAVIS
BURP
4-8

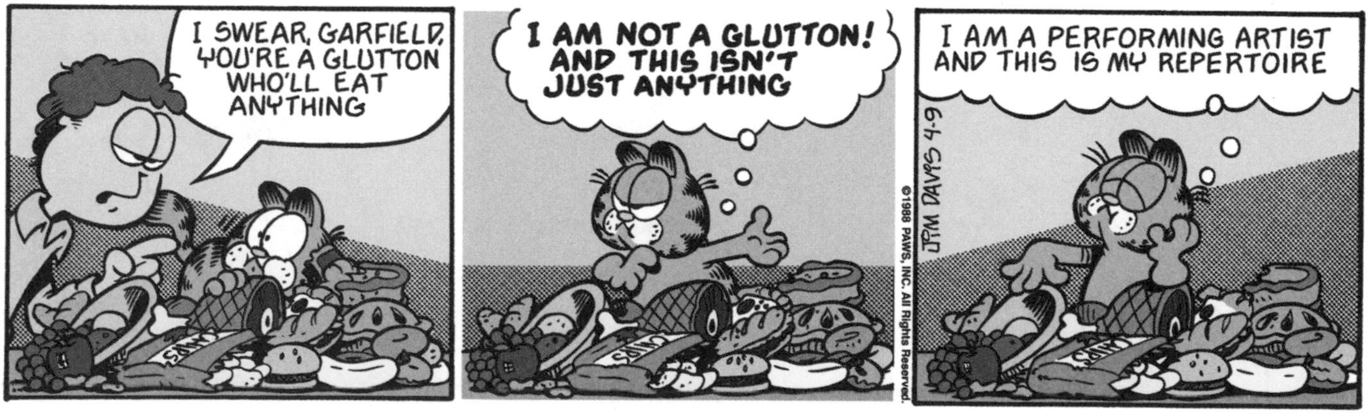
I SWEAR, GARFIELD, YOU'RE A GLUTTON WHO'LL EAT ANYTHING
I AM NOT A GLUTTON! AND THIS ISN'T JUST ANYTHING
© 1988 PAWS, INC. All Rights Reserved.
JIM DAVIS 4-9
I AM A PERFORMING ARTIST AND THIS IS MY REPERTOIRE

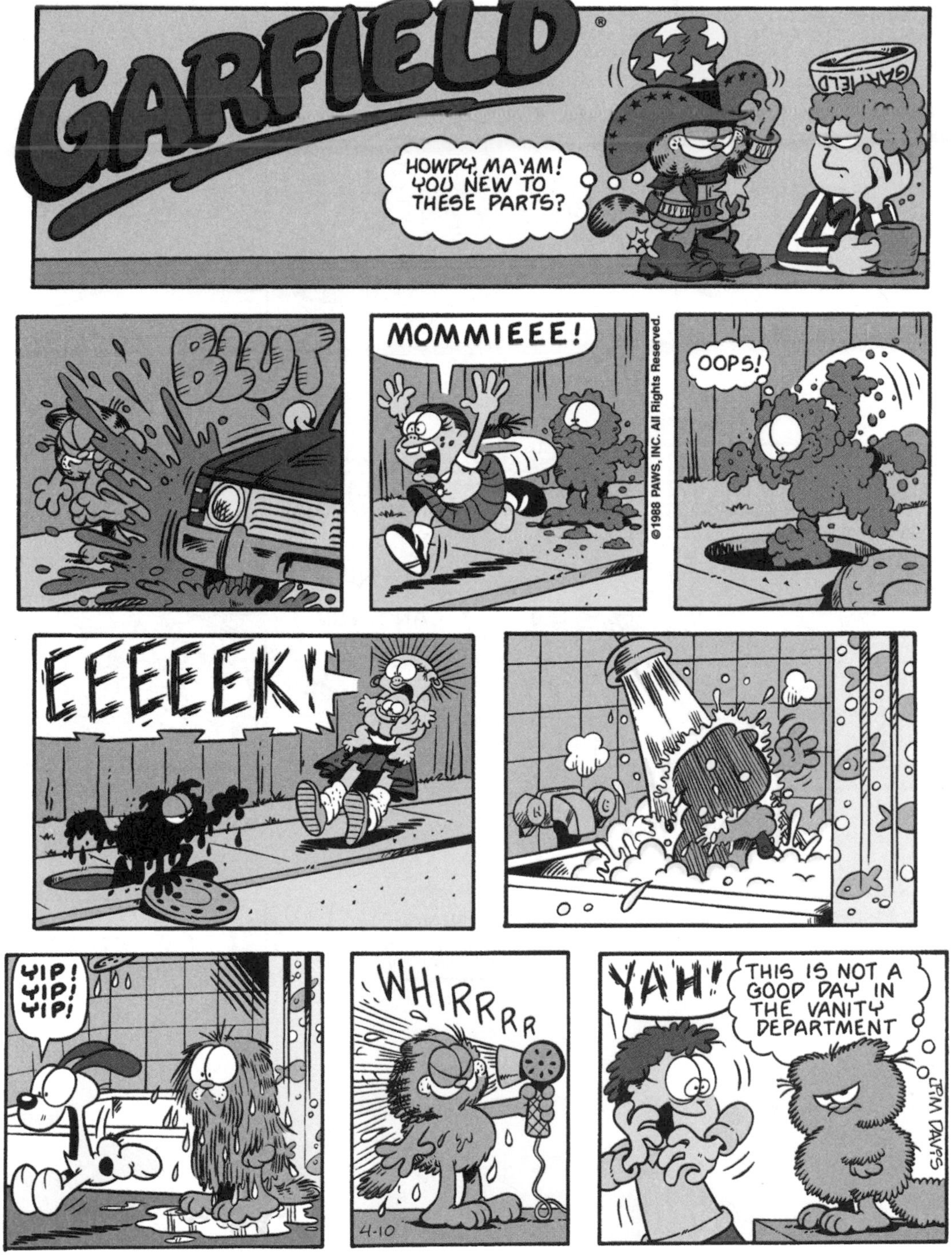
GARFIELD®
HOWDY, MA'AM! YOU NEW TO THESE PARTS?
GARFIELD
BLUT
MOMMIEEE!
©1988 PAWS, INC. All Rights Reserved.
OOPS!
EEEEEK!
YIP! YIP! YIP!
WHIRRRRR
4-10
YAH!
THIS IS NOT A GOOD DAY IN THE VANITY DEPARTMENT
JIM DAVIS

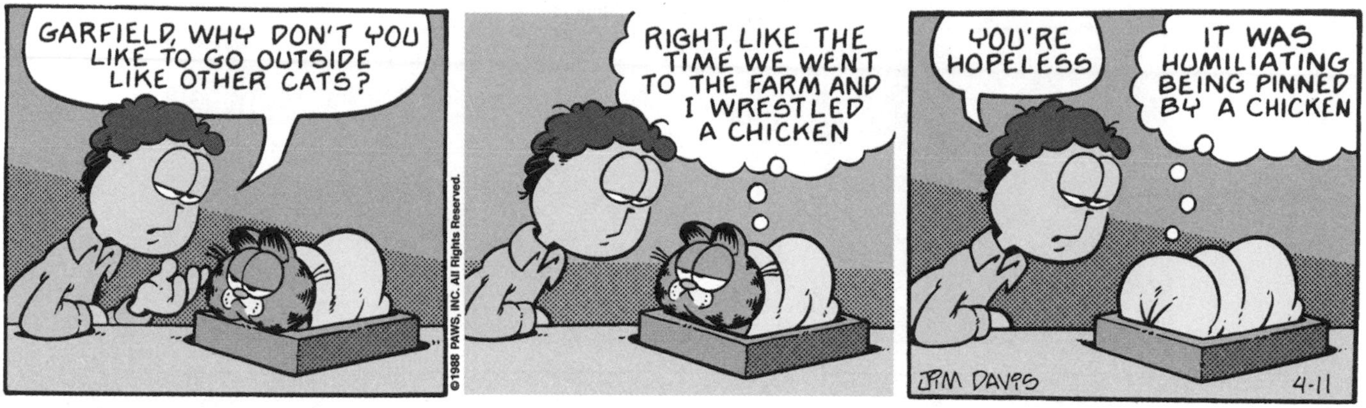
GARFIELD, WHY DON'T YOU LIKE TO GO OUTSIDE LIKE OTHER CATS?
RIGHT, LIKE THE TIME WE WENT TO THE FARM AND I WRESTLED A CHICKEN
YOU'RE HOPELESS
IT WAS HUMILIATING BEING PINNED BY A CHICKEN
JIM DAVIS
4-11
©1988 PAWS, INC. All Rights Reserved.

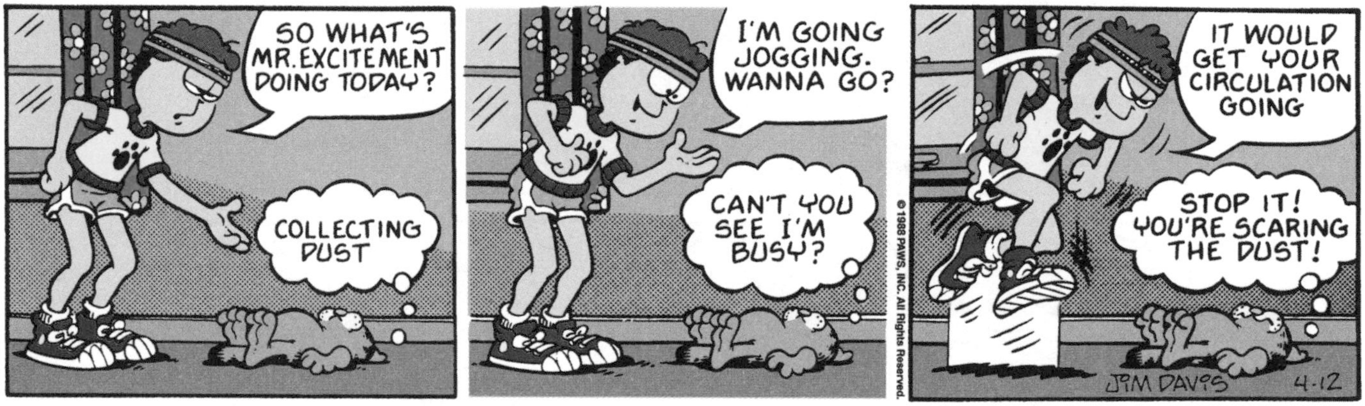
SO WHAT'S MR. EXCITEMENT DOING TODAY?
COLLECTING DUST
I'M GOING JOGGING. WANNA GO?
CAN'T YOU SEE I'M BUSY?
IT WOULD GET YOUR CIRCULATION GOING
STOP IT! YOU'RE SCARING THE DUST!
JIM DAVIS
4-12
©1988 PAWS, INC. All Rights Reserved.

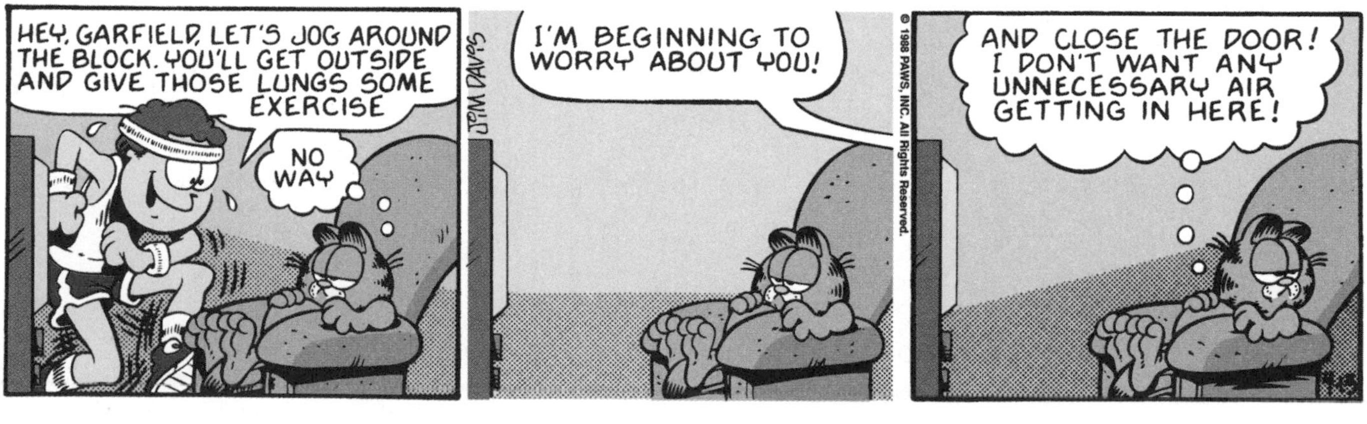
HEY, GARFIELD, LET'S JOG AROUND THE BLOCK. YOU'LL GET OUTSIDE AND GIVE THOSE LUNGS SOME EXERCISE
NO WAY
JIM DAVIS
I'M BEGINNING TO WORRY ABOUT YOU!
AND CLOSE THE DOOR! I DON'T WANT ANY UNNECESSARY AIR GETTING IN HERE!
© 1988 PAWS, INC. All Rights Reserved.

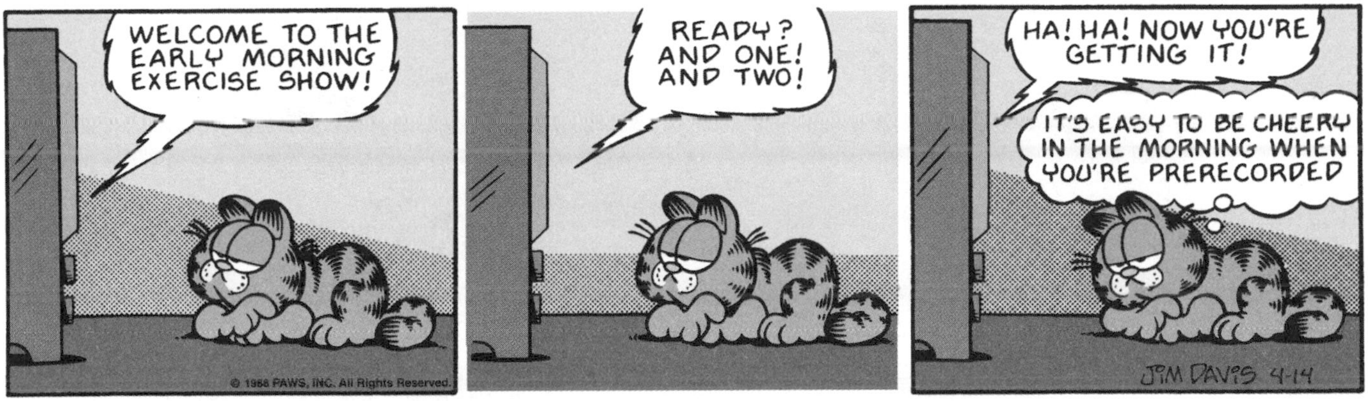
WELCOME TO THE EARLY MORNING EXERCISE SHOW!
© 1988 PAWS, INC. All Rights Reserved.
READY? AND ONE! AND TWO!
HA! HA! NOW YOU'RE GETTING IT!
IT'S EASY TO BE CHEERY IN THE MORNING WHEN YOU'RE PRERECORDED
JIM DAVIS 4-14

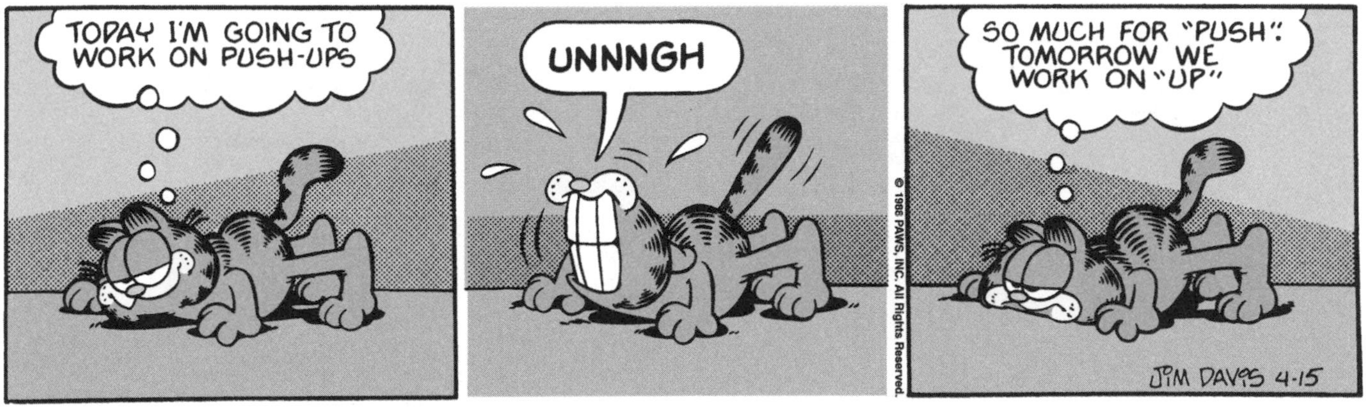
TODAY I'M GOING TO WORK ON PUSH-UPS
UNNNGH
© 1988 PAWS, INC. All Rights Reserved.
SO MUCH FOR "PUSH". TOMORROW WE WORK ON "UP"
JIM DAVIS 4-15

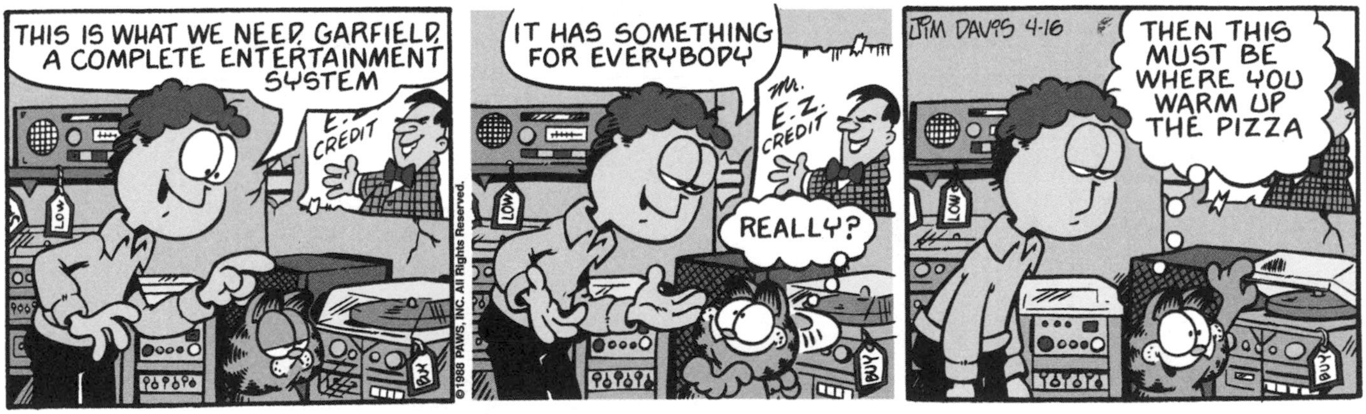
THIS IS WHAT WE NEED, GARFIELD, A COMPLETE ENTERTAINMENT SYSTEM
E.Z. CREDIT
LOW
BUY
© 1988 PAWS, INC. All Rights Reserved.
IT HAS SOMETHING FOR EVERYBODY
MR. E.Z. CREDIT
REALLY?
JIM DAVIS 4-16
THEN THIS MUST BE WHERE YOU WARM UP THE PIZZA

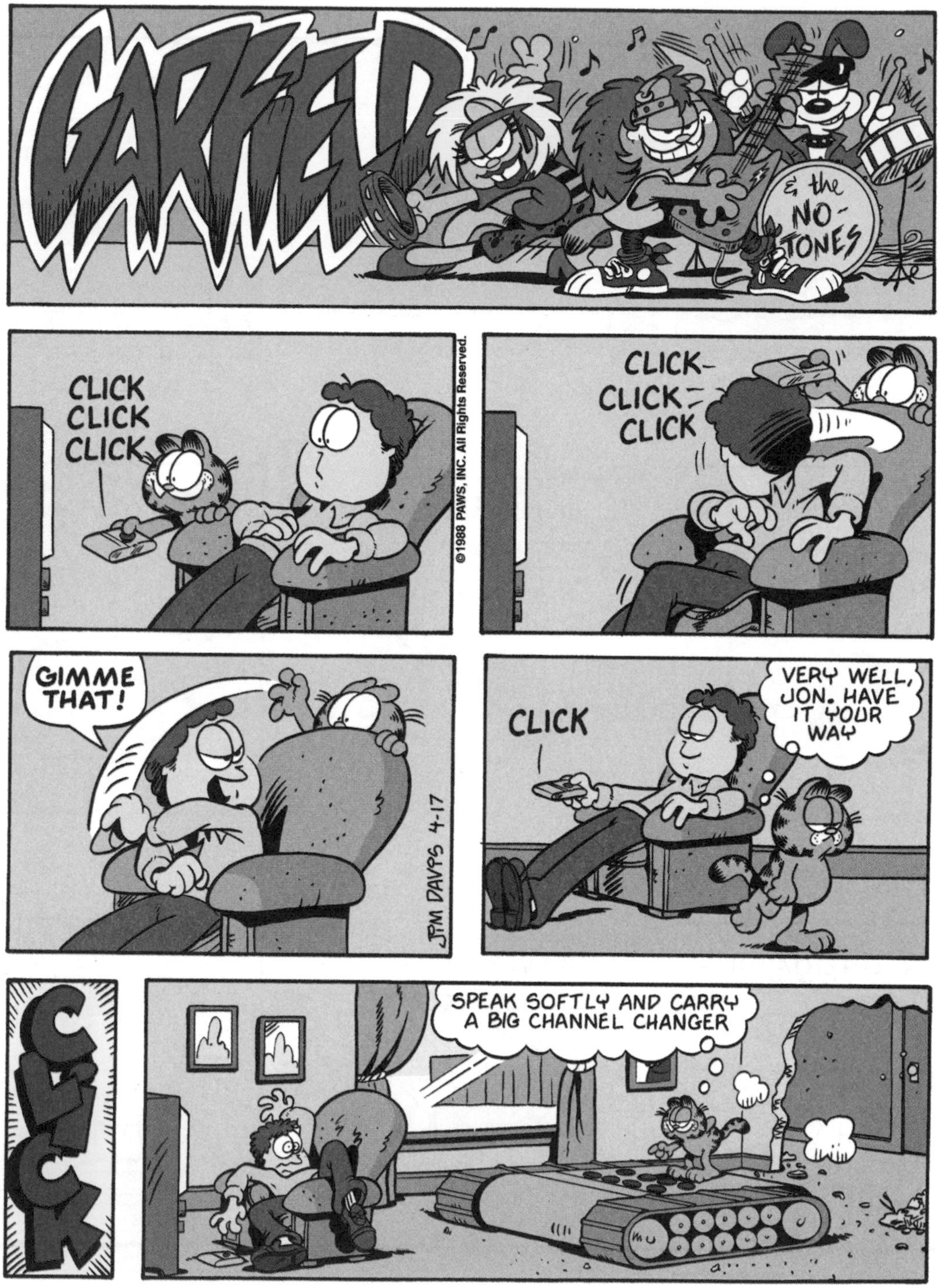
GARFIELD
& the NO-TONES
©1988 PAWS, INC. All Rights Reserved.
CLICK CLICK CLICK
CLICK- CLICK- CLICK
GIMME THAT!
JIM DAVIS 4-17
CLICK
VERY WELL, JON. HAVE IT YOUR WAY
CLICK
SPEAK SOFTLY AND CARRY A BIG CHANNEL CHANGER

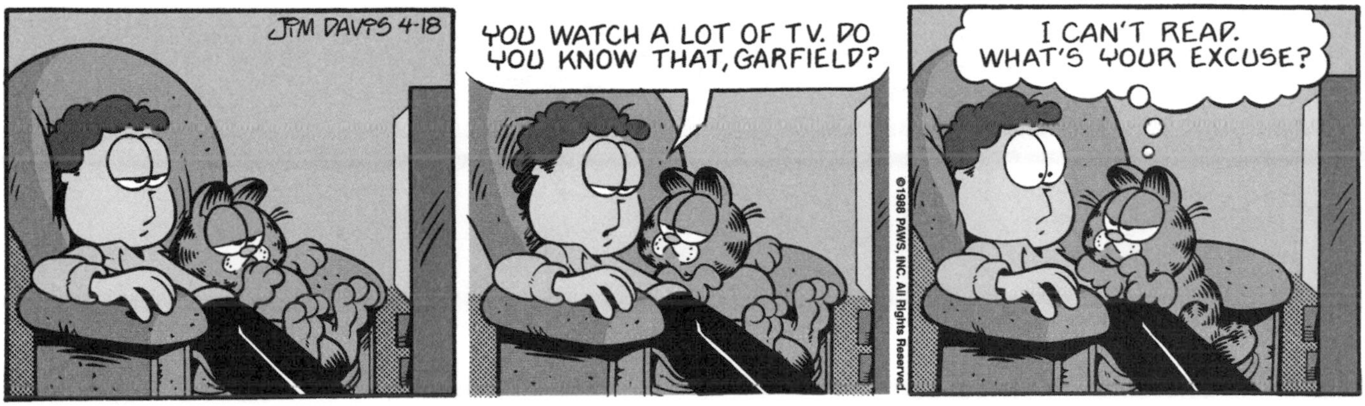
JIM DAVIS 4-18
YOU WATCH A LOT OF T.V. DO YOU KNOW THAT, GARFIELD?
© 1988 PAWS, INC. All Rights Reserved.
I CAN'T READ. WHAT'S YOUR EXCUSE?

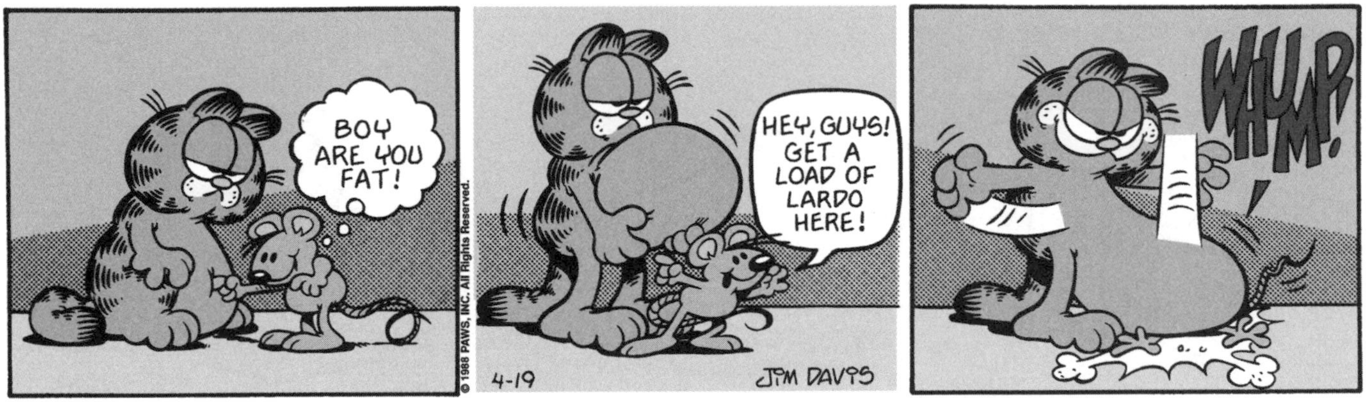
BOY ARE YOU FAT!
© 1988 PAWS, INC. All Rights Reserved.
HEY, GUYS! GET A LOAD OF LARDO HERE!
4-19
JIM DAVIS
WHUMP!

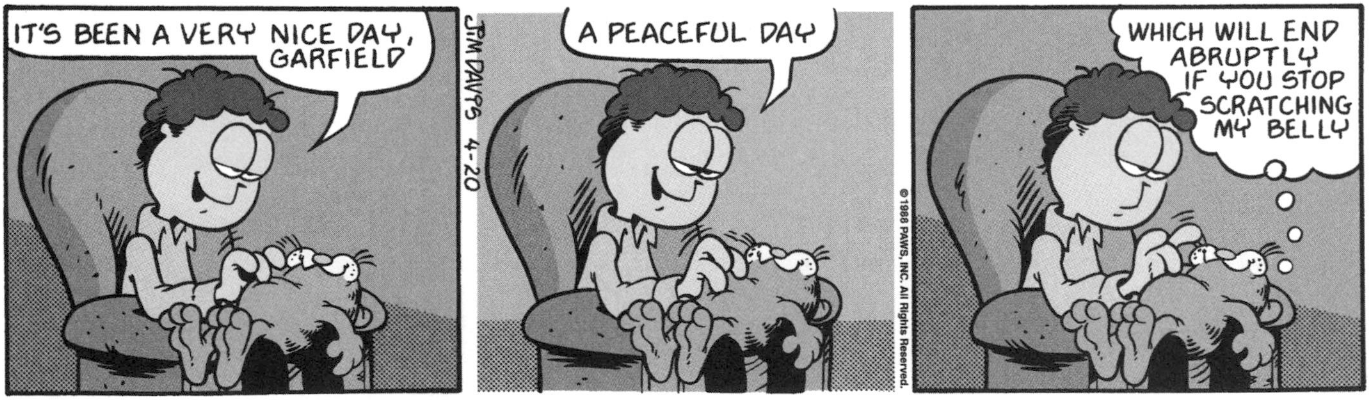
IT'S BEEN A VERY NICE DAY, GARFIELD
JIM DAVIS 4-20
A PEACEFUL DAY
© 1988 PAWS, INC. All Rights Reserved.
WHICH WILL END ABRUPTLY IF YOU STOP SCRATCHING MY BELLY

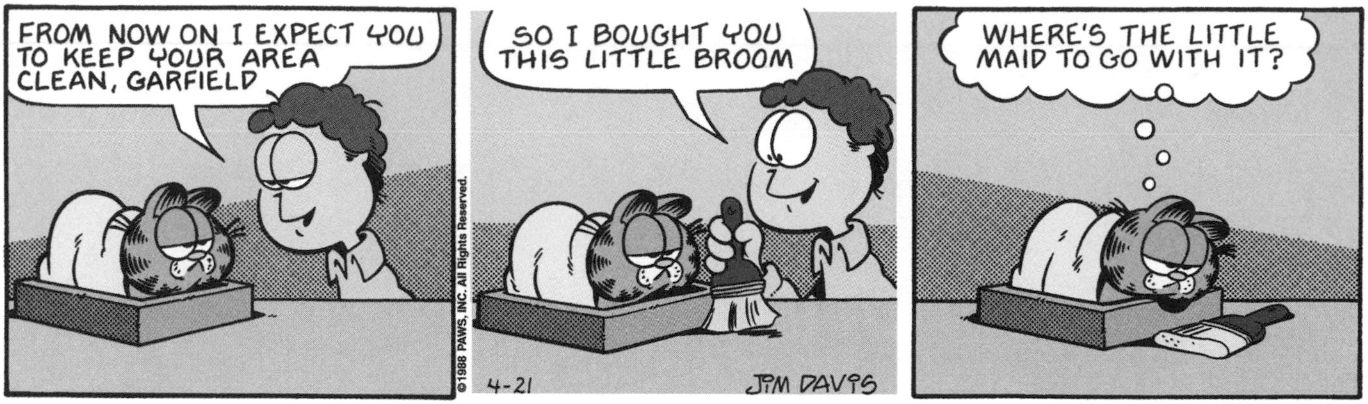
FROM NOW ON I EXPECT YOU TO KEEP YOUR AREA CLEAN, GARFIELD
©1988 PAWS, INC. All Rights Reserved.
SO I BOUGHT YOU THIS LITTLE BROOM
4-21
JIM DAVIS
WHERE'S THE LITTLE MAID TO GO WITH IT?

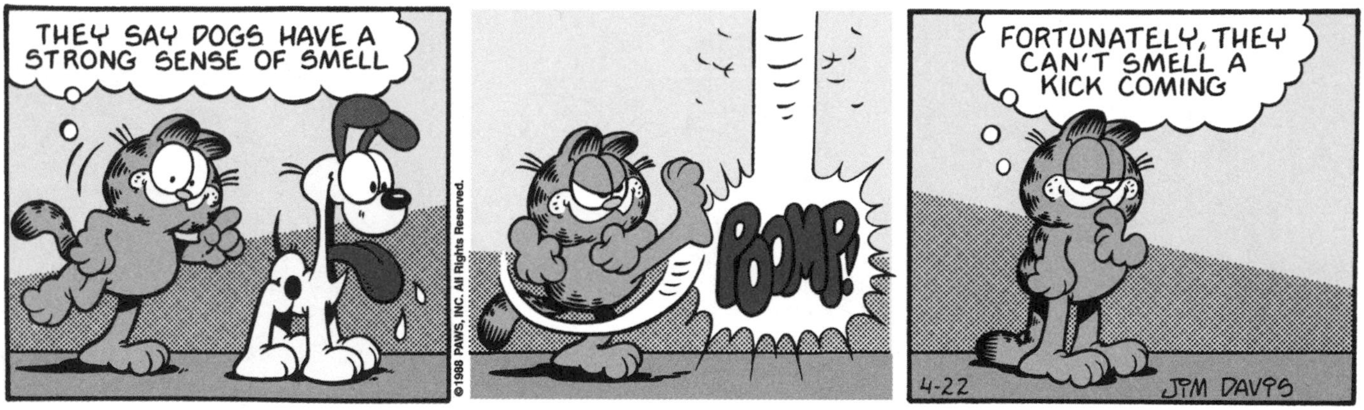
THEY SAY DOGS HAVE A STRONG SENSE OF SMELL
©1988 PAWS, INC. All Rights Reserved.
POOMP!
FORTUNATELY, THEY CAN'T SMELL A KICK COMING
4-22
JIM DAVIS

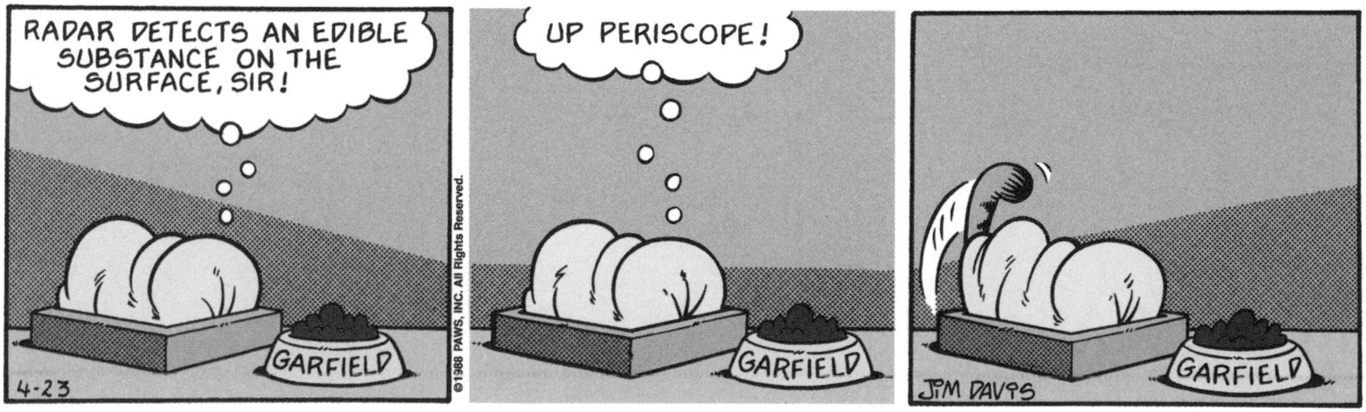
RADAR DETECTS AN EDIBLE SUBSTANCE ON THE SURFACE, SIR!
GARFIELD
4-23
©1988 PAWS, INC. All Rights Reserved.
UP PERISCOPE!
GARFIELD
JIM DAVIS
GARFIELD

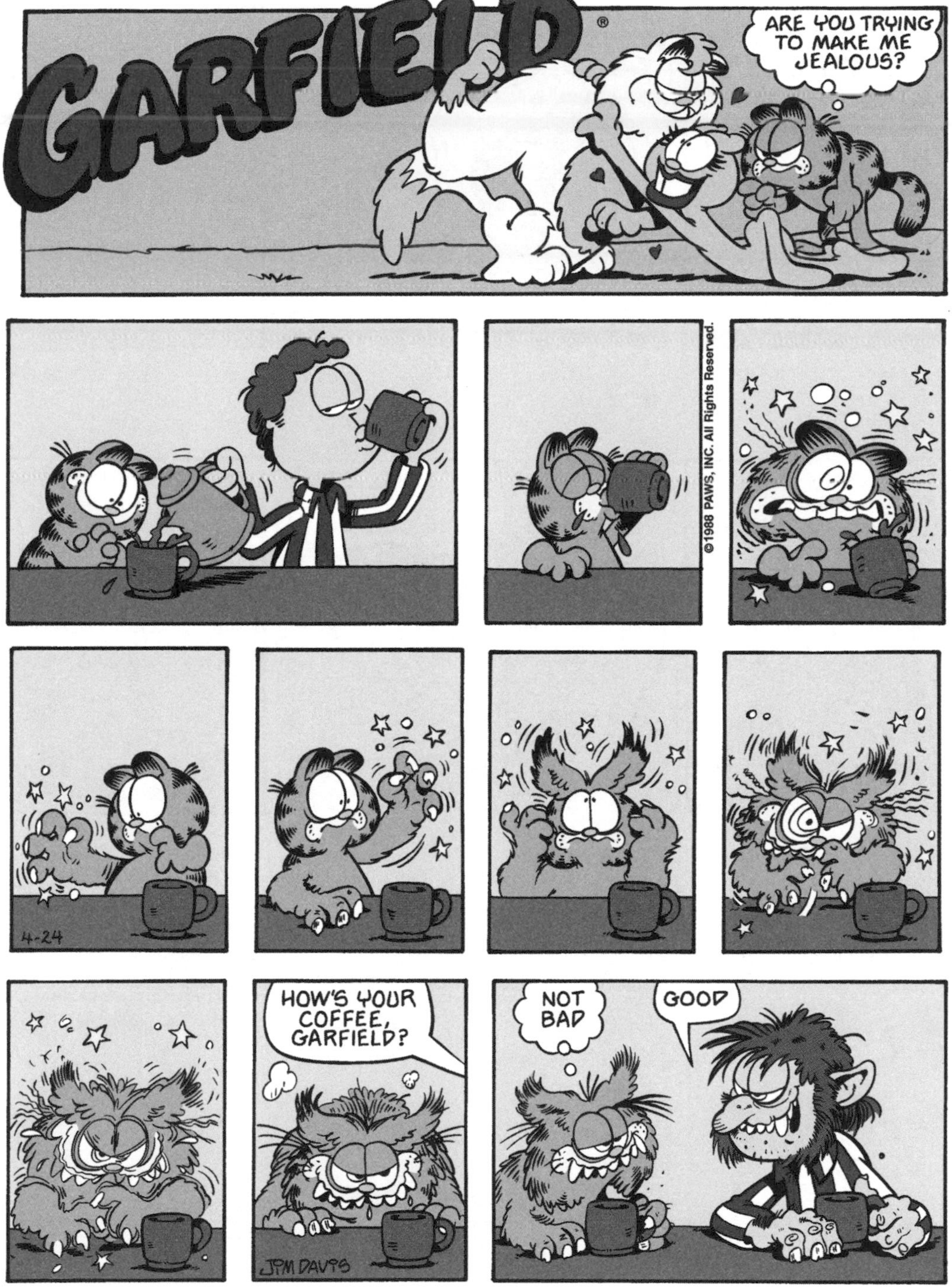
GARFIELD®
ARE YOU TRYING TO MAKE ME JEALOUS?
©1988 PAWS, INC. All Rights Reserved.
4-24
HOW'S YOUR COFFEE, GARFIELD?
JIM DAVIS
NOT BAD
GOOD

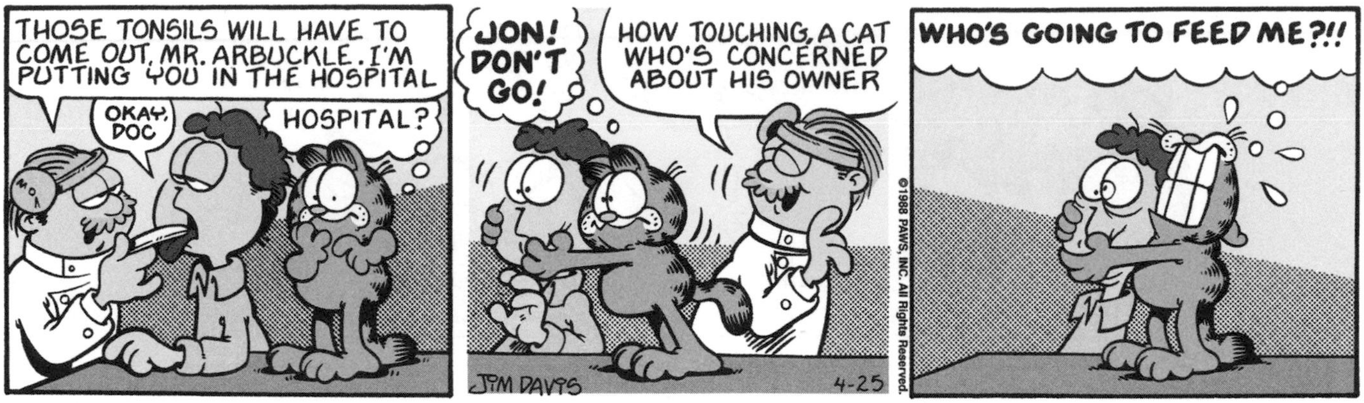
THOSE TONSILS WILL HAVE TO COME OUT, MR. ARBUCKLE. I'M PUTTING YOU IN THE HOSPITAL
OKAY, DOC
HOSPITAL?
JON! DON'T GO!
HOW TOUCHING. A CAT WHO'S CONCERNED ABOUT HIS OWNER
JIM DAVIS 4-25
©1988 PAWS, INC. All Rights Reserved.
WHO'S GOING TO FEED ME?!!

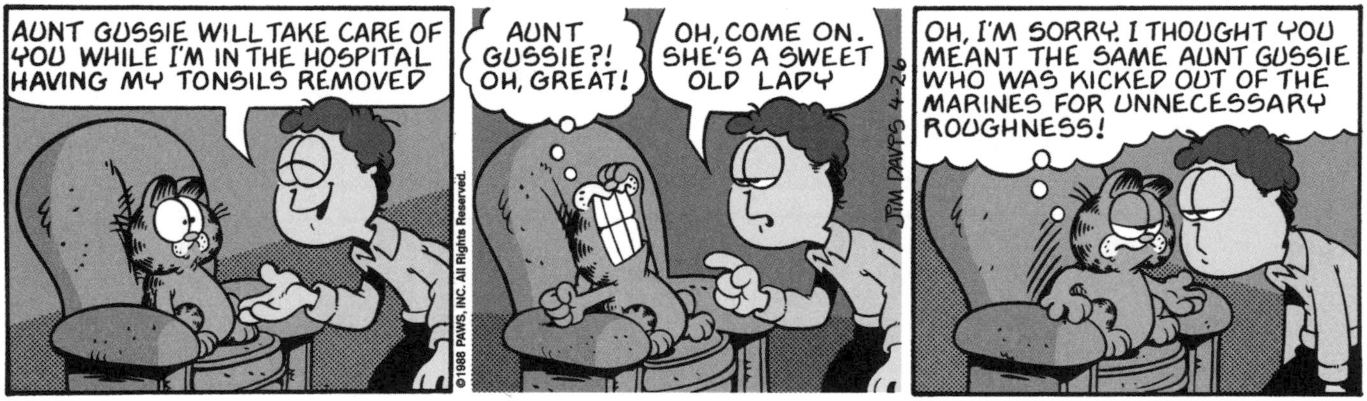
AUNT GUSSIE WILL TAKE CARE OF YOU WHILE I'M IN THE HOSPITAL HAVING MY TONSILS REMOVED
©1988 PAWS, INC. All Rights Reserved.
AUNT GUSSIE?! OH, GREAT!
OH, COME ON. SHE'S A SWEET OLD LADY
JIM DAVIS 4-26
OH, I'M SORRY. I THOUGHT YOU MEANT THE SAME AUNT GUSSIE WHO WAS KICKED OUT OF THE MARINES FOR UNNECESSARY ROUGHNESS!

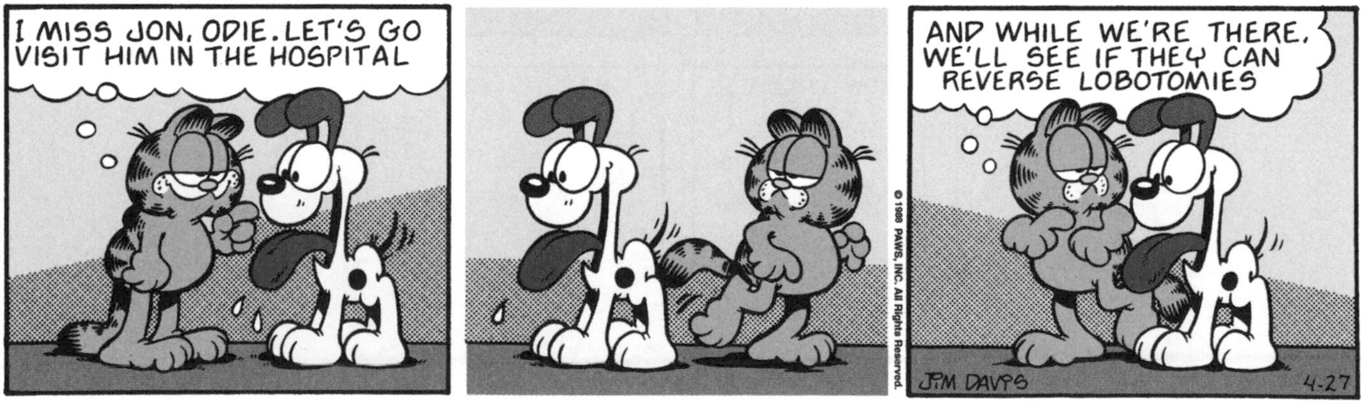
I MISS JON, ODIE. LET'S GO VISIT HIM IN THE HOSPITAL
©1988 PAWS, INC. All Rights Reserved.
AND WHILE WE'RE THERE, WE'LL SEE IF THEY CAN REVERSE LOBOTOMIES
JIM DAVIS 4-27

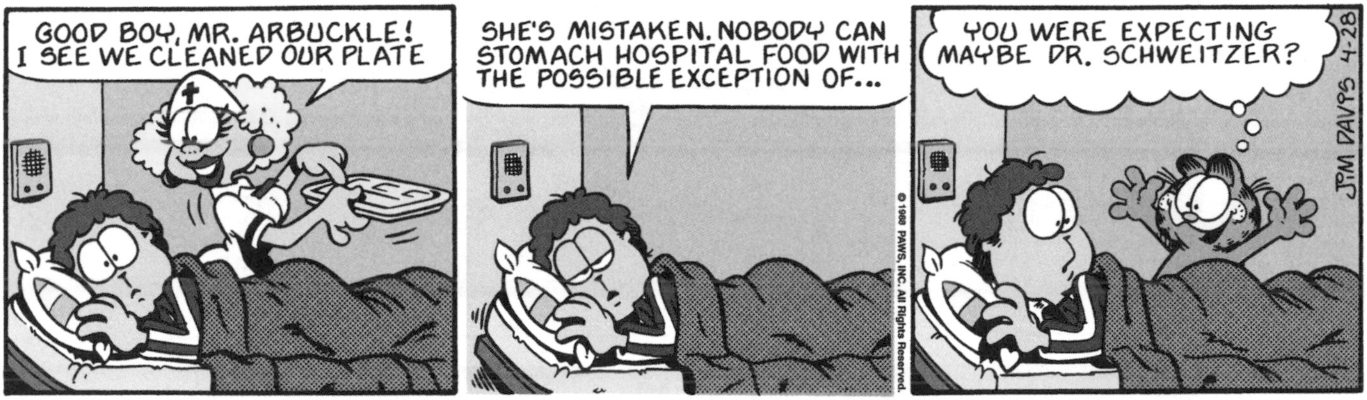
GOOD BOY, MR. ARBUCKLE! I SEE WE CLEANED OUR PLATE
SHE'S MISTAKEN. NOBODY CAN STOMACH HOSPITAL FOOD WITH THE POSSIBLE EXCEPTION OF...
© 1988 PAWS, INC. All Rights Reserved.
YOU WERE EXPECTING MAYBE DR. SCHWEITZER?
JIM DAVIS 4-28

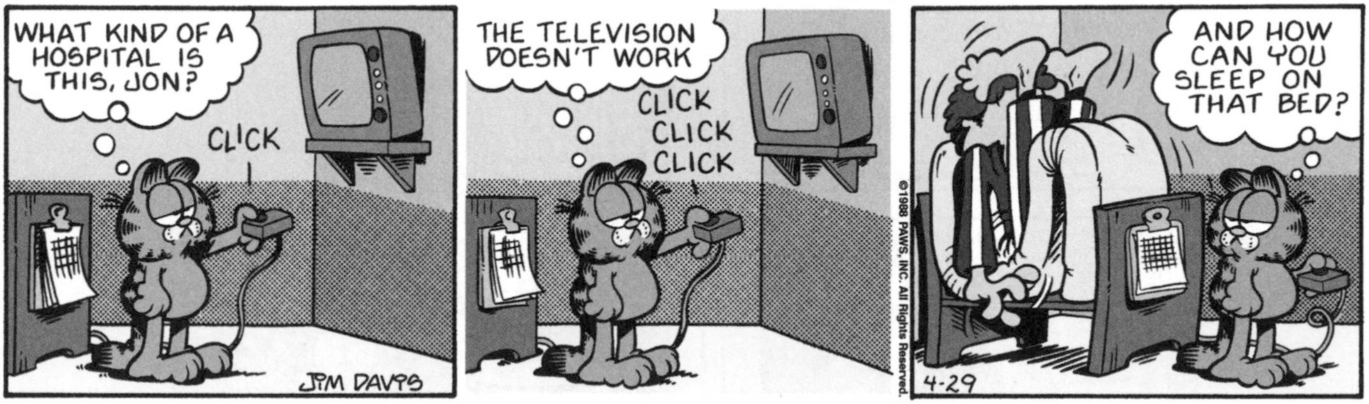
WHAT KIND OF A HOSPITAL IS THIS, JON?
CLICK
JIM DAVIS
THE TELEVISION DOESN'T WORK
CLICK CLICK CLICK
© 1988 PAWS, INC. All Rights Reserved.
AND HOW CAN YOU SLEEP ON THAT BED?
4-29

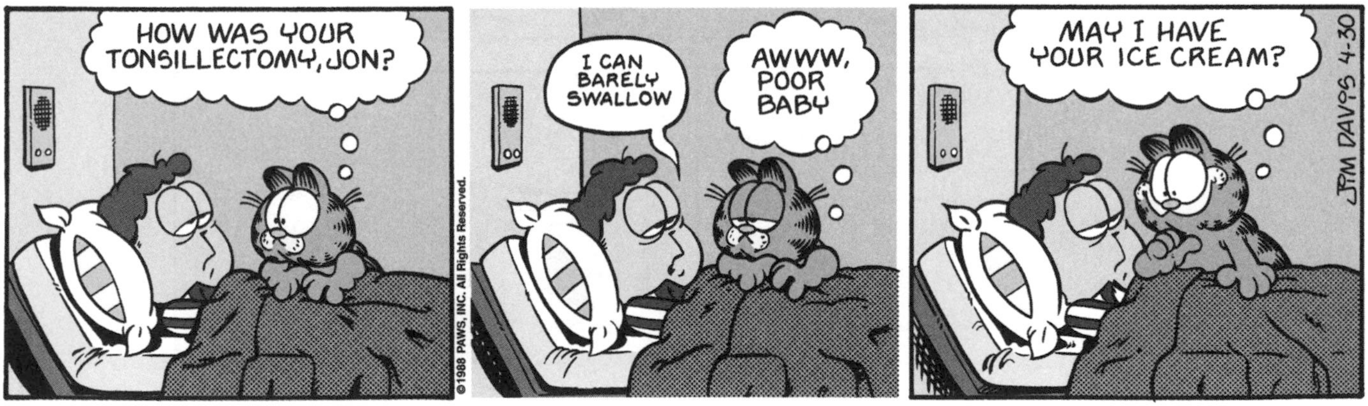
HOW WAS YOUR TONSILLECTOMY, JON?
© 1988 PAWS, INC. All Rights Reserved.
I CAN BARELY SWALLOW
AWWW, POOR BABY
MAY I HAVE YOUR ICE CREAM?
JIM DAVIS 4-30

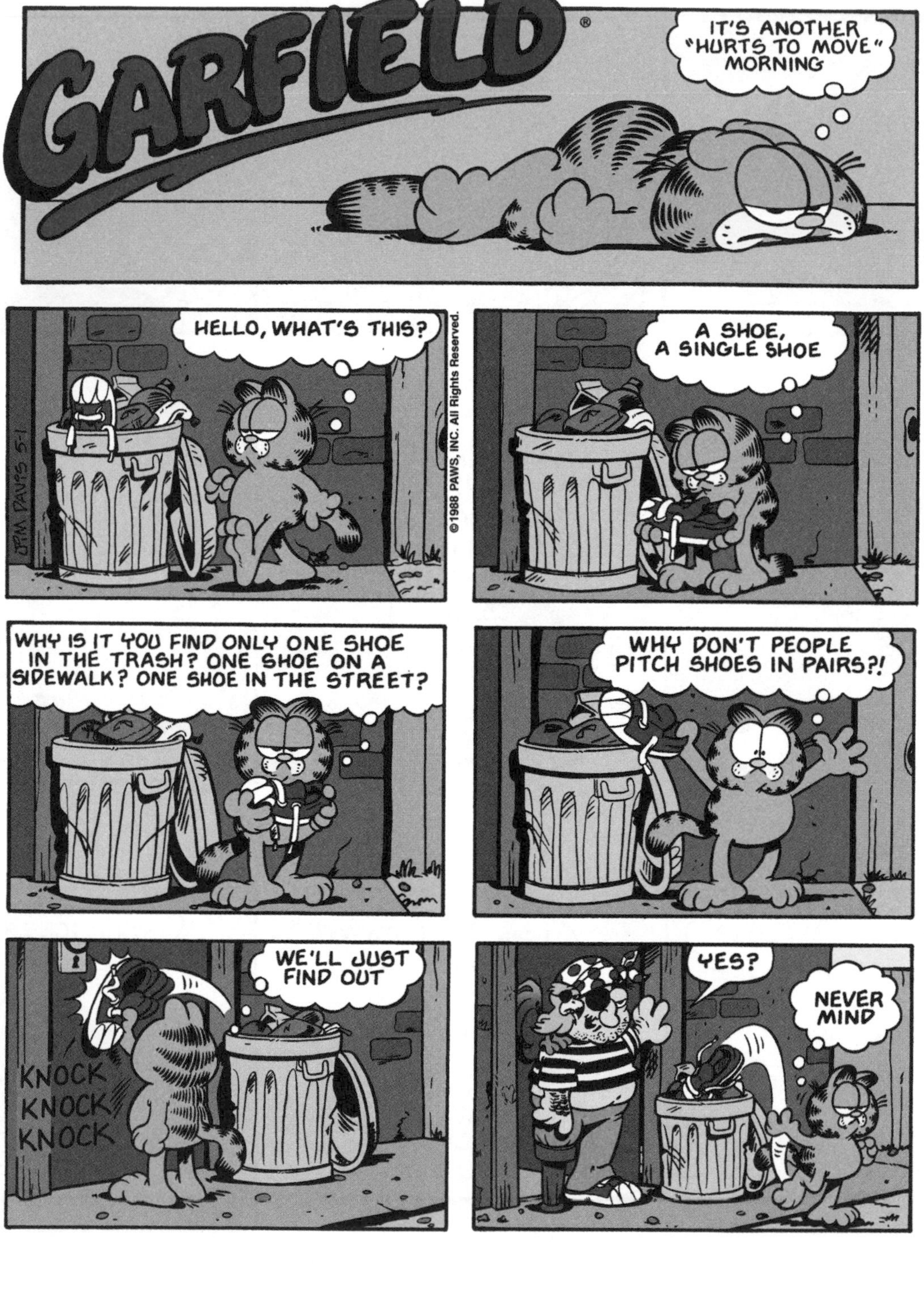
GARFIELD
IT'S ANOTHER "HURTS TO MOVE" MORNING
HELLO, WHAT'S THIS?
JPM DAVIS 5-1
©1988 PAWS, INC. All Rights Reserved.
A SHOE, A SINGLE SHOE
WHY IS IT YOU FIND ONLY ONE SHOE IN THE TRASH? ONE SHOE ON A SIDEWALK? ONE SHOE IN THE STREET?
WHY DON'T PEOPLE PITCH SHOES IN PAIRS?!
WE'LL JUST FIND OUT
KNOCK KNOCK KNOCK
YES?
NEVER MIND

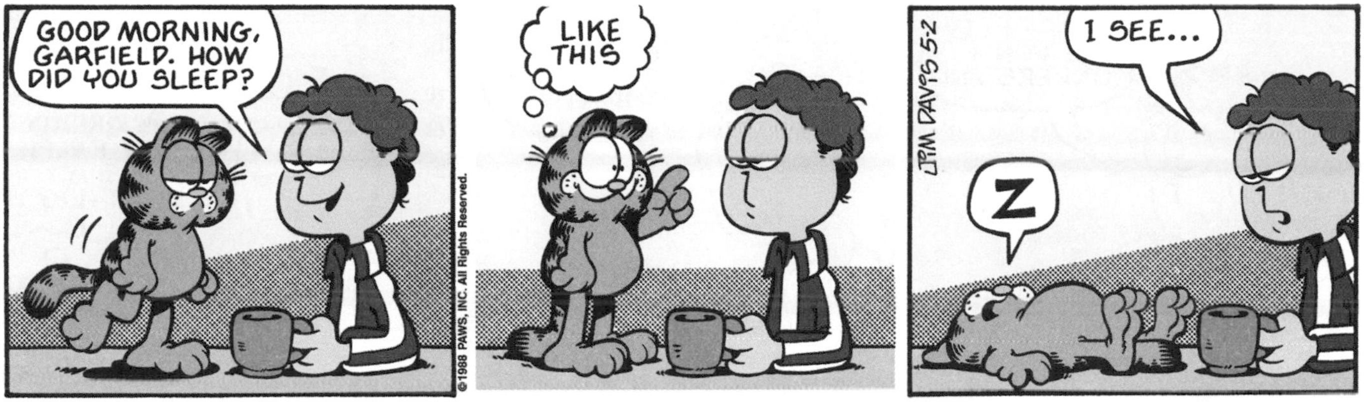
GOOD MORNING, GARFIELD. HOW DID YOU SLEEP?
LIKE THIS
I SEE...
Z
JIM DAVIS 5-2
©1988 PAWS, INC. All Rights Reserved.

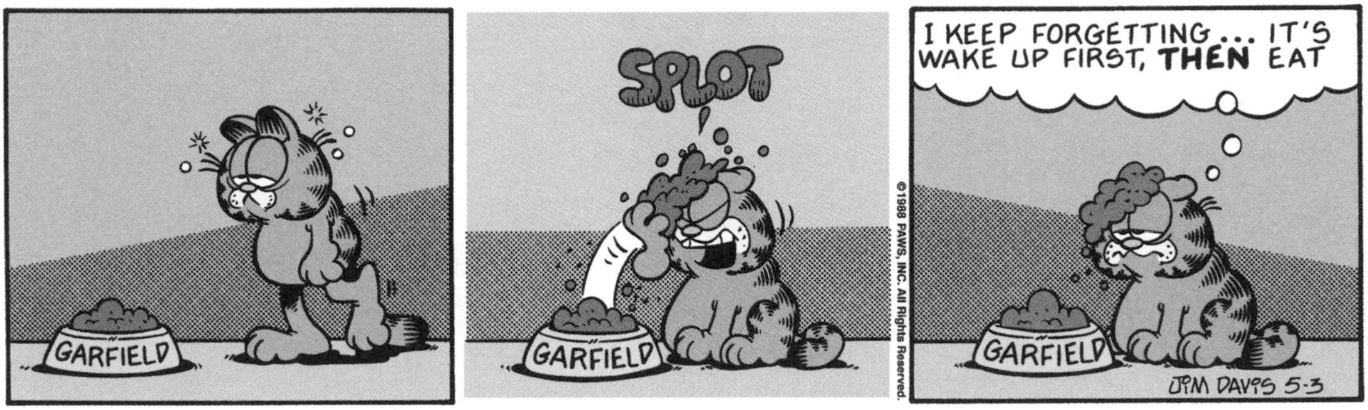
GARFIELD
SPLOT
GARFIELD
I KEEP FORGETTING... IT'S WAKE UP FIRST, THEN EAT
GARFIELD
JIM DAVIS 5-3
©1988 PAWS, INC. All Rights Reserved.

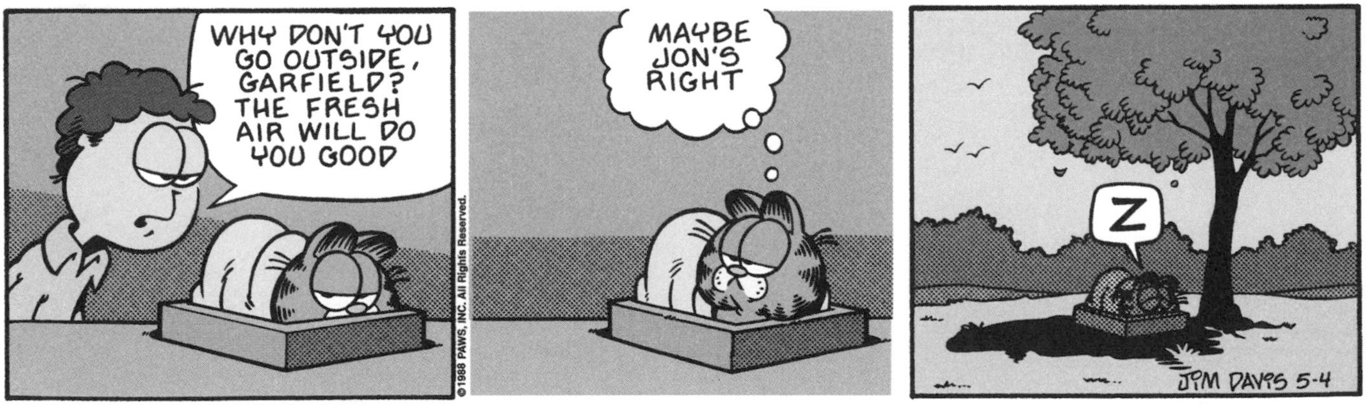
WHY DON'T YOU GO OUTSIDE, GARFIELD? THE FRESH AIR WILL DO YOU GOOD
MAYBE JON'S RIGHT
Z
JIM DAVIS 5-4
©1988 PAWS, INC. All Rights Reserved.

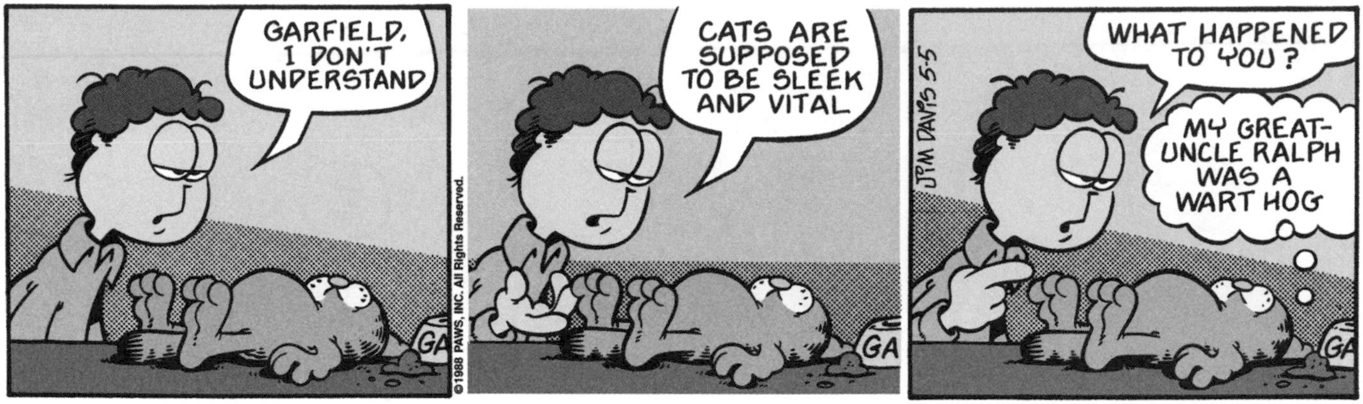
GARFIELD, I DON'T UNDERSTAND
©1988 PAWS, INC. All Rights Reserved.
CATS ARE SUPPOSED TO BE SLEEK AND VITAL
JIM DAVIS 5-5
WHAT HAPPENED TO YOU?
MY GREAT-UNCLE RALPH WAS A WART HOG

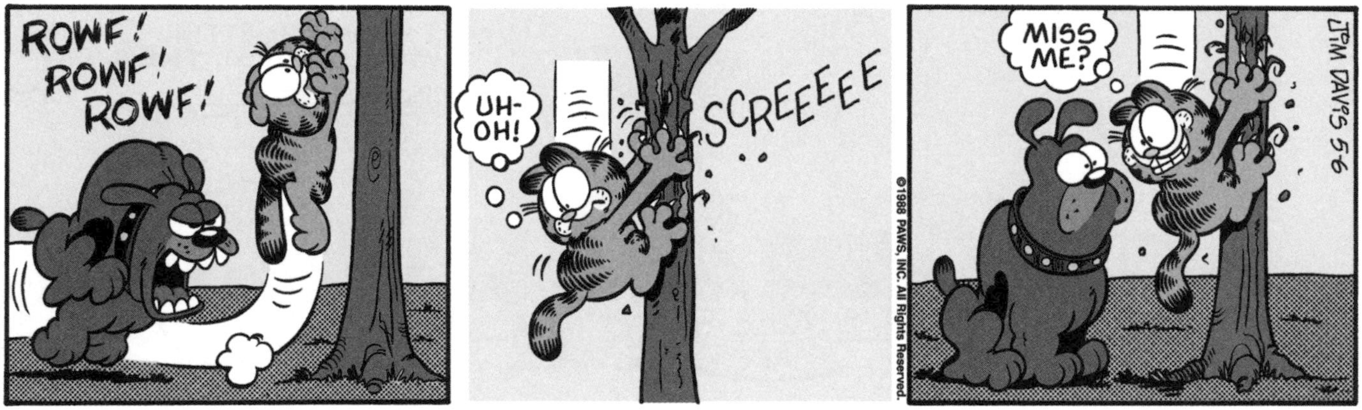
ROWF! ROWF! ROWF!
UH-OH!
SCREEEEEE
©1988 PAWS, INC. All Rights Reserved.
MISS ME?
JIM DAVIS 5-6

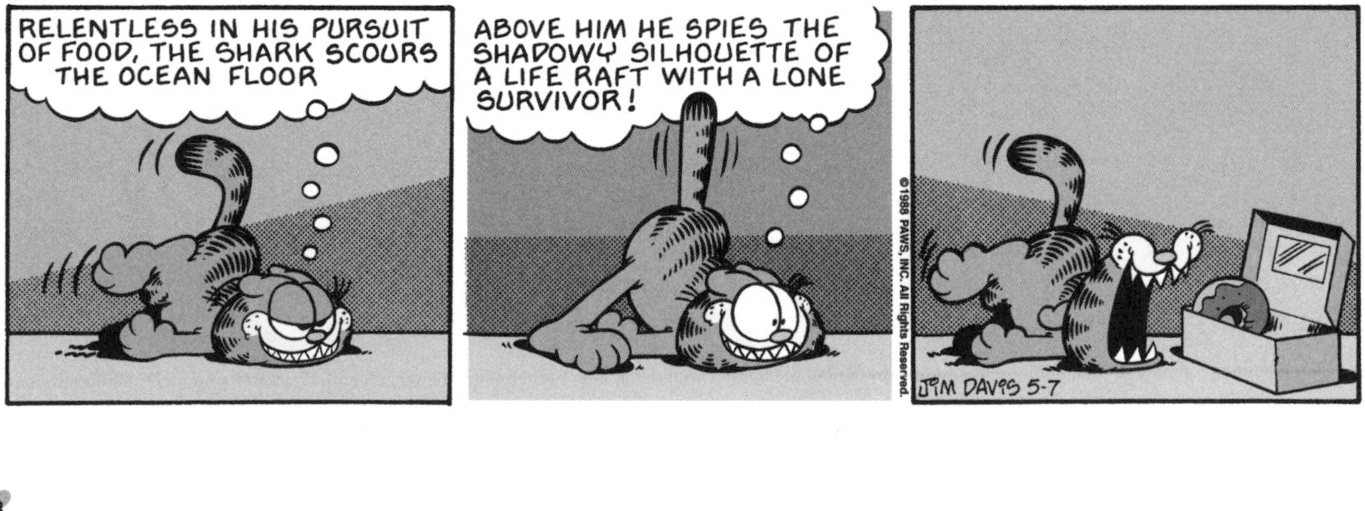
RELENTLESS IN HIS PURSUIT OF FOOD, THE SHARK SCOURS THE OCEAN FLOOR
ABOVE HIM HE SPIES THE SHADOWY SILHOUETTE OF A LIFE RAFT WITH A LONE SURVIVOR!
©1988 PAWS, INC. All Rights Reserved.
JIM DAVIS 5-7

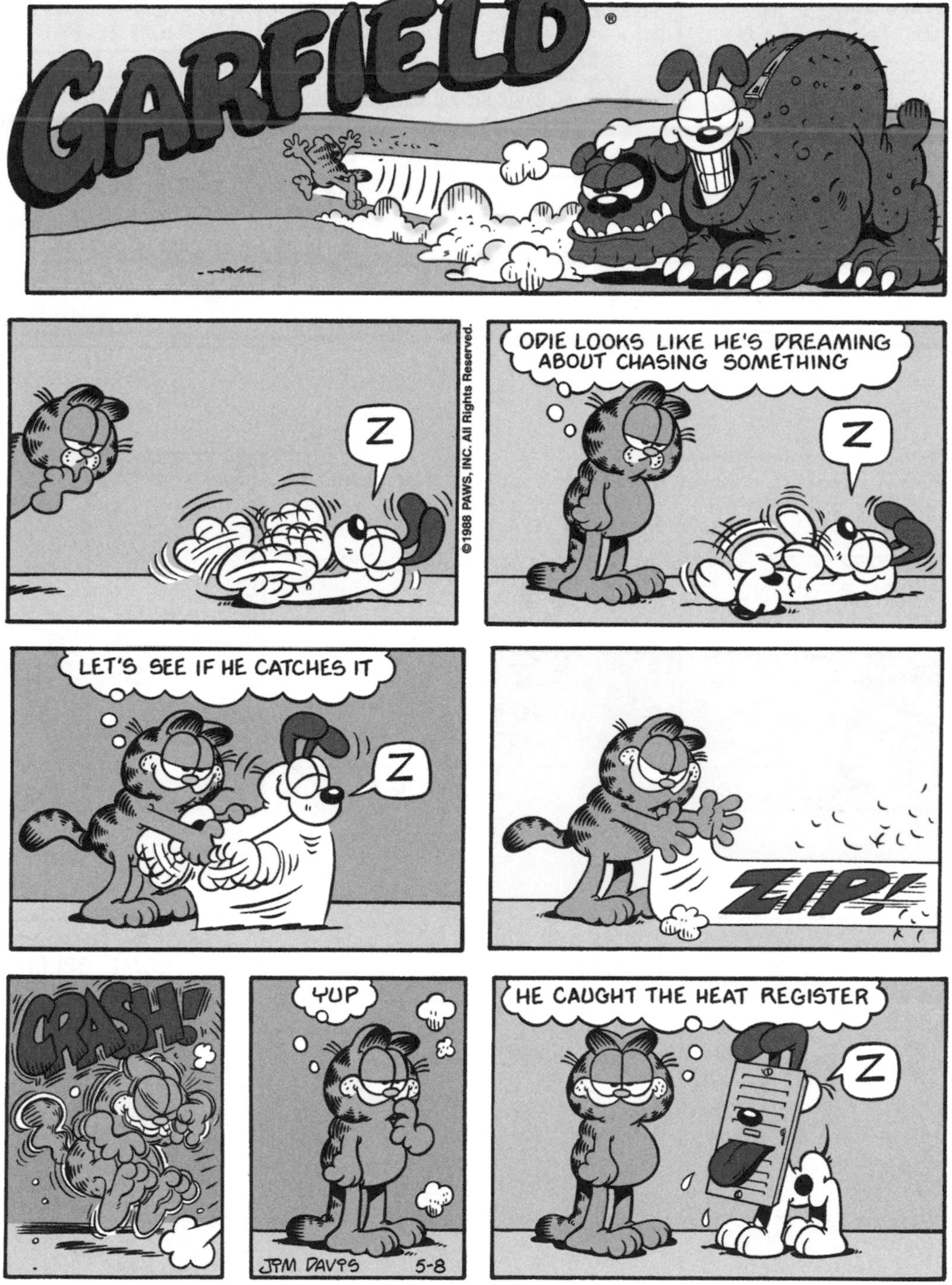
GARFIELD®
©1988 PAWS, INC. All Rights Reserved.
Z
ODIE LOOKS LIKE HE'S DREAMING ABOUT CHASING SOMETHING
Z
LET'S SEE IF HE CATCHES IT
Z
ZIP!
CRASH!
YUP
JIM DAVIS 5-8
HE CAUGHT THE HEAT REGISTER
Z

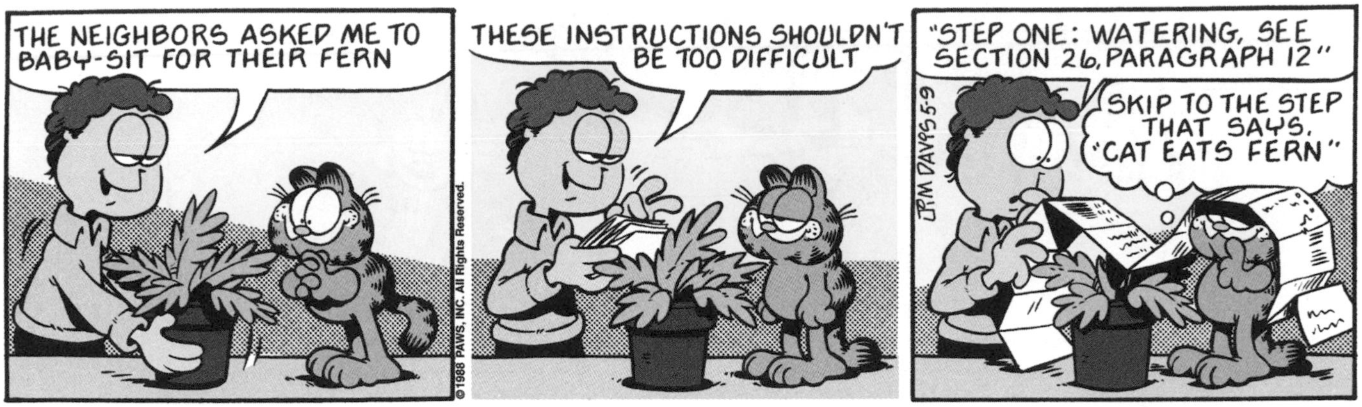
THE NEIGHBORS ASKED ME TO BABY-SIT FOR THEIR FERN
©1988 PAWS, INC. All Rights Reserved.
THESE INSTRUCTIONS SHOULDN'T BE TOO DIFFICULT
"STEP ONE: WATERING, SEE SECTION 26, PARAGRAPH 12"
JIM DAVIS 5-9
SKIP TO THE STEP THAT SAYS, "CAT EATS FERN"

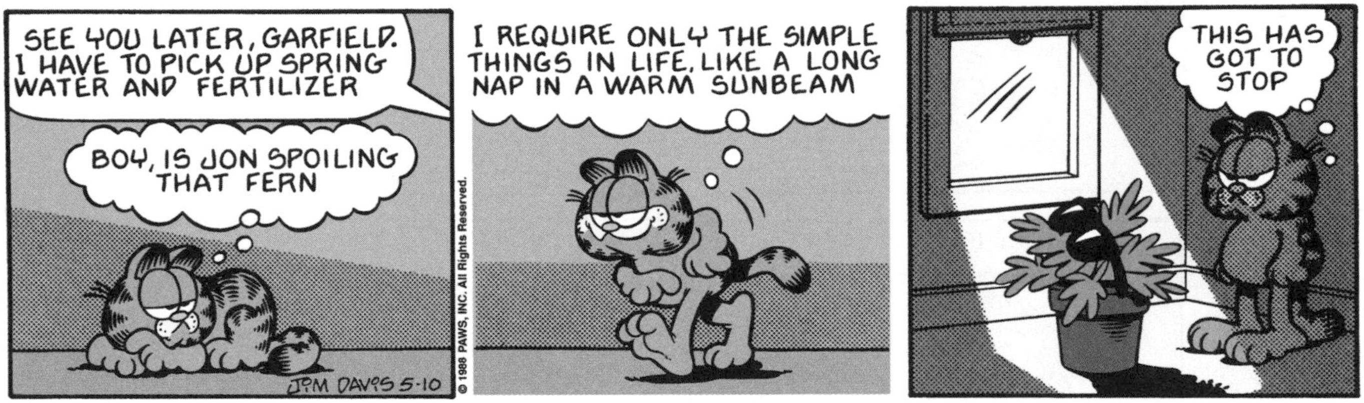
SEE YOU LATER, GARFIELD. I HAVE TO PICK UP SPRING WATER AND FERTILIZER
BOY, IS JON SPOILING THAT FERN
JIM DAVIS 5-10
©1988 PAWS, INC. All Rights Reserved.
I REQUIRE ONLY THE SIMPLE THINGS IN LIFE, LIKE A LONG NAP IN A WARM SUNBEAM
THIS HAS GOT TO STOP

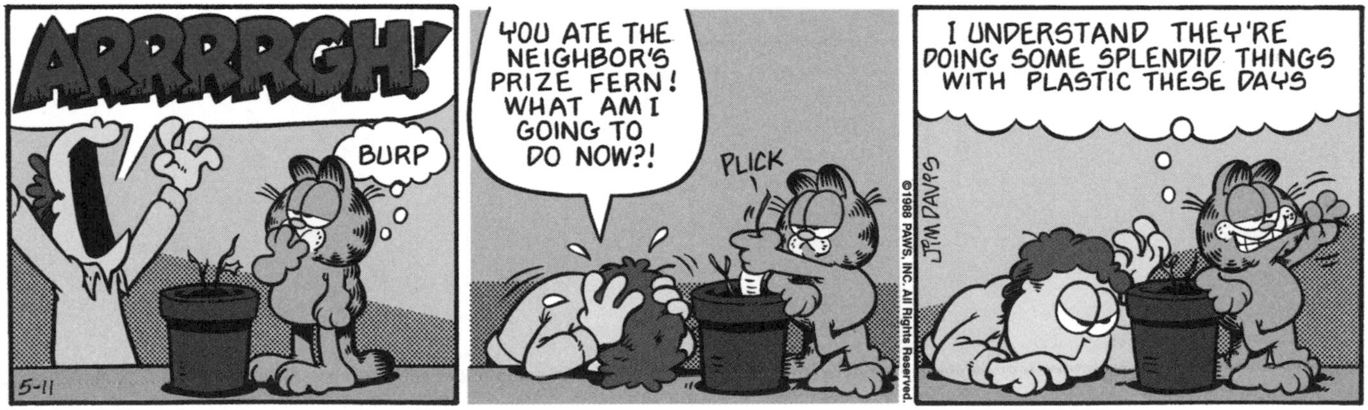
ARRRRGH!
BURP
5-11
YOU ATE THE NEIGHBOR'S PRIZE FERN! WHAT AM I GOING TO DO NOW?!
PLICK
©1988 PAWS, INC. All Rights Reserved.
JIM DAVIS
I UNDERSTAND THEY'RE DOING SOME SPLENDID THINGS WITH PLASTIC THESE DAYS

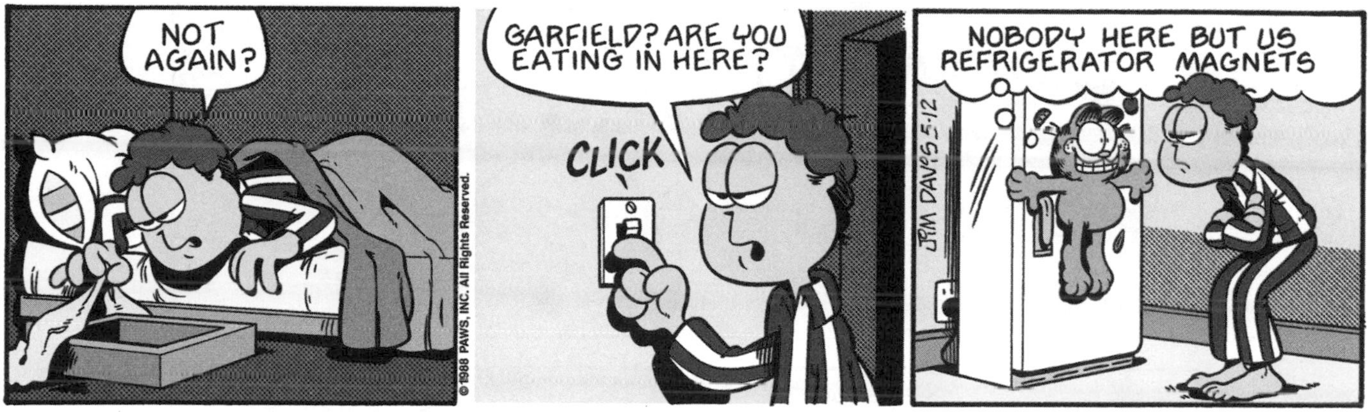
NOT AGAIN?
©1988 PAWS, INC. All Rights Reserved.
GARFIELD? ARE YOU EATING IN HERE?
CLICK
NOBODY HERE BUT US REFRIGERATOR MAGNETS
JIM DAVIS 5-12

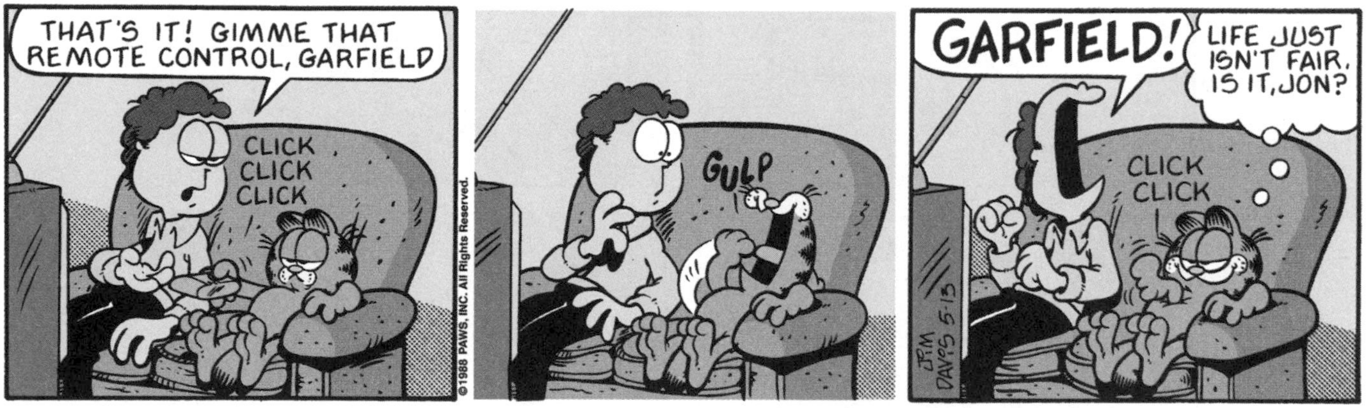
THAT'S IT! GIMME THAT REMOTE CONTROL, GARFIELD
CLICK CLICK CLICK
©1988 PAWS, INC. All Rights Reserved.
GULP
GARFIELD!
LIFE JUST ISN'T FAIR, IS IT, JON?
CLICK CLICK
JIM DAVIS 5-13

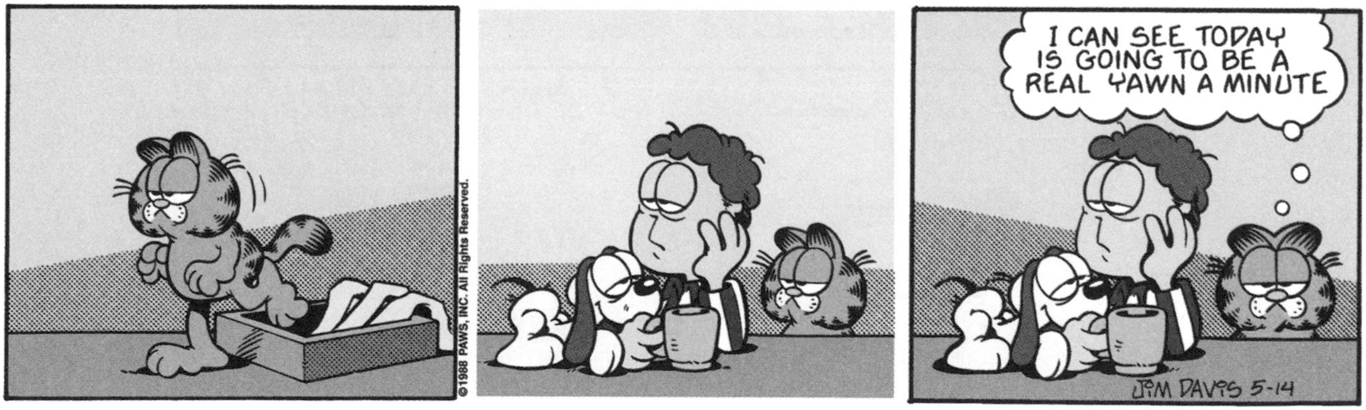
©1988 PAWS, INC. All Rights Reserved.
I CAN SEE TODAY IS GOING TO BE A REAL YAWN A MINUTE
JIM DAVIS 5-14

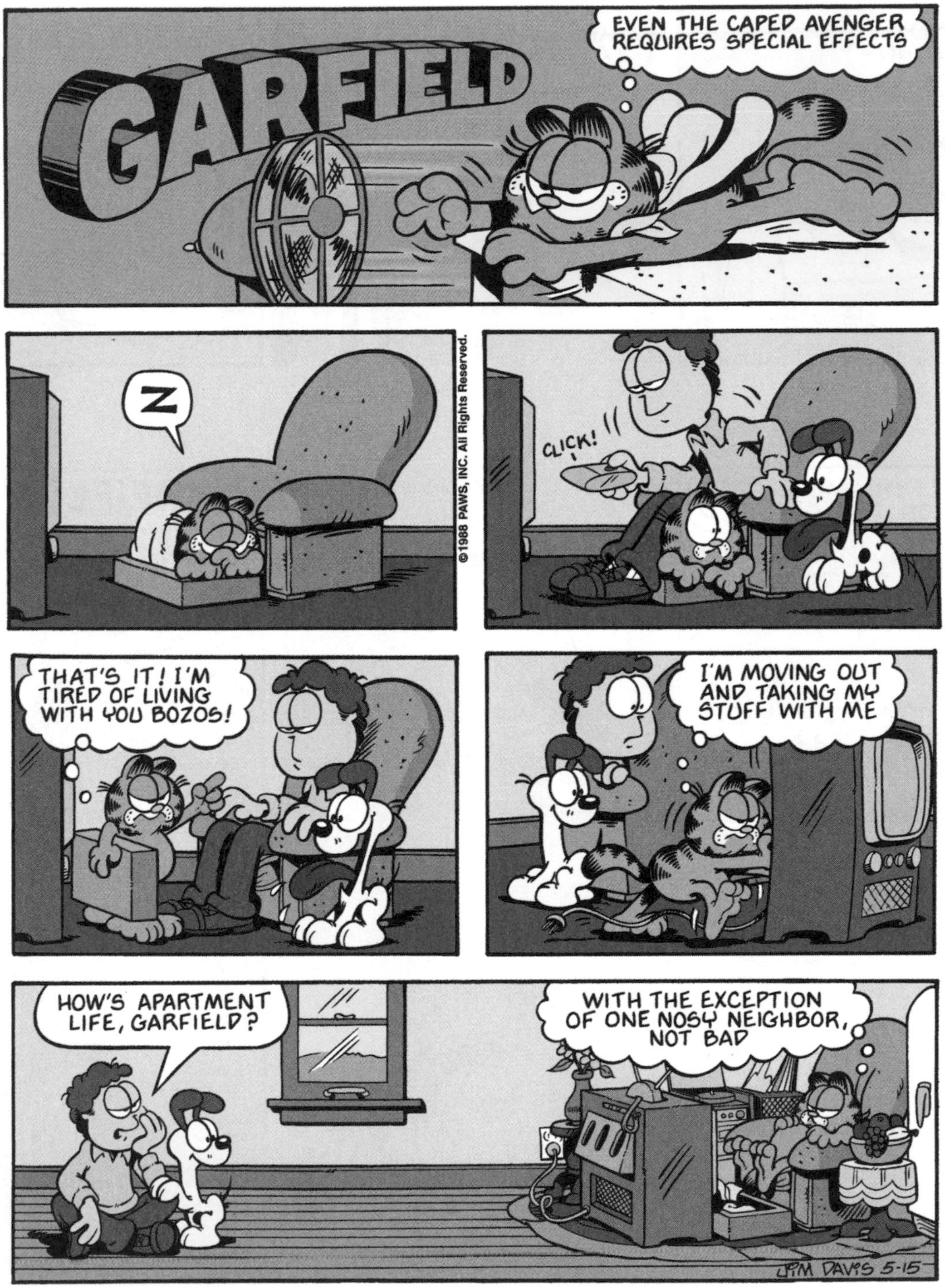
GARFIELD
EVEN THE CAPED AVENGER REQUIRES SPECIAL EFFECTS
©1988 PAWS, INC. All Rights Reserved.
Z
CLICK!
THAT'S IT! I'M TIRED OF LIVING WITH YOU BOZOS!
I'M MOVING OUT AND TAKING MY STUFF WITH ME
HOW'S APARTMENT LIFE, GARFIELD?
WITH THE EXCEPTION OF ONE NOSY NEIGHBOR, NOT BAD
JIM DAVIS 5-15

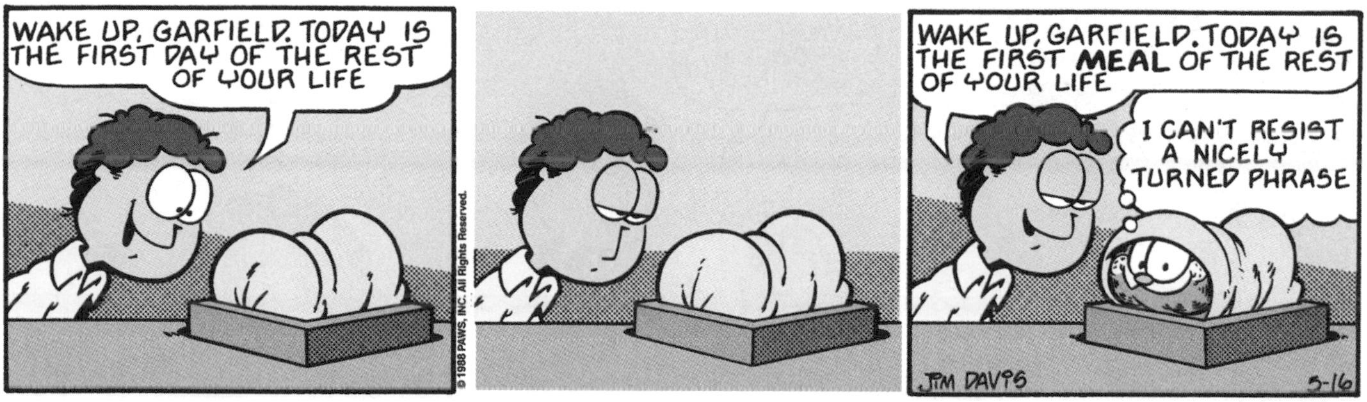
WAKE UP, GARFIELD. TODAY IS THE FIRST DAY OF THE REST OF YOUR LIFE
WAKE UP, GARFIELD. TODAY IS THE FIRST **MEAL** OF THE REST OF YOUR LIFE
I CAN'T RESIST A NICELY TURNED PHRASE
© 1988 PAWS, INC. All Rights Reserved.
JIM DAVIS 5-16

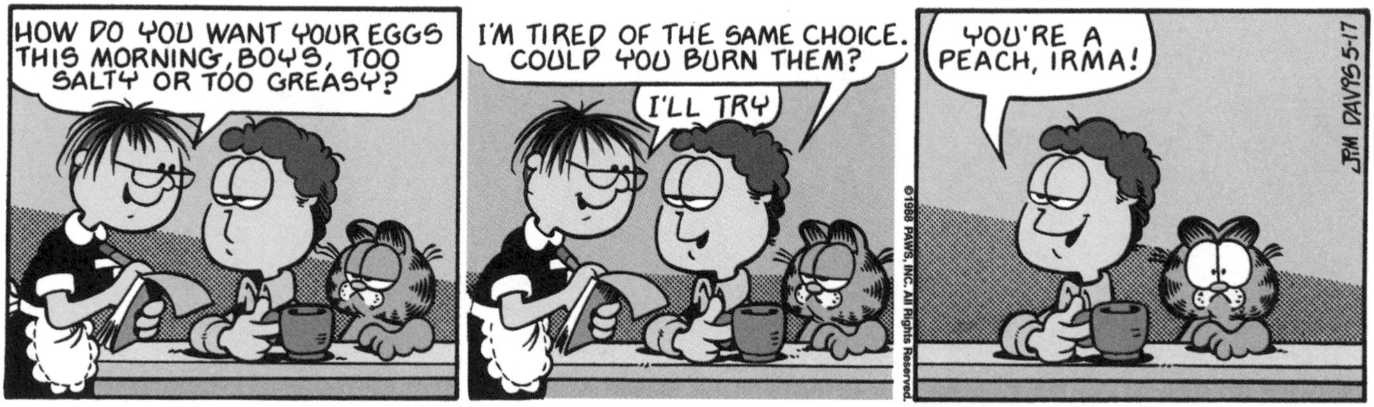
HOW DO YOU WANT YOUR EGGS THIS MORNING, BOYS, TOO SALTY OR TOO GREASY?
I'M TIRED OF THE SAME CHOICE. COULD YOU BURN THEM?
I'LL TRY
YOU'RE A PEACH, IRMA!
© 1988 PAWS, INC. All Rights Reserved.
JIM DAVIS 5-17

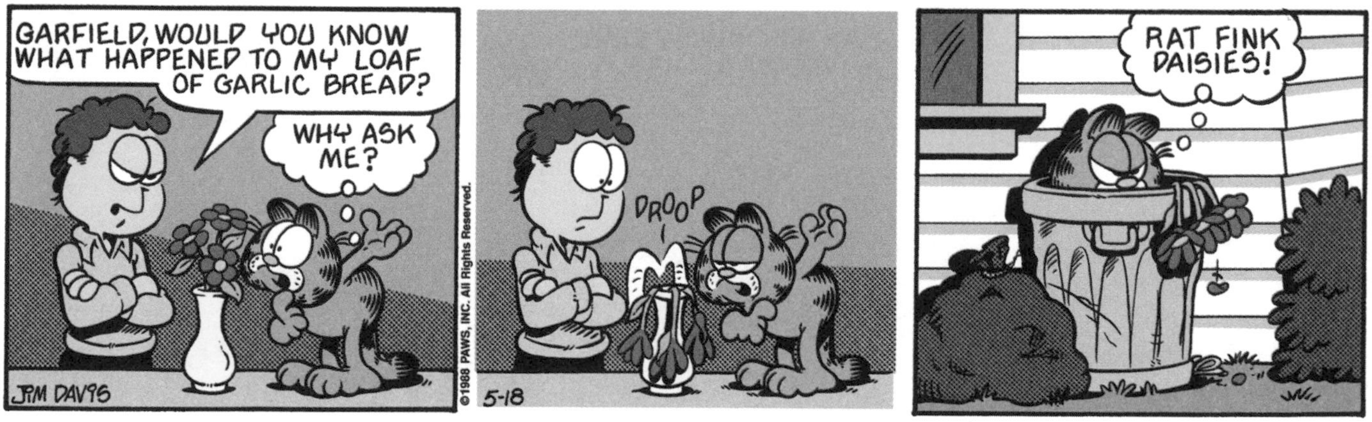
GARFIELD, WOULD YOU KNOW WHAT HAPPENED TO MY LOAF OF GARLIC BREAD?
WHY ASK ME?
DROOP
RAT FINK DAISIES!
© 1988 PAWS, INC. All Rights Reserved.
JIM DAVIS 5-18

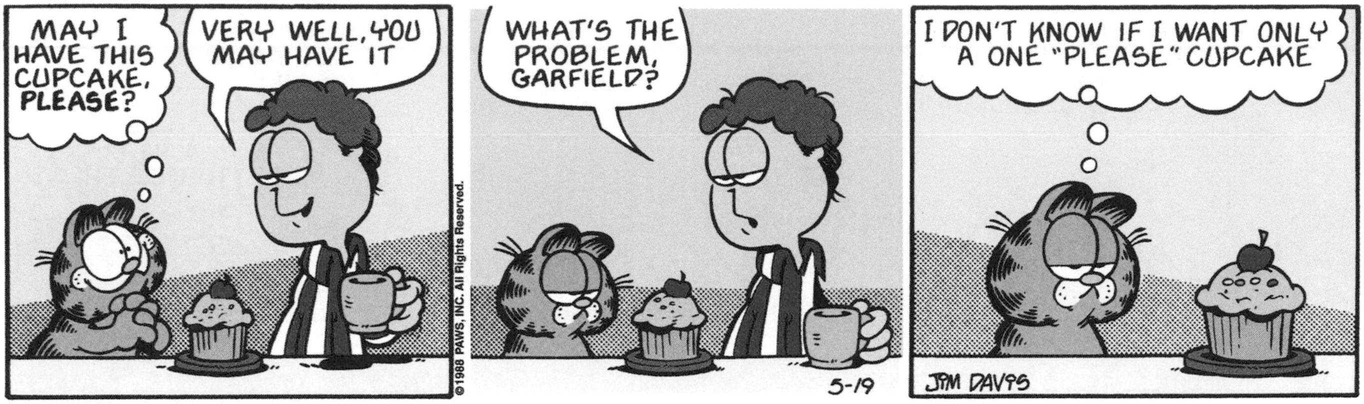
MAY I HAVE THIS CUPCAKE, PLEASE?
VERY WELL, YOU MAY HAVE IT
©1988 PAWS, INC. All Rights Reserved.
WHAT'S THE PROBLEM, GARFIELD?
5-19
I DON'T KNOW IF I WANT ONLY A ONE "PLEASE" CUPCAKE
JIM DAVIS

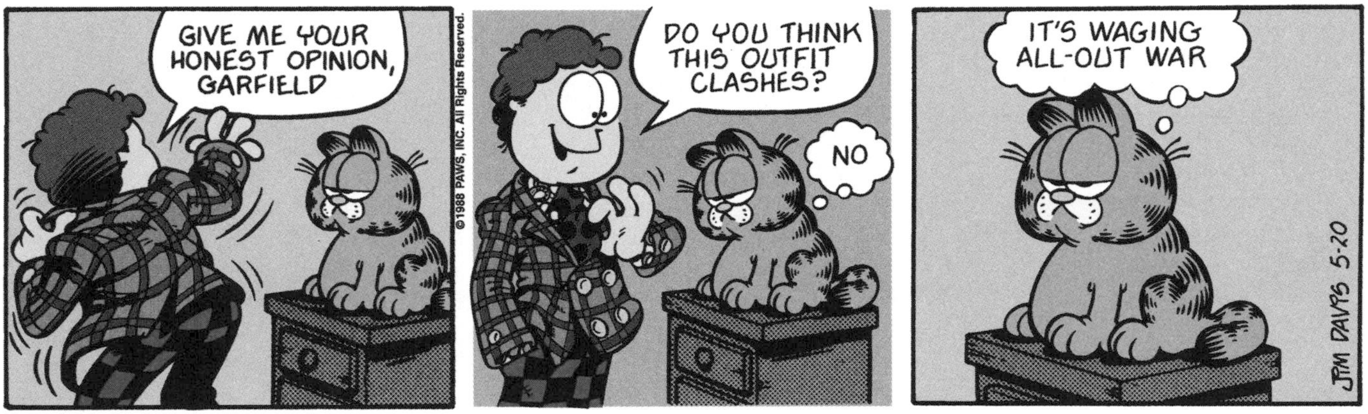
GIVE ME YOUR HONEST OPINION, GARFIELD
©1988 PAWS, INC. All Rights Reserved.
DO YOU THINK THIS OUTFIT CLASHES?
NO
IT'S WAGING ALL-OUT WAR
JIM DAVIS 5-20

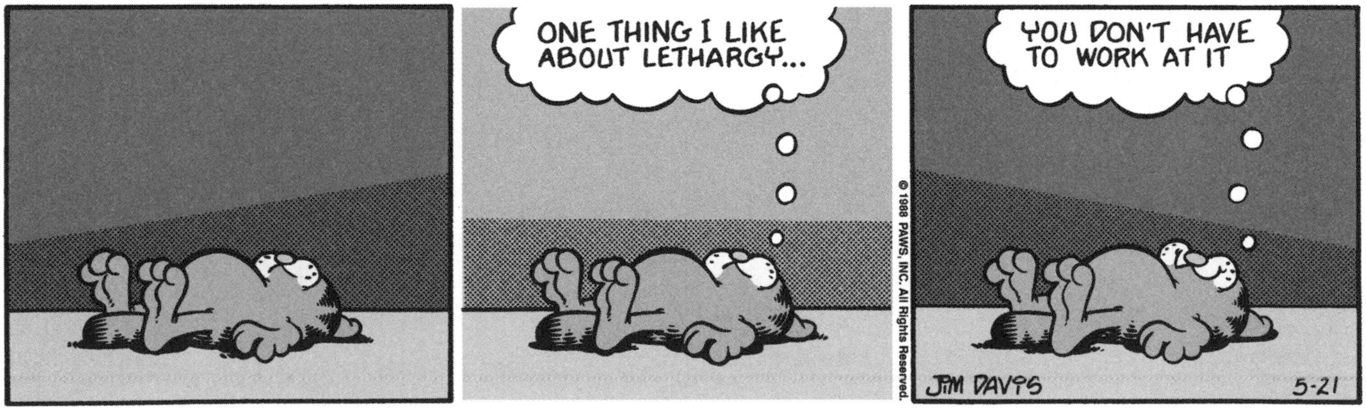
ONE THING I LIKE ABOUT LETHARGY...
© 1988 PAWS, INC. All Rights Reserved.
YOU DON'T HAVE TO WORK AT IT
JIM DAVIS
5-21

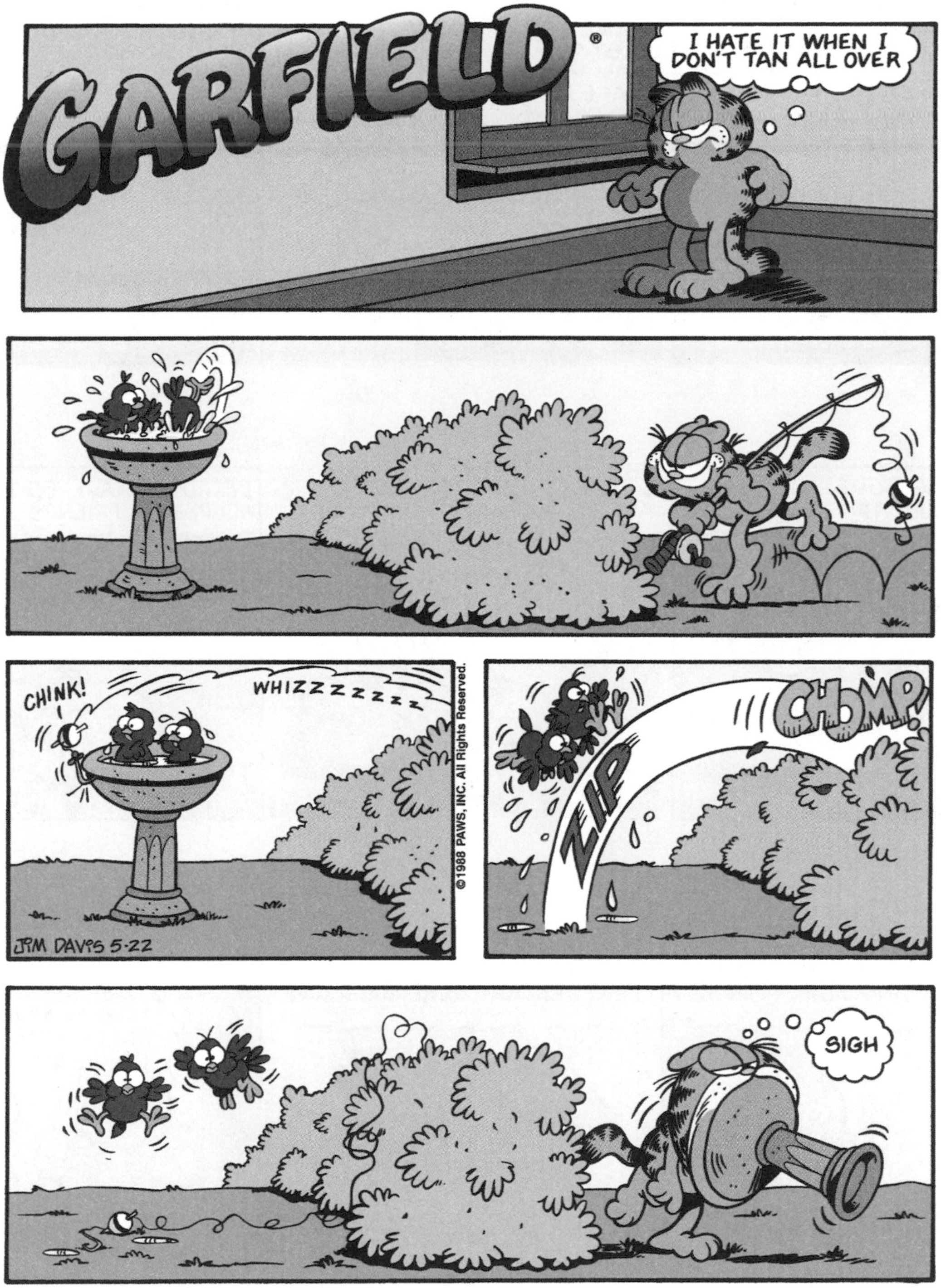
GARFIELD®
I HATE IT WHEN I DON'T TAN ALL OVER
CHINK!
WHIZZZZZZZ
©1988 PAWS, INC. All Rights Reserved.
JIM DAVIS 5-22
ZIP
CHOMP!
SIGH

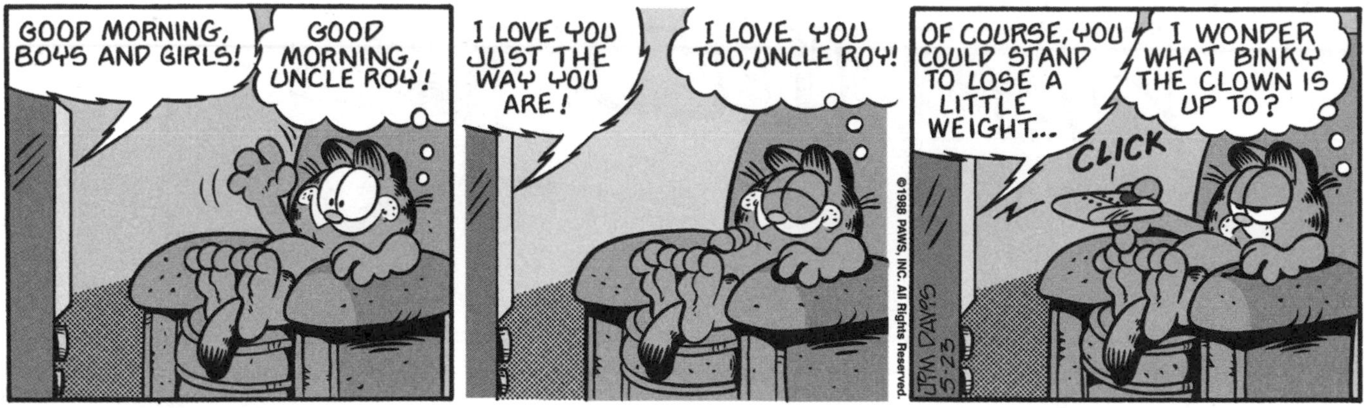
GOOD MORNING, BOYS AND GIRLS!
GOOD MORNING, UNCLE ROY!
I LOVE YOU JUST THE WAY YOU ARE!
I LOVE YOU TOO, UNCLE ROY!
OF COURSE, YOU COULD STAND TO LOSE A LITTLE WEIGHT...
CLICK
I WONDER WHAT BINKY THE CLOWN IS UP TO?
©1988 PAWS, INC. All Rights Reserved.
JPM DAVPS 5-23

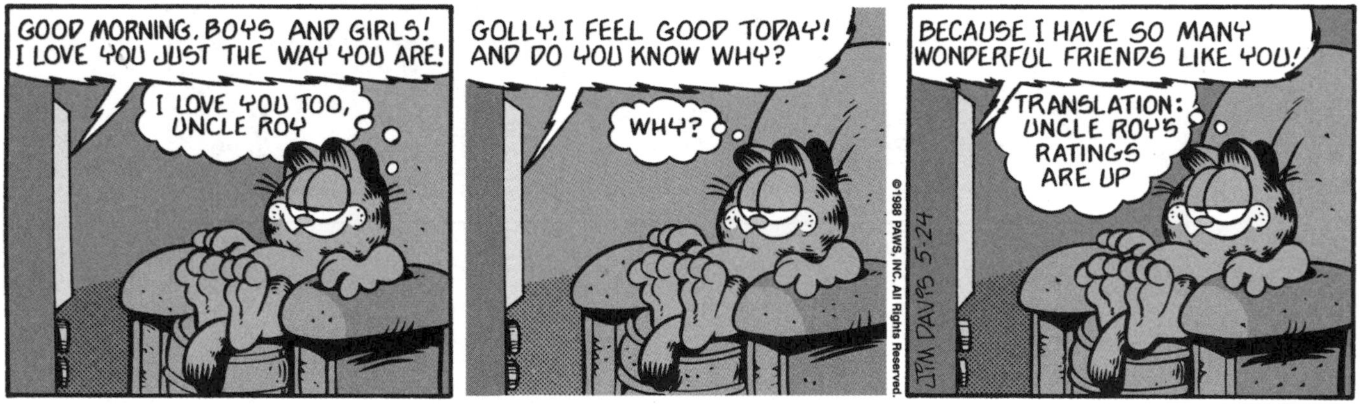
GOOD MORNING, BOYS AND GIRLS! I LOVE YOU JUST THE WAY YOU ARE!
I LOVE YOU TOO, UNCLE ROY
GOLLY, I FEEL GOOD TODAY! AND DO YOU KNOW WHY?
WHY?
BECAUSE I HAVE SO MANY WONDERFUL FRIENDS LIKE YOU!
TRANSLATION: UNCLE ROY'S RATINGS ARE UP
©1988 PAWS, INC. All Rights Reserved.
JPM DAVPS 5-24

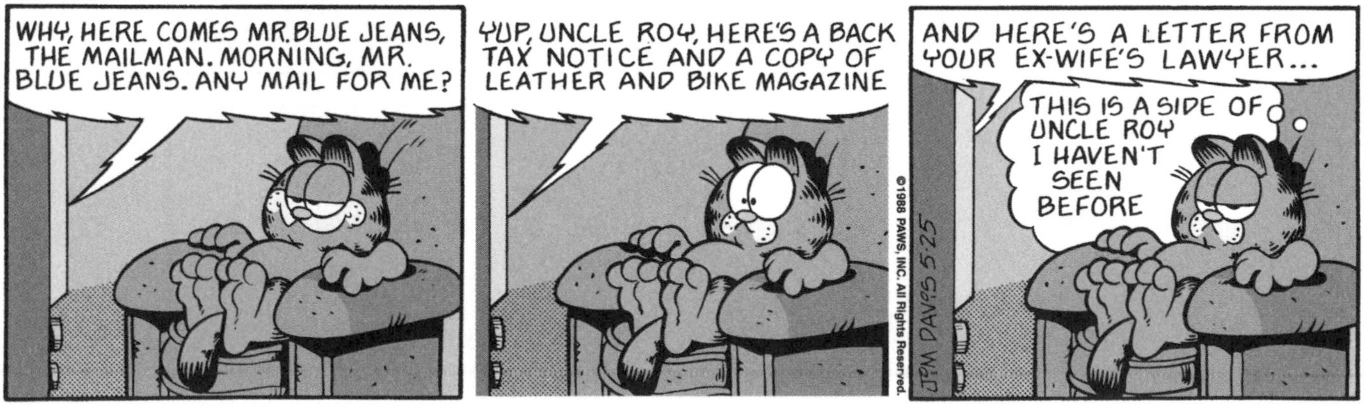
WHY, HERE COMES MR. BLUE JEANS, THE MAILMAN. MORNING, MR. BLUE JEANS. ANY MAIL FOR ME?
YUP, UNCLE ROY, HERE'S A BACK TAX NOTICE AND A COPY OF LEATHER AND BIKE MAGAZINE
AND HERE'S A LETTER FROM YOUR EX-WIFE'S LAWYER...
THIS IS A SIDE OF UNCLE ROY I HAVEN'T SEEN BEFORE
©1988 PAWS, INC. All Rights Reserved.
JPM DAVPS 5-25

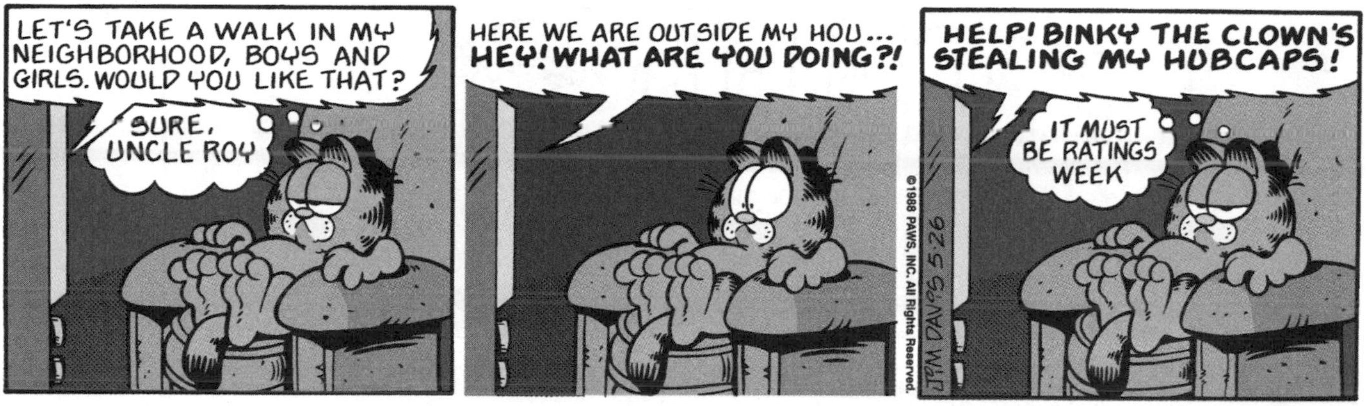
LET'S TAKE A WALK IN MY NEIGHBORHOOD, BOYS AND GIRLS. WOULD YOU LIKE THAT?
SURE, UNCLE ROY
HERE WE ARE OUTSIDE MY HOU... HEY! WHAT ARE YOU DOING?!
©1988 PAWS, INC. All Rights Reserved.
JIM DAVIS 5·26
HELP! BINKY THE CLOWN'S STEALING MY HUBCAPS!
IT MUST BE RATINGS WEEK

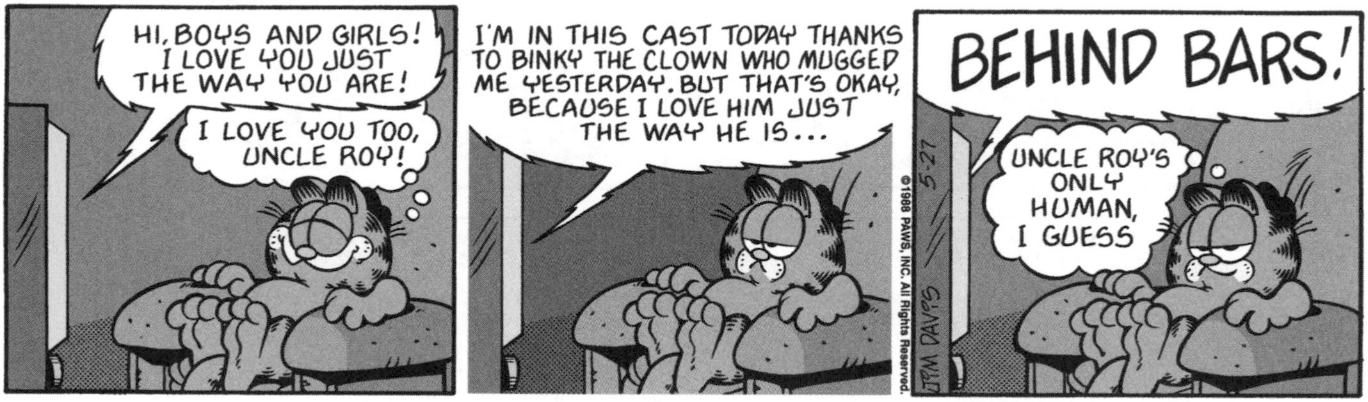
HI, BOYS AND GIRLS! I LOVE YOU JUST THE WAY YOU ARE!
I LOVE YOU TOO, UNCLE ROY!
I'M IN THIS CAST TODAY THANKS TO BINKY THE CLOWN WHO MUGGED ME YESTERDAY. BUT THAT'S OKAY, BECAUSE I LOVE HIM JUST THE WAY HE IS...
©1988 PAWS, INC. All Rights Reserved.
JIM DAVIS 5·27
BEHIND BARS!
UNCLE ROY'S ONLY HUMAN, I GUESS

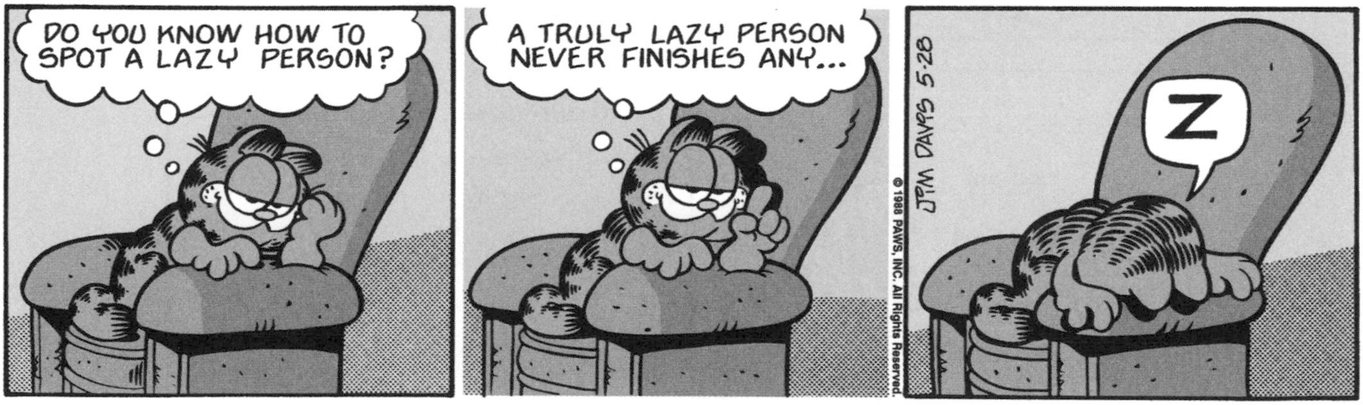
DO YOU KNOW HOW TO SPOT A LAZY PERSON?
A TRULY LAZY PERSON NEVER FINISHES ANY...
©1988 PAWS, INC. All Rights Reserved.
JIM DAVIS 5·28
Z

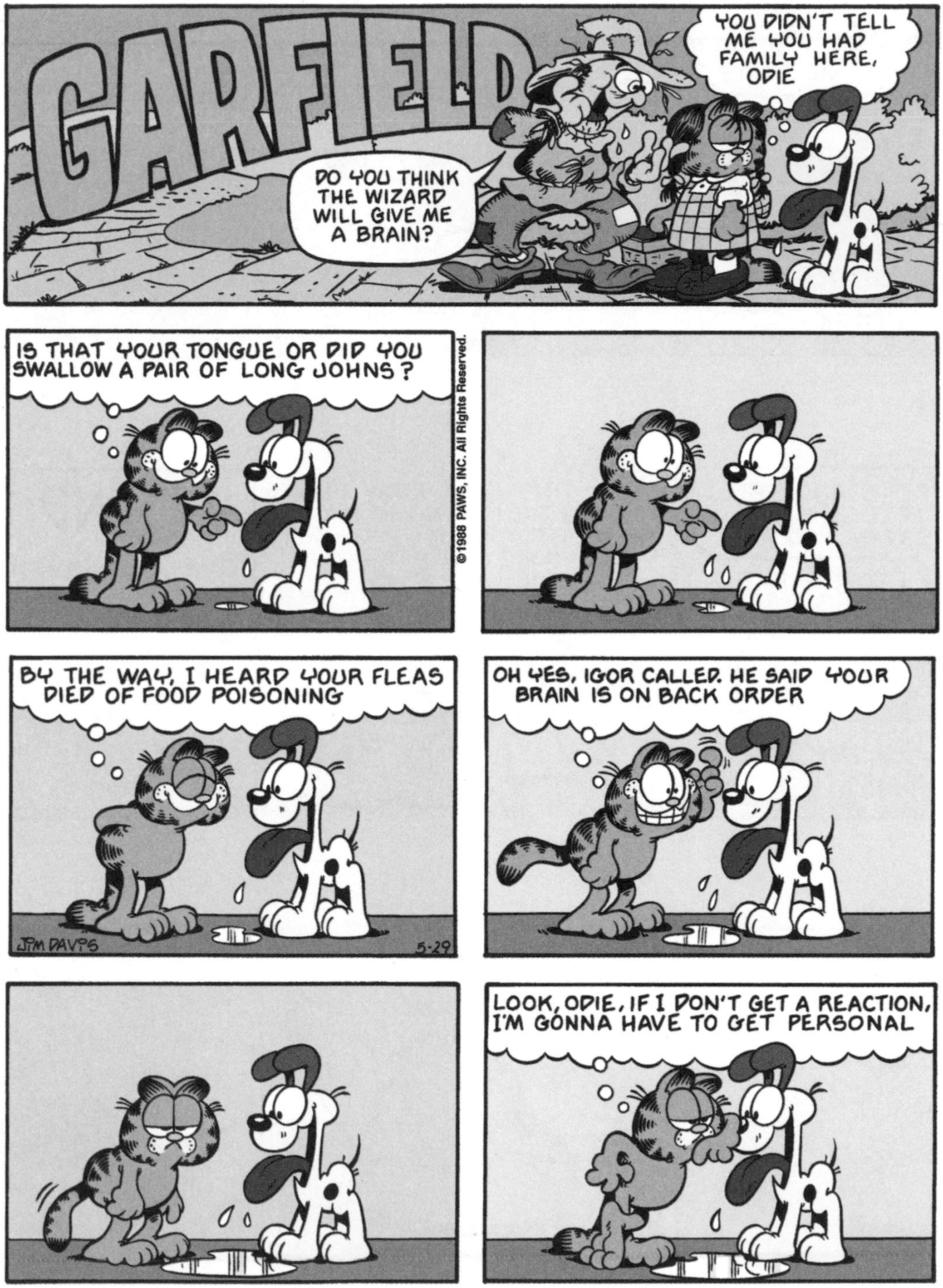
GARFIELD
DO YOU THINK THE WIZARD WILL GIVE ME A BRAIN?
YOU DIDN'T TELL ME YOU HAD FAMILY HERE, ODIE
IS THAT YOUR TONGUE OR DID YOU SWALLOW A PAIR OF LONG JOHNS?
©1988 PAWS, INC. All Rights Reserved.
BY THE WAY, I HEARD YOUR FLEAS DIED OF FOOD POISONING
JIM DAVIS
5-29
OH YES, IGOR CALLED. HE SAID YOUR BRAIN IS ON BACK ORDER
LOOK, ODIE, IF I DON'T GET A REACTION, I'M GONNA HAVE TO GET PERSONAL

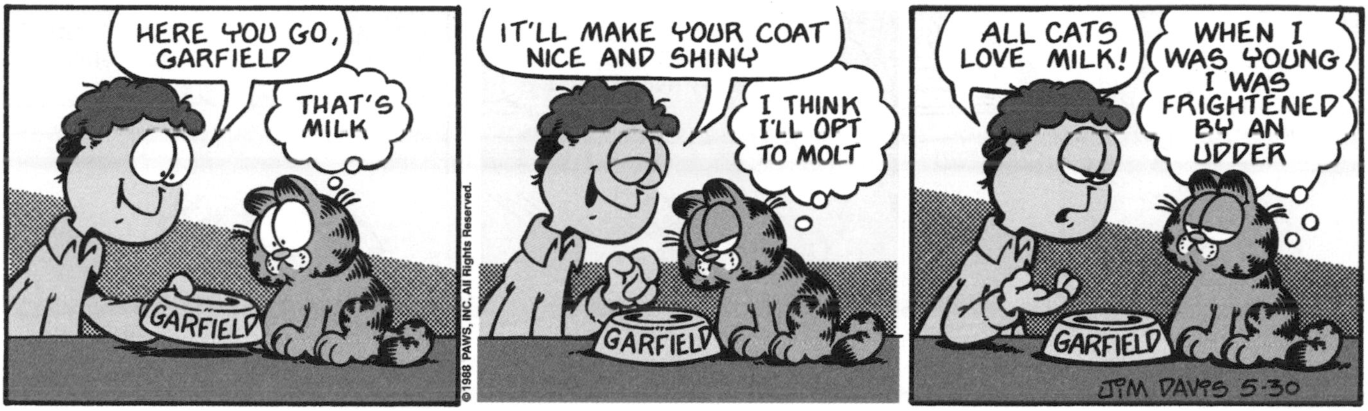
HERE YOU GO, GARFIELD
THAT'S MILK
IT'LL MAKE YOUR COAT NICE AND SHINY
I THINK I'LL OPT TO MOLT
ALL CATS LOVE MILK!
WHEN I WAS YOUNG I WAS FRIGHTENED BY AN UDDER
GARFIELD
JIM DAVIS 5-30
©1988 PAWS, INC. All Rights Reserved.

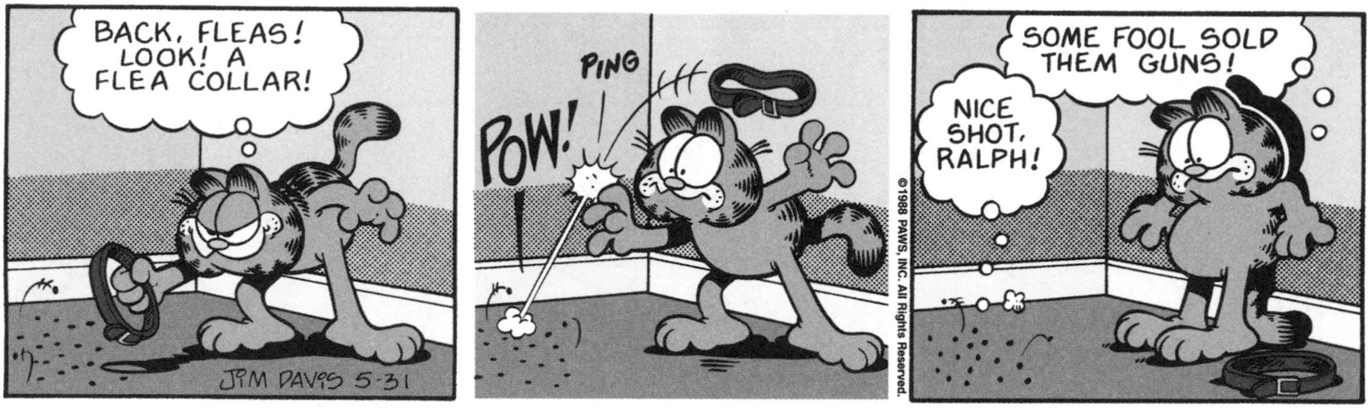
BACK, FLEAS! LOOK! A FLEA COLLAR!
JIM DAVIS 5-31
POW!
PING
©1988 PAWS, INC. All Rights Reserved.
NICE SHOT, RALPH!
SOME FOOL SOLD THEM GUNS!

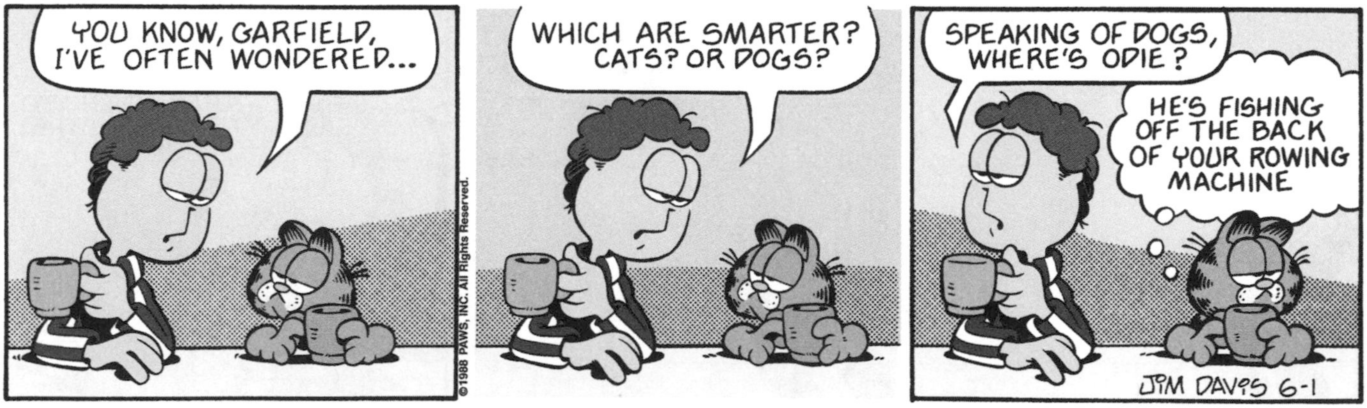
YOU KNOW, GARFIELD, I'VE OFTEN WONDERED...
©1988 PAWS, INC. All Rights Reserved.
WHICH ARE SMARTER? CATS? OR DOGS?
SPEAKING OF DOGS, WHERE'S ODIE?
HE'S FISHING OFF THE BACK OF YOUR ROWING MACHINE
JIM DAVIS 6-1

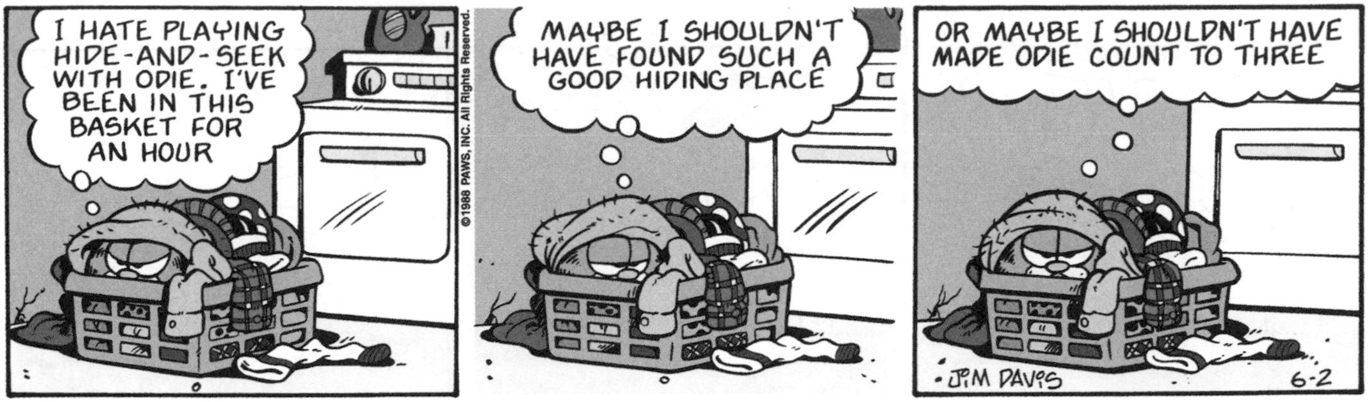
I HATE PLAYING HIDE-AND-SEEK WITH ODIE. I'VE BEEN IN THIS BASKET FOR AN HOUR
©1988 PAWS, INC. All Rights Reserved.
MAYBE I SHOULDN'T HAVE FOUND SUCH A GOOD HIDING PLACE
OR MAYBE I SHOULDN'T HAVE MADE ODIE COUNT TO THREE
JIM DAVIS 6-2

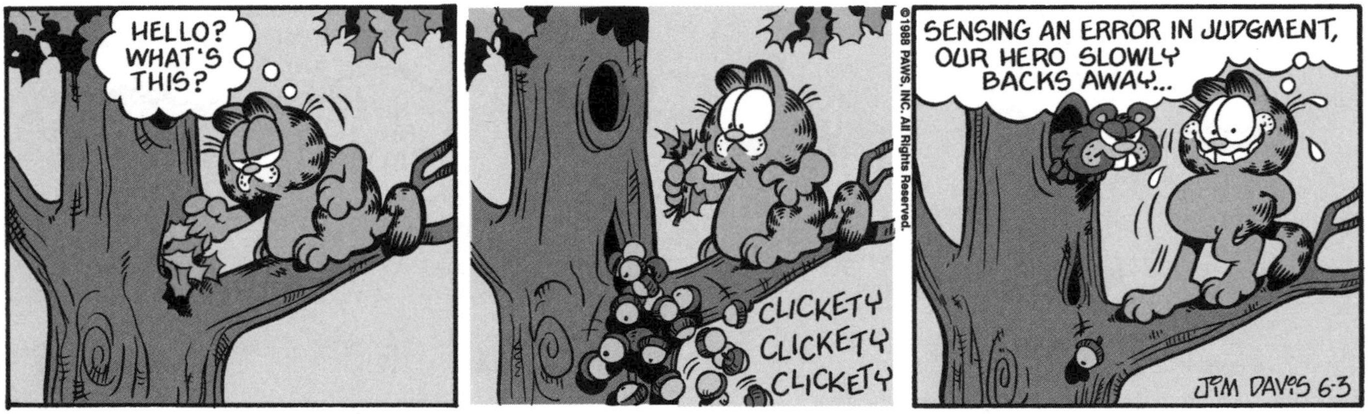
HELLO? WHAT'S THIS?
©1988 PAWS, INC. All Rights Reserved.
CLICKETY CLICKETY CLICKETY
SENSING AN ERROR IN JUDGMENT, OUR HERO SLOWLY BACKS AWAY...
JIM DAVIS 6-3

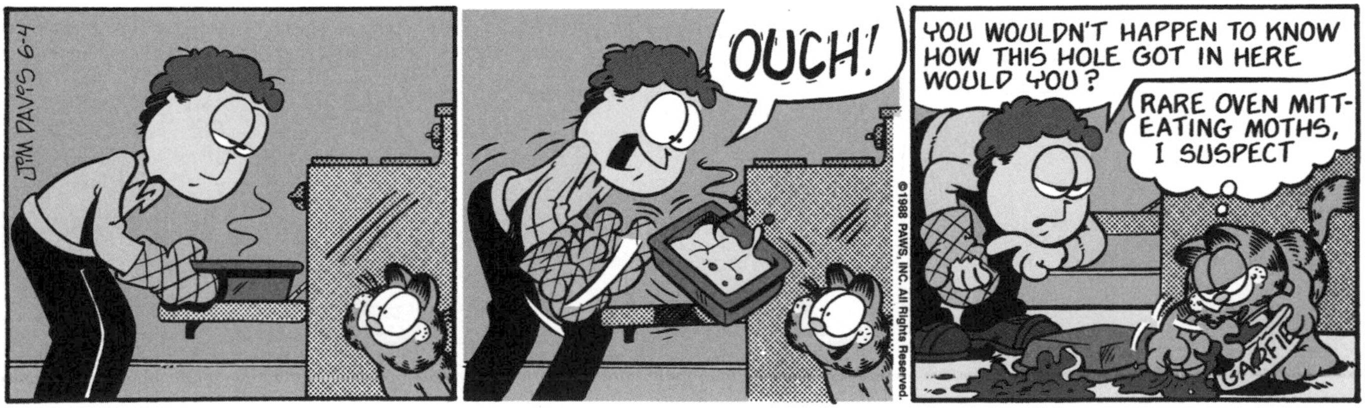
JIM DAVIS 6-4
OUCH!
©1988 PAWS, INC. All Rights Reserved.
YOU WOULDN'T HAPPEN TO KNOW HOW THIS HOLE GOT IN HERE WOULD YOU?
RARE OVEN MITT-EATING MOTHS, I SUSPECT

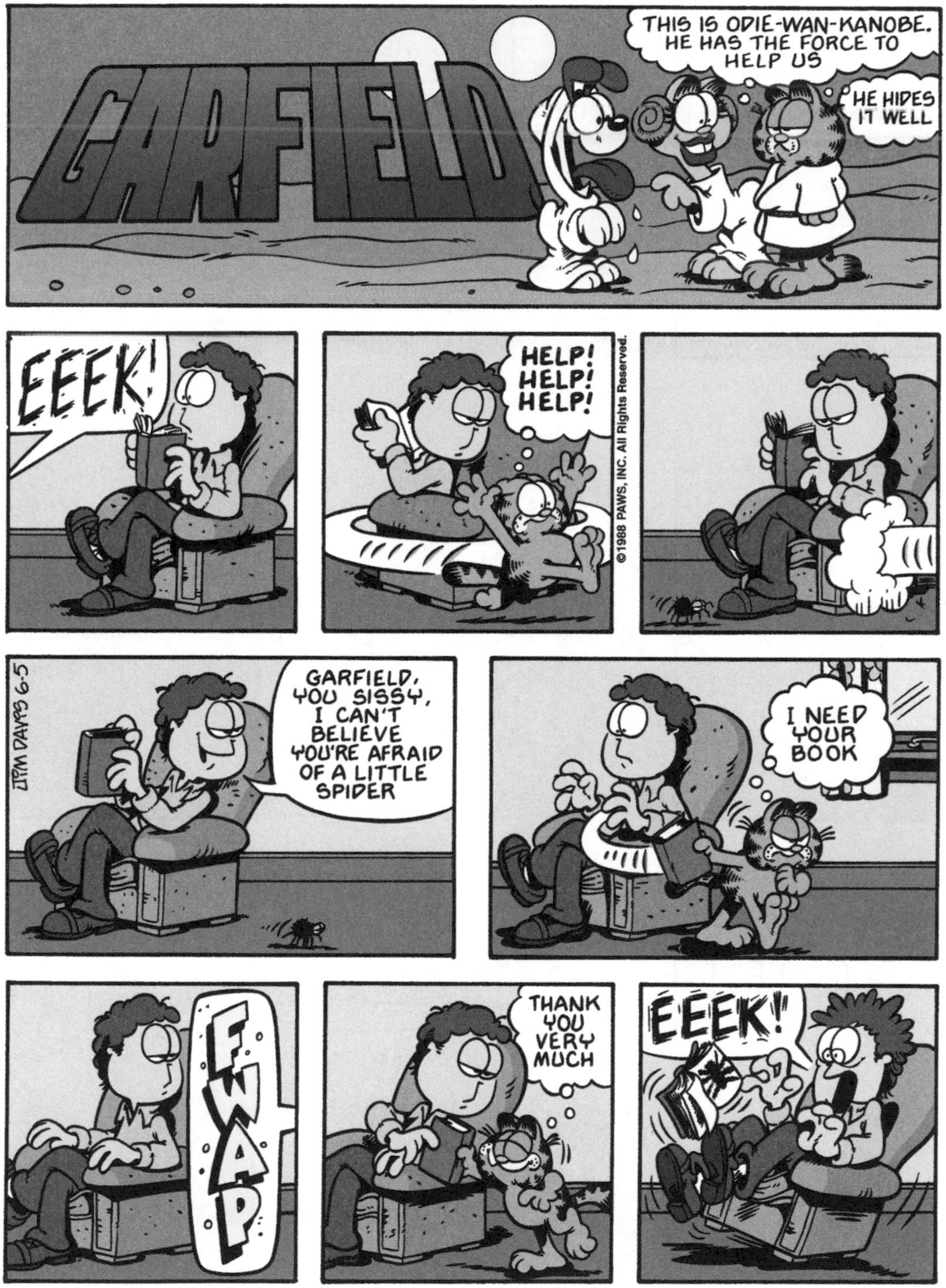

GARFIELD
THIS IS ODIE-WAN-KANOBE. HE HAS THE FORCE TO HELP US
HE HIDES IT WELL
EEEK!
HELP! HELP! HELP!
©1988 PAWS, INC. All Rights Reserved.
JIM DAVIS 6-5
GARFIELD, YOU SISSY, I CAN'T BELIEVE YOU'RE AFRAID OF A LITTLE SPIDER
I NEED YOUR BOOK
FWAP
THANK YOU VERY MUCH
EEEK!

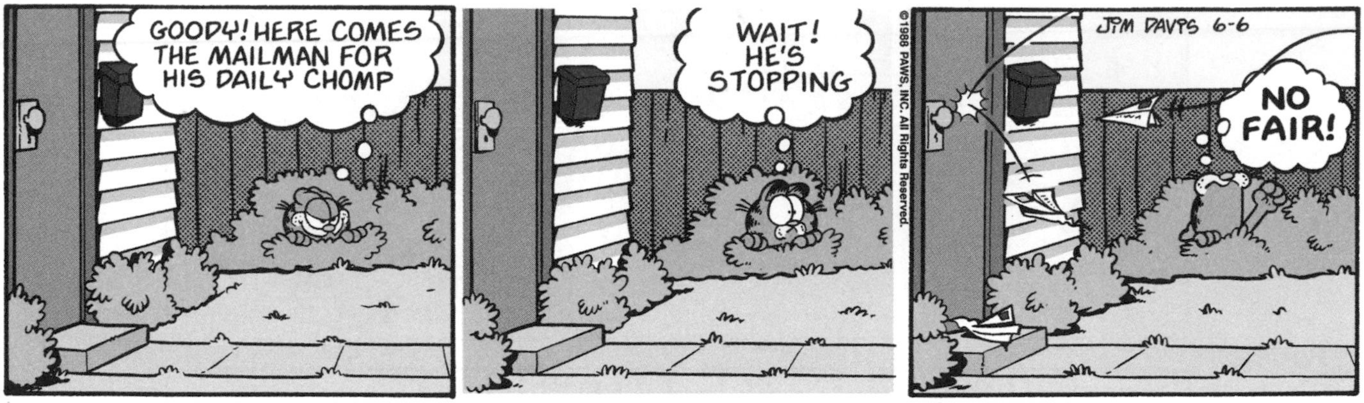
GOODY! HERE COMES THE MAILMAN FOR HIS DAILY CHOMP
WAIT! HE'S STOPPING
©1988 PAWS, INC. All Rights Reserved.
JIM DAVIS 6-6
NO FAIR!

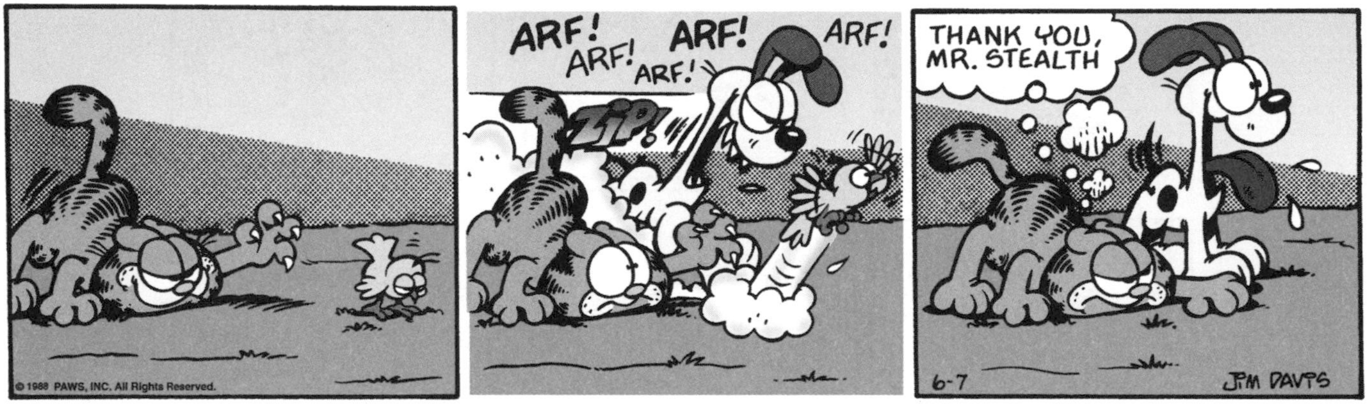
© 1988 PAWS, INC. All Rights Reserved.
ARF! ARF! ARF! ARF! ARF!
ZIP!
THANK YOU, MR. STEALTH
6-7
JIM DAVIS

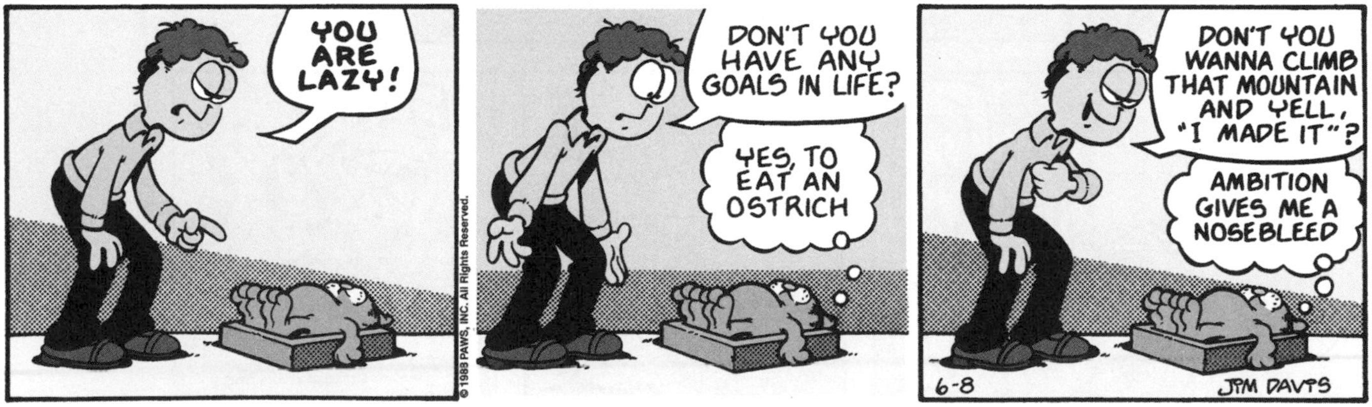
YOU ARE LAZY!
©1988 PAWS, INC. All Rights Reserved.
DON'T YOU HAVE ANY GOALS IN LIFE?
YES, TO EAT AN OSTRICH
DON'T YOU WANNA CLIMB THAT MOUNTAIN AND YELL, "I MADE IT"?
AMBITION GIVES ME A NOSEBLEED
6-8
JIM DAVIS

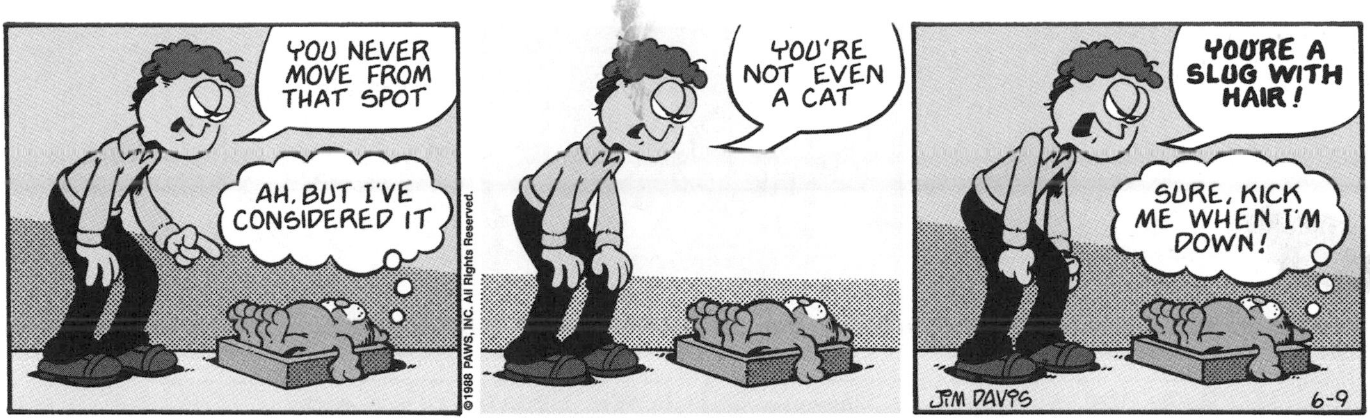
YOU NEVER MOVE FROM THAT SPOT
AH, BUT I'VE CONSIDERED IT
©1988 PAWS, INC. All Rights Reserved.
YOU'RE NOT EVEN A CAT
YOU'RE A SLUG WITH HAIR!
SURE, KICK ME WHEN I'M DOWN!
JIM DAVIS
6-9

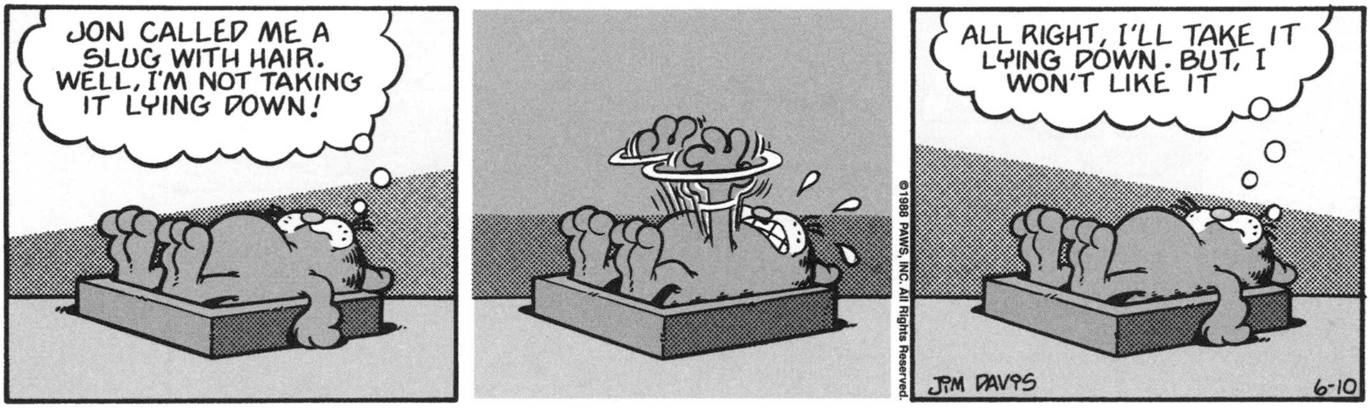
JON CALLED ME A SLUG WITH HAIR. WELL, I'M NOT TAKING IT LYING DOWN!
©1988 PAWS, INC. All Rights Reserved.
ALL RIGHT, I'LL TAKE IT LYING DOWN. BUT, I WON'T LIKE IT
JIM DAVIS
6-10

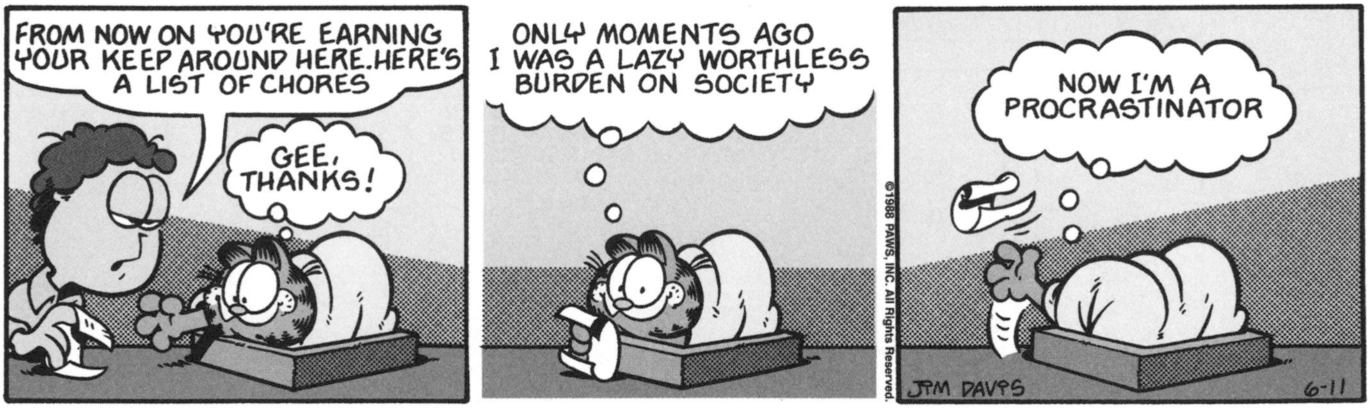
FROM NOW ON YOU'RE EARNING YOUR KEEP AROUND HERE. HERE'S A LIST OF CHORES
GEE, THANKS!
ONLY MOMENTS AGO I WAS A LAZY WORTHLESS BURDEN ON SOCIETY
©1988 PAWS, INC. All Rights Reserved.
NOW I'M A PROCRASTINATOR
JIM DAVIS
6-11

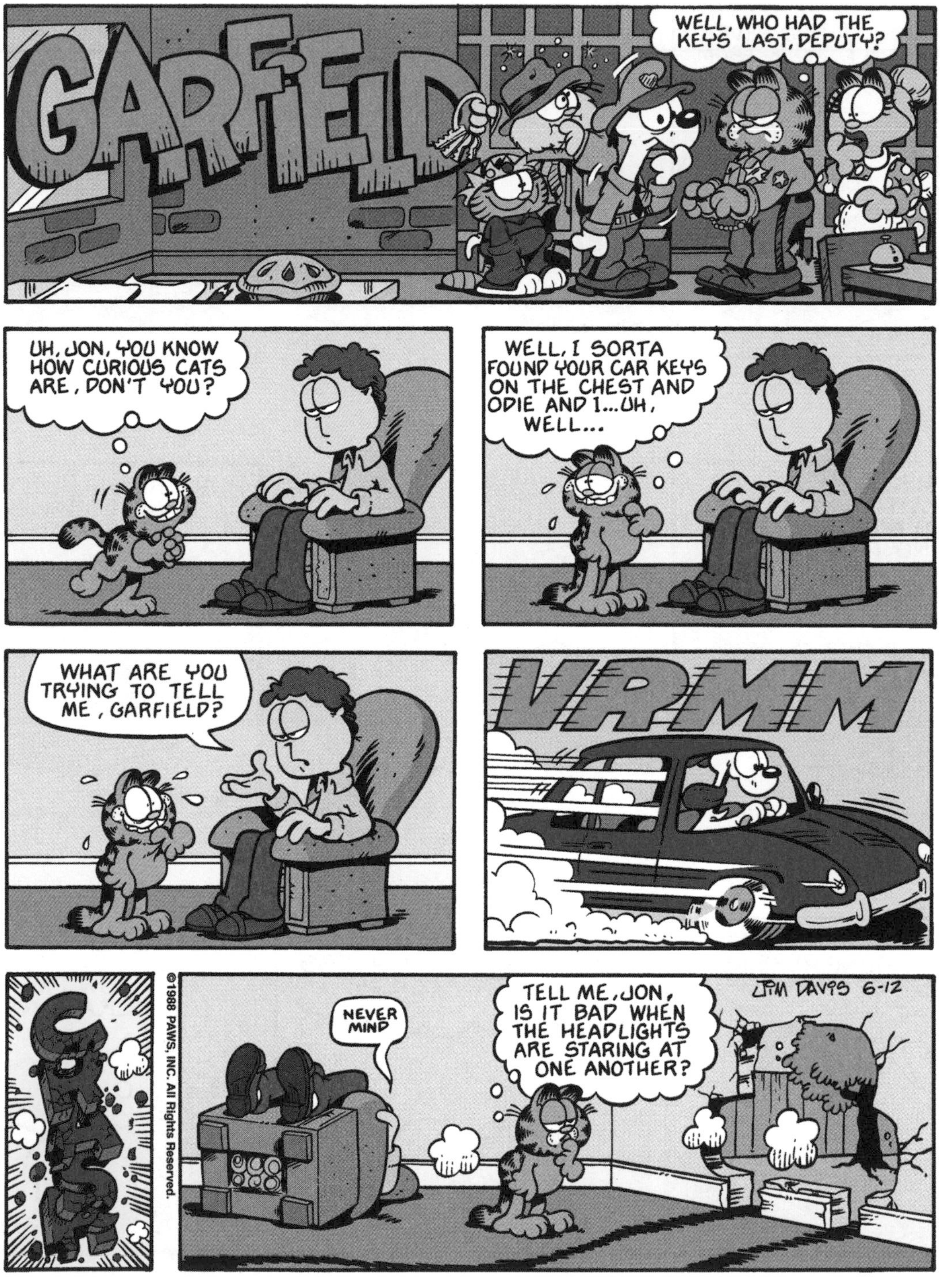
GARFIELD
WELL, WHO HAD THE KEYS LAST, DEPUTY?
UH, JON, YOU KNOW HOW CURIOUS CATS ARE, DON'T YOU?
WELL, I SORTA FOUND YOUR CAR KEYS ON THE CHEST AND ODIE AND I...UH, WELL...
WHAT ARE YOU TRYING TO TELL ME, GARFIELD?
VRMM
©1988 PAWS, INC. All Rights Reserved.
JIM DAVIS 6-12
NEVER MIND
TELL ME, JON, IS IT BAD WHEN THE HEADLIGHTS ARE STARING AT ONE ANOTHER?

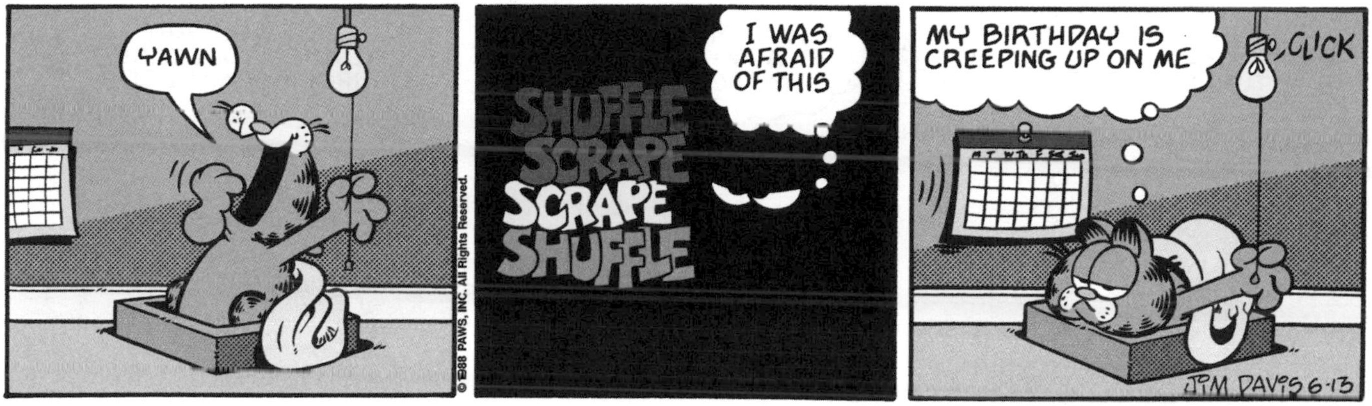
YAWN
© 1988 PAWS, INC. All Rights Reserved.
I WAS AFRAID OF THIS
SHUFFLE SCRAPE SCRAPE SHUFFLE
MY BIRTHDAY IS CREEPING UP ON ME
CLICK
JIM DAVIS 6-13

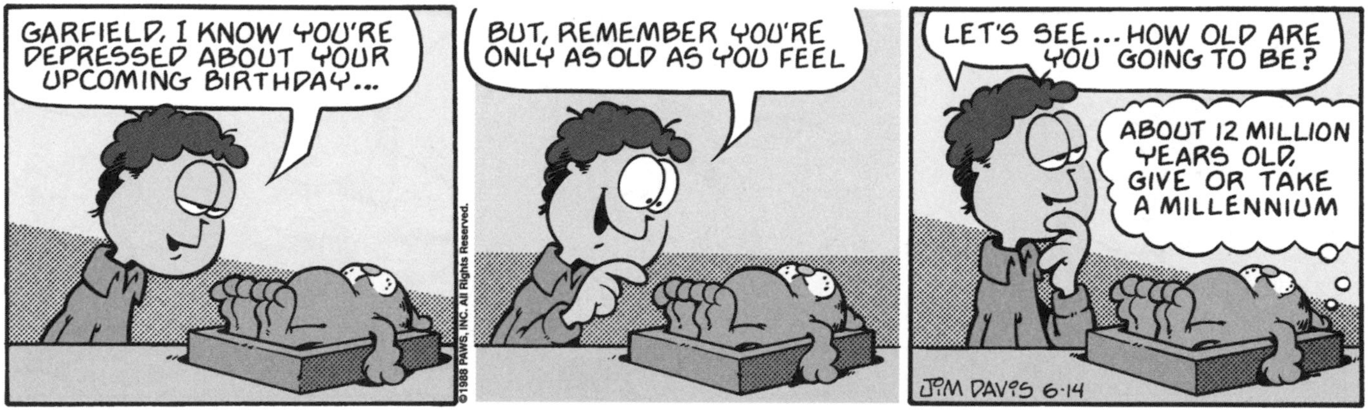
GARFIELD, I KNOW YOU'RE DEPRESSED ABOUT YOUR UPCOMING BIRTHDAY...
© 1988 PAWS, INC. All Rights Reserved.
BUT, REMEMBER YOU'RE ONLY AS OLD AS YOU FEEL
LET'S SEE... HOW OLD ARE YOU GOING TO BE?
ABOUT 12 MILLION YEARS OLD, GIVE OR TAKE A MILLENNIUM
JIM DAVIS 6-14

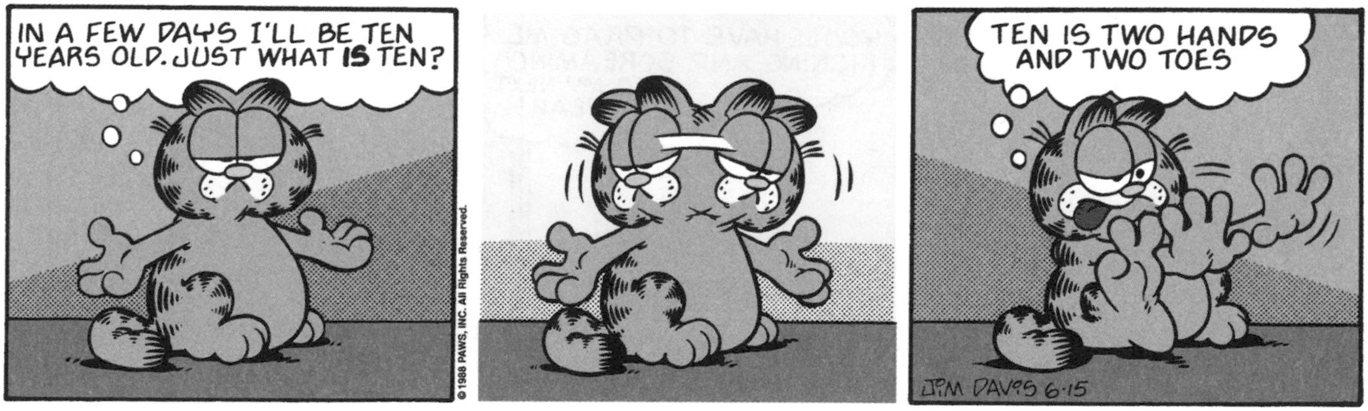
IN A FEW DAYS I'LL BE TEN YEARS OLD. JUST WHAT **IS** TEN?
© 1988 PAWS, INC. All Rights Reserved.
TEN IS TWO HANDS AND TWO TOES
JIM DAVIS 6-15

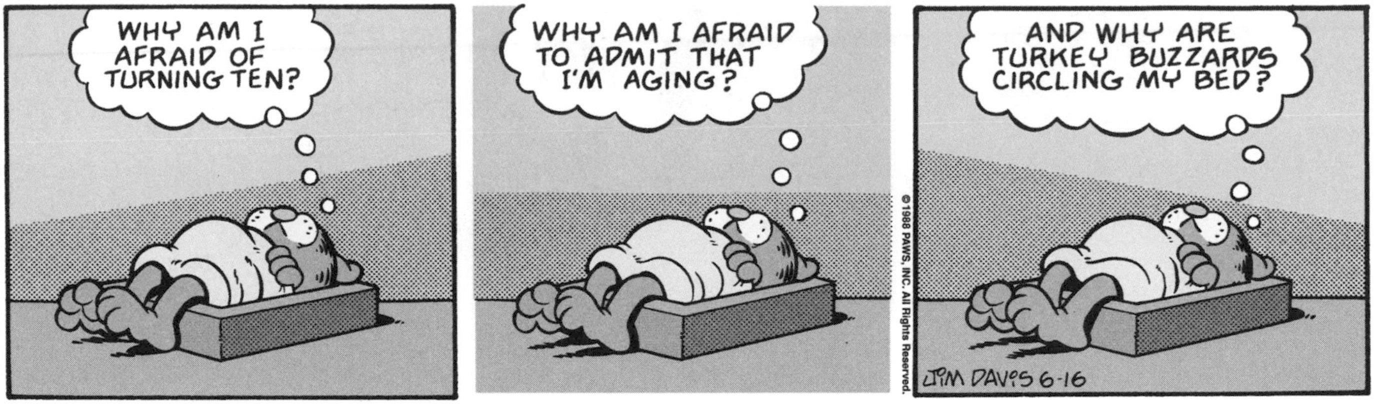
WHY AM I AFRAID OF TURNING TEN?
WHY AM I AFRAID TO ADMIT THAT I'M AGING?
AND WHY ARE TURKEY BUZZARDS CIRCLING MY BED?
© 1988 PAWS, INC. All Rights Reserved.
JIM DAVIS 6-16

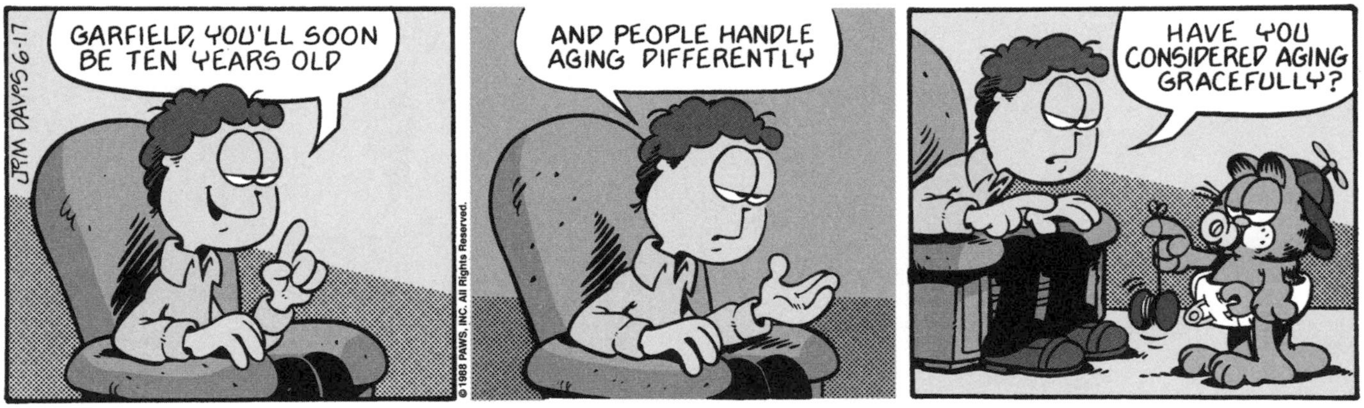
JIM DAVIS 6-17
GARFIELD, YOU'LL SOON BE TEN YEARS OLD
AND PEOPLE HANDLE AGING DIFFERENTLY
© 1988 PAWS, INC. All Rights Reserved.
HAVE YOU CONSIDERED AGING GRACEFULLY?

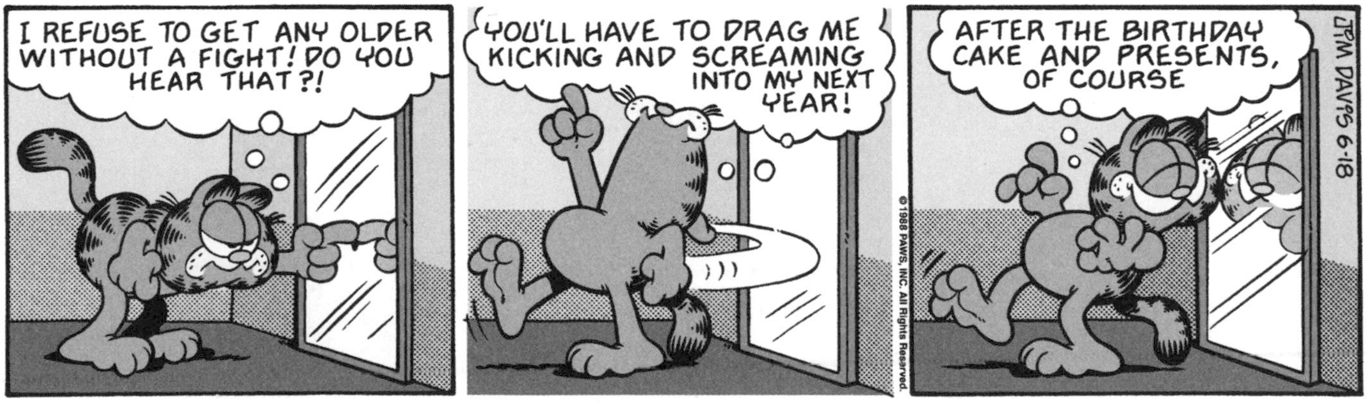
I REFUSE TO GET ANY OLDER WITHOUT A FIGHT! DO YOU HEAR THAT?!
YOU'LL HAVE TO DRAG ME KICKING AND SCREAMING INTO MY NEXT YEAR!
© 1988 PAWS, INC. All Rights Reserved.
AFTER THE BIRTHDAY CAKE AND PRESENTS, OF COURSE
JIM DAVIS 6-18

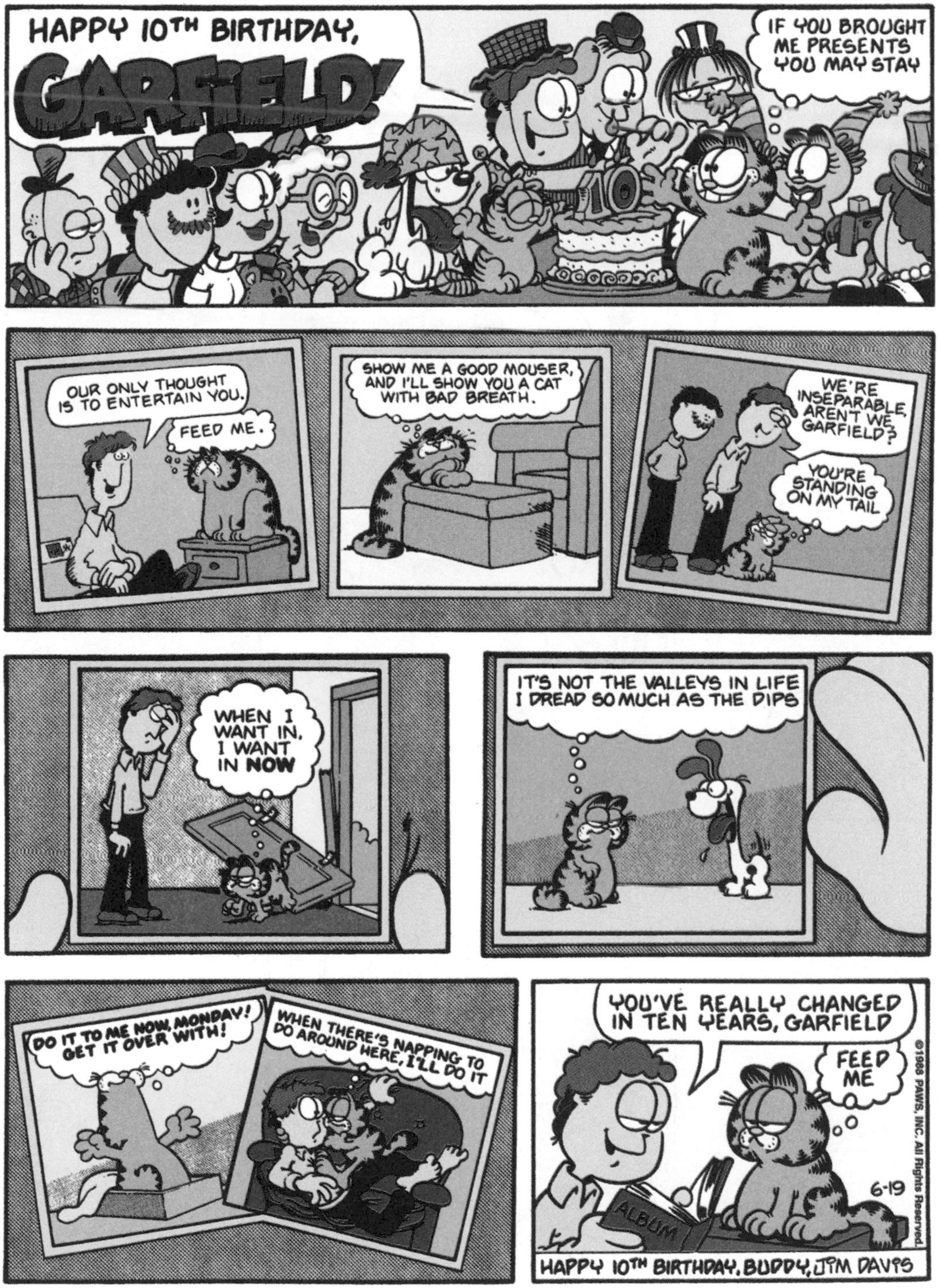

HAPPY 10TH BIRTHDAY, GARFIELD!
IF YOU BROUGHT ME PRESENTS YOU MAY STAY
OUR ONLY THOUGHT IS TO ENTERTAIN YOU.
FEED ME.
SHOW ME A GOOD MOUSER, AND I'LL SHOW YOU A CAT WITH BAD BREATH.
WE'RE INSEPARABLE, AREN'T WE, GARFIELD?
YOU'RE STANDING ON MY TAIL
WHEN I WANT IN, I WANT IN NOW
IT'S NOT THE VALLEYS IN LIFE I DREAD SO MUCH AS THE DIPS
DO IT TO ME NOW, MONDAY! GET IT OVER WITH!
WHEN THERE'S NAPPING TO DO AROUND HERE, I'LL DO IT
YOU'VE REALLY CHANGED IN TEN YEARS, GARFIELD
FEED ME
ALBUM
6-19
©1988 PAWS, INC. All Rights Reserved.
HAPPY 10TH BIRTHDAY, BUDDY, JIM DAVIS

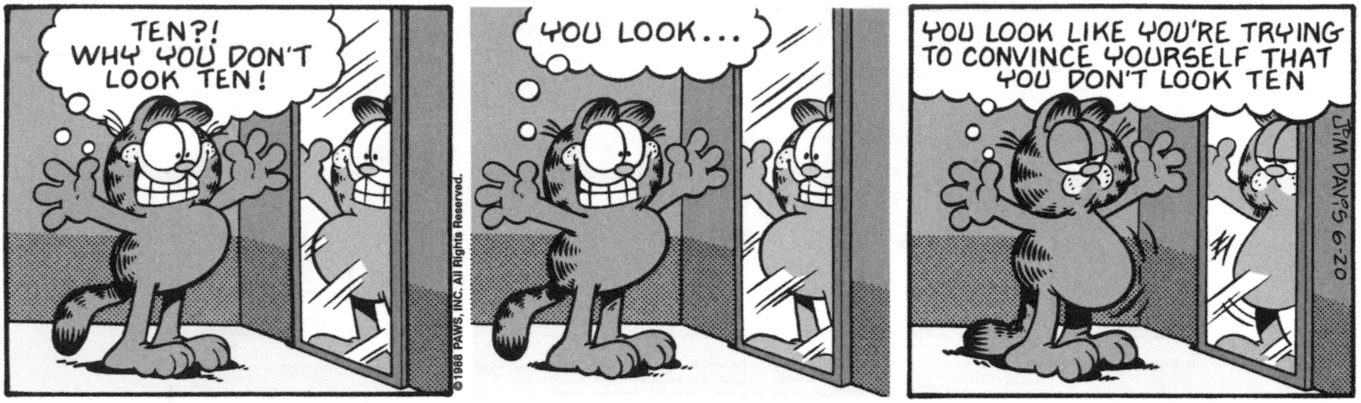
TEN?! WHY YOU DON'T LOOK TEN!
YOU LOOK...
YOU LOOK LIKE YOU'RE TRYING TO CONVINCE YOURSELF THAT YOU DON'T LOOK TEN
© 1988 PAWS, INC. All Rights Reserved.
JIM DAVIS 6-20

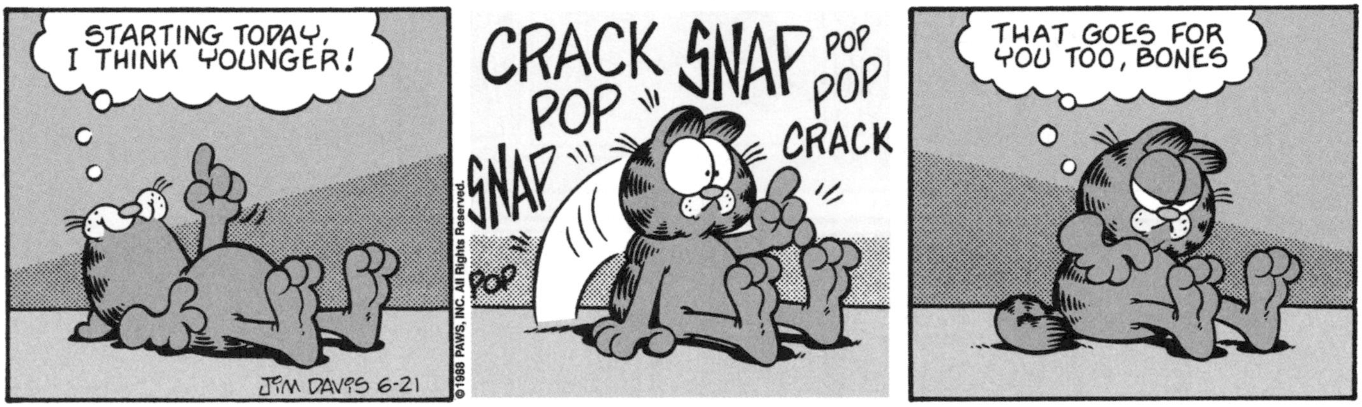
STARTING TODAY, I THINK YOUNGER!
JIM DAVIS 6-21
© 1988 PAWS, INC. All Rights Reserved.
CRACK SNAP POP POP POP CRACK SNAP POP
THAT GOES FOR YOU TOO, BONES

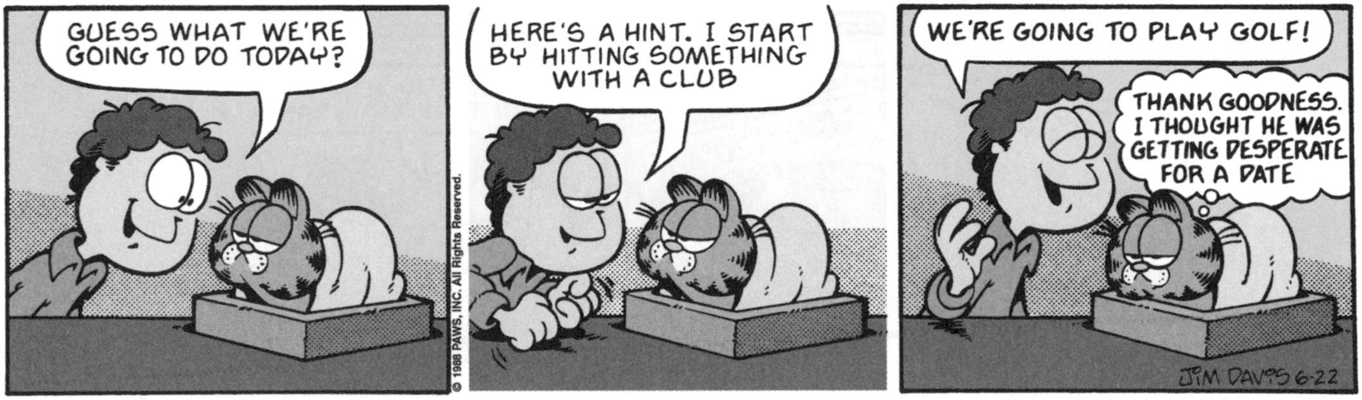
GUESS WHAT WE'RE GOING TO DO TODAY?
© 1988 PAWS, INC. All Rights Reserved.
HERE'S A HINT. I START BY HITTING SOMETHING WITH A CLUB
WE'RE GOING TO PLAY GOLF!
THANK GOODNESS. I THOUGHT HE WAS GETTING DESPERATE FOR A DATE
JIM DAVIS 6-22

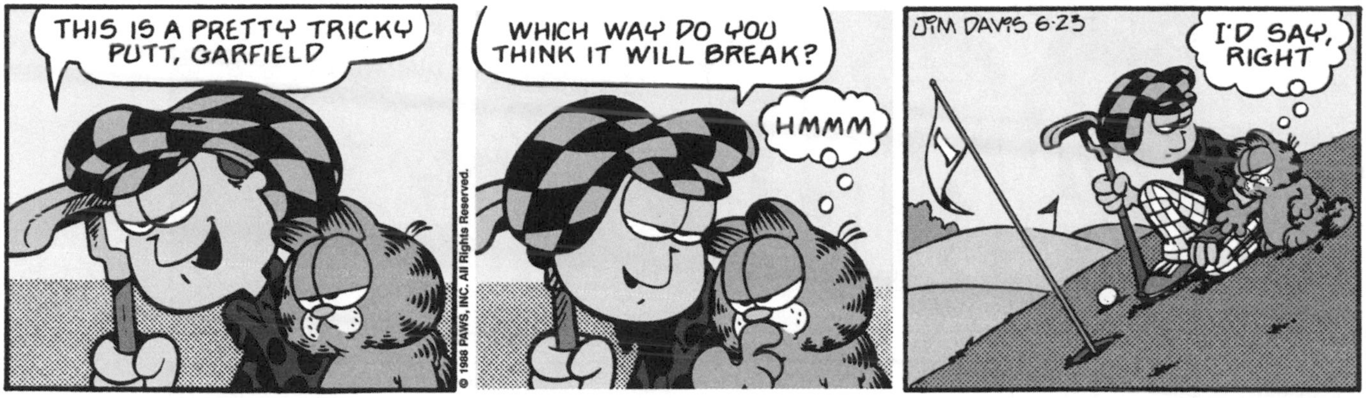
THIS IS A PRETTY TRICKY PUTT, GARFIELD
© 1988 PAWS, INC. All Rights Reserved.
WHICH WAY DO YOU THINK IT WILL BREAK?
HMMM
JIM DAVIS 6-23
I'D SAY, RIGHT

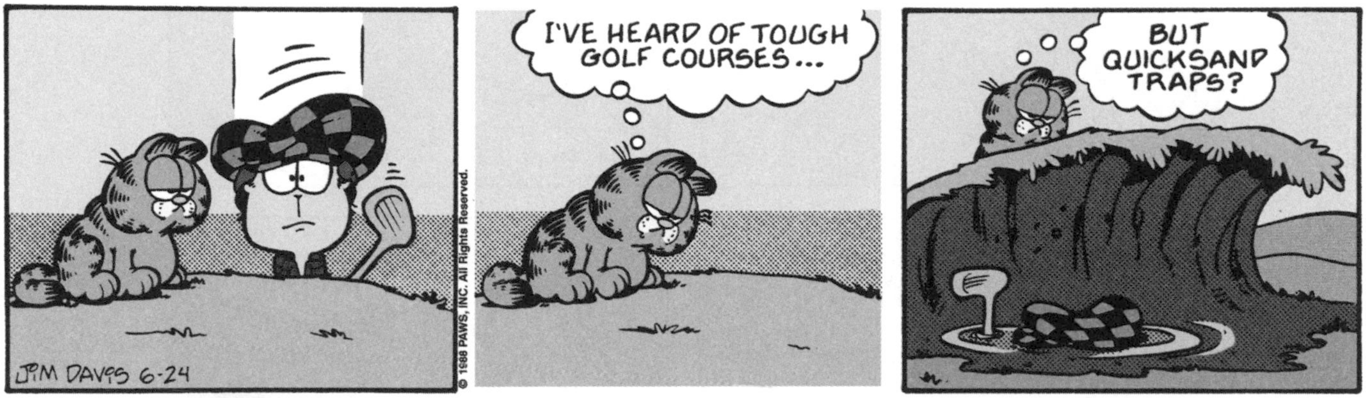
JIM DAVIS 6-24
© 1988 PAWS, INC. All Rights Reserved.
I'VE HEARD OF TOUGH GOLF COURSES...
BUT QUICKSAND TRAPS?

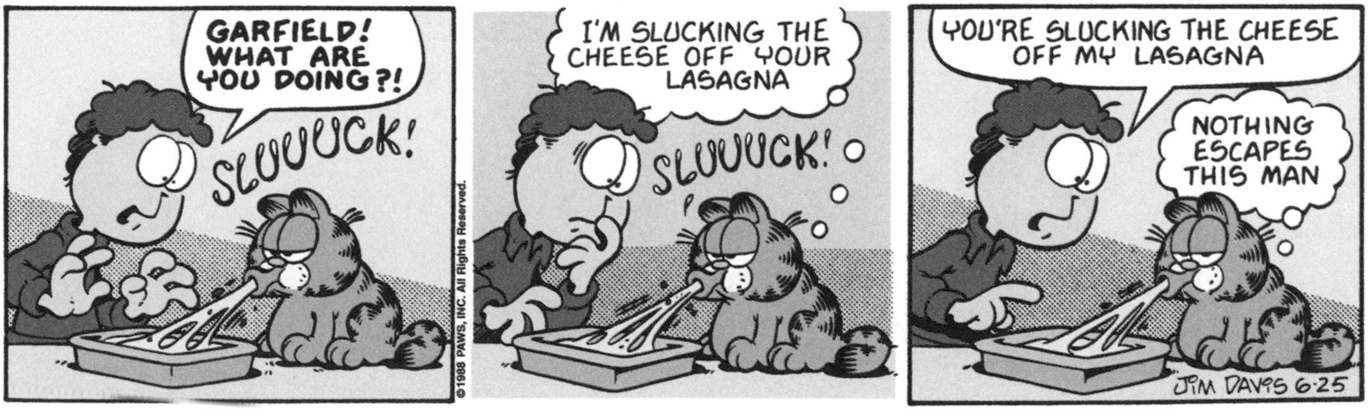
GARFIELD! WHAT ARE YOU DOING?!
SLUUUCK!
©1988 PAWS, INC. All Rights Reserved.
I'M SLUCKING THE CHEESE OFF YOUR LASAGNA
SLUUUCK!
YOU'RE SLUCKING THE CHEESE OFF MY LASAGNA
NOTHING ESCAPES THIS MAN
JIM DAVIS 6-25

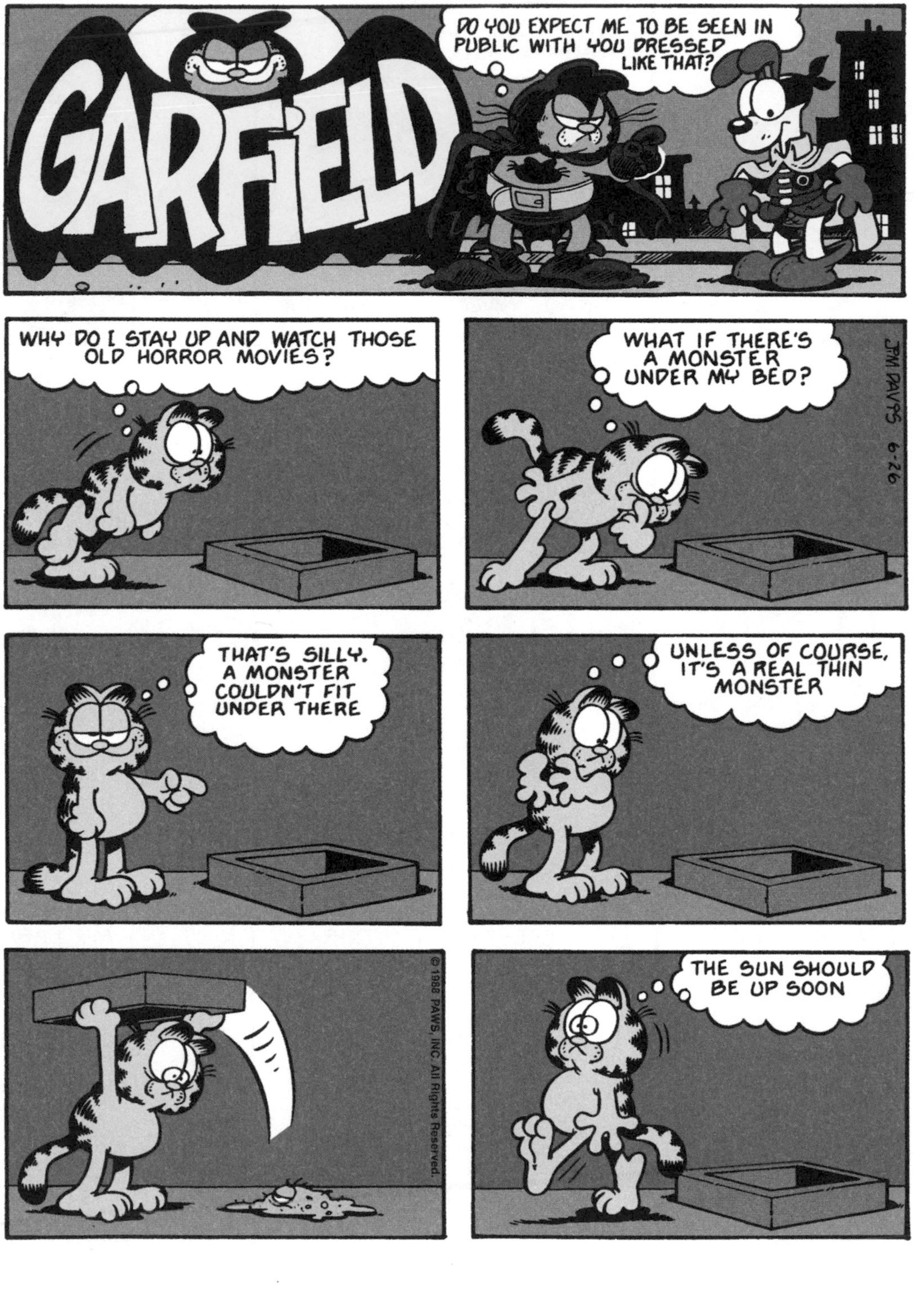
GARFIELD
DO YOU EXPECT ME TO BE SEEN IN PUBLIC WITH YOU DRESSED LIKE THAT?
WHY DO I STAY UP AND WATCH THOSE OLD HORROR MOVIES?
WHAT IF THERE'S A MONSTER UNDER MY BED?
JIM DAVIS 6-26
THAT'S SILLY. A MONSTER COULDN'T FIT UNDER THERE
UNLESS OF COURSE, IT'S A REAL THIN MONSTER
© 1988 PAWS, INC. All Rights Reserved.
THE SUN SHOULD BE UP SOON

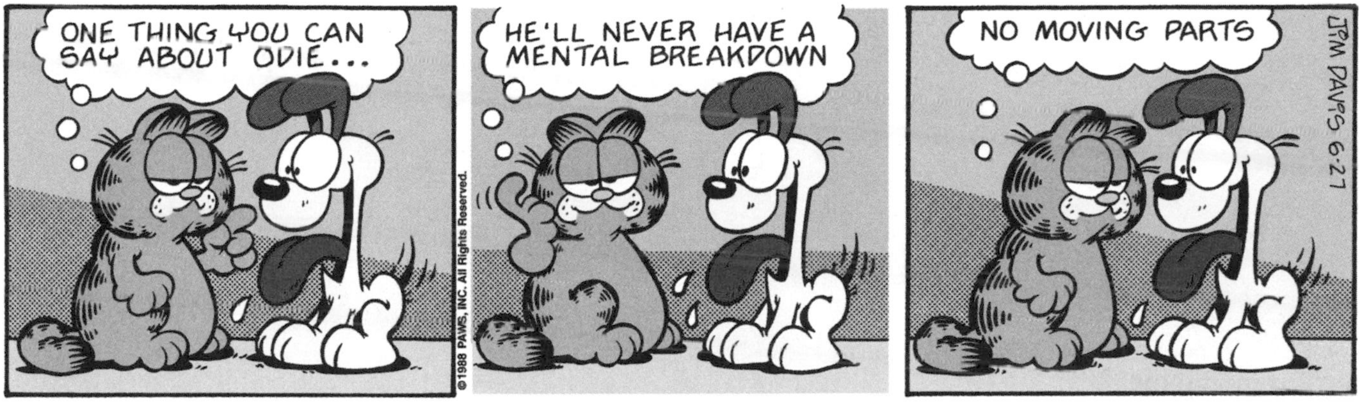
ONE THING YOU CAN SAY ABOUT ODIE...
HE'LL NEVER HAVE A MENTAL BREAKDOWN
NO MOVING PARTS
JIM DAVIS 6-27
© 1988 PAWS, INC. All Rights Reserved.

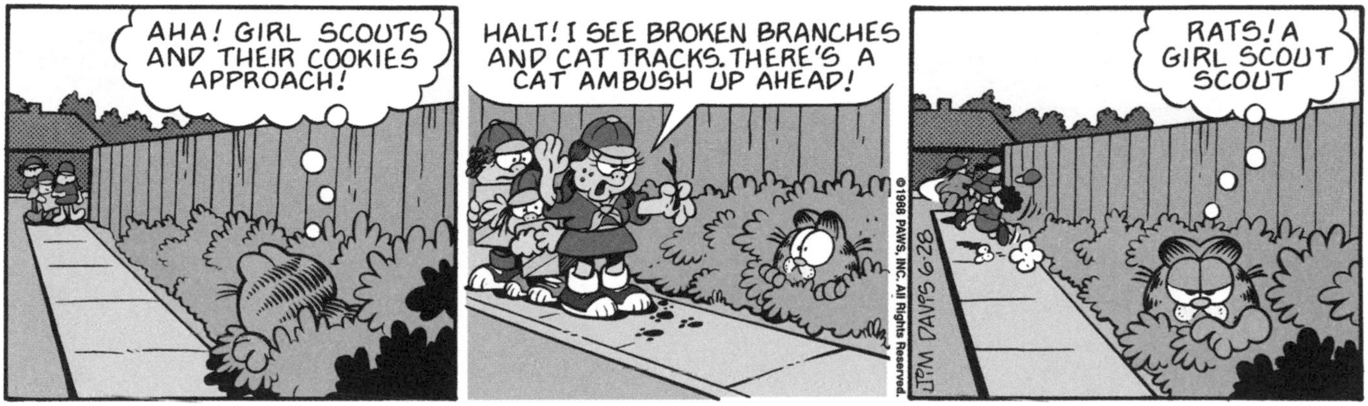
AHA! GIRL SCOUTS AND THEIR COOKIES APPROACH!
HALT! I SEE BROKEN BRANCHES AND CAT TRACKS. THERE'S A CAT AMBUSH UP AHEAD!
RATS! A GIRL SCOUT SCOUT
JIM DAVIS 6-28
© 1988 PAWS, INC. All Rights Reserved.

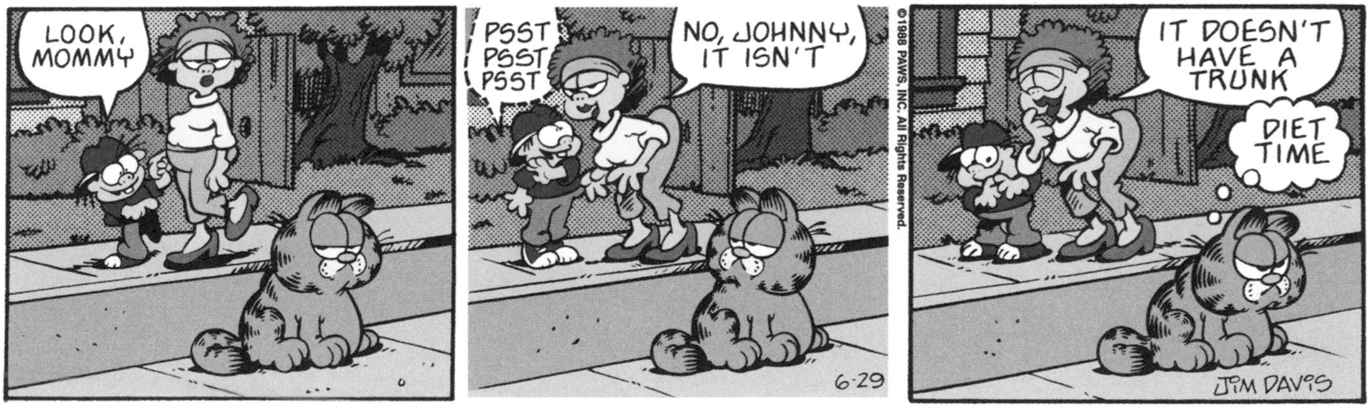
LOOK, MOMMY
PSST PSST PSST
NO, JOHNNY, IT ISN'T
6-29
IT DOESN'T HAVE A TRUNK
DIET TIME
JIM DAVIS
© 1988 PAWS, INC. All Rights Reserved.

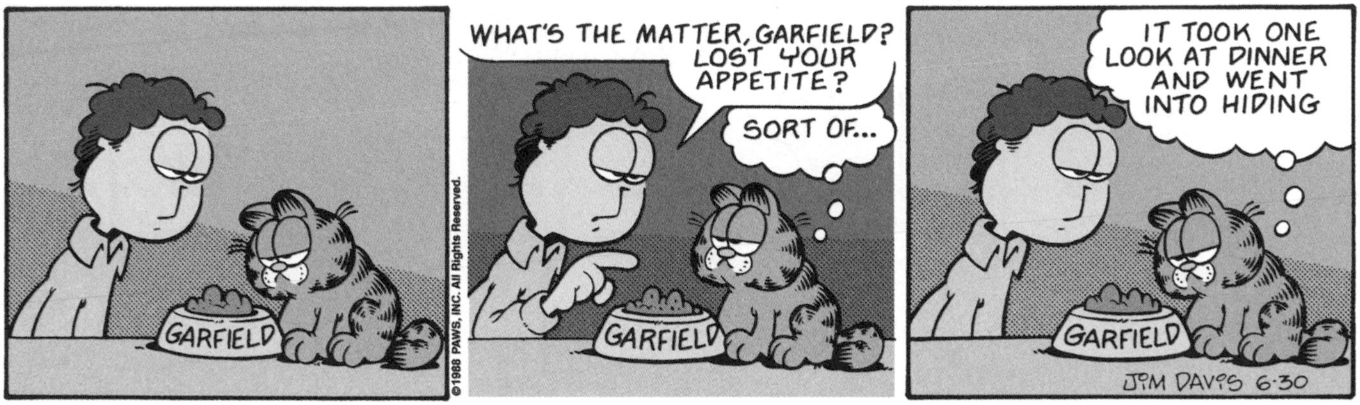
WHAT'S THE MATTER, GARFIELD? LOST YOUR APPETITE?
SORT OF...
IT TOOK ONE LOOK AT DINNER AND WENT INTO HIDING
GARFIELD
©1988 PAWS, INC. All Rights Reserved.
JIM DAVIS 6-30

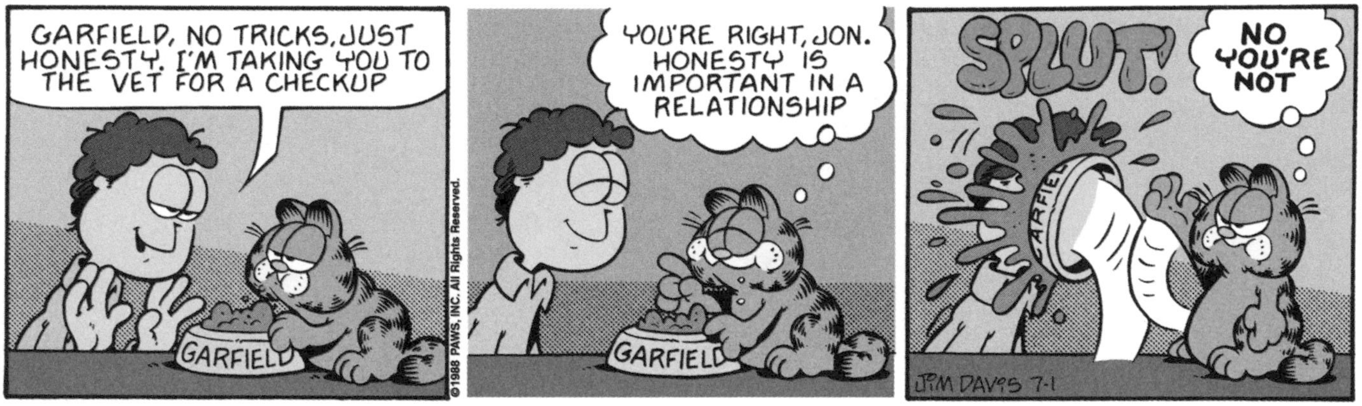
GARFIELD, NO TRICKS, JUST HONESTY. I'M TAKING YOU TO THE VET FOR A CHECKUP
YOU'RE RIGHT, JON. HONESTY IS IMPORTANT IN A RELATIONSHIP
SPLUT!
NO YOU'RE NOT
GARFIELD
©1988 PAWS, INC. All Rights Reserved.
JIM DAVIS 7-1

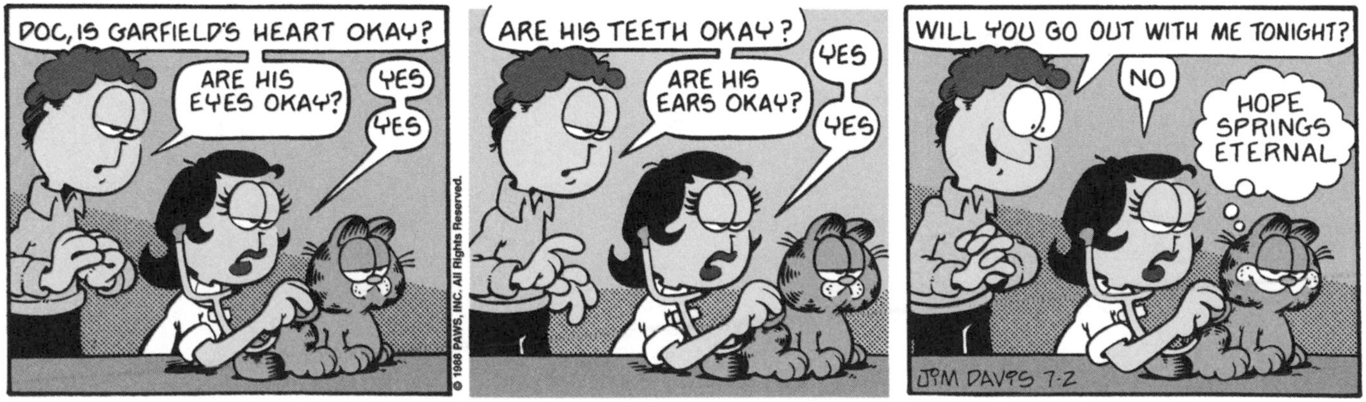
DOC, IS GARFIELD'S HEART OKAY?
ARE HIS EYES OKAY?
YES
YES
ARE HIS TEETH OKAY?
ARE HIS EARS OKAY?
YES
YES
WILL YOU GO OUT WITH ME TONIGHT?
NO
HOPE SPRINGS ETERNAL
© 1988 PAWS, INC. All Rights Reserved.
JIM DAVIS 7-2

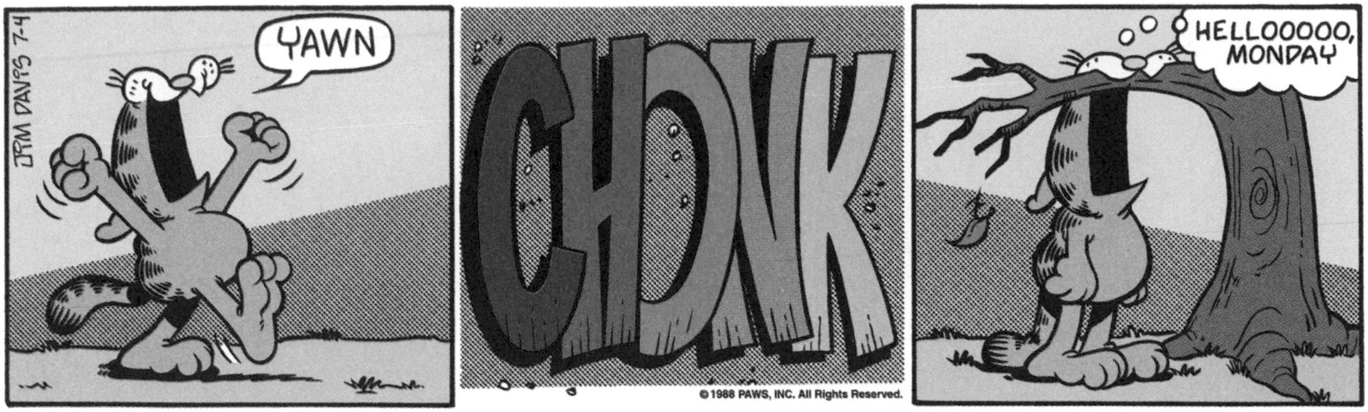
JIM DAVIS 7-4
YAWN
CHONK
HELLOOOOO, MONDAY
© 1988 PAWS, INC. All Rights Reserved.

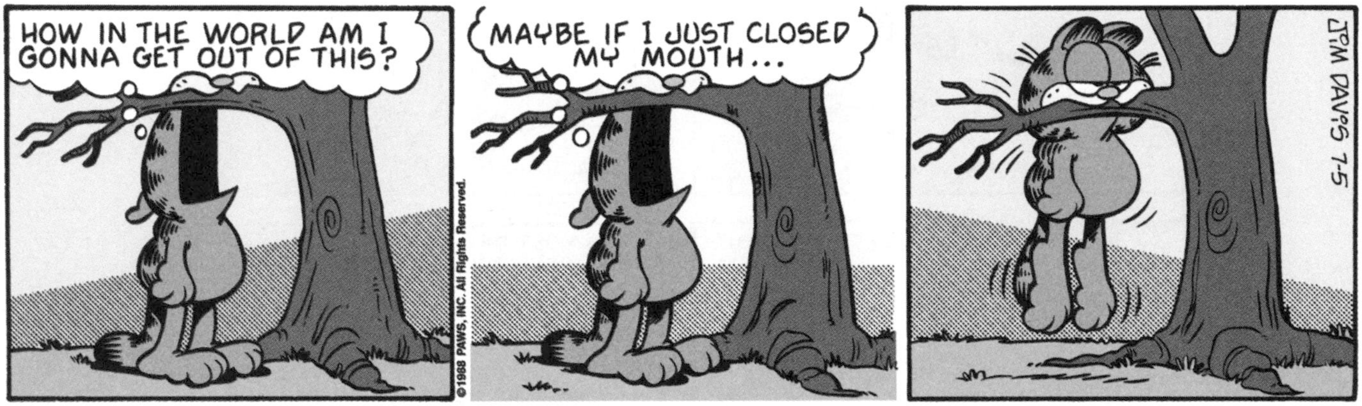
HOW IN THE WORLD AM I GONNA GET OUT OF THIS?
© 1988 PAWS, INC. All Rights Reserved.
MAYBE IF I JUST CLOSED MY MOUTH...
JIM DAVIS 7-5

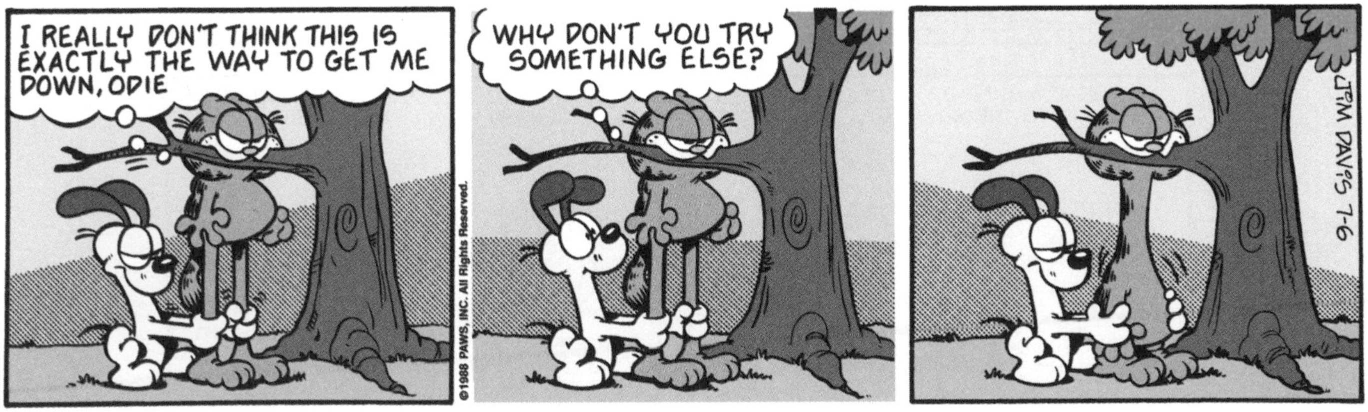
I REALLY DON'T THINK THIS IS EXACTLY THE WAY TO GET ME DOWN, ODIE
© 1988 PAWS, INC. All Rights Reserved.
WHY DON'T YOU TRY SOMETHING ELSE?
JIM DAVIS 7-6

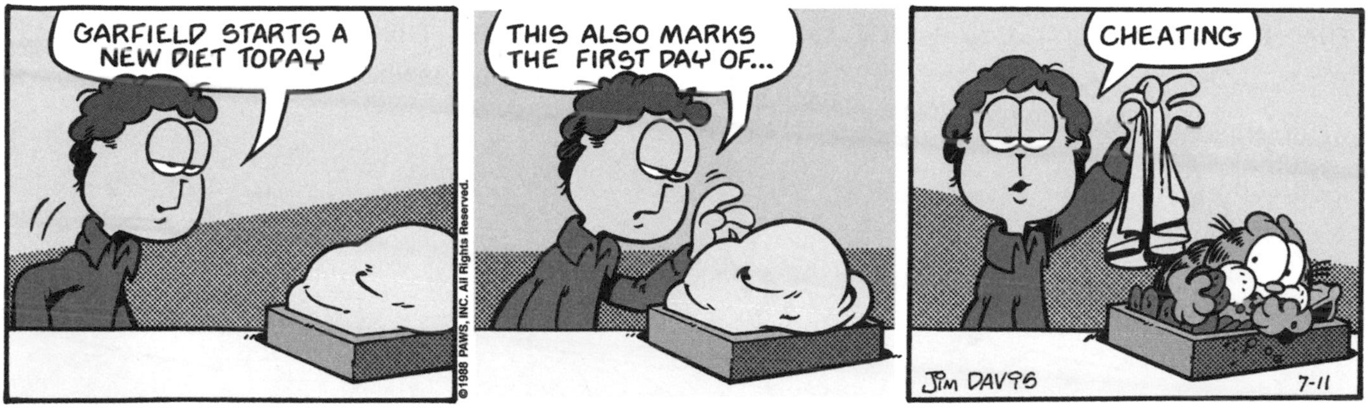
GARFIELD STARTS A NEW DIET TODAY
THIS ALSO MARKS THE FIRST DAY OF...
CHEATING
©1988 PAWS, INC. All Rights Reserved.
JIM DAVIS
7-11

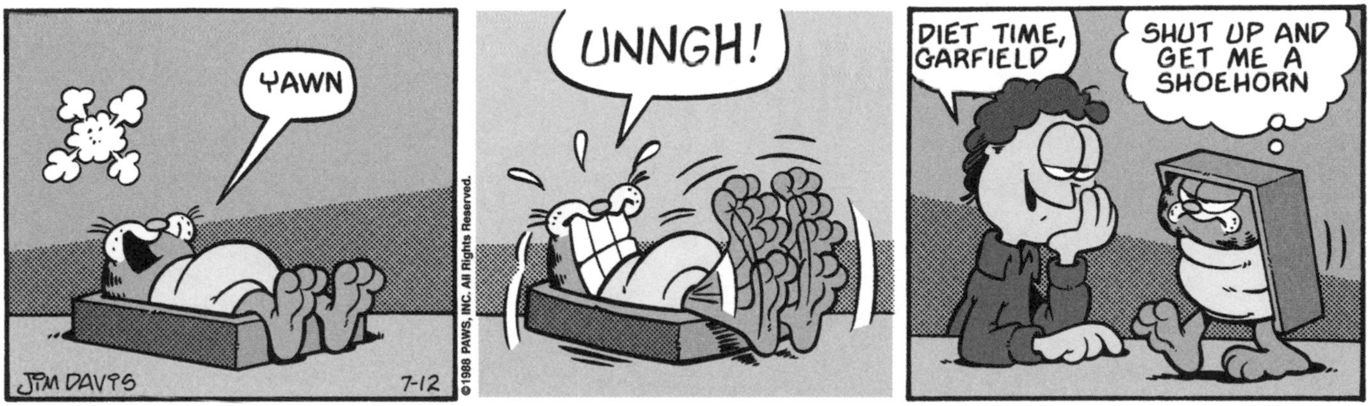
YAWN
UNNGH!
DIET TIME, GARFIELD
SHUT UP AND GET ME A SHOEHORN
©1988 PAWS, INC. All Rights Reserved.
JIM DAVIS
7-12

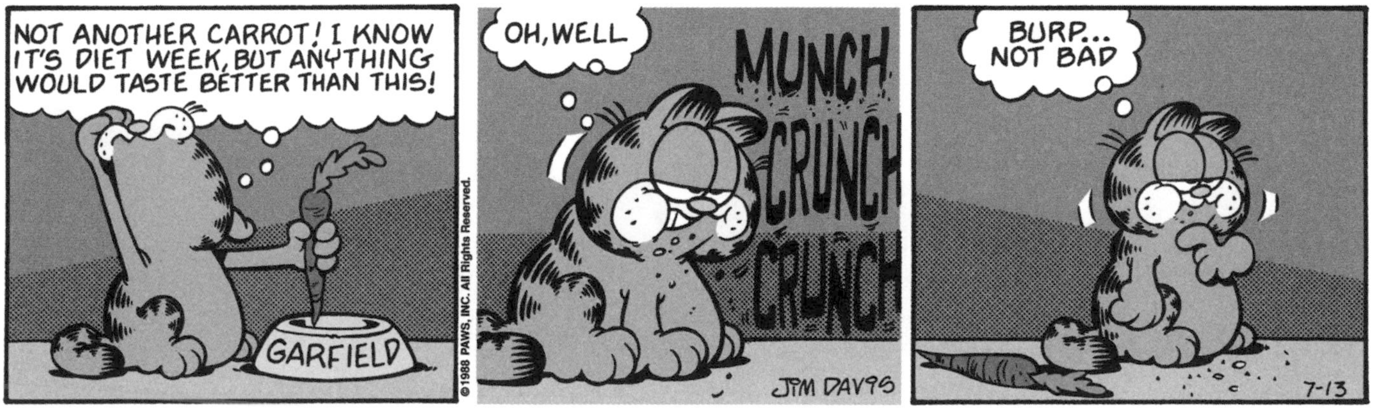
NOT ANOTHER CARROT! I KNOW IT'S DIET WEEK, BUT ANYTHING WOULD TASTE BETTER THAN THIS!
GARFIELD
OH, WELL
MUNCH
CRUNCH
CRUNCH
BURP... NOT BAD
©1988 PAWS, INC. All Rights Reserved.
JIM DAVIS
7-13

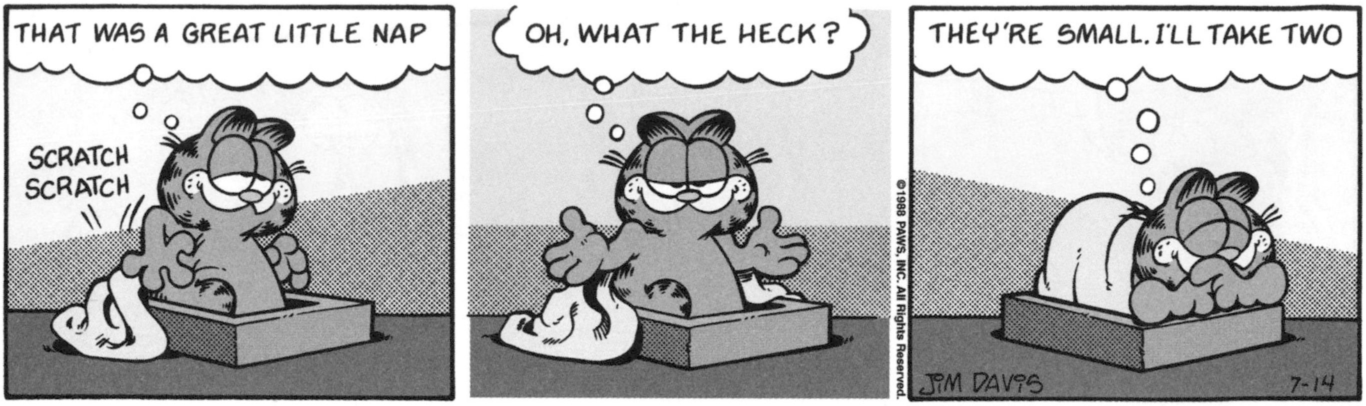
THAT WAS A GREAT LITTLE NAP
SCRATCH SCRATCH
OH, WHAT THE HECK?
©1988 PAWS, INC. All Rights Reserved.
THEY'RE SMALL. I'LL TAKE TWO
JIM DAVIS
7-14

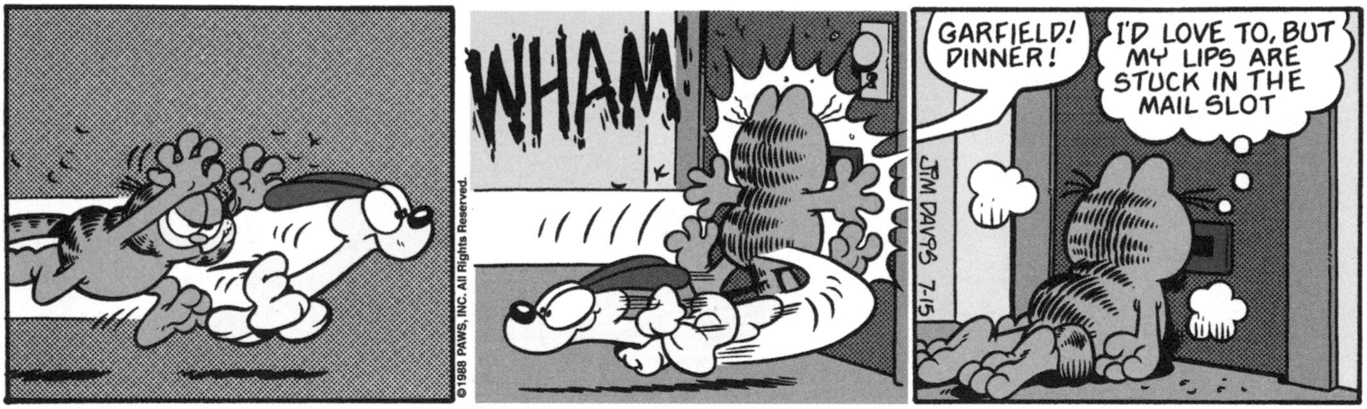
©1988 PAWS, INC. All Rights Reserved.
WHAM!
JIM DAVIS 7-15
GARFIELD! DINNER!
I'D LOVE TO, BUT MY LIPS ARE STUCK IN THE MAIL SLOT

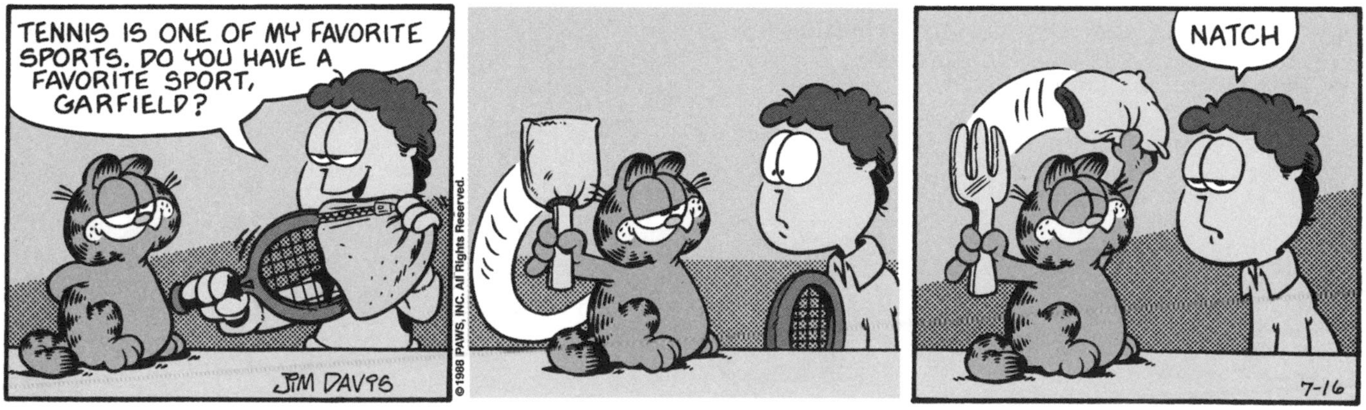
TENNIS IS ONE OF MY FAVORITE SPORTS. DO YOU HAVE A FAVORITE SPORT, GARFIELD?
JIM DAVIS
©1988 PAWS, INC. All Rights Reserved.
NATCH
7-16

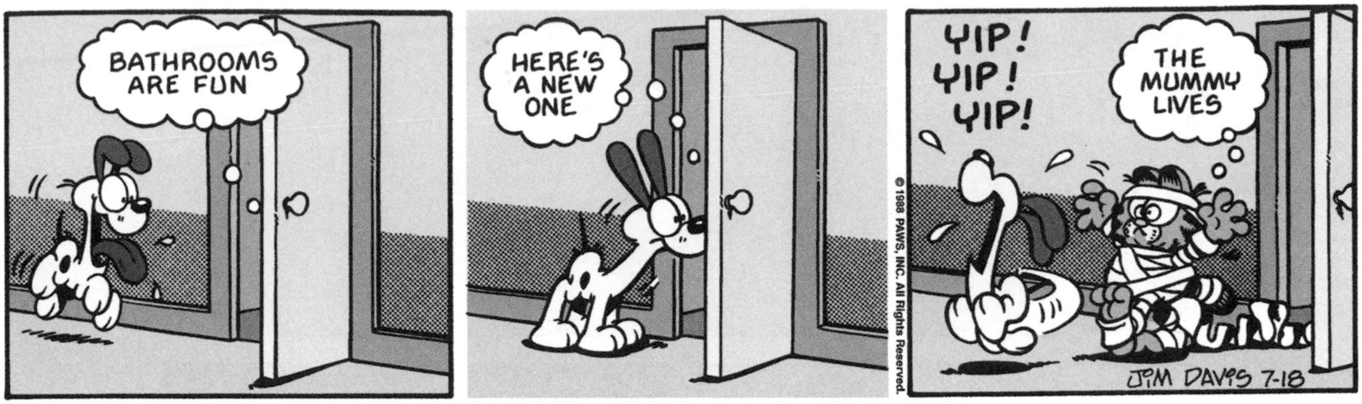
BATHROOMS ARE FUN
HERE'S A NEW ONE
© 1988 PAWS, INC. All Rights Reserved.
YIP! YIP! YIP!
THE MUMMY LIVES
JIM DAVIS 7-18

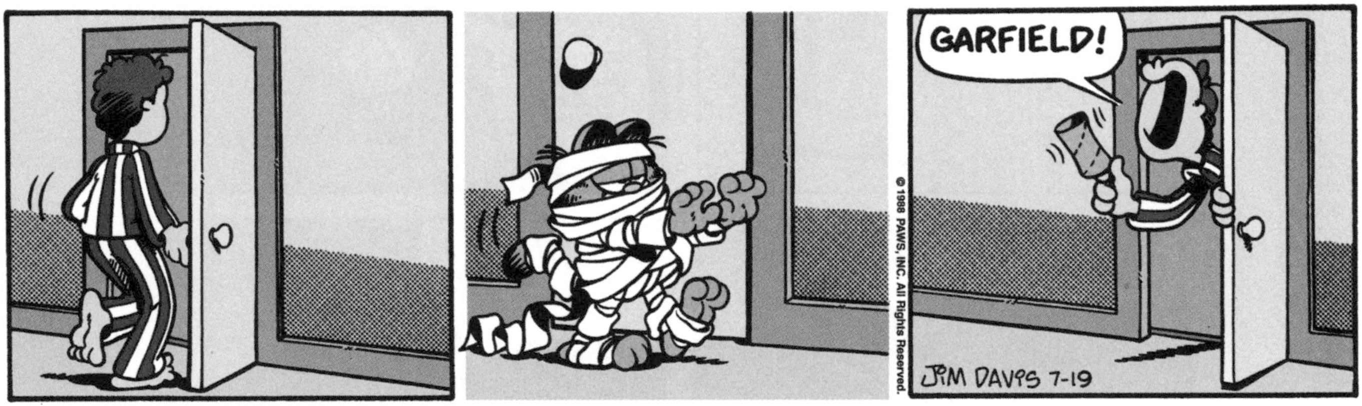
© 1988 PAWS, INC. All Rights Reserved.
GARFIELD!
JIM DAVIS 7-19

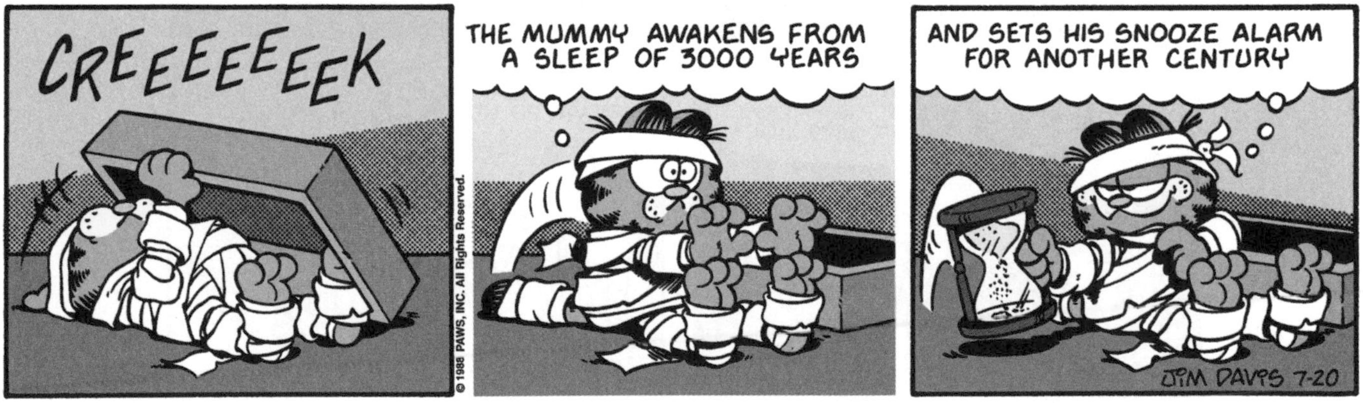
CREEEEEEEEK
© 1988 PAWS, INC. All Rights Reserved.
THE MUMMY AWAKENS FROM A SLEEP OF 3000 YEARS
AND SETS HIS SNOOZE ALARM FOR ANOTHER CENTURY
JIM DAVIS 7-20

Garfield impressions

BLIMP

BEACHED
WHALE

SMALL PLANET

COMATOSE
HIPPO

I'LL GET YOU
FOR THIS

OVERSTUFFED
SOFA

MONTANA

Garfield
goes to waist

BY JIM DAVIS

Ballantine Books ● **New York**

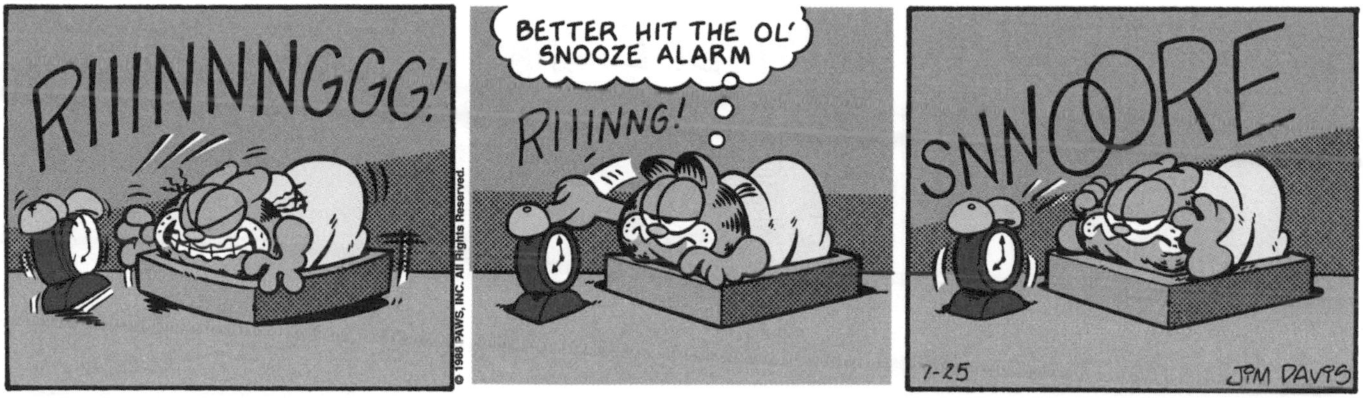
RIIINNNGGG!
© 1988 PAWS, INC. All Rights Reserved.
BETTER HIT THE OL' SNOOZE ALARM
RIIINNG!
SNNOORE
7-25
JIM DAVIS

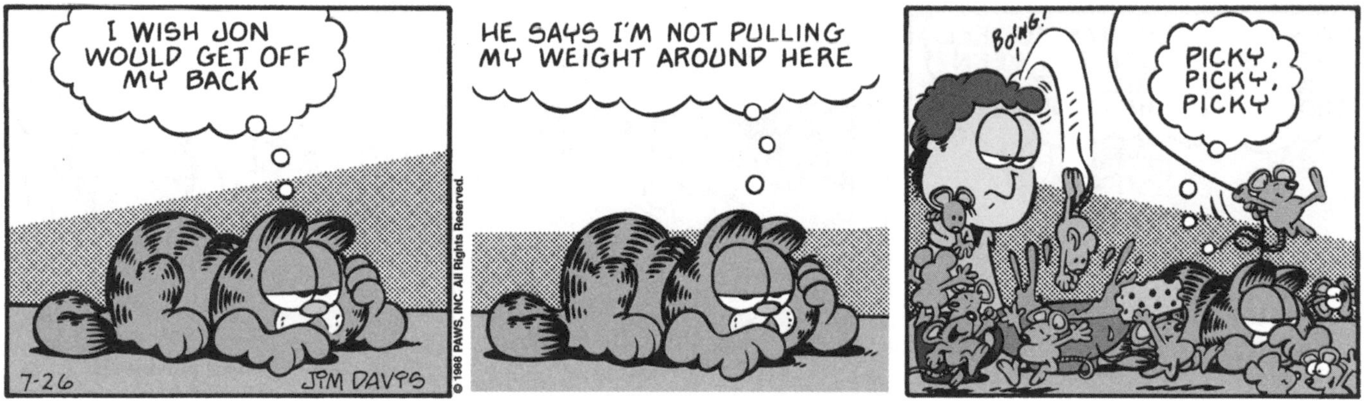
I WISH JON WOULD GET OFF MY BACK
7-26
JIM DAVIS
© 1988 PAWS, INC. All Rights Reserved.
HE SAYS I'M NOT PULLING MY WEIGHT AROUND HERE
BOING!
PICKY, PICKY, PICKY

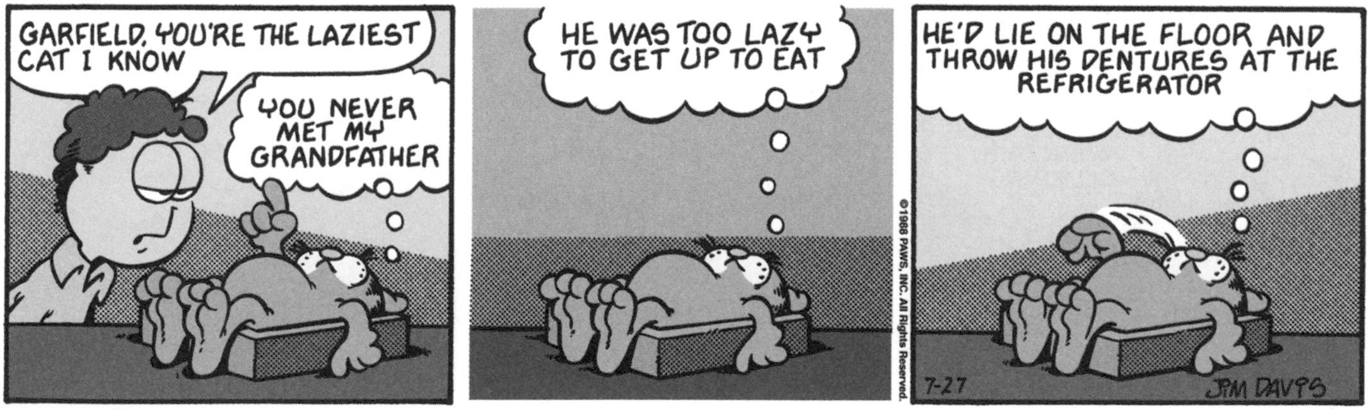
GARFIELD, YOU'RE THE LAZIEST CAT I KNOW
YOU NEVER MET MY GRANDFATHER
HE WAS TOO LAZY TO GET UP TO EAT
© 1988 PAWS, INC. All Rights Reserved.
HE'D LIE ON THE FLOOR AND THROW HIS DENTURES AT THE REFRIGERATOR
7-27
JIM DAVIS

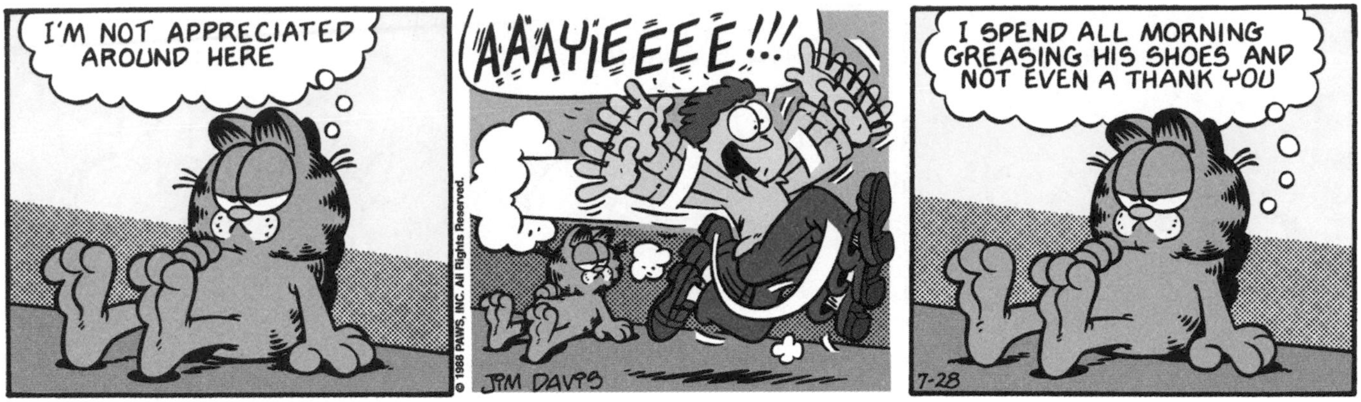
I'M NOT APPRECIATED AROUND HERE
AAAYIEEEEE!!!
© 1988 PAWS, INC. All Rights Reserved.
JIM DAVIS
I SPEND ALL MORNING GREASING HIS SHOES AND NOT EVEN A THANK YOU
7-28

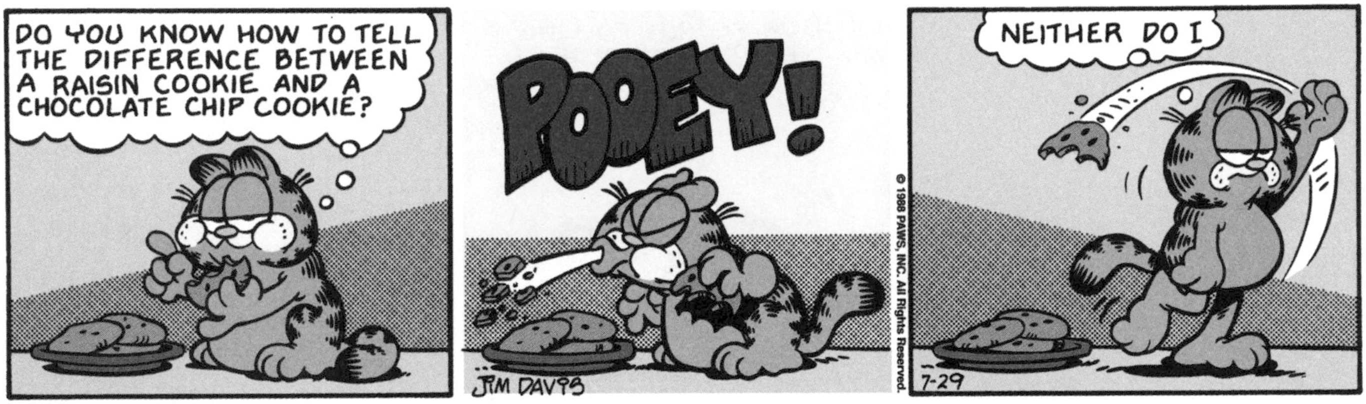
DO YOU KNOW HOW TO TELL THE DIFFERENCE BETWEEN A RAISIN COOKIE AND A CHOCOLATE CHIP COOKIE?
POOEY!
JIM DAVIS
© 1988 PAWS, INC. All Rights Reserved.
NEITHER DO I
7-29

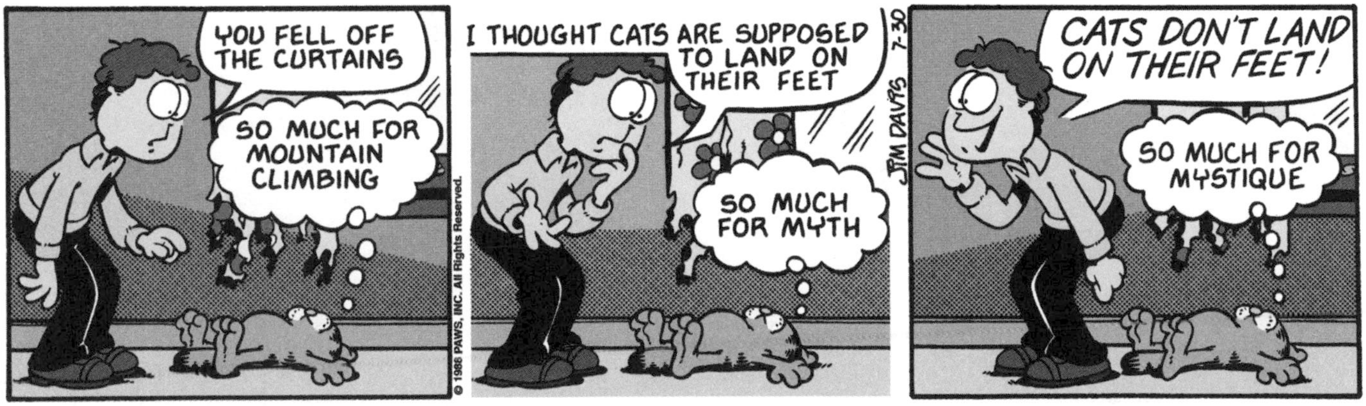
YOU FELL OFF THE CURTAINS
SO MUCH FOR MOUNTAIN CLIMBING
© 1988 PAWS, INC. All Rights Reserved.
I THOUGHT CATS ARE SUPPOSED TO LAND ON THEIR FEET
SO MUCH FOR MYTH
7-30
JIM DAVIS
CATS DON'T LAND ON THEIR FEET!
SO MUCH FOR MYSTIQUE

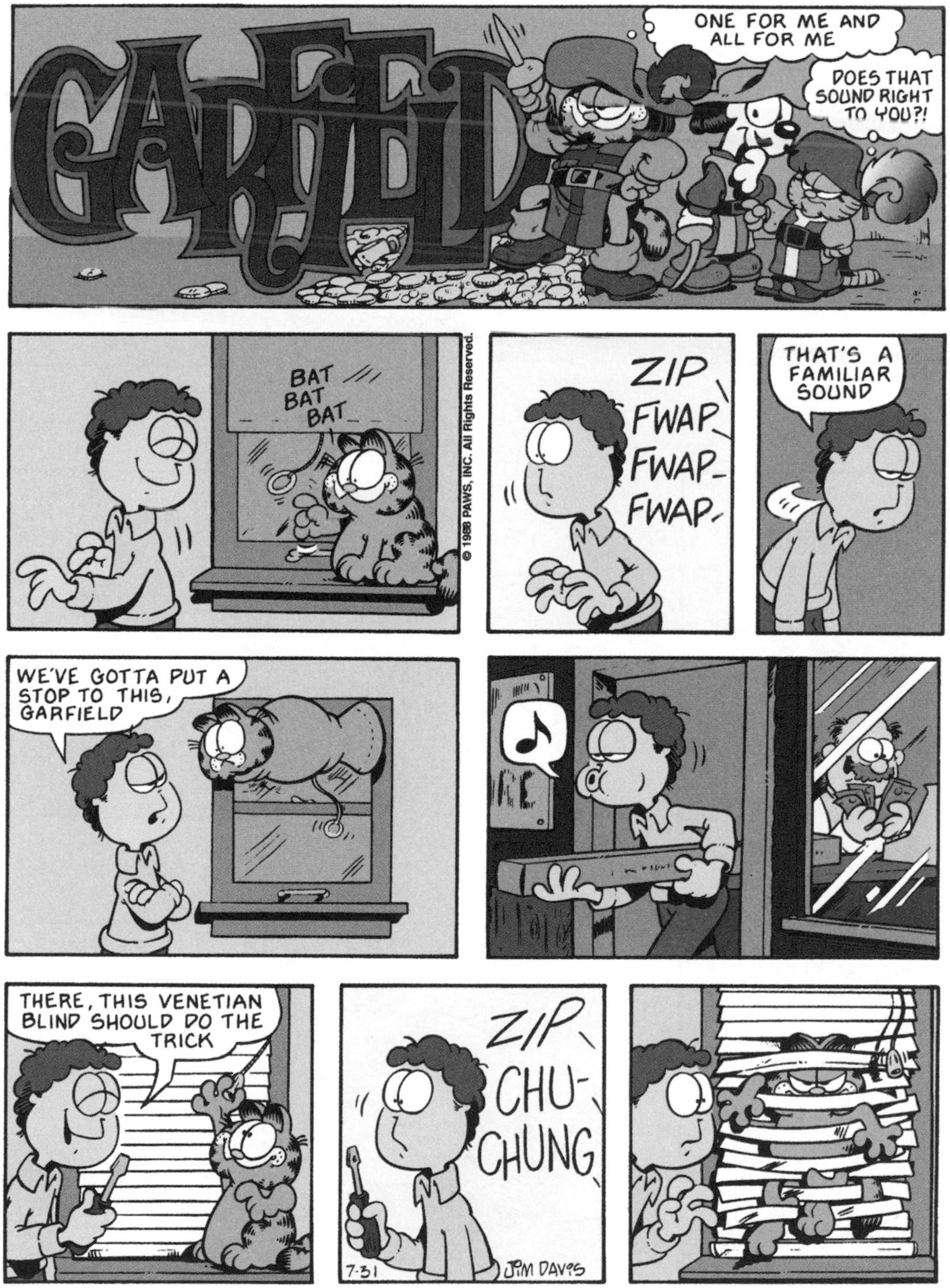
GARFIELD
ONE FOR ME AND ALL FOR ME
DOES THAT SOUND RIGHT TO YOU?!
© 1988 PAWS, INC. All Rights Reserved.
BAT BAT BAT
ZIP FWAP FWAP FWAP
THAT'S A FAMILIAR SOUND
WE'VE GOTTA PUT A STOP TO THIS, GARFIELD
THERE, THIS VENETIAN BLIND SHOULD DO THE TRICK
ZIP CHU-CHUNG
7-31
JIM DAVIS

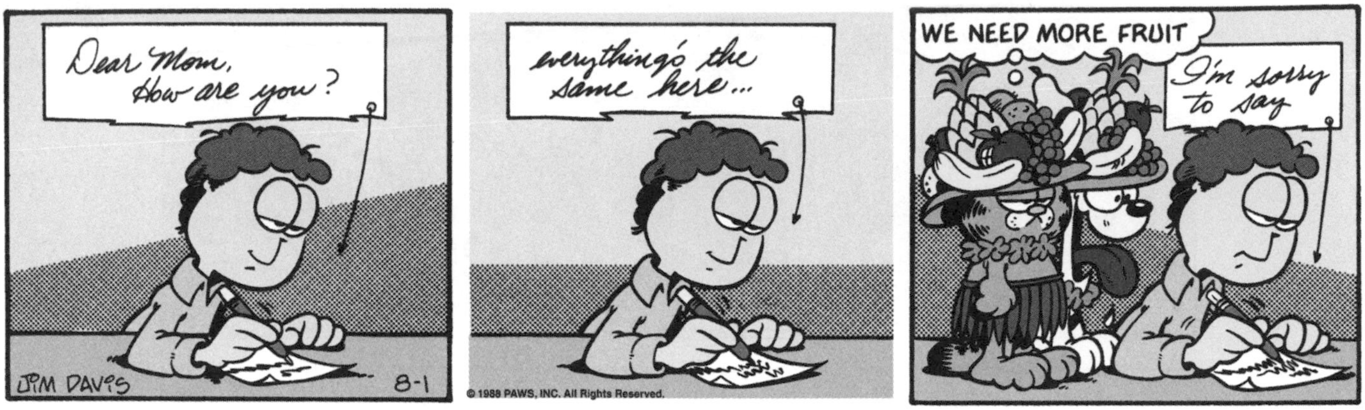
Dear Mom,
How are you?
JIM DAVIS 8-1
everything's the same here...
© 1988 PAWS, INC. All Rights Reserved.
WE NEED MORE FRUIT
I'm sorry to say

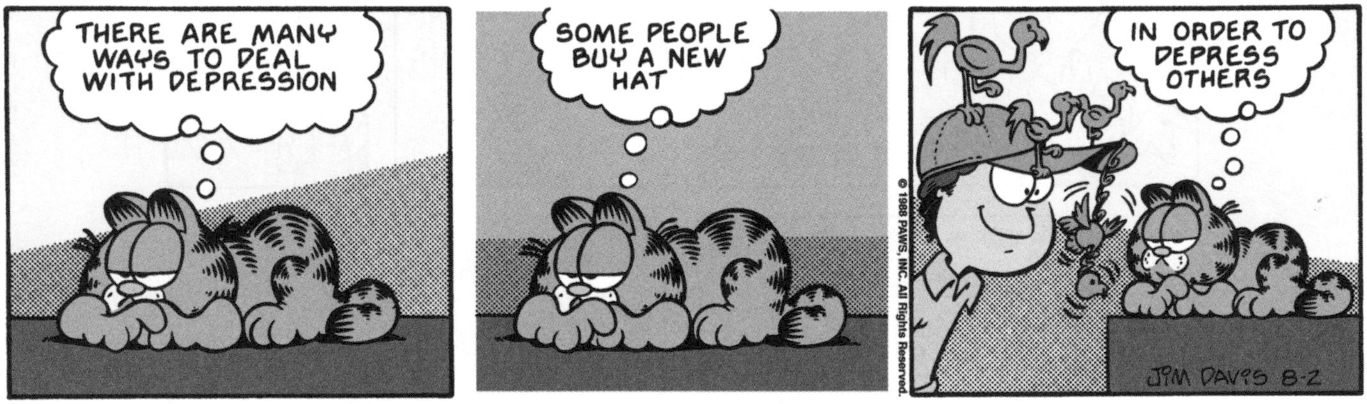
THERE ARE MANY WAYS TO DEAL WITH DEPRESSION
SOME PEOPLE BUY A NEW HAT
© 1988 PAWS, INC. All Rights Reserved.
IN ORDER TO DEPRESS OTHERS
JIM DAVIS 8-2

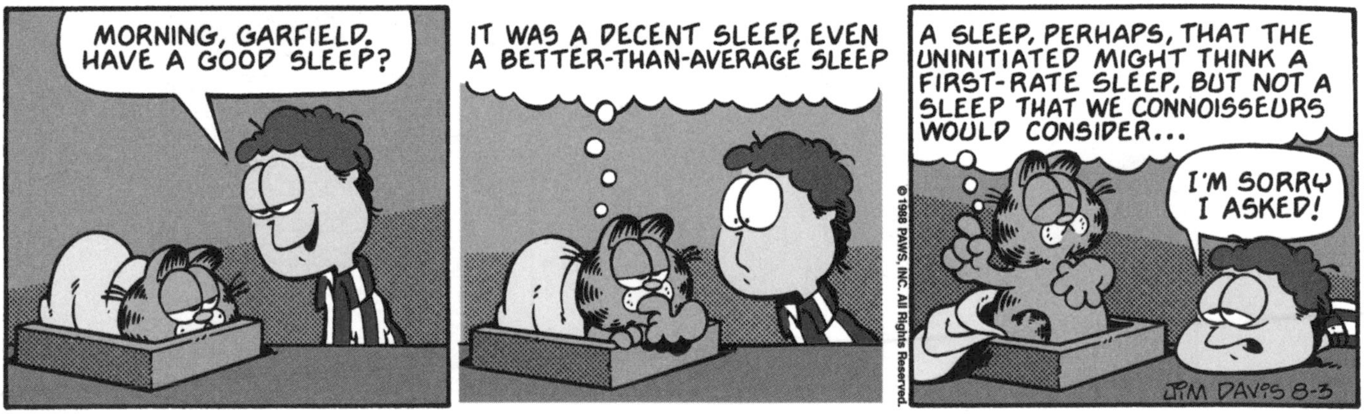
MORNING, GARFIELD. HAVE A GOOD SLEEP?
IT WAS A DECENT SLEEP, EVEN A BETTER-THAN-AVERAGE SLEEP
© 1988 PAWS, INC. All Rights Reserved.
A SLEEP, PERHAPS, THAT THE UNINITIATED MIGHT THINK A FIRST-RATE SLEEP, BUT NOT A SLEEP THAT WE CONNOISSEURS WOULD CONSIDER...
I'M SORRY I ASKED!
JIM DAVIS 8-3

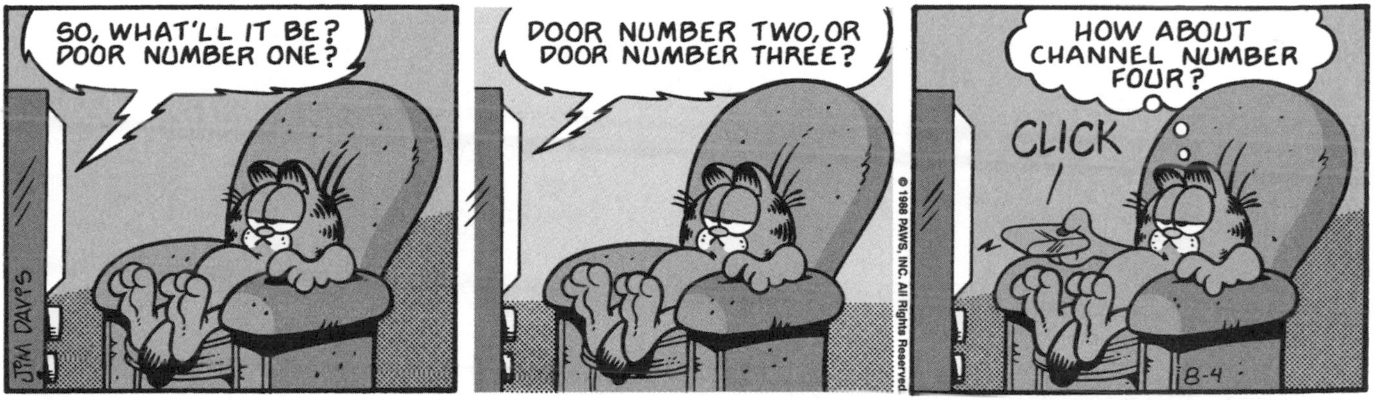
SO, WHAT'LL IT BE? DOOR NUMBER ONE?
JIM DAVIS
DOOR NUMBER TWO, OR DOOR NUMBER THREE?
© 1988 PAWS, INC. All Rights Reserved.
HOW ABOUT CHANNEL NUMBER FOUR?
CLICK
8-4

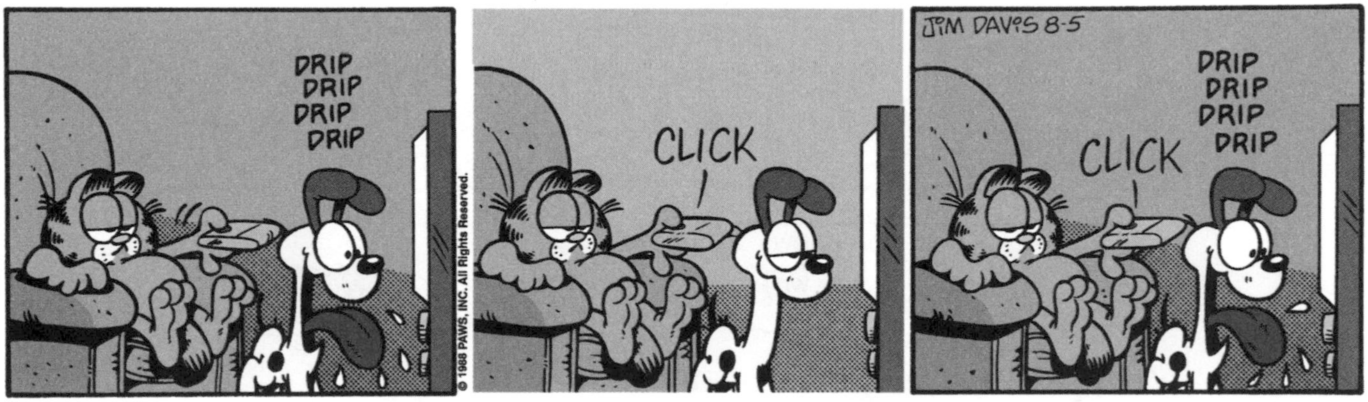
DRIP DRIP DRIP DRIP
© 1988 PAWS, INC. All Rights Reserved.
CLICK
JIM DAVIS 8-5
DRIP DRIP DRIP DRIP
CLICK

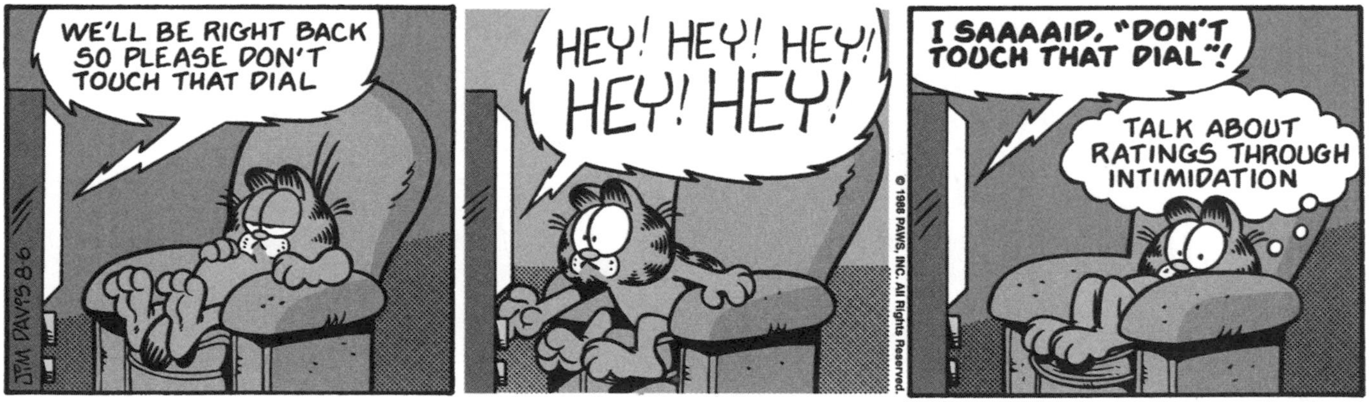
WE'LL BE RIGHT BACK SO PLEASE DON'T TOUCH THAT DIAL
JIM DAVIS 8-6
HEY! HEY! HEY! HEY! HEY!
© 1988 PAWS, INC. All Rights Reserved.
I SAAAAID, "DON'T TOUCH THAT DIAL"!
TALK ABOUT RATINGS THROUGH INTIMIDATION

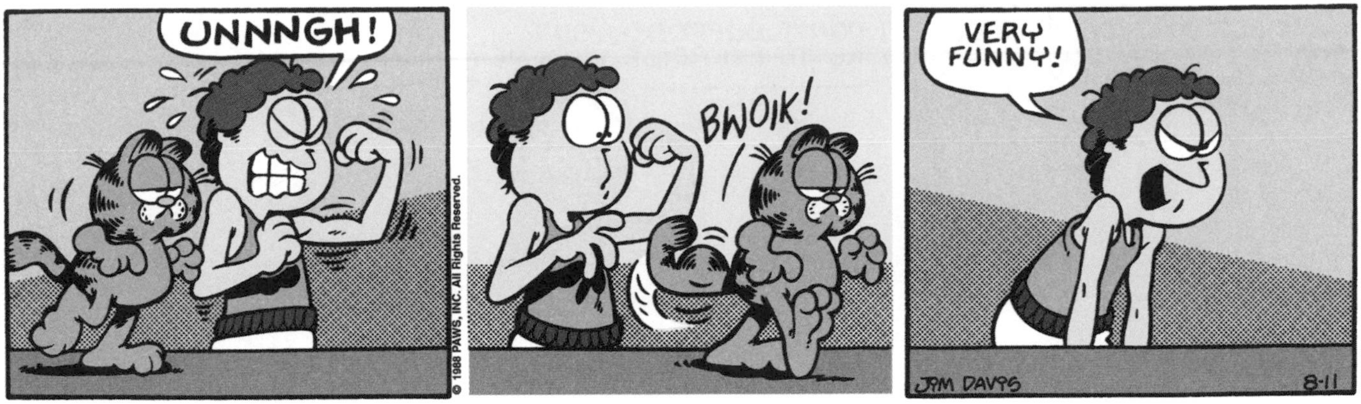
UNNNGH!
© 1988 PAWS, INC. All Rights Reserved.
BWOIK!
VERY FUNNY!
JIM DAVIS
8-11

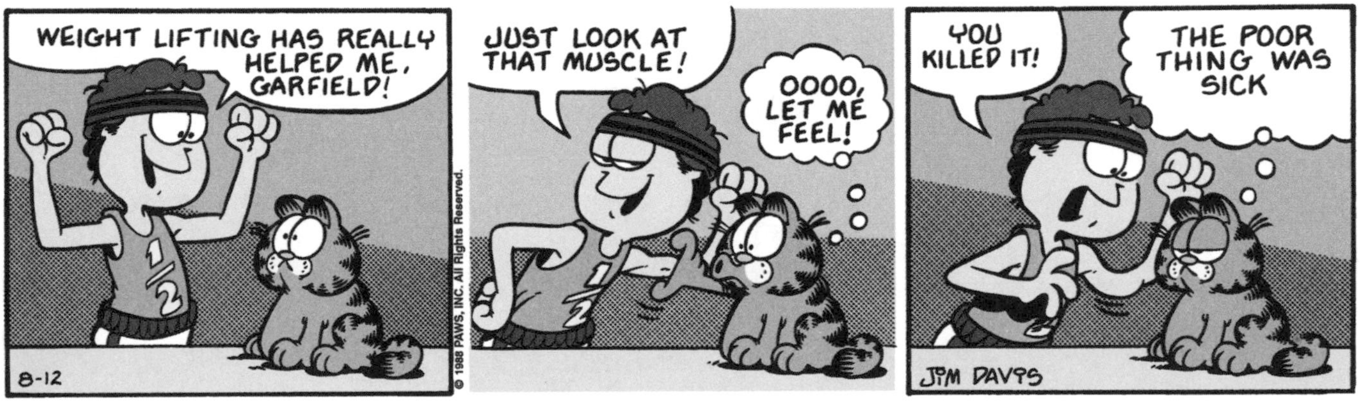
WEIGHT LIFTING HAS REALLY HELPED ME, GARFIELD!
8-12
© 1988 PAWS, INC. All Rights Reserved.
JUST LOOK AT THAT MUSCLE!
OOOO, LET ME FEEL!
YOU KILLED IT!
THE POOR THING WAS SICK
JIM DAVIS

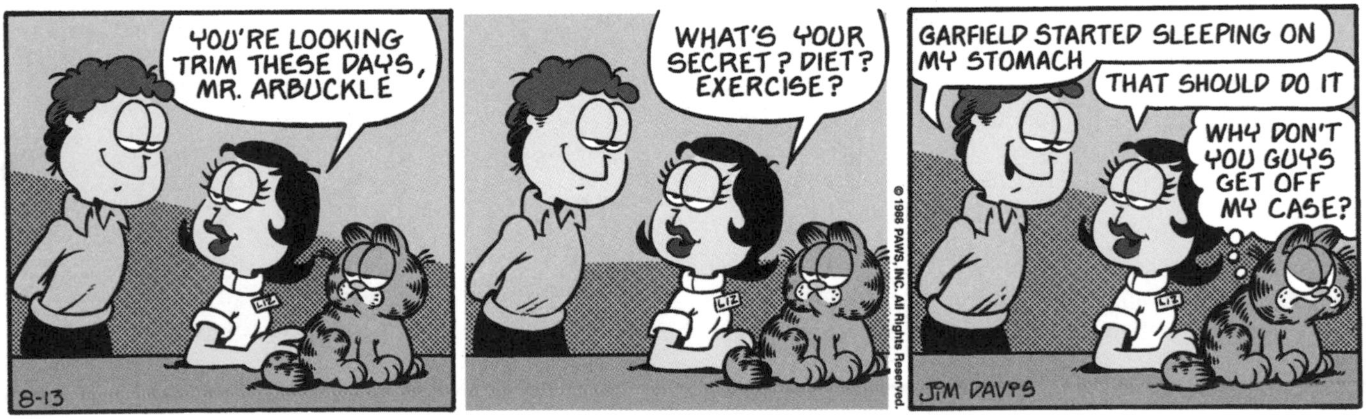
YOU'RE LOOKING TRIM THESE DAYS, MR. ARBUCKLE
8-13
WHAT'S YOUR SECRET? DIET? EXERCISE?
© 1988 PAWS, INC. All Rights Reserved.
GARFIELD STARTED SLEEPING ON MY STOMACH
THAT SHOULD DO IT
WHY DON'T YOU GUYS GET OFF MY CASE?
JIM DAVIS

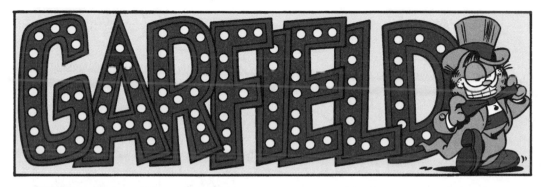

TELL YOU WHAT, GARFIELD. IF I GIVE YOU ONE OF MY HAMBURGERS, WILL YOU STOP STARING AT ME?

AGREED!

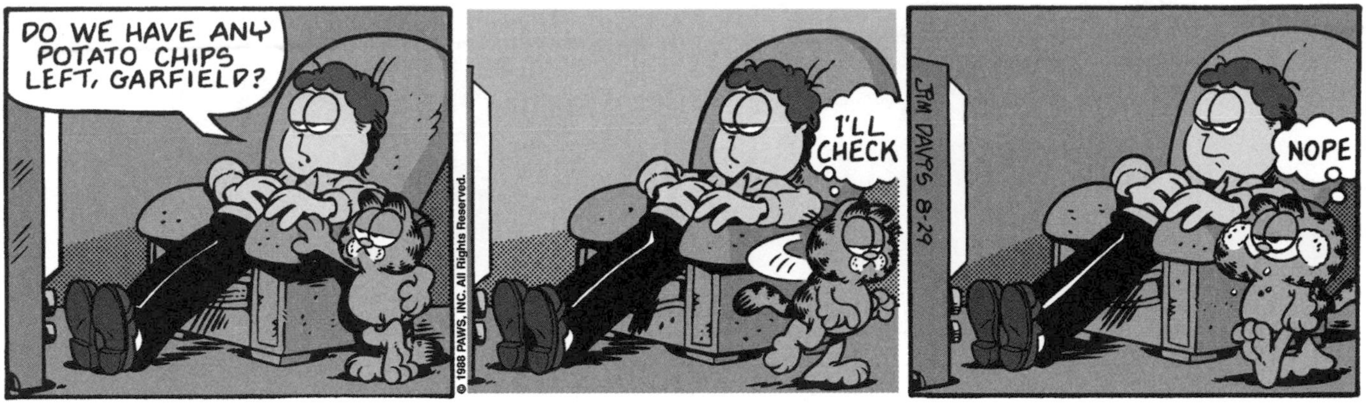
DO WE HAVE ANY POTATO CHIPS LEFT, GARFIELD?
© 1988 PAWS, INC. All Rights Reserved.
I'LL CHECK
JIM DAVIS 8-29
NOPE

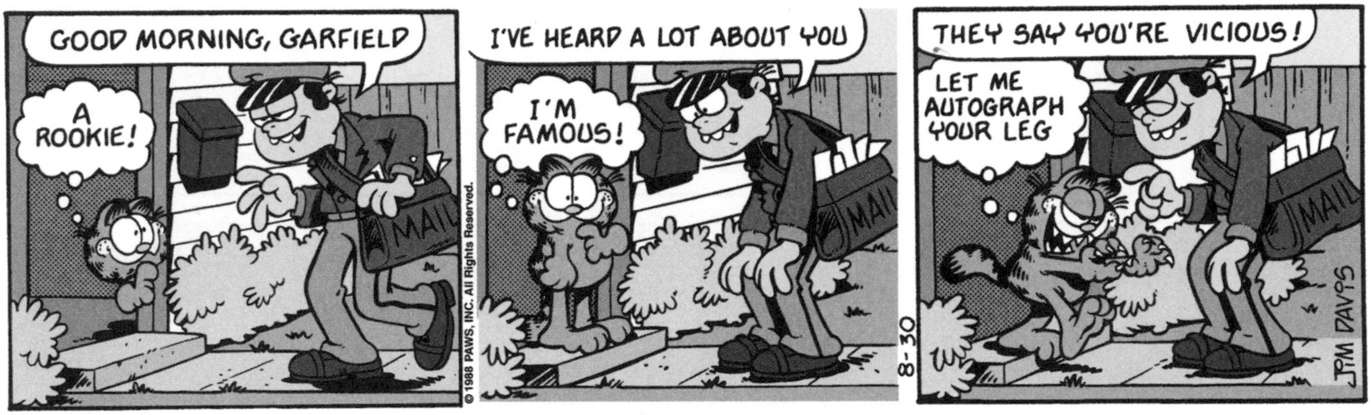
GOOD MORNING, GARFIELD
A ROOKIE!
MAIL
© 1988 PAWS, INC. All Rights Reserved.
I'VE HEARD A LOT ABOUT YOU
I'M FAMOUS!
MAIL
8-30
THEY SAY YOU'RE VICIOUS!
LET ME AUTOGRAPH YOUR LEG
MAIL
JIM DAVIS

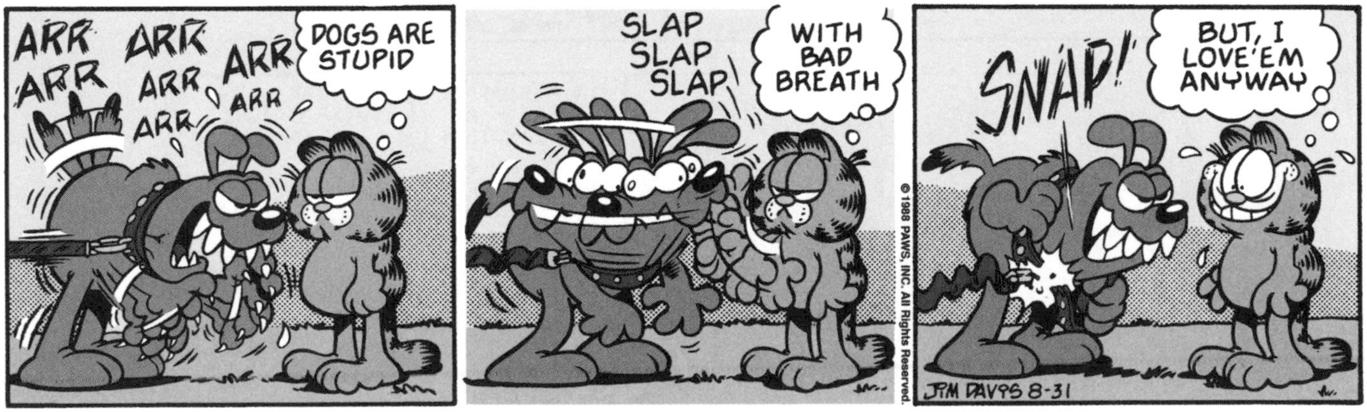
ARR ARR ARR ARR ARR ARR ARR
DOGS ARE STUPID
SLAP SLAP SLAP
WITH BAD BREATH
© 1988 PAWS, INC. All Rights Reserved.
SNAP!
BUT, I LOVE 'EM ANYWAY
JIM DAVIS 8-31

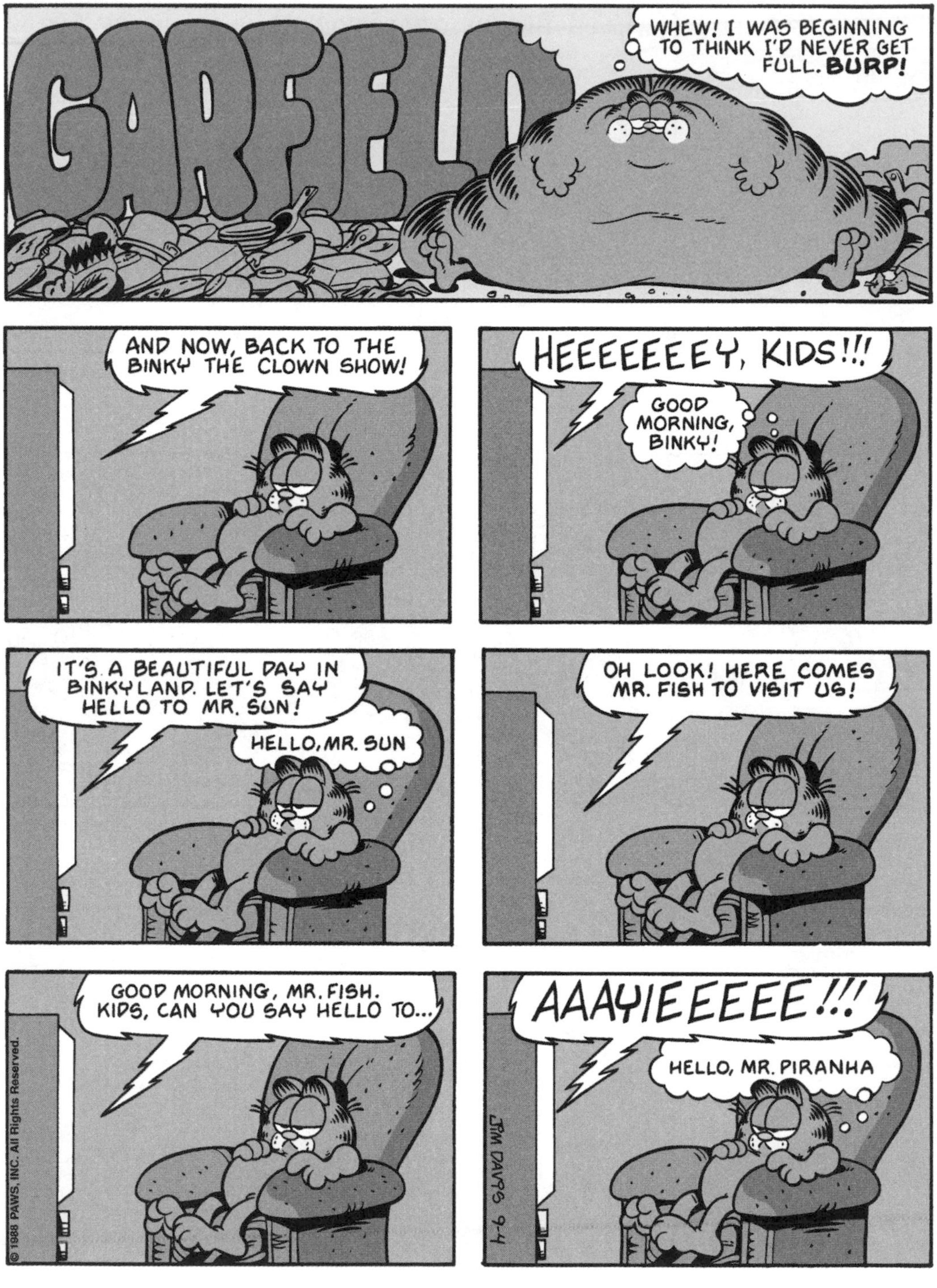
GARFIELD
WHEW! I WAS BEGINNING TO THINK I'D NEVER GET FULL. BURP!
AND NOW, BACK TO THE BINKY THE CLOWN SHOW!
HEEEEEEEY, KIDS!!!
GOOD MORNING, BINKY!
IT'S A BEAUTIFUL DAY IN BINKYLAND. LET'S SAY HELLO TO MR. SUN!
HELLO, MR. SUN
OH LOOK! HERE COMES MR. FISH TO VISIT US!
GOOD MORNING, MR. FISH. KIDS, CAN YOU SAY HELLO TO...
AAAYIEEEEE!!!
HELLO, MR. PIRANHA
JIM DAVIS 9-4
© 1988 PAWS, INC. All Rights Reserved.

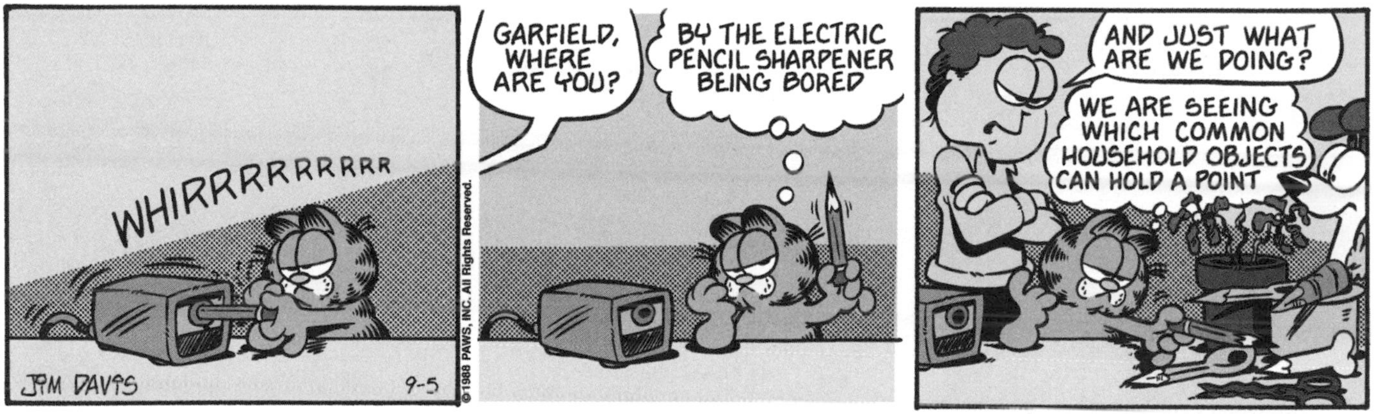
WHIRRRRRRRRR
JIM DAVIS
9-5
© 1988 PAWS, INC. All Rights Reserved.
GARFIELD, WHERE ARE YOU?
BY THE ELECTRIC PENCIL SHARPENER BEING BORED
AND JUST WHAT ARE WE DOING?
WE ARE SEEING WHICH COMMON HOUSEHOLD OBJECTS CAN HOLD A POINT

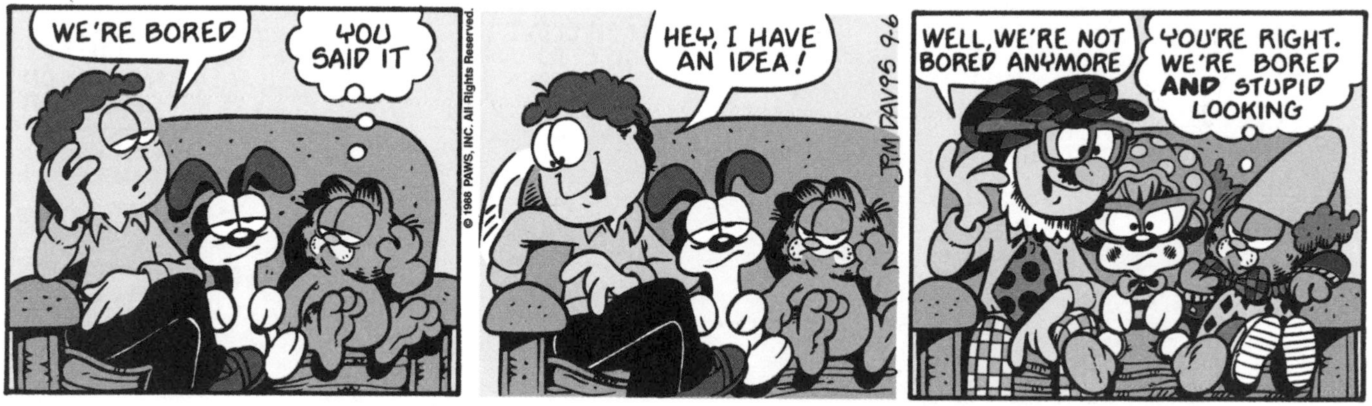
WE'RE BORED
YOU SAID IT
© 1988 PAWS, INC. All Rights Reserved.
HEY, I HAVE AN IDEA!
JIM DAVIS 9-6
WELL, WE'RE NOT BORED ANYMORE
YOU'RE RIGHT. WE'RE BORED AND STUPID LOOKING

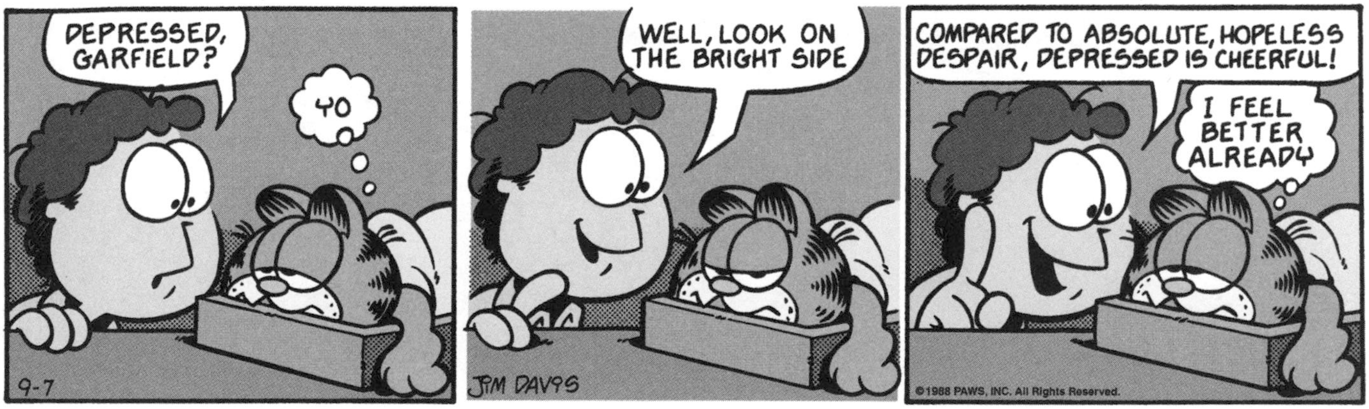
DEPRESSED, GARFIELD?
YO
9-7
WELL, LOOK ON THE BRIGHT SIDE
JIM DAVIS
COMPARED TO ABSOLUTE, HOPELESS DESPAIR, DEPRESSED IS CHEERFUL!
I FEEL BETTER ALREADY
©1988 PAWS, INC. All Rights Reserved.

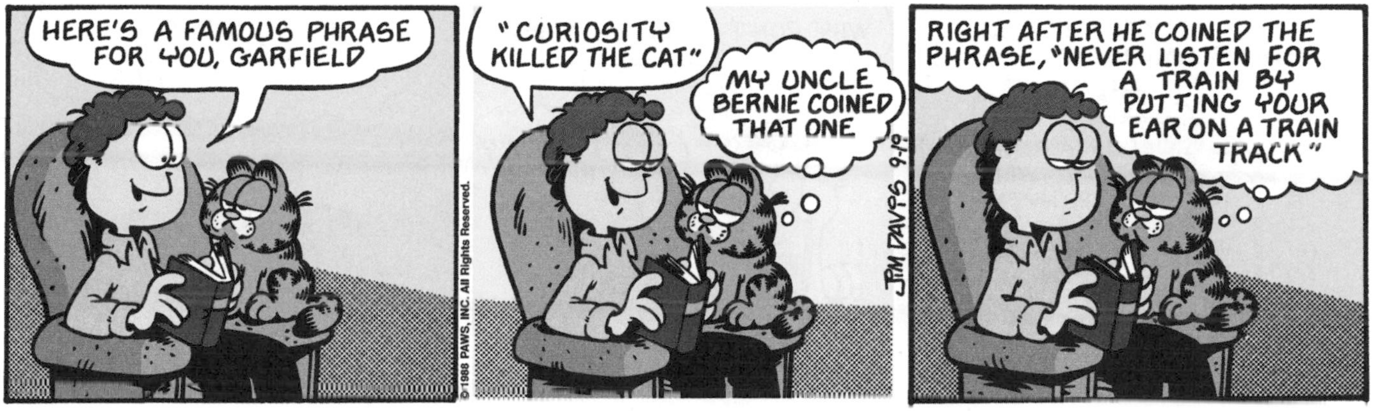
HERE'S A FAMOUS PHRASE FOR YOU, GARFIELD
© 1988 PAWS, INC. All Rights Reserved.
"CURIOSITY KILLED THE CAT"
MY UNCLE BERNIE COINED THAT ONE
JIM DAVIS 9-19
RIGHT AFTER HE COINED THE PHRASE, "NEVER LISTEN FOR A TRAIN BY PUTTING YOUR EAR ON A TRAIN TRACK"

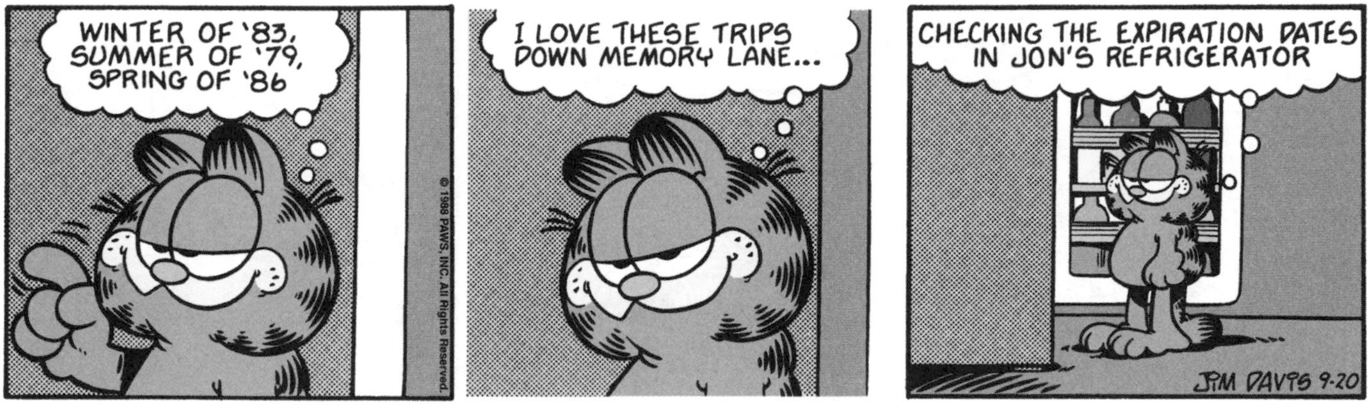
WINTER OF '83, SUMMER OF '79, SPRING OF '86
© 1988 PAWS, INC. All Rights Reserved.
I LOVE THESE TRIPS DOWN MEMORY LANE...
CHECKING THE EXPIRATION DATES IN JON'S REFRIGERATOR
JIM DAVIS 9-20

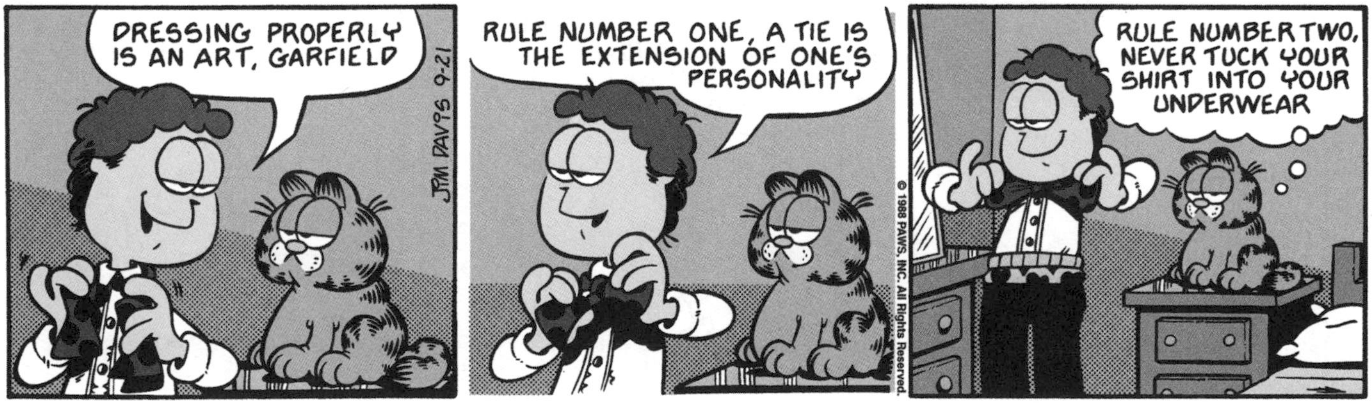
DRESSING PROPERLY IS AN ART, GARFIELD
JIM DAVIS 9-21
RULE NUMBER ONE, A TIE IS THE EXTENSION OF ONE'S PERSONALITY
© 1988 PAWS, INC. All Rights Reserved.
RULE NUMBER TWO, NEVER TUCK YOUR SHIRT INTO YOUR UNDERWEAR

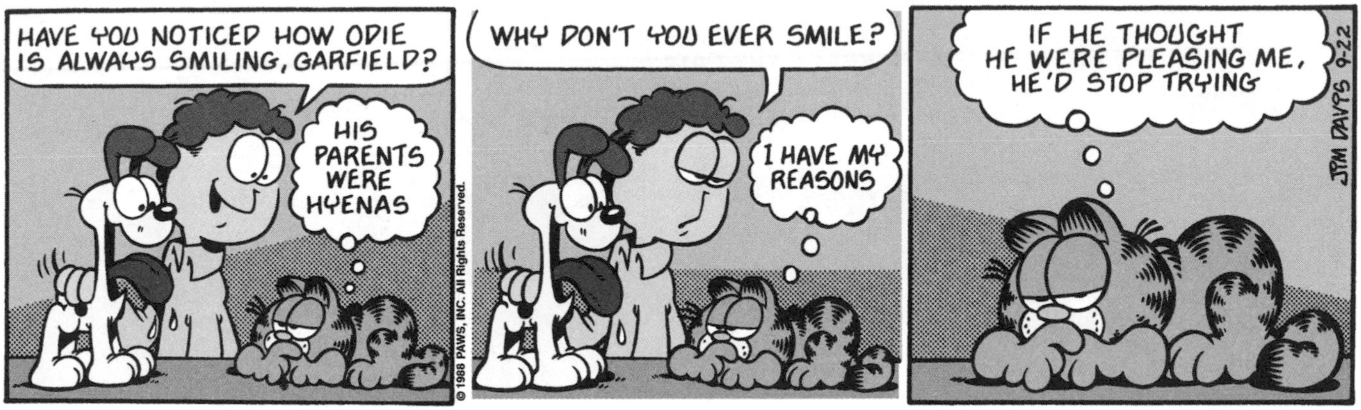
HAVE YOU NOTICED HOW ODIE IS ALWAYS SMILING, GARFIELD?
HIS PARENTS WERE HYENAS
© 1988 PAWS, INC. All Rights Reserved.
WHY DON'T YOU EVER SMILE?
I HAVE MY REASONS
IF HE THOUGHT HE WERE PLEASING ME, HE'D STOP TRYING
JIM DAVIS 9-22

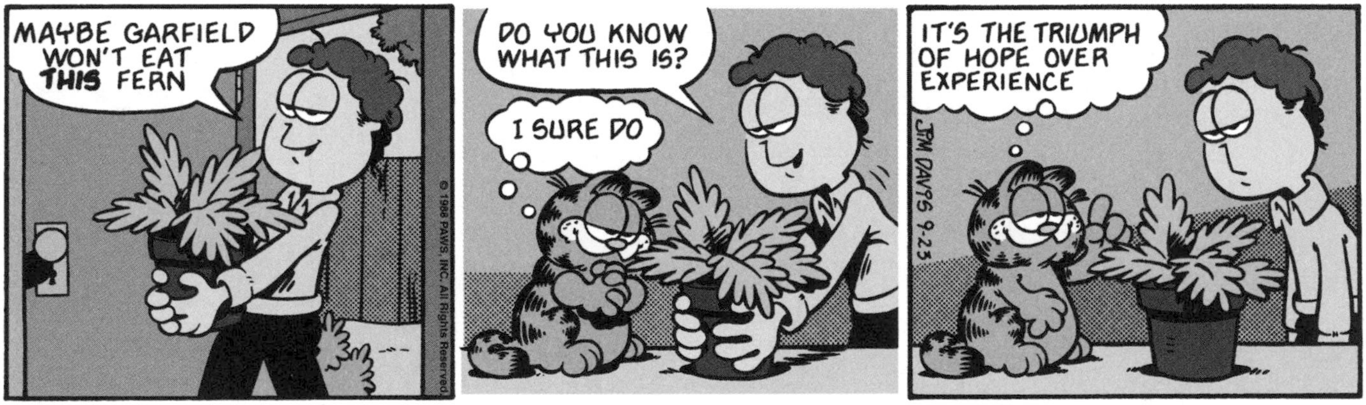
MAYBE GARFIELD WON'T EAT **THIS** FERN
© 1988 PAWS, INC. All Rights Reserved.
DO YOU KNOW WHAT THIS IS?
I SURE DO
IT'S THE TRIUMPH OF HOPE OVER EXPERIENCE
JIM DAVIS 9-23

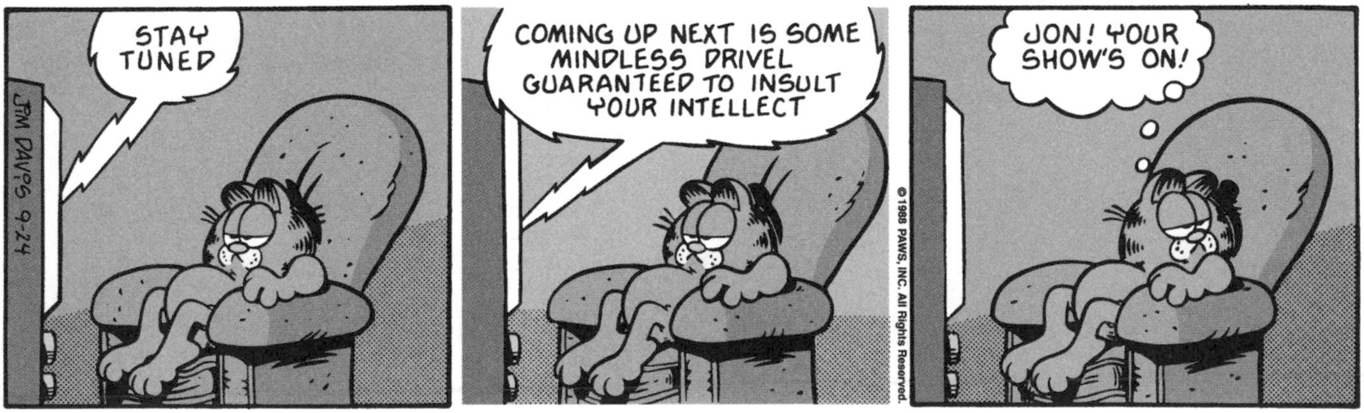
STAY TUNED
JIM DAVIS 9-24
COMING UP NEXT IS SOME MINDLESS DRIVEL GUARANTEED TO INSULT YOUR INTELLECT
© 1988 PAWS, INC. All Rights Reserved.
JON! YOUR SHOW'S ON!

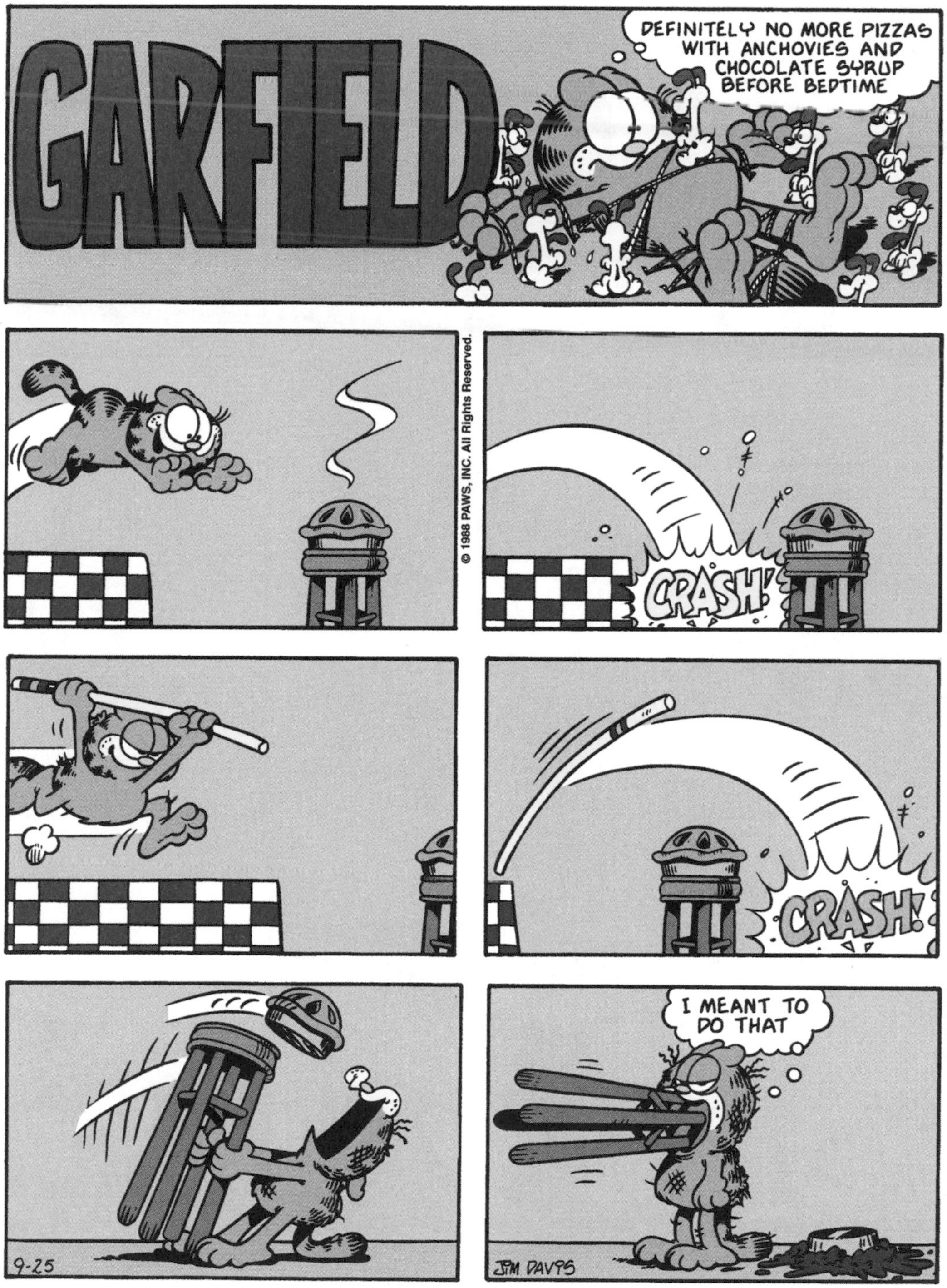
GARFIELD
DEFINITELY NO MORE PIZZAS WITH ANCHOVIES AND CHOCOLATE SYRUP BEFORE BEDTIME
© 1988 PAWS, INC. All Rights Reserved.
CRASH!
CRASH!
9-25
JIM DAVIS
I MEANT TO DO THAT

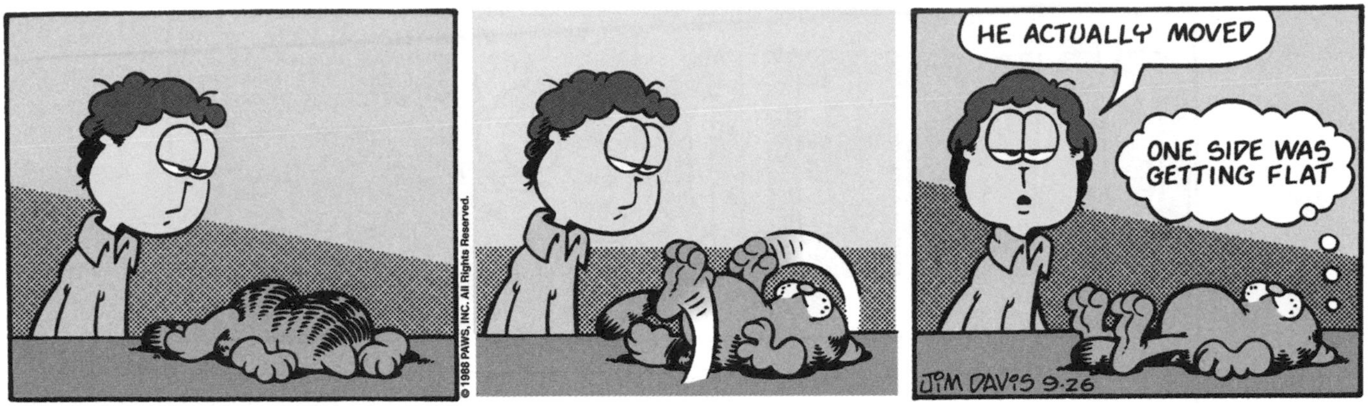
© 1988 PAWS, INC. All Rights Reserved.
HE ACTUALLY MOVED
ONE SIDE WAS GETTING FLAT
JIM DAVIS 9-26

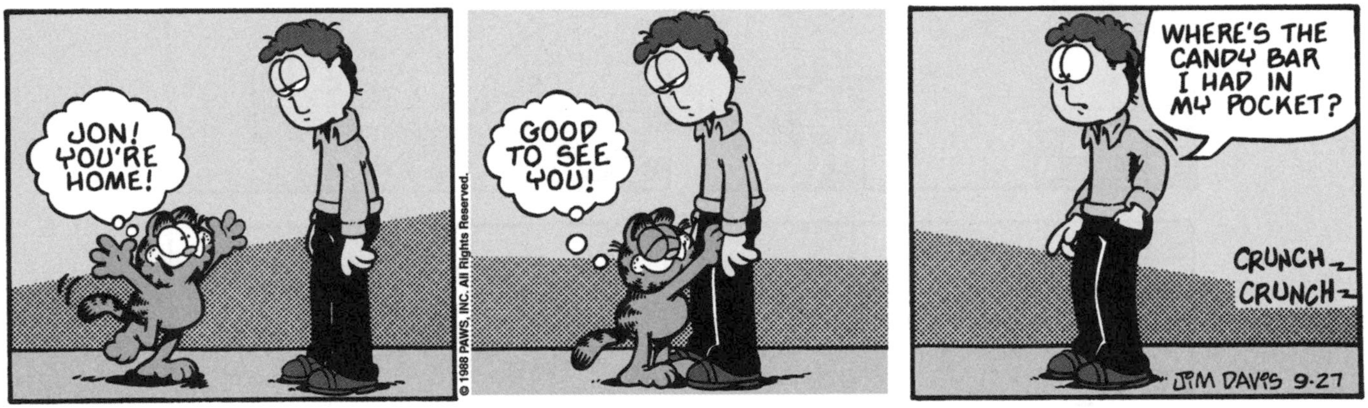
JON! YOU'RE HOME!
© 1988 PAWS, INC. All Rights Reserved.
GOOD TO SEE YOU!
WHERE'S THE CANDY BAR I HAD IN MY POCKET?
CRUNCH
CRUNCH
JIM DAVIS 9-27

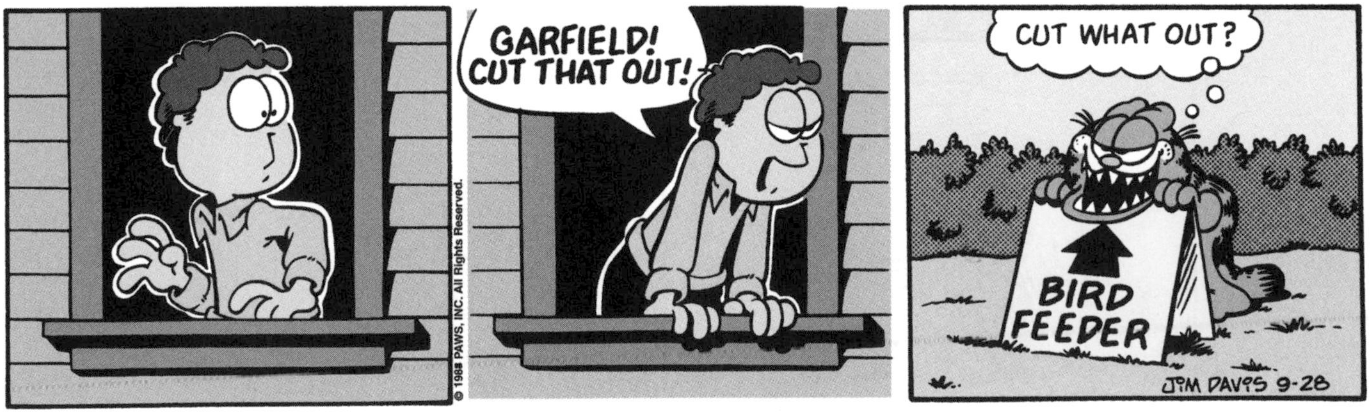
© 1988 PAWS, INC. All Rights Reserved.
GARFIELD! CUT THAT OUT!
CUT WHAT OUT?
BIRD FEEDER
JIM DAVIS 9-28

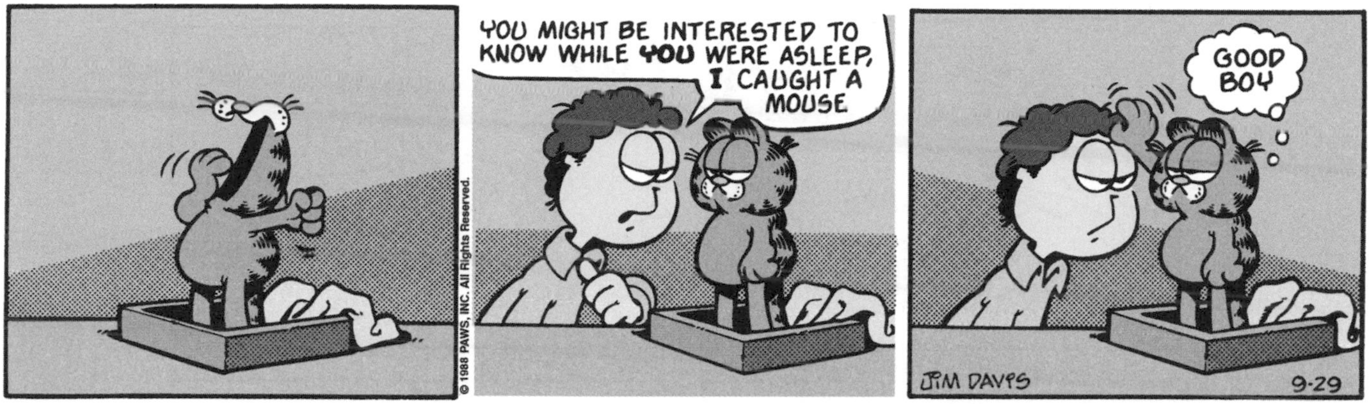
© 1988 PAWS, INC. All Rights Reserved.
YOU MIGHT BE INTERESTED TO KNOW WHILE YOU WERE ASLEEP, I CAUGHT A MOUSE
GOOD BOY
JIM DAVIS 9-29

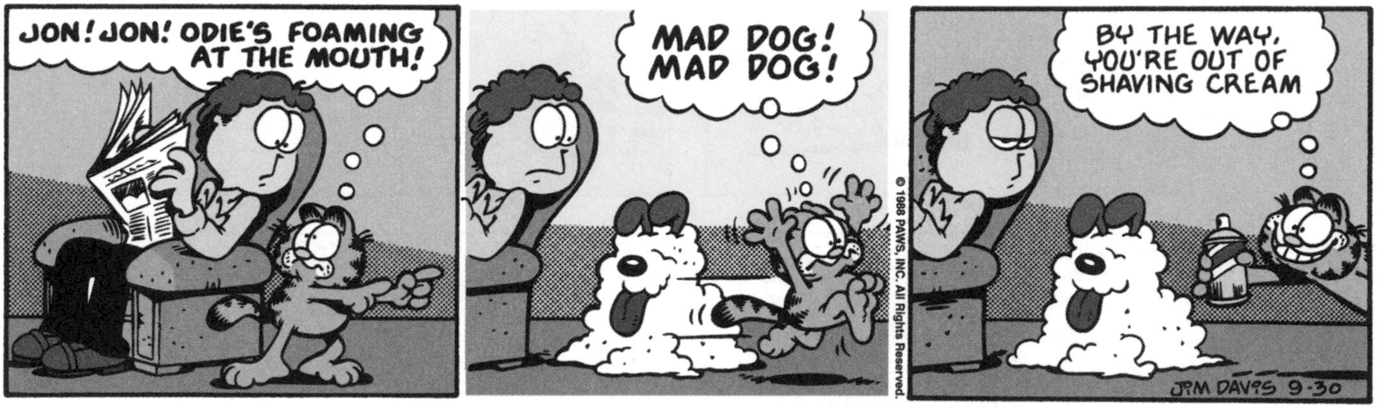
JON! JON! ODIE'S FOAMING AT THE MOUTH!
MAD DOG! MAD DOG!
© 1988 PAWS, INC. All Rights Reserved.
BY THE WAY, YOU'RE OUT OF SHAVING CREAM
JIM DAVIS 9-30

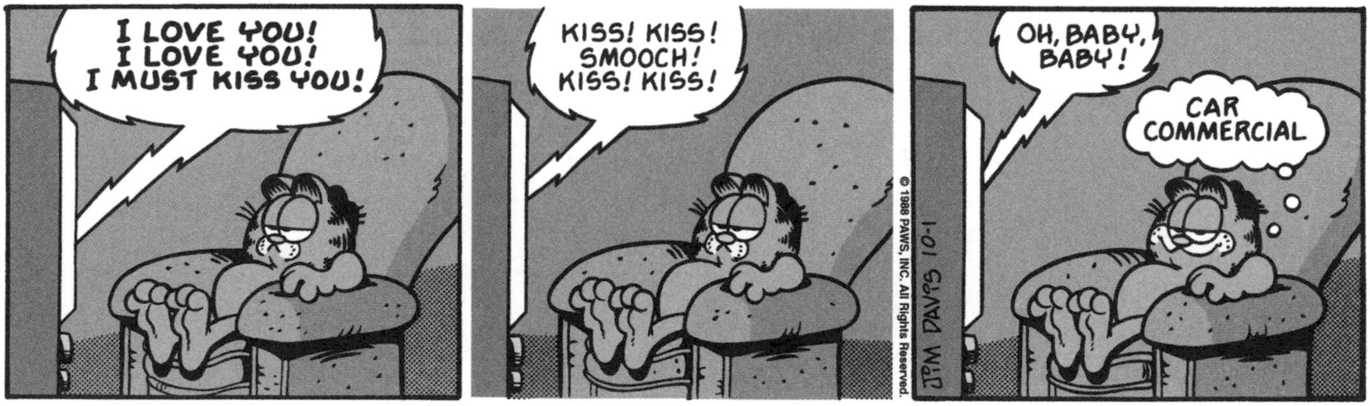
I LOVE YOU! I LOVE YOU! I MUST KISS YOU!
KISS! KISS! SMOOCH! KISS! KISS!
© 1988 PAWS, INC. All Rights Reserved.
JIM DAVIS 10-1
OH, BABY, BABY!
CAR COMMERCIAL

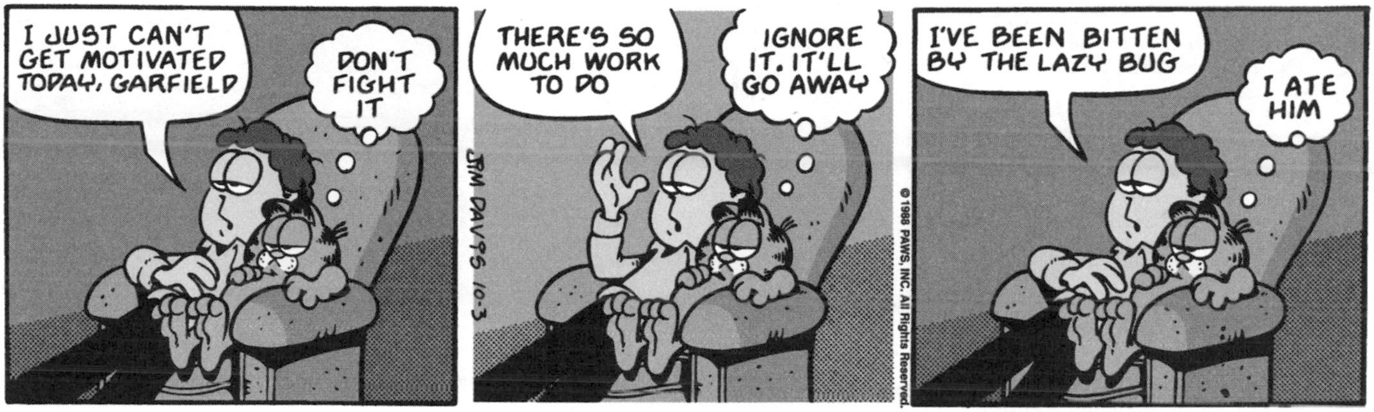
I JUST CAN'T GET MOTIVATED TODAY, GARFIELD
DON'T FIGHT IT
THERE'S SO MUCH WORK TO DO
IGNORE IT. IT'LL GO AWAY
JIM DAVIS 10-3
© 1988 PAWS, INC. All Rights Reserved.
I'VE BEEN BITTEN BY THE LAZY BUG
I ATE HIM

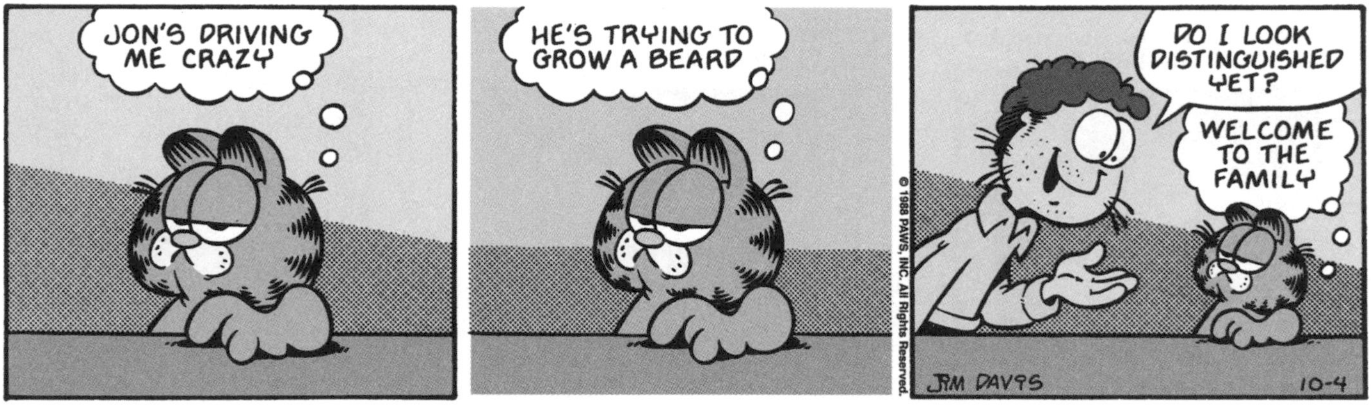
JON'S DRIVING ME CRAZY
HE'S TRYING TO GROW A BEARD
© 1988 PAWS, INC. All Rights Reserved.
DO I LOOK DISTINGUISHED YET?
WELCOME TO THE FAMILY
JIM DAVIS
10-4

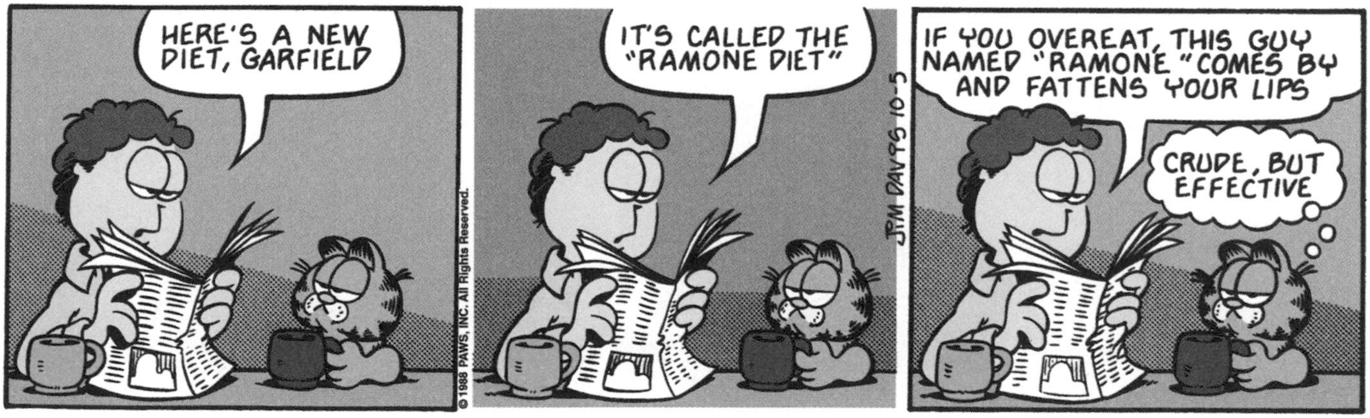
HERE'S A NEW DIET, GARFIELD
© 1988 PAWS, INC. All Rights Reserved.
IT'S CALLED THE "RAMONE DIET"
JIM DAVIS 10-5
IF YOU OVEREAT, THIS GUY NAMED "RAMONE" COMES BY AND FATTENS YOUR LIPS
CRUDE, BUT EFFECTIVE

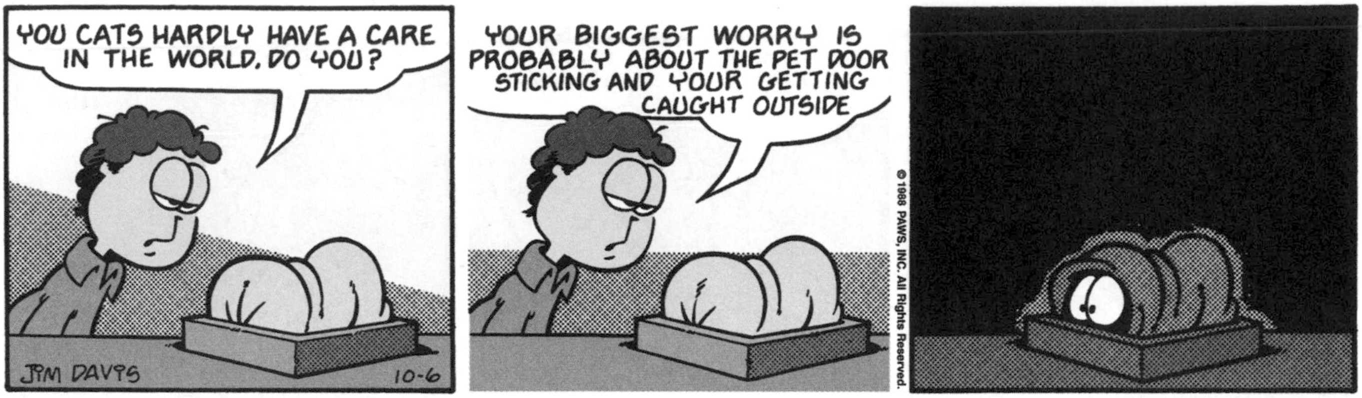
YOU CATS HARDLY HAVE A CARE IN THE WORLD, DO YOU?
YOUR BIGGEST WORRY IS PROBABLY ABOUT THE PET DOOR STICKING AND YOUR GETTING CAUGHT OUTSIDE
JIM DAVIS 10-6
© 1988 PAWS, INC. All Rights Reserved.

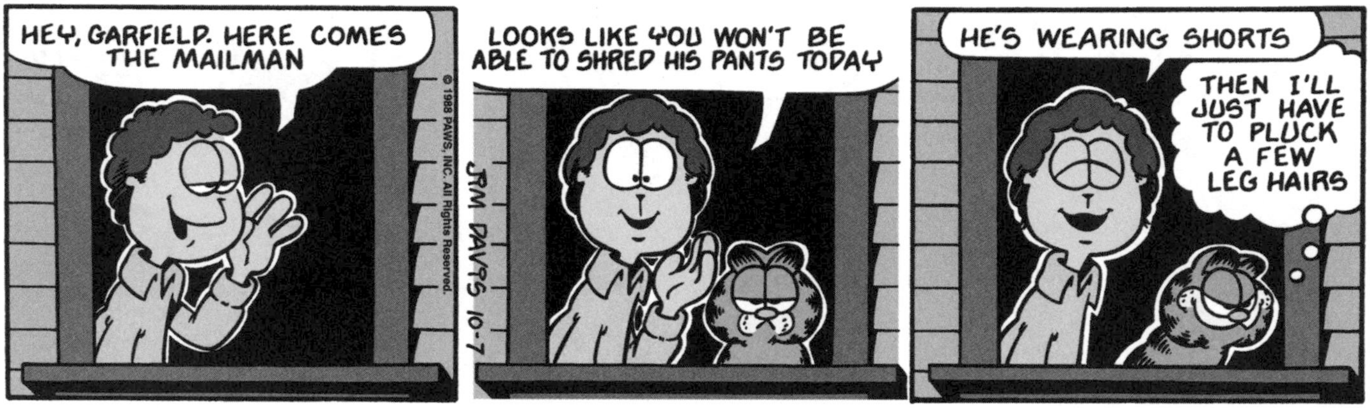
HEY, GARFIELD. HERE COMES THE MAILMAN
LOOKS LIKE YOU WON'T BE ABLE TO SHRED HIS PANTS TODAY
HE'S WEARING SHORTS
THEN I'LL JUST HAVE TO PLUCK A FEW LEG HAIRS
JIM DAVIS 10-7
© 1988 PAWS, INC. All Rights Reserved.

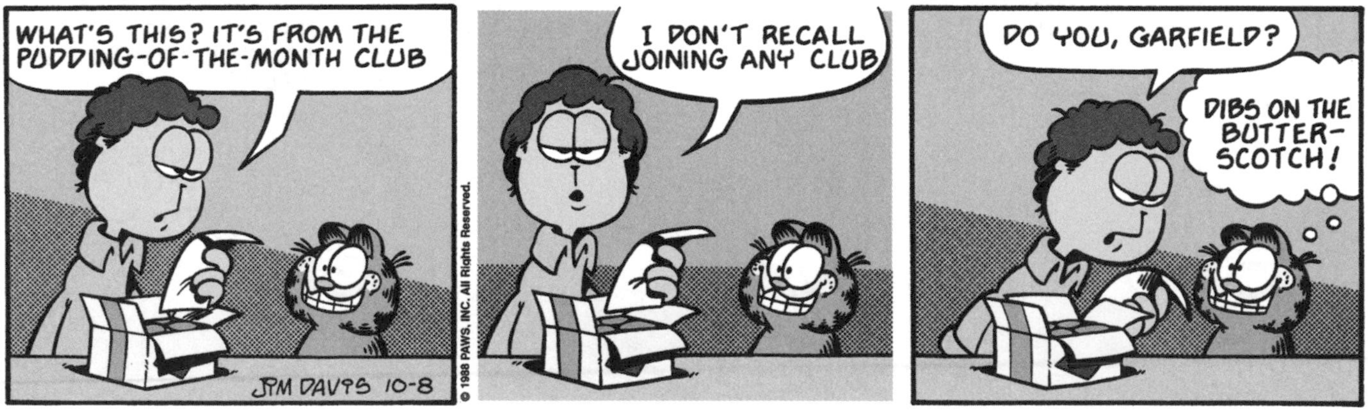
WHAT'S THIS? IT'S FROM THE PUDDING-OF-THE-MONTH CLUB
I DON'T RECALL JOINING ANY CLUB
DO YOU, GARFIELD?
DIBS ON THE BUTTER-SCOTCH!
JIM DAVIS 10-8
© 1988 PAWS, INC. All Rights Reserved.

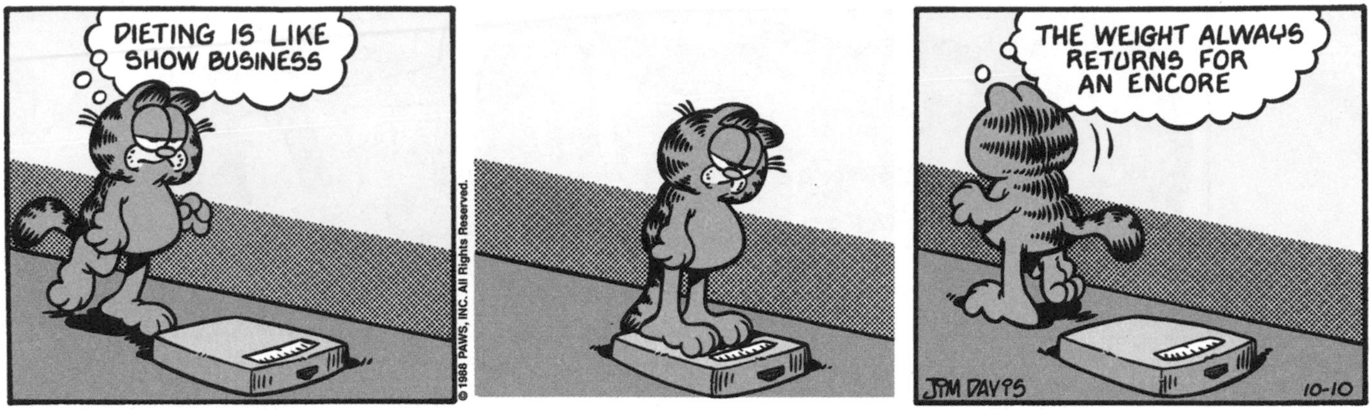
DIETING IS LIKE SHOW BUSINESS
© 1988 PAWS, INC. All Rights Reserved.
THE WEIGHT ALWAYS RETURNS FOR AN ENCORE
JIM DAVIS
10-10

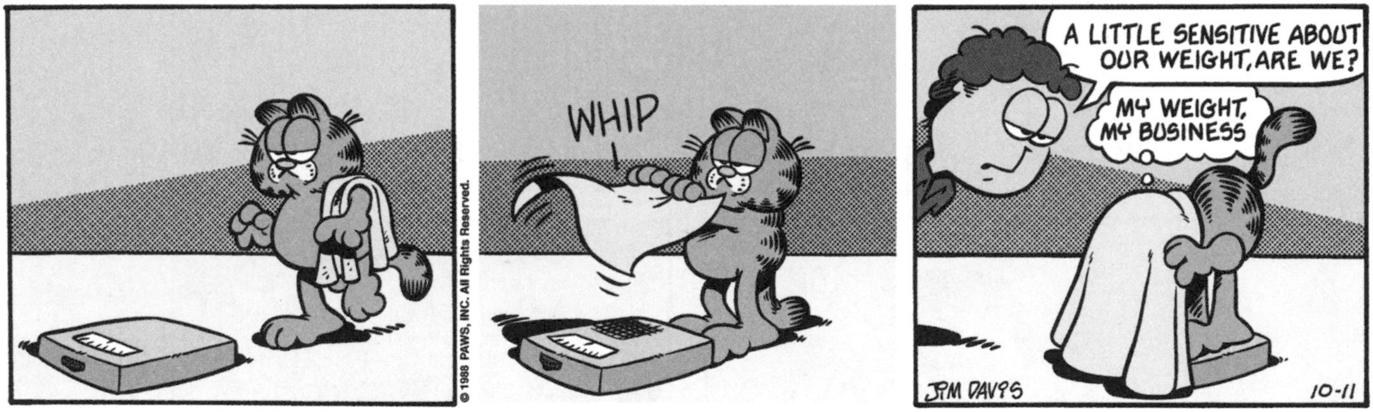
© 1988 PAWS, INC. All Rights Reserved.
WHIP
A LITTLE SENSITIVE ABOUT OUR WEIGHT, ARE WE?
MY WEIGHT, MY BUSINESS
JIM DAVIS
10-11

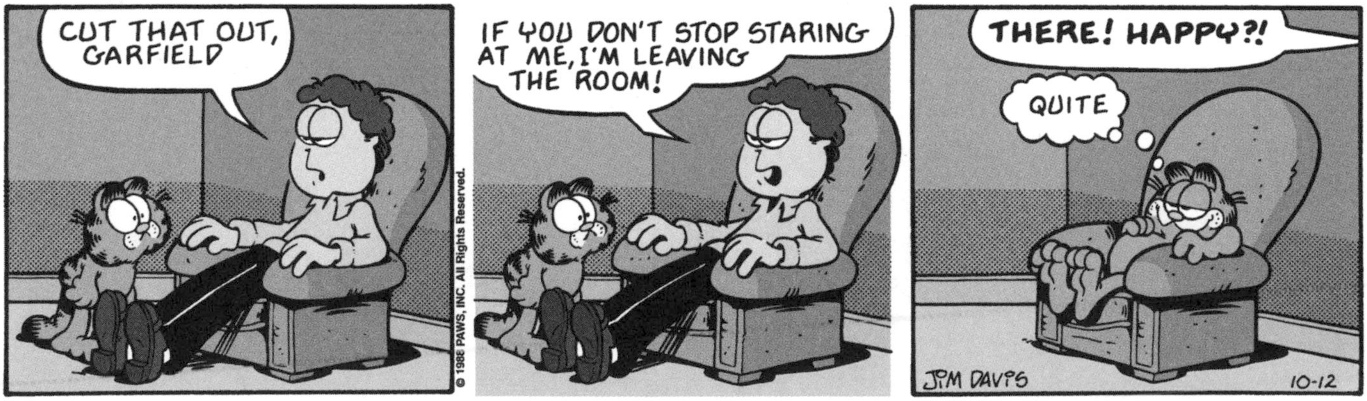
CUT THAT OUT, GARFIELD
© 1988 PAWS, INC. All Rights Reserved.
IF YOU DON'T STOP STARING AT ME, I'M LEAVING THE ROOM!
THERE! HAPPY?!
QUITE
JIM DAVIS
10-12

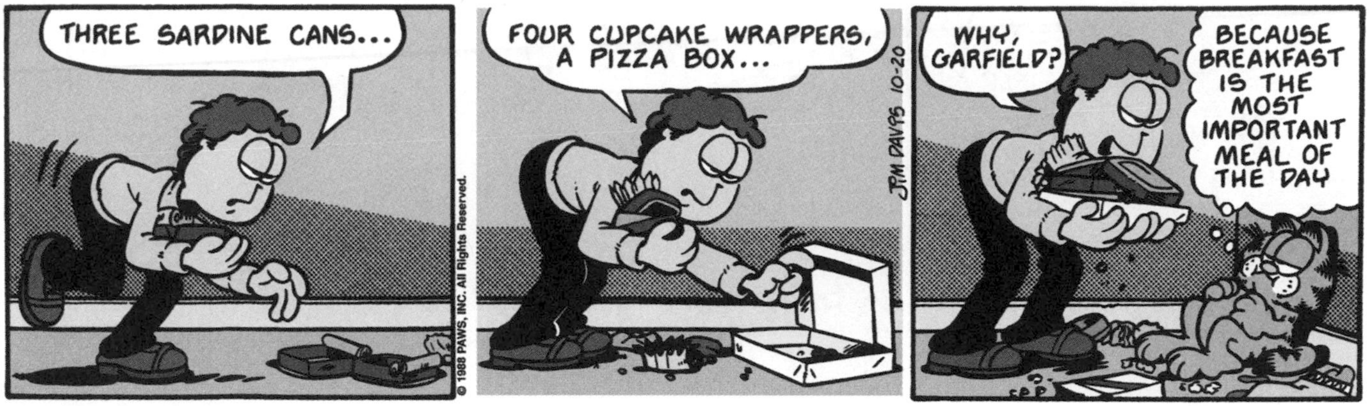
THREE SARDINE CANS...
© 1988 PAWS, INC. All Rights Reserved.
FOUR CUPCAKE WRAPPERS, A PIZZA BOX...
WHY, GARFIELD?
BECAUSE BREAKFAST IS THE MOST IMPORTANT MEAL OF THE DAY

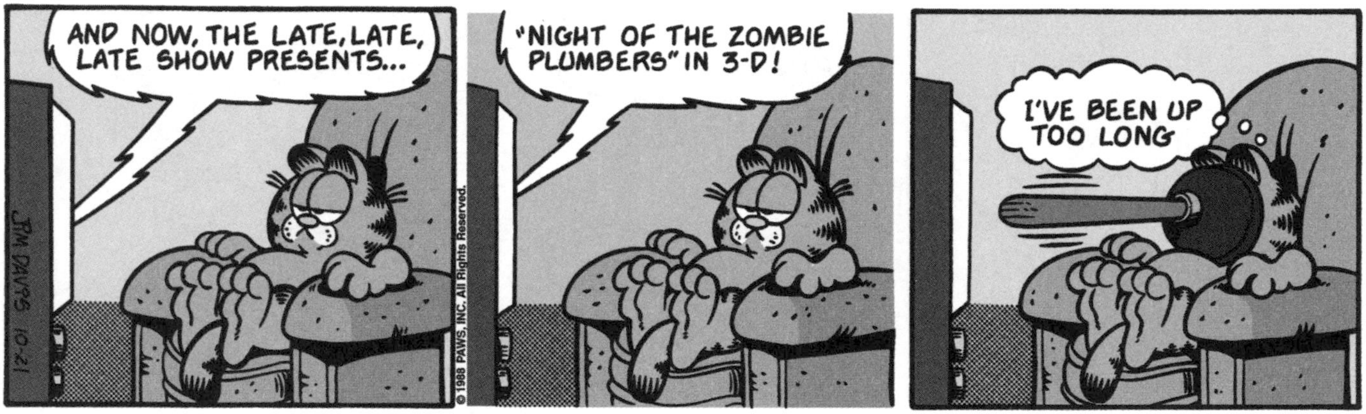
AND NOW, THE LATE, LATE, LATE SHOW PRESENTS...
© 1988 PAWS, INC. All Rights Reserved.
"NIGHT OF THE ZOMBIE PLUMBERS" IN 3-D!
I'VE BEEN UP TOO LONG

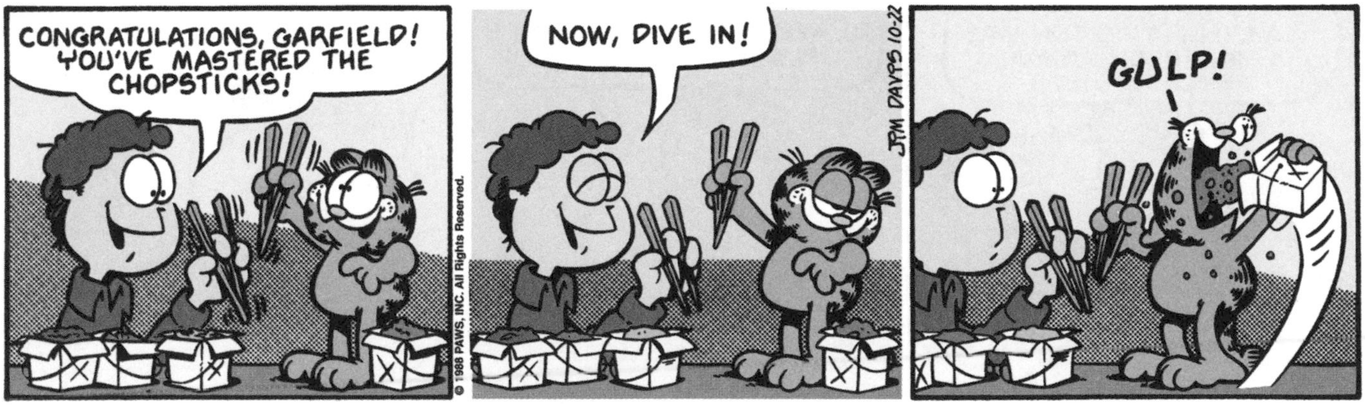
CONGRATULATIONS, GARFIELD! YOU'VE MASTERED THE CHOPSTICKS!
© 1988 PAWS, INC. All Rights Reserved.
NOW, DIVE IN!
GULP!

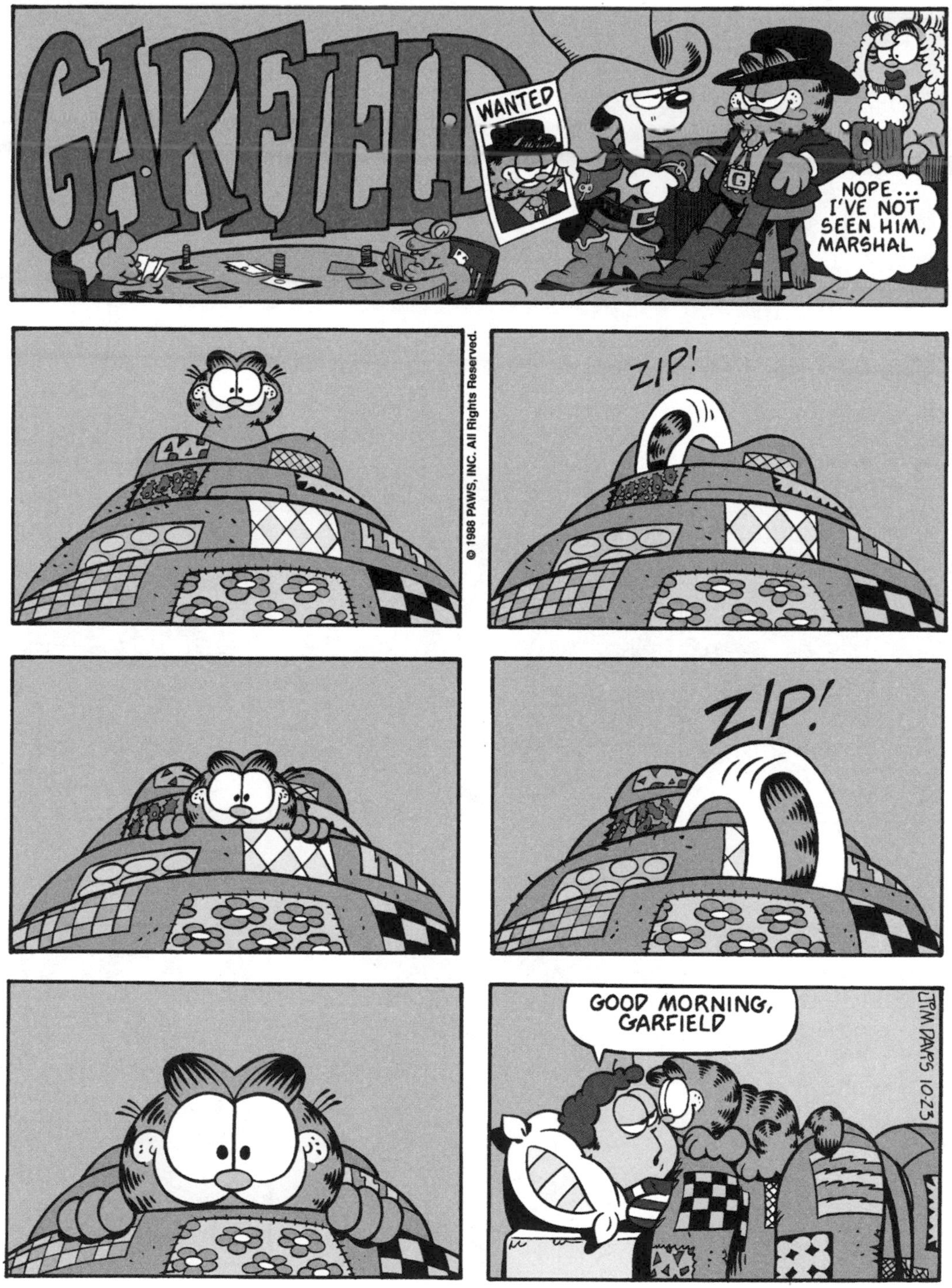
GARFIELD
WANTED
NOPE... I'VE NOT SEEN HIM, MARSHAL
© 1988 PAWS, INC. All Rights Reserved.
ZIP!
ZIP!
GOOD MORNING, GARFIELD
JIM DAVIS 10-23

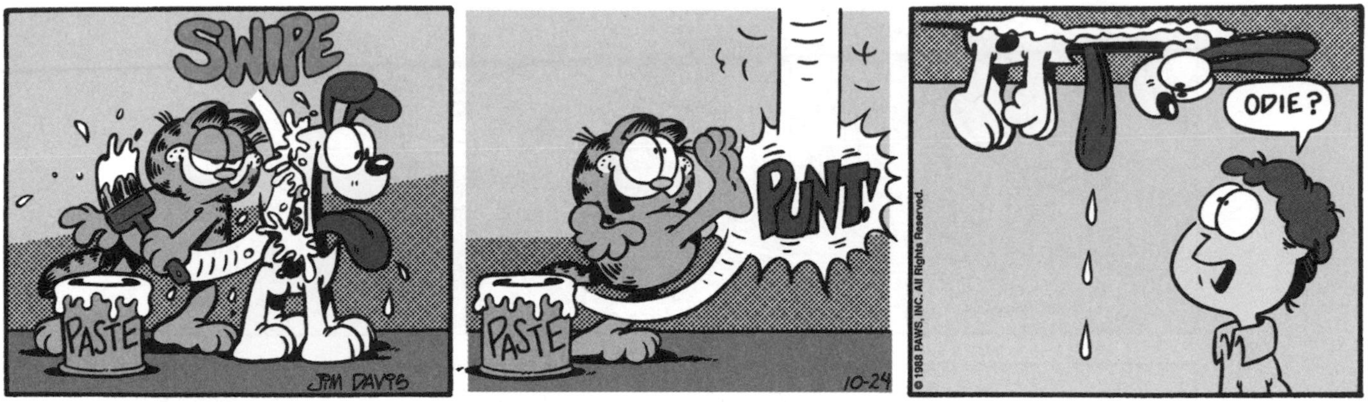
SWIPE
PASTE
JIM DAVIS
PASTE
PUNT!
10-24
© 1988 PAWS, INC. All Rights Reserved.
ODIE?

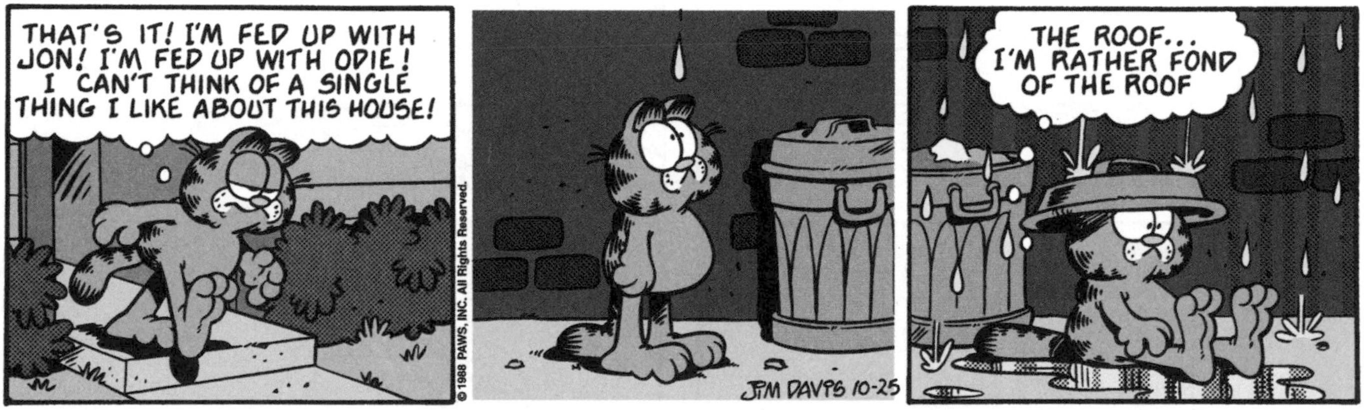
THAT'S IT! I'M FED UP WITH JON! I'M FED UP WITH ODIE! I CAN'T THINK OF A SINGLE THING I LIKE ABOUT THIS HOUSE!
© 1988 PAWS, INC. All Rights Reserved.
JIM DAVIS 10-25
THE ROOF... I'M RATHER FOND OF THE ROOF

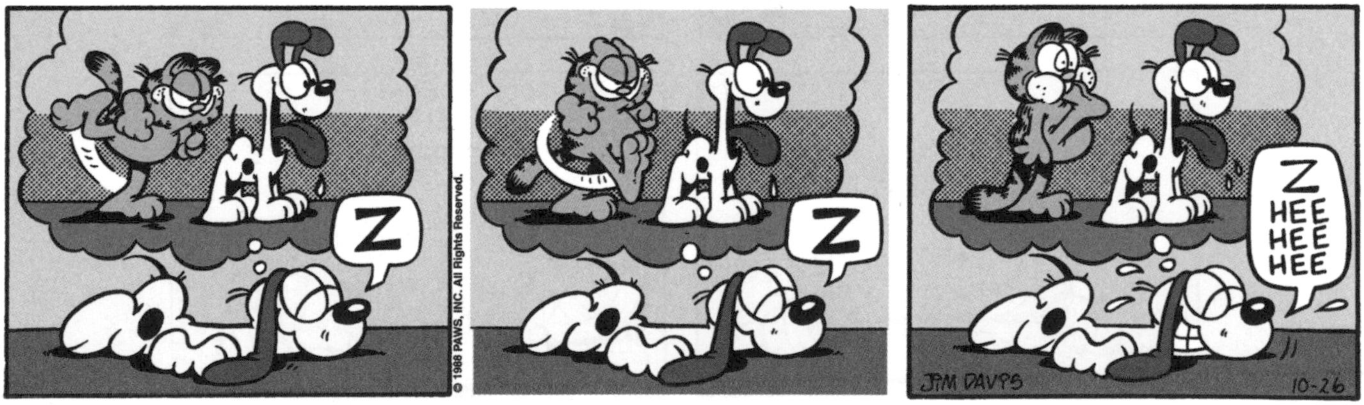
Z
© 1988 PAWS, INC. All Rights Reserved.
Z
Z HEE HEE HEE
JIM DAVIS
10-26

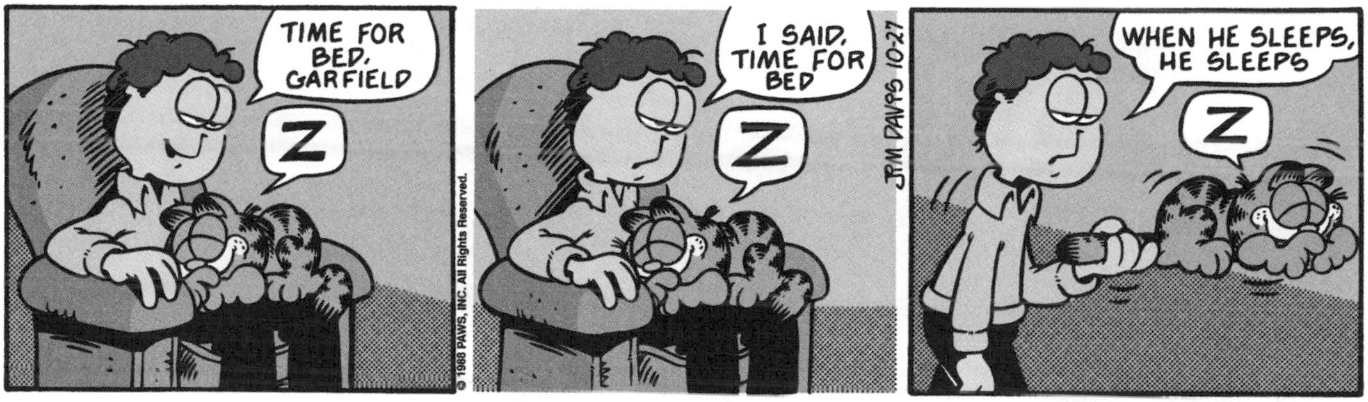
TIME FOR BED, GARFIELD
Z
© 1988 PAWS, INC. All Rights Reserved.
I SAID, TIME FOR BED
Z
JIM DAVIS 10-27
WHEN HE SLEEPS, HE SLEEPS
Z

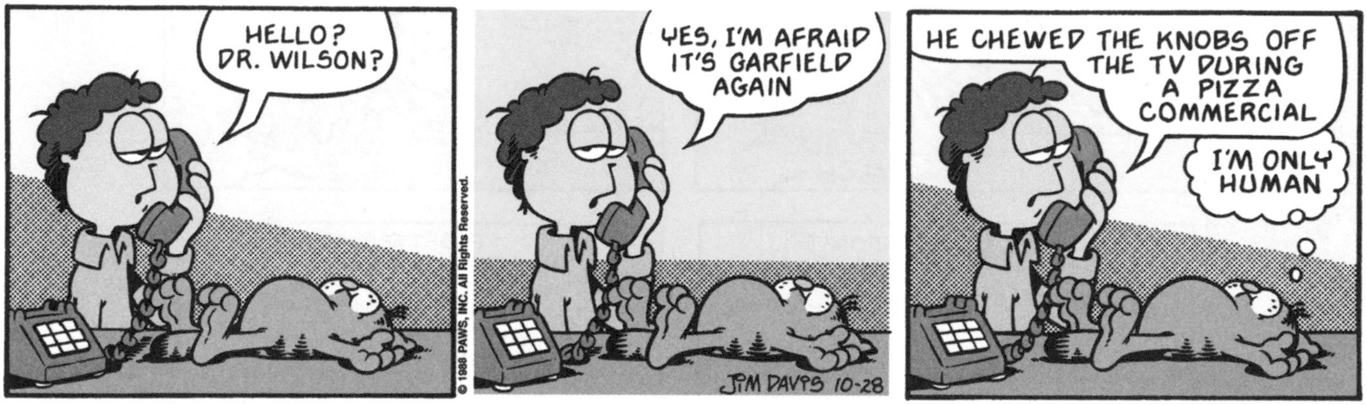
HELLO? DR. WILSON?
© 1988 PAWS, INC. All Rights Reserved.
YES, I'M AFRAID IT'S GARFIELD AGAIN
JIM DAVIS 10-28
HE CHEWED THE KNOBS OFF THE TV DURING A PIZZA COMMERCIAL
I'M ONLY HUMAN

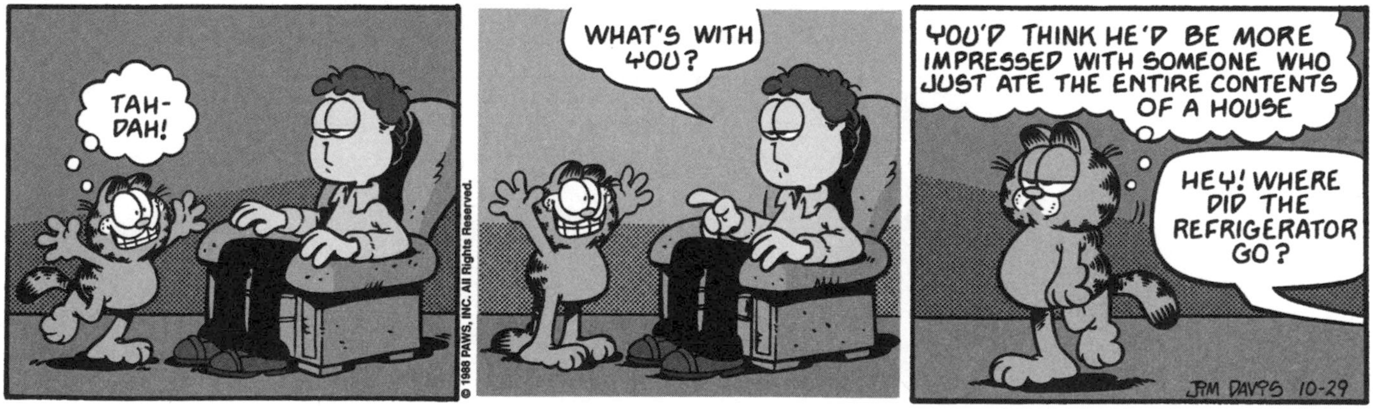
TAH-DAH!
© 1988 PAWS, INC. All Rights Reserved.
WHAT'S WITH YOU?
YOU'D THINK HE'D BE MORE IMPRESSED WITH SOMEONE WHO JUST ATE THE ENTIRE CONTENTS OF A HOUSE
HEY! WHERE DID THE REFRIGERATOR GO?
JIM DAVIS 10-29

YOU KNOW, GARFIELD, WE'RE NOT GETTING ANY YOUNGER

MAYBE WE SHOULD START PLANNING FOR OUR FUTURE

YOU'RE RIGHT

WHERE ARE YOU GOING?

TO MAKE UP A GROCERY LIST

I LIKE IT WHEN I'M HOME ALONE

11-4

THE ENTIRE HOUSE IS **MINE**

AND THIS IS **MINE**, AND THIS IS **MINE**, AND THIS IS **MINE**...

I DIDN'T KNOW YOU COULD TOUCH YOUR TOES, GARFIELD

AND YOU THOUGHT I WAS OUT OF SHAPE

ARE YOU OKAY?

DON'T JUST STAND THERE. CALL THE PARAMEDICS!

11-5

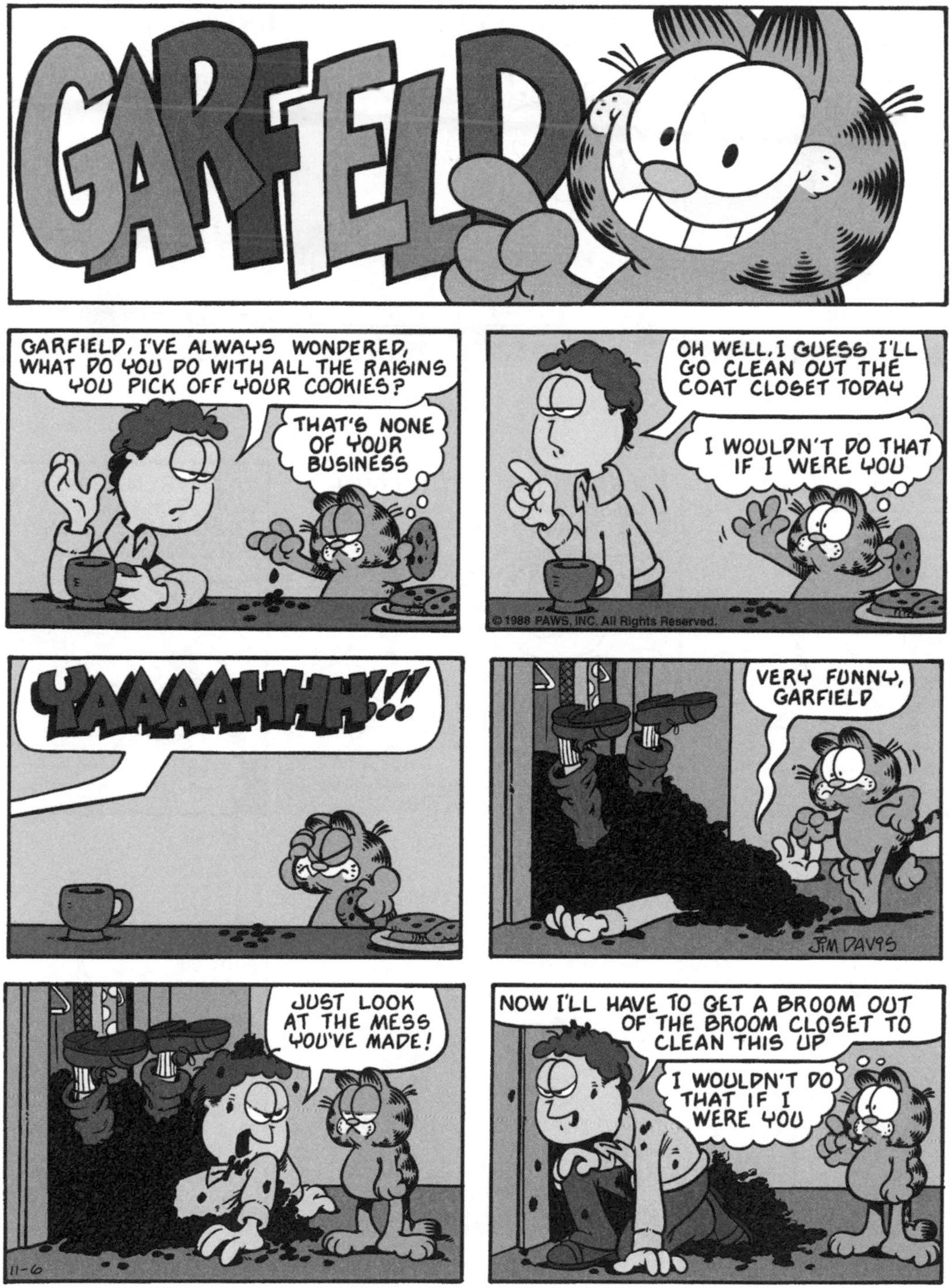
GARFIELD
GARFIELD, I'VE ALWAYS WONDERED, WHAT DO YOU DO WITH ALL THE RAISINS YOU PICK OFF YOUR COOKIES?
THAT'S NONE OF YOUR BUSINESS
OH WELL, I GUESS I'LL GO CLEAN OUT THE COAT CLOSET TODAY
I WOULDN'T DO THAT IF I WERE YOU
© 1988 PAWS, INC. All Rights Reserved.
YAAAAHHH!!!
VERY FUNNY, GARFIELD
JIM DAVIS
JUST LOOK AT THE MESS YOU'VE MADE!
11-6
NOW I'LL HAVE TO GET A BROOM OUT OF THE BROOM CLOSET TO CLEAN THIS UP
I WOULDN'T DO THAT IF I WERE YOU

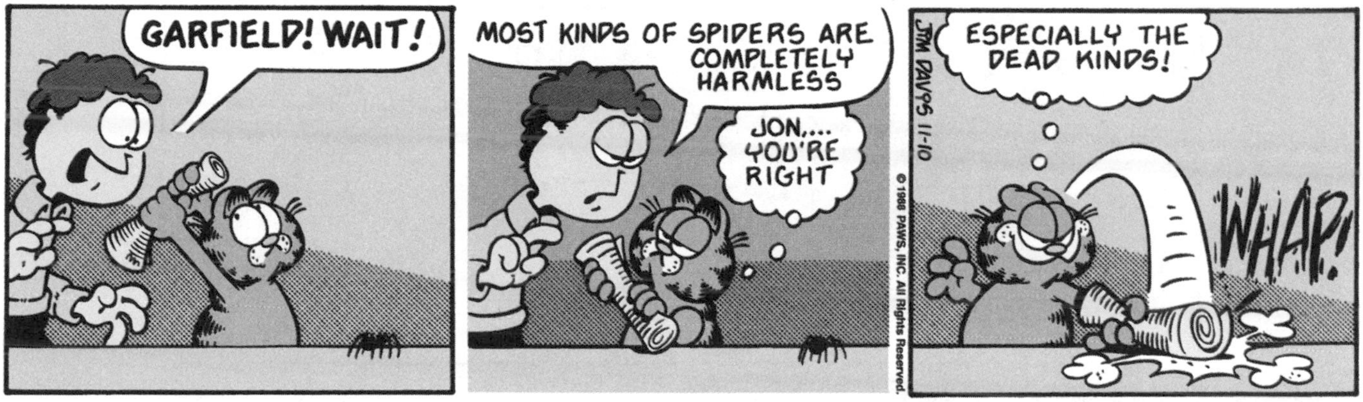
GARFIELD! WAIT!
MOST KINDS OF SPIDERS ARE COMPLETELY HARMLESS
JON,... YOU'RE RIGHT
JIM DAVIS 11-10
© 1988 PAWS, INC. All Rights Reserved.
ESPECIALLY THE DEAD KINDS!
WHAP!

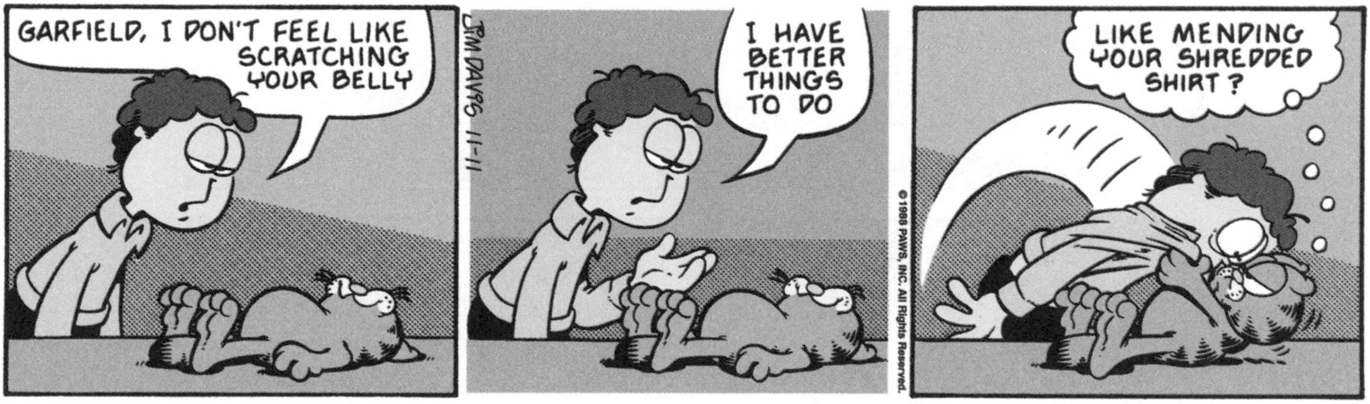
GARFIELD, I DON'T FEEL LIKE SCRATCHING YOUR BELLY
JIM DAVIS 11-11
I HAVE BETTER THINGS TO DO
© 1988 PAWS, INC. All Rights Reserved.
LIKE MENDING YOUR SHREDDED SHIRT?

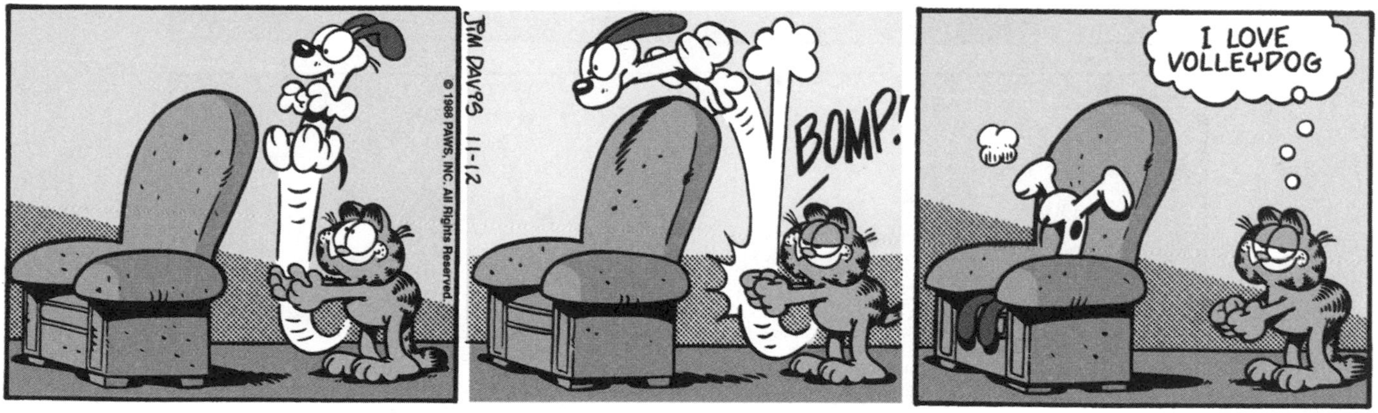
JIM DAVIS 11-12
© 1988 PAWS, INC. All Rights Reserved.
BOMP!
I LOVE VOLLEYDOG

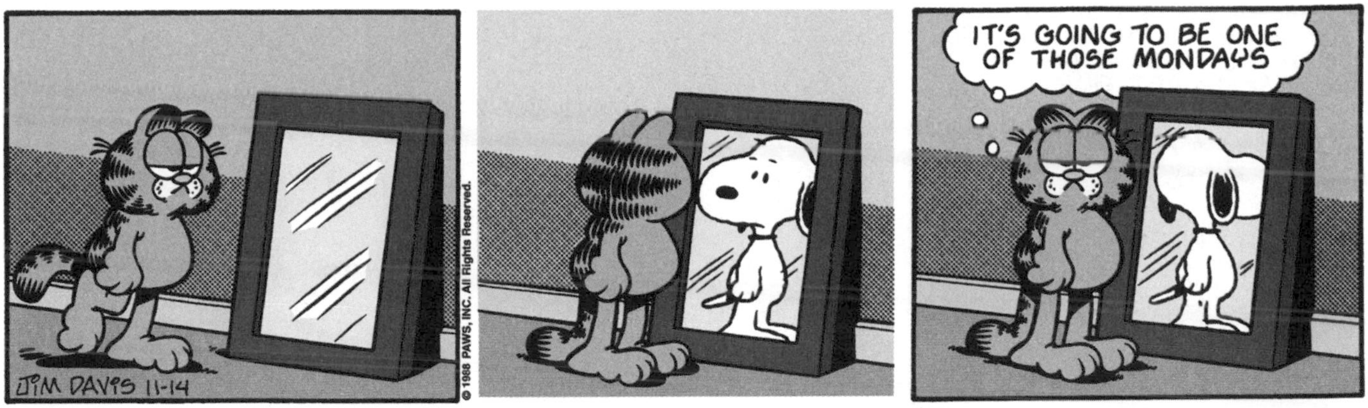
JIM DAVIS 11-14
© 1988 PAWS, INC. All Rights Reserved.
IT'S GOING TO BE ONE OF THOSE MONDAYS

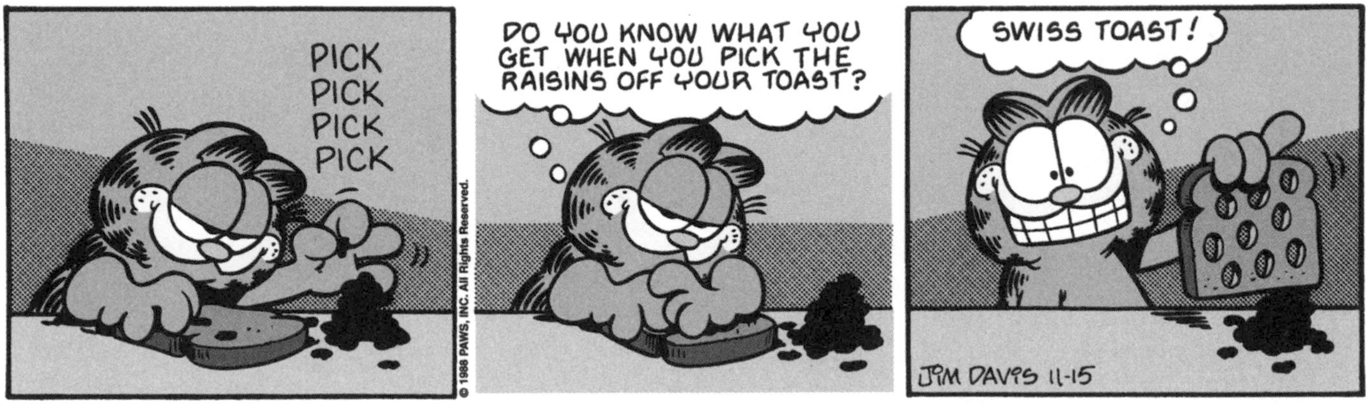
PICK PICK PICK PICK
© 1988 PAWS, INC. All Rights Reserved.
DO YOU KNOW WHAT YOU GET WHEN YOU PICK THE RAISINS OFF YOUR TOAST?
SWISS TOAST!
JIM DAVIS 11-15

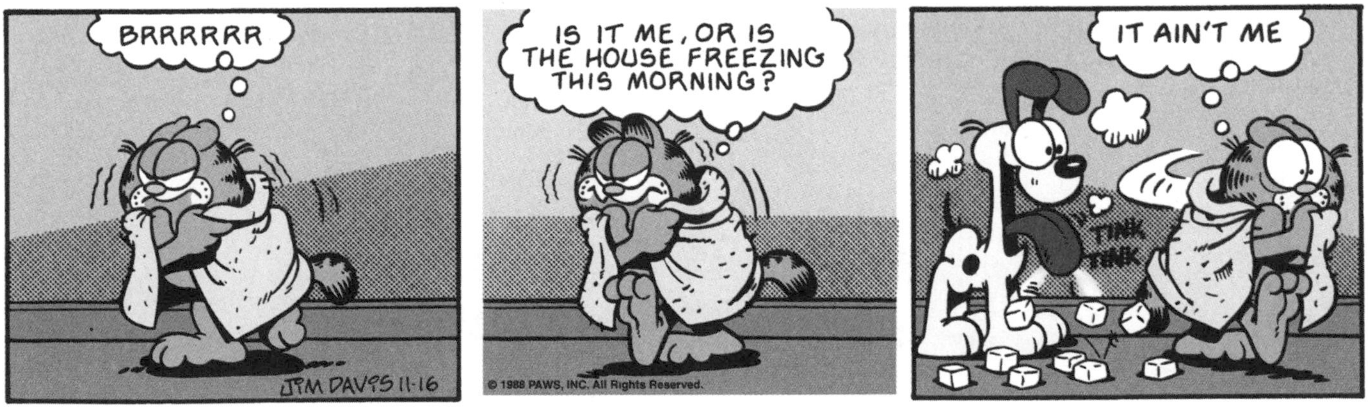
BRRRRRR
JIM DAVIS 11-16
IS IT ME, OR IS THE HOUSE FREEZING THIS MORNING?
© 1988 PAWS, INC. All Rights Reserved.
IT AIN'T ME
TINK
TINK

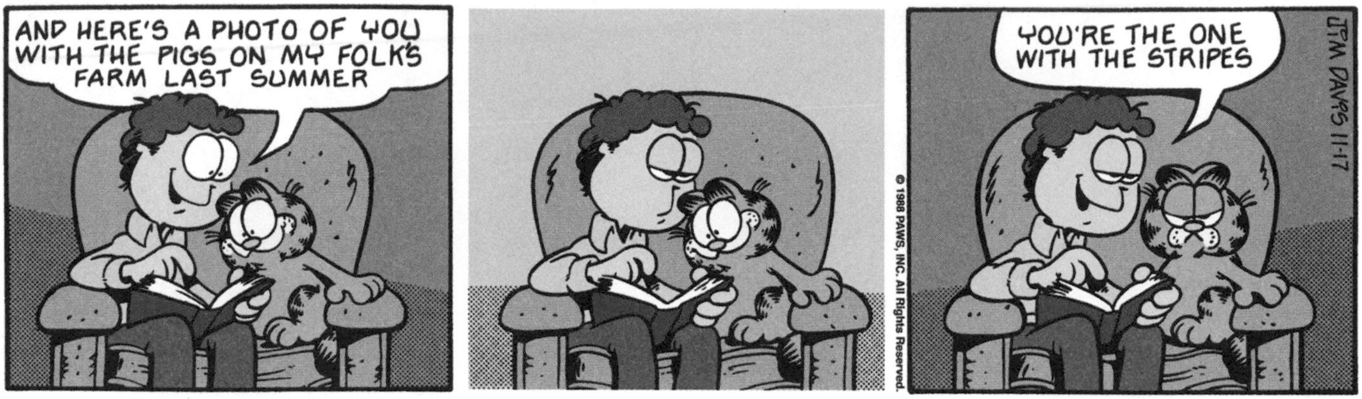
AND HERE'S A PHOTO OF YOU WITH THE PIGS ON MY FOLK'S FARM LAST SUMMER
YOU'RE THE ONE WITH THE STRIPES
JIM DAVIS 11-17
© 1988 PAWS, INC. All Rights Reserved.

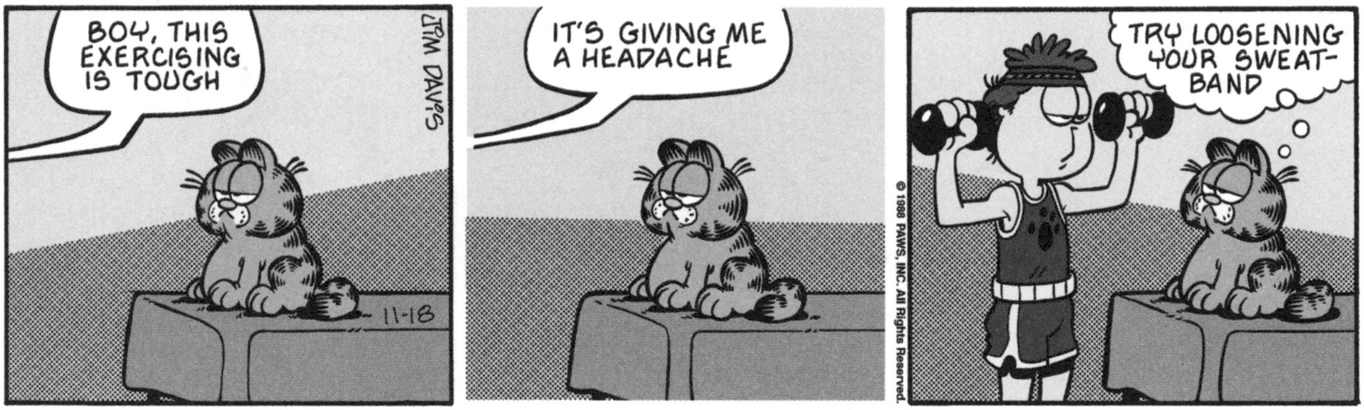
BOY, THIS EXERCISING IS TOUGH
JIM DAVIS
11-18
IT'S GIVING ME A HEADACHE
TRY LOOSENING YOUR SWEAT-BAND
© 1988 PAWS, INC. All Rights Reserved.

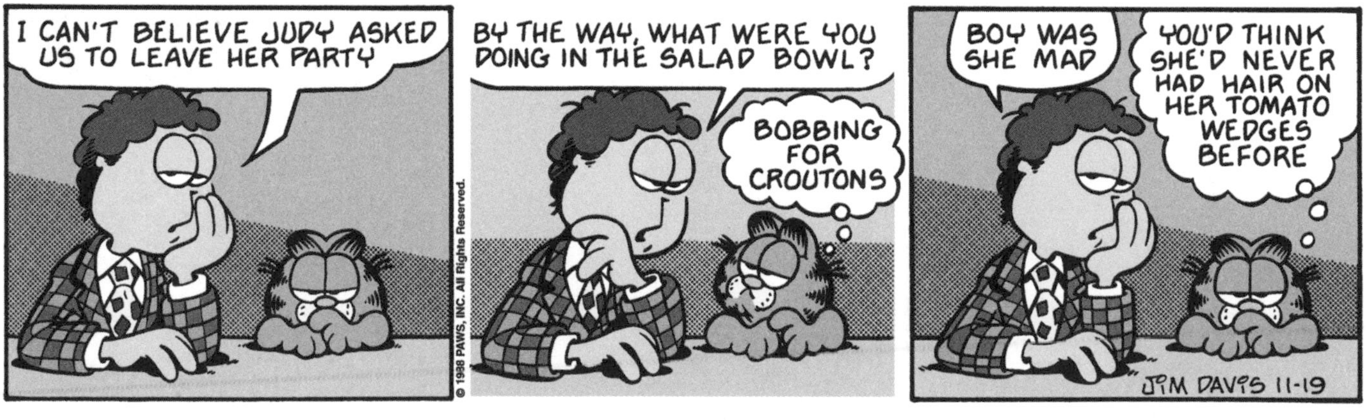
I CAN'T BELIEVE JUDY ASKED US TO LEAVE HER PARTY
BY THE WAY, WHAT WERE YOU DOING IN THE SALAD BOWL?
BOBBING FOR CROUTONS
BOY WAS SHE MAD
YOU'D THINK SHE'D NEVER HAD HAIR ON HER TOMATO WEDGES BEFORE
JIM DAVIS 11-19
© 1988 PAWS, INC. All Rights Reserved.

35 DAYS, 5 HOURS, 36 MINUTES AND 4 SECONDS TILL CHRISTMAS

Z

WHA? WHO?! ARE YOU A MONSTER?!

ODIE! IT'S YOU! SURE, YOU CAN SLEEP WITH ME

SLURP!

YAAAAH! NOW WHO ARE YOU?!

CLICK

GARFIELD!

WHAT ARE YOU TRYING TO DO? SCARE US?

JIM DAVIS 11-20

WHAT A GREAT MEAL!

ISN'T IT A SHAME THERE'S NO UNIT OF MEASURE FOR HOW GOOD FOOD TASTES?

AH, BUT THERE IS...

IT'S CALLED A CALORIE

DO YOU THINK YOU'D EVER LIKE TO HAVE A STATUE ERECTED IN YOUR MEMORY, GARFIELD?

YEAH!

IF THEY COULD MAKE IT SO IT COULD EAT PIGEONS

WAIT'LL YOU SEE WHAT I BOUGHT, GARFIELD

TAH-DAH!

IT'S AMAZING THE THINGS PEOPLE WOULD RATHER HAVE THAN MONEY

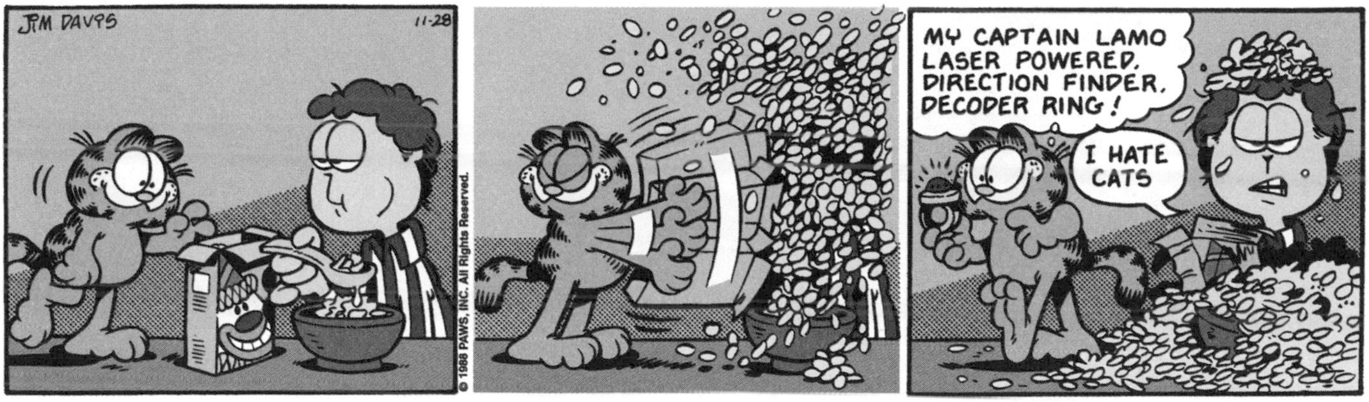
JIM DAVIS
11-28
© 1988 PAWS, INC. All Rights Reserved.
MY CAPTAIN LAMO LASER POWERED, DIRECTION FINDER, DECODER RING!
I HATE CATS

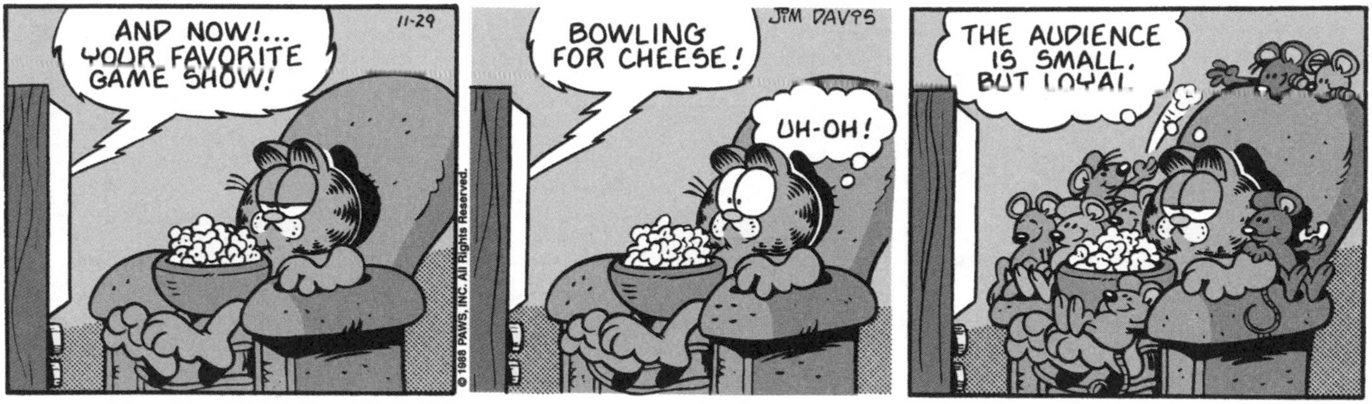
AND NOW!... YOUR FAVORITE GAME SHOW!
11-29
© 1988 PAWS, INC. All Rights Reserved.
BOWLING FOR CHEESE!
JIM DAVIS
UH-OH!
THE AUDIENCE IS SMALL, BUT LOYAL.

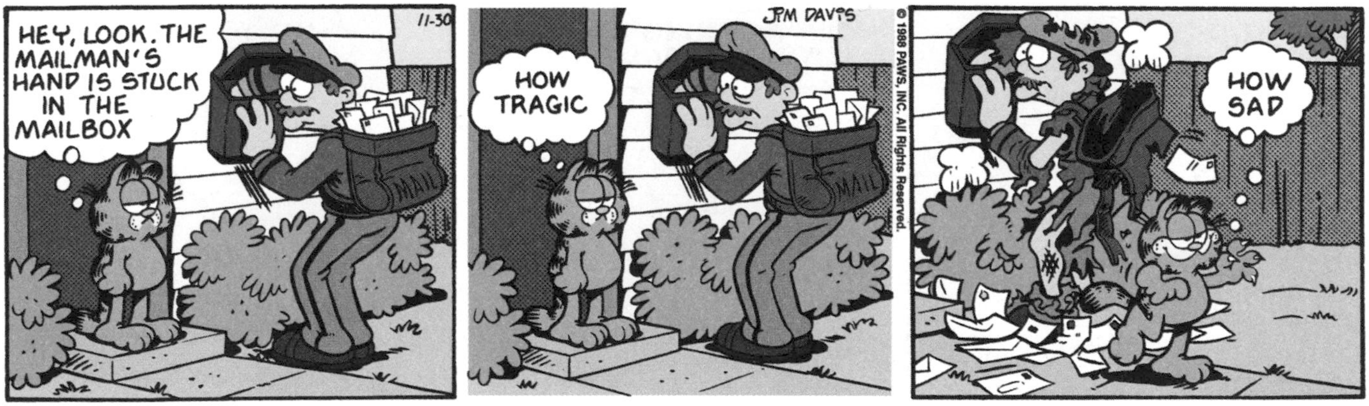
HEY, LOOK. THE MAILMAN'S HAND IS STUCK IN THE MAILBOX
11-30
HOW TRAGIC
JIM DAVIS
MAIL
© 1988 PAWS, INC. All Rights Reserved.
HOW SAD

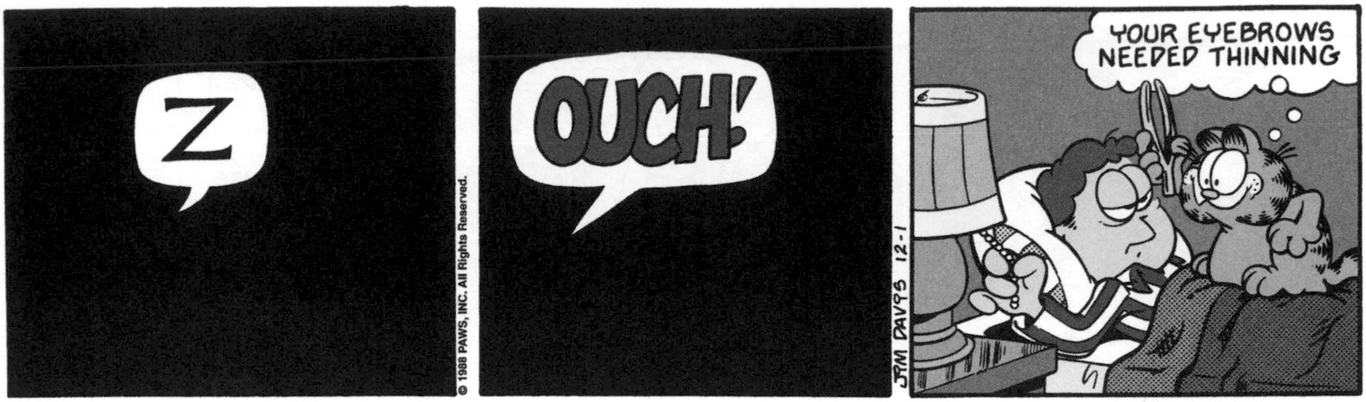
Z
OUCH!
YOUR EYEBROWS NEEDED THINNING
© 1988 PAWS, INC. All Rights Reserved.
JIM DAVIS 12-1

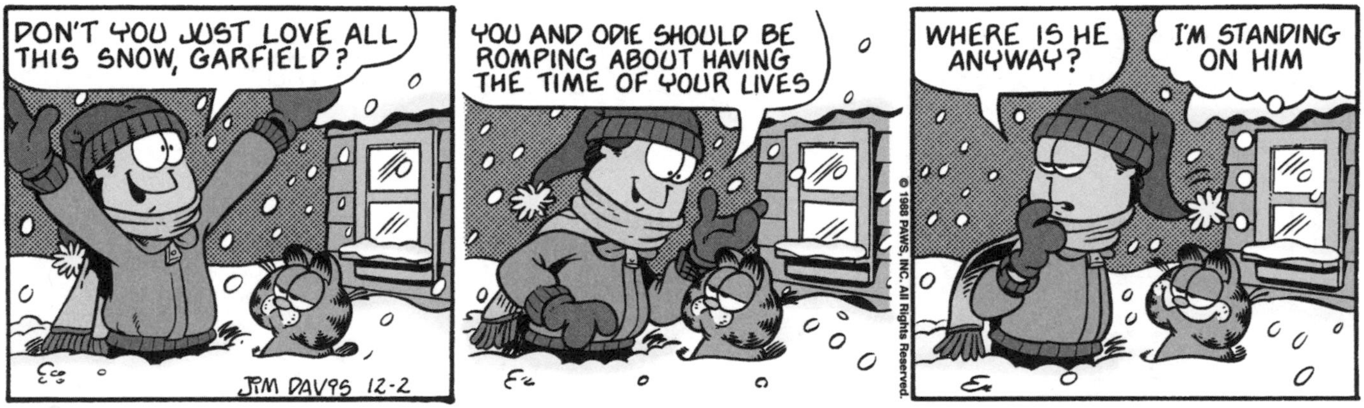
DON'T YOU JUST LOVE ALL THIS SNOW, GARFIELD?
YOU AND ODIE SHOULD BE ROMPING ABOUT HAVING THE TIME OF YOUR LIVES
WHERE IS HE ANYWAY?
I'M STANDING ON HIM
JIM DAVIS 12-2
© 1988 PAWS, INC. All Rights Reserved.

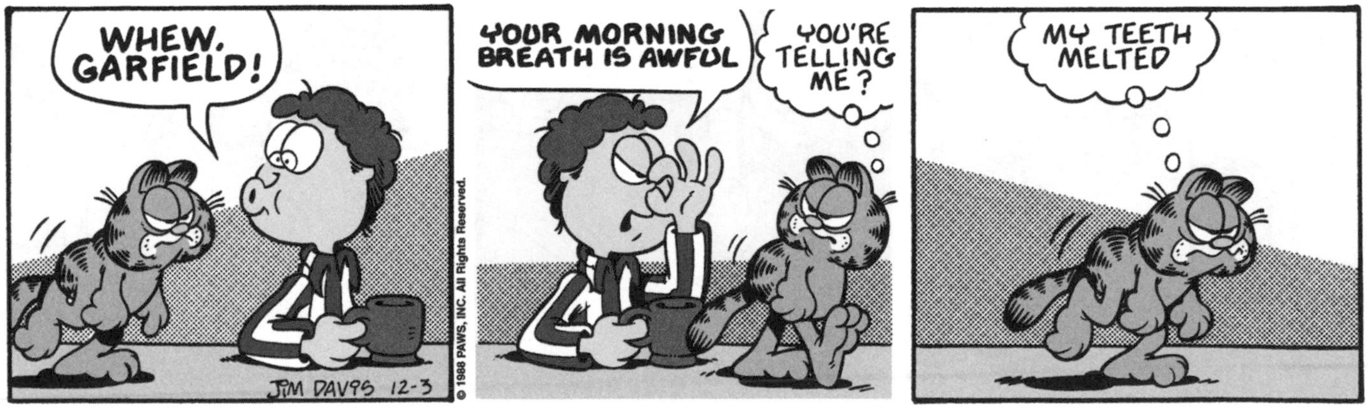
WHEW. GARFIELD!
YOUR MORNING BREATH IS AWFUL
YOU'RE TELLING ME?
MY TEETH MELTED
JIM DAVIS 12-3
© 1988 PAWS, INC. All Rights Reserved.

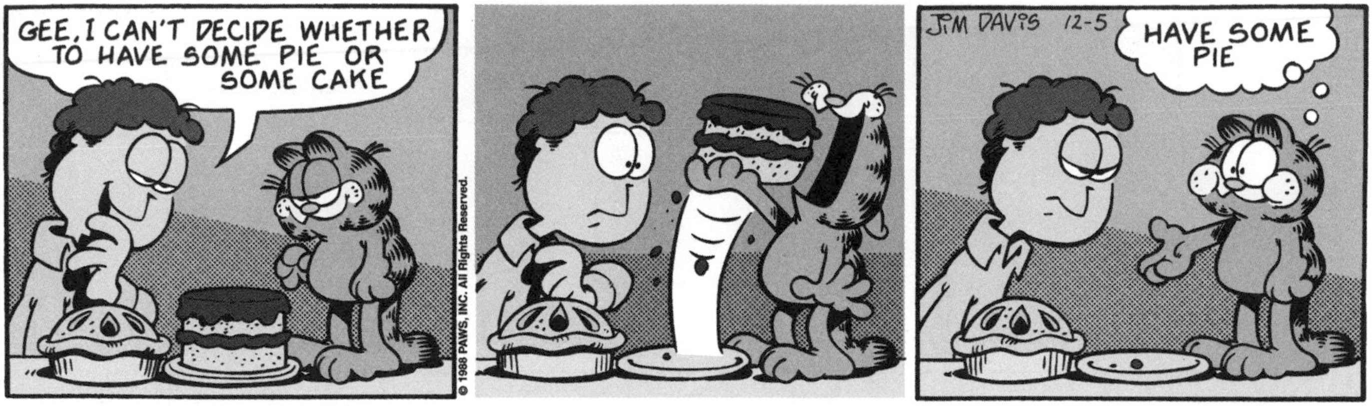
GEE, I CAN'T DECIDE WHETHER TO HAVE SOME PIE OR SOME CAKE
© 1988 PAWS, INC. All Rights Reserved.
JIM DAVIS 12-5
HAVE SOME PIE

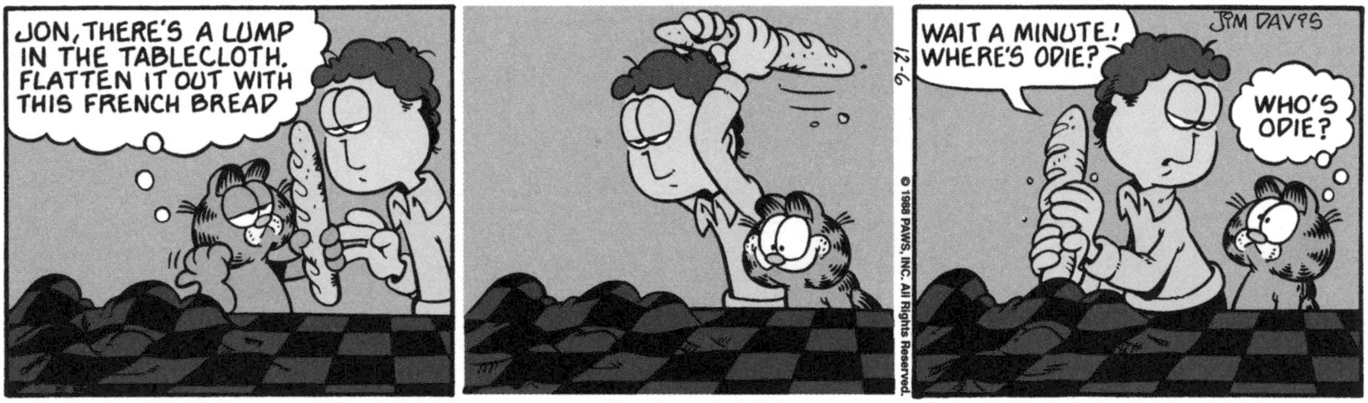
JON, THERE'S A LUMP IN THE TABLECLOTH. FLATTEN IT OUT WITH THIS FRENCH BREAD
12-6
© 1988 PAWS, INC. All Rights Reserved.
JIM DAVIS
WAIT A MINUTE! WHERE'S ODIE?
WHO'S ODIE?

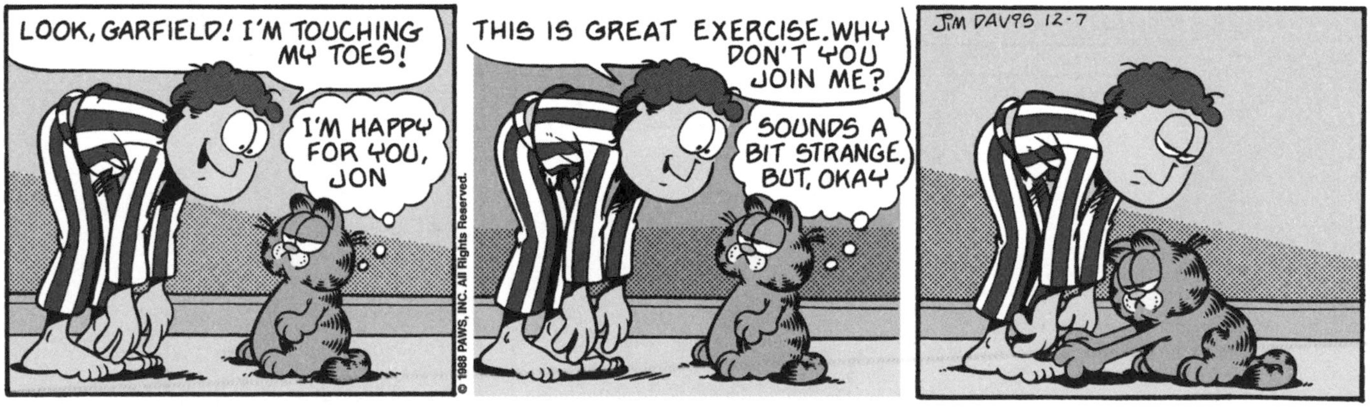
LOOK, GARFIELD! I'M TOUCHING MY TOES!
I'M HAPPY FOR YOU, JON
© 1988 PAWS, INC. All Rights Reserved.
THIS IS GREAT EXERCISE. WHY DON'T YOU JOIN ME?
SOUNDS A BIT STRANGE, BUT, OKAY
JIM DAVIS 12-7

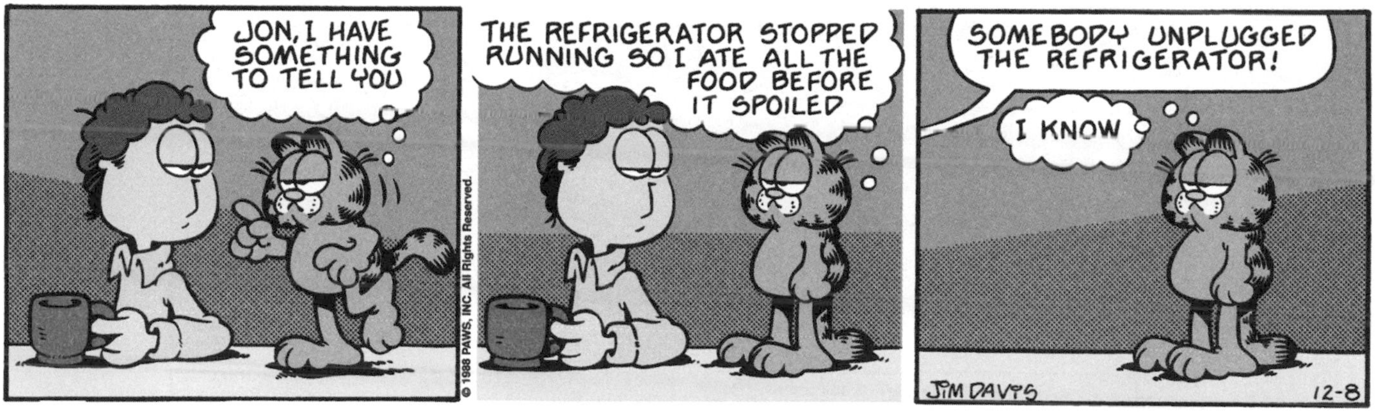
JON, I HAVE SOMETHING TO TELL YOU
© 1988 PAWS, INC. All Rights Reserved.
THE REFRIGERATOR STOPPED RUNNING SO I ATE ALL THE FOOD BEFORE IT SPOILED
SOMEBODY UNPLUGGED THE REFRIGERATOR!
I KNOW
JIM DAVIS
12-8

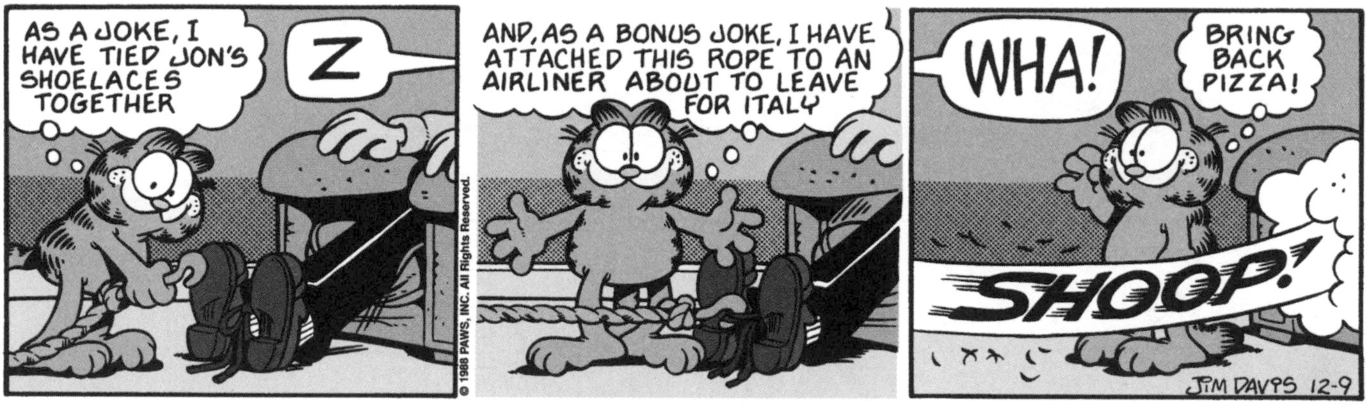
AS A JOKE, I HAVE TIED JON'S SHOELACES TOGETHER
Z
© 1988 PAWS, INC. All Rights Reserved.
AND, AS A BONUS JOKE, I HAVE ATTACHED THIS ROPE TO AN AIRLINER ABOUT TO LEAVE FOR ITALY
WHA!
BRING BACK PIZZA!
SHOOP!
JIM DAVIS 12-9

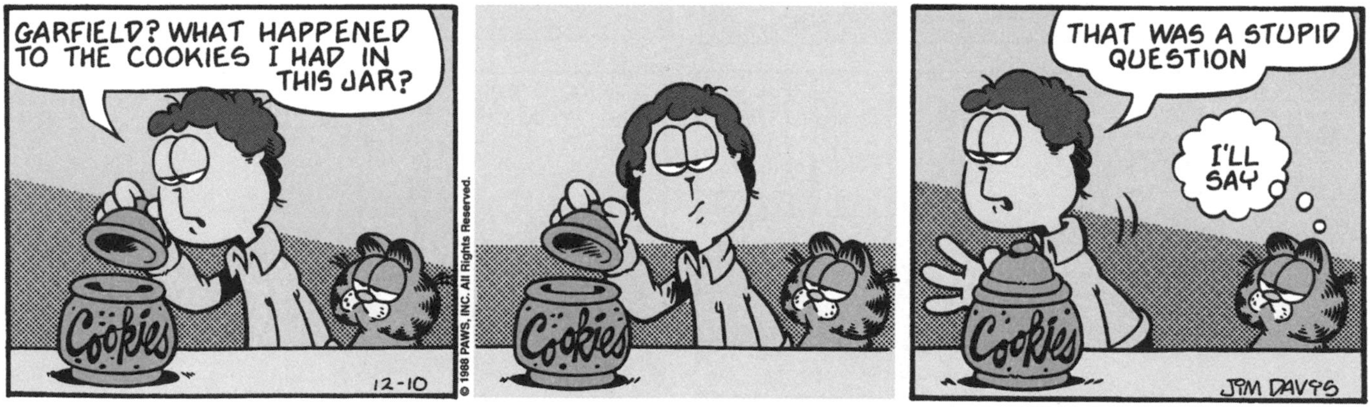
GARFIELD? WHAT HAPPENED TO THE COOKIES I HAD IN THIS JAR?
Cookies
12-10
© 1988 PAWS, INC. All Rights Reserved.
Cookies
THAT WAS A STUPID QUESTION
I'LL SAY
Cookies
JIM DAVIS

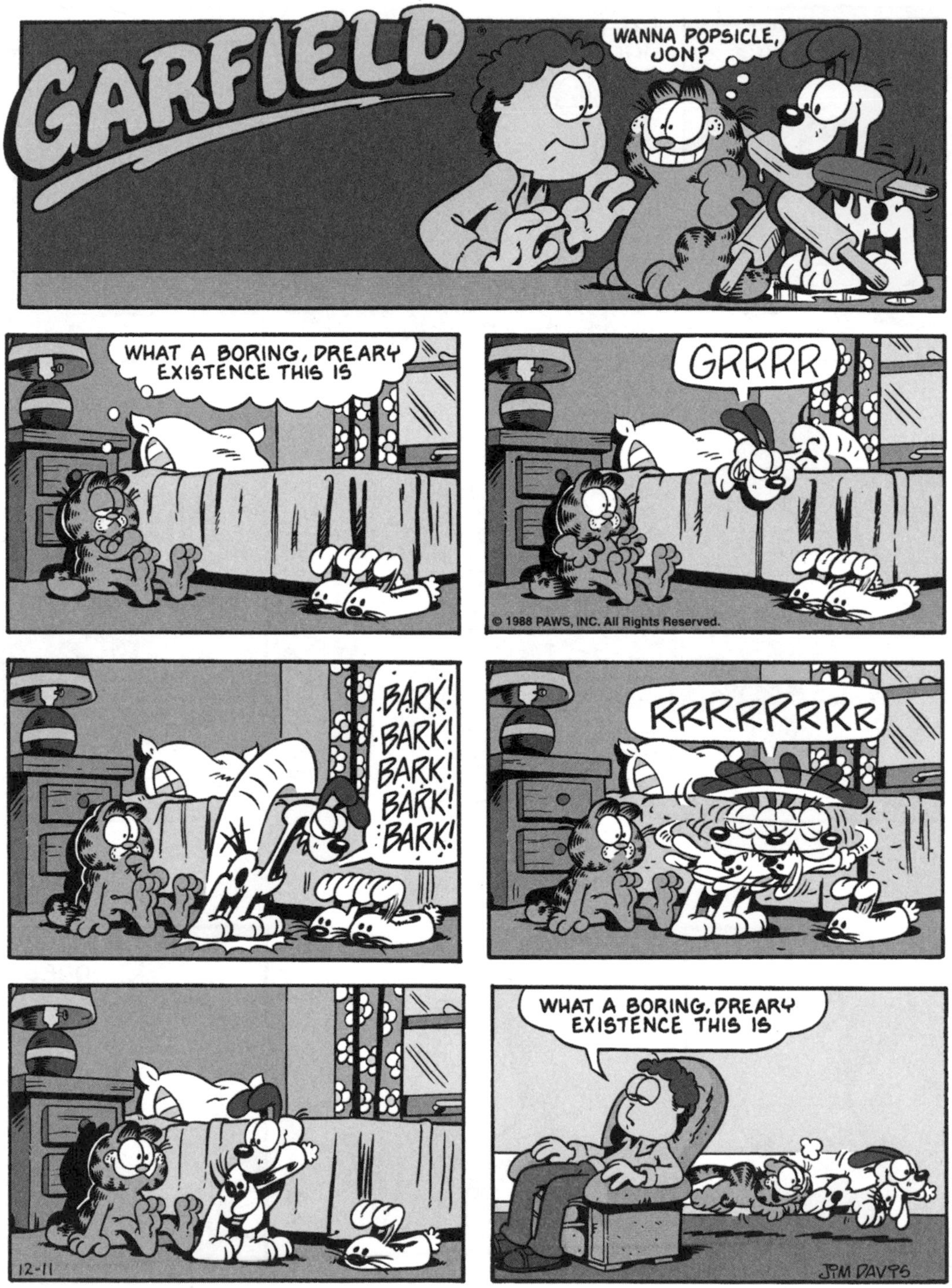
GARFIELD
WANNA POPSICLE, JON?
WHAT A BORING, DREARY EXISTENCE THIS IS
GRRRR
© 1988 PAWS, INC. All Rights Reserved.
BARK! BARK! BARK! BARK! BARK!
RRRRRRRR
12-11
WHAT A BORING, DREARY EXISTENCE THIS IS
JIM DAVIS

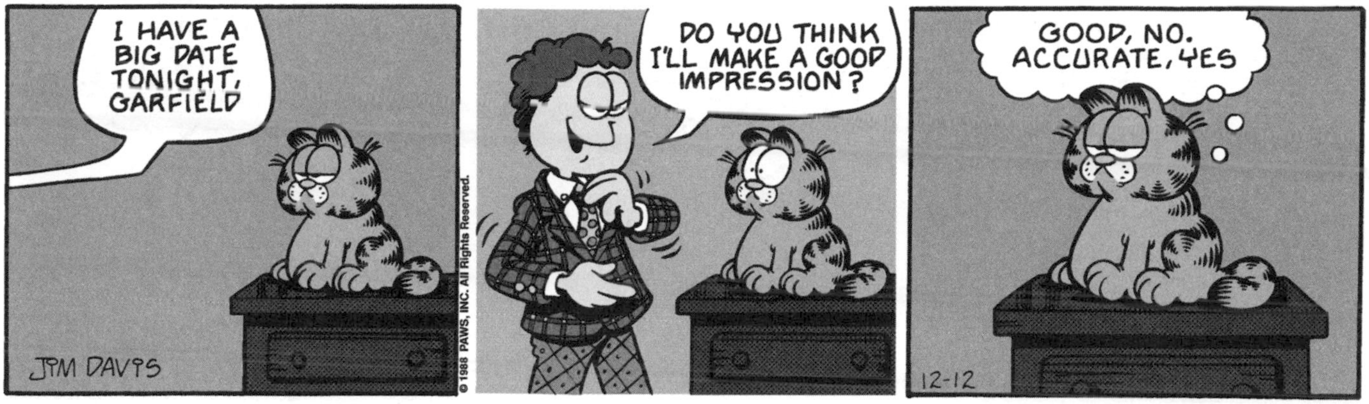
I HAVE A BIG DATE TONIGHT, GARFIELD
DO YOU THINK I'LL MAKE A GOOD IMPRESSION?
GOOD, NO. ACCURATE, YES
JIM DAVIS
© 1988 PAWS, INC. All Rights Reserved.
12-12

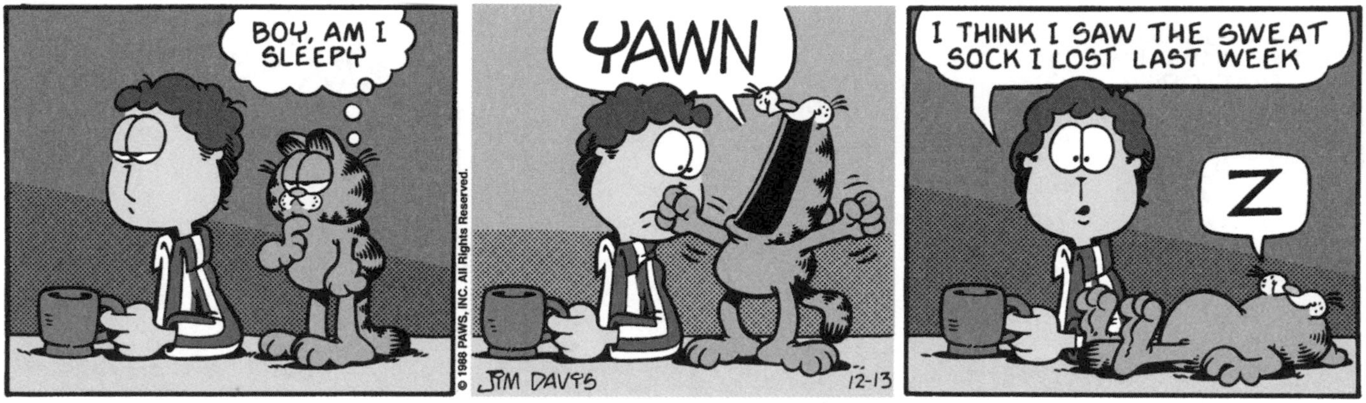
BOY, AM I SLEEPY
YAWN
I THINK I SAW THE SWEAT SOCK I LOST LAST WEEK
Z
JIM DAVIS
© 1988 PAWS, INC. All Rights Reserved.
12-13

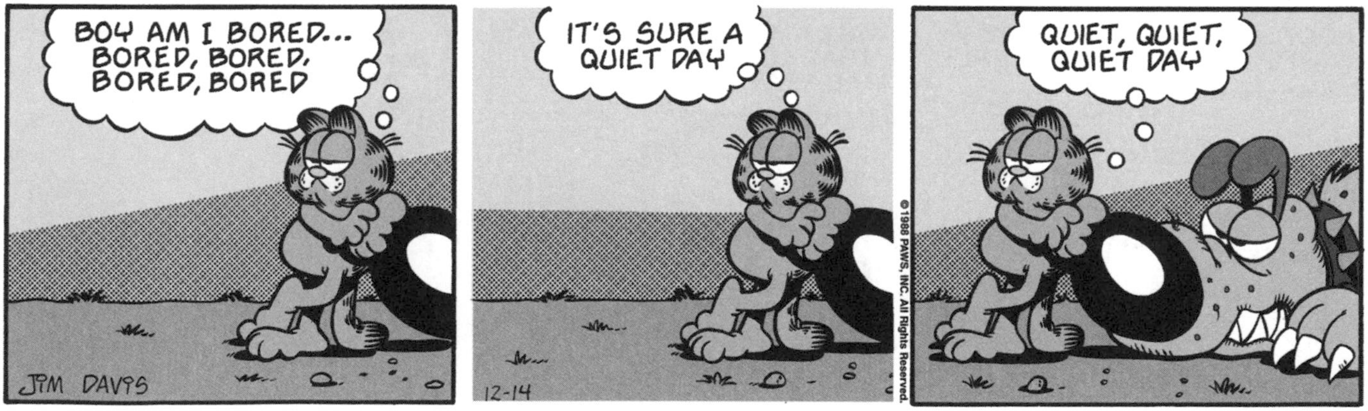
BOY AM I BORED... BORED, BORED, BORED, BORED
IT'S SURE A QUIET DAY
QUIET, QUIET, QUIET DAY
JIM DAVIS
12-14
© 1988 PAWS, INC. All Rights Reserved.

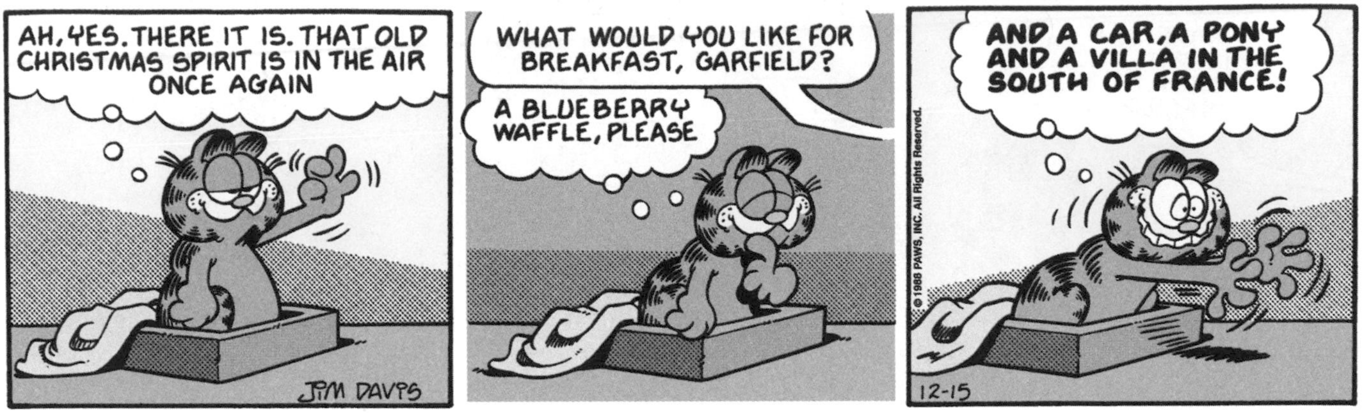
AH, YES. THERE IT IS. THAT OLD CHRISTMAS SPIRIT IS IN THE AIR ONCE AGAIN
JIM DAVIS
WHAT WOULD YOU LIKE FOR BREAKFAST, GARFIELD?
A BLUEBERRY WAFFLE, PLEASE
AND A CAR, A PONY AND A VILLA IN THE SOUTH OF FRANCE!
© 1988 PAWS, INC. All Rights Reserved.
12-15

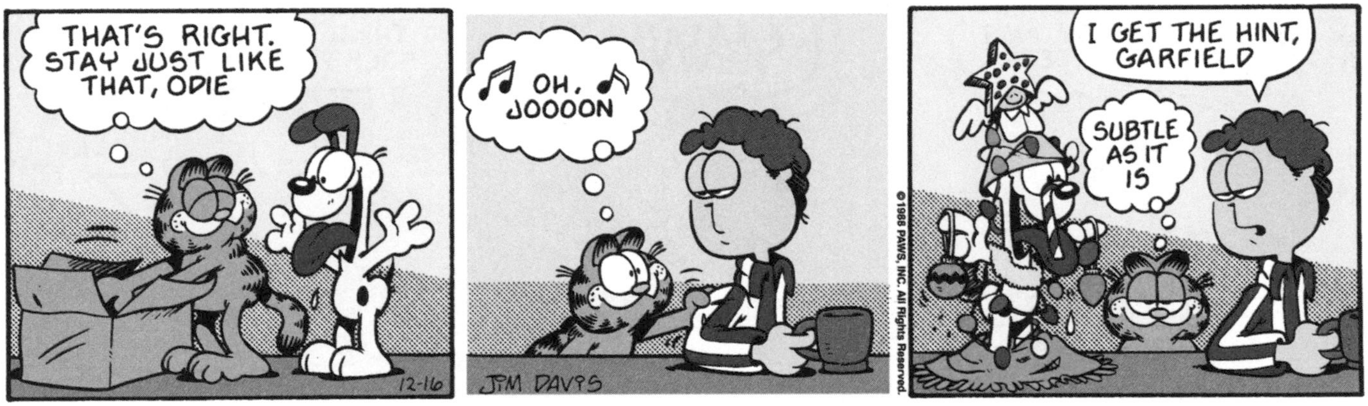
THAT'S RIGHT. STAY JUST LIKE THAT, ODIE
12-16
OH, JOOOON
JIM DAVIS
I GET THE HINT, GARFIELD
SUBTLE AS IT IS
© 1988 PAWS, INC. All Rights Reserved.

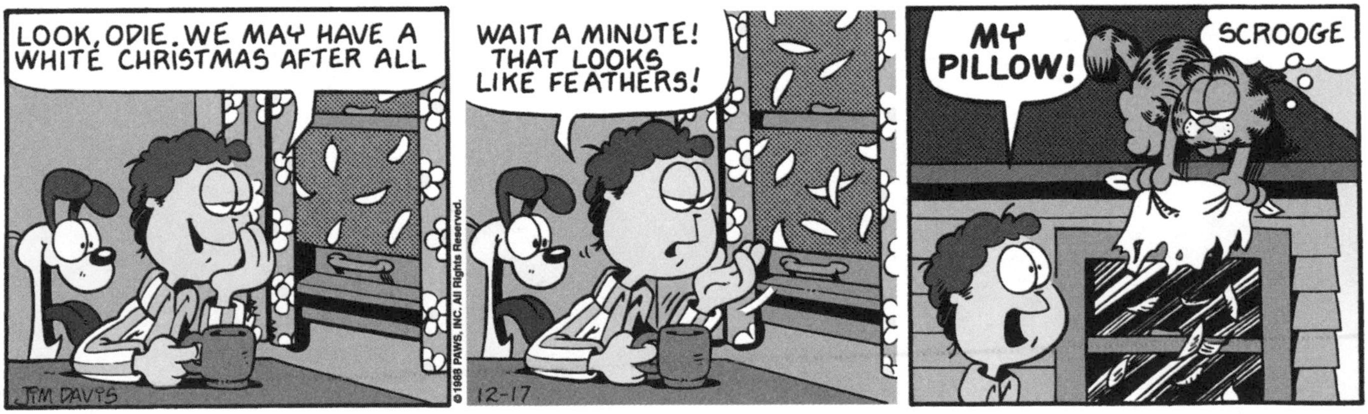
LOOK, ODIE. WE MAY HAVE A WHITE CHRISTMAS AFTER ALL
JIM DAVIS
© 1988 PAWS, INC. All Rights Reserved.
WAIT A MINUTE! THAT LOOKS LIKE FEATHERS!
12-17
MY PILLOW!
SCROOGE

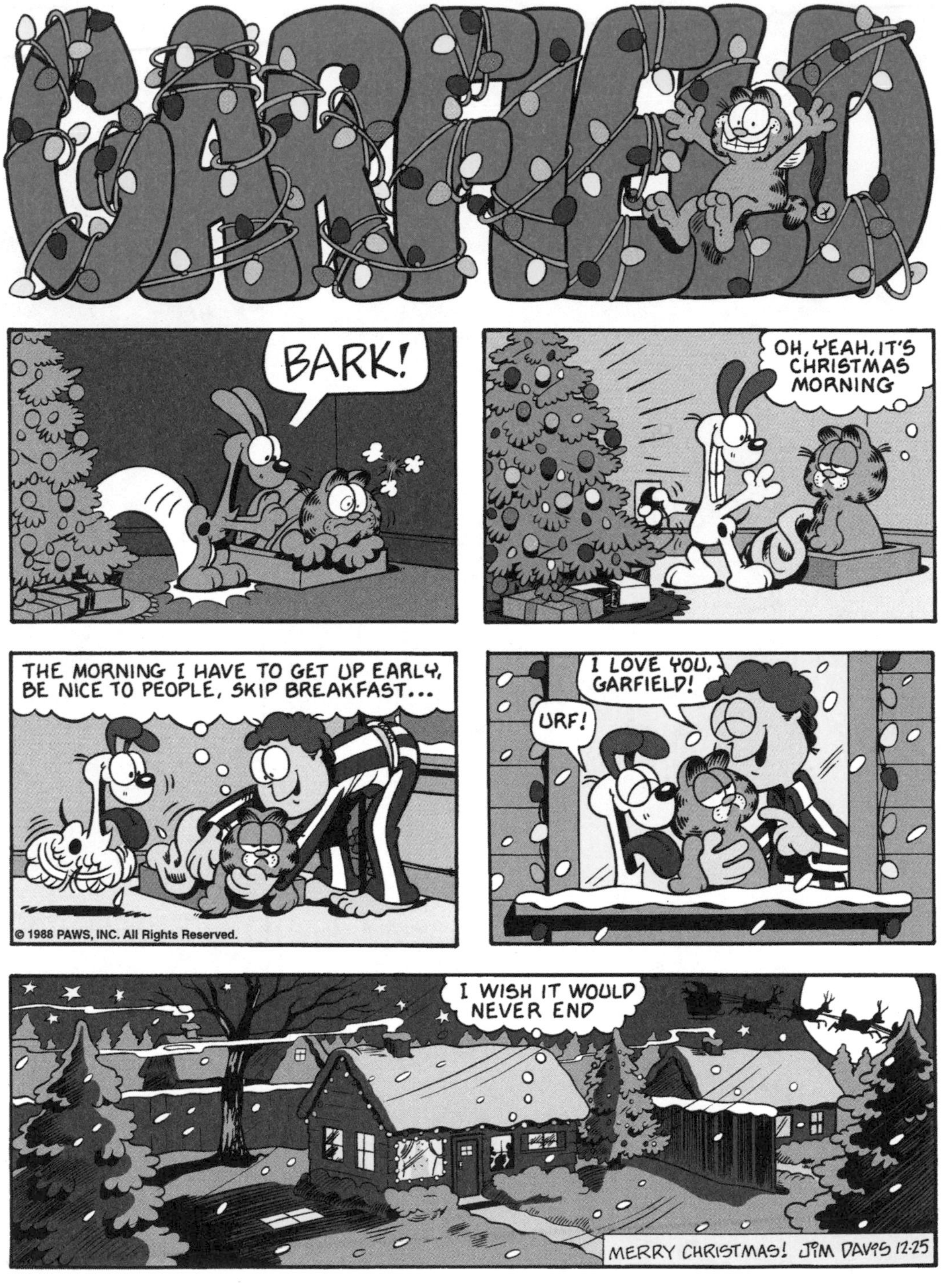
GARFIELD
BARK!
OH, YEAH, IT'S CHRISTMAS MORNING
THE MORNING I HAVE TO GET UP EARLY, BE NICE TO PEOPLE, SKIP BREAKFAST...
© 1988 PAWS, INC. All Rights Reserved.
I LOVE YOU, GARFIELD!
URF!
I WISH IT WOULD NEVER END
MERRY CHRISTMAS! JIM DAVIS 12-25

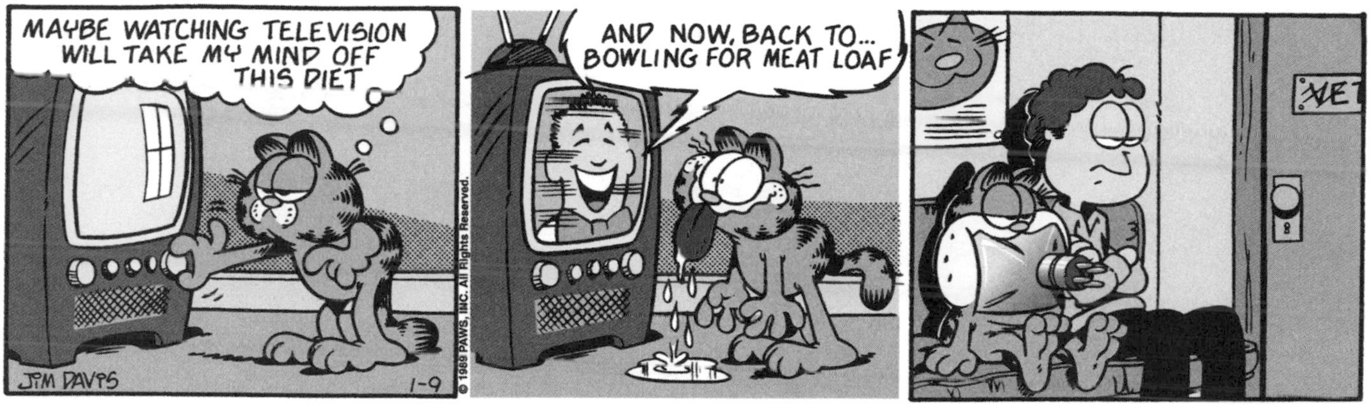
MAYBE WATCHING TELEVISION WILL TAKE MY MIND OFF THIS DIET
JIM DAVIS
1-9
© 1989 PAWS, INC. All Rights Reserved.
AND NOW, BACK TO... BOWLING FOR MEAT LOAF
VET

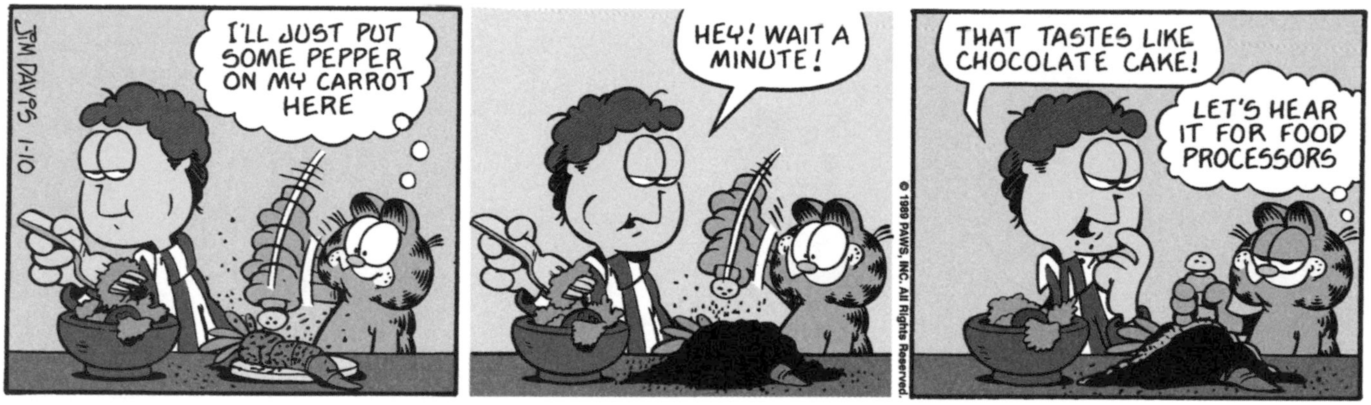
JIM DAVIS 1-10
I'LL JUST PUT SOME PEPPER ON MY CARROT HERE
HEY! WAIT A MINUTE!
© 1989 PAWS, INC. All Rights Reserved.
THAT TASTES LIKE CHOCOLATE CAKE!
LET'S HEAR IT FOR FOOD PROCESSORS

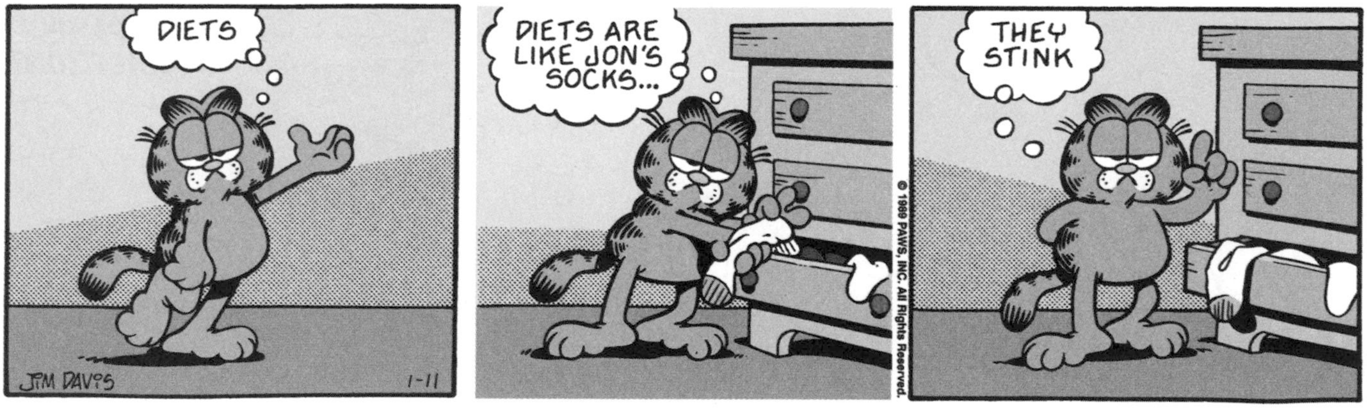
DIETS
JIM DAVIS
1-11
DIETS ARE LIKE JON'S SOCKS...
© 1989 PAWS, INC. All Rights Reserved.
THEY STINK

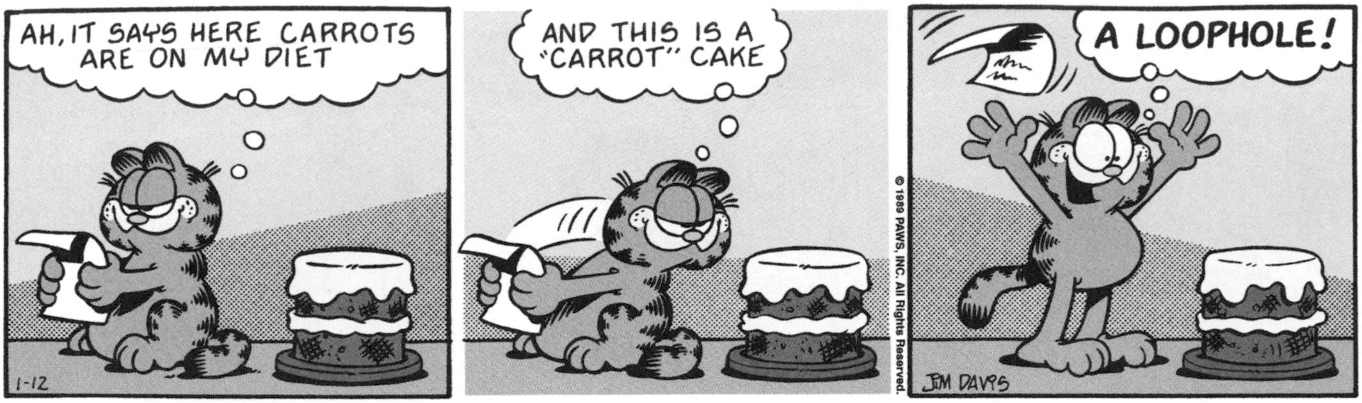
1-12
AH, IT SAYS HERE CARROTS ARE ON MY DIET
AND THIS IS A "CARROT" CAKE
© 1989 PAWS, INC. All Rights Reserved.
A LOOPHOLE!
JIM DAVIS

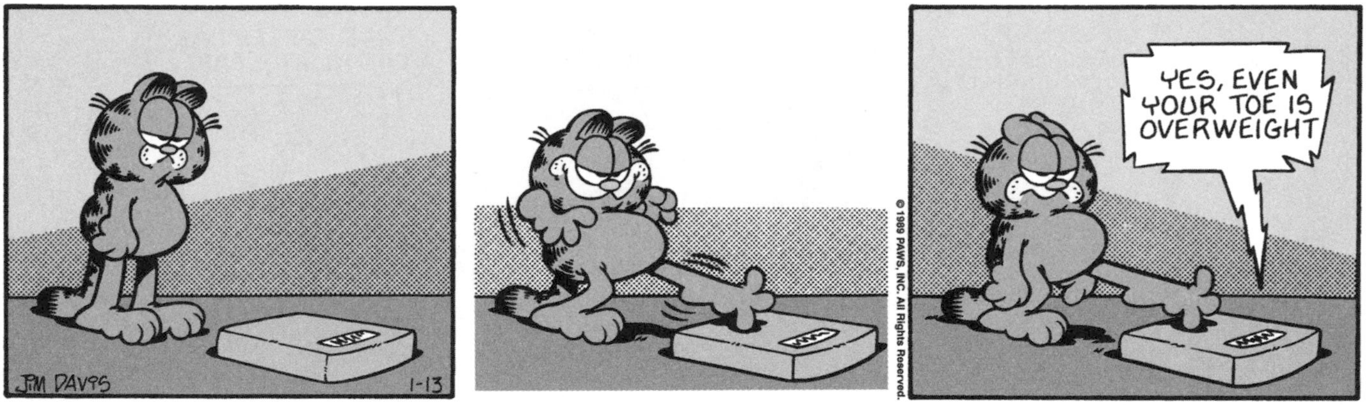
JIM DAVIS
1-13
© 1989 PAWS, INC. All Rights Reserved.
YES, EVEN YOUR TOE IS OVERWEIGHT

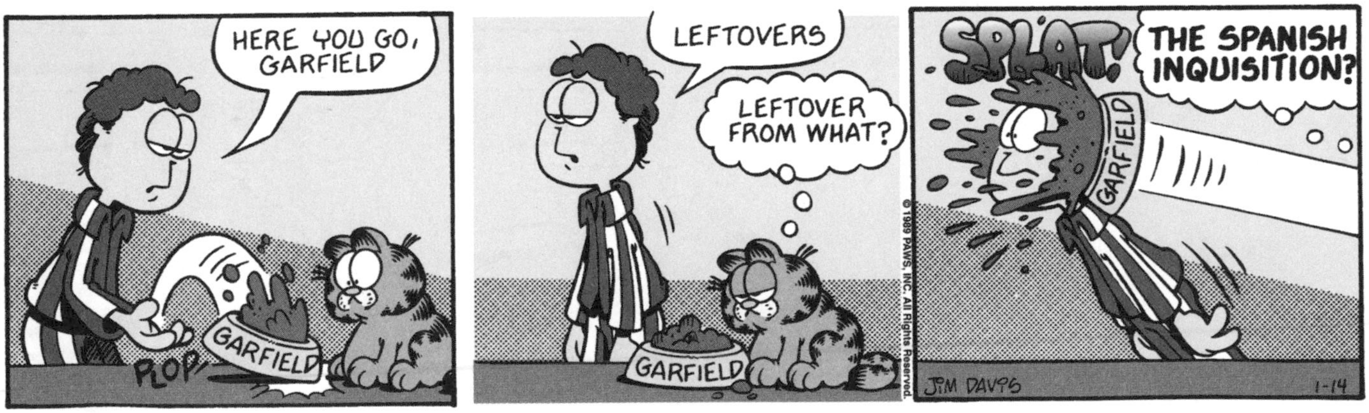
HERE YOU GO, GARFIELD
PLOP!
GARFIELD
LEFTOVERS
LEFTOVER FROM WHAT?
GARFIELD
© 1989 PAWS, INC. All Rights Reserved.
SPLAT!
THE SPANISH INQUISITION?
GARFIELD
JIM DAVIS
1-14

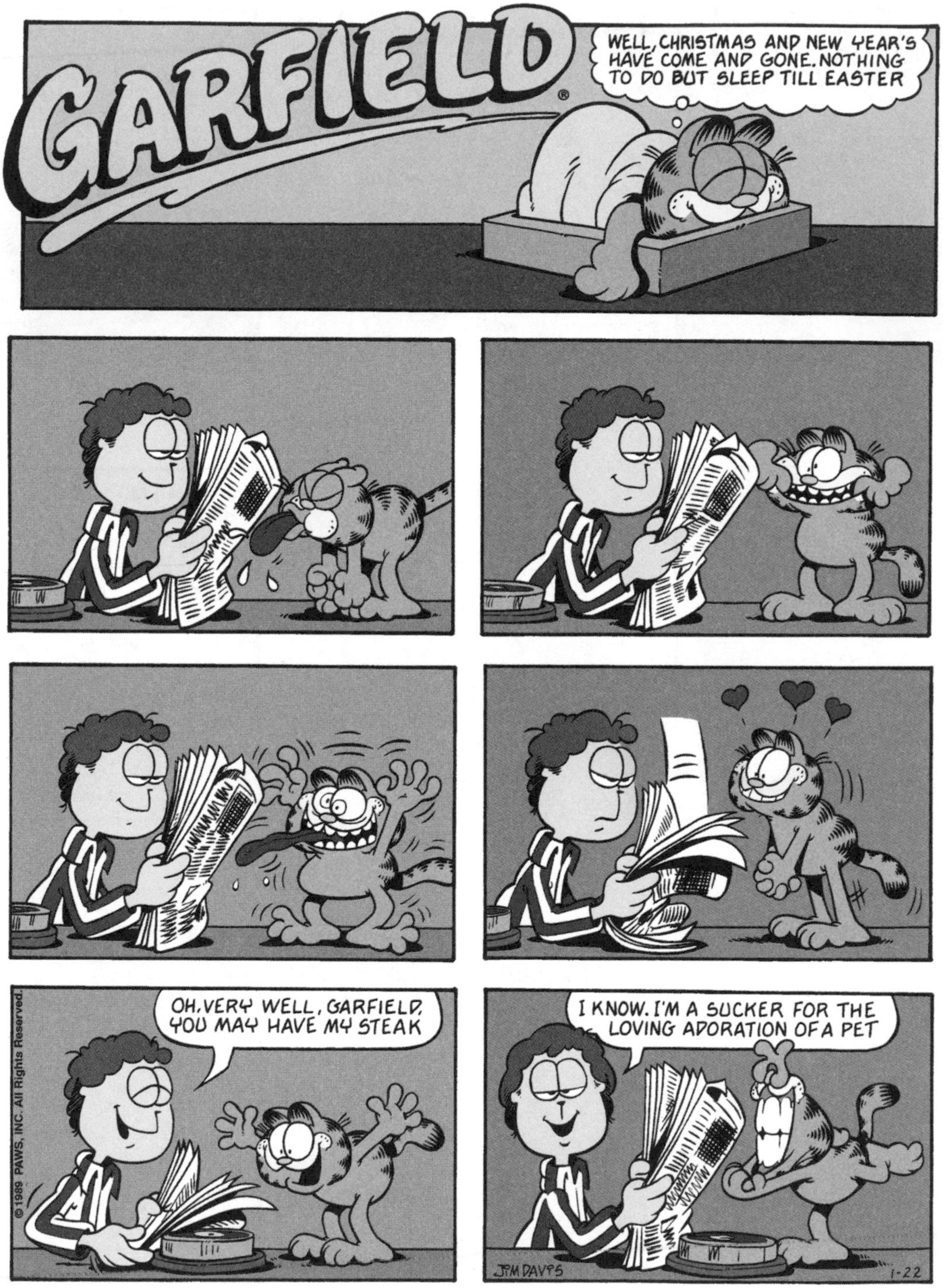
GARFIELD
WELL, CHRISTMAS AND NEW YEAR'S HAVE COME AND GONE. NOTHING TO DO BUT SLEEP TILL EASTER
©1989 PAWS, INC. All Rights Reserved.
OH, VERY WELL, GARFIELD, YOU MAY HAVE MY STEAK
I KNOW. I'M A SUCKER FOR THE LOVING ADORATION OF A PET
JIM DAVIS
1-22

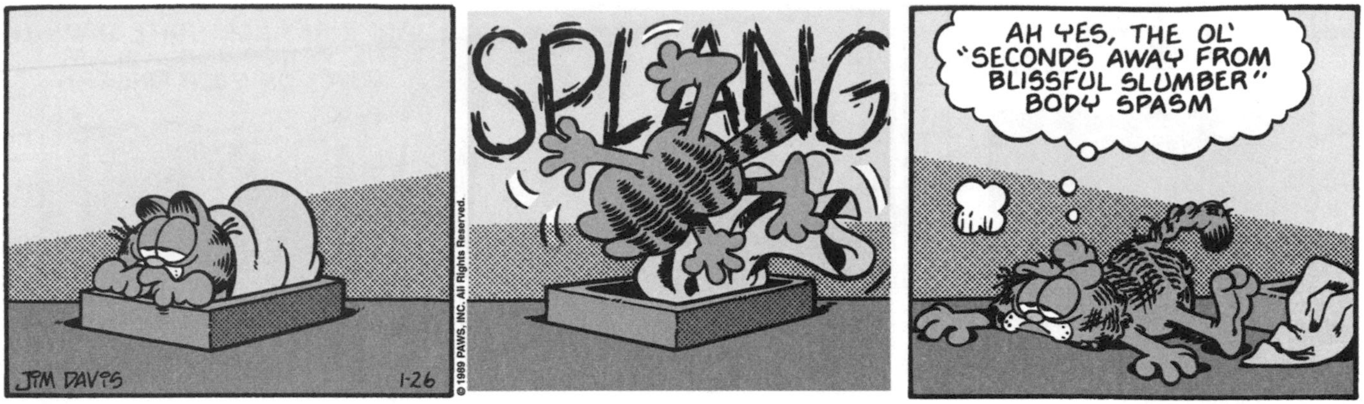
JIM DAVIS
1-26
SPLANG
© 1989 PAWS, INC. All Rights Reserved.
AH YES, THE OL' "SECONDS AWAY FROM BLISSFUL SLUMBER" BODY SPASM

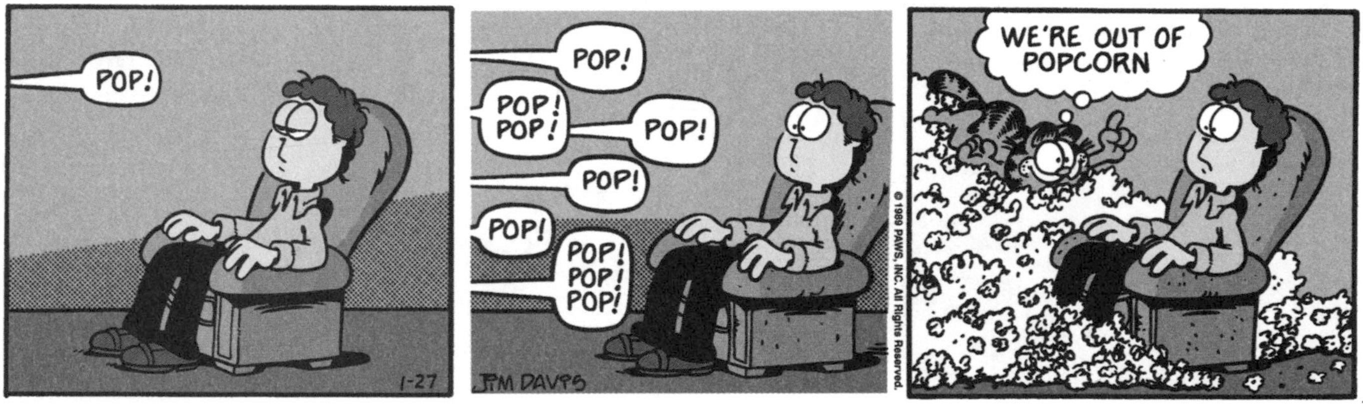
POP!
1-27
POP!
POP! POP!
POP!
POP!
POP!
POP! POP! POP!
JIM DAVIS
© 1989 PAWS, INC. All Rights Reserved.
WE'RE OUT OF POPCORN

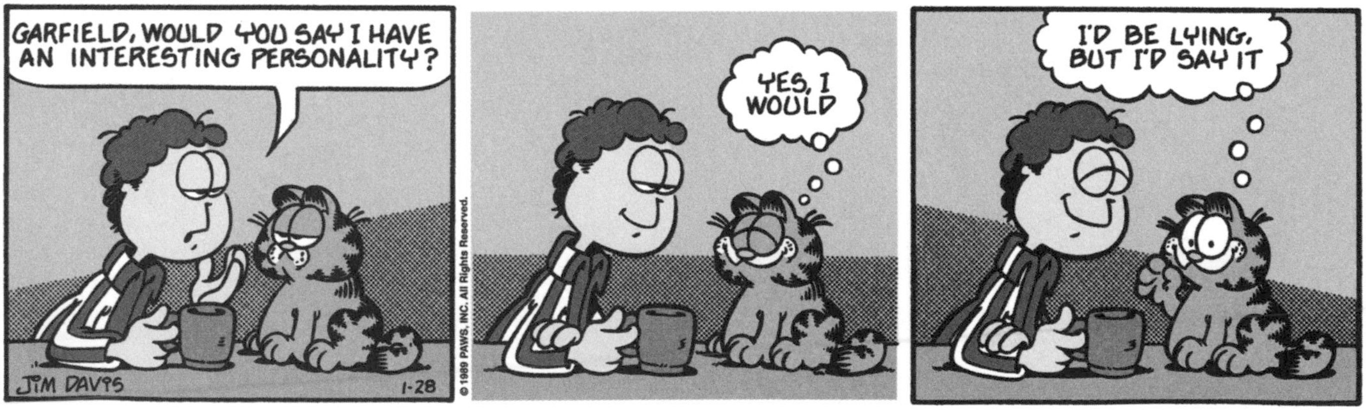
GARFIELD, WOULD YOU SAY I HAVE AN INTERESTING PERSONALITY?
JIM DAVIS
1-28
© 1989 PAWS, INC. All Rights Reserved.
YES, I WOULD
I'D BE LYING, BUT I'D SAY IT

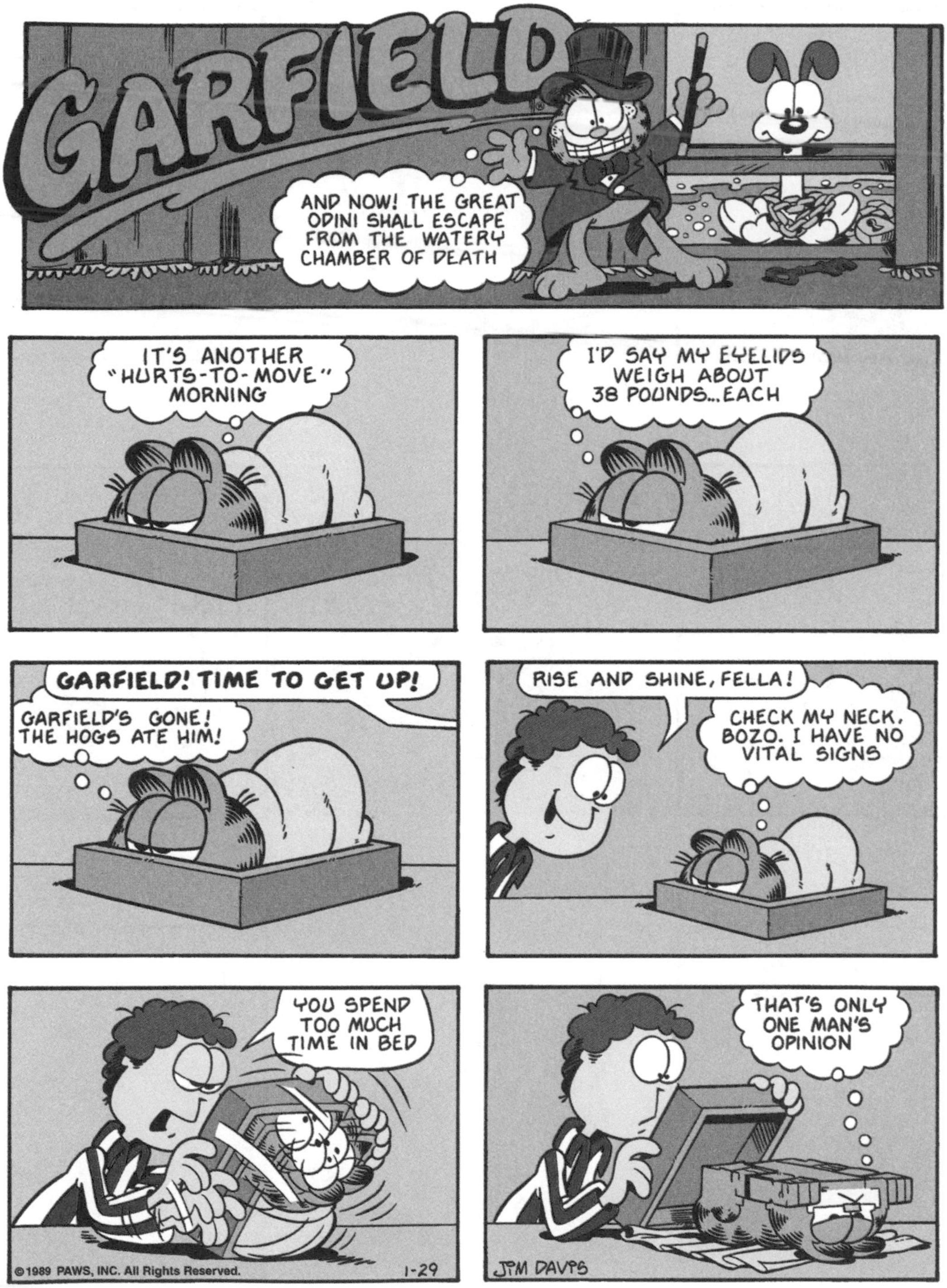
GARFIELD
AND NOW! THE GREAT ODINI SHALL ESCAPE FROM THE WATERY CHAMBER OF DEATH
IT'S ANOTHER "HURTS-TO-MOVE" MORNING
I'D SAY MY EYELIDS WEIGH ABOUT 38 POUNDS...EACH
GARFIELD! TIME TO GET UP!
GARFIELD'S GONE! THE HOGS ATE HIM!
RISE AND SHINE, FELLA!
CHECK MY NECK, BOZO. I HAVE NO VITAL SIGNS
YOU SPEND TOO MUCH TIME IN BED
THAT'S ONLY ONE MAN'S OPINION
©1989 PAWS, INC. All Rights Reserved.
1-29
JIM DAVIS

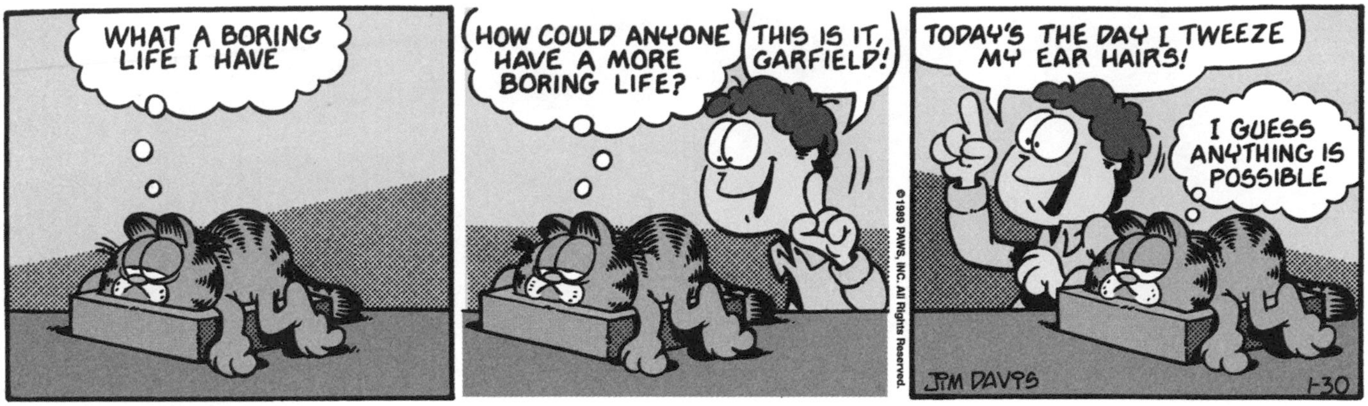
WHAT A BORING LIFE I HAVE
HOW COULD ANYONE HAVE A MORE BORING LIFE?
THIS IS IT, GARFIELD!
© 1989 PAWS, INC. All Rights Reserved.
TODAY'S THE DAY I TWEEZE MY EAR HAIRS!
I GUESS ANYTHING IS POSSIBLE
JIM DAVIS
1-30

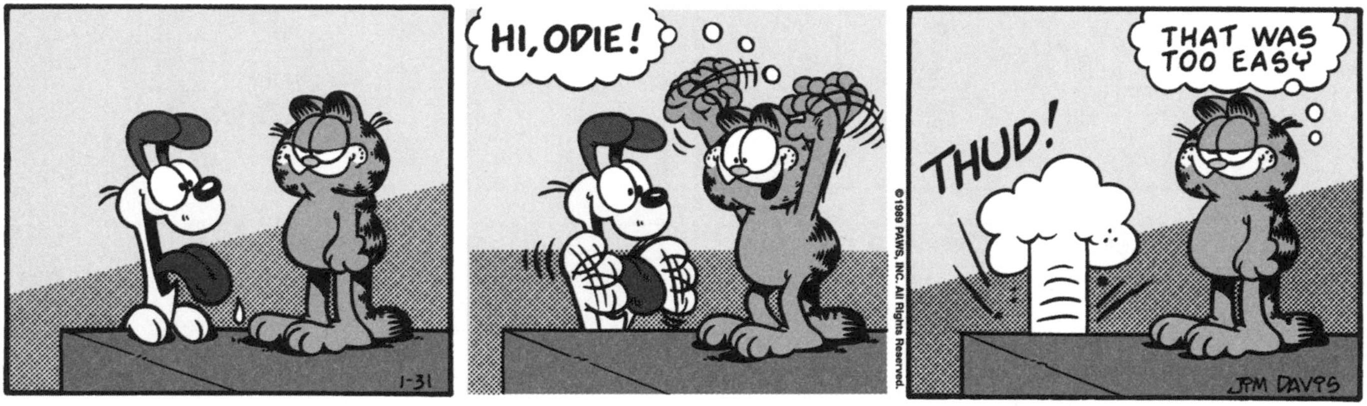
1-31
HI, ODIE!
© 1989 PAWS, INC. All Rights Reserved.
THUD!
THAT WAS TOO EASY
JIM DAVIS

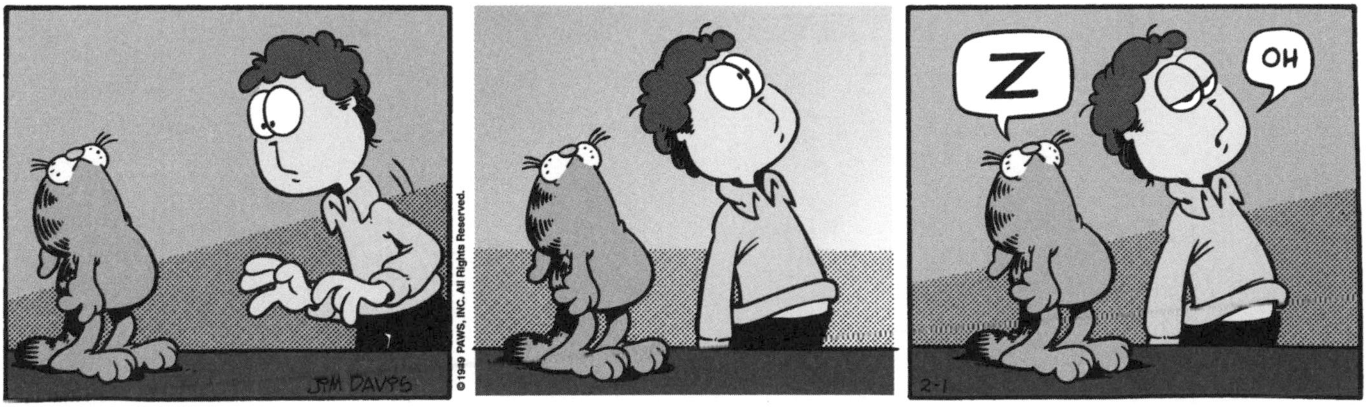
JIM DAVIS
© 1989 PAWS, INC. All Rights Reserved.
Z
OH
2-1

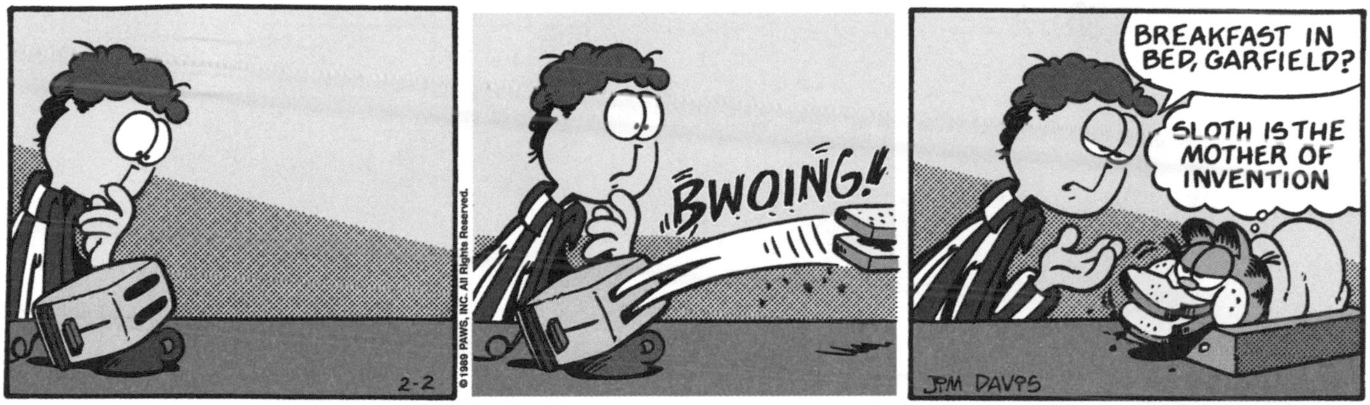
2-2
© 1989 PAWS, INC. All Rights Reserved.
BWOING!
BREAKFAST IN BED, GARFIELD?
SLOTH IS THE MOTHER OF INVENTION

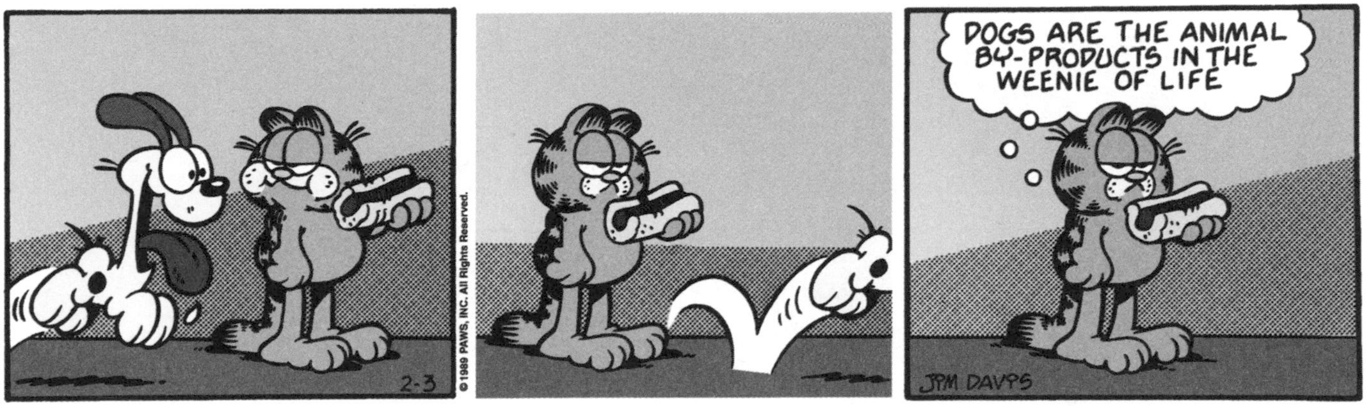
2-3
© 1989 PAWS, INC. All Rights Reserved.
DOGS ARE THE ANIMAL BY-PRODUCTS IN THE WEENIE OF LIFE

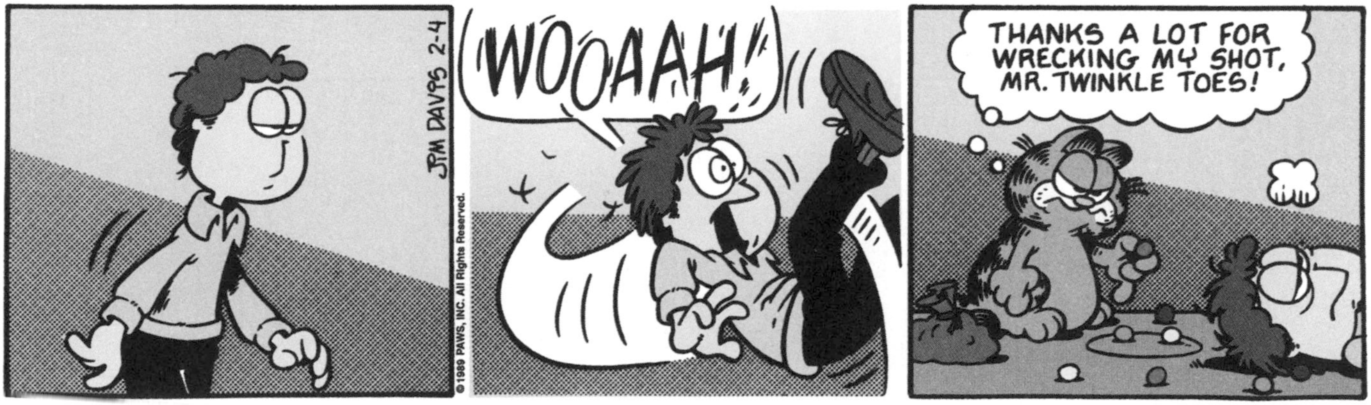
2-4
© 1989 PAWS, INC. All Rights Reserved.
WOOAAH!
THANKS A LOT FOR WRECKING MY SHOT, MR. TWINKLE TOES!

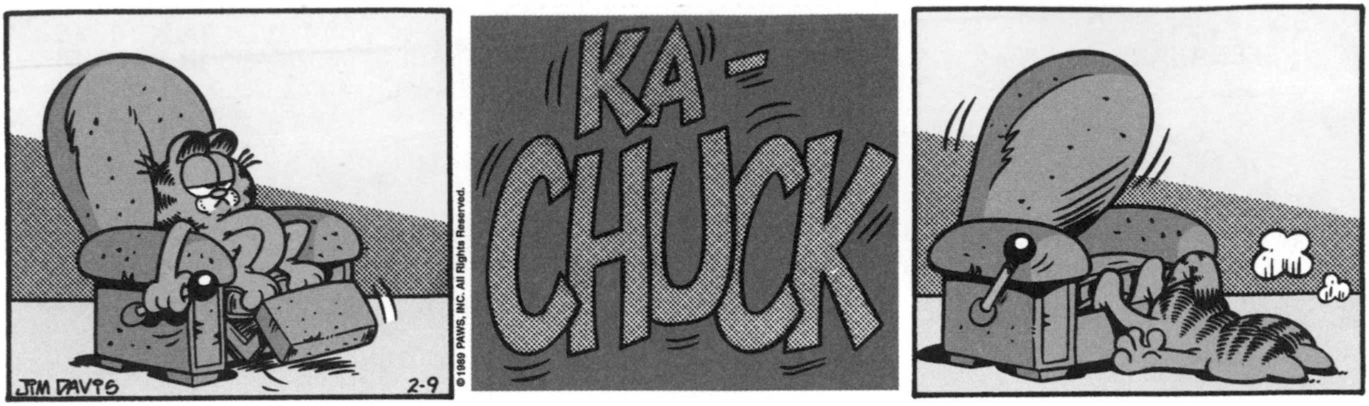
JIM DAVIS 2-9
©1989 PAWS, INC. All Rights Reserved.
KA-CHUCK

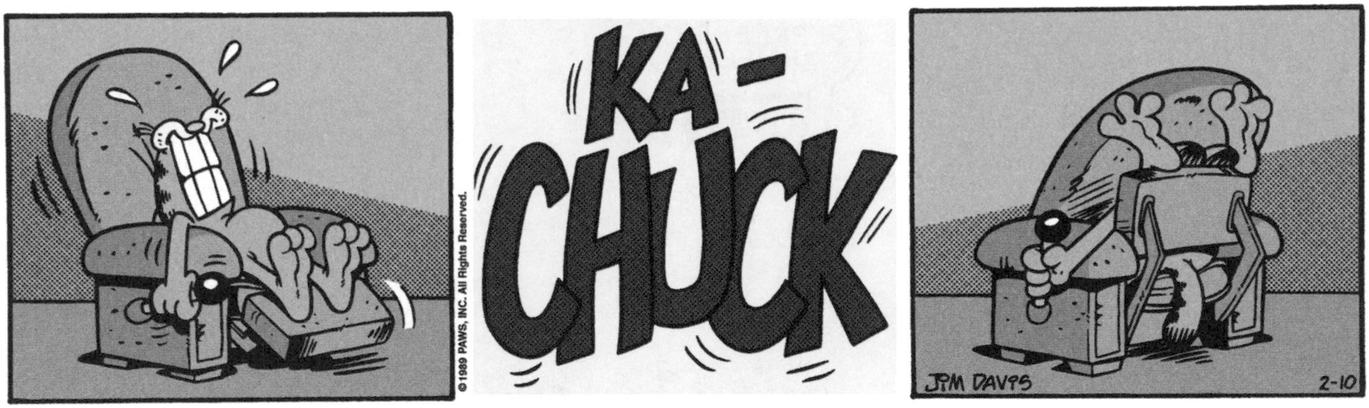
©1989 PAWS, INC. All Rights Reserved.
KA-CHUCK
JIM DAVIS 2-10

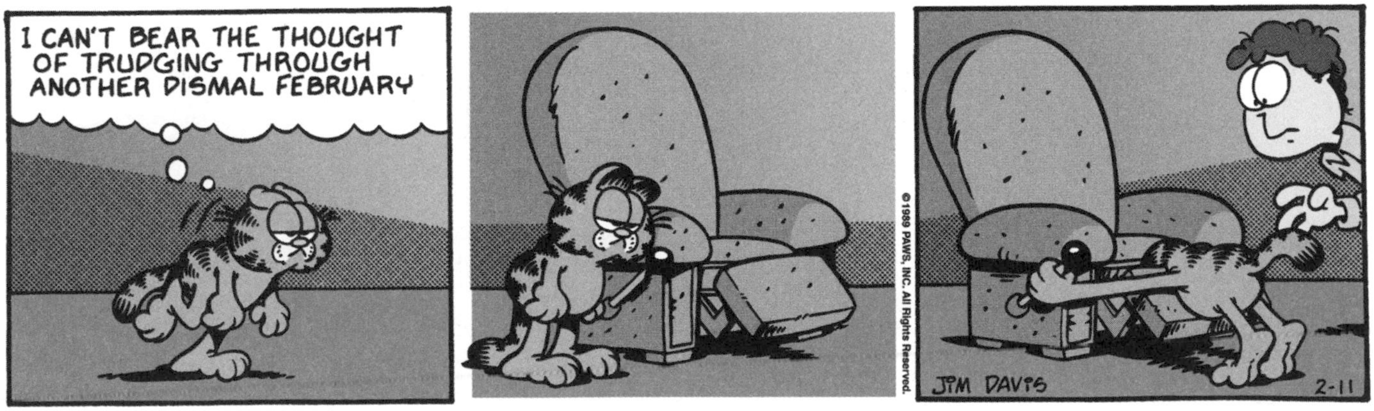
I CAN'T BEAR THE THOUGHT OF TRUDGING THROUGH ANOTHER DISMAL FEBRUARY
©1989 PAWS, INC. All Rights Reserved.
JIM DAVIS 2-11

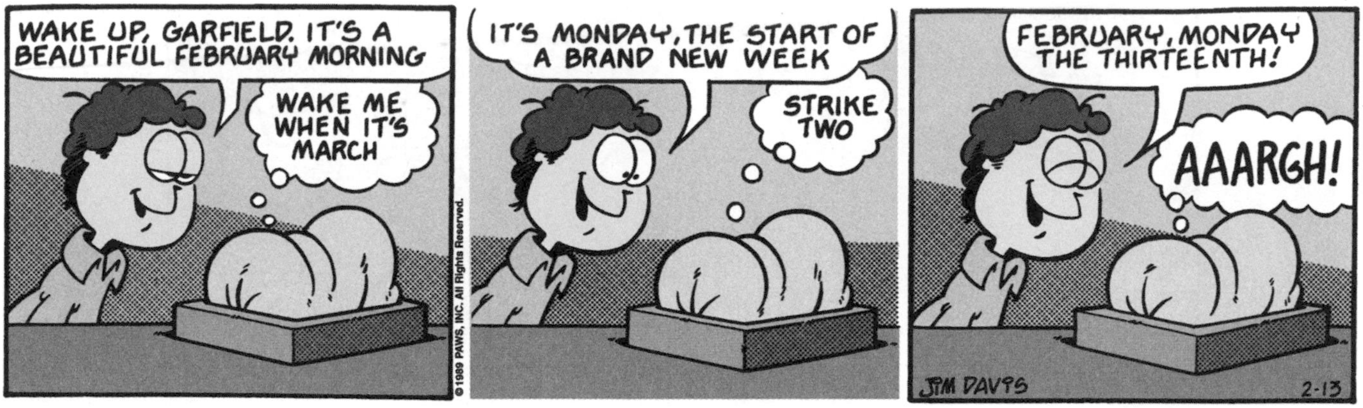
WAKE UP, GARFIELD. IT'S A BEAUTIFUL FEBRUARY MORNING
WAKE ME WHEN IT'S MARCH
IT'S MONDAY, THE START OF A BRAND NEW WEEK
STRIKE TWO
FEBRUARY, MONDAY THE THIRTEENTH!
AAARGH!
©1989 PAWS, INC. All Rights Reserved.
JIM DAVIS
2-13

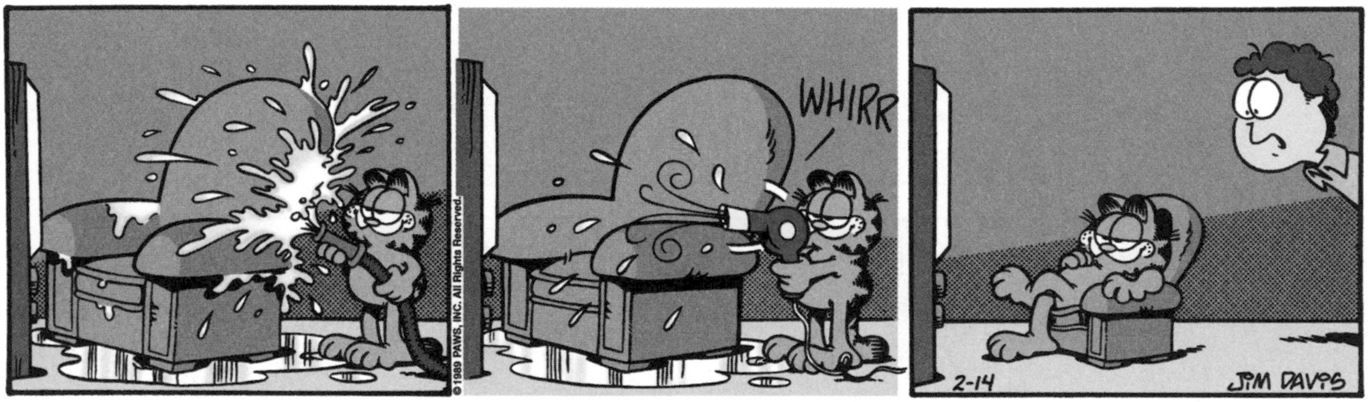
©1989 PAWS, INC. All Rights Reserved.
WHIRR
2-14
JIM DAVIS

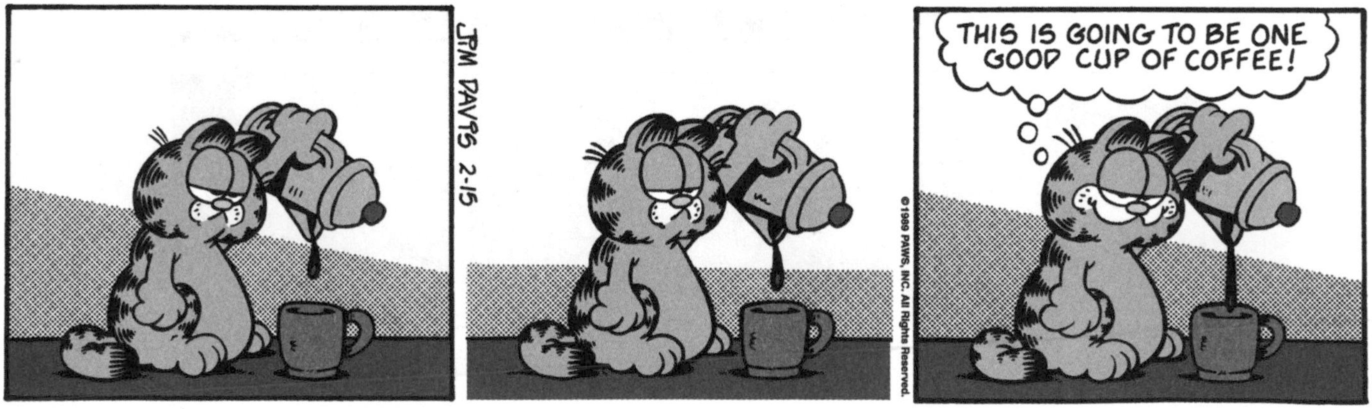
JIM DAVIS 2-15
©1989 PAWS, INC. All Rights Reserved.
THIS IS GOING TO BE ONE GOOD CUP OF COFFEE!

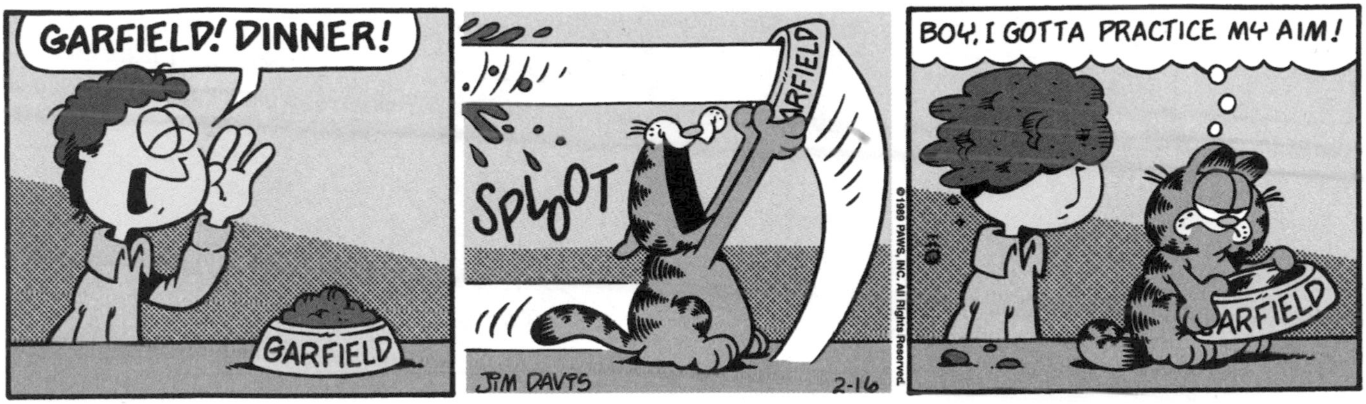
GARFIELD! DINNER!
GARFIELD
SPLOOT
GARFIELD
JIM DAVIS
2-16
© 1989 PAWS, INC. All Rights Reserved.
BOY, I GOTTA PRACTICE MY AIM!
GARFIELD

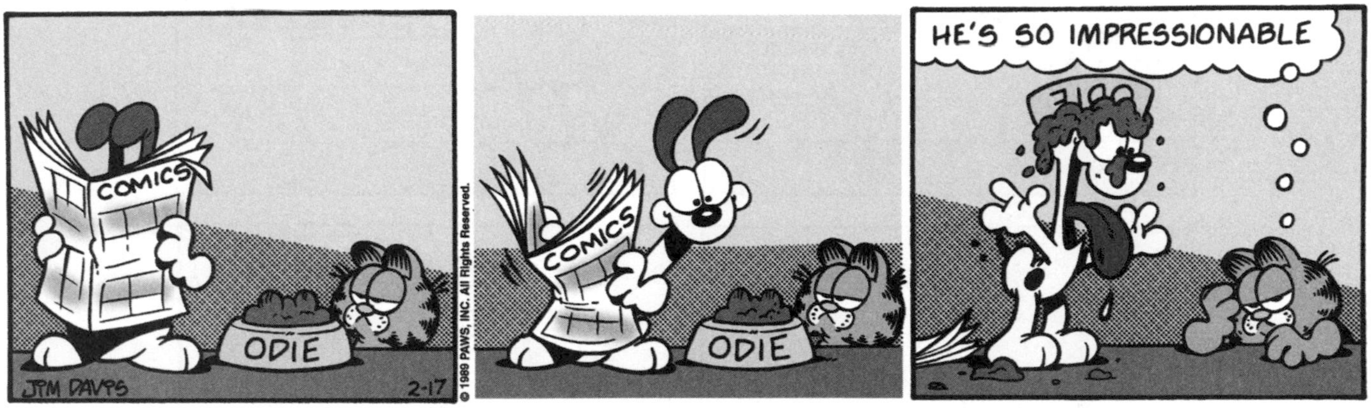
COMICS
ODIE
JIM DAVIS
2-17
© 1989 PAWS, INC. All Rights Reserved.
COMICS
ODIE
HE'S SO IMPRESSIONABLE

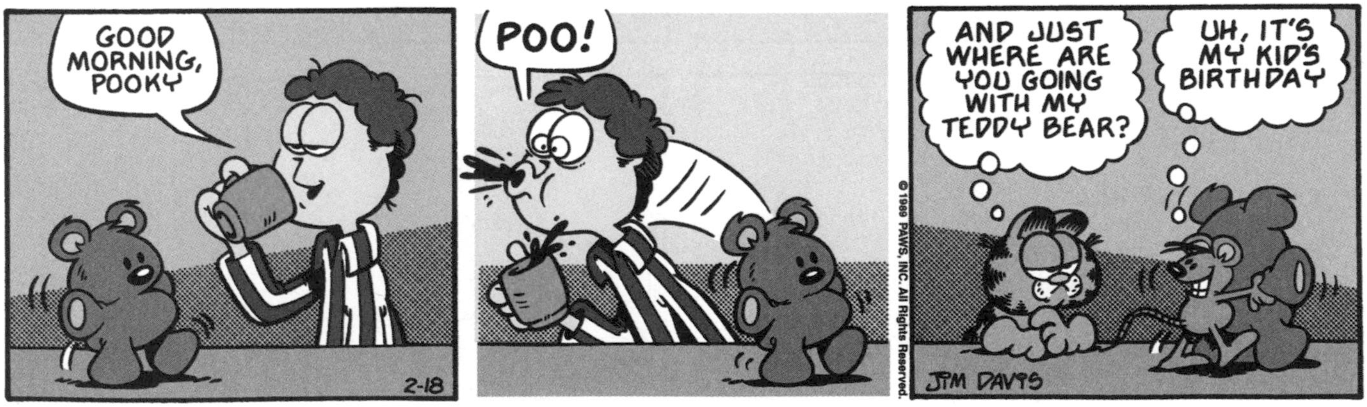
GOOD MORNING, POOKY
2-18
POO!
© 1989 PAWS, INC. All Rights Reserved.
AND JUST WHERE ARE YOU GOING WITH MY TEDDY BEAR?
UH, IT'S MY KID'S BIRTHDAY
JIM DAVIS

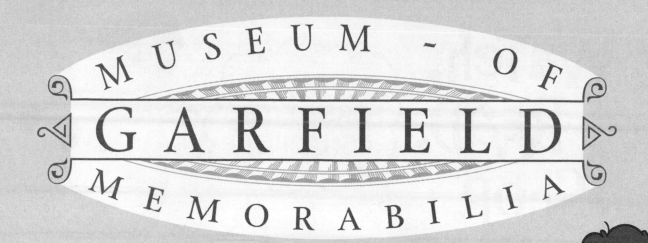

MUSEUM - OF GARFIELD MEMORABILIA

REMAINS OF FIRST SNACK

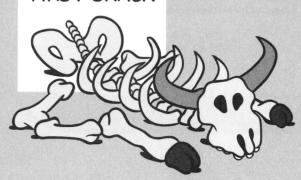

FIRST AFTER-DINNER FERN

FIRST NAP

FIRST CHEW TOY

FIRST SCRATCHING POST

FIRST HAIRBALL